International Law and Boundary Disputes in Africa

Africa has experienced a number of territorial disputes over land and maritime boundaries, due in part to its colonial and post-colonial history. This book explores the legal, political and historical nature of disputes over territory in the African continent, and critiques the content and application of contemporary international law to the resolution of African territorial and border disputes.

Drawing on central concepts of public international law such as sovereignty and jurisdiction, and socio-political concepts such as colonialism, ethnicity, nationality and self-determination, this book interrogates the intimate connection that peoples and nations have to territory and the severe disputes these may lead to. Gbenga Oduntan identifies the major principles of law at play in relation to territorial and boundary disputes, and argues that the predominant use of foreign-based adjudicatory mechanisms in attempting to deal with African boundary disputes alienates those institutions and mechanisms from African people and can contribute to the recurrence of conflicts and disputes in and among African territories. He suggests that the understanding and application of multidisciplinary dispute resolution mechanisms and strategies can allow for a more holistic and effective treatment of boundary disputes.

As an in-depth study into the legal, socio-political and anthropological mechanisms involved in the understanding of territorial boundaries, and a unique synthesis of African jurisprudence of international boundaries law, this book will be of great use and interest to students, researchers, and practitioners in African diplomacy, Public International Law, International Relations, and decision-makers in need of a better understanding of the settlement of disputes over territorial boundaries in Africa and indeed the wider world.

Gbenga Oduntan is Senior Lecturer in International Commercial Law at the University of Kent, UK.

Routledge Research in International Law

Available:

International Law and the Third World
Reshaping Justice
Edited by Richard Falk, Balakrishnan Rajagopal and Jacqueline Stevens

International Legal Theory
Essays and Engagements, 1966–2006
Nicholas Onuf

The Problem of Enforcement in International Law
Countermeasures, the Non-Injured State and the Idea of International Community
Elena Katselli Proukaki

International Economic Actors and Human Rights
Adam McBeth

The Law of Consular Access
A Documentary Guide
John Quigley, William J. Aceves and S. Adele Shank

State Accountability under International Law
Holding States Accountable for a Breach of Jus Cogens Norms
Lisa Yarwood

International Organizations and the Idea of Autonomy
Institutional Independence in the International Legal Order
Edited by Richard Collins and Nigel D. White

Self-Determination in the Post-9/11 Era
Elizabeth Chadwick

Participants in the International Legal System
Multiple Perspectives on Non-State Actors in International Law
Jean d'Aspremont

Sovereignty and Jurisdiction in the Airspace and Outer Space
Legal Criteria for Spatial Delimitation
Gbenga Oduntan

International Law in a Multipolar World
Edited by Matthew Happold

The Law on the Use of Force
A Feminist Analysis
Gina Heathcote

The ICJ and the Development of International Law
The Lasting Impact of the Corfu Channel Case
Edited by Karine Bannelier, Théodore Christakis and Sarah Heathcote

UNHCR and International Refugee Law
From Treaties to Innovation
Corinne Lewis

Asian Approaches to International Law and the Legacy of Colonialism
The Law of the Sea, Territorial Disputes and International Dispute Settlement
Edited by Jin-Hyun Paik, Seok-Woo Lee, Kevin Y L Tan

The Right to Self-determination Under International Law
"Selfistans," Secession, and the Rule of the Great Powers
Milena Sterio

Reforming the UN Security Council Membership
The Illusion of Representativeness
Sabine Hassler

Threats of Force
International Law and Strategy
Francis Grimal

The Changing Role of Nationality in International Law
Edited by Alessandra Annoni and Serena Forlati

Criminal Responsibility for the Crime of Aggression
Patrycja Grzebyk

Regional Maintenance of Peace and Security under International Law
The Distorted Mirror
Dace Winther

International Law-Making
Essays in Honour of Jan Klabbers
Edited by Rain Liivoja and Jarna Petman

Resolving Claims to Self-Determination
Is There a Role of the International Court of Justice?
Andrew Coleman

The Rise of Tamil Separatism in Sri Lanka
From Communalism to Secession
Gnanapala Welhengama and Nirmala Pillay

The United Nations and Collective Security
Gary Wilson

Justice for Victims before the International Criminal Court
Luke Moffett

Public-Private Partnerships and Responsibility under International Law
A Global Health Perspective
Lisa Clarke

Cultural Diversity in International Law
The Effectiveness of the UNESCO Convention on the Protection and Promotion of the Diversity of Cultural Expressions
Edited by Lilian Hanania

Incitement in International Law
Wibke K. Timmermann

The Cuban Embargo under International Law
El Bloqueo
Nigel D. White

Resisting United Nations Security Council Resolutions
Sufyan Droubi

The Changing Nature of Customary International Law
Methods of Interpreting the Concept of Custom in International Criminal Tribunals
Noora Arajärvi

Technology and the Law on the Use of Force
New Security Challenges in the Twenty First Century
Jackson Maogoto

International Law and Boundary Disputes in Africa
Gbenga Oduntan

Forthcoming titles in this series include:

Justice in International Law
The Legal, Political, and Moral Dimensions of Indigenous Peoples' Rights
Mauro Barelli

Means of Transportation and Registration of Nationality
Transportation Register by International Organizations
Vincent P. Cogliati-Bantz

The International Criminal Court in Search of its Purpose and Identity
Edited by Triestino Mariniello

Power and Law in International Society
International Relations as the Sociology of International Law
Mark Klamberg

The Responsibility to Protect in International Law
An Emerging Paradigm Shift
Susan Breau

Legal Accountability and Britain's Wars 2000-2014
Peter Rowe

International Law and Boundary Disputes in Africa

Gbenga Oduntan

LONDON AND NEW YORK

First published 2015
by Routledge
2 Park Square, Milton Park, Abingdon, Oxon, OX14 4RN

and by Routledge
711 Third Avenue, New York, NY 10017

Routledge is an imprint of the Taylor & Francis Group, an informa business

© 2015 Gbenga Oduntan

The right of Gbenga Oduntan to be identified as author of this work has been asserted by him in accordance with sections 77 and 78 of the Copyright, Designs and Patents Act 1988.

All rights reserved. No part of this book may be reprinted or reproduced or utilised in any form or by any electronic, mechanical, or other means, now known or hereafter invented, including photocopying and recording, or in any information storage or retrieval system, without permission in writing from the publishers.

Trademark notice: Product or corporate names may be trademarks or registered trademarks, and are used only for identification and explanation without intent to infringe.

British Library Cataloguing in Publication Data
A catalogue record for this book is available from the British Library

Library of Congress Cataloging-in-Publication Data
A catalog record has been requested for this book

ISBN: 978-0-415-83892-4 (hbk)
ISBN: 978-0-203-77684-1 (ebk)

Typeset in Baskerville by
Keystroke, Station Road, Codsall, Wolverhampton

To Prince Bola Ajibola (SAN, KBE, CFR, D. Litt) – an outstanding jurist, adjudicator and statesman for dedication to the practice of international justice and inspiring thirst for greatness in younger generations.

Contents

Acknowledgements   xvii

Introduction   1

1 **Africa: Birthing the empire of law and concept of territory**   6
    1.1 International law and Africa 8
       1.1.1 Racialism and European appropriation of the 'common law of mankind' 9
       1.1.2 Why the House always wins 14
    1.2 Eurocentricity and the applicable international boundary laws 16

2 **Sovereignty, jurisdiction, territorial integrity and territorial acquisition in international law**   23
    2.1 Concept and forms of sovereignty 23
    2.2 Globalisation vs territorial sovereignty 27
    2.3 Jurisdiction within sovereignty 31
    2.4 Westphalian vs indigenous sovereignty 33
    2.5 The principle of territorial jurisdiction 36
    2.6 Territory and territorial acquisition in public international law and international relations 38
       2.6.1 Occupation 42
       2.6.2 Cession 43
       2.6.3 Accretion, erosion and avulsion 44
       2.6.4 Conquest or annexation 44
       2.6.5 Prescription 45
       2.6.6 Renunciation or relinquishment 46
       2.6.7 Adjudication 46
       2.6.8 Abandonment and dereliction 46
       2.6.9 Discovery 46
       2.6.10 Papal grant 47

3 Frontiers and boundaries in the context of international legal framework of territorial sovereignty and jurisdiction   50
  3.1 *The functionality of frontiers and boundaries 50*
  3.2 *Natural vs artificial boundaries 52*
  3.3 *Frontier vs boundary 53*

4 Province of international boundary disputes determined   55
  4.1 *What are international boundary disputes? 55*
  4.2 *Internal boundary disputes 63*
  4.3 *Territorial vs boundary disputes 65*
  4.4 *Frontiers, borders, fences and walls in law and international relations 69*
    4.4.1 Boundaries 69
    4.4.2 Borders and borderlands 73
    4.4.3 Fences and walls 75
  4.5 *Delimitation and demarcation juxtaposed 78*
  4.6 *African delimitation and demarcation of boundaries in their historical, colonial and contemporary contexts 79*
  4.7 *High power politics: legality and illegalities of the Berlin Conference (1885) 88*
  4.8 *Classifications and nature of African boundary disputes 90*
  4.9 *Boundaries and disputes: a multidisciplinary approach 96*

5 Actual and potential role of the African Union Organisation in boundary dispute management and resolution   102
  5.1 *African Union early warning system 105*
  5.2 *The African Union Border Programme (AUBP) and the delimitation, demarcation and settlement of African boundary disputes 108*
    5.2.1 Law practice and diplomacy of the African Union Border Programme 109
    5.2.2 Implementation of the African Union Border Programme 118

6 African regional economic communities and the management of boundary disputes   126
  6.1 *Conflict resolution and management in the East African sub-region (IGAD area) 127*
    6.1.1 Role of CEWARN in detecting and managing cross-boundary disputes 127
    6.1.2 IGAD's relevance in border and boundary disputes 128
  6.2 *ECOWAS 131*
    6.2.1 Conflict resolution and management in the West African sub-region: ECOWAS area 133

      6.2.2   Rules of the ECOWAS Treaty and Protocols 134
      6.2.3   Actual and potential role of the Court of Justice of the Economic Community of West African States 140
      6.2.4   ECOWAS Early Warning System 141
      6.2.5   ECOWAS experience in boundary disputes 142
  6.3   *Conflict and dispute management in the Economic Community of Central African States (ECCAS)* *143*
      6.3.1   Assessing the early warning capabilities and performance of MARAC 148
  6.4   *Law and practice of conflict and dispute management in the SADC* *149*
      6.4.1   Political mechanisms for the resolution of boundary disputes in the SADC region 150

7 Manifestations of boundary disputes in the African geopolitical zones   155

  7.1   *East African boundaries: border disputes* *156*
      7.1.1   Sudan–Kenya: the Ilemi Triangle 157
      7.1.2   Kenya–South Sudan (Nadapal boundary) 158
      7.1.3   Tanzania–Malawi: Lake Malawi (Nyasa) 159
      7.1.4   Kenya–Uganda: Migingo Island 159
      7.1.5   Eritrea–Ethiopia 160
      7.1.6   Sudan–South Sudan border disputes 162
  7.2   *West African boundaries and borders disputes* *164*
      7.2.1   Cameroon–Nigeria: land and maritime dispute 166
      7.2.2   Gabon and Equatorial Guinea: territorial disputes on the Island of Mbanié 168
      7.2.3   Burkina Faso–Niger frontier dispute 168
      7.2.4   Benin–Niger frontier dispute 169
  7.3   *North Africa: boundary disputes and contested territories* *170*
  7.4   *Southern Africa: boundary disputes and contested territories* *171*
      7.4.1   Swaziland–South Africa 173
  7.5   *Central African states (CEMAC): boundary disputes* *176*

8 Case study: the arbitral route to settlement of African boundary disputes   177

  8.1   *The arbitral route: the* Eritrea–Ethiopia Boundary Commission Case *177*
      8.1.1   Synopsis of the Eritrean Case: statement submitted to the EEBC 178
  8.2   *Synopsis of Ethiopia's statement in accordance with paragraph 4(8) of the Agreement concluded on 12 December 2000* *184*
      8.2.1   Ethiopia's historical account of the background of the territory 184

xii *Contents*

       8.2.2 Ethiopian view of applicable law 185
       8.2.3 Ethiopian view of the methodology: the five sectors 186
       8.2.4 The Agreements pre-figuring the Treaties of 1900, 1902 and 1908 187
       8.2.5 Ethiopian view of the pertinent geography 190
       8.2.6 Ethiopian view of the changing and opportunistic attitude of Italy during key periods 190
       8.2.7 Ethiopia's position 190
       8.2.8 The disposition of the Cunama (Sector II) 191
       8.2.9 Interpretation and application of the Agreements: Sector III – along the Mareb River from the Mai Ambessa to the Belesa River 191
       8.2.10 Interpretation and application of the Agreements: Sector V – from the confluence of the Mareb and Belesa Rivers to the easternmost point defined by the Treaty of 1900 192
       8.2.11 Ethiopian view of the period 1908–present 192
       8.2.12 Incidence of disputes between the parties 194
  8.3 *Critiquing the EEBC decision and understanding the difficulties of implementation* 195
  8.4 *Eritrea–Ethiopia Claims Commission (EECC)* 203

9 Case study: mediation route to settlement: the dispute between Malawi and Tanzania over Lake Nyasa   206
  9.1 *The applicable treaties and instruments* 208
  9.2 *Malawi's position* 209
  9.3 *Tanzania's position* 211
  9.4 *HLMT: challenges, achievements and prospects* 214

10 Case study: adjudicative route – a critique of the land and maritime boundary dispute (*Cameroon v Nigeria*)   218
  10.1 *Geophysical setting of the region* 219
  10.2 *Historical provenance of the boundary and territorial problem* 220
  10.3 *The Judgment* 223
  10.4 *The law and diplomacy of the Cameroon–Nigeria Mixed Commission* 227
  10.5 *The structures of diplomacy, administration and implementation* 232
  10.6 *Identifying Eurocentricity in the jurisprudence of the World Court* 235

11 Sociology, politics, insecurity and the psychology of power in African boundary relations   240
  11.1 *Power and political differentials in the diplomacy of African boundary disputes* 246

12 Pacific settlement of international boundary disputes: a critical appraisal of the International Court of Justice 251

   12.1 Conflict resolution and cooling off mechanism functions of the ICJ in the adjudication of African boundary disputes 251
      12.1.1 Diplomatic function of international courts 253
      12.1.2 Advancing jurisprudence and elaboration of the law 254
   12.2 International adjudication of African boundary disputes: a critical appraisal of the contentious and advisory jurisdiction of the World Court 257
   12.3 Role of the International Court of Justice in relation to the struggle for self-determination and independence for the mandate and colonial territories in Africa 262
   12.4 Prospects of the African Court of Justice as a preferred option under the adjudication route 266
   12.5 International arbitration of African boundary disputes: a critical appraisal of the Permanent Court of Arbitration 267
      12.5.1 Arbitration 267
      12.5.2 The Hague Conferences and the Permanent Court of Arbitration 270
   12.6 Evaluation of alternative forms of pacific settlement of boundary disputes 279
      12.6.1 Negotiation 283
      12.6.2 Enquiry 286
      12.6.3 Conciliation 287
      12.6.4 Good Offices 289
      12.6.5 Mediation 291
   12.7 Multi-tracking and indigenising settlement of boundary disputes in Africa: a fusion of law, politics and culture 295
      12.7.1 Bona fide assisted direct negotiations 298
      12.7.2 African mediation 299
      12.7.3 The African Conciliation Commission 300
      12.7.4 The underdeveloped state of indigenous African adjudication 300
   12.8 Factors predictive of the failure of ADR and Tier 2 diplomacy in boundary matters 306
      12.8.1 Poor knowledge, incompetence or careless diagnosis of the crisis 306
      12.8.2 Poor strategy and/or poorly trained mediators 307
      12.8.3 Lack of neutrality/mediators with an interest to serve 307
      12.8.4 Unable to stay the course 308
   12.9 Identification and evaluation of best practices for pacific settlement of disputes 308
      12.9.1 Flexibility 309
      12.9.2 Visit to locus 309

12.9.3 Determination of *locus standi* 311
12.9.4 The interpretative function in boundary dispute resolution 312
12.9.5 Interim measures of protection and control 313

13 Role and scope for involvement of Africa's developed northern partners in the settlement of boundary disputes   316

13.1 Role and scope of involvement of the European Union in African boundary dispute resolution 316

13.2 Role and scope of involvement of the United States in African boundary dispute resolution 317

14 The problem of costs and the relevance of legal aid in African boundary dispute resolution: funding delimitation, demarcation and other implementation activities   319

15 Settlement of international boundary disputes by use of force   324

15.1 Retorsion, retaliation and war 326

16 Re-evaluation of the *uti possidetis* principle in light of the African experience   330

16.1 Uti possidetis in Africa: a problematic doctrine? 330

16.2 Uti possidetis within the equation of political separation and self-determination 337

17 Strategies and modalities to resolve straddling communities and resources under the African Union Boundary Programme   350

17.1 Boundary demarcation and the problem of straddling communities and enclaves 350

17.2 Varying demarcation in the interest of justice and accommodating losers' interests 357

    17.2.1 Straddling resources and hydrocarbon fields 357

    17.2.2 Straddling fisheries 359

17.3 Recognising an African customary rule in favour of sharing straddling resources 360

18 Alternative futures: strategies of negotiation and innovative methods to avoid deadlock in relation to territorial conflicts   363

18.1 Special territorial arrangements 364

18.2 Sale and purchase of territory 365

18.3 The establishment of free cities 365
18.4 Lease back options 366
18.5 Cession 367
18.6 Appropriate recourse to the use of plebiscites 367
18.7 Afrocentric solutions to the problems of delimitation and demarcation 369

19 Resolution of international boundary disputes involving African nations: alternative futures and general conclusions   371

Appendix I	389
Appendix II	391
Appendix III	392
Appendix IV	398
Appendix V	400
Index	403

Acknowledgements

Anyone who has written at least a page of meaningful literature will understand the imperative of intellectual borrowing as the very building block of the exercise. In the construction of this 388 page work I have had to rely on my contact with, as well as the intellectual and other influence of a vast number of people too numerous to list seriatim. I will, however, hazard a few names just so that I am not paralysed by the impossibility of the task and will do so in no particular order of importance.

Many thanks to colleagues and experts involved with the African Union Border Programme with whom I have had the rare opportunity of working closely, particularly: Dr Wafula Okomu, Professor Anthony Ashiwaju, Dr Mohammed Ahmed, Dr Paul Nugent, Tim Daniel, Professor Martin Pratt, Dr John W. Donaldson.

Mr El Ghassim Wane (Director of Peace and Security of the African Union Commission) has been both a brother and a teacher. He has given me a very unique insight to the workings (actual and potential) of this most important African international organisation. Their contributions and influences are inextricably part of the intellectual DNA of this work. Special thanks also to Sven M. G. Koopmans with whom I worked on the proposed African Union Border Programme Boundary Dispute Settlement Mechanism (BDSM). His intellectual influences are replete in important sections of this work.

Much gratitude to my colleagues assisting the High Level Mediation Team (HLMT) under the Malawi–Tanzania process – Judge Raymond Ranjeva (ICJ), Prof. George Kanyeihamba, Dr Dire David Tladi, Judge Barney Afako, Dr Miguel Alberto Chissano, (President of the National Institute for Maritime and Border Affairs, Republic of Mozambique) and Judge Abdul Koroma (ICJ). I owe especial gratitude for exposure to their doctrinal soundness on international law and vast experience in international judicial practices. My exposure to them opened up new vistas in my appreciation of the suitability of international law to the tasks of catering for all eventualities and nuances that international relations can generate in relation to the boundaries separating independent nations and states.

My understanding of the whole field of boundary delimitation and especially practical demarcation activities was built upon my decade-long and very unique exposure as well as close involvement with the Cameroon–Nigeria Mixed Commission (CNMC). My gratitude, therefore, goes to many important personalities on the Cameroonian, Nigerian and United Nations sides to this August body. Specific mention is to be made here to Mrs Nella Andem-Ewa (SAN); Barrister Mohammed Monguno; Lt General A. F. K. Akale OFR (rtd); Amb. Femi George; Alhaji Dahiru Bobbo, OFR; I. A. Adewola; Mr S.M. Diggi; Al-Kaleel Al-Ahamad; Professor Oye Chuwurah (Late), H.E. Ahmadu Ali; H. E. Martin E. Belinga; H. E. Prof. Maurice Kamto; Gen. Pierre Semengue, H. E. John Dion Ngute, Mr Ernest Bodo Abanda (Late), Ambassador Said Djinnit; H. E. Ahmedou Ould-Abdallah, Robert Mckay and Mr Vladimir Golytsyn.

In researching this book the author benefitted from trips funded by the *Deutsche Gesellschaft für Technische Zusammenarbeit* (GTZ) under the AUBP allowing two consultants to visit the various RECS in Africa. Thus, the author undertook field trips to the Economic Community of West African States (ECOWAS) Commission in Abuja, the African Union headquarters as well as to CEWARN (a Regional Office of the Intergovernmental Authority on Development (IGAD)) all based at Addis Ababa in Ethiopia in 2011 and 2012. The discussion in this work relies partly on the findings of the field trips and incorporates an analysis of the interviews consulted with pertinent officials of the aforementioned organisations.

I owe a debt of gratitude to the staff and services of the Templeman Library, the Kent Law School and the entire staff and administration of the University of Kent at Canterbury who have provided excellent facilities for me to engage in this research under the best of collegial traditions.

And to my children, Jimi, Fela, Duntan and Bosola many thanks also. Oh! the joys of academic writing to the accompaniment of kids climbing on one's back. Loving thanks to their mother Obianuju for constant understanding and support.

For any and all errors/controversies that are actually certain to exist in any work of this nature, I gladly accept sole responsibility.

Gbenga Oduntan
Canterbury, August 2014

Introduction

> Frontiers are indeed the razors edge on which hang suspended the modern issues of war and peace, life or death of nations.[1]

> Spatial boundaries have ambiguous features: they divide and unite, bind the interior and link it with the exterior, are barriers and junctions, walls and doors, organs of defence and attack and so on. Frontier areas (borderlands) can be managed so as to maximise any of these functions. They can be militarised, as bulwarks against neighbours, or be made into special areas of peaceful interchange.[2]

Where best to study the central questions of sovereignty, jurisdiction, territory, war and dispute resolution and their relations to boundary conflicts than Africa where it all began? This book dispels popular myths about the endemic nature of boundary disputes in Africa and critiques the content and application of contemporary international law to the resolution of African territorial and border disputes. Apart from principles of public international law and aspects of international relations theory, this book is informed by current debates and influences in socio-legal studies, politics, critical legal studies and general social theory. Outside the social sciences the book identifies and incorporates into its analysis pertinent scientific theories in surveying, geography, space sciences and the geosciences. The book, therefore, enquires into a variety of substantive, theoretical and normative issues surrounding boundary academic discourse such as migration, nationalism, citizenship, security, ethnic identity, alternative dispute resolution and anthropology. In this way the book engages in an ambitious project of synthesising an African jurisprudence of international boundary law.

In spite of its active history, authoritative legal literature on African international boundary is not in abundance; Brownlie's *African Boundaries* remains the *locus*

---

1 Lord Curzon of Kedleston, Viceroy of India 1898–1905 and British Foreign Secretary 1919–1924, 1907 Romanes Lecture, Oxford.
2 R. Strassoldo, "The State of the Arts in Europe" in A. I. Asiwaju and P. O. Adeniyi (eds), *Borderlands in Africa: A Multidisciplinary and Comparative Focus on Nigeria and West Africa* (Lagos: University of Lagos Press, 1989), p. 359.

classicus – so to speak – on the subject. In terms of historical atlas, J. F. Ade Ajayi and Michael Crowder's *Historical Atlas of Africa* (1985) is considered to enjoy immense prestige.[3] The absence of a successor to Brownlie's book may be because of the fact that its topic is so vast and its theme so potentially contentious that only a writer with magisterial sagacity like Brownlie could have contemplated to embark on such a journey in the first place. Our book does not even attempt to replace his work nor does it have any hope of so doing. Both books are written in different eras to serve different purposes and to meet differing ends within the general purpose of providing useful legal discourse of African boundaries.

The significance and import of the study is that it will perhaps be the first major effort by an African scholar in this century to interrogate the disciplines of international law and diplomacy in relation to their relevance, specifically to African boundary disputes. By so doing the work will aid researchers and scholars of African boundaries and international relations in formulating useful answers to the many problems that continue to arise in this area. Furthermore, the work will hopefully be of help to those practitioners charged with the task of aiding boundary disputants in Africa to come to a multidisciplinary resolution of their cases based on conformity with the general principles of public international law.

Africa as a continent since the era of political emancipation from debilitating colonialism is no stranger to border problems, conflicts and territorial disputes of all descriptions. Military skirmishes around borders are near common place although the vast majority go unacknowledged. Cattle rustling, terrorism, smuggling, ethnic violence, prostitution, people trafficking, drug trafficking, agrarian revolts, straddling villages and communities are just some of the issues that afflict African states in their border areas and boundary zones. In consequence of this social wreckage, human rights abuses, discrimination, political exclusion and economic stagnation have attended very many African states, especially in those areas that are at the forefront of territorial or boundary disputes.

Statesmen, diplomats, lawyers, mediators and other skilled adjudicators have for just over a century exerted considerable effort in devising various means for promoting the peaceful settlement of international disputes. In furtherance of this, institutions of considerable variety and sophistication have also been conjured up to enable states and international organisations to create appropriate means of dispute settlement.[4] What is, however, conspicuously missing is a body of specialised literature and perhaps even experts in the area of African boundaries dispute resolution. Nearly at the vanishing point of existence is the *corp* of qualified legal expertise on boundaries relating to specific geopolitical regions within Africa. Indeed African legal and political scholars are just beginning to wake up to their

---

3 Alan R. H. Baker, *Geography and History: Bridging the Divide* (Cambridge: Cambridge University Press, 2003), p. 200.
4 A particularly useful work exists in the Report of a Study of the David Davies Memorial Institute of International Studies titled *International Disputes: The Legal Aspects* (London: Europa Publications Limited, 1972).

historic role and to realise that 'being knowledgeable of the nature, purposes and functions of international boundaries is very helpful when dealing with disputes relating to their location, management and administration'.[5] We argue in this book that the development of viable political, diplomatic and legal mechanisms and institutions in which African scholars, jurists, technocrats, leaders and elders of repute participate as the main engines of decision making in resolving African boundary disputes is imperative for the future. It is argued that the predominant use of foreign-based adjudicatory mechanisms in attempting to deal with African boundary disputes alienates those institutions and mechanisms from African people and is perhaps a cause for the recurrence of conflicts and disputes in and among African territories even in relation to disputes to which legal decisions had already been taken. The frequent decisions emanating from the International Court of Justice, situated far away at The Hague, have often failed to holistically resolve the dispute. Although the vast majority of international judgments have in fact, to the credit of African states, been implemented oftentimes through actual demarcation, in reality continuing political divisions and historical grievances have prevented genuine 'resolution' of the disputes. Hence the perennial recurrence of tensions and new dangers along the boundary lines that have been decided upon and in other places that were not previously affected.

Yet the story of the African international boundary is not simply that of a place of conflict or despondency. The vast majority of African boundaries and borders are maintained in a constant state of peacefulness. The African international boundary is predominantly a place of immense intercultural exchange, multiculturalism, international trade, tourism, economic opportunities and peaceable interactions. All these positive aspects, successes and especially best practices must also be accounted for in academic and legal literature on the topic. By focusing on the law and practices of the Regional Economic Communities (RECs) and the African Union (AU), the book unearths evidence of many progressive practices indigenous to Africa and worthy of further study, development and fine-tuning. Our research, thus, establishes many points of positive practice that are unique to Africa and ought to be recommended to other regions and areas of the world, even the developed western world. The hypothesis to be tested includes whether the physical and cultural distance between the key institutions and personnel that usually decide over African disputes and the continent itself contribute to the perception of dissatisfaction with the justice meted out by international tribunals. The current situation whereby sovereign African states may under certain situations have to submit themselves to the supervisory jurisdiction of Dutch domestic courts in the resolution of their

---

5 Wafula Okomu, "The Purpose and Functions of International Boundaries: With Specific Reference to Africa" in *Boundary Delimitation and Demarcation: AUBP Practical Handbook* (Addis Ababa: African Union, 2010), p. 31.

boundary cases is apparently dissatisfactory.[6] The combination of non-African venues, judges, arbitrators and experts as well as the application of a suspiciously Eurocentric, modern public international law, appear to have created a widespread impression that the justice in relation to African international boundary disputes continues to be handled in an unsatisfactory and biased manner. It remains to be determined whether the lack of ownership of the processes for resolution of international disputes in Africa generally has contributed to the increasing porosity of the continent to foreign intervention by other technologically advanced countries and corporate interests.

The principles of public international law continue to provide the ground rules for determination of sovereignty, jurisdiction and control over territory. They are also the primary rules that are used to determine the merits of boundary cases. To this extent the book identifies the major principles of law at play in relation to territorial, and boundary, disputes. The treatment of the topics herein will hopefully offer a running critique of the content and practice of international law especially where the applicable principles of law are deemed to work against the interests of developing states, particularly those of Africa. The weaknesses of contemporary international law and in the general framework of international relations and diplomacy are highlighted and corrective measures are suggested. Only the most optimistic account of boundary research will ignore pointers to an urgent need for improvements to regional and international institutions that regulate border activities as well as the legal instruments that they operate under. Hence our work will focus at some length on evaluation of aspects of the legal and political competences as well as practices of the major RECs and regional groupings in Africa, especially in relation to border conflict management. Indeed, six African regional organizations, namely the Economic Community of West African States (ECOWAS),[7] the Economic Community of Central African States (ECCAS), the Southern African Development Community (SADC)[8] and the continental body, the African Union (AU)[9] will be focused upon in our analysis. The most worthy aspiration of the book is to provide a multidisciplinary discussion

---

6 As Brooks Daly correctly put it:

> In the Abyei arbitration such jurisdiction would have been exercised by Dutch courts pursuant to the Netherlands Arbitration Act 1986 in view of the choice of The Hague as the place of arbitration in Article 6 of the Arbitration Agreement 28. It is unclear whether the parties were conscious of this procedural difference in the PCA Rules, as no application was made to Dutch courts at any stage in the proceedings.
>
> See Brooks Daly, "The Abyei Arbitration: Procedural Aspects of an Intra-state Border Arbitration", Vol. 23, *Leiden Journal of International Law* (2010), No. 4, p. 808.
> See also our discussion in Section 12.5: International arbitration of African boundary disputes: a critical appraisal of the Permanent Court of Arbitration.

7 Information and materials about the ECOWAS are on the website of the organisation, available at www.ecowas.int/.
8 Information and materials about the SADC are on the website of the organisation, available at www.sadc.int/.
9 Information and materials about the AU are on the website of the organisation, available at www.au.int/en/.

of the problems afflicting African boundaries and particularly to identify necessary changes to the way African boundary disputes are handled. It will inevitably provide multidisciplinary analysis for the purposes of strengthening the knowledge base and understanding of African boundary related institutions and mechanisms and those of their experts and judges.[10]

On the whole our approach will be critical and will invite the reader to 're-imagine' international law and certainly to reconceptualise aspects of the doctrine to African states. If the work is seen as unique and provocative in several aspects it would have achieved its purpose. Some of the positions and conclusions will be decidedly Afrocentric. We remain acutely aware that Afrocentric critical approaches to academic literature often tend to be controversial. As explained with exasperation by Cheikh Anta Diop:

> When they explain their own historical past . . . that seems normal. Yet, when an African does likewise to help reconstruct the national personality of his people, distorted by colonialism that is considered backward or alarming. We contend that such a study is the point of departure for the cultural revolution properly understood.[11]

The justification for a critical legal approach to international law and international relations, particularly in areas such as delimitation and demarcation of boundaries that are widely regarded as value neutral, is the same for other areas of academic discourse. It lies in the fact that African 'truths' will remain suspended in the air and cannot be written correctly until African scholars dare to connect the dots across their disciplines and across the continent.

---

10 Social science theorists generally have developed an interest in international borders which regards borders as motive forces in the development of nations and states. They also correctly treat borders as zones of culture contact that often extend some distance from a borderline. Disciplines, such as history, politics, geography and sociology, have increasingly perceived border culture as problematic, and a key way to understand the international dimensions to a borderlands' development. All these influences impinge on both national and international law, hence our analysis will be incomplete if it does not delve into and cull knowledge from many other areas of academic discipline that have interrogated boundary problems. A nation may be taken as a population group that defines itself based on a common cultural identity. The term 'nation' is often interchangeable with 'state' in academic literature. However, 'nation' is normally used in reference to identity whereas 'state' is normally used in reference to a defined territorial entity. See Tim Daniel, "The Lexicon of Boundary-Making" in *Boundary Delimitation and Demarcation: AUBP Practical Handbook* (Addis Ababa: African Union, 2010), p. 234.
11 Cheikh Anta Diop, *The African Origin of Civilisation Myth or Reality*, Mercer Cook (ed.) (Chicago: Lawrence Hill Books, 1974), pp. xiii–xiv.

1 Africa: Birthing the empire of law and concept of territory

> Why not study the acculturation of the Whiteman in a Black milieu, in ancient Egypt for example[1]

In most academic literature, it would seem as if international laws have never had roots in Africa. More so, it seems as if international law only tangentially relates to Africa as a continent. Nothing in reality can be further from the truth. It has been demonstrated quite convincingly that much of what forms the basis of thinking in international ordering had its roots in Africa, with the influences of African thinking and legal practices to be found in what have developed into notions of sovereignty, jurisdiction, territorial control, war, truce, capitulation etc. The fact that this is not much acknowledged and discussed in academic literature is perhaps related to Diop's admonition that 'the West has not been calm enough and objective enough to teach us our history correctly without falsifications'.[2] International law and, by extension, the wealth of principles and jurisprudence relating to international boundaries' law, was born in Africa. International law has at least since antiquity and perhaps before, been continuously practiced in Africa and has involved its peoples, territories and political states in a number of fundamentally important ways. This assertion will certainly be controversial in some quarters but that itself is not a problem; for as Diop stated 'the essential factor is to retrace the history of the entire nation (of mankind)'.[3]

First, the primogeniture of law generally, and international law by extension, in primitive terms is naturally African. The monogenetic thesis of humanity even

---

1 Cheikh Anta Diop, *The African Origin of Civilisation Myth or Reality*, Mercer Cook ed. (Chicago: Lawrence Hill Books, 1974), p. xvi.
2 Diop, op.cit., p. xiv.
3 Parenthesis added. Ibid p. xvi. Many other authors have vociferously argued, and quite correctly so, that the history of international law remains incomplete until recognition of the contributions of non-western societies are engaged with in a more meaningful manner. See U. O. Umozurike, *International Law and Colonialism in Africa* (Enugu. Nigeria: Nwamife Publishers. 1979); J. Levitt (ed.), *Africa: Mapping New Boundaries in International Law* (Oxford and Portland: Hart Publishing, 2010); James Gathii, A Critical Appraisal of the International Legal Tradition of Taslim Olawale Elias, 21 *Leiden Journal of International Law*, (2008) p. 318; T.O. Elias, *Africa and the Development of International Law* (Leiden: Sijthoff Dobbs Ferry, NY: Oceana, 1972).

at the stage of the 'homo sapiens-sapiens' and the scientific conclusions about filiation deriving from DNA science makes compelling the argument that all other races in the world descended from black Africans.[4] Africa is the birth place of mankind and inevitably the forum for the first meaningful intercultural exchanges between nations. Various nations and peoples over thousands of years logically must have related to each other at various levels in legally relevant situations, ranging from the organisation of trade and negotiation of disputes to the surrendering of one group's territory and peoples to another. International legal practitioners and scholars like Adama Dieng have begun the tedious task of correctly recognising the pioneering importance of the continent in confident terms. He wrote:

> Africa is the world's oldest continent and her nations, institutions and peoples are humanity's first. Ancient African civilisations are responsible for founding the original logic, structure and method of statecraft for which modern human civilisation is structured. Africa's contributions to human civilisation are indisputable and vast, spanning, for example, the areas of agriculture, arts, government, law, medicine, monotheistic religion and science.[5]

Others like Professor Levitt, a respected scholar of international law and Africa, contemplates Africa as a subject and not simply an object of the field of international law – as a market place not a basket case.[6]

Second, apart from primitive connections, the continent of Africa as a geophysical reality is host to ancient Egypt and the other neighbouring nations and political groups to which it was most closely related at all points of its historical development. Egypt, by nearly all universally recognised studies and across many disciplines, is the home of the ideas, concepts and practices in art, science, literature, law, politics and government that gave birth to Pythagorean mathematics, the theory of the four elements of Thales of Miletus, Epicurean materialism, Platonic idealism, Judaism, Islam and modern science. Letters of credit, for instance, existed among the black civilisations along the Nile including ancient Egypt. In time the concept spread through the ancient Greek to Roman civilisations, the Islamic civilisations and ended up in the modern manifestations we have in the world today.[7] The origins of many of the world's religions upon

---

4 Ibid., p. xv. Both *homo sapiens* and our primordial ancestors, the australopithecines, who were a zoological group of small-brained erect running creatures originated from the high African Savannahs between one or two million years ago. Robert Ardrey, *The Territorial Imperative: A Personal Inquiry into the Animal Origins of Property and Nations* (London: Collins, 1969).
5 Adama Dieng in his foreword to J. I. Levitt, *Africa: Mapping New Boundaries in International Law* (Portland, Oregon: Hart, 2010), p. vii.
6 See Dieng, ibid., p. viii.
7 See generally J. Braithwaite and P. Drahos, *Global Business Regulation* (Cambridge University Press, 2001), pp. 45–7; see also M. M. Postan, *Medieval Trade and Finance* (London: Cambridge Univ. Press, 1973), p. 57; R. J. Trimble, 'The Law Merchant and the Letter of Credit', *Harvard Law Review* (1948), pp. 982, 984.

8 *Africa: Birthing the empire of law*

which much of the content of morality is determined and from which most of the world's legal systems, including international law, derive their inspiration, are African. Persuasive research reveals that:

> One needs only to meditate on Osiris, the redeemer-god, who sacrifices himself, dies, and is resurrected to save mankind, a figure essentially identifiable with Christ. A visitor to Thebes in the Valley of the Kings can view the Moslem inferno in detail (in the tomb of Seti I, of the Nineteenth Dynasty), 1700 years before the Koran. Osiris at the tribunal of the dead is indeed the 'lord' of revealed religions, sitting enthroned on Judgment Day, and we know that certain Biblical passages are practical copies of Egyptian moral texts.[8]

African participation in international relations indeed did not start with the pre-eminence of Egyptian empires; and obviously did not end with it. Before the age of European expansion to other continents and the Portuguese circumnavigation of Africa, Renaissance Italy had already become a common and frequent destination for scores of Ethiopian monks and dignitaries. These purveyors of the Ethiopian age of exploration approached European peoples as '. . . active agents of transcontinental discovery: interested in learning more about a region they regarded as the ultimate center of organized Christianity'.[9] Historical facts like this ought not to be ignored in as much as they run counter to ideas of African and black inferiority that have quite unfairly represented legal epistemolology for much of the modern period.[10]

1.1 International law and Africa

African concepts of justice have been sophisticated for several millennia. Few lawyers today are aware of the African origins of human legal ordering and foundations of inter-nation diplomacy. Fewer still are aware that the now famous statue of justice (depicted by the figure of a Greek goddess blindfolded and holding in one hand the balancing scale and on the other hand a sword) was for many centuries preceded by an Egyptian Goddess who also balances in one hand scales of justice and in the other hand a feather with which it weighs against the soul of all mortals when they face divine judgment. The similarities and conceptualisation of ideas are so striking that today's copyright, design and patent lawyers will find no problems in identifying the intellectual property trail that suggests itself here.[11]

---

8 Ibid., pp. xiv–xv.
9 Matteteo Salvadore, 'The Ethiopian Age of Exploration: Prester John's Discovery of Europe, 1306–1458', Vol. 21, *Journal of World History*, No.4, (2011) p. 593.
10 Cf. Ibid. pp. 593–4.
11 A correct understanding of the connections runs thus: 'Justice stands as a quasi-religious, quasi-political icon. Of course, Justice is not a solitary icon in the Western tradition. Rather, she is one

1.1.1 Racialism and European appropriation of the 'common law of mankind'

Despite the abundance of evidence, intellectual accounts of the contributions of Africa to the empire of human laws and international relations have been austere. This continuing situation was, however, carefully cultivated through concerted efforts at maintaining an 'otherness' by certain aspects of western scholarship and political leadership as part of the justification for the project of colonialism and latterly neocolonialism. Davidson pointed out:

> In retrospect, the whole great European project in Africa stretching over more than a hundred years, can only seem a vast obstacle thrust across every reasonable avenue of African progress out of the preliterate and prescientific societies into the 'modern world'. It achieved the reverse of what occurred in a Japan made aware of the need to 'catch up with the West'. It taught that nothing useful could develop without denying Africa's past, without a ruthless severing from Africa's roots and a slavish acceptance of models drawn from entirely different histories . . . Africa's own experience and achievements could teach nothing: it was 'only evil and evil continually . . .'.[12]

It is important to note that the concept of the exclusivity of international law to European thinking is an engineered falsehood, conveniently deployed as part of the general imperial project of Western Europe in the past few centuries. There is incontrovertible evidence that the predominant position from as far back as the seventh century until the nineteenth century – even among European classical writers – was that international law is universal, based on natural law and is applicable to all nations. The writings of Grotius,[13] Vitoria[14] and Vattel[15] clearly express the organic nature of international law as arising from shared universal values and traditions, emanating from various human civilisations. The classical

---

of a series of images, most in the female form, associated with powerful concepts of virtues and vices. Justice, like many of these images, traces her ancestry to goddesses. Her forerunners seem to have been Ma'at in Egyptian culture . . .', Dennis E. Curtis and Judith Resnik, Vol. 96, *The Yale Law Journal*, No. 8 (Jul., 1987), p. 1729. Herodotus indeed correctly observed that the Greeks got the names of their gods from the Egyptians: S. Todd Lowry and Barry Lewis and John Gordon (eds.), *Ancient and Medieval Economic Ideas and Concepts of Social Justice* (Brill, 1998), p. 11. See generally Anna Mancini, *Maat Revealed, Philosophy of Justice in Ancient Egypt* (U.S.: Buenos Books, 2004).

12 Basil Davidson, *The Blackman's Burden Africa and the Curse of the Nation State* (Ibadan: Spectrum Books, 1992), pp. 42, 43.
13 Grotius himself treated international law as universal and secular. See E. Nys, *Les Origines du Droit International* (1894), at pp. 151–9; A. Nussbaum, *A Concise History of the Law of Nations* (1954), at p. 86; Alexander Orakhelashvili, "The Idea of European International Law", vol. 17 *European Journal of International Law*, 2 (2006), p. 316.
14 Vitoria pleaded that non-Christian nations in America were not to be treated as objects of conquest but ought to be regarded as nations with legitimate princes and that wars against them could only be waged against them only for just causes.
15 E. de Vattel, *The Law of Nations or the Principles of Natural Law Applied to the Conduct and to the Affairs of Nations and of Sovereigns*, Sixth American Edition, (Philadelphia: T & J. W. Johnson, Law Booksellers, 1844) pp. v, vii–viii, xiii, 148–149.

European writers also perceived public international law not as a law of domination but as a law of order and the means of avoidance of anarchy and strife. It was realised that European imperialism had the potential to create both. In addition, the idea that international law had a specifically European character was most actively and fully developed in and around the nineteenth century on cue for the acceleration of an ongoing imperialist project of subjugation of other independent peoples and continents who were largely unaware of the full intentions of European rulers. It was at such a stage that the 'satanic verses' of European jurisprudence were penned by the likes of Wheaton,[16] Westlake[17] and Lorimer who amplified imperialistic thinking into what was regurgitated as facts. Lorimer wrote:

> The sphere of plenary political recognition extends to all the existing States of Europe, with their colonial dependencies, in so far as these are peopled by persons of European birth or descent; and to the States of North and South America which have vindicated their independence of the European States of which they were colonies. The sphere of partial political recognition extends to Turkey in Europe and Asia, and to the old historical States of Asia which have not become European dependencies –*viz.*, to Persia and the other separate States of Central Asia, to China, Siam, and Japan. The sphere of natural, or mere human recognition, extends to the residue of mankind, though here we ought, perhaps, to distinguish between the progressive and non-progressive races. It is with the first of these spheres alone that the international jurist has directly to deal. [However, he] must take cognisance of the relations in which civilised communities are placed to the partially civilised communities which surround them. He is not bound to apply the positive law of nations to savages, or even to barbarians, as such; but he is bound to ascertain the points at which, and the directions in which, barbarians or savages come within the scope of partial recognition. In the case of the Turks we have had a bitter experience of extending the rights of civilisation to barbarians who have proved to be incapable of performing its duties, and who possibly do not even belong to the progressive races of mankind.[18]

---

16 H. Wheaton, *Elements of International Law* (London: The Clarendon Press, 1866), at pp. 17–18.
17 J. Westlake, *International Law* (Cambridge, MA: The University Press, 1904), Pt 1, at pp. 40.
18 J. Lorimer, *The Institutes of the Law of Nations* (Edinburgh: William Blackwood and Sons, 1883), at pp. 101–02. We were also able to find such unbecoming inscriptions of 'otherness' in other unexpected quarters. Hegel had occasion to vituperate: 'The Negro, exhibits the natural man in his completely wild and untame state. We must lay aside all thought of reverence and morality – all that we call feeling – if we would rightly comprehend him; there is nothing harmonious with humanity to be found in this type of character . . . . They have no knowledge of the immortality of the soul . . . the devouring of human flesh is altogether consonant with the general principles of the African race': Georg Wilhelm Friedrich Hegel, cited in V. L Poliakov, *The Aryan Myth: A History of Racist and Nationalist Ideas in Europe* (New York: Basic Books, 1974), p. 241. For more discussion of the inscription of the 'other'. see N. Chabani Manganyi, 'Making Strange: Race, Science and Ethnopsychiatric Discourse' in Francis Barker *et al.*, *Europe and its others*, Vol. 1, *Proceedings of the Essex Conference on the Sociology of Literature July 1984* (Essex: University of Essex, 1985), p. 152ff.

It is astonishing, however, to note that it was indeed a civilised Africa with recognisable states, kingdoms, cities, towns, villages, clans and spheres of influence that the pioneer European explorers and traders encountered; hence, it was possible for them to enter into mutual treaties, agreements and complex arrangements. As Walter Rodney correctly maintained, 'When Cecil Rhodes sent in his agents to rob and steal in Zimbabwe, they and other Europeans marvelled at the surviving ruins of the Zimbabwe culture, and automatically assumed that it had been built by white people'.[19] Even today there is a lasting tendency to consider evidence of significant achievements of every major African group with a sense of wonder rather than with the calm acceptance that it was 'a perfectly logical outgrowth of human social development within Africa, as part of the universal process by which man's labour opened up new horizons'.[20] Nothing defeats the idea that Europe brought civilisation to all of Africa (or that without European intervention the destiny of Africa till date would have been one of barbarism) than the account of forthright pioneer Europeans who came in contact with African peoples before the ideology of racism, deemed necessary for the subjugation of colonial peoples took root.[21] One such valuable account was given by the Dutch who visited the city of Benin in present day South-Western Nigeria; they described a highly civilised town with sophisticated tastes and advanced citizenry:

> The town seems to be very great. When you enter into it, you go into a great broad street, not paved, which seems to be seven or eight times broader than the Warmoes street in Amsterdam...
>
> The king's palace is a collection of buildings which occupy as much space as the town of Harlem, and which is enclosed with walls. There are numerous apartments for the Prince's ministers and fine galleries, most of which are as big as those on the Exchange at Amsterdam. They are supported by wooden pillars encased with copper, where their victories are depicted, and which are carefully kept very clean.
>
> The town is composed of thirty main streets, very straight and 120 feet wide, apart from an infinity of small intersecting streets. The houses are close to one another, arranged in good order. These people are in no way inferior to the Dutch as regards cleanliness; they wash and scrub their houses so well that they are polished and shining like a looking-glass.[22]

Despite glaring evidence that there were very many advanced cultures and political systems in Africa prior to the era of colonialism some of the direct

---

19 Walter Rodney, *How Europe Underdeveloped Africa*, (London: Bogle-L'Ouverture Publications, and Tanzanian Publishing House, Dar-Es-Salaam, 1983), p. 55.
20 Ibid.
21 Ibid., p. 61.
22 Ibid., p. 62.

participants in European colonisation chose to record a different reality. As one writer impressively reports:

> In the battle for the empty spaces of Africa – the so called 'Dark Continent' – France and Britain Germany, Belgium, Portugal resort not only to force but a whole slew of theories and rhetoric to justifying their plunder. The Most famous of such devices is the French notion of the civilising mission – *la Mission Civilisatrice*, a notion underlying which is the idea that some races *and cultures* have an higher aim in life than others. This gives the more powerful, the more developed, the more civilised, the higher, the right to colonise others not in the name of brute force or plunder both of which are standard components of the exercise, but in the name of a noble ideal.[23]

Conrad's narrative in his *Heart of Darkness* contains a brutally honest appraisal of the colonial enterprise. He wrote: 'The conquest of the earth, which mostly means the taking it away from those who have a different complexion or who have slightly flatter noses than us, is not a pretty thing when you look into it too much'.[24] In other words colonialism and the creation of modern African state territories was simply the result of the self-reinforcing theories of predestined pre-eminence held by competing imperial powers. These mainly Western European empires used a narrow international law that applied mostly among them to arrogate, sometimes fraudulently, the territory and destinies of others. In other words the international law that was allowed to operate and flourish was the sort which gave sanctimony to acts of plunder and subjugation. In essence a new international law was effectively created to permit the grand schemes of colonialism in the nineteenth and twentieth centuries. International law in this way became the handmaiden of oppression. More unfortunately the international law created in this period among European states is largely regarded as the real beginnings of contemporary international law as we know it today.

Christopher Fyfe, a reputable historian of Sierra Leone, wrote about the creeping racialism that accompanied colonialism throughout Africa. He observed that in the large new protectorates that were tacked on to existing small British colonies in West Africa there was no place for literate Africans. Whites ruled and blacks obeyed. Inexorably the racial rule of the protectorates seeped into the colonies. Perhaps one of the most pernicious effects and legacy of this period has been the way it has sanctified the 'airbrushing' of history in such a way that the very nations that meted out the extreme violence of the colonial project have somehow emerged as the custodians of a pure discipline of international law. Whereas in truth much of the actions of the Western colonial powers were indeed

---

23 Edward Said, "The Myth of 'The Clash Of Civilizations'" (Northampton: Media Education Foundation, 1998), p. 5 available at http://www.mediaed.org/assets/products/404/transcript_404.pdf, accessed 5 August 2014.
24 Joseph Conrad, "Heart of Darkness," in *Youth and Two Other Stories* (Garden City: Doubleday, Page, 1915), pp. 50–51.

incompatible even with the existing law among nations of the period as well as inter-civilizational engagements and understandings. The sudden manner in which protectorate agreements and trade pacts were twisted around and turned into legal basis for colonialism came as a rude shock to the vast majority of African ethnic groups, and kingdoms and wars were fought over the issue although most dissenters were beaten back into submission. These forms of conduct caused severe upset among the comity of nations in Africa and the world over. The very spectacular success of the grand scheme of colonisation across the globe and in favour of the Western patrons is a strong indication that most precolonial societies literally could not believe the audacity let alone the legality of what went on. The military might and various strategic advantages retained by the colonisers made it impossible for most parts of Africa and other areas of the developing world to meaningfully resist; and they serially lost their sovereignties. Ironically the architects of the policy of colonisation have emerged to proclaim authorship of the law of nations and have been accorded the status of civilisers of mankind. Europe is, therefore, apparently credited not only with originating and evolving international law but also with engaging in colonialism for higher motives and with a civilising mission.[25] Historical facts, however, do not bear this as correct. As a distinguished commentator reiterated:

> It is within the continent of Africa that the Great Pharaohs of Egypt lived in decadent splendour while Europe and many parts of the world wallowed in primitivity and the dark ages. It was within the territorial boundaries of Africa that some of the key elements of the present world civilisations have developed.[26]

By most accounts, records of Western culture in Europe more or less began with Ancient Greece and Ancient Rome. Christianisation furthered the development of Western culture during the Middle Ages and the reform and modernisation triggered by the Renaissance led to the onset of globalisation by successive European empires, by which the major tenets of European ways of life and European legal methods spread around the world between the sixteenth

---

25 Levitt, op.cit. p. viii. As Hochschild correctly observed: 'Underlying much of Europe's excitement was the hope that Africa would be a source of raw materials to feed the Industrial Revolution, just as the search for raw materials – slaves – for the colonial plantation economy had driven most of Europe's earlier dealings with Africa. Expections quickened dramatically after prospectors discovered diamonds in South Africa in 1867 and gold some two decades later. But Europeans liked to think of themselves as having higher motives. The British, in particular, fervently believed in bringing "civilisation" and Christianity to the natives; they were curious about what lay in the continent': Hochschild, *King Leopold's Ghost: A Story of Greed, Terror, and Heroism in Colonial Africa* (Oxford: Macmillan, 1999), p. 27.
26 Remarks made by Commander O. P. Fingesi, President of the Second World Black and African Festival of Arts and Culture, Nigeria's Federal Commissioner for Special Disputes at the Opening Colloquium of the Second World Black and African Festival of Arts and Culture, Lagos, Nigeria, on Monday 17 January 1977 at the National Theatre, Lagos. A. U. Iwara and E. Mveng (eds.), *Colloquium on Black Civilisation and Education Colloquum Proceedings*, Vol. I (Lagos, 15 January. 2012, 1977), p. 14.

and twentieth centuries. Immense influence has been exerted by European westernisation over the world and extremely impressive human progress has in many fields been championed in this way. However, to claim authorship over the very idea of international legal framework among nations and peoples is an idea colossal in its shortcomings. For instance, this view does not account for abundant records of the contributions of other races and peoples to important doctrines like international boundary marking, bilateral and multilateral treaties, diplomatic representation, asylum practice, cease-fire agreements and declarations of war and peace. Examples of these dating back thousands of years are replete in the practice of African, Asian, and Middle Eastern and other places in the so-called old world. Ngenda persuasively describes such insidious appropriation of international law as: 'the violence and nature of law by which distinction and definition is constituted by difference from the "other" while, incongruously, still encompassing the very being of the "other".'[27]

1.1.2 Why the House always wins

The suspicion with which African scholars and statesmen continue to regard the fields of modern international law and contemporary international courts is justified on many levels – not least the fact that it was the tool by which their entire lands were taken over.[28] This is discernible in at least three ways. First, there was highly effective use of concocted international legal principles against the interest of weaker states many of which are in Africa. International legal principles were concocted to introduce and legitimise colonisation ranging from annexation to various forms of protectorates. In time, even when the colonial era began to recede, new techniques of neocolonisation were introduced to neutralise charges of colonisation while conserving its advantages. There were dubious military pacts and trading rights, the pressure of public loans, large-scale private firms and open door policies that really worked in one direction. Egypt, Morocco and the Congo among others were forced to lower their tariffs under a liberal

---

27 Akalemwa Ngenda, 'The Nature of the International Intellectual Property System: Universal Norms and Values or Western Chauvinism?', Vol. 14, *Information and Communications Technology Law*, No. 1, (2005) p. 2. For more on this theme of intellectual appropriation see John M. Hobson, *The Eastern Origins of Western Civilisation* (Cambridge University Press, 2004), pp. 11, 102, 296. Reg Little, 'Review of John M. Hobson *The Eastern Origins of Western Civilization*', Vol. 7, *The Culture Mandala* (1) (2007); John A. Hall, 'Review of The Eastern Origins of Western Civilization', Vol. CXIII, *English Historical Review*, No. 495 (2007).

28 Many of the early European explorers mischievously construed Africa as essentially empty and an 'unpeopled country'. The British American explorer of central Africa, Morton Stanley, exposed this unsatisfactory mindset in statements attributed to him in Hochschild's work: 'There are plenty of . . . Pilgrim Fathers among the Anglo-Saxon race yet, and when America is filled up with their descendants, who shall say that Africa . . . shall not not be their next resting place?'. In the true tradition of the European instinct of aggrandisement of his day, Stanley also said: 'What a settlement one could have in this valley! See, it is broad enough to support a large population. Fancy a church spire rising where that tamarind rears its dark crown of foliage, and think how well a score or two of pretty cottages would look instead of those clumps and gum trees!', Adam Hochschild, op. cit. p. 31.

agenda which the colonial powers essentially were not equally prepared to suffer at home.[29]

It has, thus, for long been argued that much of western law, including international law (selectively codified and applied since Grotian scholarship), has developed in response to requirements of western trade, business and politics.[30] Judge Amman in the *Barcelona Traction Case* noted that '. . . certain customs of wide scope became incorporated into positive law when in fact they were the work of five or six powers.' Eminent African jurists and even African judges on the Bench of the International Court of Justice have drawn attention to this credibility gap.[31] As one commentator put it, 'a major research theme that unites this diverse anti-colonial intellectual tradition is its primary focus on arguing about the limits within which the newly independent nations of Africa would embrace an international law that was Eurocentric in its geographic origin.'[32]

Second, there was the effective application of 'carrot and stick' stratagems and successful manipulation of the entire African continent through the resort to the 'game theory' and other cooperative synchronisation of interests – that typify the actions of the western states. This aspect of Western European international relations has been particularly devastating on African peoples as very little was 'off the table' in the coercion of their nations and subjugation of their interests. Hochschild's brilliant study of the Congo, for instance, reveals how all Europe and the USA contributed to the making of King Leoplold's holocaust of the Congolese people.[33] Similar disregard for the sovereign interests of the Congolese people survived well into the era of political independence when the decision to assassinate the premier democratically elected Prime Minister of the Country, Patrice Lumumba was taken by several Western countries.[34]

Third, there was the effective arrogation of authorship and the liberal use of the 'power of inscription' which have contributed to the literal perception of ownership of international law by powerful western states. Where *lex lata* is sufficiently in favour of an African State as against its Western counterpart,

---

29 Reuter, *International Institutions*, trans. J.M. Chapman (London: George Allen & Urwin Ltd, 1958), p. 59.
30 O. J. Lissitzyn, 'International Law in a Divided World', *International Conciliation*, 37 (March 1963).
31 *Barcelona Traction* Case (*Belgium* v *Spain*), 1958 ICJ REP. 308. Materials on all ICJ cases are available online at http://www.icj-cij.org. For wider perspectives of this issue see the following: Wade Mansell *et al.*, *A Critical Introduction to Law*, (London: Cavendish, 1995), pp. 1-27 *et passim;* Surya P. Sinha, *Legal Polycentricity and International Law*, (Durham, NC: Carolina Academic Press, 1996); Siba N'zatioula Grovogusi, *Sovereigns, Quasi Sovereigns and Africans: Race Self Determination in International Law* (Minneapolis, MN: University of Minnesota Press, 1996).
32 James Thuo Gathii, 'Review Essay': *International Law and Eurocentricity: Introduction*, 9 *European Journal of International Law*,185 (1997).
33 Hochschild, op.cit.
34 The casual manner in which African destinies are wittingly and unwittingly being altered is described by Hochschild in a personal account, thus: 'In an Leopoldville apartment, I heard a CIA man, who had too much to drink, describe with satisfaction exactly how and where the newly independent country's prime minister, Patrice Lumumba, had been killed a few months earlier. He assumed that any American, even a visiting student like me, would share his relief at the assassination of a man the United States government considered a dangerous leftist troublemaker', ibid., p. 3.

development of the law is arguably accelerated to reverse the advantage.[35] When *lex feranda* is postulated in the interests of justice by African states, the formal and substantive qualities of international law is affirmed. Much more telling is the contemporary evidence of all three even in relation to territorial control, international boundary law and international relations.

1.2 Eurocentricity and the applicable international boundary laws

The game theory principle was introduced primarily as a doctrine within the field of theoretical economics. Yet, this principle, arguably, also has applications within the fields of international law and international relations. It can be used to explain the behaviour of the leading western states in their interactions and engagements with the rest of the world. There is little doubt that the western powers continue to rely on each other in the creation of the perfect conditions for an unequal world. This was true of the colonial period, and continues unabated as a general principle of relations with the developing world to date. Very few limits exist in terms of the human or legal interests of other states or peoples that may be sacrificed in furtherance of the cooperative game behaviour of the powerful states. Justice Gibbs takes judicial notice of this philosophy in his judgment concerning the emptying and 'unpeopling' of the African peoples of Chagos Island by the UK, in favour of the creation of US military bases, and in gross violation of the principles expressed in Articles 8 and 13 of the Universal Declaration of Human Rights, (UDHR),[36] as well as the provisions of the much celebrated Magna Carta.[37]

> It is unarguable that the purposes of the BIOT Order and the Ordinance were to facilitate the use of Diego Garcia as a strategic military base and to restrict the use and occupation of that and the other islands within the territory to the extent necessary to ensure the effectiveness and security of the base. Those purposes were (or could at least reasonably be described as) of great benefit to the United Kingdom and the western powers as a whole.[38]

---

35 Note the eagerness of Lord Denning to depart from precedence in favour of finding liability for the Central Bank of Nigeria in the *Trendtex* case: 'Ought we not to act now? Whenever a change is made, some one some time has to make the first move. One country alone may start the process. Others may follow. At first a trickle, then a stream, last a flood . . . I would use of international law the words, which Galileo used of the earth: "But it does move." International law does change: and the Courts have applied the changes without the aid of any Act of Parliament'. See Lord Denning's judgment, *Trendtex Trading Corporation v. Central Bank of Nigeria* [1977] 1 All E.R. 881 at 889.
36 Universal Declaration of Human Rights, G. A. res. 217A (III), UN Doc A/810 at 71, adopted 10 December 1948.
37 Article 39 of the 1215 version; Article 29 of the next versions. Sir Paul Gore-Booth, senior official at the Foreign Office, wrote to a diplomat in 1966: 'We must surely be very tough about this. The object of the exercise is to get some rocks which will remain ours . . . There will be no indigenous population except seagulls', BBC News, 'The Chagos Islands: A Sordid Tale', 3 November, 2000. Available at http://news.bbc.co.uk/1/hi/uk_politics/1005064.stm, accessed 27 April 2013.
38 *R. (on the application of Bancoult) v Secretary of State for the Foreign and Commonwealth Office* [2001] QB 1067.

Clearly, thus, one Western state will rely on legal principles and its own national laws and courts to protect the interests of another Western state against the very existence and territorial interest of an African state. Perhaps even more fascinating is the emerging picture that one European state (Spain) would soften claims to its own territorial jurisdiction against another European state where it is clear that doing so would enable it to continue to exercise territorial jurisdiction over territories in Africa. Declassified documents from the 1980s released by the UK Foreign Office reveal that King Juan Carlos of Spain told Britain that Spain 'did not really want' Gibraltar back as it would lead to claims from Morocco for Spanish territories of Ceuta and Melilla in North Africa.[39]

By far the greatest disappointment collectively perceived by African boundary scholars in relation to contemporary international law is in relation to the Eurocentricity of the applicable international boundary laws. African countries have repeatedly been short-changed in terms of the justice meted out to them by international courts and international arbitral tribunals. This trend is particularly disturbing when the courts in issue are the major international courts such as the International Court of Justice (ICJ)[40] and the Permanent Court of Justice (PCA).[41] It is probably correct to add that many of the issues that would be treated by the ICJ and the PCA when dealing with disputes involving African states would not necessarily call for specialised knowledge of African affairs or indeed require sensitivity towards developing states issues.[42] Yet it is important to stress that since most of the cases that come before these institutions involve boundary and territorial disputes emanating from situations created by their colonial experience, it becomes incumbent on the courts to develop a special competence in these matters and to develop a critical jurisprudence.

This is why it is particularly disconcerting that the ICJ (also known as the World Court) has not developed a clear jurisprudence in this area taking into account the particular interests of African states. This tendency has prompted Judge Ajibola to attest in his separate opinion to the *Territorial Dispute* (Libyan Arab

---

39 The King of Spain was said to have admitted privately in a meeting with the then British ambassador to Madrid, Sir Richard Parsons, that it was 'not in Spain's interest to recover Gibraltar in the near future'. If it did so, 'King Hassan would immediately reactivate the Moroccan claim to Ceuta and Melilla.' Spain, however, continues to reiterate calls for sovereignty over Gibraltar: Fiona Govan, 'Spain's King Juan Carlos told Britain: "we don't want Gibraltar back"' *The Telegraph*, 7 January 2014, available at http://www.telegraph.co.uk/news/worldnews/europe/gibraltar/10554172/Spains-King-Juan-Carlos-told-Britain-we-dont-want-Gibraltar-back.html (accessed 8 January 2014).
40 Materials on all ICJ cases and information about the World Court itself are available online at www.icj-cij.org.
41 Cases and materials of the PCA are available online at www.pca-cpa.org.
42 For instance, the proceedings Guinea-Bissau instituted against Senegal in *Case Concerning The Arbitral Award of 31 July 1989* was in respect of a dispute concerning the existence and the validity of the Arbitral Award delivered on 31 July 1989 by an Arbitration Tribunal consisting of three arbitrators and established pursuant to an Arbitration Agreement concluded by the two states on 12 March 1985. Available at http://www.icj-cij.org/icjwww/idecisions/isummaries/igbssummary911112.htm, accessed 15 December 2014.

18 Africa: Birthing the empire of law

Jamahiriya/Chad) that it appeared as if territorial issues relating to Africa are constantly being judged from Eurocentric eyes.[43] Professor Allott's remark in his work, *Boundaries and Law in Africa* betrays the perplexities that afflict most judges and arbitrators when confronted with complicated African boundary and territorial disputes. He wrote: 'I feel that one can very easily lose one's way in a discussion on political problems in Africa, minority problems, territorial disputes, imperialism etc.' This is precisely what appears to have been the fate of most of the judges of the leading international courts in attempting to resolve these disputes.[44]

In light of this reality, it is indeed a wonder that developing states generally, and African states in particular, continue to express tremendous support for international laws and that they respect the decisions of international courts and tribunals in the vast majority of cases. The acceptance of the reality of international law by African states is important in refuting the proposition that international law is not law. African states have always been among those states that are said to have developed a 'law habit' as noted by a host of writers including Morgenthau, Brierly and Shaw.[45] This is equally true of most developing states in the international system. The vigour displayed by Robert Mugabe to avert the suspension of Zimbabwe from the Commonwealth in 2002 attests to the importance attached by states to even largely symbolic sanctions. International law has indeed also worked in favour of African states such as when international sanctions helped to bring about the end of the evil system of apartheid in South Africa. When Saddam Hussein ordered the invasion and 'annexation' of Kuwait in 1990, he did not claim that he was intent on breaking the law but he attempted rather unsuccessfully to justify what he had done in terms of international law. In fact he claimed that what he had done was consistent with international law, arguing that it was an act of self-defence and that historically Iraq had irrefutable claims to Kuwait. China in its claim to Taiwan and Tibet continues to elaborate its position from a legal point of view. The erstwhile Apartheid regime and the Israeli occupation of the West Bank and Gaza are some of the difficult *de facto* situations in relation to which attempts have been made to justify questionable State conduct using arguments under international law rather than denial of its application. In this way the great majority of the rules of international law are generally observed by all nations without actual compulsion, for it is generally in the interest of all nations concerned to honour their obligations under international law.

---

43 Territorial Dispute (Libyan Arab Jamahiriya/Chad), Judgment of 13 February 1994, Separate Opinion of Judge Ajibola, para. 8, available at www.icj-cij.org/icjwww/icases/idt/idt_ijudgments idt_ijudgment_19920203_separateAjibola.pdf, (accessed 1 April 2013).
44 A. Allott, 'Boundaries and the Law in Africa', in C.G Widstrand (ed) *African Boundaries Problems* (1969), p. 9.
45 Morgenthau, *Politics Among Nations* 6th ed. (New York: McGraw Hill, 1985), pp. 312–13; Brierly, *The Law of Nations*, revised by H. Waldock 6th ed., (Oxford: Clarendon Press, 1963), pp. 41–2, 68–76; G. Schwarzenberger, *A Manual of International Law*, 3rd ed. (London: Stevens and Sons., 1952), p. 3; M.N. Shaw, *International Law*, 4th ed. (Cambridge: Cambridge University Press, 2001), pp. 1–3.

This realisation explains the submission of African states to the corpus of international law. It also explains the commitment of African states to resolving their boundary disputes under the rule of international law. Resolution by reference to international legal principles and processes is one of the commendable features of African diplomacy and international legal practice. Rather than resorting to open armed conflict in a systematic manner they have largely adopted the resort to open judicial settlement of the disputes principally by extensive negotiations and where that failed reference to the World Court based at The Hague. They have done so on such a regular basis that one writer aptly notes, 'Anyone hoping to learn about Africa's positive contributions to international law might begin by scoffing at the proposition that a chapter in such analysis could be found in the continent's resolution of boundary dispute.'[46] It is indeed true that the situation by many projections ought to be worse. In 1983 the erstwhile Algerian President Chadly Benjedid problematised the inherited boundaries of the continent as '. . . delayed action bombs left by colonialism'.[47] Older nations like China and its neighbours in East Asia continue to have volatile interruptions to their foreign relation as a result of differences over their land and maritime boundaries. In contrast, the faith of African states in the ICJ (and more often than not willingness to abide by its decisions), despite an initial scepticism arising out of the *South West Africa* cases, has helped to legitimise the ICJ as an arbiter of disputes between states.[48]

The readiness and record of African states to adopt the adjudicatory route for the settlement of boundary disputes will be discussed quite extensively later in this book. It must, however, be noted that this does not mean that any law of oppression must be unquestionably given effect to. International Courts, arbitral tribunals as well as mediators, can free themselves from the shackles of mechanistic loyalty to an oppressive applicable law in relation to boundary matters. Particularly in relation to adoption and application of colonial law *per se*, a more confident tone is gradually emerging from the jurisprudence of certain judges in relation to African cases. One such view was expressed by Judge *ad hoc* Abi-Saab, in his separate opinion appended to the judgment in the case concerning the *Frontier Dispute* (Burkina Faso/Republic of Mali). Rejecting the imperative of always granting unquestioning sanctimony to colonial laws, he noted that the Chamber had been led into 'an excessively detailed analysis of French colonial law, a task which is not, in my view, a fitting one for an international court and was largely superfluous'.[49] It is becoming generally clear especially to non-western judges that precautions ought to be taken in judgments when considering colonial law. As the learned Judge added: '. . . there can therefore be no question of even circuitously finding in contemporary international law any retroactive legitimation whatever

---

46 J. H. Samuels, 'Redrawing the Map: Boundary Dispute Resolution in Africa', in Levitt, op.cit., p. 226.
47 Cited in V. Prescott and G. D. Triggs, *International Frontiers and Boundaries: Law, Politics and Geography* (Leiden: Martinus Nijhoff, 2008), p. 313.
48 Ibid p. 228.
49 *ICJ Reports*, 1986, p. 659, para. 3.

of colonialism as an institution.'[50] The World Court has indeed in relation to African cases sought to clarify the function conferred on colonial law. Colonial law 'may play a role not in itself (as if there were a sort of continuum juris, a legal relay between such law and international law), but only as one factual element among others, or as evidence indicative of what has been called the 'colonial heritage.'[51]

In fact, it is not a question of legitimating *a posteriori* an institution which law and history have definitively classed among those which have been profoundly violent and unjust because of their violation of the dignity and freedoms of entire populations. The question is whether, when drawing frontiers, contemporary international law can rely on law produced by such an institution, even though it involved only administrative boundaries which, moreover, attached little importance to the populations concerned and their historical and sociological relationships. In many ways the way forward may lie in courageous policy suggested by Judge *ad hoc* Abi-Saab. He sought to qualify this paradox by advocating recourse to 'considerations of equity *infra legem*'. For instance, when applying the controversial *uti possidetis juris* doctrine, a court should take account of the intertemporal law but should not ignore the fate of the populations concerned. This in the words of Judge Bennouna is how to ensure that the same injustices that were perpetrated by artificial and brutal frontiers, at times following parallels or meridians, are not 'legitimated' by an international judicial organ operating in the twenty-first century.[52]

Unfortunately, much of the pertinent literature has given little credit for the collective approach and legalism of African states to the management of their inherently flawed inherited colonial boundaries. The relative peace over boundaries is on the other hand quite surprisingly attributed even in recent literature to the doubtful proposition expressed by Prescott and G. D. Triggs that colonial boundary making was exceptional and that if the European powers were guilty of anything it was to have hurriedly brought the colonial projects to an end.[53] In the

---

50 Ibid., para. 4.
51 *Case concerning the Frontier Dispute* (Burkina Faso/Republic of Mali), Judgment, ICJ Reports 1986, p. 568, para. 30.
52 Declaration Of Judge Bennouna available at http://www.icj-cij.org/docket/files/149/17308.pdf, accessed 3 April 2014.
53 This strand of conservative thinking needs to be debunked. It is premised on the idea that perhaps, African states got their independence too quickly. Others in this school of thought also ascribe the hurried nature of the independence epoch for the insensitive stitching together of African states especially where there is evidence of careless mapping of African territories. The argument that the withdrawal of colonial administration from Africa should have been slower may actually be offensive to the very idea of liberty and justice. The idea deserves a strong rebuttal based as it is on the presumption that Africans are actually so bereft of understanding of civilisation that independence and political freedom ought to have eluded them for much more time. Given the global nature of the practice of colonialism at its height it will appear that this argument supports the idea that the European colonisers indeed had set out to civilise the world. According to this logic, therefore, colonised territories and peoples would never have achieved civilisation as we know it but for the fact of their colonisation. Such claims are best dismissed as ludicrous and offensive to correct reason in agreement with nature.

condescending and depressing tradition of a large part of post-colonial academic commentary on Africa, the authors declared:

> The colonial powers were diligent in delimiting and even demarcating agreed boundaries and as colonies became independent states, most had a clear understanding of their territorial extent. There have been boundary disputes but only a few, considering that there are 102 bilateral boundaries. This situation has only been greatly assisted by all members of the Organisation of African Unity, making a pledge to respect the boundaries existing on the achievement of national independence. Indeed it can be argued, that the colonial powers acted much more responsibly in delimiting the territories of colonies than they did in managing their progress to independence. The scramble of European powers to divest themselves of expensive and troublesome colonies was not well managed in the period after 1956. In 1975 the dereliction of duty by the Portuguese authorities, in the decolonisation process in Africa can be judged disgraceful. Post-colonial African history has been marked and marred by civil wars, tribal massacres, political dictatorships and financial corruption on a grand scale. The most recent example involves Zimbabwe.[54]

The idea that colonial delimitation was largely competent and satisfactory is simply not true. As an exercise in self-aggrandisement, colonial delimitation of African territories was no more competent and satisfactory than the accomplishments of any conqueror in carving out and parcelling his prize into convenient units for the sole purpose of enjoying the benefits. From the contemporary African point of view moreover, and with the benefit of hindsight, the delimitation of the colonialists is not satisfactory as a matter of fact for the following reasons. First the evidence is clear even in case law as to the shoddy delimitation arrangements done by ill-informed colonial geographers and administrators. Second, the evidence is also clear that there were a lot of bad faith dealings even among colonial powers themselves in relation to their efforts to appropriate territories by inventive mapping and rescinding on delimitation agreements. Third, colonial territories, protectorates and mandates were not treated in any clear manner in relation to delimitation exercises. Hence delimitation was done mainly according to the political convenience of the concerned colonial power thereby creating boundaries that made no meaning in reality even by reference to intertemporal law. The African continent is replete with dormant and active boundary 'questions' some of which have matured into disputes and some which are left dormant in the quest of the states concerned not to disturb the peaceful relations among them and in a fear not to unduly swim against the tide of the wisdom expressed in the *quieta non movere* principle of international law. Nevertheless every couple of years after independence African states declare open border disputes between

---

54 Prescott and G. D. Triggs, op.cit., p. 313.

themselves. The expired docket of the International Court of Justice stands as irrefutable evidence of these. The African Union Boundary Programme has unearthed quite a number of these ambiguities and border questions. It is quite easy to predict that many more disputes will become apparent by the middle of this century. It is to the credit of African diplomacy that a lot of problems are being settled quietly through bilateral diplomacy and negotiations.

2 Sovereignty, jurisdiction, territorial integrity and territorial acquisition in international law

The concepts of sovereignty, jurisdiction and territory have incredibly important relevance in time and space. In this chapter we will seek to establish the centrality of these concepts to international law as well as the social, natural and environmental sciences.

2.1 Concept and forms of sovereignty

Sovereignty is the absolute and perpetual power of a commonwealth, which the Latins call *majestas*; the Greeks *akra exousia, kurion arche* and *kurion politeuma*; and the Italians *segnoria* – a word they use for private persons as well as for those who have full control of the state; while the Hebrews call it *tomech shevet* – that is, the highest power of the command. We must now formulate a definition of sovereignty because no jurist or political philosopher has done so, even though it is the chief point, and the issue that most needs to be explained.[1]

Sovereignty in law and political science is a concept of universal significance – with application across human cultures and with manifestations in time and space. Its relevance to African state territories has been expressed both in antiquity and in this period of late modernity. Sovereignty in one form or another will no doubt be applicable to Africa and across all other continents until the very end of history. Therefore, we must begin by elaborating upon and interrogating this critical concept in relation to state territories and the disputes over their boundaries. Only in this way can a thorough understanding of the current challenges confronting the independent states of Africa in occupying and defending their territories be meaningfully achieved.

Sovereignty in law encapsulates the essence of the state and explains the powers of a state over its entire territories and its inhabitants. The normal complements of state rights, including the typical case of legal competence, are described commonly as sovereignty.[2] The concept is political in conception and is popularly

---

1 Julian H. Franklin (ed.), *Jean Bodin, On Sovereignty: Four Chapters from the Six Books of the Commonwealth* (Cambridge: Cambridge University Press, 1992), p. 1.
2 Ian Brownlie, *Principles of Public International Law* (Oxford: Clarendon Press, 1998), p. 106.

symbolised by the Leviathan of Hobbes. It implies the supreme authority of a state, which recognises no higher authority in the region.[3] Bodin developed the concept in terms of internal strength and external limitation of power.[4] He took the view that sovereignty is not only absolute; it was also indivisible. Accordingly, he expressed the idea that concentration of power in the ruler is an essential condition of the state. Bodin's conclusion about the King of France in 1576 as an absolute power in relation to whom any apparent restraints are mere recommendations and definitely not constitutional arrangements, was among the reasons why Bodin's account of sovereignty was both a source of confusion and at the same time 'a major event in the development of European political thought'.[5] To the African mind, however, the naked pre-eminence of the concept of sovereignty has always been there and clearly understood by ruler sovereigns and their subjects. Royal absolutism over the territorial extents that a people occupy is a central feature of many African societies and precolonial states. The African King is exemplified by the Yoruba King -an *Oba*, who is referred to as '*Alase Ikeji Orisa*' and '*Iku baba Yeye*' (overall commander, partner of the gods; and owner of the very rights to life and death). This conceptualisation of sovereignty is not to say that the power of the King to rule is not shared or delegated to other chieftains and persons with magisterial authority within the realm such as the *Baales* nor does it mean that the followership and the entire people do not appreciate that sovereignty flows from them collectively upwards to the King. What is collectively realised is the need to secure their collective sovereignty by means of giving prerogative to a political authority that must hold it exclusively without acknowledging any other superior or equal in its territory. To defend territory is to retain sovereignty and to conquer other territories is to increase the reach of the territorial sovereign. Hence the many wars over territorial acquisition replete in the precolonial histories of African states and societies. The concentration of high powers of government in a single individual or group as an embodiment of collective right to sovereignty over a specific territory is not only African but very much part of universal legal history.[6]

Jowitt picks up on this theme and defines sovereignty as: '[t]he power in a state to which none other is superior'.[7] As the respected jurist Max Huber wrote in his opinion in the *Island of Palmas Arbitration* between the US and the Netherlands, '[s]overeignty in the relations between states signifies independence. Independence in regards to a portion of the globe is the right to exercise therein to the exclusion of any other the functions of a state ...'.[8] In modern literature the term

---

3 G. S. Sachdeva, "Sovereignty in the Air – A Legal Perspective", 22 *Indian Journal of International Law* (1982), p. 398.
4 Imre Anthony Csabafi, *The Concept of the State Jurisdiction in International Space Law: A Study in the Development of Space Law in the United Nations* (Hague: Martinus Nijthoff, 1971), p. 50.
5 Franklin, op.cit., p. xii.
6 Ibid., p xv.
7 *Jowitts Dictionary of English Law*, 2nd edn, Vol. 2, John Burke (ed.), (London: Sweet and Maxwell, 1977), p. 1678.
8 *Island of Palmas Case* (1928) RIAA; Vol. 2, p. 829.

'sovereignty' has been employed in four different ways: not necessarily overlapping, in the sense that a state can have one and not necessarily the other. They are –

- international legal sovereignty
- Westphalian sovereignty
- domestic sovereignty, and
- interdependence sovereignty.

Reference to international legal sovereignty denotes the practices that are associated with mutual recognition, usually between territorial entities that possess formal juridical independence. Westphalian sovereignty refers to political organisation, which is based on the exclusion of external actors from authority structures within a specific territory. Domestic sovereignty explains the ability of a state to exercise effective control within its territory and the competence to construct formal organisation of political authority within the polity. Lastly, interdependence sovereignty is used in reference to the ability of public authorities to regulate the flow of information, ideas, goods, people, pollutants, or capital across the borders of their state.[9]

The principle of sovereignty is also embodied in various important treaties. Article 2(1) of the UN Charter gives effect to the concept.[10] It is further elaborated upon in the provisions of the 1970 UN General Assembly Declaration on Principles of International Law concerning Friendly Relations and Co-operation among States in accordance with the Charter of the United Nations, as follows: 'All states enjoy sovereign equality . . . Each state enjoys the right inherent in full sovereignty . . .'.[11] However, Schwarzenberger rightly describes this emphasis on complete independence as 'negative sovereignty'. Negative sovereignty means non-recognition of any superior authority. On the level of legal relations, this situation may be expressed in terms of a right, or freedom not to have to recognise any superior.[12] It is indeed true that the limitation of sovereignty to its absolute extreme is as little justified as the attribution of a necessarily absolute character to

---

9 International legal sovereignty and Westphalian sovereignty centre upon issues of legitimacy and authority but exclude control. However, they are both based on what Krasner calls 'certain distinct rules or logic of appropriateness'. The rule for international legal sovereignty is that recognition is extended to territorial entities which possess formal juridical independence while the rule for Westphalian sovereignty is the exclusion of external actors both *de facto* or *de jure*, from state territory. On the other hand, domestic sovereignty involves both authority and control in the sense that it encompasses the specification of legitimate authority within a given state and the extent to which that authority may be exercised. Interdependence sovereignty is exclusively concerned with control and not authority since it explains the inherent capacity of the state to regulate movements across its borders. See Stephen D. Krasner, *Sovereignty: Organised Hypocrisy*, (New Jersey: Princeton University Press, 1999), pp. 3–4.
10 It reads thus: 'The Organization is based on the principle of the *sovereign* equality of all its Members'. Charter of the United Nations San Francisco, 26 June 1945. In force 24 October 1945. Documents on the UN Conference on International Organisation, vol. 15, p. 336.
11 Adopted by resolution 2625 (XXV) of 24 October 1970. See UNGA Official Records: Twenty-Fifth Sess., Supp. No. 28 (A/8028).
12 G. Schwarzenberger, "The Forms of Sovereignty", Vol. 10, *Current Legal Problems*, (1957) p. 264.

any other notion. In fact '... the very contrast of sovereignty of God with any form of worldly sovereignty powers proves sufficiently the necessarily relative character of any type of sovereignty claimed by a temporal authority'.[13] Social theorists like Freud, Feuerbach and Nietzsche have suggested that the very idea of religious sovereignty, in terms of a supreme, infinite and supervenient power, is born of the human experience of smallness and vulnerability in a huge and overwhelming universe and that it is this experience that drives the need for containment into political and territorial units.[14] The dictates of our modern day international society seem to incline towards interdependence of states more than unduly rigid exercise of sovereign powers. For this reason, some writers insist that political sovereignty has always been something of a fiction. This is said to be especially so in the case of democracies where the pre-eminence of sovereign power slides in favour of sovereignty of the people rather than sovereignty in the autonomous state.

Yet the association of sovereignty with God deserves some elaboration.

> The state can be divided, disunified, subordinated, even captured, and still survive. Not so political sovereignty, which, like God, is finished as soon as it is broken apart. Political sovereignty may be a secularised theological concept, but secularization, we need remember, does not mean the end of religion. Rather, secularization produces religion without the sword, religion located and deployed apart from direct political purposes does not lose its religious structure or bearing, even as it ceases to have the direct authority of God at its heart. As 'secular' political authority is substituted for God's, the religious modality of the authority persists. Paradoxically, religion indirectly recovers its sword as it re-emerges in the form of political sovereignty.[15]

Ultimately, therefore, the imperative of loyalty to state within its territorial constraints was always meant to be akin to the demand of loyalty to God. This fiction is so important to the human project of societal organisation that it survives perhaps unchallenged to date, despite developments of secularisation, globalisation or interdependence and despite disagreements as to the conceptualisation of God even in the multi-faith religious states that most African states are today.

On another level of legal relations, a complete lack of sovereignty over a territory or environment may be dictated by international law. For instance, Article 137 of the Convention on the Law of the Sea 1982,[16] states that no state shall claim or exercise sovereignty or sovereign rights over any part of the Area or its resources, nor shall any state or natural juridical person appropriate any part thereof. Thus, while Schwarzenberger speaks of *negative sovereignty* in terms of absolute and complete independence, modern day international law actually

---

13 Ibid., p. 276.
14 Wendy Brown, *Walled States, Waning Sovereignty* (New York: Zone Books, 2010), p. 71.
15 Wendy Brown, op.cit., p. 70.
16 UN Doc A/CONF. 62/122; (1982) 21 ILM 1261.

moves in the direction of *negativing* sovereignty. However, wherever sovereignty cannot be exercised, jurisdiction is not excluded.

The Chinese view on state sovereignty is that it is tantamount to territorial integrity and that ascertainment of territorial boundaries is a factor necessarily 'conducive to the sound development of relations with neighbours' and 'peace and stability in the border regions'.[17] A likely model in terms of legal and political attitude to boundary cooperation and management is that expressed by one Chinese delegate to the 2nd International Symposium on Land, Maritime, River and Lake Boundaries held in Maputo, who asserted:

> We would continue to uphold the policy of friendship and partnership with all neighbours and concurrently promoting security and development in the border regions, so as to create an East Asia of everlasting peace and common development.[18]

This Westphalian conceptualisation of sovereignty constitutes the predominant approach of African states and is in many ways based on their shared history of colonial experience and hard fought independence struggles.

2.2 Globalisation vs territorial sovereignty

It is a trite observation that in as much as sovereignty remains an abstraction, serious impact has been made upon the principle by a host of factors in modern day international society. Thus, international lawyers are beginning to speak more in terms of 'globalisation'. The term globalisation is one which until fairly recently was unknown to international law but which it may in fact be argued is a natural consequence of the development of that body of law itself. Wherever we look, the omnipotent nature of sovereignty is in recession. Whether the focus is on human rights, exchange rates, monetary policy, arms control, chemical weapons, landmines, warfare, environmental control or minority rights, the policy options open to states in any real sense have become increasingly constrained. Challenges to the traditional international law system of sovereignty can be seen in increases in depth and density of rules promulgated by intergovernmental organisations. These organisations are becoming more assertive *vis-à-vis* individual sovereign states both in rule-making and in implementation. National courts, administrative agencies, and perhaps even parliamentary bodies are said to increasingly function as parts of cooperative regulatory and enforcement transgovernmental networks and no longer simply as parochial national institutions.[19]

---

17 Fu Fengshan, "China's Experience in Settling Boundary Disputes and its Border Management Practice". Paper Presented at 2nd International Symposium on Land, Maritime River and Lake Boundaries: Maputo, Mozambique, 17–19 December 2008, p. 14.
18 Ibid., p. 56.
19 See Phillip Alston, "The Myopia of the Handmaidens: International Lawyers and Globalisation", *European Journal of International Law*, No. 3 (1997), p. 435. See also Benedict Kingsbury, 'Sovereignty and Inequality', Vol. 9, *European Journal of International Law*, No. 4 (1998), p. 611.

Even in Africa where governments still very much guard state sovereignty, globalisation seems to imply that territoriality is losing out as an organising principle of the modern world. On the other hand some writers think that globalisation inadvertently facilitates, if not actually encourages, separatism. Ironically, however, by creating new sovereign territories globalisation on the continent could be interpreted as an affirmation of territoriality. With the emergence of new states in Africa such as South Sudan territorial sovereignty simply replicates itself in a new political space and immediately looms large.[20] Hence the following interesting set of queries:

> Under the pressure of globalisation . . . Is the territorial state doomed while nations will prosper? Will the Westphalian system adapt to globalisation or will it be overwhelmed by it? If the latter should be the case, would the outcome resemble a globalised Columbia or a universalised Switzerland?[21]

As nation-state sovereignty wanes, it produces effects and pressures on national life which have now started to manifest internationally through religious tensions. Even with respect to advanced economies it has been noted that:

> . . .open borders are (falsely) held responsible for growing refugee and immigrant populations and border fortifications are (falsely) imagined capable of stemming this tide, porous borders are also commonly figured as the scrim through which terror slips. The two dangers, of course, are frequently twinned in the figure of the Arab Muslim. No matter that the vast majority of terror episodes in the United States have been home grown, carried out by white male citizens and aimed at state heartland, and the guns and explosives used in these attacks . . . also sourced domestically.[22]

The tensions are felt globally and in Africa it manifests in hundreds of international border skirmishes and protracted religious crises with groups like Boko Haram in northern border areas of Nigeria and the Lord's Army in Uganda.[23] Elsewhere

---

20 The Republic of South Sudan became the world's newest nation and Africa's 55th independent state on 9 July 2011, following a peaceful Referendum held in January 2011. The referendum was foreseen as part of the 2005 Comprehensive Peace Agreement (CPA) signed by the Government of the Republic of the Sudan and the then southern-based rebel group, the Sudan People's Liberation Movement, after decades of conflict. See further the World Bank website 'South Sudan Overview' available at http://www.worldbank.org/en/country/southsudan/overview, accessed 5 August 2014.
21 M. Albert and L. Brock, "What Keeps Westphalia Together? Normative Differentiation in the Modern System of States", in M. Albert, D. Jacobson and Y. Lapid (eds.) *Identities, Borders, Orders: Rethinking International Relations Theory* (Minneapolis: University of Minnesota Press, 2001), pp. 30–31.
22 Wendy Brown, op.cit, p. 69.
23 The Lord's Resistance Army (LRA) conflict affects tens of thousands of people. Originating in northern Uganda in the late 1980s, it has spread to the neighbouring countries of South Sudan, the Democratic Republic of Congo (DRC) and the Central African Republic (CAR), where continuing political instability contributes to the perpetuation of violence. See more at: http://www.c-r.org/our-work/lords-resistance-army#sthash.IjOamED.dpuf, accessed 5 August 2014.

groups like Hamas also stand in the vanguard of movements to gain sovereignty in their lands and reflect a sense of Muslim discontent with the present world order as it impacts directly on their societies. Globalisation whittles down the control of the traditional custodians of sovereignty in societies and many religious adherents resent the hegemony that seeks to impose western cultural templates on their cultures, while masquerading as universal values of freedom, justice and good governance. The problem the traditionalists have is not with the concepts themselves but 'they reject the idea that the West enjoys some sort of cultural copyright on how these values should be implemented; how they should be made part of everyday life'.[24]

The call for states to close and secure national borders is fuelled by populations anxious about everything from their physical security and economic wellbeing to their psyche of 'I' and 'we'. Today, xenophobia is so over-determined by the economic and political insecurities generated by globalisation that even politicians cognizant of the limited efficacy of border fortifications lack discursive points of entry for discussing them.[25]

The view that the nature of sovereignty has changed to the extent that we may be approaching the beginnings of a borderless world has not been unchallenged. Scholars like Krasner believe that international legal sovereignty and Westphalian concepts of sovereignty have always been characterised by 'organised hypocrisy'. He agrees with the mainstream view that with changes to the basic nature of the international system, the scope of activities over which states can effectively exercise control is declining. These include atmospheric pollution, terrorism, the drug trade, currency crisis, and acquired immunodeficiency syndrome (AIDS). He agrees that technological changes have drastically reduced the costs of transportation and communication, and that this has in turn prompted independent states to enter into binding conventions and contracts, some of which have led to a compromise of their Westphalian sovereignty by establishing external authority structures like international institutions. He, however, thinks that treaties are indeed a manifestation of international legal sovereignty possessed by states and that contemporary scholars have consistently overstated the novelty of globalisation. He reminds us that:

> Rulers have always operated in a transnational environment; autarky has rarely been an option; regulation and monitoring of transborder flows have always been problematic ... There is no evidence that globalisation has systematically undermined state control or led to the homogenisation of policies and structures. In fact, globalisation and state activity have moved in tandem.[26]

---

24 The words of Alastair Crooke of the *Conflicts Forum* in his preface to Azzam Tamimi, *Hamas: Unwritten Chapters*, (London, C. Hurst & Co.), p. x.
25 Wendy Brown, op.cit., p. 69.
26 Krasner, op. cit., pp. 12, 222–3.

It has been persuasively argued by other theorists of globalisation from a multiplicity of disciplinary backgrounds that rather than preside over the death of sovereignty and the nation state, globalisation itself will succumb to the stronger logic of human individualistic and group instinct. The features of this eventuality are identifiable in international relations. Globalisation has paved the way for unprecedented increase in economic activities as well as free liberal economic agenda. A necessary part of this agenda appears to be increasing privatisation. Privatisation, however, creates an 'age of uncertainty' whereupon the various peoples of the world react by resorting to individualistic strategies and a return to the reassurances of tribal strategies. The prediction, therefore, is that the search for stability and security will lead people to rediscover old certainties and stability in the form of ethnic, racial and national identities wherever possible within national sovereignties.[27] For African countries the neoliberalism and privatisation agenda has followed global patterns and is likely to have similar rebounding effects on the doctrine of state sovereignty.[28]

In view of these arguments it certainly must not be assumed that the death knell has been sounded on the doctrine of state sovereignty. Sovereignty remains a crucial element in today's world and its manifestation is tri-dimensional in the land, maritime and air spaces. Conceptualisation of sovereignty is definitely not a zero-sum game. What a state loses in one respect in the exercise of its sovereignty it obviously gains in some other respect. For instance, the *Lockerbie case* shows that the reach of a foreign state's power to deal with the perpetrators of aerial crimes

---

27 Hopper, *Living with Globalization* (London: Bloomsbury Academic, 2006), p. 39; Hopper in this case aligns himself with other theorists like Zygmunt Bauman who claim that '[t]he dissipation of the social rebounds in the consolidation of the tribal. As identities go, privatisation means tribalization', Zygmunt Bauman, 'From Pilgrim to Tourist – or a Short Story of Identity', in Stuart Hall and Paul du Gay (eds.), *Questions of Cultural Identity* (London: Sage), p. 57.

28 Keynesianism cultural and economic forces also had their run in Africa via the dictat of neo-colonial institutions of western nations such as the IMF, the World Bank and the OECD. In conjunction with the ascendancy of the neoliberal agenda (J. Rapley, *Understanding Development and Practice in the Developing World*, (3rd ed., New York: Lynne Rienner, 2007), p. 3) Privatisation refers to the transfer of the ownership (and the entire incidence of ownership, including management) of a public enterprise to private investors. (E. Iheme, *The Incubus: The Story of Public Enterprise in Nigeria* (Lagos: Helmsman Associates, 1997), p. 27). Colonial governments in Africa owned most agencies across Africa. The task of providing infrastructural facilities such as railways, roads, bridges, water, electricity and port facilities fell on the colonial government due to the absence of indigenous companies with the required capital as well as the inability or unwillingness of foreign trading companies to embark on these capital intensive projects. This involvement was expended and consolidated by the Colonial Welfare Development Plan (1946–56) formulated when the Labour Party came to power in the United Kingdom. (O. Igbuzor, 'Privatization in Nigeria, Critical Issues of Concern to Civil Society' (3 September 2003), paper presented at a Power Mapping Round Table Discussion on The Privatization Programme in Nigeria organised by the Socio-Economic Rights Initiative in Abuja available at http://www.dawodu.com/otive2.htm, accessed 9 December 2013. In Nigeria such enterprises include the Nigerian Railway Corporation (NRC), Nigerian Telecommunications (NITEL), Nigerian Postal Services (NIPOST) and other enterprises. E. C. Ugorji, 'Privatization/Commercialization of State-Owned Enterprises in Nigeria: Strategies for Improving the Performance of the Economy', Vol. 27, *Comparative Political Studies*, (1995), pp. 537–60.

has become more formidable even as we lament the decline of sovereignty.[29] This paradox is aptly captured in the interesting submission of one academic writer who comments that sovereignty should not be thought of 'as the object of some kind of zero sum game, such that the moment "x" loses it, "y" necessarily has it. Let us think of it rather more as of virginity, which can in at least some circumstances be lost to the general satisfaction without anybody else gaining it'.[30]

2.3 Jurisdiction within sovereignty

The doctrine of jurisdiction emerged in the seventeenth century from the concepts of sovereignty and territoriality. Its development led through the *statute theory* to the *Huber Storyan maxim* and it became fully established in the nineteenth century.[31] Jurisdiction in a strict legal sense denotes the particular rights or accumulation of rights quantitatively less than the norm, which the omnibus term of sovereignty covers. In other words, while the term 'sovereignty' covers the total legal personality of a state, jurisdiction refers to particular aspects of the substance, especially rights (or claims), liberties and powers.[32] Thus, jurisdiction is the authority a state exercises over natural and juristic persons and property

---

29 *Questions of Interpretation and Application of the 1971 Montreal Convention arising from the Aerial Incident at Lockerbie (Libyan Arab Jamahiriya v. United Kingdom) (Libyan Arab Jamahiriya v United States of America).* On 3 March 1992, Libya filed in the Registry of the Court two applications instituting proceedings against the UK and the US concerning disputes on the interpretation or application of the Convention for the Suppression of Unlawful Acts against the Safety of Civil Aviation signed in Montreal on 23 September 1971. Libya referred to charges made by the Lord Advocate of Scotland and an American Grand Jury against two Libyan nationals suspected of having caused the destruction of Pan Am flight 103 over the town of Lockerbie, Scotland, on 21 December 1988, in which 270 people died. Following these charges, the UK and the US demanded that Libya surrender the suspects for trial either in Scotland or in the US. The Security Council of the United Nations subsequently adopted three resolutions (731, 748 and 883, two of which imposed sanctions) urging Libya 'to provide a full and effective response' to the requests of the UK and US 'so as to contribute to the elimination of international terrorism'). After a protracted case, the parties agreed to a novel procedure, which is a significant victory for the long arms of national courts. This witnessed the transfer to the Netherlands, for trial by a Scottish court, of the two Libyan nationals suspected of having caused the Lockerbie incident. See also *infra*, chapter 3.
30 Alston, op. cit., p. 435, note 4. For further discussions on the shrinking of the concept of sovereignty in modern day international relations see Neil MacCormick, 'Beyond the Sovereign State', Vol. 56, *Modern Law Review*, (1993), pp. 1–18; Walter B. Wriston, *The Twilight Of Sovereignty: How The Information Revolution Is Transforming Our World* (New York: Maxwell Macmillan International, 1992); J.-M. Guehenno, *The End of the Nation State*, (Minneapolis: University of Minnesota Press, 1995), p. 435.
31 One of the leading Roman jurisconsults of the early third century AD, J. Paulus, formulated the term 'statute theory' which has long influenced the doctrine of jurisdiction. In Italy the concept '*statutum non ligat nisi subditos*' became accepted around 1200 AD. In effect it denied the absolute power of *lex fori* and around the 16th century writers like Bertrand d'Argentre spelt out the essence of the *statute theory* by distinguishing between *potestas* and jurisdiction. The 'Huber Storyan maxim' refers to the theory developed in Ulricus Huber's work titled *De Conflictu legum diversarum in diversis imperiis*, which was written in 1948. In terms of the Storyan maxim, territorial jurisdiction means that each state has exclusive jurisdiction within its own territorial domain over persons, property, things and legal transactions done within it, including the extraterritorial activities of such persons. See Csabafi, op. cit., pp. 49–51, notes 51–2.
32 Brownlie, op. cit., p. 85.

within it. It concerns mostly the exercise of this power on a state territory or quasi-territory; however, some states exercise a measure of their jurisdiction both ex-territorially and extra-territorially. States which claim ex-territorial jurisdiction threaten punishment for certain acts either against the state itself, such as high treason, forging bank notes, and the like or against its nationals, such as murder, arson, libel and slander.[33] States that claim extra-territorial jurisdiction, chiefly the United States, have taken the view that whenever activity abroad has consequences within the state which are contrary to local legislation then that state may make orders requiring such things as the disposition of patent rights and other property of foreign corporations, the reorganisation of industry in another country, or the production of documents.[34] It need only be said that this sort of jurisdiction (mostly in the context of economic issues) is a source of serious controversy between the very few states that practice it or acquiesce to its exercise and the majority of states which are opposed to it.[35]

Beale narrowly defined the concept of jurisdiction in the following words: 'The power of a sovereign to affect the rights of persons whether by legislation, by executive decree, or by judgement of a Court'.[36] This definition is narrow in that it restricts jurisdiction to powers over persons alone. In *McDonald v Mabee*,[37] Justice Holmes said that the ultimate basis of jurisdiction is 'physical power' and in *Wedding v Meyler*[38] he equated jurisdiction with 'authority'. It can, thus be said that state jurisdiction refers to the capacity of a state to exercise certain powers. That is the state's right to regulate or affect by legislative, executive or judicial measures the rights of persons, property acts or events within its borders. But such actions are not always entirely and exclusively of domestic concern.[39] Fawcet, thus correctly noted that in exercise of its sovereignty a state has the jurisdiction to forbid the entry into any part of its territory any person or thing such as aircraft or pesticide.[40] In equal manner, such jurisdiction is forbidden outside territorial

---

33 See L. F. L. Oppenheim, *International Law: A Treatise*, Vol. I, 8th edn (London: Longmans, 1963), p. 331. See also U. O. Umozurike, *Introduction to International Law*, (Lagos: Spectrum, 1993), p. 85.
34 See for example the case *U.S. v Aluminium Co. of America*, 148 F. 2d 416 (1945) and *U.S. v Watchmakers of Switzerland Information Center Inc.*, 133 F. Supp. 40 (1955); 134 F.
35 See Brownlie, op. cit., pp. 310–12; M. N. Shaw, *International Law*, 4th edn (Cambridge: Grotius Publication, 1997), pp. 483–4.
36 Joseph Beale, "Jurisdiction of a Sovereign State", Vol. 36, *Harvard Law Review* (1922–3), p. 24.
37 90 US 230 (1916).
38 192 US 573, 584 (1904).
39 Csabafi, op. cit., p. 49.
40 Ivory Coast closed its 700km (450-mile) land, sea and air border with Ghana in 2012 after several people were killed in an attack on an army checkpoint by what was described as an attack from 'armed elements from Ghana' who carried out the attack in the border town of Noe. In 2014 some West African nations imposed travel restrictions in a last-ditch attempt to stop the worst ever outbreak of Ebola, a disease with a mortality rate of up to 90 per cent that killed hundreds in Liberia, Sierra Leone and Guinea. BBC News, 'Ivory Coast closes Ghana border after Deadly Attack' 22 September 2012, available at http://www.bbc.co.uk/news/world-africa-19683708, accessed 5 August 2014; Javier Blas, 'Borders closed to tackle Ebola outbreak', *Financial Times*, 28 July 2014 available at http://www.ft.com/cms/s/0/8feaa158-1662-11e4-93ec-00144feabdc0.html#axzz39Y2FAhJA, accessed 5 August 2014; J. Fawcett, "Domestic Jurisdiction", 132 *Recueil Des Cours* (1971), p. 431.

limits especially within the jurisdiction of another state without its consent.[41] These assertions inevitably bring us to a discussion of state territory within the context of the principle of state territorial supremacy or sovereignty.

2.4 Westphalian vs indigenous sovereignty

The idea peddled in some Western literature that Europe is the birthplace of both the nation and the state is disappointing and ill-conceived.[42] Since the principle of sovereignty could only have had its origins in the 1648 Treaty of Westphalia that recognised a new form of political organisation in Western Europe then it is no more than a relatively new phenomenon, and just another form of arrangement of political life in Europe following the *Res publica Christiana* of the Middle Ages. The question is why is the inherent sovereignty of tribal peoples and indigenous precolonial African states not to be regarded as sovereignty? Numerous African indigenous political systems were headed by sovereigns who answered to no one. Sovereignty in our view is ancient as a legal and political concept. It is, thus, both a cause and symptom of human civilisation in Africa. Its manifestations in Africa date back to antiquity and predate the Westphalian conceptualisation found in modern literature. The idea that sovereignty as a juridical concept is beyond African political conceptualisation is not convincing. Much of such reasoning is based on impatience in studying African history –a quite difficult field of research but one that is very fulfilling in its enrichment of interdisciplinary research. The following account of an encounter with one of Sub-Saharan Africa's greatest cities by a Western scholar is revealing.

> There came to me through that distance the outline of a wall both tall and long, a city wall. Very big was this wall, said our navigator-sergeant. It was built of mud and timber, and it went right round a city lost in this African nowhere. One day, he said he was going to get himself inside that city. All he could tell about it, meanwhile, was its name. 'Kano, K-a-n-o. Ever heard of it? Of course you haven't. It's there though . . . It's old they say. Five hundred years old, they claim. Don't see how it can be though.' I found out later. Kano was seven hundred years old, If not a lot more. But even five hundred years meant history, and there wasn't any history in Africa, as far as I'd ever been taught. Perhaps one should find out.[43]

Europeans of the nineteenth century believed that Africans had never built their own nations. At best Africans are said to be grouped only into tribes. In an intellectual tradition that doubts the existence of cities in an entire continent there is little hope of thorough application of socio-legal and historical research to the

---

41 Fawcet, ibid., p. 431.
42 See, for instance, Hastings Donnan and Thomas M. Wilson, *Borders: Frontiers of Identity, Nation and State* (Oxford and New York: Berg, 1999), p. 7.
43 Davidson, op.cit., pp. 6–7.

understanding of its legal jurisprudence. Conceptualisation of sovereignty in relation to national territory is in fact prevalent in nearly all African cultures. African political systems pre-dating extensive contact with Arabs and Europe are of course familiar with nation states as a philosophy of societal organisation. The continent's people produced nations, nation states and states in their classical senses before the advent of any form of colonialism on the continent. Archaeological evidence of clearly demarcated early states in Yoruba land within the forest zone of West Africa date back to the fourteenth and sixteenth centuries which was around the same time comparable states were formed in the savannah regions of Northern Africa.[44] The very idea that important legal concepts are only conceivable by certain cultures or that they were first discovered by legal families that are in many cases less than 2000 years old is somewhat offensive to reason.

The history of early states of Western and Central Sudan is replete with properly constructed state territory that experienced and coped with both internal and external threats and conflicts. A military historian cites some examples:

> Ghana, the earliest known state of western Sudan, which fell in 1076 to the Almoravids following a long period of tension between it and its northern neighbours, the Sanhaja, but Ghana regained its independence following the collapse of the Almoravid movement in about 1087 and maintained its position as the greatest kingdom in the Western Sudan. Ghana was finally subdued and crushed, however by the Sosso, their Sudanese neighbours. The next state which is known to have experienced internal and external conflicts was the kingdom of Mali, which became the next notable state in Western Sudan after it vanquished the Sosso ... The Songhay Empire succeeded the Mali ... There were similar scenarios in Central Sudan. Here the Kanuri Empire of Kanem had emerged as an imperial power in the thirteenth century with its base on the eastern side of Lake Chad ... The succeeding second Kanuri state of Bornu on the west of Lake Chad also saw violent conflicts. The new state built a walled capital at Ngazargamu.[45]

Historical facts like these have, however, not influenced the definitions found in public international law which appear to exclude the concept of statehood from precolonial Africa. One of the most under-reported facts of academic legal literature is the near total monopoly that Western writers, scholars, diplomats and statesmen have in recording the history of international relations and the evolution of the international legal order. This monadic control affords Western intellectualism the near singular advantage of cultivating the international legal agenda, as well as opportunities to nurture, amend and abrogate principles of international law in accordance with Western regional and group expediencies.

---

44 See Peter G. Stone, *Cultural Heritage, Ethics and the Military* (England: Boydell Press Series, 2011), p. 158;
45 Ibid., pp. 158–9.

At the root of such considerable influence is a deliberate arrogation of the power to declare, to define and to recognise. This influence, in its purest form, is expressed in Anglo-Saxon scholarship, and is guarded jealously through the processes of economic, diplomatic and political hegemony.[46] Perhaps an example of such arrogation may be found in the politico-legal formulation of the concept of 'failed states' which started as a rhetorical tool of exclusion of certain states by leading Western politicians but which has been picked up even by legal scholars. Hence leading international scholars like James Crawford believe perhaps quite unfortunately that '... apparently much of Africa and swathes of Asia are covered by the term (failed states)' [parenthesis added].[47] By such broad and careless classifications the opportunities and international relevance that ought to be available to large swathes of mankind resident in places like Africa are whittled down by sheer exercise of the power to declare. Not many writers care to mention that the history of formation of European states was not perfectly linear and that the processes were slow and difficult. The rhetoric on occasion is in fact predictive of future dangers to the independence of African states. As Wedgwood explains, 'At times there is almost an intimation that sovereignty does not properly belong to people who cannot employ it well'.[48]

The prevalence of ethnocentricity and/or sheer tribalism in the interactions within and between nations and states in Africa has created the impression in Western literature that Africa is organised into tribes whereas other countries particularly of the Western extraction have nationalism. But the human need for a sense of belonging is universal phenomena. In Africa as in every continent in the world, tribalism exists and is 'driven by fear and confusion and fed by the reassuring "sameness" of others in the group'.[49] Basil Davidson, for instance, in comparing what is often described as African tribalism to Hungarian nationalism in the 1950s found little or no difference between the two. Both, he noted, contain the perversities of nationalism. There is in both cases a reliance on the Janus-like nature of the national spirit that demands freedom with one face and denies it with the other. He concludes, therefore, that 'the nation state in Eastern Europe – but just as in Africa – has failed to meet the high claims of its promoter and the promises of its propagandists'.[50]

At any rate at the end of the period of collapse of the colonial empires in Eastern Europe and later in Africa about a dozen new nation states took shape in Europe out of the collapsed old internal empires and above 50 new states emerged

---

46 See generally Gbenga Oduntan, "International Law and the Discontented: How the West Underdeveloped International Laws", in Parashar, Archana and Amita Dhanda (eds), *Decolonisation of Legal Knowledge* (India: Routledge, 2009).
47 James Crawford, *The Creation of States in International Law*, 2nd edn (Oxford: Clarendon Press, 2006), p. 721.
48 Ruth Wedgwood, "The Evolution of United Nations Peacekeeping", 28 *Cornell International Law Journal* (1995), pp. 631, 636, cited in Crawford, op.cit., p. 721.
49 Horsman and Marshall, *After the Nation-State: Citizens, Tribalism and the New World Disorder* (London: Harper Collins, 1995), p. x; see also Hopper, p. 39.
50 Davidson, op.cit., p. 18.

in Africa. These states all appeared to have adopted the sovereign models found in the history of Western states like England and France.[51]

2.5 The principle of territorial jurisdiction

The land Resource is the first essential to any state.[52]

Territorial jurisdiction is seen as the sum total of the state's powers in respect of a portion of *terra firma* under its governmental authority including all persons and things therein, and the extra-territorial activities of such persons.[53] It denotes the power of legislation, executive and judicial competence over a defined territory.[54] It is generally derived from territorial sovereignty, but it may also be derived from treaties, as in the case of mandated, trust or leased territories. It may also derive from *occupatio pacifica* or *bellica*.[55] The principle of territorial supremacy arises from the view that a state has absolute and exclusive authority over people, things and events within its own territory and, therefore, may exercise jurisdiction over them in all cases.[56] It is in exercise of territorial jurisdiction that the sovereign mints currency – hence the anachronistic connotation of the gold coin as the 'Sovereign' in England around the reigns of Henry VII and Charles I.[57] But the problem of what may properly be considered state territory for purposes of jurisdiction is not always clear. This brings us to the concept of territory itself.

The corpus of state territory and its appurtenances (airspace and territorial sea together with the population and government), comprise the physical and social manifestations of the state, which is the primary type of an international legal person.[58] The territory of a state is separated from those of other states by boundaries. A boundary may be natural or artificial.[59] Apart from land territory, which is permanently above low-water mark, territorial sovereignty may be exerted over all the geographical features associated with or analogous to land territory.

---

51 Ibid., p. 267.
52 Lucie Carlson and Allen K. Philbrick, *Geography and World Politics* (NJ: Prentice-Hall, Inc., 1958), p. 56.
53 B. Cheng, "The Extra-Territorial Application of International Law", *Current Legal Problems* (1965), p. 135.
54 Umozurike, op. cit., p. 86.
55 Cheng, op. cit., p. 135.
56 Some authors like Starke choose to refer to these overwhelming powers as territorial sovereignty. The question then arises as to whether there is a possible distinction between territorial sovereignty and territorial jurisdiction. Oppenheim seems to have effectively answered this query by stating that he sees 'Independence and Territorial as well as personal Supremacy (which Starke seems to have referred to as territorial sovereignty) as aspects of Sovereignty' (brackets added). cf. Brownlie, op. cit., pp. 105–6. See J. G. Starke, *Introduction to International Law* (London: Butterworths, 1984), pp. 151–2. Oppenheim, op. cit., p. 286. See also D. H. Ott, *Public International Law in the Modern World* (UK: Pitman, 1987), p. 135.
57 Wendy Brown, op.cit., p. 57.
58 Brownlie, op. cit., p. 107.
59 Umozurike, op. cit., p.107.

Permanence, accessibility and natural appurtenance are naturally essential qualities. Furthermore, it is clear that, no one knowledgeable in international law can deny that the territory of a state including its earth surface ('... a sector of the earth below and a sector of space above')[60] are within the areas of exercise of jurisdiction permitted by international law. Indeed, the tri-dimensionality of state territory is recognised in customary international law. A state's territory is considered to consist of three sectors:[61]

1. legitimately owned land mass within its borders, including the internal water territories, rivers, lakes, reservoirs, canals and the territorial sea;
2. the land mass below the surface of the soil (including its mineral resources) down to the centre of the earth and;
3. the airspace and atmosphere above the ground level up to an extent which is still the subject of intense debate in academic circles.

In spatial terms the law knows two other types of regime, which must be highlighted. They are the *res nullius* and the *res communis*. The *res nullius* is that land territory or environment legally susceptible to acquisition by states but not as yet placed under any state's territorial sovereignty. The European powers made use of this concept which though legal in form was often political in application in that it involved the occupation of large areas in Asia and Africa which were often in fact the seat of previously well-organised communities.[62] There have also been some unsuccessful attempts to forge a link between this concept and outer space territory. In fact it would appear that with or without the use of the technicality of *res nullius*, certain states are set to embark on the introduction of property rights over outer space-based resources for national and private ends despite the position of current international law on this issue. The *res communis* is that territory or environment such as the high seas or Antarctica, which is not capable of being legally placed under state sovereignty. In accordance with customary international law and the dictates of practical convenience, the airspace above and subsoil below each of the three categories, state territory, *res nullius* and *res communis* are included in each category.[63]

The tri-dimensionality theory of territorial jurisdiction received judicial assent in relation to African situations in the reasoning of the ICJ in the *Frontier Dispute* (Benin/Niger) 2002. The Chamber took note of Niger's claim that its boundary with Niger in a particular sector is situated at the middle point of each of a set of bridges given that the construction and maintenance of these structures has been financed by the parties on an equal basis and that the bridges are their joint property. Benin, for its part, submitted to the court that a difference between the

---

60 J. C. Cooper, "High Altitude Flight and National Sovereignty", *Explorations in Aerospace Law: Selected Essays*, (Montreal: McGill Univ. Press, 1968), p. 157.
61 G. I. Tunkin, (ed.), *International Law* (Moscow: Progress, 1988), p. 400.
62 Ian Brownlie, *Principles of Public International Law* (Oxford: Clarendon Press, 1966), p. 118.
63 Ibid., p. 98.

location of the boundary on the bridges and the course of the boundary in the river beneath would be incoherent. The Chamber observed that, in the absence of an agreement between the parties, the solution would be to extend vertically the line of the boundary on the watercourse and noted that this solution accords with the general theory that a boundary represents the line of separation between areas of state sovereignty, not only on the earth's surface but also in the subsoil and in the superjacent column of air.[64] Moreover, the solution consisting of the vertical extension of the boundary line on the watercourse avoids the difficulties which could be engendered by having two different boundaries on geometrical planes situated in close proximity to one another. Following this line of reasoning, the Chamber concluded that the boundary on the bridges between Gaya and Malanville follows the course of the boundary in the river.[65]

It suffices to mention that territorial jurisdiction also determines the appropriate forum in civil actions and service of court papers can only be served out of the boundaries of a state (i.e. jurisdiction) by leave of court. A total lack of territorial connection may remove a dispute from the competence of a state.

2.6 Territory and territorial acquisition in public international law and international relations

> The territorium is the sum of the lands within the boundaries of a community [*civitatis*]; which some say is so named because the magistrate of a place has the right of terrifying [*terrendi*] that is exercising jurisdiction, within its boundaries.[66]

Territory is both a political and legal term and concerns the relation between sovereignty, land and people.[67] Territory derives its roots from the Latin *terra* meaning land or terrain and the compound – *territorium* – which by the prefix

---

64 Gbenga Oduntan, *Sovereignty and Jurisdiction in the Airspace and Outer Space Legal Criteria for Spatial Delimitation* (Oxon: Routledge, 2012) pp. 11–39, 169.
65 This finding was made without prejudice to the arrangements in force between Benin and Niger regarding the use and maintenance of the road in issue. The Chamber specifically observed in particular that the question of the course of the boundary on the bridges is totally independent of that of the ownership of those structures, which belong to the parties jointly. The logic of the court's jurisprudence in this area is particularly useful for those tasked with the role of demarcation according to the court's decision. This is in that even where the delimitation achieved by the court deprives a state of the ownership of a boundary road, bridge or maintained track, it may still access that feature for the purposes of maintenance and/or use. Similar issues have cropped up at the demarcation stages of the Cameroon–Nigeria process in relation to the implementation of the Court's judgment in the Northern sector.
66 Pomponius Manual in the Digest of Justinian cited in Stuart Elden, *Terror and Territory: The Spatial Extent of Sovereignty* (Minneapolis: London), p. v.
67 A critical interpretation of the basis for the emergence of this concept in the way it is recognised has been explored elsewhere: see Stuart Elden, "Missing the Point: Globalisation, Deterrritorialisation, and the Space of World", in *Transactions of the Institute of British Geographers*, Vol. 30, No. 1 (2005), pp. 8–19, and 'Governmentality, Calculation, Calculation, Territory', in *Environment and Planning D: Society and Space*, 25, p. xxvi ff.

'*orium*' denotes 'the place of something' or surrounding something. Although the etymology of *territorium* according to the *Oxford English Dictionary* is 'unsettled', Awe or *Majestas* 'has always been a synonym of sovereignty'.[68] It is described as:

> ... usually taken as a deriv[ative]: of terra earth, land (to which it was certainly referred in popular [Latin]. When altered to *terratorium*); but the original form [*territorium*] has suggested derivation from *terrere* to frighten.[69]

Territory is, therefore, both spatial and locational in referring to 'the place surrounding an area'.[70] In this sense we can envisage that the location of such an 'area' at least in our modern world can indeed be maritime, aerial or celestial as long as it is a space, place or sphere of physical activities capable of being occupied by use or for passage. It is interesting that territory has in time, however, acquired a popular meaning of a 'bounded space'. One of the problems that emanate from such a view has been adduced to by the query 'what is space?', and 'how is it bounded?'[71] It is for this reason that one author concluded quite persuasively that:

> A properly critical political theory of territory needs to investigate the quantification of space and the role of calculative mechanisms in the commanding of territory, and the establishment of borders.[72]

René Descartes also helpfully suggested that geometry is the science that best allows us to conceptualise spatial territory. Analytical geometry and the entire gamut of scientific methodology of spatial measurement have indeed provided the techniques to map out the various terrains known to mankind including deserts, arctic, polar and even celestial bodies and the geostationary orbit.[73] It is for this reason that this book proceeds from the *a priori* position that determination of territorial extents by objectively verifiable criteria is both human instinct and a legally obligatory act. It makes good policy both in the domestic and international legal orders for there to be distinct territories and a fundamental understanding of the juridical nature of all forms of physical and extra-terrestrial territories. A corollary position of this view is that wherever possible the precise distinction in terms of delimitation and demarcation of all territories must be attempted if not achieved.

---

68 Jacques Derrida, *Rouges: Two Essays on Reason*, trans. Pachale-Anne Brault and Michael Naas (Stanford, CA: Stanford University Press, 2005), p. 81.
69 J. A. Simpson and E. S. C. Weiner, *The Oxford English Dictionary*, 2nd edn (Oxford: Clarendon Press, 1989), Vol. XVII, Su-Thrivingly, 819.
70 Elden, op.cit, p. xxix.
71 Elden, ibid., p. xxvii.
72 Ibid., p. xxvii.
73 Ibid., p. xxvi. Elden points out that advances in the time of Descartes including analytic geometry (which he pioneered using algebra and equations), partnered with developments in cartography and land surveys, as well as more accurate means of measuring time, allowed for the accurate determination of longitudes and latitudes.

There are at least 267 separate geographic entities in the world today. This includes 195 independent states.[74] 'Independent states' are constituted by peoples politically organised into separate sovereign states with definite territories.

Furthermore, there are dependencies and areas of special sovereignty connected to states like Australia (Ashmore and Cartier Islands, Christmas Island, Cocos (Keeling) Islands, Coral Sea Islands, Heard Island and McDonald Islands, Norfolk Island); China (Hong Kong, Macau); Denmark (Faroe Islands, Greenland); France (Clipperton Island, French Polynesia, French Southern and Antarctic Lands, New Caledonia, Saint Barthelemy, Saint Martin, Saint Pierre and Miquelon, Wallis and Futuna); the Netherlands (Aruba, Curacao, Sint Maarten); New Zealand (Cook Islands, Niue, Tokelau); Norway (Bouvet Island, Jan Mayen, Svalbard); the UK (Akrotiri, Anguilla, Bermuda, British Indian Ocean Territory, British Virgin Islands, Cayman Islands, Dhekelia, Falkland Islands, Gibraltar, Guernsey, Jersey, Isle of Man, Montserrat, Pitcairn Islands, Saint Helena, South Georgia and the South Sandwich Islands, Turks and Caicos Islands); and the US (American Samoa, Baker Island, Guam, Howland Island, Jarvis Island, Johnston Atoll, Kingman Reef, Midway Islands, Navassa Island, Northern Mariana Islands, Palmyra Atoll, Puerto Rico, Virgin Islands, Wake Island (consolidated in United States Pacific Island Wildlife Refuges entry)).[75]

In addition to independent states and dependent territories there are other geographic entities of contested existence like Taiwan; sector claims in Antarctica, Gaza Strip, Paracel Islands, Spratly Islands, West Bank, Western Sahara; as well

---

74 The 195 independent states are as follows: Afghanistan, Albania, Algeria, Andorra, Angola, Antigua and Barbuda, Argentina, Armenia, Australia, Austria, Azerbaijan, The Bahamas, Bahrain, Bangladesh, Barbados, Belarus, Belgium, Belize, Benin, Bhutan, Bolivia, Bosnia and Herzegovina, Botswana, Brazil, Brunei, Bulgaria, Burkina Faso, Burma, Burundi, Cambodia, Cameroon, Canada, Cape Verde, Central African Republic, Chad, Chile, China, Colombia, Comoros, Democratic Republic of the Congo, Republic of the Congo, Costa Rica, Cote d'Ivoire, Croatia, Cuba, Cyprus, Czech Republic, Denmark, Djibouti, Dominica, Dominican Republic, Ecuador, Egypt, El Salvador, Equatorial Guinea, Eritrea, Estonia, Ethiopia, Fiji, Finland, France, Gabon, The Gambia, Georgia, Germany, Ghana, Greece, Grenada, Guatemala, Guinea, Guinea-Bissau, Guyana, Haiti, Holy See, Honduras, Hungary, Iceland, India, Indonesia, Iran, Iraq, Ireland, Israel, Italy, Jamaica, Japan, Jordan, Kazakhstan, Kenya, Kiribati, North Korea, South Korea, Kosovo, Kuwait, Kyrgyzstan, Laos, Latvia, Lebanon, Lesotho, Liberia, Libya, Liechtenstein, Lithuania, Luxembourg, Macedonia, Madagascar, Malawi, Malaysia, Maldives, Mali, Malta, Marshall Islands, Mauritania, Mauritius, Mexico, Federated States of Micronesia, Moldova, Monaco, Mongolia, Montenegro, Morocco, Mozambique, Namibia, Nauru, Nepal, Netherlands, New Zealand, Nicaragua, Niger, Nigeria, Norway, Oman, Pakistan, Palau, Panama, Papua New Guinea, Paraguay, Peru, Philippines, Poland, Portugal, Qatar, Romania, Russia, Rwanda, Saint Kitts and Nevis, Saint Lucia, Saint Vincent and the Grenadines, Samoa, San Marino, Sao Tome and Principe, Saudi Arabia, Senegal, Serbia, Seychelles, Sierra Leone, Singapore, Slovakia, Slovenia, Solomon Islands, Somalia, South Africa, South Sudan, Spain, Sri Lanka, Sudan, Suriname, Swaziland, Sweden, Switzerland, Syria, Tajikistan, Tanzania, Thailand, Timor-Leste, Togo, Tonga, Trinidad and Tobago, Tunisia, Turkey, Turkmenistan, Tuvalu, Uganda, Ukraine, United Arab Emerites, United Kingdom, United States of America, Uruguay, Uzbekistan, Vanuatu, Venezuela, Vietnam, Yemen, Zambia, Zimbabwe: see the CIA, *The World Factbook* available at https://www.cia.gov/library/publications/the-world-factbook/docs/notesanddefs.html, accessed 10 December 2013.
75 Ibid.

as territories of unfolding juridical nature such as the European Union. The land boundaries in the world total add up to approximately 251,060km (and that is where effort has been expended to prevent the counting of shared boundaries twice). Most states share boundaries with multiple land or maritime neighbours.[76] Nearly a quarter of all independent states are landlocked. Liechtenstein and Uzbekistan are in fact doubly landlocked. Africa has two interesting examples – Zambia which is completely surrounded by eight states (Congo DRC, Angola, Malawi, Zimbabwe, Mozambique, Tanzania, Namibia and Botswana) and Lesotho which is not only landlocked but country locked as it is completely surrounded by South Africa.[77] Fortunately, however, virtually all states have access naturally to their airspace and a potential direct access to outer space depending only on their level of rocket technological acquisition or interest in procurement of launches through spacecraft in their own states or through the airspace of other states.

Territory may be acquired by many means and there is much truth in the statement of Brownlie that the student of the materials on the acquisition of title to territory is apt to erroneously feel that he is studying the history of a class of disputes, instances of which are unlikely to arise in future. He wrote:

> ... [i]n one sense at least law is history and the lawyer's appreciation of the meaning of rules relating to acquisition of territory and of the manner of their application in historical cases will be rendered more keen by a knowledge of the historical development of the law ... In other words, the principles developed in relation to the normal territorial areas provide useful analogies for those engaged in building a legal regime for any international space.[78]

In reality there is a continuing relevance of the classical modes of territorial acquisition and the entire question of modes of territorial acquisition is of current legal significance. This will remain so for a considerable length of time. A cursory glance at the work of the International Court of Justice (ICJ) in the last ten years alone will reveal that the Court is occupied with disputes arising out of territorial questions. Many of these are as a result of controversy over the applicable root of title and can only be resolved with reference to them.[79] It would appear that a

---

76 China and Russia, for instance, each border 14 other countries.
77 The list of presently recognised 45 landlocked states and territories is as follows: Afghanistan, Andorra, Armenia, Austria, Azerbaijan, Belarus, Bhutan, Bolivia, Botswana, Burkina Faso, Burundi, Central African Republic, Chad, Czech Republic, Ethiopia, Holy See (Vatican City), Hungary, Kazakhstan, Kosovo, Kyrgyzstan, Laos, Lesotho, Liechtenstein, Luxembourg, Macedonia, Malawi, Mali, Moldova, Mongolia, Nepal, Niger, Paraguay, Rwanda, San Marino, Serbia, Slovakia, Swaziland, Switzerland, Tajikistan, Turkmenistan, Uganda, Uzbekistan, West Bank, Zambia and Zimbabwe.
78 Ian Brownlie, *Principles of Public International Law*, 5th edn (Oxford University Press, 1970), pp. 125–6.
79 Those territorial and boundary-related disputes that have been litigated before the court in the last decade are as follows: *Proceedings jointly instituted by Burkina Faso and the Republic of Niger* (Burkina Faso/Republic of Niger) *Maritime Dispute (Peru v Chile*; 2010); *Dispute regarding Navigational and Related Rights*

surprising proportion of frontiers taken for granted as settled are actually dormant disputes waiting to erupt. States may at any time be called to prove territorial title or defend their territorial sovereignty. The need to do so may in fact be on the increase in the twenty-first century for many reasons. These include conflict over natural and energy resources, challenge of inchoate titles and the consequences of rapid and previously unimaginable changes in technological advancements.[80] Developments in shipping technology, aviation, space technology and even global warming continue to break down zones of inaccessibility to mankind and put valuable resources within the reach of corporations and businesses. All these make it necessary for the modern-day lawyer, statesman and decision-maker to remain very familiar with the issues and nuances surrounding the legal modes of territorial acquisition including of course the possible causes of loss of sovereignty over territory.

Even the ancient concept of *terra nullius* (i.e. land belonging to no one), which arguably can no longer rear its head in modern times having been exposed as a political tool for acquisition of territory by stealth in Africa and Asia by the European powers, rather unfortunately remains relevant in legal analysis as root of previous titles and in the resolution of disputes between states.[81]

Territory may be transferred or acquired in one of several ways but the methods are now restricted by current international law. Some methods are now of completely historical interest and some that are still employed are quite controversial and are reminiscent of 'the old international law'.

2.6.1 Occupation

This is one of the oldest means of acquisition of territory. Under this method a territory that is not controlled by another state is taken over by way of occupation.

(*Costa Rica v Nicaragua*; 2005); *Maritime Delimitation in the Black Sea* (*Romania v Ukraine*; 2004); *Sovereignty over Pedra Branca/Pulau Batu Puteh, Middle Rocks and South Ledge* (*Malaysia v Singapore*; 2003); *Application for Revision of the Judgment of 11 September 1992 in the Case concerning the Land, Island and Maritime Frontier Dispute* (*El Salvador v Honduras: Nicaragua intervening*; 2002); *Armed Activities on the Territory of the Congo* (*New Application: 2002*) (*Democratic Republic of the Congo v Rwanda*; 2002); *Frontier Dispute* (*Benin v Niger*; 2002); *Territorial and Maritime Dispute* (*Nicaragua v Colombia*; 2001). Note also celebrated cases such as *Land and Maritime Boundary Between Cameroon and Nigeria*; *Territorial and Maritime Dispute* (*Nicaragua v Colombia*); *Sovereignty over Pulau Ligitan and Pulau Sipadan* (*Indonesia v Malaysia*; 1998).

80 According to International Energy Agency (IEA) forecasts, global energy demand will grow 45 per cent between 2006 and 2030. See Communication and Information Office, "New Energy Realities – WEO Calls for Global Energy Revolution Despite Economic Crisis", 12 November 2008 (London) available at https://www.iea.org/press/pressdetail.asp?PRESS_REL_ID=275, accessed May 2010; cf. International Energy Agency, World Energy Outlook 2008, Executive summary, p. 13, available at http://www.worldenergyoutlook.org/docs/weo2008/WEO2008_es_english.pdf, accessed 6 May 2008. Aside from territorial sovereignty there may also be issues of indigenous rights and control to consider. See also Al Gedicks, *The New Resource Wars: Native and Environmental Struggles against Multinationals* (Boston: South End Press, 1993), pp. 13–15, 156–60.

81 Note, for instance, that the *terra nullius* doctrine came to be tested and was mentioned directly 16 times in the determination of Singapore's sovereignty over Pedra Branca in the case *Sovereignty over Pedra Branca/Pulau Batu Puteh, Middle Rocks and South Ledge; Malaysia v the Republic of Singapore*, ICJ Reports, 2008.

Up until the nineteenth century, Europeans denied statehood to territories outside Europe with a few exceptions. Thus, if they did not have the military power to adequately defend themselves, they could be subjugated and their territory occupied by the first European power, which moves in that direction. The Permanent Court of International Justice (PCIJ) later laid down the constituent ingredients of effective occupation in the *Eastern Greenland Case* as:

(i) the intention to act as sovereign;
(ii) adequate exercise of display of sovereignty.[82]

An issue of current relevance regarding this mode of acquisition relates to the contiguity theory advanced by the US and Canada to claim sectors in the Arctic. In 2008 Russia dramatically staked a claim to parts of the Arctic by planting a flag at the bottom of the sea. The penchant for flag-planting by states continued in 2010 when China staked its flag at the bottom of the contentious South China Sea.[83] This theory as well as that of historical ties has traditionally been used to explain situations in which it is not clear exactly how much territory was subject to occupation. It is, however, clear that the theory as well as the maintenance of sector claims over an area increasingly regarded as international common remains controversial. The legal theory of prior discovery and occupation was established and followed in the *Western Sahara Case*.[84] An advisory opinion was requested by the UN General Assembly on the question of whether Western Sahara was *terra nullius* as at the time Spain colonised the territory. The ICJ established that the Western Sahara territory was actually inhabited by peoples who though were of a nomadic nature were also socially and politically organised into tribal groups under the suzerainty of chiefs who represented them. Crucially the Court also concluded that the fact that Spain concluded treaties with local chiefs also indicated that Spain could not have viewed the territory as *terra nullius*.

2.6.2 Cession

This is where right to possess certain territory as a sovereign is conferred by agreement between intending grantor and grantee. Cession may take the form of a treaty, sale, gift exchange or grant provided sovereignty is transferred. A ceding state cannot give more than it has; defects in title as well as servitudes and other rights survive the cession.[85] Spain ceded the Caroline Island to Germany in 1899;

---

82 Norway–Denmark, PCIJ, Ser A/B (1933), No. 53.
83 Council of Foreign Relations, "China's Maritime Disputes" available at http://www.cfr.org/asia-and-pacific/chinas-maritime-disputes/p31345#!/, accessed 6 August 2014; Arthur Zhu, "South China Sea Crisis: Invasion of Spratly Islands", Policy Paper, Washington, DC, available at blogs.yis.ac.jp/14zhua/files/2013/11/Policy-paper-FINAL-2hwa1as.docx, accessed 6 August 2014.
84 *Western Sahara* Case, 1975 ICJ at 39.
85 *Island of Palmas* case 2 R.I.A.A. (1928), See also Lee Seokwoo, "Continuing Relevance of Traditional Modes of Territorial Acquisition in International Law and Modest Proposal", 16 *Connecticut Journal of International Law* 8 (2000–01), p. 89.

France ceded Louisiana to the US in 1803 for 60 million Francs and Lombardy to Italy in 1859 gratuitously. In 1902 and 1926, Britain made interval transfers of Ugandan territory to Kenya, both under British rule. There is no reason to believe that this form of territorial transfer will not remain relevant even in the twenty-first century. Indeed the right to transfer territory is an attribute of sovereignty. It is, however, clear that if such cession is acquired by duress or force other rules of international law will operate to nullify it.

2.6.3 Accretion, erosion and avulsion

All three refer to the changes to territory through geographical or geological formations. Thus, in the simple case, deposits on a seacoast may result in an extension of sovereignty. In the case of avulsion the change comes through sudden, forcible and significant changes in river courses. In relation to these sorts of geological events, no formal acts of appropriation are required. However any addition will relate to areas already under effective occupation. Indeed because of the slow and gradual nature of the process involved, it is clear that it is only a matter of time before discussion of this mode returns to relevance in particular cases. For instance, echoes of accretion and avulsion are to be found in the arguments presented before the boundary commission in the *Eritrea-Ethiopia Boundary Dispute Arbitration*, which began in 2000.[86] Erosion of Tanzanian shores of Lake Malawi/Nyasa is also one of the reasons which aggravate the dispute between Malawi and Tanzania since this geological change allegedly decreases Tanzanian territory and in effect increases that of Malawi.[87]

2.6.4 Conquest or annexation

This is the acquisition of enemy territory after its conquest and a declared intent to annex. For this mode of title to be effective, military conquest is not enough; it must be followed by the intent to annex. There must be the declaration or other act of sovereignty by duly authorised and competent persons intended to provide unequivocal evidence of annexation. Italy formally annexed Ethiopia after its conquest in 1936. The Allies expressly disclaimed this act after their victory in the Second World War. Japan, for instance, established total control over Korea through a gradual process that began at the end of the nineteenth century and accelerated in the early years of the twentieth century, leading to the 1905 Protectorate Convention and to formal annexation in 1910. Questions as to the legality of this under international law divided lawyers for decades as many claimed that the position will have to include examination of both the state of

---

86 Submitted under the aegis of the Permanent Court of Arbitration as a result of the 12 December 2000 Agreement between the Government of the Federal Democratic Republic of Ethiopia and the Government of The State of Eritrea.
87 See discussion below relating to the Malawi–Tanzania mediation.

international law at the time at which these events took place and international law as exists today.[88] The question will appear to have been well answered by the unequivocal apology made by Japan in 2010. In more recent times Iraq invaded Kuwait for the purposes of annexation in 1990 but UN resolutions and enforcement actions under Chapter VII of the Charter were brought to nullify and correct the illegality. It is perhaps safe to conclude that the current state of international law does not permit the use of this mode of acquisition any longer. As the case of Israeli occupation of Palestinian territories demonstrates and has been restated in countless UN resolutions, occupation of conquered territory no matter for how long cannot confer legitimate title to the occupied territories. Conquest as a legal mode of acquisition is, therefore, of purely historical value.

2.6.5 Prescription

This results from peaceful exercise of *de facto* sovereignty for a long time, which either confirms an existing title or extinguishes a prior title. Some jurists express doubt as to whether prescription confers a good title. The *Island of Palmas Case*[89] the *Anglo-Norwegian Fisheries Case*[90] and the *Eastern Greenland Case*[91] do, however, support this principle. Prescription has featured regularly in recent African cases although several states have discovered that it is actually difficult to use expressly or impliedly in support of occupation. Prescription featured strongly in the arguments of Nigeria in its claims over the Bakassi Peninsula but the claims failed.[92] Similarly in awarding Kaskili/Sedudu to Botswana, the ICJ took the view that the necessary conditions for prescription cited by Namibia fell short of the 'necessary degree of precision and certainty' in that '. . . even if links of allegiance may have existed between the Maubia and the Caprivi authorities, it has not been established that the members of this tribe occupied the Island a *titre de souverain* . . .'; in other words that they exercised functions of the state authority there on behalf of those authorities.[93] Johnson stressed in support of prescription, that the territory must be held under a claim of sovereign title, peacefully, publicly and uninterruptedly for a long time.[94] Fifty years was regarded long enough in the British Guyana–Venezuela dispute.[95]

---

88 This raises the problem of 'intertemporal law': see Jon M. Van Dyke, 'Reconciliation between Korea and Japan', Vol. 5 *Chinese Journal of International Law*, No. 1, pp. 215–39.
89 Op.cit., p. 829.
90 ICJ Rep (1951) 116.
91 PCIJ, Ser. A/B (1933), No. 53.
92 See below our criticism of the ICJ judgment on the Bakassi Peninsula.
93 Case Concerning Kaskili/Sedudu Island (*Botswana v Namibia*) 94, 13 December 1999, at 95–9.
94 D. H. N. Johnson, 'Acquisitive Prescription', in *British Yearbook of International Law* (1950), p. 345. He identified four conditions which must be present for acquisitive prescription to operate. They are: (i) the possession of the prescribing state must be exercised *a titre de souverain*; (ii) the possession must be peaceful and uninterrupted; (iii) the possession must be public; and (iv) the possession must endure for a reasonable length of time; see pp. 343–8.
95 Britain–USA, 89 BFSP (1896) 57.

2.6.6 Renunciation or relinquishment

A state may readily relinquish territory or deny continuous or further sovereignty or ownership over it. This may take the form of recognition that another state now has title. It may be by agreement to confer territory or exercise of a power of disposition to be exercised by another state or group of states. It is clear that an option open to the state of Israel in the future with regard to the occupied territories under its control is that of renunciation or relinquishment. This may be appropriate in the face of international consensus expressed through widely supported UN Security Council and General Assembly Resolutions, particularly Resolutions 242 of 22 November 1967 and 348 of 22 October 1973 affirming Israel's obligation to withdraw from occupied territories.

2.6.7 Adjudication

The award of a tribunal is certainly a valuable root of legal title to territory but the award is not of itself dispositive. In other words the existence of a pre-existing root of title acquired through another mode is presumed.

2.6.8 Abandonment and dereliction

This is the negative counterpart of effective occupation in that in the face of competing activity and claims by another; a State by conduct or by express admission acquiesces to the extension of its competitor's sovereignty. In very rare situations a State may intend to abandon as well as formally and expressly renounce its title to a piece of territory.

2.6.9 Discovery

Whereas mere discovery (i.e. visual apprehension) could not give a valid title, symbolic acts of taking possession could have this result.[96] This mode would seem quite adaptable to the realities of outer space exploration but will in fact be counter to the letter and spirit of Space Law based as it is on the principle of Common Heritage of Mankind. In practice discovery may be accompanied by symbolic acts like the planting of a flag. The Americans actually did plant their flag on the moon but according to present-day international law act that does not give them title to the moon. It may be suggested, therefore, that flag planting exercises may have lost their potency as proof of occupation or first landing as it may have had in antiquity. Today flag-planting appears to serve no more a value than to express love for the motherland.

---

96 Brownlie, op.cit., p. 127.

2.6.10 Papal grant

> Among other works well pleasing to the Divine Majesty and cherished of our heart, this assuredly ranks highest, that in our times especially the Catholic faith and the Christian religion be exalted and be everywhere increased and spread, that the health of souls be cared for and that barbarous nations be overthrown and brought to the faith itself . . . we (the Papacy) command you (Spain) . . . to instruct the aforesaid inhabitants and residents and dwellers therein in the Catholic faith, and train them in good morals.[97]

Papal grants though controversial were recognised in the fifteenth century as root to title over territories some of which by size were several times bigger than Spain and Portugal its principal beneficiaries. The Pope had power to grant or transfer territory. This took place principally through the Bulls of Donation or the so-called Alexandrine Bulls (*Inter Caetera* of 4 May 1493; *Eximiae devotionis* of 3 May 1493 and *Dudum siquidem* of 26 September 1493) – three papal Bulls of Pope Alexander VI delivered in 1493. These documents purported to grant overseas territories to Portugal and the catholic monarchs of Spain. The papal Bulls were the basis for negotiation between Portugal and Spain and are the basis upon which the Treaty of Tordesillas of 1494, dividing the non-Christian world beyond Europe between them, was concluded. At first these arrangements were respected by most other European powers, but as the Protestant Reformation proceeded the states of Northern Europe came to consider them as a private arrangement between Spain and Portugal.

Papal grant had some effect in Africa. By a Bull of 1454 Nicholas V granted Alfonso V of Portugal the discoveries made and to be made on the West coast of Africa. By the Bull of 25 September 1492, the Pope opened up the entire field of oceanic space to Portugal and Spain. The Spaniards, however, were allowed only to sail westward and not infringe the African monopolies of Portugal. By 1494 Portugal and Spain in the Treaty of Tordesillas, fixed their mutual limits at a line drawn 370 leagues west of the Cape Verde Islands and in 1506 Pope Julius II confirmed the treaty.[98]

Ultimately Papal grants are part and parcel of the generational fraudulence and violent acquisitive philosophy encapsulated in the colonial project. It is little

---

97 English Translation of The Bull Inter Caetera (Alexander VI), 4 May 1493, Frances Gardiner Davenport, ed., *European Treaties bearing on the History of the United States and its Dependencies to 1648* (Carnegie Institution of Washington, 1917, Washington, DC), at p. 75. Also available at http://www.nativeweb.org/pages/legal/indig-inter-caetera.html, accessed 20 December 2013. See further H. Vander Linden, "Alexander VI and the Demarcation of the Maritime and Colonial Domains of Spain and Portugal 1493–4", *The American Historical Review*, 22 (1916).
98 William Edward Hall, *International Law* (Cambridge: Cambridge University Press, 1990), pp. 96–7, available at http://books.google.co.uk/books?id=P_I8AAAAIAAJ&printsec=frontcover&source=gbs_ge_summary_r&cad=0#v=onepage&q&f=false, accessed 18 August 2014.

wonder then that various indigenous peoples particularly of the Americas have increasingly questioned the legality of the papal Bull *inter caetera* which led to the subjugation of their peoples, and called for their repeal.[99] It will be interesting to see if similar questions will be raised in Spanish and Portuguese-colonised Africa. This mode of title is clearly obsolete in modern times and its return to relevance is highly unlikely if not impossible. As such papal grants will (*deo volente*) never apply to Africa again in the future.[100]

It must be noted that international law no longer confines itself to recognition of state territory. The notion of territory today encompasses; sea territories, Antarctic territories, polar territories, outer space territories (including celestial *terra firma*), orbital territories and lunar territories etc. Some of these territories fall under the jurisdiction and sovereignty of states while others are under the category of 'international spaces'. The unifying factor is that all are subject to international law. The emerging concept of 'common heritage of mankind' along with other formula like the 'province of mankind', operate to prevent many of the traditional modes of acquisition from operating in relation to the high seas, Antarctica and outer space. While there are useful analogies some of the traditional modes like conquest and occupation stand rather more as relics of the past and reminders of how the law must not be allowed to develop.

Orthodox analysis indeed does not account for the full range of interaction between the various categories of territorial acquisition. There is always the danger of doctrinal confusion over the modes of acquisition which may lead to miscarriage of justice in present and future international territorial adjudication. This is more so when the question relates to any of the newer and common territories such as Antarctica, Polar regions, and within very strict legal limits, outer space. Therefore, lawyers must remain knowledgeable about the older categories. On the other hand a rigid attachment to the classic five 'models' without recognising any relationships and connections they may have to each other may lead to confusing analysis. In fact the issue of territorial sovereignty or title over territory is by its very nature complex and involves the application of various principles of law both historical and modern. The process of reconciling them cannot be ascribed to any single dominant rule or mode of territorial acquisition. Disputes arising from the various means of territorial acquisition are not entirely unlikely to repeat themselves, even if in new and novel contexts such as in Antarctica and (in certain respects) outer space.

It must be stated that there is no rule that state territory must at all times be contiguous and there have indeed been many cases of small and large non-contiguous sovereign territories. The territorial state in such instances will enjoy the full complements of coterminous territorial jurisdiction. This was certainly

---

99 John L. Allen Jr, "Indigenous Demand Revocation of 1493 papal bull", *National Catholic Reporter*, 27 October 2000.
100 'God willing' (in Latin).

true of Germany's right over East Prussia (1919–45), East and West Pakistan (before 1971), and of US territory of Alaska. Fragmentation may be an indication of other debilitating disability but it is not determinative of statehood. Neither does fragmentation affect the full complements of the tri-dimensional nature of territory. As aptly summed up by James Crawford 'Sovereignty comes in all shapes and sizes'.[101]

---

101 Crawford, op.cit. (2006), p. 47. States like Sao Tome and Principe consist of many small land areas separated by vast amounts of maritime territory.

3 Frontiers and boundaries in the context of international legal framework of territorial sovereignty and jurisdiction

It is necessary to set the ambition of Africa to successfully demarcate and delimit its independent and sovereign territories within the context of international law and international relations. Terms like 'boundaries', 'border', 'frontiers', 'delimitation demarcation' and 'territory' are often used interchangeably in language without much deference to their technical and legal connotations. It is necessary to formulate clear distinctions between these terms, which sometimes even in legal literature, are treated as synonyms and are virtually indistinguishable to the layman while recognising at the same time the interconnectedness of the pertinent concepts.

3.1 The functionality of frontiers and boundaries

As explained earlier sovereignty and territorial sovereignty are key concepts of public international law that are aspects of the basic constitutional doctrine of the law of nations. The presence of sovereignty imposes a duty of non-intervention in the exclusive jurisdiction of other states. In this way territorial integrity is an integral part and a 'necessary corollary to the principle of territorial sovereignty'.[1] Very importantly, the existence with respect to a state of 'territorial sovereignty extends to the mineral resources in the soil and subsoil of their land territory and territorial sea to an unlimited depth'.[2] It follows, therefore, that no state may exercise rights over mineral resources of other states without their consent.[3] For state sovereignty and territorial jurisdiction to have any practical meaning there must be a way to ascertain territorial extents of states – hence the development of the primordial concepts of boundaries, borders and frontiers.

The multiplicity of states and their rich diversity have led to a variety of conflict situations ranging from traditional bilateral boundary disputes to unilateral claims of one sort or another. Adjudication over disputes relating to international terrestrial and maritime boundaries has occupied the attention of numerous international courts and tribunals particularly in the last hundred years.

---

1 Rainer Lagoni, "Oil and Gas Deposits Across National Frontiers", 73 *American Journal of International Law*, 215–16 (1979), p. 217.
2 L. Oppenheim, *International Law* (H. Lauterpacht, 8th edn 1955), at p. 462; see also P. Fauchille, *Traite De Droit International Public* 99 (H. Bonfils, 8th edn 1925); Lagoni, op. cit., p. 216.
3 *North Sea Continental Shelf Cases*, 1969 ICJ. at 22.

Nevertheless a staggering number of wars and military conflicts have arisen due to border, frontier and territorial questions. Because many of these remain unresolved and as a result of pending geopolitical questions, or irredentist issues the following comment attributed to Verzijl remains apposite. He wrote:

> Political reality shows *ad nauseam* how much weight is still in the present time attached to the frontier as a strict line of separation between territorial sovereignties and how necessary it remains to keep arms at the ready with the object of defending the national territory against treacherous foreign invasions, intrusion of spies, infiltration of subversive propaganda etc. Frontiers as defensive partitions remain indispensable.[4]

Boundaries whether natural, geographic, strategic, secure or artificial should at all points in time remain ascertainable. They should be difficult to violate and strongly defensive and verifiable in character as nature, art, agreement or convention can make them. The importance of international boundary delimitation, however, transcends the defence and security factor. In the long run a boundary may determine for millions the language to speak and the laws that govern their lives. Even mundane aspects of municipal existence such as the books and newspapers which people will be able to buy and read, the kind of money they shall use, the markets in which they must buy and sell and perhaps the kinds of food they may be permitted to eat are all factors of the territorial boundaries in which they belong.[5] The boundaries of a state also determine the lateral limits of the airspace appertaining to that state. However, the inherent difficulties that attend human attempts at developing final and infallible boundaries or frontiers is revealed in the accounts in legal and political literature of border villages in South East Asia which indulge in removing or shifting boundary pillars at the time tax collectors of their own government arrive in autumn and voluntarily and temporarily placing their area in a neighbouring country. Many such opportunistic approaches to boundary beacons also exist in Africa. In the tripoint between Cameroon, Nigeria and Chad around the area of the Lake Chad the local populations simply moved along with the increasingly declining valuable resource of the Lake water without regard to national sovereignty.[6]

---

4 J.H.W. Verzijl, *International Law in Historical Perspective*, Vol. III (Netherlands: A.W. Sijthoff Leyden, 1970) pp. 516–7.
5 S.W. Boggs, *International Boundaries: A Study of Boundary Functions and Problems* (New York: Columbia University Press, 1940) p. 5; Cukwurah, *The Settlement of Boundary Disputes in International Law* (Manchester University Press, 1967), pp. 228–9.
6 Nigeria handed 31 villages in the Lake Chad area to Cameroon. The Nigerian population had been following the receding water in the direction of Cameroon. The villages are: Aisa Kura, Ba Shakka, Chika'a, Darak, Darak Gana, Doron Liman, Doron Mallam, Dororoya, Fagge, Garin Wanzam, Gorea Changi, Gorea Gutum, Jibrillaram, Kafuram, Kamunna, Kanumbari, Karakaya, Kasuram Mareya, Kalti Kime, Kolaram, Logon Labi, Loko Naira, Mukdala, Murdas, Naga'a, Naira, Nimeri, Njia Buniba, Ramin Dorina, Sabon Tumbu and Sokotoram. Nigeria also gained the village of Dambore in this sector. All these exchanges and transfers between the two countries took place in December 2003 as a result of the judgment of the ICJ in the Cameroon–Nigeria

It is in fact common in many parts of Africa that boundary communities engage in some fair level of forum shopping between different jurisdictions for governmental services. Political boundaries experts like Okomu note: '[m]any borderland communities have benefited from the borders in different ways. They can evade taxes on one side of the border, enjoy services such as health care and education on the other side, and have access to goods that are reasonably priced on either side of the border'.[7] Despite the many years of boundary tensions in certain sectors and particularly in relation to Bakassi Peninsula, Cameroonian and Nigerian boundary villages are known to engage in such opportunistic use of their mutual public services especially primary schools, dysentery centres, clinics, mosques and churches. Peninsula children from the boundary communities attended schools that are based in the neighbouring country without let or hindrance and farmers relied on regular vaccination of their livestock from whichever state that was close enough. In 2004, some 17,000 Nigerian refugees were reported to have fled ethnic conflicts between pastoralists and farmers and found refuge in Cameroon where many of them then took permanent residence.[8] The phenomenon of international border as refuge appears to have been taken to a new level in 2014 when more than 600 Nigerian soldiers abandoned the battle for Bama and a few other Nigerian border towns and fled across the border into Cameroon. Cameroonian officials later on helped in repatriating the troops.[9]

3.2 Natural vs artificial boundaries

The placement or misplacement of borders has traditionally presented grave problems. To date there exists no consensus as to what constitutes a boundary in international law. Neither is there clear guidance as to the criteria for measurement or delimitation. There is, however, a distinction between 'boundary' and 'frontier' which is necessary to mention here because of its possible relevance in the emerging African process. In its geographical sense a natural boundary consists of such features as water, a range of rocks or mountains, deserts, forests and the like.[10] In contrast 'artificial boundary' includes such signs as have been purposely put up to indicate the way of the imaginary line. Natural boundaries would apply mostly to land territories, whereas artificial boundaries are prima facie more suited for the delimitation of airspace and maritime zones. However, the distinction between natural and artificial boundaries in the geographical sense has

---

case. See UNOWA, Cameroon–Nigeria Mixed Commission: Background (www.un.org/Depts/dpa/prev_dip/africa/office_for_srsg/cnmc/bkground.htm), accessed 14 December 2008.
7 Okomu (2010); See also our pictures of African borders and border crossings in Appendix III.
8 See the discussion on Nigeria transnational issues in *World Fact Book* available at http://www.cia.gov/cia/publications/factbook/geos/ni.html, accessed 2 April 2006.
9 Associated Press, "Hundreds Flee Homes in Northern Nigeria as Boko Haram Move In", *The Guardian*, 5 September 2014, available at http://www.theguardian.com/world/2014/sep/05/hundreds-flee-homes-nigeria-islamic-extremists-boko-haram accessed 06 September 2014. For pictures of refugees on the move in Africa see Appendix III.
10 Oppenheim and Lauterpacht, *International Law*, Vol. 1, 8th edn (1955), p. 531.

been criticised on the ground that it is not sharp, in so far as some natural boundaries can be artificially created. Thus, a forest may be planted and desert may be created, as was the frequent practice of the Romans of antiquity for the purpose of marking frontiers. In essence, qualities, which really belong merely to the surveyor's lines of demarcation, have been attributed to boundaries as political lines of separation and given legal significance.

In reality the regional movements of civilisation have not in fact conformed themselves in all cases to the physical contour line of nature.[11] This is particularly true of African states. The utility of natural features as a marker of natural boundaries breaks down irretrievably in the delimitation of certain environments such as great ocean expanses, air space and outer space. Indeed natural boundaries are difficult to determine in a totally natural environment where there are no visually perceptible differences in features. Thus, most boundaries today result from conscious and arbitrary delimitation exercises. For this reason certain jurists are of the view that nowadays no boundaries can be regarded as 'natural' boundaries and that consequently all boundaries are artificial. According to this view, rivers, mountains, deserts etc. are 'derived artificial boundaries' as distinct from the more commonly referred to 'artificial boundaries' – such as parallels of latitude and meridians of longitude. These latter categories are, therefore, artificial boundaries properly so called.[12] It is important to highlight the limitations of reliance on natural boundaries. Simply because a line is marked along natural or geographical lines does not necessarily imply that it is a 'natural' line of separation between neighbouring peoples or territories. There are a host of other considerations, which must be given effect to in arriving at a consensus with legal significance.

3.3 Frontier vs boundary

A necessary technical distinction must be made between frontiers and boundaries in legal literature. A boundary denotes a line whereas a frontier is more properly a region or zone having width as well as length and, therefore, merely indicates, without fixing the exact limit, where one state ends and another begins. In effect a boundary girds a frontier and more often than not, it is the expansion of a frontier owing to pressure from within which so frequently renders a boundary necessary.[13] A frontier is but a vague and indefinite term until a boundary is set putting a hedge between it and the frontier of a neighbouring State. The term 'boundary', therefore, denotes a line such as may be defined from point to point

---

11 C. Fenwick, *International Law* 4th edn, (New York: Appleton-Century-Crofts, 1965), p. 437.
12 See Paul de Lapradelle, *La Frontiere* (Paris: Les Éditions Internationales, 1928) p. 175; see Yehuda Z. Blum, *Secure Boundaries and Middle East Peace: In the Light of International Law and Practice* (Jerusalem: Hanakor Press, 1971).
13 O. Cukwurah, op. cit., p. 11. For the distinction between boundaries and frontiers see further Surga P. Sharma, *Delimitation of Land and Sea Boundaries between Neighbouring Countries*, (New Delhi: Lancers Books, 1989). See also Blum, ibid., p. 15.

in an arbitral award, treaty, boundary commission report agreement, etc. Therefore, delimitation and then demarcation of a boundary were the central tasks before the EEBC and EECC (*Eritrea v Ethiopia* dispute) and ICJ and CNMC (*Cameroon v Nigeria* dispute) respectively.[14] It is perhaps more apt to speak at the present only in terms of the frontiers of airspace and outer space – for at present no specific boundaries exist between the two in international law.[15] It may, however, be observed that the wide acceptance of the existence of a frontier would make the establishment of a boundary possible but not necessarily easy. In fact in many instances it may be the seeming impossibility of establishing a boundary or the lack of satisfactory technical details that makes states and international lawyers settle for the recognition of frontiers. It is in this category that majority of African 'frontier–boundaries' exist.

The importance of clearly defined borders, boundaries and frontiers becomes more discernible when 'boundary disputes' or 'frontier disputes' occur. As a matter of principle the determination of the location in detail of boundaries is distinct from the issue of title to territory. This is because considerable dispositions of territory may take place in which the grantee enjoys the benefit of a title derived from the grant although no determination of the precise frontier line is made. On the other hand precise determination of the frontier may be made a suspensive condition in a treaty of cession. On occasion the distinction between cession and the fixing of a boundary involves considerations of convenience rather than logic. Nevertheless there is no gainsaying the fact that questions of territory and frontiers or boundaries are quite interrelated and at times it may be difficult, and perhaps serve no useful purpose to determine whether a frontier or boundary dispute is in fact a territorial one or vice versa in as much as the relevant legal criteria are applicable to either class of the dispute.

---

14 See Progress Report of the Secretary-General on Ethiopia and Eritrea to the Security Council of 13 December 2001, available at http://www.pca-cpa.org/PDF/UNSG%20Report3.pdf
15 For further on this issue see Gbenga Oduntan, "The Never Ending Dispute: Legal Theories on the Spatial Demarcation Boundary Plane between Airspace and Outer Space", *Hertfordshine Law Journal* (2003), pp. 64–83 available at http://www.herts.ac.uk/fms/documents/schools/Law/HLJ_V1I2_Oduntan.pdf visited 10 December 2008.

4 Province of international boundary disputes determined

Pertinent questions here include whether it is indeed possible to identify the basic kernel of what constitutes an international dispute. Disputes over territory come in various forms and shapes and are usually entwined together with other issues of law and politics, sometimes making it near impossible to isolate the strictly legal issues that may be treated in resolving the dispute.

4.1 What are international boundary disputes?

The boundaries between nations (land, maritime and air) present many opportunities for international disputes. Land boundary disputes may involve disagreement over interpretation of applicable treaties that delimit the boundaries between two or more states. It may involve trespass by nationals of another state which occur advertently or inadvertently (such as the way in which up to 33 Nigerian small villages shifted and followed a receding lake, thereby crossing into Cameroonian territory without any governmental involvement).

Deliberate incursion by military personnel would nearly always create serious contention and reaction from the territorial state (Djiboutian–Eritrean border conflict).[1] In relation to the sea; adjacent or opposite states may disagree over the boundaries separating their respective maritime zones (e.g., *Qatar v Bahrain Maritime Delimitation and Territorial Questions* and the evolving situation in the Gulf of Guinea). One state may claim the right to conduct naval manoeuvres in the EEZ of another state whilst the latter would typically deny the existence of such rights.[2] Another state may seek to exclude fishermen from neighbouring states and

---

1 The Djiboutian–Eritrean border conflict between the forces of Djibouti and Eritrea occurred between 10 June and 13 June 2008. Djibouti reported that on 16 April 2008, Eritrean armed forces penetrated deep into Djiboutian territory and dug trenches on both sides of the border. Armed clashes have since broken out between the two armed forces in their common border areas. "Djibouti–Eritrea Border Skirmishes Subside as Toll Hits Nine", Agence France-Presse, 13 June 2008; BBC, "US condemns Eritrea 'aggression'", *BBC News*, 12 June 2008, at http://news.bbc.co.uk/1/hi/world/africa/7450075.stm, accessed June 2008.
2 R. R. Churchill and A. V. Lowe, *The Law of the Sea*, 3rd edn (Manchester: Manchester Univ. Press, 1999), p. 447. States like Bangladesh, Brazil, Cape Verde, Malaysia, India and Pakistan have all expressed concern over the ability of foreign military vessels to engage in certain activities within the EEZ. Jing Geng, 'The Legality of Foreign Military Activities in the Exclusive Economic Zone

exercise powers of arrest over them for many miles from its coast (Africa–European Union disputes; Namibia–South Africa).[3] The right of a sovereign to continue fishing in the waters of a separatist territory may be called into question (Morocco–Western Sahara).[4] In the air, on an annual basis, states experience dozens of contentious disagreements over the trespass of aircraft, drones and other aerial vehicles into national territory.[5] Although not as prevalent as it is of the case in the Middle East and Europe, the African continent has recorded many aerial trespass disputes of its own.[6] Invariably disagreement over ownership of a territory will extend to a contest over the airspace above that territory. There is also the possibility of dispute over the spatial demarcation problem in international law

under UNCLOS', Vol. 28, *Merkourio: Utrecth Journal of International and European Security Law*, No.74 (2012), p. 25.

3 The agreement, framed in a renewable annual protocol drawn up by the European Commission, cost €36 million and gave access to more than 100 European boats. In the1970s Namibia's waters were fished for hake (mainly by South African vessels) to the point of depletion. As a result and the legacy of losses the country 'has since Namibianized its fisheries', and provided for exclusive enforcement methods. U. TharaSrinivasan, Reg Watson, U. Rashid Sumaila, "Global Fisheries Losses at the Exclusive Economic Zone Level, 1950 to Present", *Marine Policy* 36 (2012), p. 547 available at http://www.ecomarres.com/downloads/Loss3.pdf, accessed 13 July 2014.

4 Fishing has become the most politically sensitive industry in terms of the Western Sahara debate, and the EU has become closely associated with this issue largely because of a fishing agreement between Morocco and the EU introduced in 2006. It has been alleged that Morocco maintains fisheries agreements with the EU to legitimise Morocco's illegal occupation of Western Sahara by making the EU an accomplice to the fact. Aidan Lewis, "Morocco's Fish Fight: High Stakes over Western Sahara", *BBC News*, 15 December 2011 available at http://www.bbc.co.uk/news/world-africa-16101666, accessed 13 July 2014.

5 The problem of airspace trespass remains one of the bugbears of international relations and threatens only to escalate in frequency and severity of consequences given technological developments and the prevalence of intractable political differences that surround the practice. The mischief is very prevalent and affects states irrespective of size, relative military importance, ideology or population.

6 One of the earliest disputes dates back to 21 February 1973 when a Libyan Airlines Boeing 727 civil aircraft scheduled flight from Tripoli to Cairo overflew Cairo and was shot down 12 miles into occupied Sinai costing 108 lives. There were disagreements as to whether warnings were given. Israel justified its action stating the flight was over a highly sensitive Israeli controlled area but the International Civil Aviation Organisation (ICAO) passed a Resolution on 4 June 1973 condemning Israeli action. More recently, at 08.00 hrs on 16 July 2009 two Chadian Sukhoi fighter jets and a Chadian helicopter were alleged to have engaged in an aerial bombardment of the Um Dukhun area which is within the borders of the Sudan. A Chadian helicopter also bombarded that city at 11:00 hrs on the same day, dropping two bombs that fell some 500 metres from the market. Sudan reserved its unrestricted and legitimate right to respond decisively to this attack and to previous trespass, aggressions and violations in a letter dated 16 July 2009 from the Chargé d'affaires of the Permanent Mission of the Sudan to the United Nations and to the President of the Security Council. Similar incidents were said to have occurred on 18 and 27 June 2009 at 08:30 hrs when two Mirage and two Jaguar fighter jets belonging to Chad violated Sudanese airspace over a distance of several dozen kilometres. They allegedly circled at medium altitude east of the city of Kulbus in Darfur (coordinates 1422–2246). The Government of the Sudan reserved its full, sovereign and legitimate right to respond to those violations in such a manner as to preserve the sovereignty and national security of the country and addressed a letter dated 13 July 2009 from the Permanent Representative of the Sudan to the United Nations and to the President of the Security Council. S/2009/355. Between 1951 and January 2011 a total of 1,403 written state protestations including some refutations) were reported to the United Nations concerning trespass in airspace. Some states are particularly susceptible to the tensions and occurrences of aerial trespass. These

(i.e. the height at which other states must steer clear of national territory in aerial or space flight in order not to violate airspace). At least two African states – Nigeria and Tunisia – have already expressed a clear opinion on this problem which may put them potentially in conflict with developed states.[7]

Evidently the causes, types and manifestation of boundary dispute are legion. Tim Daniel, a lawyer with many years of boundary disputes litigation involving African states, draws attention to the hazards of attempting a definition of disputes. He wrote:

> Ordinarily, one would think that it is relatively easy to know whether or not a dispute exists. It is, however, a requirement under the rules both of the ITLOS and of the ICJ that a dispute must first exist before the parties can refer the subject-matter to the Court/Tribunal. It is not uncommon, in cases where a unilateral application is made, for the defending state to argue, by way of preliminary objection, that there is no dispute capable of adjudication by the Court/Tribunal.

The definition of an international dispute – just as the celebrated English writer T. S. Eliot said of the naming of cats – is 'a difficult matter' and is not 'just one of your holiday games'.[8] Literature in the area tends to lump too many issues into a single category of 'boundary dispute'. Where, for instance, two neighbouring states are in agreement on the alignment of 99.9 per cent of their boundary but disagree over the thalweg (the centre of the navigable channel) in relation to the last 800 meters in a river, would it be reasonable or accurate to classify this as a 'dispute' in the same category as a 'dispute' over an entire Peninsula? It is obviously easier to use the term 'boundary dispute' in relation to the Bakassi dispute or a significant area of territory such as the Hala'ib Triangle; but is it technically correct to call these boundary disputes given that it is the territory that is actually in dispute and not just an alignment?[9] What if there are five sections of a long boundary which are disputed for different reasons: can we call this one boundary dispute or should it be five disputes? Is it proper to still classify the Eritrea–Ethiopia

---

include Cyprus–Turkey, India–Pakistan, Iraq–USA, Cuba–USA, Lebanon–Israel (and possibly, UK–France). Gbenga Oduntan, *Sovereignty and Jurisdiction in the Airspace and Outer Space Legal Criteria for Spatial Delimitation* (Oxon: Routledge, 2012), pp. 150–51.

7 Nigeria and Tunisia both belong to the school of thought that there is a pressing need to define the spatial demarcation boundary plane between airspace and outer space. Tunisia goes on further to believe that the ability to maintain aerial security or the need to do so should be considered in arriving at a suitable height. Nigeria for its part further believes that delimitation in the air will add to the sovereignty and equality of states principles inherent in international law and to which the country subscribes to in entirety. The technologically developed states such as the US and the UK deny the need for such spatial delimitation. Oduntan, ibid., pp. 359–60; Daniel, op.cit., pp. 224–5.

8 'The Naming of Cats' is a poem by T. S. Eliot from *Old Possum's Book of Practical Cats* (Faber and Faber, 1939).

9 The *Hala'ib* Triangle is an area of land measuring 20,580 sq. km (7,950 sq miles) located on the Red Sea's African coast. The area takes its name from the town of Hala'ib. The triangle is created by the difference in the Egypt–Sudan border between the 'political boundary' set in 1899 by the Anglo-Egyptian Condominium, which runs along the 22nd parallel north, and the 'administrative

boundary as one of the African boundary disputes? Delimitation and demarcation of this boundary has taken place to wide acclaim by the international community and by a boundary commission which was given authority to make final and binding decisions by the parties. This was preceded by a final and binding arbitration by the EEBC – hence, the inherent difficulty with the opinion that there remains a legal basis for a dispute between the parties in relation to their territorial extents. Yet the two countries are clearly not entirely at peace with regard to the line that the Arbitral Commission defined for them. At what point does an un-delimited maritime boundary in an area where there is clear overlapping jurisdictional entitlements become a disputed maritime boundary? The list of possible points of factual and conceptual confusion is nearly endless. Counting disputes is an interesting and challenging exercise; and many writers and even governmental websites engage in this exercise but an academic that seriously pinpoints any number engages in hazardous activity and would perhaps raise as many questions as he hopes to answer.

The late Sir Ian Brownlie reflected eloquently on the nature of boundary disputes in his introduction to *African Boundaries: A Legal and Diplomatic Encyclopedia*. He wrote:

> As a matter of political fact, as reflected in international law, the concept of a 'dispute' involves certain specific elements. It involves a disagreement between two states on a point of law or fact, which disagreement is normally manifested by the making of a claim or protest. The claim or protest should be expressed by properly authorized agents at the appropriate level and in the appropriate form: in diplomatic exchanges, in applications sent to the Registry of the International Court of Justice, at a session of a diplomatic conference, or at a session of a meeting of an international organization. The claim or position expressed in the form of a protest must be opposed by the other state concerned.[10]

As a result only a proportion of the situations catalogued by some authors technically qualify in law as 'disputes'. That, however, is not the end of the matter. Eminent jurists like Brownlie have always insisted on a more precise and more technical conception of boundary disputes. One outcome of this is the setting aside in legal textbooks of a proportion of issues which are either not concerned with delimited boundaries or do not qualify as disputes. A further outcome is the

---

boundary' set by the British in 1902, which gave administrative responsibility for an area of land north of the line to Sudan, which was an Anglo–Egyptian client at the time. Since the independence of Sudan in 1956, both Egypt and Sudan have claimed sovereignty over the area. See Office of Geography, Sudan–Egypt (United Arab Republic) Boundary International Boundary Study #18, Bureau of Intelligence and Research, US Department of State (27 July 1962); "Sudan's Bashir reiterates sovereignty over disputed border area of Halayeb", *Sudan Tribune* (1 July 2010), available at http://www.sudantribune.com/spip.php?article35542, accessed 12 January 2013.

10 Ian Brownlie, *African Boundaries: A Legal and Diplomatic Encyclopaedia* (C. Hurst & Co., 1979), pp. 13–14.

inclusion of a large range of issues often involving very restricted points of principle relating to alignments, including the location of tripoints, or to demarcation of boundaries. To lawyers adopting the more precise form a 'dispute' does not necessarily involve hot blood, threats to use force and the like. They note that states may and do pursue claims against a background of normal and even close relations. Journalists and political scientists are seen as tending towards the dramatic and 'conflict'-seeking, and in so doing may not appreciate the normal and the undramatic. Furthermore and particularly in relation to issues affecting boundaries, there is the question of scale. While many of the disputes and issues relating to boundaries in places like Africa involve small areas and restricted technical points, disproportionate attention appears to be given to disagreements over large territories and politically charged boundary disputes. Of course, even small areas may generate heat when questions of rights are in issue and even a small area may allow access to a valuable mineral deposit. The current dispute over Lake Nyasa is a case in point where, by and large, the governments concerned seem to have shown little sense of proportion from the perspective of outside observers.

States are also not always trigger happy in finding a reason for quarrelling over territory. If anything they are mostly slow and reluctant to act for various reasons. Even when map and other items of evidence held and presented by various authors and even foreign countries show anomalies and confusing details which could trigger potential disputes (at least in a technical sense), in many cases little or no reaction is elicited from the affected state(s). Such anomalies do not always immediately invoke concepts of 'dispute' or 'conflict'. In many cases in which such anomalies come to light, they are settled by administrative action on the basis of informal agreement between the governments concerned. Even when anomalies come to light they are commonly settled by administrative action on the basis of informal agreement between the governments concerned. It is in this light that it is concluded here that the term 'boundary dispute' belongs to the definer and the discipline he espouses. Boundary dispute to an international lawyer may have a different sense from its meanings to a political scientist, a diplomat, a geographer or a journalist. These professions all have useful and viable conceptualisations of boundary dispute. They may be useful for different purposes in real life situations as well. While the journalist's and political scientist's connotations may fall short of evidence capable of seizing an international court of jurisdiction in a case, it is very possible that it is only in their own sense that the dispute may be resolved at the end of the day by negotiation, mediation or other peaceful means.

Nonetheless we should proceed by identifying and delineating what is meant by the term 'international disputes' at least in relation to the justiciable issues that could be submitted to the contentious jurisdiction of courts such as the ICJ. It suffices to mention that without international disputes there would be no need for the contentious jurisdiction of international courts. Curiously though even within the field of public international law there is no generally accepted definition of 'international disputes' anywhere in treaties or literature. Yet legal consequences for States arise from the existence of such disputes. However, the PCIJ attempted a definition in the *Marvrommatis Palestine Concession Case* (1927).

Here 'international dispute' was defined as 'a disagreement on a point of law or fact, a conflict of legal views or of interests between two persons'. The ICJ has since accepted this but as Judge Fitzmaurice said in the *Cameroons case* (1963), 'a dispute must involve more than a mere difference in opinion'.[11] The term 'dispute', thus, has a technical connotation in international law. This is more so in the determination as to what can and cannot be submitted to the contentious jurisdiction of the ICJ. The Court has on occasion noted that whether an international dispute exists or not is a matter for objective determination, and that an international dispute will be held to be in existence when two sides 'hold clearly opposite views concerning the question'. The essential element of a dispute being 'a divergence of views between the parties on definite points' (*Peace Treaties Case* (1950) and *Asylum Case* (Interpretation (1950)).

International lawyers stress that there is such a thing as the justiciability of disputes, with reference to the accepted distinction between legal and political questions. Thus, it could happen that a demand to settle a particular dispute made by a state is rejected by the ICJ. For instance, if a developing state demands preferential treatment from a developed state, such a claim based as it is on moral and supposedly non-legal grounds could be rejected by the ICJ. A political question in the true sense may translate into a demand for the development of international law beyond existing law. Many disputes submitted to the Court over the last 69 years have involved such demands. There is nothing inherently wrong in this, particularly in the sphere of advisory opinions. The UN Secretary General's Report to the General Assembly in 1991 wisely counsels that questions which seem entirely political, but which 'have a clearly legal component' could be usefully referred to the Court for an advisory opinion, 'if for any reason the parties fail to refer the matter to Court'.

The German government's claims for delineation of non-defined borders in the *Continental Shelf Cases* (1967), for instance, pushed to extreme limits the issue of justiciability. But the compromise achieved between the parties kept it within legal limits so that the Court was able to decide the issue.[12] In these cases the Netherlands and Denmark were shown to have convex coasts whereas the Germany's North Sea coast is concave. The equidistance rule allows for 'drawing a line each point of which is equally distant from each shore'. If the delimitation had been determined by this rule *simplicta*, Germany would have received a smaller portion of the resource-rich shelf – relative to the two other states. Germany argued

---

11 Fitzmaurice, Separate Opinion Northern Camaroons Case, ICS Rep. (1963), p. 109.
12 Articles 1–3 of the Special Agreement between the Governments of Denmark and the Federal Republic of Germany founded the Court's jurisdiction stating; 'Article 1 (1),The International Court of Justice is requested to decide the following question: What principles and rules of international law are applicable to the delimitation as between the Parties of the areas of the continental shelf in the North Sea which appertain to each of them beyond the partial boundary determined by the above-mentioned Convention of 9 June 1965? (2),The Governments of the Kingdom of Denmark and of the Federal Republic of Germany shall delimit the continental shelf in the North Sea as between their countries by agreement in pursuance of the decision requested from the International Court of Justice.' See *North Sea Continental Shelf*, *Judgment*, ICJ Rep (1969), p. 3.

forcefully that the length of the coastlines be used to determine the delimitation. Accordingly Germany wanted the ICJ to apportion the continental shelf to the proportion of the size of the state's adjacent land and not by the rule of equidistance. The Court ultimately urged the parties to 'abat[e] the effects of an incidental special feature [Germany's concave coast] from which an unjustifiable difference of treatment could result.' Germany succeeded in subsequent negotiations with the other states to secure their acceptance that it should receive the additional shelf it sought.[13] The *Continental shelf Cases* are, thus, viewed in legal commentary as prime example of the application of 'equity *praeter legem*'. In such instances judges go 'beyond the law' – and supplement the law with equitable rules necessary to decide the case at hand. In such cases the worlds of law and politics align in the clear night sky of justice and in the interest of peace. In other words what appears to be a lack of legal rights to a boundary line claim or a territory may still be the subject of a legal dispute and the basis of an international court's exercise of jurisdiction.

There is yet another type of political question, namely those that could be legally decided, but which a state may not wish to have legally decided by an international court. This refers to the age old problem of 'vital issues', questions of honour or domestic jurisdiction. These are questions of international concern and which an international court could settle but on which an independent state is unwilling to accept an international court's judgment. Whether an international court will accept such arguments or objections to its jurisdiction will depend on the statute upon which it operates.

It is, therefore, not possible to isolate any single principle of justiciability even for boundary disputes and an attempt to do so will only produce controversy and perhaps unsound legal reasoning. There are certainly cases of functional non-justiciability, for example where the parties have not properly presented the issues to the international court. Yet even in such cases it is within the competence of international courts to deal with the relevant issues whether or not the parties had pleaded or argued the cases accordingly. In this manner justiciability is ultimately a matter of policy and this may be measured (but is definitely not necessarily limited) by the standard assumptions of the legal persons most closely affected. International courts such as the ICJ would in all cases steer clear of the application of municipal law.

The distinction between legal and political disputes is particularly crucial with respect to Article 36(2) of the ICJ Statute, which establishes the system of compulsory jurisdiction. The jurisdiction over 'legal disputes' enumerated in paragraphs (a)–(d) is not at all easy to identify. Some writers argue that in the strict sense of the term a dispute means only a dispute as to the existence on the basis of law, of an obligation of one state in relation to another state. In short, only legal disputes are in fact true disputes. Other writers take a broader view and

---

13 Mark W. Janis, *An Introduction to International Law*, 4th ed. (New York: Aspen, 2003), pp. 70, 73; 1969 ICJ Rep 4, 50.

maintain that the existence of the political dimension is not a bar to classifying a dispute as a legal dispute. It may be concluded then that although not all disputes are legal, all legal disputes are political to some extent. Moreover, in actual practice, states regard international disputes as fundamentally political in nature and invariably treat all disputes in a political sense. This is certainly the case with most boundary disputes whether territorial, political, or land- or maritime-based. This perhaps accounts partly for the phobia of the majority of states to submit fully to the compulsory jurisdiction of the ICJ or even to avail themselves sufficiently of the services of the Court. In practice, however, the Court hardly if ever concludes that it lacks jurisdiction ostensibly because the dispute was not legal in nature.

There is no dispute which is inherently immune to legal treatment once the parties are agreed to depoliticise it and provide the Court with the means to act. The distinction between justiciable and non-justiciable disputes seems to be borne out of practicability and politics rather than compelling theoretical necessities. The important things to look for are whether or not the pronouncement of the Court is likely to form the basis for the ultimate settlement of the problems and relax rising tensions.

The question may still be posed, does 'dispute' and 'difference of opinion' or 'divergence of views' mean the same thing as has been assumed by some writers, or is the concept of 'difference of opinion' used to indicate a milder form of disagreement? Some writers believe that it would help ease the tension among states and improve the prospects of settling the dispute if the divergent assessment of a point of law were to be brought as soon as possible before a neutral body – without even waiting for an actual case to arise and before the difference had a chance to become unnecessarily entrenched in the course of protracted diplomatic negotiations.[14] Hasty referral to an international court may on the other hand thicken the plot and bury the chances of negotiated peace and genuine reconciliation. It appears, however, to have been established that a purely theoretical difference of opinion as to a question of law or fact is not enough to constitute a 'dispute' in the legal sense. An international dispute has, therefore, a conception narrower than 'case' or 'matter' which may relate not to a dispute, but to what the parties may choose to call a 'difference'; that is to say, to something broader and perhaps less than a dispute.[15]

In the last three decades of African international relations, the international implications of insurgency and even more the pressure of liberating and separatist movements blur even further the dividing line between international and internal disputes. With the end of the Cold War and its super power rivalries and alignments, African states have tended to generate such serious intra-state

---

14 Hans Von Mangoldt, "Arbitration and Conciliation" in Max Planck Institute for Comparative Public Law and International Law, *Judicial Settlement of International Disputes* (Berlin and New York: Springer Verlag, 1974), p. 520.
15 Shabtai Rosenne, *The International Court of Justice: An Essay in Political and Legal Theory* (Netherlands: A. W. Sijthoff-Leiden Oceana, 1957), p. 307.

conflicts, now reshaping the definition of international disputes. The recent events in Liberia, Democratic Republic of Congo, Sierra Leone, Libya, Nigeria (Boko Haram), the breakaway republics of the former USSR, Yugoslavia, Somalia, Angola, Mozambique, Rwanda, Burundi and Yemen typify such a development. To effectively cope with such situations it is necessary to give a broad interpretation to the concept of international dispute. It may be observed that since the whole purpose of defining an international dispute is the maintenance of peace, the terms should not be too narrowly construed nor made too elastic. Article 33 of the Charter, which states that an international dispute is 'any dispute the continuance of which is likely to endanger the maintenance of international peace and security', provides a useful guide. Civil wars, however, have not traditionally been considered international disputes. What makes a civil war develop into international conflict is the decision reached by different states about which is the legitimate government and which group should be regarded merely as insurgents. It is when the outsider intervenes not on the side of the legitimate government but on the side of insurgents that the conflict becomes international.[16] In other words, a civil war where the *casus belli* includes the desire to break the polity into two or more territories is not an international dispute. This is despite the fact that the eventual breakdown of the pre-existing state and the emergence of new one(s) will have repercussions on international boundaries.

The distinction drawn in the UN Charter between situation and disputes is more important in relation to some Charter Articles than to others. For instance, the duty of arbitration imposed on the Security Council under Article 37(2) applies only to disputes. In other Articles the term 'situation' does not form a contrast to disputes but as the wider term, is intended to include disputes: as in Articles 11(3) and 14 of the UN Charter. In interpreting the meaning of the term 'dispute' in jurisdictional clauses both the ICJ and the proceeding PCIJ had always given it a liberal construction to define it in its widest sense as any disagreement between parties. It is suggested that the proposed African Court of Justice will not find it difficult to follow this practice. Perhaps it could be safely concluded that an international dispute is a contentious disenchantment between two or more states over points of law and/or fact, the continuance of which can endanger international peace and security.

4.2 Internal boundary disputes

Though this work concerns itself primarily with international boundaries it is important to note that internal boundary delimitation and sometimes demarcation within independent states can be as fraught with difficulties and complexities

---

16 As a writer explains '[w]hatever its precise form, external intervention has the effect of making the conflict a matter of international concern.' Sydney D. Bailey, *How Wars End: The United Nations and the Termination of Armed Conflict 1946–1964*, Vol. 1 (Oxford: Clarendon Press, 1985), p. 20; As Reuter correctly notes, 'war takes on many forms: civil wars merge into international law', Raul Reuter, op. cit., p. 32.

as international boundaries. Internal boundary disputes occurring within independent African states ravage the entire continent. It is fair to say they constitute the vast majority of boundary disputes within the continent. Internal boundaries are drawn up according to national laws and regulations and constitute the very core of political decision making, often revealing the liveliest dramas of nationhood. It may in fact be suggested that more violence and humanitarian crises have been caused by internal boundary disputes within African states than have been caused by the delimitation and demarcation of external boundaries. It is also the case that many decades after independence, internal boundaries are still very much a reflection of colonial efforts. Herein lies the roots of many of the conflicts afflicting African nations. The internal boundaries even more than the external boundaries were drawn up for the administrative and political convenience of the colonial powers. Hence client ethnic groups would have been favoured and those deemed as recalcitrant, resisting or irredentist would have been ingeniously disfavoured in both overt and covert methods of internal boundary delineation.

The question that will appear in the minds of the non-African reader will be why not redraw the boundaries to reflect local realities? In reality the tasks can be extremely difficult and, in some instances, maybe even more so than in the case of external boundary disputes. There are of course more boundaries within states and, therefore, more potential and actual flashpoints. Indeed European political theory recognises that choices about sub-national organisation are inherently controversial. Such choices would often involve power-sharing arrangements and the carving up of a territory into smaller jurisdictions. Of these choices and their inherent susceptibility to conflict it has been well noted that:

> sometimes choices are based on well researched recommendations with easily grasped consequences. More often territorial choices are fuzzy affairs with numerous battlefronts and bewildering claims of benefits and pitfalls associated with the various options. Is a unitary urban authority better for a large conurbation than retaining a number of smaller jurisdictions? Better for whom, or for what purposes or functions? .... And then there is the related issue of finances: how are jurisdictions to be delineated so that local authorities are financially viable? Territorial choice also impacts on political chances and careers. One way of carving up the territory may ensure the permanence of left-wing strongholds, another way of cutting the pie may yield right-wing bastions.[17]

It is, therefore, clear as in the case of international boundaries, that decision making and action relating to the perseverance and/or modification of internal boundaries are to be precipitated by intelligent choices, carefully made in the very

---

17 Harald Baldersheim and Lawrewnce E. Rose, "A Comparative Analysis of Territorial Choice in Europe–Conclusions" in Harald Baldersheim and Lawrence E. Rose (eds.), *Territorial Choice: The Politics of Boundaries and Borders* (New York: Palgrave Macmillan, 2010), p. 234.

best tradition of deliberate diplomacy. In a lot of cases the dispute will arise on the same scale as the *uti possidetis* argument in the sense of where was the internal line drawn as at independence? It is usually on the basis of this that understanding of where a province or local government boundary should lie even if it has been changed more than once since independence. This is because the initial boundaries on independence would have been the reference point upon which subsequent changes would have been based and if the question is where are the territorial extents of the new division lines, the older delimitation will still be of relevance.

Preserving the existing lines can be difficult enough. Now if the task administrators are facing is to reform existing boundaries, local governments or wards, the job becomes at least tenfold more precarious. As succinctly put by one authority, 'One of the reasons why reforms of this magnitude are difficult to carry through is that they always involve confiscation of privileges in the form of money, status, positions and access, and often a major reshuffling of identities'.[18] The presence or discovery of significant mineral resources tends to exacerbate internal boundary disputes particularly in African federations such as Nigeria.

Internal boundary disputes may literally down the line involve another independent state or its interests and this may easily internationalise the dispute. Many of the solutions discussed and recommendations given in this book are also relevant and useful to the resolution of land and maritime disputes that arise within one state.

4.3 Territorial vs boundary disputes

Sometimes the distinction between disputes concerning international boundaries and disputes arising out of the acquisition of territory are blurred. Indeed both boundary and territorial questions are part of the larger question of territorial sovereignty;[19] In the *Temple of Preah Vihear* (Cambodia v Thailand) even though the dispute in principle involved conflicting claims to sovereignty over the disputed regions, the ICJ nevertheless dealt at length in its decision on the legal boundary line between the two.[20]

From a strict legal point of view, however, factual and legal differences exist between the two types of disputes. Boundary issues are involved when two (or more) adjacent governmental entities dispute the line to be drawn between their respective territorial domains. In such cases it is common ground that both (or more) states have lawful claims to adjacent territory. The real question to be decided is how the territory can be divided between them. For instance, in accordance with the provisions of the 12 December 2000 Agreement Between the Government of the Federal Democratic Republic of Ethiopia and the Government of the State of Eritrea, the mandate of the *Eritrea–Ethiopia boundary*

---

18 Ibid., p. 39.
19 Surya P. Sharma, "Boundary Dispute and Territorial Dispute: A Comparison", Vol. 10, *Indian Journal of International Law*, No. 2 (1970).
20 ICJ Rep. 1962, p. 14.

Commission is to delimit and demarcate the colonial treaty boundary based on pertinent colonial treaties of 1900, 1902 and 1908 and applicable international law (*Eritrea–Ethiopia boundary Commission Arbitration* 2000).

On the other hand, territorial disputes may not always involve the drawing of lines between adjacent territorial communities. In fact disputes relating to territorial acquisition will involve the intent by one party to exercise sovereignty and jurisdiction over either the entire territory or large parcels of it. It would normally involve a denial of the rights of the competing party to that territory. Even though disputes about the acquisition of territory are strictly competitive as between the claimants (in the sense that one must lose completely), a boundary dispute on its own would involve a disagreement over alignment of lines in relation to the particular region. There is the possibility of a boundary dispute involving more than two parties in a region. The Somali claims in the 1970s incorporating as it did all Somali-dominated adjoining areas involved a four-way controversy between Kenya, Ethiopia, the French and Somali land. Similarly disputes relating to territorial control may involve more than one independent state and may occur in a territory, which historically belongs to no state, such as the overlapping claims over Antarctic sectors made by Chile, Argentina and the United Kingdom.

Territorial questions would ordinarily involve a determination of the applicable root of title including which of the traditional rules governing modes of acquisition of title applies (e.g. discovery, occupation, conquest, cession or prescription). In a sense territorial contests are part and parcel of a dispute between a sovereign state and a separatist movement within its territory striving for separate existence. It is indeed in this sense that Africa at present appears to be more exposed to territorial questions.[21] Boundary questions on the other hand would involve only those rules which are relevant to specifying functions performed in the fixation and maintenance of boundaries (e.g. determination, delimitation, demarcation and administration). The Iraqi attempt to annex Kuwait in 1990 is a classic case of a dispute relating to territorial acquisition.[22] So also is the continuous challenge in recent times by Turkey of the sovereignty of several hundred Greek islands, Greek territorial waters, and of Greek national airspace.[23] The *Land and Maritime Boundary between Cameroon and Nigeria* case (discussed at length below) is an example of a boundary dispute that involves territorial (Bakassi Peninsula) and boundary (land and maritime) aspects.

Certain principles assist international courts and tribunals in the resolution of boundary and territorial disputes. In the words of the arbitrator in the *Island of*

---

21 See below at 16.2: *Uti Possidetis* within the equation of political separation and self-determination.
22 George K. Walker, "The Crisis Over Kuwait, August 1990 – February 1991", Vol. 25 *Duke Journal of Comparative & International Law* (1991), pp. 29–33; Oscar Schacher, 'United Nations Law in the Gulf Conflict', Vol. 85 *American Journal of International Law*, no. 3 (1991), pp. 452–73.
23 International Crisis Group, Turkey and Greece: Time to Settle the Aegean Dispute *Crisis Group Europe Briefing* N°64, (19 July 2011), p. 1. Available at www.crisisgroup.org, accessed 06 September 2014.

Palmas Case, 'the act of peaceful and continuous display (of sovereignty) is still one of the most important considerations in establishing boundaries between States'.[24] To this extent territorial disputes and boundary or frontier disputes are interrelated. In most cases boundary changes imply the diminution or enhancement of territory and jurisdiction for the affected states. The principle of *uti possidetis* operates to ensure that boundaries have a compelling degree of continuity and finality. In order to avert numerous boundary conflicts and wars among the African states in 1963 and 1964, the founding fathers of the Organization of African Unity (OAU) adopted the principle so as to preserve the territorial *status quo*.[25] The Permanent Court of Arbitration (PCA) established as far back as 1909 in the *Grisbadarna* that 'it is a settled principle of the law of nations that a state of things which actually exists and has existed for a long time should be changed as little as possible.'[26] The International Court of Justice has followed this principle in the *Temple Case*[27] as well as in the *Frontier Land Case*.[28] Furthermore a party's statements and actions with respect to a boundary may preclude it from asserting inconsistent claims or contesting the sovereignty over the territory at a later stage.[29] Acquiescence, however, is not to be lightly presumed and each case is examined individually with due consideration of all the facts (*La Palena Case*).[30]

The fear of statelessness and its consequences are as real as they are dire for affected populations if their states do not properly manage the transition periods and remain determined to be fair to the populations well into the future. The African continent indeed already provides a worrying share of the international problem of statelessness. Whereas the late creation of modern political boundaries in all regions of Africa has caused the prevalence of transborder communities, the governments of some states continue to adopt a social disciplinarian attitude to these communities in furtherance of political aims. Recent studies have shown that:

> As if in punishment for a lifestyle that suggests that belonging to two states at the same time is possible, indeed, necessary, states usually resist granting basic identification documents to these populations. They therefore live in constant threat of statelessness and face a significant risk of mass expulsion by one or the other state in which they reside.[31]

Examples of ambiguous or tenuous citizenship status of transborder communities arise on the borders between Chad and Sudan, Uganda and the Democratic

---

24 J. B. Scott, ed., The Hague Court Reports (Washington: Carnegie, 1916), p. 122.
25 See Article III (3) of the OAU Charter and resolution AHG/Res. 16(1) adopted by the OAU Summit in Cairo in 1964.
26 Scott, op. cit., p. 122.
27 ICJ Reports 1962, p. 6.
28 ICJ Reports 1959, p. 209.
29 See *Legal Status of Eastern Greenland*, 1933 PCLJ (ser. AB) No. 53, at 193–4.
30 *La Palena Case (Argentina–Chile)*, 38 ILR 10 (1966).
31 Open Society Justice Initiative, "The Face of Statelessness: A Call for African Norms on the Right to Citizenship" (February 2007), p. 5, available at http://www.citizenshiprightsinafrica.org/Assets/PDFs/The%20Face%20of%20Statelessness.pdf, accessed 11 September 2007.

Republic of Congo, Guinea and Sierra Leone, Tanzania and Rwanda, Zimbabwe and Mozambique. In all of these instances, governments are prone to argue that transborder communities largely harbour illegal immigrants that are, therefore, subject to expulsion.[32]

> Lacking state protection, stateless individuals exist in a state of permanent vulnerability to government actions. Denied access to birth certificates, passports, or other identification documents, stateless persons become, in effect, 'nonpersons' with no claim on governments to protect their most basic rights. As a result, they are systematically denied access to the full range of public goods and services essential to a decent existence – from freedom of movement and police protection, to healthcare, education, housing, and employment. Groups suffering protracted statelessness usually suffer poverty as well, throughout successive generations.[33]

Since the general rule is that nationality is an attribute granted by the territorial sovereign, changes to the territory of states often necessitates the reallocation of nationality. Note may be taken of the exception in relation to the Bakassi population in the Cameroon–Nigeria case (below). Article 3(a) of the Green Tree Agreement provides that Cameroon will 'not force Nigerian nationals living in the Bakassi Peninsula to leave the Zone or to change their nationality'.[34] In such cases it is best that the allocation of citizenship should take place between the concerned states by virtue of express agreements probably in the form of bilateral treaties. After the Netherlands recognised the independence of Indonesia, a Convention to assign citizens was concluded in 1949 between the two states: Agreement concerning the Assignment of Citizens between the Kingdom of the Netherlands and the Republic of the Netherlands and the Republic of the United States of Indonesia.[35] All citizens of the Netherlands were thereby divided between the two states. Some categories of persons so affected who obtained the nationality of Indonesia, had a right of option to the nationality of the Netherlands. See also Agreement Concerning the Assignment of Citizens between the Kingdom of the Netherlands and the Republic of Surinam.[36] Similarly certain categories of persons who got the nationality of Surinam could use an option-right in order to re-acquire their Netherlands' nationality. It appears, however, that in

---

32 Open Society Justice Initiative, Ibid., p. 5.
33 Open Society Justice Initiative, p. 4.
34 Cameroon is also enjoined in subparagraph (b) to 'respect their culture, language and beliefs'. Agreement Between the Republic of Cameroon and the Federal Republic of Nigeria Concerning the Modalities of Withdrawal and Transfer of Authority in the Bakassi Peninsula UNTS, Vol. 2542, 2008 I-45354 also available on the website of the UN Office for West Africa (UNOWA) at http://www.peaceau.org/uploads/cn-agreement-12-06-2006.pdf, accessed 6 September 2014.
35 69 UNTS, p. 3. The Republic of the United States of Indonesia, usually abbreviated as RUSI, was the federal state to which the Netherlands formally transferred the sovereignty it possessed over the Dutch East Indies on 27 December 1949. This followed the Dutch–Indonesian Round Table Conference.
36 997 UNTS, p. I-14598.

the Cameroon–Nigeria process the possibility of such reacquisition of nationality was not a feature of the considerations – possibly because the national laws of both states permit dual nationality.[37]

In sum, it is clear that matters of delimitation and demarcation of boundaries and frontiers between territories are important in law and in fact. The saying that 'good fences make good neighbours' holds true in international relations and has particular significance in terms of territorial sovereignty and jurisdiction. Settling disputed borders on a mutually acceptable basis removes an important irritant to relations and the means and methods as to which this can be achieved must continue to receive scholarly attention.

4.4 Frontiers, borders, fences and walls in law and international relations

Border is Fate[38]

It is important to set out the meanings of the central concepts we are dealing with in this book. Definitions are in essence problematic and, thus, we will aim to describe in as clear terms as possible the legal connotations and collocations of essential terms. Many studies have addressed with varying levels of success, the issues of definition, distinguishing between: boundaries and borders from frontiers, boundaries from borders, borders from borderlands and political frontiers from settlement frontiers. Boundaries and borders were initially conceived as being no more than lines separating sovereign territories, while frontiers were assumed to constitute the area in proximity to the border whose internal development was affected by the existence of the line. The political frontier may be differentiated from the settlement frontier, the former is affected by the existence of the international boundary, the latter constituting the, as yet, uninhabited region lying within the state territory and representing the spatial margin of the state's ecumene.[39] We hope to address a few of these definitions and distinctions below.

4.4.1 Boundaries

'Boundary' in this work refers to the physical limits of a state's geographic, territorial and, usually, national jurisdictional extents.[40] We have, however, used the term 'boundary disputes' to also cover disputes over territory and disputes over territorial extents of contested frontiers or borderlines. The term 'territorial

---

37 Gerard–Rene de Groot and Carlos Bollen, "Nationality Law of the Kingdom of The Netherlaands in International Perspective", Vol. XXXV, *Netherlands Yearbook of International Law* (2004), p. 212.
38 Julius Varsanyi, *Border is Fate: A Study of Mid-European Diffused Ethnic Minorities* (Sydney: Australian Carpathian Federation, 1982).
39 David Newman and Anssi Paasi, "Fences and Neighbours in the Postmodern World: Boundary Narratives in Political Geography", Vol. 22, *Progress in Human Geography* 2 (1998), p. 189.
40 See Daniel, op.cit., p. 218.

claim' would be more precise when used to cover large contested areas or pieces of territory; whereas 'boundary' in technical use should refer to the linear point of contact with other states. We have chosen for convenience of discussion to adopt the general meaning of the word boundary. Boundaries in modern parlance can be *de jure* or they can be *de facto*. The former is used to denote a boundary with legal backing typically in the form of a binding agreement, such as a treaty; and the latter refers to boundaries established by virtue of a set of facts which so to speak exist on the ground. A *de facto* boundary is usually observed by the local people and sometimes respected by states themselves.[41]

The best record of the world's oldest boundary treaty is contained in a cuneiform pronouncement,[42] and refers to the original border treaty between Umma and its rival Mesopotamian state of Lagash dating back to about 2550–2600 BC. Some authorities estimate that this treaty – one of the world's earliest treaties – indeed itself records earlier boundary agreements that occurred dating back up to 3100 BC.[43] The original treaty fortunately survives in its physical form even now and may be viewed at the Louvre Museum in Paris. The large clay peg with inscriptions on the sides contains the formal pronouncement of the historical record of the Lugash ruler Entemena, around 2400 BC and refers to the original border treaty between Umma and Lagash as having been set by Mesilim (who was known to be alive in 2550 BC).[44]

In 2400 BC, according to another archaeological document known as the Stele of Vultures, the King of Lagash, Eannatum (also Ennatum) warred with Umma and won. He forced the Umma King to take an oath that his inhabitants would respect the agreed boundaries and restrict themselves to their side of the dividing canal. According to the treaty, the kingdoms of Lagash and Umma agreed to a precise boundary between their two adjoining territories, with a boundary marker known as a *stele* –a large stone marker or stone pillar) placed at a spot.

Reminiscent of modern-day bloody boundary battles, the Stele of Vultures[45] derived its name from the sight of vultures feeding on the bodies of the 3,600 dead Umman soldiers. A reference to the treaty of 2550 BC survived in statements of religious celebration and pronouncements of the victory of Eannatum in 2450 BC. The Stele of the Vultures was again placed in a prominent position on the ancient dike-border where the destroyed stele of Mesilim had stood a hundred years earlier, and included this admonition: 'Let the man of Umma never cross the border of Ningirsu! Let him never damage the dyke or the ditch! Let him not

---

41 Daniel, op.cit., p. 223.
42 On the sides of a clay peg.
43 The Louvre Museum in Paris dates Mesilim's tenure as ruler of the city of Kish around 2550–2600 BC. The reasons for dating it in this period includes the fact that historians accept that Mesilim lived during the period.
44 Because historians have records of when Mesilim lived, the date of the treaty is placed at about 2550 BC, although some authorities set the date of the world's first treaty as 2600 BC or even 3100 BC.
45 Was discovered at Telloh, on the site of what used to be Girsu, but in fragments only.

move the stele! If he crosses the border, may the great net of Enlil, king of heaven and earth, by whom he has made oath, fall upon Umma!'

Eventually, the historic border succumbed to another monumental development in the form of the invasion and defeat of most of the Sumerian cities by the Akkads who forcefully brought them into a new kingdom called the Babylonian Empire, after their capital city of Babylon. The virulent nature of boundary disputes is given expression by the fact that Lagash and Umma continued to fight intermittently for hundreds of years and the border between them continued to move with the fortunes of war.[46]

Having discussed boundaries generally it is important to introduce their factual synonyms – frontiers and borders. It needs to be mentioned that among boundary scholars, it is recognised that these terms are generally technical terms which ought to be deployed carefully in discourse with a full understanding of their differences and nuances. As Prescott and Triggs rightfully maintain, '[t]here is no excuse for geographers who use the terms "frontier" and "boundary" as synonyms'.[47] Frontier zones tend to be zones of blending and are of varying widths and shapes. Even in the case of boundaries that are marked by sharply defined natural barriers, the barrier-region itself will form the transition zone between one area and another.[48] A boundary is best represented by a line while a frontier and a border are distinctly different types of boundary areas.[49] Frontiers can generally be political frontiers i.e. 'neutral ground' separating ethnic groups, kingdoms, or independent states or they can be settlement frontiers (i.e. ground within a larger country at the edge of a settled area or a settlement on the frontier of civilisation, such as in Australia or the US). It is in the former sense that the term is mostly used in this book. Africa has a rich history of frontiers and examples of African political frontiers abound. These range from the many frontiers in the Niger–Benue region to the unstable and peaceful frontiers regulating and maintaining contact between political groups in the south of modern-day Nigeria. Where boundaries are unprotected, weaker political groups appear to suffer the effects the most. The frontier between colonists and the Xhosa in southern Africa witnessed savage events many British citizens will not be proud of today. In 1812, for instance, the British adopted a scorched earth policy. Mostert described the policy thus:

> The only way of getting rid of them is by depriving them of the means of subsistence and continually harrying them, for which purpose the whole force is constantly employed in destroying prodigious quantities of Indian corn and millet which they have planted . . . taking from them the few cattle

---

46 Lloyd Duhaime, 2550 BC "The Treaty of Mesilim", available at http://www.duhaime.org/LawMuseum/LawArticle-1313/2550-BC--The-Treaty-of-Mesilim.aspx accessed 17 June 2012; George A. Barton, "Inscription of Entemena #7", *The Royal Inscriptions of Sumer and Akkad* (New Haven, CT: Yale University Press, 1929), pp. 61–65; Re 3100 BC, Charles Phillips and Alan Axelrod, *Encyclopedia of Historical Treaties and Alliances*, 2nd Ed. (New York: Facts on File Inc., 2006), Vol. 1, p. 6.
47 See V. Prescott and G. D. Triggs, op.cit., p. 22.
48 Carlson and Philbrick, op.cit., p. 11.
49 See V. Prescott and G. D. Triggs, op.cit., p. 1, 12.

which they conceal in the woods with great address, and shooting every man who can be found. This is detestable work . . . we are forced to hunt them like wild beasts.[50]

In 1818 a British commander attacked and stole 23,000 cattle from the Xhosa in cross-frontier raids. These sorts of incidents expose the dangers of frontiers as devices of separation because of their penchant for harbouring vagrants and dangerous elements.[51]

It will be useful to identify some of the various classifications of international boundaries and consider their manifestation in Africa. Various classifications have been suggested in academic literature such as the Boggs, Jones and Hartshorne classifications. Boggs' classification identifies physical or natural boundaries (following natural features such as rivers, watersheds, range of mountains); geometric boundaries (following straight lines, arcs of a circle – longtitude and latitude); anthropolgical-geographical boundaries (relating to human settlements, culture and language) and compounded boundaries (comprising a combination of the above features). S. B. Jones divided boundaries into five categories, namely: natural boundaries; national boundaries; contractual boundaries; geometrical boundaries; and power-political boundaries.[52] Others like Richard Hartshorne, from a geographer's perspective divided boundaries into five categories: pioneer boundaries; antecedent boundaries; subsequent boundaries (drawn up after the development of the cultural landscape to coincide with social, economic, cultural and linguistic lines); superimposed boundaries (drawn after the development of the cultural landscape but without regard to possible cultural boundaries); and relict boundaries (such as the Great Wall of China, the Berlin Wall and Hadrian's Wall).[53]

Yet it is recognisable that there is a wealth of literature that argues for the de-emphasis of boundaries and borders. In this supposedly new brave world created in liberal academic discourse it is as if boundaries and borders acquire an ignoble meaning and belong to a savage past.

---

50 N. Mostert, *Frontiers: The Epic of South Africa's Creation and the Tragedy of the Xhosa People* (New York: 1992), p. 39, quoted in Prescott and Triggs, op.cit., p. 45.
51 Prescott and Triggs, ibid., pp. 34 and 45.
52 S.B. Jones, "The Description of International Boundaries", *Annals of the Association of the American Geographers* 33: 99–117; "Boundary concepts in Setting Time and Space", *Annals of the Association of American Geographers* 49 (3), pp. 99–117.
53 Relict boundary refers to antecedent boundaries which have been abandoned for political purposes but are still evident in the cultural landscape. Relict boundaries manifest themselves in space among others by direct border remains such as border stones, mounds, ancient walls, border roads, clearings, customs houses, watchtowers. See generally R. Hartshorne, "Suggestions on the Terminology of Political Boundaries", Vol. 26, *Annals of the Association of American Geographers* (1936), pp. 56–57; David Newman, "Boundaries, Borders, and Barriers: Changing Geographic Perspectives on Territorial Lines", in Albert, Mathias (et al.) *Identities, Borders, Orders: Rethinking International Relations Theory* (Minneapolis: University of Minnesota Press, 2001), pp. 137–151, p. 140; Marek Sobczynski, "Studies On Relict Boundaries and Border Landscape in Poland", paper presented at the Università degli Studi di Trento, pp. 1 and 3 available at http://web.unitn.it/archive/events/borderscapes/download/abstract/SOBCZYNSKI_paper.pdf, accessed 17 August 2014.

In truth, however, the disappearance of boundaries thesis is largely a Western European and North American discourse. This idea reflects the trend towards globalisation by which many (although by no means all) of the boundaries in Northern regions have become increasingly permeable as a result of both technological and political changes that have taken place within the past three decades.[54]

Although there are undeniable shifts away from the physical and intellectual conception of boundaries as we know it, Nugent's observations (below) remain apposite and a reflection of the status quo in this first quarter of the twenty-first century. He wrote:

> Territorial lines remain partial barriers to the physical movement of people. Fences, walls and customs posts retain their function of preventing the movement of people who do not possess the correct documents or are defined as undesirable elements, although this too, is changing as the technology of transportation becomes increasingly sophisticated, as borders are removed from the territorial periphery of the state into the heart of the metropolitan airfields...[55]

4.4.2 Borders and borderlands

Border and borderland are regarded as synonymous in boundary literature and they both refer to the zones of indeterminate width that form the outmost parts of a country that are also bounded on at least one side by national territory.[56] Sovereignty may create boundaries, and the recreation of boundaries is also an exercise of sovereignty.[57] Indeed nation states usually set out quite early to participate in the creation of their landscape just as much as landscapes have themselves been agents in the construction of national images.[58] The creation and recreation of boundaries and borders is inevitably the source of tensions, hostilities and conflicts between states and peoples. This will no doubt remain so till the end of history. In Africa, as in most other continents, borderlands are sites

---

54 See generally Newman (2001), ibid., pp. 137–151.
55 Newman (2001), op. cit. p. 143. For an example of the positive exercise of removal of fences in furtherance of cross-boundary joint maintenance and exploitation of eco tourism/conservation see Appendix III which contains a picture of the cutting of 15km of fence between Kruger National Park (KNP) and Limpopo National Park (LNP).
56 Prescott and Triggs, op.cit., p. 12.
57 Wendy Brown, op.cit., p. 71.
58 Baker, op.cit., p. 153. African states are particularly adept at creating symbolic depictions of their territorial landscape in art, cultural items, flags, national dress and romanticising their landscapes and physical environments as distinct places. The Nigerian flag in its simplicity – green-white-green – is redolent of the agrarian past of the land and its peoples. The current Kenyan flag adopted on 12 December 1963 (Independence Day), was based on the flag of KANU (Kenya African National Union), the political party that led Kenya to independence. The original flag of Kenya had three equal stripes of black, red and green, symbolising the indigenous Kenyan people;the blood that was shed in the fight for independence; and Kenya's rich agricultural land and natural resources. See the website of the Kenyan embassy in Paris available at http://www.kenyaembassyparis.org/about-kenya/national-symbols, accessed 10 January 2012.

and symbols of power. Guard towers, fences of all descriptions, moats, ridges and all sorts of artificially constructed monuments have from time immemorial been used to inscribe territorial limits on the surface of the earth and in maps of varying providence. Despite all the utopian models that have been touted in history both by fantasists as well as well-meaning intellectuals, a world without sovereign states is not only unattainable – it is in fact undesirable. Anyone who seriously wants a stateless planet can only be encouraged to leave the earth and settle on any other planet in this solar system or beyond. It is equally true that with the explosion in the number of states and an even more explosive increase in human population comes the inevitability of border wars. Hence Horsman and Marshall's position that '[t]here has always been a tension between the fixed, durable and inflexible requirements of national boundaries and the unstable, transient and flexible requirements of people' is sufficiently premised on universal experience.[59] It has been provocatively suggested that border wars are a requirement of state- and nation-building in the post-imperial age and that it serves a useful function in inspiring protagonists to greater nationalist endeavours. Border wars according to this view are in fact necessary to fire the imaginations of peoples everywhere to understand the nature of minority rights and defend the rights of small states to defend themselves.[60]

The argument in this work is that without prejudice to the imperatives of the narrative of cooperation between states, borders are a necessary part of international relations. Borders are a logical necessity of reality of boundaries. If borders did not exist they would literally have to be invented – for how else would people be allowed safe conduct as they move between nations and peoples? Given national policy commands and the need for information and control over terrorism and organised crime, policing and public safety, sustainable tourism and other general immigration and international policies, borders are a *sine qua non* of civilisation even in a globalised world.[61] The functions of properly delimited and demarcated international boundaries include the following:

- A specific delineation of the sphere of sovereignty and territorial jurisdiction. It is on these bases that the whole system of municipal law – upon which human civilisation is organised – is primarily founded. In this way taxes are collected, criminal and civil laws are instituted and enforced. The prescription of internal boundaries is also determined by the territorial sovereign.
- Determination of the precise scope for which physical security must be provided for by the state.

---

59 M. Horsman and A. Marshall, *After the Nation-State: Citizens, Tribalism and the New World Disorder* (London: Harper Collins, 1995). See also Paul Hopper, *Living with Globalization* (London: Bloomsbury Academic, 2006), p. 39.
60 Hastings and Thomas Wilson, op. cit., p. 3.
61 Cf. Mark Sedwill, *UK Border Agency Annual Report and Accounts 2012–13* (UK: The Stationery Office, 2013), p. 5 available at http://www.ukba.homeoffice.gov.uk/sitecontent/documents/aboutus/annual-reports-accounts/, accessed 9 December 2013.

- Determination of the precise scope of where national resources may be derived and exploited. It is good international policy that the precise areas upon which states may conduct and organise their economic activities be identifiable. Conversely, contested boundaries are bad for international relations as they often lead to territorial contests, gun-boat diplomacy and threats to international peace and stability.
- Determination of the scope of responsibility of the national and provincial governments for the welfare of nationals and sharing of national resources.
- Determination of the points of interaction with neighbouring independent states. International boundaries are crucial to the 'strenthening of territorial integrity' a *sine qua non* of peaceful cohabition of geographical contiguous nations and peoples from time immemorial and an antidote to irredentism, separatism and inordinate adventurism.
- Clarification and stabilisation of point of interaction with other states and transnational economic as well as social actors. International law works upon the basis of the equality of states. The whole essence of this principle is that clearly identified independent territories with perpetual existence should be granted international legal personality.
- International boundaries are important points of contact between states. They serve as bridges between peoples, cultures and nations. In the vast majority of cases in Africa and elsewhere border areas stimulate economic activities, innovation dynamism, and complementarism and growth. With the right political will expressed and practiced by governments boundary zones can spark impressive regional growth and corridors of success.[62]

The existence of borders does not preclude innovative transnational de-territorialised cooperation in Africa. The advent of such cooperation such as the Kavango Zambezi Trans-frontier Conservation Area (KAZA) is greeted with palpable interest among scholars. African borders must like most other borders around the world serve as barriers and bridges. It must, however, be ensured that African borders should not become generally hostile to human migration or become points of extinction of the developing African *lex mercatoria*.

4.4.3 Fences and walls

It is particularly hoped that the increasing resort to the building of actual fences between countries will find no further expression on the African continent.[63] Gradually this expensive and inefficient phenomenon has been regaining entry in

---

62 Okomu, op.cit., pp. 39–42; B.A. Simmons, "Rules Over Real estate: Territorial Conflict, and International Borders as Institutions", *Journal of Conflict Resolution* (2005), p. 38; Douglass Cecil North, *Structure and Change in Economic History*, (London: Norton, 1981), pp. 201–2.
63 For more on the poisoning effects of fences between state territories see Derek Gregory, *The Colonial Present* (Oxford: Blackwell, 2004), pp. 76–106. For an example of the positive exercise of removal of fences in furtherance of cross-boundary joint maintenance and exploitation of eco tourism/conservation see Appendix III.

and around Africa. Botswana initiated the construction of an electric fence along the border with Zimbabwe in 2003, claiming that it was necessary to prevent the spread of foot and mouth disease among livestock. The European Union is contributing to this unfortunate feature of African international relations as it sponsored triple-layer walls around Spanish enclaves in Morocco. Morocco also maintains a long berm feature which it uses to secure the resources of the long-disputed Western Sahara. There is a wall between Egypt and Gaza and Israel has just completed a 245-mile security fence along the Sinai Border with Egypt replacing an older fence.[64] It is predicted that more walls are coming across the world even though writers on the subject reveal the interesting paradox that higher and stronger walls do not guarantee the integrity of a boundary.

Fences say much more about the party erecting the fence than it does about those sought to be excluded. Niccolò Machiavelli, not generally known for being liberal or soft on matters of state security was correct to observe that '[f]ortresses are generally much more harmful than useful.'[65] He explains further by stating that: '. . . if you make fortresses, they are useful in times of peace because they give you more spirit to do evil . . . but they are very useless in times of war because they are assaulted by the enemy and by subjects; nor is it possible for them to put up resistance to both the one and the other.'[66] Indeed it is a hardly recognised fact among boundary scholars that perhaps the most ardent opponents of walled borders are statesmen who support strong defence and crime control policies. Shimon Peres had occasion to remind his country that 'we need soft borders, not rigid impermeable ones . . . At the threshold of the twenty-first century, we do not need to reinforce sovereignty'.[67] Ariel Sharon cynically turned the logic on its head but essentially exposed the short-sightedness of fenced boundaries between peoples. He wrote, 'don't build fences around your settlements. If you put up a fence, you put a limit to your expansion. We should place the fences around the Palestinians and not around our places'.[68]

It is hoped that third party arbiters and courts of whatever description will see it as part of their duties to steer states and disputants away from the practice of building walls. Not because walls may not serve a short-term purpose of assuaging feelings and fears or even deterring security threats successfully but because they are in the long run an unreliable and unsustainable way of managing human affairs relating to frontiers between peoples. In modern times they often replicate and amplify hate and provide a physical summation of the lack of imagination

---

64 Wendy Brown, op.cit., pp. 8 and 19. Christian Fraser, "Egypt Starts Building Steel Wall on Gaza Strip Border", *BBC News*, 9 December 2009 available at http://news.bbc.co.uk/1/hi/8405020.stm, visited 10 December 2013; Joshua Mitnick, "Israel Finishes Most of Fence on Sinai Border", *The Wall Street Journal* available at http://online.wsj.com/news/articles/SB10001424127887324374004578217720772159626, visited 8 December 2013.
65 Niccolò Machiavelli, *Discourses on Livy* (Chicago: Univ. of Chicago Press, 1996), p. 185.
66 Ibid., 185.
67 Daniel Byman, *A High Price: The Triumphs and Failures of Israeli Counterterrorism* (Oxford: Oxford University Press, 2011), p. 71.
68 Ariel Sharon quoted in Neve Gordon, *Israel's Occupation* (California: University of California Press, 2008), p. 116.

towards peaceful ordering of international relations. Fences and physical barriers between nations are reminiscent of a more primordial past in the story of human societal evolution. They are ultimately wasteful of resources and inefficient, damaging to the environment and pervert the soul of the builder and the excluded. Perhaps no further proof is needed of how the practice goes against the enterprise of humanity than the treatment of walls in art and popular literature as well as the euphoria and sensationalism that the masses exhibit when such walls come tumbling down as they inevitably do again and again.[69] Example may be made here of the breaking of the Berlin Wall in 1989. Judicial disapproval has also been voiced in the hallowed jurisprudence of the World court in the *Legal Consequences of the Construction of a Wall in the Occupied Palestinian Territory*.[70]

> One place these tensions nest is in the new walls striating the globe, walls whose frenzied building was underway even as the crumbling of the old bastilles of Cold War Europe and apartheid South Africa was being celebrated. . . . Brazil plans to build a steel–and–concrete wall along its border with Paraguay. . . United Arab Emirates is designing a wall for its Oman border. Kuwait has a fence, but wants a wall in the demilitarised zone approximating its border with Iraq. Serious proposals have been floated to allow completion of the U.S.–Mexico wall with one along the Canadian border. . .Thailand insurgency and to deter illegal immigration and smuggling, Thailand and Malaysia have cooperated to build a concrete and steel border wall. . .Iran is walling out Pakistan. Brunei is walling out immigrants and smugglers coming from Limbang. China is walling out North Korea to stem the tide of Korean refugees, but parallel to one section of this wall, North Korea is also walling out China.[71]

---

69 Walls have featured in biblical cities like Jericho, which is now the West Bank and which had its walls erected around 8000BC. China built parts of its Great Wall by 700BC and Hadrian's Wall which was built to separate Romans from the Barbarian world was built in 129AD. Works of fiction that reveal the human horror that the Berlin Wall represented include Peter Schneider, *The Wall Jumper* (1984; German edn, *Der Mauerspringer*, 1982); 'Holidays In The Sun', a song by the English punk rock band The Sex Pistols prominently mentions the wall, specifically singer Johnny Rotten's fantasy of digging a tunnel under it. 'Over de muur', a 1984 song by Dutch pop band Klein Orkest, about the differences between East and West Berlin during the period of the Berlin Wall; 'Chippin' Away' a song by Tom Fedora, as performed by Crosby, Stills & Nash on the Berlin Wall appeared on Graham Nash's 1986 solo album 'Innocent Eyes'. Fictional films featuring the Berlin Wall include: *The Boy and the Ball and the Hole in the Wall* (Spanish–Mexican co-production, 1965); *The Wicked Dreams of Paula Schultz* (1968 Cold War spy farce about an Olympic athlete who defects, director George Marshall); *Funeral in Berlin* (1966; spy movie starring Michael Caine, directed by Guy Hamilton); *Casino Royale* (1967; featuring a segment centred around a house apparently bisected by the wall; *The Spy Who Came in from the Cold* (1965; Cold War classic with plot set on both sides of the Wall, from John le Carré's book, directed by Martin Ritt).
70 In this case the Court not only disapproved of the route of the wall but also of its humanitarian and socio-economic impact on the Palestinian population. *Legal Consequences of the Construction of a Wall in the Occupied Palestinian Territory*, Advisory Opinion of 9 July 2004.
71 Wendy Brown, op.cit., pp. 8 and 19.

The proliferation of walls offends international morality and the statistics are obviously depressing and should not continue.[72] It is necessary to conclude along with Wendy Brown that rather than emitting the symbolism of sovereignty of the nation state, the new walls signal the loss of the nation state's sovereignty, legal authority, unity and settled jurisdiction.[73]

4.5 Delimitation and demarcation juxtaposed

It is important at this stage to introduce the technical differentiation between delimitation and demarcation of boundaries and to explain the manifestation of these concepts in precolonial, colonial and post-colonial Africa. This task is important given the generality of opinion to the effect that precolonial Africa was so bereft of legal standards that it had no respectable system of delimitation, demarcation, management or reaffirmation of boundaries. Prescott, following the scholarship of Lapradelle and Jones delineates up to four stages of boundary-making: allocation; delimitation; demarcation; and administration of a demarcated line. He, however, admits that few international boundaries have been established as result of the full stages he suggested.[74]

Allocation explains the initial political division between at least two states. Delimitation in legal literature generally refers to the delineation of a boundary line by appropriate and legally acceptable description. According to Prescott and Triggs, delimitation means the selection of a boundary site and its definition.[75] It is modern practice that a given set of coordinates are supplied specifying the applicable datum relating to boundary delimitation. A horizontal datum positions a mathematical model of the earth (normally a spheroid) as closely as possible to the actual earth (the geoid). This is how the coordinate system is defined. When computing survey observations are done on different datums, this will produce small but often significant differences in latitude and longitude. Over the last half century individual states have adopted different datum systems but nowadays WGS 84 is most commonly used in land and maritime delimitation. A vertical datum provides the basis for heights and is usually defined by a series of readings from tide gauges taken to determine mean sea level.

The establishment of international boundaries would usually involve a two-stage process. First there is the delimitation achieved either through agreements

---

72 India/Bangladesh Length: 2100 miles started in the 1990s with concrete and barbed wire. Western Sahara/Morocco has a length of 1700 miles and a height of 2 metres and started in 1980. Saudi Arabia–Yemen wall has a length of 1100 miles and is 3 metres high. This wall is built with material of concrete filled pipes. The US–Mexico wall started in 2006 is 670 miles long and has a height of 5 metres. In 2002 the West Bank wall was built extending 440 miles using concrete, steel and razor wire. The Greece/Turkey wall extends for six miles and was built with concrete and thermal sensors. See Jon Henley, "Forget Hadrian, Berlin and China. This is the Age of the Wall", *The Guardian*, 20 November 2013, p. 23.
73 Wendy Brown, op.cit., p. 84.
74 See J. V. Prescott, *Map of Mainland Asia by Treaty*, (Carlton (Vie.): Melbourne University Press (in association with the Australian Institute of, 1975), p. 3; Prescott and Triggs, op.cit., p. 12.
75 Prescott and Triggs, op.cit., p. 12.

or as a result of adjudication which specifies the location of the boundary line. Second there is the exercise of actual demarcation through the exercise of detailed description, production of a final map and/or ideally by the placement of boundary pillars or other physical markers evidencing the boundary on the ground by a joint commission.[76] To Professor Cukwurah (*The Settlement of Boundary Disputes in International Law*), the definition of demarcation should be limited to the physical marking of the boundary on the ground. A descriptive report of such marking is also seen as part of the process.[77] Demarcation, therefore, refers to the construction of physical structures like boundary markers in the landscape.[78] The distinction between the two terms is exemplified by the experience of China which has delimited up to 90 per cent of its 22,000km-long international boundary with a total of 14 states but of which it has demarcated only about ten boundary lines.[79] Administration as a concept here refers to the maintenance of the boundary markers for as long as the relevant boundary lines run.

4.6 African delimitation and demarcation of boundaries in their historical, colonial and contemporary contexts

Much has been written about the idea that African peoples had little or no practice or conceptualisation of strict and linear boundaries, both in Western and African authorship. Wafula Okomu, for example, concludes that in traditional African societies land was neither individually owned nor used, making physical boundaries almost non-existent. There was a general understanding of the span of the area in which the community could either grow its food or graze its animals. He reiterates the popular opinion that 'this was the state of things until populations started to increase and Europeans arrived with an ideology of private ownership'.[80] According to such views, prior to European contact, delineation of one kingdom to another did not in fact exist but Africans relied on indigenous zones of separation. Such zones are usually typified in the following manner:

(a) zones or frontiers of contact, that operated between political groups that are close to each other. Example of this is that between the Yorubas and the Dahomey and those between the Buganda and their East African neighbours;

---

76 Melissa Anne Perry, "State Succession, Boundaries and Territorial Regimes", dissertation submitted for the degree of Doctor of Philosophy, University of Cambridge.
77 Oye A. Cukwurah, *The Settlement of Boundary Disputes in International Law* (Manchester: Manchester UP; Dobbs Ferry, NY: Oceana 1967), pp. 27–9.
78 Prescott and Triggs, op.cit., p. 12.
79 China is said to have inherited a boundary line full of problems when founded in 1949 and has had to settle up to 12 territorial disputes with its neighbours. Fu Fengshan, "China's Experience in Settling Boundary Disputes and its Border Management Practice", paper presented at the 2nd International Symposium on Land, Maritime River and Lake Boundaries: Maputo, Mozambique, 17–19 December 2008, pp. 10–13.
80 Okomu, op.cit., p. 32. Okomu appears to contradict himself when he admits: 'However, this does not mean that Africans generally did not have linear boundaries, as even pastoralists had a conception of the limits of their pastures'. Okomu, at p. 33.

(b) frontiers of separation through which communities separated themselves with the device of buffer zones such as 'evil forests' or wild frontiers, barren land or deserts (Fulani versus the central Sudanese states and Bornu Kingdom); and
(c) enclave delineation consisting of diverse nations and groups as in the case of the Tuaregs, Masais and the Somalis.[81]

There are many reasons to differ from the conclusion that traditional Africa did not possess any sophisticated delimitation and/or demarcation. To begin with, the position appears to be supported by too little research directly on the issue. To deal with all the peoples of Africa with their various stages of political development and organisation in one broad generalisation is insufficient and reminiscent of the popular misconception found in much of Western commentary on the continent that Africa is just one big single jurisdiction. Such views also tend to echo the prejudiced positions of commentators foreign to Africa with too little time and resources to understand precolonial history. First, historical studies about land tenure systems all around the world generally refer to their social and administrative conceptual manifestations. They tend not to dwell on the physical or geographical concepts.[82] Thus, early studies and reports of African boundaries were naturally scanty on this important point. Furthermore it was part and parcel of the political strategy of the colonialists to downplay recognition of pre-existing indigenous sovereign arrangements as much as possible. Since the legal instinct of colonialism was to usurp power over as much territory as quickly as possible it was preferable to pronounce as much land as possible as *terra nullius*. Recognition of precolonial geography of African states and empires was mostly denied and dismissed as indeterminate.[83] This thinking is betrayed in McEwen's position when he wrote that:

> the concept of linear boundary was alien to Africa [due to an] absence of centralized 'state' structures or entities. *Some areas remained unappropriated by any clan or state* . . . There was a general (but not total) absence of modern methods of physical marking of alignments.[84]

Notably even this account acknowledges that there were modern methods of marking boundary alignments.

Second, the 'non-linear contemplation of boundaries in indigenous Africa' view ignores the pre-modern and modern influences of measurements and architecture that African empires were exposed to by virtue of their interactions with other cultures including the Baroque, Arab, Chinese, Turkish and Indians.[85]

81 A. Ajala, "The Origin of African Boundaries", *Nigerian Forum* (1981), pp. 7 and 8.
82 Gebeyehu usefully examined the factors that made land measurement in Shashemene District of Ethiopia possible. Temesgen Gebeyehu, "A History of Land Measurement in Shashemene (Ethiopia), 1941–1974", Vol. 1, *African Journal of History and Culture (AJHC)*, No. 4, October 2009, pp. 67–75.
83 A. C. McEwen, *International Boundaries of East Africa*, (London: Oxford University Press, 1971), p. 8.
84 Ibid.
85 David Keys, "Medieval Houses of God, or Ancient Fortresses?", Vol. 57, *Archaeology*, No. 6, (2004).

It is true that generally in Africa, the most ancient system of land holding is the communal land tenure system. This system has indeed survived to this day in many parts of the continent. It is also true that with the formation of independent African states after the colonial era, the ancient form of land tenure changed drastically in many places for the political contraption of the state and to a large extent for the peoples and sub-parts of the state. The newly independent states of Africa inherited the land they had from their colonial powers along with the fiction of snapshot of the territory including its linear form and tridimensionality. New forms of land right inexorably emerged and additional claims on the ownership of land came into being.[86] Nevertheless it is the case that the law and practice of communal land ownership endures to date all over Africa.

The most important thing to note, however, is that many African cultures were as much as focused on linear boundary lines and/or could easily conceptualise it as other cultures anywhere else. There is impressive evidence in anthropology and history to show that linear and strict delimitation of territories between communities, families, individuals, kingdoms and states existed among African peoples and they utilised it when considered necessary. Disagreeable as colonial partitioning and delimitation of African territories may be, it does not offer an opportunity to reject the usefulness of delimitation as a means of separating territories. It certainly does not permit scholars to disregard the abundant evidence that African states and cultures did understand the existence of boundaries and borders between their various peoples. It also does not mean the continent should in this modern age discard the necessity for frontiers and borders in Africa. In Ethiopia, for instance, land measurement has been traced to at least the Gondarine period and from the fifteenth century, although it was in the nineteenth and twentieth centuries of the Shewa Kingdom within the Ethiopian Empire that land measurement between the regions reached its height and continued until the collapse of the imperial regime in 1974.[87]

The historical institution of the Yoruba '*Oni ibode*' and '*aso ibode*' (the border lord and border guard) as a professional class predates European contact and goes back to antiquity. According to linguistic evidence they in fact date back into the deepest recesses of Yoruba history and are found in the corpus of *Ifa* religious texts.[88] The border guard watches over borders based on an understanding of

---

86 Cf. Gebeyehu, ibid.
87 Ibid.; see also Richard K.P. Pankhurst, *History of Ethiopian Towns: From the Middle Ages to the Early Nineteenth Century*, Vol. 1 (Wiesbaden: Franz Steiner Verlag, 1982), pp. 114–18.
88 Oral history showing early evidence of borders and boundaries among the Yoruba people is reflected in a very recent account about the origins of a festival in one of the towns in Yorubaland in South Western Nigeria. The account goes: 'During our ancestors' period, there was an Ifa called Owonriwonsa, there was this warrior called Ayedu, he was a great warrior who won every battle and he came to Ila with the intention of taking us into captivity but Orangun was a great warrior – and it is also a tradition in Ila that nobody has ever confronted Ila and succeeded. Our fathers consulted the Ifa oracle which directed them on what to do. The oracle instructed that Ayedu should be given food and they prepared pounded yam for him. After eating, Ayedu was hypnotised, confused and scattered. After five days of being in the state of confusion, he decided to take his exit from the town. The people consulted Ifa again on what to do. Ifa again instructed them to clothe

where the boundaries are. This at the very least shows the need to maintain strict boundary lines as against foreign claims and intruders. The '*ibode*' (or border) as in many other African cultures relies on city walls and other boundary markers such as mounds, moats and natural geographical features. Towns and cities around Africa had borders, fences and gates and this is incontestable and reflected both in oral and written literature.

It is fortunate that evidence emanating from recent satellite imagery and orthorectified imagery as well as archaeological studies have been providing overwhelming evidence for very precise boundary markers separating precolonial African political groups. For instance, it has been discovered that between Lake Chad and the Atlantic Ocean in West Africa there are about 10,000 town walls, 25 per cent or more of them on presently deserted sites. Although only a handful have been surveyed so far, this is said to represent the largest concentration of past urban civilisation in black Africa. Old aerial photographs and other more modern remote-sensing methodologies continue to offer an opportunity to record much of this evidence all over Africa. Although the Kano City walls, with their 24km long, 20m-high perimeter, were considered the most impressive monument in West Africa as at 1903, their achievements pale into absolute insignificance in comparison with other recent discoveries of older demarcated boundaries. Fieldwork surveys and inspections have revealed 1,600km of the 16,000km-long Benin earthwork complex. There is the 160km-long Sungbo's Eredo wall; the 45km-long Orile Owu walls; the walls of Old Oyo; Old Egbe wall; and walls completely surrounding pre-European influence cities of Kwiambana, Old Ningi, Gogoram, Pauwa, Old Rano, Old Sumaila.[89]

The emerging picture is that since at least the eighth century AD enormous systems of walls and ditches have been used to demarcate state territorial control in the area of contemporary Benin and Western Nigeria. The total length of the discovered fortifications in this area alone is said to exceed 6,000 kilometres.[90] It

---

him and after *escort him out to the border of the town* (emphasis added). After seeing him off the town, our people prayed, rejoiced and thanked God for successfully ex-communicating war, sorrow, hunger, confusion and crisis and ushering in harmony, love, peace and development. And that is the genesis of what we are celebrating today.' Wale Ojo-Lanre, "Orangun of Ila Celebrates Isinro, Marks 10th Anniversary", *The Tribune*, 8 October 2013. Available at http://tribune.com.ng/news2013/index.php/en/tourism/item/23468-orangun-of-ila-celebrates-isinro,-marks-10th-anniversary.html, accessed 12 January 2014.

89 Stone, op.cit., p. 158; African Legacy – School of Conservation Sciences, Bournemouth University, "Hausaland Walled Cities & Towns – remote sensing studies", available at http://apollo5.bournemouth.ac.uk/africanlegacy/kano_walls.htm, accessed 15 January 2013; E. A. Ayandele, 'Ijebuland 1800–1891: era of spendid isolation' in G. O. Olusanya, ed., *Studies in Yoruba History and Cultures: Essays in honour of Professor S. O. Biobaku* (Ibadan, 1983) pp. 88–105; P. Darling, "1975 Benin earthworks: some cross-profiles", Vol. 40, *Nigerian Field* No. 4: pp. 164–5; P. J. Darling, 'Sungbo's Eredo, Southern Nigeria', *Nyame Akuma*, No. 48 (June 1998), pp. 55–61.

90 Eredo represents a system of walls and ditches dug in laterite, a typical African soil consisting of clay and iron oxides. The total length of these fortifications is approximately 160km. The height difference between the bottom of the ditch and the upper rim of the bank on the inner side can reach 20m. The diameter of this enormous fortification in a north–south direction is approximately 40km and in an east–west direction, 35km. The walls of the ditch are unusually smooth. The system of walls encircle the ancient Ijebu state. See further African Legacy – School of

was not just that Kings of Benin such as Ewuare built and maintained secure walls it is more importantly significant that they maintained their empire very much in the tradition of civilised knowledgeable civilisations much like progressive and sophisticated societies elsewhere in Asia, Europe and the Americas. By the time the Portuguese arrived on the Benin coast, the city of Benin had broad streets, impressive architecture, modern town planning and was advanced in terms of art and trade.[91] In view of such evidence it is indeed curious that writers like Engelbert and colleagues hold on to the position that in relation to Africa, 'the concept of territorial delimitation of political control was by and large culturally alien.'[92] In support of this it is argued that the concept of territorially defined statehood is a European import and contrasts with the relative survival of local traditions of political authority and social interaction. In support of this the example of the Chewa and Nagoni of Zambia, Mozambique and Malawi, were cited, as they have retained stronger ties among themselves than they have developed with their respective states, and traditional Chewa migratory patterns have endured despite the post-colonial borders. The fact that the great demarcating walls found in parts of Africa could only have occurred after some technical criteria for delimitation and that they conveniently fit into the classification of relict boundaries recognised by writers like Hartshorne is lost to many.[93] It would appear that what has happened is that scholars have begun to confuse the dissatisfaction of African peoples and nations with colonial-inspired boundaries with the idea that African peoples and states did not generally recognise delimited boundaries.[94] Scholars holding such views are indeed guilty of fudging issues in much the same way that they think African conceptualisation of boundaries is blurred at the edges. How then do Western writers and African writers both arrive at the same watering hole in terms of the 'no linear or strict boundaries in African history' school of thought? This is accounted for by gross oversimplification of the demands of their intellectual interests. The former are intent on sanctifying the colonial effort even when they do agree that it was grossly inequitable at least from the perspective of the colonised states. The latter also hold similar views because they find disagreeable the very basis of much of colonial boundary-making and seek its modification and sometimes removal. In a sense this is a form of throwing the baby away with the bathing water.

Walls, linear boundaries, borders and frontiers have always been needed and useful from time immemorial in African history as much as everywhere else. It was not till around 1900 that linear boundaries became recognisably predominant

Conservation Sciences, Bournemouth University, "Sungbo's Eredo – Africa's Largest Single Monument", available at http://apollo5.bournemouth.ac.uk/africanlegacy/sungbo_eredo.htm, accessed 15 January 2013.
91 S. Kasule, *The History Atlas of Africa* (New York: Macmillan, 1998), p. 293.
92 Engelbert, Tarango and Carter, "Dismemberment and Suffocation– A Contribution to the Debate on African Boundaries", Vol. 35, *Comparative Political Studies*, No. 10 (December 2002), p. 1095.
93 See Richard Hartshorne, *A Survey of the Boundary Problems of Europe (Lectures on the Harris Foundation)*, (University of Chicago Press, 1937) p. 164.
94 S. H. Phiri, "National Integration, Rural Development, and Frontier Communities", in A. I. Asiwaju (ed.), *Partitioned Africans* (New York: St Martin's, 1985), pp. 105–25.

around the world.[95] But walls, fences, precise boundaries and borders are as much of African history as that of any other part of the world. It would be surprising if this were not so. Precolonial Africa was not the particularly peaceful era that is romanticised in much of new literature. It was a dangerous era for indigenous political groups and their leaders. Slave-raiding was happening on a systematic nearly genocidal basis and internecine wars were rampant. Empires rose and fell with equal ease around the continent. For security reasons the establishment of precise national boundaries would have been more necessary in precolonial Africa than they are today. It is indeed true that in many cases not only the entire national boundary had to be established and maintained but the regions, cities and towns also needed sophisticated boundary-markers and boundary maintenance.

The following account typifies the precolonial Africa encountered by the British in precolonial West Africa:

> Old Ningi was a nineteenth century cult settlement opposing Kano, Zaria and Bauchi from its hill fortress base using up to 4,000 cavalry. Its mud walls were built on stone-based parapets and presented a complex defence strategy, which the larger kingdoms were unable to breach. It was captured by the British using a local traitor to show a secret way in near the beginning of the twentieth century.[96]

Having said this, it is necessary to agree that modern African boundaries 'are of relatively recent origin and thus, do not even possess the sanctity that derives from age. The majority of African boundaries were delimited between 1884 and 1904 and the definitive partition was completed in 1920.'[97] It is now, therefore, possible to recognise that the making of African boundaries can be divided into five distinct phases. The first and last phases are rarely ever recognised in international legal theory while the next three often find expression in boundary research literature.

i. Phase I: The era of delimitation and demarcation by indigenous African nation states, vassal states, communities, cities and towns.
ii. Phase II (1850–86): This phase involved the conquering and mischievous acquisition of territories by the British, French, Belgians, Portuguese, Germans and Italians. Of this period Okomu aptly stated: 'Colonial mischief in territorial acquisition and boundary making included deceit, fraud, intimidation, bribery and confusion of the African rulers'.[98] Where the territory of European interests in Africa possesses great mineral resources, European countries would even make efforts to cheat and outwit each other.

---

95 See V. Prescott and G.D. Triggs, op.cit., p. 1.
96 African Legacy, op.cit.
97 J. Herbst, "The Creation and Maintenance of National Boundaries in Africa", Vol. 43, *International Organization*, No. 4, (Autumn, 1989), p. 692.
98 Op.cit., p. 34.

iii. Phase III (1886–1900): This witnessed the formal creation of colonial states. Although there was a fairly common use of maps and treaties, it is of this era that Lord Salisbury lamented that Europeans were 'drawing lines upon maps where no white man's feet ever trod'.[99] The inception of most of the confusion currently afflicting African boundaries was created in this era.
iv. Phase IV (1900–1930): This phase included elaboration, finalisation and conclusion of cartographic and geographic surveys of territories by colonial boundary commissions that enabled the total usurpation of the sovereignties of pre-existing African states and societies.
v. Phase V (1945–Present): This phase includes the delimitation and demarcation arising out of bilateral activity between African states after attaining independence or as a result of the decsision of a Court, negotiated solutions or as a result of mediation and other ADR efforts.

The problem with much of delimitation and demarcation work achieved by the colonial powers is that it is much less the product of disciplined colonial record-keeping romanticised by the leading international courts and some Western scholars but has proven to be far less accurate and useful by courts and demarcators in practice. Chukwurah wrote particularly with reference to evidence and records in relation to colonial Latin America that '[i]n the chaotic state of things, it is not unusual to find documents partially supporting both claimants'.[100] Walter Benjamin's thesis that 'there is no document of civilisation which is not at the same time a document of barbarism' rings particularly true of much of the colonial maps on the basis of which treaties sharing out African lands were drafted.[101] His conclusion, '[a]nd just as such a document is not free of barbarism, barbarism taints also the manner in which it was transmitted from one owner to another' – applies to the provenance of many maps delineating African territories and upon which international courts and tribunals rely today.[102]

This credibility gap is yet to receive the required attention it deserves in much of legal writing on African boundaries save by few (if highly respected and candid) writers and commentators from those peoples at the receiving end of the injustices perpetrated by colonial boundary-making. The problem is arguably complicated further by the conspiracy of silence involving both foreign and African writers and statesmen regarding the provenance of the maps made by various colonial authorities presumably on the assumption that silence is necessary if the myth of *uti possidetis* is to have any meaning at all. There is, however, no reason to believe that the policy and determination of the African Union (AU) expressed several times in the past to keep states faithful to the territory they inherited after colonialism will be irreversibly damaged if scientific methods are employed to

---

99 See Memorial of Libya in the *Territorial Dispute* (Libyan Arab Jamahiriya/Chad), Vol.1, 25, para.3.01, quoted from *The Times*, 7 August 1890.
100 Cukwurah, op.cit., p. 115.
101 Walter Benjamin, "Theses on the Philosophy of History" in *Illuminations*, Hannah Arendt (ed.) (New York: Schocken, 1968), p. 256.
102 Ibid.

verify boundaries. Those charged with delimitation and demarcation ought to be aware that they must remain watchful of the possibility that shoddy surveying and cartography may have become fossilised into boundary reality and there ought to be a healthy debate as to how to deal with this reality. It in fact accords with the true interests of all concerned not to be seen to give effect to absurdities. After all it is recognisable that the documents and provisions were products of previous centuries where scientific attainments was far more modest than at present. Brownlie in his seminal work African boundaries noted of the Benin–Niger border as follows:

> The alignment depends upon certain French arrêtes, of December 8, 1934, December 27, 1934, and October 27, 1938. The entire boundary consists of sectors upon the rivers Mekrou and Niger but the precise division of the rivers, and thus, the allocation of islands, remains the subject of doubt since the relevant French instruments are not sufficiently precise.[103]

It is also fair to note that where there is good political will and determination much can be achieved in considerably little time even by African states. Example may be made here of the tremendous successes in the Gulf of Guinea even in the highly technical field of maritime delimitation. Complex maritime demarcation has already been achieved between and among Nigeria, Benin, and Ghana, Equatorial Guinea, Nigeria and Sao Tome and Principe. Recent examples of progress made in peaceful delimitation and demarcation of contested African territories may be found in the *Cameroon–Nigeria Case* (dealt with in greater detail below) and the *Botswana–Namibia Case*. In both cases the delimitation was attained in consonance with the provisions of colonial treaties and agreements and the implementation stage of the judgments was achieved through the establishment of joint Commissions among other indigenous platforms of diplomacy.[104]

The modus operandi of the parties in giving effect to the judgments of the court in both processes is widely regarded as the gold standard in contemporary post-boundary dispute demarcation work.[105] The Namibia–Botswana process was much shorter in time-frame but of course the issues involved in the implementation

---

103 Ian Brownlie, *African Boundaries: A Legal and Diplomatic Encyclopedia* (Berkeley: University of California Press, 1979), p. 161.
104 Important working documents adopted for the demarcation exercise in the Botswana–Namibia case include the: Eason Survey report of 1912; Kalahari Reconnaissance of 1925; 1925 aerial photography; Kalahari Reconnaissance of 1943; Kalahari expedition of 1945; 1943 aerial photographs of the area; 1897 map by Schultz and Hamar; 1905 map of Ngamiland by Franz Seiner and Stigands, compiled between 1910 and 1922; 1987 mosaic with flight index and photography from shaile up to Lake Liambezi; Swampy Island correspondence of 1910.
105 See Said Djinnit, 'Opening Speech by the Chairman of the Mixed Commission' – 23rd Meeting of the Mixed Commission, Yaounde, 9 October 2008; Amadou Ali Chef De La Delegation Du Cameroun A L'Ouverture De La 23eme Session De La Commission Mixte Yaounde, 9 October 2008; See also G. O. Uzochukwu Okafor, "Namibian Boundary: Experience With Delimitation and Demarcation", paper presented at the Regional Workshop on African Border Programme (Windhoek, 22–23 October 2009).

exercise were different and perhaps not as complex as Cameroon–Nigeria. The agreement for the establishment and the Terms of Reference of the Joint Commission of Technical Experts for the delimitation and demarcation of the boundary between Namibia and Botswana along Kwando/Linyanti/Chobe River was signed in 1999. A team of eight Commissioners divided equally between both countries was appointed. The Commissioners consisted of permanent secretaries and directors from the relevant agencies. The Commissioners were supported by a technical team consisting of surveyors, lawyers and hydrologists. The first meeting was held on 8 March 2000 in Windhoek. The meetings (just as latter became the practice in the Cameroon–Nigeria process) alternated between the two countries and a total of 23 meetings were held before the conclusion of the process at the 23rd meeting, which was held from 22 to 23 June 2002.[106]

The mandate of the Joint Commission was to use scientific methods to best interpret the provision of the original colonial boundary treaty based on the Berlin Conference of 1884. The difficulties before a demarcation tribunal charged with the technical and politically fraught task of transforming legal judgments into reality was exposed in many ways in both processes. With regard to a major river feature in the Namibia–Botswana process the Berlin 1884 treaty documents indicate the river boundary as the middle of the river. However, on this river there are multiple channels and in some cases the river is not visible (no water flowing on the surface). The Commission took a reconnaissance trip, by helicopter, over the area. The joint technical support team inspected the reference beacons along the river, after which they drew up an action plan that was approved by the Commission. Aerial photos/orthophotos of 0.5 resolution were acquired. Apart from the master negatives all other documents were delivered in duplicates. Where stripes of negatives fall entirely on either country, that particular country takes custody of the complete strip of negatives. In case of overlaps, negatives are shared such that one party takes the odd numbered negatives while the other takes the even ones.[107]

It is, thus, clear that the task of demarcation of boundaries in Africa much like that of demarcation anywhere in the world is difficult and complex in nature. The work is very sensitive and should not be rushed.[108] It is notable that the establishment of joint commissions and mixed implementation working groups on a multi-layered level is now a standard practice of boundary-making and management on the African continent and elsewhere. It may be necessary for one single state to engage in such arrangements with all its neighbours and to operate them simultaneously. Indeed the requirement to do so has become unavoidable

---

106 Okafor, op.cit., pp. 13–24.
107 Ibid., pp. 13–24.
108 The Namibia–Botswana process was perhaps quite expeditious in comparison with the Cameroon–Nigeria process. It included: Ground Marking (26 July 2000–20 August 2000); Photography (20 August 2000–31 August 2000); Mapping (31 August 2000–15 January 2001); Delimitation and Digitising (01 September 2000–15 March 2001); Study Report (Technical) (15 March 2001–15 April 2001); Study Report (Commission) (15 April 2001–25 May 2001); Report Approval by the Commission (1 June 2001); Demarcation (25 June 2001–24 August 2001); Commission Draft Report (24 August 2001–14 September 2001); Commission Final Report (30 September 2001).

for many states as a result of the AUBP.[109] Note may be taken of the experience of Burkina Faso in the maintenance of its approximately 3,500km common boundary with six other states –Benin Republic, Cote-d'Ivoire, Ghana, Mali, Niger and Togo. Although the argument is advanced here that the AU Border Programme appears to be ambitious in terms of time-frame it is hoped that this is not taken to mean that its intentions are not based on the noblest intentions of the pertinent policymakers or not laudable.

4.7 High power politics: legality and illegalities of the Berlin Conference (1885)

The partitioning of Africa at the Berlin Conference in the mid-nineteenth century marked the beginning of renewed interest in the continent of Africa by the imperialist powers of Europe. Of particular interest to them at the time were the hitherto unexplored central African regions, comprising modern-day Zaire, Zambia and Zimbabwe. This interest was based on the relentless rush for raw materials and investment that these territories provided for Europe's continuing industrialisation. Competition between the European powers was severe as they coveted the opportunities that colonial subjugation assured. Much interest was concentrated on the Congo region (modern Zaire) upon which King Leopold II of Belgium had set his sights (it later turned out to be a lucrative source of rubber). However, the old colonial nation of Portugal, with African interests in Angola and Mozambique extending back over three centuries, also saw the Congo region as its historical sphere of influence. International rivalry and diplomatic conflicts between the principal European powers prompted France and Germany to suggest the notion of a European conference to resolve contending claims and provide for a more orderly 'carving up' of the continent. This conference convened at Berlin from November 1884 to February 1885 and resulted in an important agreement entitled The Berlin Act of 1885. The participating states sending representatives were Austria–Hungary, Belgium, Denmark, France, Germany, Great Britain, the Netherlands, Portugal, Russia, Italy, Spain, Sweden, Turkey and the USA.

It would take a very bold scholar to stand behind the proposition that the Berlin Conference achieved a meaningful delimitation of the African continent. Indeed accurate delimitation or demarcation was never the intention of the participating states. Nevertheless the resulting treaty from the conference delimited spheres of influence between various powerful states, unfairly granting them rights over many African territories which became the *de jure* colonial and then post-colonial boundaries of the continent. As Lord Salisbury admitted not only was the delimitation largely arbitrary but the mapping exercise was far from a precise art.[110]

---

109 Claude Obin Tapsoba, *La Politique De Gestion Des Frontieres AU Burkina Faso 2eme Symposium International Sur La Gestion Des Frontieres Terrestres, Maritimes, Fluviales Et Lacustres*, Maputo, Mozambique, 17–19 December 2008, p. 3.
110 Note again Lord Salisbury's lamentation that Europeans have been drawing lines upon maps where no white man's feet ever trod. See Joshua Castellino, "Territoriality and Identity in

As Botswana successfully advanced in relation to the maps in *Kasikili Sedudu Case*; early maps show too little detail, or may be too small in scale, to be of value. The World Court significantly also admitted of colonial maps that: 'maps merely constitute information which varies in accuracy from case to case; of themselves, and by virtue solely of their existence, they cannot constitute a territorial title.'[111] As alleged by Nigeria in its written submissions to the ICJ in the land and maritime dispute, it was not unknown for colonial surveyors 'to round things up' in order to save themselves from further bother or the embarrassment of doing a shoddy job and coming up with unsupportable maps.

The signing of the Berlin Conference was primarily for the benefit of the European powers that sent delegates to the conference. The conference was convened for the mutual interests of the colonial powers as a means of conducting a systematic takeover of the world's second largest continent. Via the conference they secured unfettered access to the interior of Africa principally for themselves and of course without any contribution or participation by the African peoples and states. From a strictly legal point of view, even by the standards of the times, freedom of trade in the whole of the Congo (the so-called 'conventional basin'), a key point in the programme was really only threatened by the avarice and greed of the competing European powers and not by any illegality or protectionism by the African kingdoms or peoples. Vacuous statements from leading political figures of the period like Bismarck that the participating states had showed 'much careful solicitude' for the moral and physical welfare of the native races and that they were engaging in the partitioning to help introduce the populations to the advantages of civilisation must also be judged against the general record of colonialism. The next century after Berlin indeed witnessed genocidal events, massacres and repressions in the Congo, Kenya and Nigeria, to mention just a few cases. Kidnapping of African monarchs who sought to exercise their sovereignty was common. In many such cases the brutal sanction of deposition was meted out not because they endangered trade but (as in the case of monarchs such as Jaja of Opobo), because they championed the right to open trade on the same terms with Europeans and resisted monopolies that operated in favour of European states and trading companies. Officially backed or tolerated 'brigandry' and land seizures without compensation were rife in all colonies. Notable examples of these are replete in the colonial history of Zimbabwe and South Africa. There was destruction of cities in Benin as well as brutal and violent gender repression (e.g., the Aba women's riot). Infrastructural development in Africa consisted mostly of thinly disguised efforts to make the removal of resources from the interior to the ports easier to operate. The very idea that the colonial project was engaged in for the noble and exemplary purpose of a civilising mission is a self-delusionary myth sponsored mainly by the designers of colonialism and other apologists of

---

International Law: The Struggle for Self-Determination in the Western Sahara," *Millennium: Journal of International Studies* 28 (3) (1999): 529.
111 *Frontier Dispute* (Burkinu Faso/Republic of Mali), ICJ Rep (1986), p. 582.

colonialism. This idea continues to be rebutted well into the twenty-first century not only in Africa but all around the world.[112]

In many ways the Berlin Conference was the anti-climax of the scramble for Africa. Pakenham incisively marshals this argument view when he wrote:

> It was Berlin that precipitated the Scramble. It was Berlin that set the rules of the game. It was Berlin that carved up Africa. So the myths would run. It was really the other way round. The Scramble had precipitated Berlin. The race to grab a slice of the African cake had started long before the first day of the conference. And none of the thirty-eight clauses of the General Act had any teeth. It had no rules for dividing, let alone eating the cake.[113]

The view that '[t]he Scramble was not a sprint' but 'the final stages of a marathon'[114] is important because it helps to illuminate the emerging picture of the Berlin Conference as 'bad law'. The conference and the ensuing Act were in a sense *ab hominem* in that it was designed to grant legality *ex post facto* to a host of individual acts of depredation against African societies and precolonial states. The initial context and legal principles upon which contact between African monarchs and Europeans took place was that of free and unfettered freedom. This was in many cases guaranteed by 'treaties of protection' brought about usually at the insistence of European states. The view ought to have been taken much earlier in academic writing that the Berlin treaty was simply a 'treaty contract' between the participating states and not a law-making treaty that binds African peoples and their states. In this sense there is an arguable case for the illegality of colonisation from the perspective of African international law.

4.8 Classifications and nature of African boundary disputes

> How and why does one get oneself into a long and difficult work, even a life's work: trying to understand and tell truths, in my case, about a huge and hugely complex continent?[115]

---

112 Recent legal actions for colonial killings include those brought by descendants of the Mau Mau in Kenya and the Malaysian descendants of the Batang Kali massacre. See Ian Cobain, Richard Norton-Taylor and Clar Ni, "Mau Mau Veterans Win Right To Sue British Government", 5 October 2012, available at http://www.theguardian.com/world/2012/oct/05/maumau-court-colonial-compensation-torture, accessed 21 March 2014; Cahal Milmo, "Relatives of Malaysians killed by British troops in the Batang Kali massacre vow to take their fight to the Supreme Court", *The Independent*, 19 March 2014, available at http://www.independent.co.uk/news/ukv/home-news/relatives-of-malaysians-killed-by-british-troops-in-the-batang-kali-massacre-vow-to-take-their-fight-to-the-supreme-court-9202912.html, accessed 21 March 2014.
113 Thomas Pakenham, *The Scramble for Africa* (George Weidenfeld & Nicolson, 1991), p. 254.
114 Prescott and Triggs, op.cit., p. 291.
115 Davidson, op.cit., p. 3.

Boundary disputes have been used in this work in a very general sense. There will be considerable hesitation on the part of anyone with legal or even diplomatic sensitivity to come to a precise assessment of the number of boundary disputes that exist in any given region. A lot will, for instance, depend on how the word or concept of 'dispute' is defined. One of the unique features of boundary disputes as a genre of international disputes is that the existence of many such disputes are in fact disputed and may be denied by governments for diplomatic reasons or to give room for required political manoeuvring. During the field visit stage of the writing of this book it was revealed that the numbers of flashpoints in Africa identified by our interviewees across the various Regional Economic Commissions (RECs) are much more than the acknowledged disputes by African Union member states. Interviews with civil servants and other international observers brought up many specific situations involving intense fighting and deaths between governmental forces, private militia and border communities locals, that were hitherto unacknowledged by states. The informants themselves attached caveats as to the fact that some problematic areas identified would not even at this stage be publicly acknowledged by any of the state parties concerned. Indeed a surprisingly high number of the problematic situations have arisen out of the actions of private persons, ethnic communities, pastoral and artisanal groups. There is general agreement among those spoken to that the present effort to develop a mechanism for the prevention and resolution of boundary disputes through the African Union Border Programme (AUBP) is a timely and commendable effort. Our research reveals that the actual number of problematic situations and contested land borders as at 2010 across Africa may be up to 44 separate instances and that is without counting existing or emerging maritime delimitation disputes as well as separatist claims.

To set the following discussions in context, it may be necessary to suggest certain distinctions and classifications in relation to the various kinds of disputes that may be found in Africa. There are outright territorial disputes such as that currently experienced over the Migingo Island in Lake Victoria between Kenya and Uganda; the Mauritius and Seychelles conflicting claims over the Chagos Islands[116] or the erstwhile Nigerian claim over the Bakassi Peninsula. Territorial disputes raise questions relating to sovereignty over a specific territory and may take two forms: (a) competing claims by two or more existing states to a territory that is already under the control of one of the concerned states[117] or (b) a claim to

---

116 The Island is currently a UK-administered British Indian Ocean Territory. Mauritius also claims French-administered Tromelin Island. See Disputed Territories: Tromelin Islands available at http://www.disputedterritories.com/territory/tromelin_island.html, accessed 30 April 2012.
117 Note the case of the Mayotte (Departmental Collectivity of Mayotte) which is an overseas collectivity of France. It consists of two main islands, and many smaller islets around them. These islands are geographically part of the Comoros Islands, and they are claimed by Comoros. Note also the interesting case of Glorioso/Glorieuses Islands (Archipel des Glorieuses) which is operated as a nature reserve, and manned by the French Foreign Legion. The Glorioso Islands are, however, the subject of territorial claim by Madagascar, the Seychelles and Comoros. While Madagascar is a close neighbour, the disputed Islands are geographically part of both the Comoros Archipelago and the Seychelles Archipelago. Note as well the Mauritian claim over

an independent homeland or territory which the territorial state and/or a neighbouring state has refused to accept involving an area which is in fact counter contested.[118] There are boundary delimitation disputes *simplicta* such as the *Frontier Dispute* between Burkina Faso and Niger[119] or the dispute between Malawi and Tanzania over their common boundary in relation to Lake Nyasa. There are also disputes of a mixed nature such as the territorial, land and maritime disputes between Cameroon and Nigeria which involved disputes over the Bakassi Peninsula in the South; and extends to disputes over many points of boundary alignment along a 2000-kilometre boundary and extending also to a maritime delimitation dispute in the waters of the Gulf of Guinea. It may need to be mentioned that disputes may also relate to the delimitation, demarcation or management of boundaries and borders and may involve all three. The problematic issues of sovereignty, jurisdiction and control over territories and boundaries are sometimes of such a mixed nature that it is impossible to classify them into neat categories. Boundary problems are indeed as rife in interstate relations as they are in intra state affairs.[120] We have considered above the phenomena of intrastate boundary disputes and noted that they can be even more intense in human terms and produce higher casualty rates than international boundary disputes.

In discussing the above classifications – territorial, boundary, mixed (territorial and boundary), land or maritime, terrestrial or aerial it may also be helpful to state that apart from those that have been settled and/or resolved; they may all be divided into three possible categories:

(a) Disputes of an academic or dormant nature. These sort of disputes are essentially and usually not likely to endanger international peace. They may,

---

Bassas da India, Europa Island and Juan de Nova Island (part of the French overseas territory of the French Southern and Antarctic Lands). Note also Moroccan claims over Plazas de Soberanía (which translates as 'Places of Sovereignty' and formerly known as Spanish North Africa).

118 Note, for instance, the case of the *Western Sahara* (Saharawi Arab Democratic Republic/SADR). Somaliland (Republic of Somaliland) which pronounced itself independent since the 1991 collapse of the central government in Somalia. Somalia, however, also claims sovereignty. No states or international organisations currently recognise Somaliland, but it continues to diplomatically press for recognition. Puntland, another Somali region presents a similar declaration as an autonomous region, but it does not seek full independence from Somalia. Things are complicated further by the fact that Puntland's claims also overlap some of the territory under Somaliland claims. Another example but one arguably with even less success than Western Saharawi and Somaliland is the Republic of Cabinda. When this part of Africa was decolonised in the 1960s, Cabinda was assimilated into greater Angola, even though it had been governed as a separate state until then. Cabinda has since sustained a claim to independence. This claim is vigorously denied by Angola which exercises sovereignty and control over the territory Cabinda claims. Cabinda is not recognised by any other states, but many of its independence-seeking groups continue a military struggle against Angola. There are reports of thousands of Cabinda citizens currently in Congolese refugee camps due to such conflicts. See Disputed Territories available at http://www.disputedterritories.com/territory/cabinda.html. See also our discussions below on Africa's separatist movements; 16.2: *Uti Possidetis* within the equation of political separation and self-determination.

119 *Frontier Dispute (Benin/Niger)*, (*Benin v Niger*), 2005 ICJ Rep., p. 90.

120 As a result of many long-lasting internal boundary disputes the Nigerian National Boundary Commission (NBC) has embarked upon plans towards the monumental project of building boundary pillars between the borders of its 35 states and Federal capital territory.

however, be based on a myriad of factors and experience transfiguration into (b) and (c) below. What was previously a position of principle may become a contentious point due to political changes in one or all of the states involved. A swell of nationalist sentiments, electoral calculations and even interference from foreign states may change the character of the dispute gradually or very rapidly.

(b) Disputes which have led or may lead to a breach of the international peace or cause severe tension between states. This may take the form of a pattern of brief border skirmish(es) involving small armed groups which are either officially or unofficially sanctioned. This is unfortunately quite common in Africa and a lot of the evidence of armed skirmishes is buried away from the watchful eyes of the international community and even the majority of the population of both states.

(c) Disputes which have already led to armed conflict. This would typically involve the acknowledgment of a state of war by both states and the main participants in this kind of conflict will be the armed forces of the countries involved. Such wars may be long and protracted; short-lived war; or indeed intermittent armed conflict (see below on settlement of international boundary disputes by use of force, Chapter 15).[121]

In relation to all the above categories it may not be so easy to spot the exact stage a boundary conflict actually is in and a conflict may accelerate very quickly from 'a' to 'b' and then 'c'. It may move from 'a' to 'b' and never get to 'c' before being resolved. It may move from 'a' to 'b' and return to 'a' (with all the potential of progressing again unless it is resolved). It may move intermittently between all three categories before being eventually resolved. It is unfortunately a sad fact of international life that even where such a dispute has been finally resolved by the parties, there is always the chance that the dispute is merely dormant again and may, therefore, be reignited by malicious or disgruntled elements from within and foreign to the concerned states.[122]

The dispute settlement procedures to be used to cope with a boundary dispute may have to be adjusted to match the different stages or categories that the dispute is in, as identified above. For instance, in relation to category (c) i.e. where military dispute has commenced, the first essential step that any institution or persons seised with the dispute must achieve is to try and bring about an immediate

---

121 Cf. the classifications attempted by Francis Vallat in Report of a Study Group, op.cit., p. xi.
122 Dissatisfaction with the World Court's decision has made staple reading in much of the Nigerian Press and even among some academics. A similar occurrence raised its head in Nigeria when powerful voices in the country mounted a failed last-ditch effort to persuade the Nigerian President Goodluck Jonathan to stop the implementation of the judgment of the ICJ in relation to the Bakassi Peninsula and even appeal the judgment of the World Court. This is despite the fact that there is no provision for such appeals to an ICJ judgment. See V. Akanmode, "Bakassi Peninsula: Nigeria vs. Cameroun at last, the Judgment," *Punch*, (12 Oct., 2002), p. 4. See also Elizabeth Embu, "Why Nigeria did not Appeal ICJ Ruling on Bakassi", *Daily Times*, 24 June 2013, available at http://www.dailytimes.com.ng/article/why-nigeria-did-not-appeal-icj-ruling-bakassi, visited 30 December 2013.

cease-fire. As a writer correctly notes: '[t]he settlement of the outstanding issues falls in a sense into a secondary place though the means for dealing with the issues may well be one of the most important factors in any negotiations either during the continuation of hostilities or after a cease-fire'.[123]

It needs, however, to be mentioned that territorial, boundary and border disputes are not unique to Africa and that they are indeed of global dimensions.[124] Since 1945 alone disputes and armed conflicts over territorial sovereignty as well as boundary delimitation have proliferated on a yearly basis in the Middle East, Europe and Asia. Severe problems are currently being faced by many of the states that were in the former USSR as a result of the dissolution of Yugoslavia, in Northern Ireland and in the Basques area of the Franco–Spanish Border. There is also a persuasive argument which is not usually encountered in literature that holds assiduously to the view that Africa is far from being the lawless, warfaring and chaotic continent of border disputes regularly depicted in Western conception. Such thinkers point to the fact that since 1950, boundary disputes *per se* have been the cause of virtually very few hostilities on the African continent. Indeed the Ethiopia and Eritrea war which followed Eritrea's move to independence in 1993 without clearly delimited boundaries with Ethiopia is perhaps the only real boundary war in Africa. Furthermore the fact that this particular dispute ended up in a celebrated arbitration case only goes to show the impressive and sophisticated African spirit of dispute resolution.[125]

This interesting view is helpful in understanding the possibility of exaggeration of the number and severity of boundary conflicts in Africa. However, in many respects it is an oversimplification of the issue. Rarely do boundary issues come neatly wrapped only in strict legal arguments over maps, delimitation and demarcation alone. Boundary disputes more commonly have roots in other factors, such as political, socio-economic, sociological, historical and economic disagreement and ethnic divisions. The truth is that African states appear to be dangerously frayed around the edges. It is notable that the activities of militants and armed groups as well as downright cross-border criminality are both symptoms and causes of boundary problems across the African continent. Guinea, Liberia and Sierra Leone continue to trade accusations of boundary incursions (some involving aerial raids) and many civilians have lost their lives.[126] Abductions have for long taken place along the Angolan–Namibian border and not even aid workers are not spared violence.[127] The Republic of Guinea experiences conflicts in its territory and along boundaries with rebel groups, warlords and youth gangs from neighbouring states resulting in domestic instability. Kenya provides shelter

---

123 Report of a Study Group, op.cit., p. xi.
124 See also Samuels, op.cit., p. 228.
125 Samuels, op.cit., p. 228.
126 *BBC Online*, "Guinean forces shoot Liberian Helicopter", 18 October 2000, available at http://news.bbc.co.uk/2/hi/africa/977835.stm, accessed 25 August 2014.
127 *BBC Online*, "Hundreds killed in Guinea attack", 7 December 2000, available at http://news.bbc.co.uk/2/hi/africa/1059818.stm, accessed 25 August 2014.

to almost a quarter million refugees, including Ugandans who flee across the border periodically to seek protection from Lord's Resistance Army rebels; Kenya directly feels the impact of incursions and tensions with clans and militia fighting in Somalia and spreading across the border, which has long been open to nomadic pastoralists. Similar problems exist between Chad–Sudan, Mali–Mauritania,[128] Burundi–Tanzania, Equatorial Guinea–Gabon, Eritrea–Sudan, Ethiopia–Kenya[129] etc. Togolese rebels create refugee problems for Ghana by shelling border villages, problems between Congo and Zaire, Sudanese Lord's Resistance Army, frequently attack Ugandan border villages. Since 2003, *ad hoc* armed militia groups and the Sudanese military have driven hundreds of thousands of Darfur residents into Chad. In addition to the above there are also numerous armed conflicts and civil wars within Burundi, Cote d' Ivoire, Chad, Ethiopia, Liberia, Nigeria (the Biafran War), Rwanda, Somalia, Sudan, Sierra Leone, Rhodesia/Zimbabwe which invariably involve issues of sovereignty, territorial jurisdiction and control. The Boko Haram scourge which is mainly manifested in the North-eastern part of Nigeria also affects Nigeria's border regions with Cameroon, Niger and Chad leading to immense problems for the region.

In essence without succumbing to sheer sensationalism it is safe to say that the years following the independence of African states have seen no shortage of armed conflicts, many of which arise out of disputes over territorial control and disagreements over boundary alignment. Identity does, in fact, play a huge part in African boundary disputes. Boundaries in time translate to or become closely linked to group identities and the relationship between spatial boundaries and the formation of ethnic and national identities is one of the strongest primal instincts celebrated by mankind. As Newman explains it:

> Not only do the social and ethnic boundaries that enclose groups create the Us and the Other, but so, too, do territorial boundaries as the lines within which state activity takes place and that determine the spatial locus around which national identities are formed through processes of social construction.[130]

It is indeed true that territory itself becomes part of the national identity, with places and spaces taking on historical and, in many cases, mythical significance in the creation of the nation's historical narrative. The African continent's case becomes complicated because of the shared reality that precolonial consolidation

---

128 Joe Bavier, "Chadians Concerned over Growing Tensions with Sudan", *Voice Of America*, 28 December 2005, available at http://www.voanews.com/english/2005-12-28-voa35.cfm, acccessed 25 August 2014. See Appendix III for a regional overview of the Lord's Resistance Army affected Areas.
129 "Troops Deployed On Border", *Kenya Times*, 25 March 1999, (FBIS-AFR-1999-0325). See Appendix III for pictures of refugees on the move in Africa.
130 Newman, op.cit., p. 146; see also A. Paasi, *Territories, Boundaries, and Consciousness: The Changing Geographies of the Finnish–Russian Border*, (Chichester: John Wiley, 1996); T.M. Wilson and H. Donnan, "Nation, State, and Identity at International Borders" in T. M. Wilson and H. Donnan (eds), *Border Identities: Nation and State at International Frontiers* (Cambridge: CUP, 1998).

of 'territory-people' relationships (complicated as they were as a result of indigenous warfare and empire adventures) was thrown into a thousand violent rebirths by insensitive colonial treaties and acts of delimitation and demarcation. Thus, while newer realignment of destinies and group identities began inexorably in some states after the independence era in the 1960s, the strong pull of precolonial territory-people cultural affinities dating back sometimes to over a millennia continues to produce effects. For illustration purposes reference may be made to the Israel–Palestine conflict and its multi-dimensionality. This sort of complexity afflicts many African state boundaries whereas these group identity crises find expression in boundary conflict without of course enjoying the same attention and status of recognition in contemporary international relations. This is why issues surrounding African boundaries will remain lively for at least another century.

4.9 Boundaries and disputes: a multidisciplinary approach

> Of the wide range of problems that falls within the scope of political geography, that of boundaries comes up for closest scrutiny. Neighbouring nations – some friendly, some hostile – face each other across some 100,000 miles of international boundaries. What are the current boundary problems of the world, and how can they be solved?[131]

The above quote penned in 1958 by political geographers reflects the multidisciplinary problem that boundary issues have become in the modern world. The concern for the razor's edge nature of boundaries and frontiers as the pivot upon which the modern issues of war or peace, of life and death of nations turn upon remains topical. Indeed the only change of note is that since the 1950s there has been an approximate tripling of international boundaries to around 300,000 as a result of the creation of scores of newer states. Much criticism has been levied at the field of international law for its perceived unpreparedness for these massive increases. Criticisms have emerged in particular of the reliance of the discipline of international law on old, static and perhaps tired notions of state sovereignty, territorial jurisdiction, nationality and territorial control in the postmodern world we now live in. A work like this must, therefore, interrogate the fields of international relations, history, anthropology, geography, sociology etc. for deeper under-standing of the issues and even solutions. But quite perplexingly it has been acknowledged by writers in international relations that, '[w]hat is interesting is that international relations theory is also underdeveloped in this area.'[132] Similar allegations have been levied against geography which in its classic sense can be compared to political studies and which concerns itself with the

---

131 Carlson and Philbrick, op.cit., p. 11.
132 Chris Brown, Borders and Identity in International Political Theory in M. Albert, D. Jacobson and Y. Lapid (eds), op. cit., pp. 117–36.

controversies concerning the role of territory in general as well as the relationship between territory and conflict.[133]

One area of multidisciplinary approaches to boundary studies which we find troubling is the perception that anthropological, sociological and other multidisciplinary studies largely support a deterritorialisation of peoples or deborderisation of the world.[134] In relation to African territories particularly, a de-emphasis of boundaries is romanticised in much of non-legal literature. It is true that various sociocultural dimensions of borders do not necessarily coincide with the literal borderline which is fetishised in legal writing, but it is far from the truth that at a general baseline strict borders are regrettable realities. In a sense the story(ies) of boundary communities and their acceptance or rejection of territorial boundaries and borders is not a simple one because of the clashes of ethnic, national and historical interests that occur around boundaries. As David Newman helpfully explains there is the chicken-and-egg question of which comes first – the boundary or the identity. In truth the germane question that has to be answered in many regions of the world is whether boundaries are simply drawn up, in modern state systems as a means of reflecting existing national and territorial identities, or conversely whether it is the partition of territory which eventually acts as a catalyst towards the creation of separate identities.[135] In relation to Africa, it is clear that although some attention may have been paid to identity in determining some boundaries, it was not one of the obsessions of colonial administrators to be faithful to the task of ensuring identity-territory correlation.

To some it will be a fortunate thing that whenever national groups are divided by international boundaries such as in North and South Korea; East and West Germany and the Arab–Palestinians (after the creation of the state of Israel) the core elements of national identity remain strong. In fact in some cases mutual affinity heightens particularly when it relates to minority populations.[136] It is, however, true that this reality of continued and enduring identity is the source of tension in many countries and territories.

At any rate it is becoming obvious that the story of regulation of boundaries is and ought to be multifaceted. Eminent jurists like James Crawford correctly concede the multidisciplinary and universal phenomenon inherent in the study of ethnic identity and territory. He wrote that:

> The consciousness of a 'people' or 'nation' that they constitute a separate entity has always been a factor in international relations: its importance

---

133 Newman (2001), op. cit. p. 141.
134 Historical sociologists like Abbott advocated that 'It is wrong to look for boundaries between pre-existing entities. Rather, we should start with boundaries and investigate how people create entities by linking these boundaries into units. We should not look for the boundaries of things, but for the things of boundaries', Andrew Abbott, *Time Matters: On Theory and Method* (Chicago: University of Chicago Press, 2001), p. 261. See also Kenichi Ohmae, *The Borderless World* (London: Collins 1990); Mathias Albert and Lothar Brock, "Debordering the World of States: New Spaces in International Relations", *New Political Science*, no. 35 (1996) pp. 69–106.
135 Newman, op.cit., p. 141.
136 Ibid., p. 142.

increased substantially in the nineteenth and early twentieth centuries, and it has come to have a certain juridical or quasi-juridical consequences.[137]

Although ethnographic studies of African borders abound in literature the complexities of understanding a continent with literally thousands of languages, ethnicities and social groups make theorising about borders and border conflicts a terribly exacting if not hazardous task.[138] Moreover, the connections between boundary and identity are still being interrogated in many of the social sciences. The interactions between boundaries, culture and ethnicity can be confusing and extremely difficult to put into typologies. One of the riddles surrounding African boundaries (both internal and international) is that the passage of time does not appear to assuage ethnic differentiation whereas the popular conception is that wherever people are in contact, their cultures will merge. Anthropological writers like Barth, however, argue that cultural differences are products of contact rather than the result of isolation. This analysis is persuasive in that contact between different peoples may increase points of conflict especially in relation to the sharing of scarce resources. This argument, however, does not account for the construction of boundaries and acquiescence thereto when the people are the same culturally and ethnographically on either side.[139] Example may be given of the creation of boundaries between Germans on either sides of the Iron Curtain. Although it is usual and it is logical to start enquiries into lines that demarcate territories, it is equally crucial to recognise that borders are created, sustained and altered as much 'from the inside out as the outside in'.[140] Borders created by people who are distant to the line may in time solidify into ethnographic reality. Indeed as Pelkmans explains:

> we need to pay particular attention to the ways in which state representatives as well as local actors conceptualize, mobilize and consume cultural stuff to understand their significance in assertions of difference and commonality. In other words, we should take a more organic view of the relation between borders and 'cultural stuff', looking at the ways they mutually constitute each other over time.[141]

---

137 Crawford (2006), p. 449.
138 Whereas the first widely acknowledged ethnographic study of socialist borders appeared in 1992 in the form of John Borneman's leading study (*Belonging in the Two Berlins: Kin, State, Nation*, Cambridge Studies in Social and Cultural Anthropology (Cambridge: Cambridge University Press, 1992)), both foreign and African writers have looked at the Anthropology of African boundaries for many more decades. Examples of these include the works of Basil Davidson, op.cit.
139 Frederick Barth, ed., *Introduction to Ethnic Groups and Boundaries: The Social Organisation of Culture Difference* (Boston: Little, Brown, 1969), pp. 9–10 and 15.
140 Henk Driessen, "The 'New Immigration' and the Transformation of the European–African Frontier" in *Border Identities: Nation and State at International Frontiers*, T. Wilson and D. Donnan (eds), (Cambridge: CUP, 1998), p. 99.
141 Mathijs Pelkmans, *Defending the Border: Identity, Religion, and Modernity in the Republic of Georgia* (London: Cornell University Press, 2006), p. 13.

Thus, for continents like Africa that have been violently balkanised into administrative units in the image of their colonisers the answer may not necessarily lie in a relaxation of borders or even a return to precolonial boundaries if at all those can be determined. It is indeed not to be easily presumed that populations are hostile to the existence of the boundary line or that they would rather have them removed. The removal of problematic borders certainly does not mean affected populations will embrace themselves wholeheartedly. Insight into the fossilising effect of boundaries may be found in an ethnographic and sociocultural study conducted into the divided border village of Sarpi situated between Turkey and (the former USSR, now) Georgia. It was discovered that:

> Changes in government rhetoric and renewed border permeability did not mean, however that the contrasting dimensions had simply evaporated. Although, the border had become easier to cross than before, it continued to regulate movement and communication in ways that could not have been anticipated beforehand. In the midst of new dangers the inhabitants created new divides, fortified them with stereotypes, and solidified them with ethnicized versions of culture and religion. These processes had the paradoxical effect of creating a contemporary divide that in some regards was more impermeable than the Iron Curtain had been. The fortification of identity offers an important antidote to views of hybridity and intermingling on and across state borders. It suggests that in a world that is characterised by transnational contact and the absence of grand ideological divides between states, it may be cultural boundaries that become more rigid and less permeable.[142]

In essence it is not irrefutably certain that Yoruba populations spread as they are over many existing independent states across West Africa would in fact welcome unification under the same boundaries in the twenty-first century.[143]

In other words it is our position in this book that national boundaries do matter and are of consequence in their manifest reality. Where they are sensibly imposed they are a good in themselves and they may be a means to an end while not necessarily being an end in themselves. Where insensitively imposed they are still a necessity in the ordering of international affairs but the problematic nature of the delineation may be ameliorated or removed by various legal and political strategies which we will be discussing throughout this work (see particularly Chapter 18 and the discussion on appropriate recourse to the use of plebiscites at 18.6). It is also suggested that it is the lack of a settled acceptance of the

---

142 Pelkmans, op.cit., p. 224.
143 Studies show that 'The homeland of Yoruba Culture is West Africa. Due to the European colonial policy of partitioning, this homeland spans the four West African countries of Nigeria, Benin Republic, Togo, and Ghana (Although the culture is also found in the West African countries of Sierra Leone'. It is estimated that the population of the Yoruba in West Africa around 2005 was 25 million with at least 2 million situated outside the shores of Nigeria their principal home. Carol R. Ember, Melvin Ember, Ian Skoggard (eds), *Encyclopedia of Diasporas: Immigrant and Refugee Cultures Around the World* (New York: Springer, 2005), p. 318.

reality and unforgiving 'hardness' of national boundaries on the one hand and pragmatism to work with existing boundaries or change them through overt peaceful means assented to by all parties concerned on the other hand, that causes perennial disputes among states. This philosophical divergence over the true nature of boundaries afflicts many disciplines that intertwine with boundary law and practice.

The author observes and is intrigued by the way many boundary experts (especially at conferences and sometimes during boundary delimitation/ demarcation exercises (usually consisting of joint teams of technical experts) imbue lawyers with the cloak of unhelpfulness and conservative rigidity. Lawyers are often in such situations perceived as legalistic, fatalistic and even obsessed about the significance of boundary lines and the full complements of territorial sovereignty where applicable. In truth few experts in international relations theory and even less in other social sciences (apart from security and strategic studies fields) share this strict and legalistic approach to international boundaries. Non-liberal approaches favoured mostly by lawyers are characterised as focusing more explicitly on the community and the state which in principle necessitates a greater awareness and importance of borders. International relations experts on the other hand are perceived as more liberal on the crucial question of the sanctity of arbitrary borders. International relations theory started to change rapidly towards the idea of softening borders as it grappled with the reality of globalisation and events such as the end of the Cold War and the collapse of the erstwhile Soviet Union's borders. The development of the principle of free movement within the European Union was significant in this direction as it reduced the importance of borders within the community. What is often overlooked is the fact that the European Community developments hardened borders in relation to the exterior of the EU. The declining costs of international transportation are indeed one of the real driving forces behind globalisation and borders are at the forefront of the pressure created by globalisation.[144] Certainly within Africa a lot of the tension that exists in relation to borders emanates from the increasing access and ease of illegal entry into national territory through manned and unmanned borders. Borders will, thus, for a long time be a flashpoint in interstate relations although the brunt of the problems surrounding the usage of borders such as its effects on boundary communities will be felt more by non-state entities.

It is by no means true that international relations experts are uniform in their conceptualisation of boundaries and border issues. Within international relations discourse there is a difference between the liberal-cosmopolitans who are in the majority and the communitarian particularistic position which is conservative and gives more attention to the primacy of borders and separateness of identities.[145]

---

144 Frank Broeze, "The 1990s: Globalisation", *Research in Maritime History: The Globalisation of the Oceans Containerisation from the 1950s to the Present*, No. 23 (Newfoundland: Int Maritime Economic History Association, 2002), p. 116.
145 Chris Brown, "Borders and Identity in International Political Theory" in M. Albert, D. Jacobson and Y. Lapid, op.cit., pp. 117–19.

Despite a remarkably less conservative if not less legalistic view of boundaries and borders it has been correctly recognised that international relations theory is still far from a whole scale abandonment of borders. It has been noted that:

> Liberal political theory is Janus-faced in its approach to the political significance of boundaries and identity. On the one hand, liberals are generally universalities who approach politics from the perspective of a belief in a common humanity and whose commitment to notions such as human rights, religious tolerance, the rule of law, representative and responsible government are, in principle universal. At a first approximation, liberals are 'cosmopolitan'. . . . Given this general position, the expectation would be that liberals/cosmopolitans will be sceptical of any account of borders and frontiers that attempts to assign to them more than provisional and instrumental significance . . . A liberal who wished to sustain this position would presumably promote the establishment of the borderless world of some theorists of globalisation, a world in which peoples, goods, and information would flow freely and frontiers would become of trivial importance. Some do take this position, but surprisingly few.[146]

In essence, therefore, even though liberal approaches to international relations recognise that borders can be legitimated solely on pragmatic grounds, it is nevertheless appreciated that these pragmatic grounds may actually be too wide. Borders and boundaries are therefore, very useful constructs even within the liberal construction of international relations theories. It is not surprising that international relations theory wrestles with the boundary issue in this way. It is a central feature of the discipline that communities in general are entitled to defend themselves. In this principle lies the necessity of retaining a power of exclusion of others from national territory even though a writer like O'Neill believes that boundaries are not acceptable when they 'systematically inflict injustices on outsiders'.[147] International relations theory as a result also concludes that borders and frontiers have a deep significance in identity information and frontiers in that 'borders are what make community possible in the first place'.[148] As a result the essential contribution of international relations is to adopt an interpretation of sovereignty and boundaries that does not constitute an arbitrary limit to the scope of justice.[149]

---

146 Brown, op. cit., pp. 120–21.
147 Onora O'Neill, "Justice and Boundaries", in *Political Restructuring in Europe*, Chris Brown (ed.), (London: Routledge), p. 86.
148 Brown, op.cit., p. 129.
149 O'Neill, op.cit., p. 122.

5 Actual and potential role of the African Union Organisation in boundary dispute management and resolution

Within the African Union the most relevant department to detect and originate action with respect to boundary problems is the Peace and Security Department.[1] The Peace and Security Department (PSD) of the Commission of the African Union (AU) provides support to the efforts aimed at promoting peace, security and stability on the continent.[2] The Peace and Security Council currently rests upon certain pillars. They are: the African Standby Force; the African Commission; the AU Panel of the Wise;[3] the Continental Early Warning System (CEWS) and the Peace Fund.[4]

---

1 Interviews were held with Director of Peace and Security, Mr El Ghassim Wane, Director of Political Affairs; Amb. Ognimba L. Emile; Wafula Okomu of the AUBP, Head of the Situation Room, among others.
2 Its activities cover the following areas: implementation of the Common African Defence and Security Policy (CADSP); operationalisation of the Continental Peace and Security Architecture as articulated by the Protocol Relating to the Establishment of the Peace and Security Council (PSC) of the AU, including the Continental Early Warning System (CEWS) and the African Standby Force (ASF); support to the efforts to prevent, manage and resolve conflicts; promotion of programmes for the structural prevention of conflicts, including through the implementation of the AU Border Programme (AUBP); implementation of the AU's Policy Framework on Post-Conflict Reconstruction and Development (PCRD); and coordination, harmonisation and promotion of peace and security programmes in Africa, including with the Regional Economic Communities (RECs)/Regional Mechanisms for Conflict Prevention, Management and Resolution (RMs), the United Nations and other relevant international organisations and partners.
3 The Protocol Relating to the Peace and Security Council (PSC) of the African Union entered into force on 26 December 2003, having been ratified by the required majority of Member States of the AU. It is made up of 15 Member States. In order to fully assume its responsibilities for the deployment of peace-keeping and quick intervention missions to assist in cases of genocide, war crimes and crimes against humanity, the PSC could consult a Panel of the Wise comprising five African public figures so as to take action on the distribution of the military on the field ; VOA, "AU Launches 'Panel of the Wise'", 18 December 2007, available at http://www.voanews.com/english/news/a-13-2007-12-18-voa47-66814662.html, accessed 14 May 2012.
4 Indeed the PSD is comprised of four divisions: (a) the Conflict Management Division (CMD), which focuses on aspects of the African Peace and Security Architecture (Continental Early Warning System – CEWS, the Panel of the Wise, the Memorandum of Understanding between the AU and the RECs/RMs). The CMD supports and coordinates activities relating to conflict prevention and management, as well as to PCRD. The CMD also supervises and coordinates the work of the AU Liaison Offices; (b) The Peace Support Operations Division (PSOD), which works towards the full actualisation of the operations of the ASF and the Military Staff Committee, (MSC, as provided for in the Protocol relating to the Establishment of the PSC). Its remit includes

The AU of course has the entire continent in its purview in relation to efforts to prevent and resolve boundary conflicts. By some estimates it has had to deal with scores of boundary disputes and situations over the last few decades, some of which are still ongoing. They include the Cameroon–Nigeria, Libya–Chad, Sudan–Kenya, Tanzania–Malawi, Namibia–Zimbabwe–Zambia and Ethiopia–Eritrea, with the AU engaging with the parties to these problematic boundary situations. There are situations when the AU intervenes directly and others where it does so merely as an observer or facilitator in conjunction with another body or authority that has the acceptance of the parties. For instance, in the continuing Djibouti–Eritrea situation, the AU is partnering with IGAD in a supportive role while the Emir of Qatar, Ahmed El Khaifa Alshani is the main mediator. To some, this particular instance, in fact, reveals the limitations of the usefulness of the AU in certain contexts. Eritrea is said to prefer a mediator from outside the continent because of its obvious suspicion of any efforts emanating from Addis Ababa, Ethiopia where the AU headquarters is based – especially since Eritrea and Ethiopia have a subsisting and long-lasting boundary dispute. Another very recent role of the AU has been to support parties in the South Sudan–North Sudan situation where the AUBP has been assisting the Mbeki Panel to help bring about resolution to the parties.

Senior officials of the AU confirmed indications that the African Union usually responds to conflicts by offering mediation. If that does not succeed the organisation favours recommending international arbitration (such as was done between Ethiopia and Eritrea). The AU also responds by giving timely warnings to parties who are in danger of entering into conflict over boundaries. Specific recommendations as to what to do to bring back normalcy are also communicated to the parties. In reaction to the escalating conflict between Sudan and South Sudan in April of 2012, the AU promptly called upon both parties to exercise restraint and to respect each other's territorial integrity. It also called upon the parties to withdraw any armed forces that may be in the territory of the other state with immediate effect and bring an end to all aerial bombardment and the harbouring of rebel forces and movements. Furthermore, the AU called for implementation of the Joint Political and Security Mechanism, which established the Joint Border Verification and Monitoring Mission (JBVMM) between the states and which also mandates the UN Interim Security Force for Abyei to support the JBVMM. The AU, however, continued to seise the African Union

---

the elaboration of relevant policy documents and coordination with relevant African structures and AU partners. The PSOD plans, mounts, manages and supports AU peace support operations; (c) the PSC Secretariat provides the operational and administrative support required by the PSC to enable it and its subsidiary bodies to effectively perform their designated functions. The Secretariat acts as the builder and custodian of the institutional memory on the work of the PSC and facilitates its interaction with other organisations/institutions on issues of peace and security; (d) The Defence and Security Division (DSD), addresses long-term cross-cutting security issues and is in charge of issues relating to arms control and disarmament, counter-terrorism and other strategic security issues, including security sector reform. Information about the PSD and other organs and agencies of the AU are available online at http://au.int/en/dp/ps/.

High Level Implementation Panel (AUHIP) with the dispute and urged the parties to continue to cooperate with it.[5]

A recurring theme in our interviews at the African Union is the expression of regret that the African Court of Justice envisaged by the AU Charter has not been brought into existence as a permanent institution.[6] High expectations of the Court appear to exist even among the principal officers of the PSD department. The absence of the Court, it has been argued, is one of the reasons why foreign international and even foreign national courts attempt many times successfully to exercise jurisdiction over matters of African concern or matters that ought to be dealt with by an African court because the facts of the matter or dispute relate to the local situation in Africa. It is arguable that the many instances of recourse made to the ICJ by African states in relation to their boundary problems is indicative of the existence of this lacunae.

The AU, to its credit however, has assisted states in several successful negotiations in relation to complex boundary delimitation and demarcation exercises. An example of this is the recent tripartite maritime agreements reached between Tanzania, Mozambique and Comoros.[7] A similar maritime delimitation success was achieved between Tanzania and Madagascar.

Where a maritime boundary dispute involves a non-AU member state such as a country based on another continent, the AU can still be closely involved in the resolution of such disputes. The AU, for instance, has a continuing partnership with the Arab League, AESEAN, the Organisation of Islamic Countries and the United Nations, empowering it to address any dispute within these channels wherever appropriate.

It is notable that the AU has so far not had to intervene in the enforcement of a boundary decision directly. However, it does have power and capacity to engage in military action where needed. Furthermore the AU has been known to apply

---

5 See below. AU Press Release, "African Union Deeply Alarmed by the Escalating Conflict between Sudan and South Sudan", April 2012, available at http://www.au.int/en/sites/default/files/auc%20com%20sudan%2011%2004%202012.pdf, accessed 10 April 2012.

6 The African Court of Justice (ACJ) is in charge of civil matters particularly with regards to the protection of human rights and consolidation of good governance in Africa. Upon its implementation it will serve as a court of wide jurisdiction including criminal matters for the Continent. The ACJ was merged with the African Court of Human and People's Rights (ACHPR) to become what is now known as 'The African Court of Justice and Human Rights'. This union happened during the AU Summit of Heads of State and Government on 1 July 2008 in Sharm El Sheikh, Arab Republic of Egypt. It is expected to act as the principal judicial institution of the AU. See AU, "The African Court of Justice", available at http://www.au.int/en/organs/cj, accessed 15 May 2012.

7 On 17 February 2012, in Victoria, Seychelles, and as part of the implementation of the African Union Border Programme (AUBP), the Governments of the Comoros, the Seychelles and Tanzania signed Agreements on the delimitation of their maritime borders. These include: an Agreement on the delimitation of the maritime border between the Republic of Seychelles and the Union of the Comoros; and an Agreement between the Republic of Seychelles, the Union of the Comoros and the United Republic of Tanzania on the Indian Ocean triple point. Tanzania's Ministry of Foreign Affairs and International Cooperation, "The African Union Welcomes The Signing By Seychelles, The Comoros and Tanzania of Agreements on the Delimitation of their Maritime Borders", *Foreign Affairs*, 19 February 2012, available at http://foreigntanzania.blogspot.co.uk/2012/02/seychelles-comoros-and-tanzania-signed.html, accessed 26 August 2014.

sanctions on states. Examples include the sanction against Madagascar in reaction to unconstitutional change of government in relation to developments in Cote d'Ivoire.[8]

5.1 African Union early warning system

The Early Warning Unit is very likely to be first to take notice of an emerging crisis in a boundary area. Watching out for boundary disputes and conflicts is a specific part of the duty of the desk officers of the PSC department. The EWU has indeed over the years identified several instances of border tensions, situations and disputes. But it is crucial to note that it has no dedicated officers on boundary matters. The EWU is also currently understaffed. It has a total of ten officers who operate 24 hours and there are only three analysts in the unit – although the AU has plans to recruit five more analysts and four more Situation Room staff. The Situation Room itself has been operating continuously since 1998.[9]

Steps taken after an emergency that falls within the remit of the EWU duties are as follows:

(a) Flash messages are sent out. This may take the form of 'News Desk text messages' and emails to the Directors, Commissioner of Peace and Security, Deputy Chairperson of the Commission, and Chairperson of the Commission and PSC members. A call may in addition be placed by the EWU to the Director of the PSC.

(b) Simultaneously or after the appropriate alerts, Early Warning Reports are prepared in which analysis, projected scenarios and response options are communicated.

(c) The Director may call a PSC meeting over the issue, situation or conflict where specific responses will be identified.

---

8 AU Sanctions have been levied principally for two reasons: unconstitutional changes in government (by the Peace and Security Council); and refusal to make budgetary contributions. For sanctions in relation to Coup d'États and unconstitutional changes in Government examples include those against the Central African Republic (March 2003–June 2005); Mauritania (August 2008–June 2009); Guinea (December 2008–December 2010); Niger (August 2009–March 2011); Madagascar (March 2009); Madagascar (2009), Cote d'Ivoire (December 2010–April 2011). See Konstantinos Magliveras, "The Sanctioning System of the African Union: Part Success, Part Failure?", revised version of paper presented to an expert roundatable on "The African Union: The First Ten Years", a conference organised by the Institute of Security Studies, Addis Ababa, Ethiopia, 11–13 October 2011. Available at http://aegean.academia.edu/KonstantinosMagliveras/Papers/1159844/THE_SANCTIONING_SYSTEM_OF_THE_AFRICAN_UNION_PART_SUCCESS_PART_FAILURE, accessed 11 May 2012.

9 It is notable that the European Union has as recently as 2011 established a similar EU 'Situation Room' under the new External European Action Service (EEAS). On this development one commentator observed that the newer EU Situation Room may 'prompt questions as to whether the EU might have copied the AU–but never admit it!', adding, 'Let's see the dates: 1998 and 2011. Some 13 years down the line? I do not think anyone can convince me that the bilaterals that have taken place over the years between the AU and the EU Commissions might not have touched on peace and security and, by extension, the situation rooms!'; see "The African Union's 'Situation Room' compared to the EU's newly created 'Situation Room'", *Critiquing Regional Integration, Regions Watch*, available at http://critiquing-regionalism.org, accessed 12 April 2012.

(d) A Communiqué is issued with respect to findings, decisions and recommendations.

Areas of possible improvement with the Early Warning System fall under two clear themes. First the early warning unit should be able to enhance data-gathering mechanisms by focusing on border issues. This may take the form of an assignment of dedicated officers on border matters attached to the Unit – either to report or to form part of the AUBP unit within the AU. Second, the Early Warning Unit could develop a list of indicators which can be used to predict imminence of boundary conflicts such as presence of illegal poaching and trans-border crime which could be very useful in the prediction of likely disputes and flashpoints.

Generally the AU is quite top-down in its diplomatic approach to conflict prevention and management. It is recognised that some bottom-up approaches that are seen to be succeeding in the RECs may be of benefit to the AU. Examples of these mass mobilisations for peace strategies include the institution of Council of Elders of IGAD and ECOWAS, and peace radios and peace newspapers in the ECOWAS region. Such approaches will certainly make the AUBP more effective and responsive even within the framework of its terms of reference. Although the AU itself has a Panel of the Wise, the grassroots reach of the RECs' Council of Elders is observably better, and their numbers are at any rate greater. What is canvassed here is not an abandonment of the rich and varied practice of the AU – commendable in its own right – but a better approach to complementarity between the AU and the African sub-regional RECs in relation to boundary dispute management.

Indeed note should be made of the extensive work and capabilities of the RECs in the area of conflict management and prevention. If the AU is to fulfil its sacred duties of maintaining peaceful conduct of international relations in Africa it must be seen to work even closer and in a more strategic manner with the various RECs on the continent. It is important that existing mechanisms are recognised and retained. The general feeling among staff and officials of the various RECs visited in the writing of this book was that the AU need only get involved to strengthen their efforts through targeted assistance. The officials of IGAD, for instance, made it known that it would be appreciated if the AU can assist them in setting up local offices to deal with conflicts. They insist that conflicts can only be properly understood at the local level. Thus, the AUBP mechanism could be adapted to include secondment of officials to the RECs.

One of the suggestions made by the international civil servants sampled in our interviews was to incorporate the names of experts on the mediation councils of the existing RECs in Africa into a dedicated list, to be maintained by the AUBP, which would form the basis of a pool of experts to be used for boundary disputes. This position is reasonable but it is important to note that the members of the existing mediation councils by the laws of the RECs that set them up are usually not specifically trained in boundary issues and typically will have very little if any appreciable expertise in that field. Furthermore, at least some of the existing

Mediation Council members such as the Mediation and Security Council of ECOWAS appear to consist of current governmental officials of member states. This may appear to compromise their independence from the perspective of those countries facing border arbitration and/or mediation. Furthermore, the availability of such important personalities for service when they are no longer in national office cannot not be guaranteed. It must, however, be conceded that experience within the Mediation Council of any of the RECs would certainly benefit anyone called in to assist the AUBP in handling the various crises that arise on the continent in relation to boundary conflicts.

Feedback from interviews conducted at the AU including particularly the Office of the Director of Peace and Security, Mr El Ghassim Wane, attest to the institutional enthusiasm of the AU to provide a one-stop specialisation for the continent of Africa in the resolution of future boundary disputes. There is also a clear indication that it is realised that the AUBP as an existing structure needs to be further strengthened in capacity. Indications are also to the effect that beyond the AUBP Unit specifically created for the boundaries programme, the Peace and Security Council structure would benefit from targeted measures to strengthen its capacities in this area. This at the very least should involve the addition of boundary specialists to its pool of experts. It is recognised that bureaucrats who generally address conflict situations within the AU still need to be advised on what to do when boundary problems arise. This will further increase the confidence of member states in the AU mechanisms as an alternative to foreign resolution of boundary conflicts. The idea of the development of a typology of specific steps to be followed by experts and bureaucrats in dealing with boundary crises received particular support. There also appears to be a demand within the AU for standardisation of the terms of reference and competences to be given to those charged with resolving border problems.

Yet there is a strand of responses which represent a radical proposal for the creation of an independent body like the ACHPR to handle boundary disputes as a court, with the option of being constituted as a standing mediation panel. The belief is that such a body will in time develop an advanced specialism in an area where Africa is in dire need of expertise. Their argument is that a permanent, standalone institution funded by member states may be created as long as it works within the existing framework of the PSC. This view, however, does not preclude the use of lists of experts that can be called upon to work *ad hoc*, as and when needed, in the furtherance of the duties of the proposed mechanism. It was also suggested that there may indeed be a good reason for the proposed mechanism to be situated a healthy distance away from the AU headquarters in order to project impartiality from the politics of the African Union. This may involve affiliation with existing influential diplomatic structures such as the Mbeki Panel. The proposed structure may also be based in an influential member state's territory such as Nigeria or South Africa and depend a lot on the patronage of influential backers.[10]

---

10 Interviews at the Early Warning Unit.

There was also consensus among another group of interviewees both at the AU and ECOWAS that RECs should be encouraged to have similar bodies to the AUBP mechanism. The proposed specialist bodies within the RECs acting in concert with the existing AUBP would feed into the continental peace and conflict architecture. A particularly interesting view expressed by one ECOWAS official is that the ECOWAS Commission should be assisted in developing expertise in boundary issues in order to be able: (a) to handle all the issues that may crop up in relation to boundary matters; and (b) that this expertise may thus be used to also assist in intrastate boundary disputes such as the many disputes among the component states and units particularly in African federations. Another useful output identified from the interviews is the reminder that maritime delimitation conflicts would become more prevalent as the exploitation of the resources of the seas increase. Thus, it is suggested that it is in this area that the RECs that have extensive maritime territory (such as the Gulf of Guinea) should focus their attention. A good start in this area would be the development of specialist maritime law and natural resources advisers who may then provide assistance to African states in the process of delimiting and/or demarcating maritime or riparian territories.

The use of 'thematic reflection' was also recommended by the interviewees. The technique was adopted by the Panel of the Wise (in relation to the Kenyan conflict over a controversial election that led to violence) around the time it was relatively newly set up. This was seen as successful and the adoption of 'thematic reflection' on border disputes by the Panel of the Wise at the AU level may also be proposed. Indeed the suggestion that thematic conferences on boundary conflicts may be held every three years is particularly persuasive.

Responses from the PSC department in the AU are indicative of the fact that for the AUBP to work effectively and indeed for the AU to become more relevant in this direction three things are crucial: (a) more money will have to be provided; (b) more manpower will have to be brought to the task; and (c) additional studies will have to be undertaken.

5.2 The African Union Border Programme (AUBP) and the delimitation, demarcation and settlement of African boundary disputes

The AUBP is an epoch-making development in African international law and international relations. It is based on an audacious move to finalise the delimitation and demarcation of all African territories within an ambitious timetable in order to forestall further territorial and boundary disputes in and around the continent. In a sense, therefore, it is impossible to conceptualise the future of dispute resolution on the continent without recognising the influence (positive or negative) the AUBP would have had by the time it is considered complete. The following section, therefore, will examine the law and practice of the AUBP and evaluate its chances of successful completion.

5.2.1 *Law practice and diplomacy of the African Union Border Programme*

It is probably fair to say that since the Berlin Conference of 1885 no comprehensive and collective political effort has been made to study the legal and political provenance of African boundaries. The imprecision of the delimitation and the inordinate apportionment of territory principally along the lines of mere convenience of colonial rule have produced untold confusion, conflict, tensions and wars among African peoples. The effects of these have reverberated around the continent at least in the last five decades to the present day.[11]

Prior to the implementation of the AUBP, coordination and collaboration around international boundary issues was in the hands of African binational boundary commissions and was largely within the remit of foreign affairs ministries. African joint boundary commissions come in many shapes and sizes. In West Africa Benin Republic and Equatorial Guinea respectively have national boundary commissions. Cameroon–Nigeria is mixed and was established in 2002. It deals with transboundary and riparian issues. Similarly Ethiopia and Kenya share a binational commission which considers boundary development and general cooperation. Individually some African countries have moved towards establishing their own national boundary commissions. Each boundary commission is a product of the constitutional and administrative culture of the country. Mozambique and Niger Republic also have national boundary commissions. Mozambique's Commission has the major function of boundary development and aims to foster general cooperation with the country's neighbours.[12] Niger Republic's Commission was formed in 1987 but became fully operational in 1989, its main task being to maintain the country's boundaries. The Nigerian Boundary Commission is quite mature in many respects when compared with many other African states.[13]

---

11 Indeed it is widely recognised that European colonialism continues to underlie most territorial disputes in Africa. Recent examples include the Nigeria–Cameroon dispute over the Bakassi Peninsula; the Gabon–Equatorial Guinea dispute over the islands of Mbanié, Cocotiers and Conga in the Corisco Bay; the Mauritius–UK dispute over the Chagos Archipelago; and the Comoros–France situation. Mi Yung Yoon, 'European Colonialism and Territorial Disputes in Africa: The Gulf of Guinea and the Indian Ocean', Vol. 20, *Mediterranean Quarterly*, No. 2, Spring 2009, pp. 77–94.
12 Mozambique's *Instituto do Mar e Fronteiras* (IMAF) was established in 2001 and also coordinates and collaborates in its role with the Ministries of Interior, Defence, State Administration, Agriculture, Fisheries, Transport & Communication, Mineral Resources, Environmental, Coordination, Justice, Finance, Minister at Presidency, for Diplomatic Affairs.
13 The Commission works in close collaboration with the Ministries of Interior, Defence, State Administration, Agriculture, Fisheries, Transport & Communication, Mineral Resources, Environmental, Coordination, Justice, Finance, Minister at Presidency, for Diplomatic Affairs. The body also collaborates with the pertinent border authorities with its neighbours in Niger, Benin, Cameroon, and the Lake Chad Basin Authority. The departments that make up the NBC include: Research and Policy Analysis; Border Regions; Development; Legal Services; International Boundaries; Internal Boundaries; Maritime Services and Geo-information; and the Administration Supplies Department.

When the AU Assembly of Heads of State and Government at their eighth ordinary session in January 2002 mandated the AU Commission[14] to pursue efforts towards the structural prevention of conflicts particularly through implementation of the AUBP delineation and demarcation of borders, they commendably opened a new and illustrious chapter in the history of African relations and perhaps international peace and stability.[15] The Commission, in furtherance of the border programme, produced a 2004–2007 'Plan of Action' which aimed *inter alia* to identify trans-border areas that would serve as a basis for cross-border cooperation, consolidation of trade, and free movement of people and goods. Pursuant to this ministers in charge of border issues in the member states deliberated on means and measures geared towards achievement of greater unity and solidarity among African countries and peoples and the reduction of the burden of borders separating African states. This ministerial body drew up a Declaration on the African Union Border Programme and its Implementation Modalities in 2007.[16]

A component of the Commission's border programme as set out in the 2004–2007 Plan of Action is the identification of trans-border areas that would serve as a basis for cross-border cooperation, consolidation of trade and free movement of people and goods. The Commission correctly noted that the transformation of border areas could be achieved through effective demarcation and monitoring by way of control logistics and infrastructure capacity-building at both national and regional levels. Other objectives of the border programme include: harmonisation of the integration policies of regional and sub-regional organisations; strengthening the capacity of decision-makers in the area of border management and regional integration; and funding of cross-border development projects. These noble aims rest on: (i) the principle of the respect of borders existing on achievement of national independence, as enshrined in the Charter of the Organization of African Unity (OAU), Resolution AHG/Res.16(I) on border disputes between African states,[17] and Article 4 (b) of the Constitutive Act of the African Union;[18] (ii) the principle of negotiated settlement of border disputes, as provided for notably in Resolution CM/Res.1069 (XLIV) on peace and security in Africa through negotiated settlement of boundary disputes.

---

14 Hereinafter referred to as 'the Commission'; materials relating to the AU are available at www.africa-union.org.
15 "AU moves to ease border conflicts in Africa", *The Guardian* (Nigeria), 23 May 2007.
16 Declaration on the African Union Border Programme and its Implementation Modalities as adopted by the Conference of African Ministers in Charge of Border Issues held in Addis Ababa (Ethiopia), on 7 June 2007, available at http://www.africa-union.org/root/au/publications/PSC/Border%20Issues.pdf.
17 Adopted by the 1st Ordinary Session of the Assembly of Heads of State and Government of the OAU, held in Cairo, Egypt, in July 1964.
18 This provision reiterates the age-old directive philosophy of African states regarding territorial boundaries by protecting, '[r]espect of borders existing on achievement of independence'; Constitutive Act of African Union, 11 July 2000. The Organization for African Unity (OAU) was officially replaced by the African Union on 9 July 2002. See Charter of the Organization of African Unity, 479 UNTS 39 (entered into force 13 September 1963).

The declaration on the AU border programme and its implementation modalities as adopted by the conference of African ministers in charge of border issues is potentially, therefore, one of the most significant legal events of the last century in relation to the African continent. The declaration is quite clear on the imperatives of the AUBP particularly regarding the demands of an Africa-wide delimitation and demarcation exercise. It also very significantly appears to have set a very ambitious timetable for the implementation of the programme. The AUBP stated:

> The delimitation and demarcation of boundaries depend primarily on the sovereign decision of the States. They must take the necessary steps to facilitate the process of delimitation and demarcation of African borders, including maritime boundaries, where such an exercise has not yet taken place, by respecting, as much as possible, the time-limit set in the Solemn Declaration on the CSSDCA. We encourage the States to undertake and pursue bilateral negotiations on all problems relating to the delimitation and demarcation of their borders, including those pertaining to the rights of the affected populations, with a view to finding appropriate solutions to these problems.[19]

This statement originated earlier in the propositions and work of the Preparatory Meeting of Experts on the African Union Border Programme.[20] This body of experts was in turn attempting to give life to the Memorandum of Understanding on Security, Stability, Development and Cooperation in Africa (CSSDCA) adopted in July 2002, which provided for the delimitation and demarcation of African boundaries, where such an exercise has not yet taken place, by 2012 latest. That particular instrument was, however, not followed up by any concrete plan to facilitate the implementation of the ambitious plan. The audacious and noble aims expressed in the 2002 MOU were, thus, set against an ambitious timetable which envisioned the completion of the programme by 2012. The idea that the AUBP could significantly achieve its desired aim of delimiting and demarcating African boundaries in a decade was indeed a case of runaway optimism.

It is recognisable that for lawyers, surveyors, cartographers, geographers and other social and natural scientists there is an attraction for the certainty and specificity of clearly demarcated boundaries rather than vagueness of mere frontiers.[21] But the optimism around generating more precise boundaries across Africa must be balanced against the realism of the vastness of the frontiers

---

19 Paragraph 5 (a)(i), Declaration on the African Union Border Programme, *supra* n. 3.
20 The meeting of government experts preparatory to the Conference of African Ministers in charge of Border Issues, scheduled for 7 June 2007, was held in Addis Ababa from 4 to 5 June 2007.
21 The near esoteric discussion of the spatial demarcation between airspace and outer space has not escaped heated academic discussion. Hence the present writer has been moved to consider this issue elsewhere. See Gbenga Oduntan, (2003), op.cit.

that potentially have to be covered. Africa has approximately 28,000 miles of international boundaries. The national boundaries are recognisably highly porous with up to 109 of its international boundaries characterised by permeability. It is significant that experts agree that up to 25 per cent of African international boundaries are completely undemarcated.[22] Although less than 50 per cent of the world's maritime boundaries have been agreed upon, in Africa that figure is even lower than that average. Africa has 27 mainland coastal states and their maritime boundaries are – except in a few cases – never far from controversy. There are also seven sets of island states whose geographical locations in various ways impact on the maritime fortunes of some of the mainland coastal states.[23]

With the above considerations in mind the initial idea of completing the AUBP in just about half a decade (albeit extended to a decade later) shows a disappointing under-assessment of the demands of this sensitive programme (see Appendix IV: Status of African National Boundaries as at 2011). Maritime delimitation negotiations alone would prove challenging to complete in the initial time-frame allowed for the AUBP. Apart from the sheer financial cost implication of continental shelf claims, there are considerable time implications. It is relevant that up to eight African states have utilised the avenue created under the law of the sea to make applications in order to extend their continental shelf by making technical submissions, through the Secretary-General of the United Nations, to the Commission on the Limits of the Continental Shelf, pursuant to Article 76(8) of the United Nations Convention on the Law of the Sea of 10 December 1982 (LOSC).[24] African states have, increasingly, shown avid interests in securing the valuable energy/natural resources that are found in the seabed for national development.[25]

Following the submission of a continental shelf claim to the UN Division of Ocean Affairs and Law of the Sea, and to the Commission on the Limits of the

---

22 For examples of Africa's porous borders see pictures in Appendix III. African international boundaries are 'protected' by about 350 official road crossing points – one for every 80 miles of boundary. Wafula Okumu, 'Border Security in Africa', presentation to the African Union Border Programme Regional Workshop, Windhoek, Namibia, 22–23 October 2009, p. 3.
23 Tim Daniel, "African Maritime Boundaries", in Jonathan I. Charney, David A. Colson, Robert W. Smith (eds), *International Maritime Boundaries*, Vol. V (Martinus Nijhoff, 2005) p. 3429.
24 UNCLOS III ILM 1245 (1982). Joint submission by the Republic of Mauritius and the Republic of Seychelles – in the region of the Mascarene Plateau, Côte d'Ivoire, Ghana; Joint submission by France and South Africa, Kenya, Mauritius – in the region of Rodrigues Island, Namibia; Nigeria, South Africa – in respect of the mainland of the territory of the Republic of South Africa.
25 A geomorphological description of the continental shelf encompasses the gently sloping platform of submerged land surrounding the continents and islands, normally extending to a depth of approximately 200m or 100 fathoms at which point the seabed falls away sharply. The legal definition of the continental shelf as contained in Article 76 of the LOSC (1982) reads: 'The continental shelf of a coastal State comprises the sea-bed and subsoil of the submarine areas that extend beyond its territorial sea throughout the natural prolongation of its land territory to the outer edge of the continental margin, or to a distance of 200 nautical miles from the baselines from which the breadth of the territorial sea is measured where the outer edge of the continental margin does not extend up to that distance'. Note that according to paragraph 3, the coastal state

Continental Shelf (CLCS),[26] the deliberations and negotiations may involve a waiting period of up to two-and-a-half years. During this time, the concerned African state will have to maintain a core team of experts at the UN offices. A fully fledged and equipped office will have to be maintained in New York and there will be several rounds of technical deliberations and question-and-answer sessions, where the submitting state will be asked to defend portions of its submissions. Presumably this again is one of the areas in which the AU and indeed the AUBP will prefer an early rather than later finalisation of claims. The ambitious dates set for the completion of the AUBP were, therefore, unrealistic on this point as well.

There is a possible argument that an inordinate and poorly executed rush towards strict demarcation in a continent that apparently is held together by a controversial Latin American construct of *uti possidetis* (roughly described as 'snapshot of territory at independence') can produce potentially dangerous consequences. The issue of a continent-wide simultaneous delimitation and demarcation exercise based on an unquestioning loyalty to the legal fiction of *uti possidetis* should be handled with the utmost care. This is so especially because it is often the question of exactly what was inherited at independence that is in issue.[27] There is an undue optimism in academic writing that *uti possidetis* is a magic wand that can resolve every territorial and boundary contest in ex-colonial settings. There is indeed a certain danger that if the AU Border Programme is not

---

may also establish the outer edge of the continental margin wherever the margin extends beyond 200 nautical miles from the baselines from which the breadth of the territorial sea is measured, by either: (i) a line delineated in accordance with paragraph 7 by reference to the outermost fixed points at each of which the thickness of sedimentary rocks is at least 1% of the shortest distance from such point to the foot of the continental slope; or (ii) a line delineated in accordance with paragraph 7 by reference to fixed points not more than 60 nautical miles from the foot of the continental slope. In the absence of evidence to the contrary, the foot of the continental slope shall be determined as the point of maximum change in the gradient at its base. Aware of the immense resources that lay buried in the continental shelf, certain coastal states from the mid-1940s, introduced declarations to secure a beneficial utilisation regime for themselves over this maritime zone.

26 Materials relating to the CLCS are available at http://www.un.org/Depts/los/clcs_new/submissions_files/submission_rus.htm.

27 The ascendancy of the *uti possidetis* principle in the jurisprudence of African international law and relations via its manifestation as a Latin American principle and as enshrined in Article paragraph 3 of the OAU Charter has theoretically transfixed African boundaries. Yet there is some merit to the argument that the limits of *uti possidetis* as policy must be recognised. The true target of the principle is the doctrine of protection of boundaries and borders. *Uti possidetis* was not even in the Latin American sense designed to answer neither back to separatists nor to trump the right of self-determination. It definitely should not be an incantation against well-founded exercise of the rights of a people to self-determination. For critical views on *uti possidetis* see Ratner's excellent article, "Drawing a Better Line: Uti Possidetis and the Borders of New States", Vol. 90, *American Journal of International Law*, No. 4, pp. 590–624, See also Crawford, *The Creation of States in International Law* (1979). Ardent supporters of the principle like Santiago Torres Bernardez, admit the *uti possidetis* doctrine still has to be reconciled with developments in law and 'the evolution of the rules of international law governing, for example succession, self-determination, acquisition of title to territory, frontiers and other territorial regimes, treaty law, intertemporal law, etc.' See e.g. Torres Bernárdez, "The '*Uti Possidetis Juris* Principle' in Historical Perspective", in K. Ginther *et al.* (eds), *Festschrift für Karl Zemanek* (1994), p. 436. International Crisis Group, "Central Asia: Border Disputes and Conflict Potential", p.6. Reports of the International Crisis Group are available at www.crisisgroup.org, accessed 5 June 2007.

successfully prosecuted events may conspire to endanger the delicate balance achieved under the *uti possidetis* principle in Africa.[28]

Perhaps instead of the present effort towards simultaneous consideration of all undelimited and undemarcated territories across the continent more or less at the same time, it may be better to proceed by adoption of a phased regional approach (compare Appendix IV: Status of African National Boundaries as at 2010). Thus, for instance, West Africa may be the focus of the next 10 years' border programme efforts, moving on thereafter to six African regions – North Africa, West Africa, Central Africa, North East Africa, East Africa, Southern Africa.[29] A phased approach reduces the severity of costs, risks and the overall demands on the institutions and experts involved. Lessons may be learnt from earlier phases and the experience would prove valuable during latter stages. The phased implementation option in fact accords with international practice of demarcation and consideration of delimitation tasks by international courts. Sectorial analysis and demarcation in phases was in fact applied by both the courts and implementation bodies in the Cameroon–Nigeria and Eritrea–Ethiopia processes.[30]

For the AU Border Programme to succeed the input of a large number of experienced experts to undertake the enormous tasks ahead would be required. These include competent and independent geologists, surveyors, hydrographers, cartographers, linguists and lawyers. There is also a need for capacity development in the requisite African international courts and tribunals in order to be able to competently handle complex boundary matters, particularly of a maritime nature, and to be able to develop a regional jurisprudence that will be able to cope with the possible upsurge in delimitation and demarcation disputes. It is fair to say that the required institutional and skilled capacity may be lacking presently unless drastic strategies are adopted. The choice is not really between allowing sleeping dogs lie and waking them up. It is arguably more a case of waking them up selectively and managing events in a controlled fashion and to deal with unexpected cases of rabid reactions not only among states but even within them.[31]

---

28 The merits and demerits of the *uti possidetis* doctrine are beyond this section and will be explored further below.
29 It has been suggested that the African border programme itself emanated from the desire to expand on achievements of the West African region. It may be that what is needed is to consolidate this further and then move on sequentially to other areas. OECD, *Cross-Border Diaries West African Borders And Integration Bulletin On West African Local-Regional Realities*, Issue 6 June 2007. *The Cross-border Diaries* are published both in French and English and are available on www.oecd.org/sah; www.afriquefrontieres.org, visited 21 December 2008.
30 The EEBC adopted the three-sector delimitation of the international boundary between Eritrea and Ethiopia.
31 One of the consequences of changes and shifts in international boundaries is that it may create traumatic and irreversible changes within national boundaries. This phenomenon may be hardest hitting on resource-rich federal states. As a result of the recent handover of Bakassi Peninsula to Cameroon by Nigeria in 2008, the Revenue Mobilisation, Allocation and Fiscal Commission (RMAFC) redefined the entire maritime territory of the federal states abutting the pertinent section of the Gulf of Guinea. As a result the entire maritime territory of Cross River State became ceded to its neighbouring Akwa Ibom state. The former state became declassified as a littoral state and was required to transfer 76 oil wells in favour of the latter. Cross River

In relation to the above it is reasonable to raise three queries. Could it be said that the dates set in 2002 by the Assembly of Heads of State and Government allowing for a ten-year period to complete such a major programme was in the first place very ambitious? Could that inscription have been an expression of a desire to begin to address seriously the issue and put in place a credible programme of action by 2012? Considering that the programme only became meaningfully addressed around 2012 it is now imperative that a more realistic implementation approach be set up by the AU.[32] Indeed the period from 2002 to 2012 would perhaps be best recognised as the consultative period for the Border Programme. Deep studies and sociological, scientific and legal enquiries into the nature of the important tasks before African states in terms of the delimitation and demarcation of international boundaries must continue both at the national, regional and continental levels.

Perhaps a more practical strategy, and one which in a very cynical world will present the AU as a competent intergovernmental organisation, is to cast the Border Programme within a 30-year completion period. As will be argued below, the delimitation of territory and the subsequent demarcation are complex tasks, the seriousness of which may be sacrificed by underestimation and under-preparation by the parties and interests involved. Assuming for argument's sake that all factors necessary for achieving delimitation of remaining and yet to be demarcated African boundaries are presently available (including scientific data, adequate funds, reliable satellite imagery, cartographic evidence, appreciable political will etc.), it would hardly be possible to complete the task even within 10 years simply on the grounds of a dearth of qualified and experienced surveyors. Employment contracts will have to be developed, qualified and adequately experienced staff attracted into Africa from abroad. They will be relocated with their families, language and logistic problems will be significant and questions of impartiality required in international survey work will have to be reconciled in the employment pattern. Local realities may also make progress extremely difficult if not impossible. Example may be made of boundary areas that need to be cleared of mines from previous wars and conflicts before any reaffirmation or reconnaissance surveying work can be done. This is certainly the case in some boundary areas between Mozambique and Zimbabwe.[33]

State Government, "RMAFC, Imoke Receives Report, Frowns at Data Collection". News & Press Releases, 8 July 2009, see http://crossriverstate.gov.ng/portal/modules/news/article.php?storyid=49, visited 8 January 2010; News & Press Releases: "Elders Condemn Delisting of Cross River as Oil Producing State", 1 July 2009, available at http://crossriverstate.gov.ng/portal/modules/news/article.php?storyid=44 visited 8 January 2010.

32 After the inception of the programme in 2002 about 5 years appear to have been lost whilst the infrastructure and funding for the programme was sought and put in place. Thus, the period of serious activity by the AUBP is quite recent although its productivity in that short time is clearly commendable given the immense tasks before it.

33 A writer notes of this zone 'these are bombs - not time bombs so much as timeless bombs - that have been strewn recklessly across the path of development in countries like Angola and Mozambique, a deadly legacy of the region's long agony of war. And they are primed, quite literally, to go off: again . . . and again'. Alex Vines, "The Southern Africa Minefield", vol. 11,

Since negotiations are the prescribed means by which Maritime delimitation is achieved it is clear that negotiating the important multi-layered jurisdictional zones known to the law of the sea are not events that can be meaningfully rushed. The LOSC 1982 recognised 12 nautical miles (nm) for the territorial sea, 24nm for the contiguous zone, 200nm for the EEZ, and a 350nm maximum for the extended continental shelf. Delineating these zones in the special circumstances and under the influence of opposing coasts, competing islands, rocks, reefs etc. have been known to last for decades between some countries. There is no doubt that this will also be the case in the African maritime setting.

Indeed the question that suggests itself is why the policy took so long in coming. The continent has had more than its fair share of international disputes and boundary-related problems, such that the policy was near universally welcomed.[34] It goes without saying that the AU Border Programme if it is to succeed at all must complement the exercise of sovereignty among African states through mutual respect for national governments.

It is necessary to note that in the African experience, the end of judicial and arbitral proceedings in relation to boundary conflicts does not necessarily indicate the end of the danger to the affected population. For instance, the Ethiopia–Eritrea Border situation remains volatile and dangerous to the population therein, despite the award of the Eritrea–Ethiopia Boundary Commission (EEBC) on 13 April 2002.[35] Severe disagreements and occasional conflict still attend the Cameroon–Nigeria land boundary, the October 2002 ICJ decision and the apparent cooperation of the parties in implementing the judgment notwithstanding.[36]

It needs, however, to be remembered that territorial, boundary and border disputes are not unique to Africa and that they are indeed global phenomena.[37] There is no shortage of condemnable practices to be found outside of Africa. The AUBP and the proposed mechanism for prevention of boundary disputes must actively seek to avoid such practices from taking root in Africa.

Southern Africa Report Archive, no. 1, p. 19. Available at http://www.africafiles.org/article.asp?ID=3915 Visited 14 December 2008.

34 Department of Public Information, News and Media Division, "Secretary-General Pledges Support for African Union Border Demarcation Efforts", in *Message to Seminar on Implementation of Regional Programme* SG/SM/11309AFR/1626, New York, available at http://www.un.org/News/Press/docs/2007/sgsm11309.doc.htm, visited 8 December 2008; Federal Foreign Office, "Speech by Dr Frank-Walter Steinmeier, Federal Minister for Foreign Affairs, at the luncheon for African Heads of Delegation" (New York, 23 September 2008), available at http://www.auswaertiges-amt.de/diplo/en/Infoservice/Presse/Rede/2008/080924-BM-UN-DelegationsleiterAfrika.html, visited 12 December 2008.

35 VOA News, "UN: Ethiopia-Eritrea Border Remains Potentially Volatile", 29 December 2005 available at http://www.voanews.com/english/2005-12-29-voa43.cfm, accessed 14 January 2006.

36 *Land and Maritime Boundary between Cameroon and Nigeria (Cameroon v Nigeria: Equatorial Guinea intervening)*. Cases and materials relating to the ICJ are available at www.icj-cij.org.

37 Severe problems are currently been faced by many of the states that were in the former USSR, as a result of the dissolution of Yugoslavia, in Northern Ireland and in the Basque area of the Franco–Spanish Border.

Such identifiable 'bad practices' along boundary communities include the creation of impenetrable barriers,[38] the use of armed village militias,[39] inordinate creation of visa regimes,[40] and intermittent exchange of gunfire at frontier positions.[41] Other unsupportable antecedents which have been employed with debilitating effect include policies which serve to freeze the natural development and spread of people in a region. Negative strategies that have been employed include restrictive use of building permits, selective house demolitions, arrests, fines and daily harassment – all designed to confine the population in small enclaves.[42]

It is hoped that in place of the negative strategies the AU Border Programme would actively promote and where possible help arrange international funds for bilateral and multilateral projects designed to bridge the border regions into regenerative zones of economic and cultural revival. Examples include the joint

38 On 9 January 1999 the state government of West Bengal (India) set the target of fencing 900km of the border with Bangladesh. 500km out of the total of 1600 km had been fenced with barbed wire, with central government funding. The West Bengal state government also favoured the creation of a 150-mile 'no man's land', affecting 450 villages in the border area, in its attempts to stem the influx of migrants from Bangladesh. India is currently building a fence along its 4,000-km (2,500 miles) border with Bangladesh. See 'Border tense over push-in, fence erection bids by BSF', *New Age Dhaka*, 6 March 2005 available at http://www.newagebd.com/2005/mar/06/front.html, visited 30 December 2005; M. Rama Rao, 'India's interior ministry favours fencing more stretches of border with Bangladesh', *Asian Tribune*, New Delhi, available at http://www.asiantribune.com/show_news.php?id=11656, visited 30 December 2005. The Russian border with Estonia was also fortified with watchtowers and barbed wire presenting problems among people who were accustomed to moving freely across the border, 'Estonian-Russian Border Troubles', *The Baltic Observer*, 13 March 1994, p. 5. It may be noted that despite a long history of enthusiastic self-preservation strategies and irredentism, at least within the last century, the idea of boundary fences and walls between states have not retained any appreciable acceptability in law and public perception.
39 Consider the reports of Turkish Militia actions against Kurdish populations along the Iraq–Turkey border, Owen Bowcott, 'Buffer Zone Proposal', *The Guardian* (London), 11 February 1997, p. 11.
40 Witness the introduction of a visa regime between Russia's Baltic enclave of Kaliningrad and its neighbouring states with which it had coexisted in peace prior to their joining the European Union. *Peoples Daily Online*, 'Russia Criticizes Visa Regime between Kaliningrad, Neighbouring States', 11 June 2002 http://english.people.com.cn/200206/11/eng20020611_97585.shtml, visited 30 December 2005. Similarly a visa regime was introduced for persons travelling between Russia and Poland on 1 October 2003 consequent upon Poland's upcoming entry into the EU. Prior to this time the rural populace in both Russia and Poland conducted large-scale formal and informal trade across their common boundaries freely. The resultant situation is long and debilitating queues and the hampering of trade between the neighbours. See further RIAN, 'Russia, Poland introduce visa regime', Pravda, 1 October 2003, available at http://newsfromrussia.com/world/2003/10/01/50268.html.
41 Exchange of fire between Indian and Bangladeshi border guards at a frontier outpost has for long been a feature of the tense border relations between the two countries since the partition of the subcontinent into India and Pakistan in 1947. The ownership of several villages on both sides of the border are disputed and claimed by both countries. *BBC News*, 'India-Bangladesh border battle', 18 April, 2001, available at http://news.bbc.co.uk/2/hi/south_asia/1283068.stm, visited 1 January 2006. Note also long-standing Isreali–Lebanon problems. See *BBC News*, 'Fighting erupts on Lebanon border', 26 November 2000, available at http://news.bbc.co.uk/2/hi/middle_east/1041319.stm, visited 1 January 2006.
42 Such an unfortunate regime has been described as the matrix of control in relation to Palestinian villages bordering Israel (i.e. within the context of Isreali dominance). See Jeff Halper, 'The Key To Peace: Dismantling The Matrix of Control', 28 June 2002, available at http://www.jerusalemites.org/facts_documents/peace/28.htm; see also "Habitat International Coalition, Housing and Land Rights", Committee Statement before the Committee on Economic, Social and Cultural Rights, 24th Session, Geneva, 13 November 2000, Follow-up Procedure (Israel), available at http://www.cesr.org/programs/palestine/hicgeneva.pdf.

development of resorts, parks, and 'international villages' along part(s) of the common boundary of states. Other viable options include the unitisation of the straddling oil fields (discussed below), joint eco-tourism, territorial trade-off, and land for oil trade-off, among others.[43]

5.2.2 Implementation of the African Union Border Programme

The implementation of the AUBP was designed to be effected at several levels – national, regional and continental. It is also notable that the responsibility of each of these levels should be determined on the basis of the principle of subsidiarity and respect for the sovereignty of states. In this regard, the Declaration specifies the respective roles to be played by member states, the Regional Economic Communities and the AU with respect to the various components of the AUBP, namely border delimitation and demarcation, local cross-border cooperation and capacity building. With respect to resource mobilisation and partnership, the Ministers requested the AU Commission to coordinate and implement the AUBP on the basis of an inclusive governance involving the member states, RECs, locally elected representatives, parliamentarians and civil society, as well as organisations regulating European border movement, particularly the Association of European Border Regions (AEBR),[44] the United Nations and other AU partners having experience in cross-border cooperation.[45]

---

43 See representation of the transfrontier conservation area (TFCA) Transfrontier park in Appendix III. See also *infra* note 1012. One such laudatory example which may be adopted with respect to one or more of the straddling communities is the International Peace Garden created to commemorate over 150 years of peace between the United States and Canada. This feature straddles the world's longest unguarded international boundary and is situated in the scenic Turtle Mountains between North Dakota and Manitoba, halfway between the Atlantic and Pacific coasts. Situated at the mouth of this feature are the flags of both nations, and on a boundary marker is inscribed, 'To God in his glory, we two nations dedicate this garden and pledge ourselves that as long as man shall live, we will not take up arms against one another'. The most prominent structure, the Peace Tower, with its four pillars, stands over 100 feet tall astride the exact geographical coordinates separating the international boundary. Inspiration for the idea came through the private efforts of a certain academic (Dr Henry Moore of Islington, Ontario) and culminated in the gathering of 50,000 people on 14 July 1932 to dedicate the territory to peace. Spreading over 2,339 acres, the territory displays a spectacular mosaic of flowers, trees, fountains, and paths. Visitors can stroll through the formal gardens, camp under aspen and oaks, or even get married in the Peace Chapel. Concerts, arts festivals, and renowned youth summer camps for music and athletics are also held in there. Over 250,000 people visit the Garden during the summer months alone to help renew the pledge of friendship between Canada and the US. See Sheldon Green, 'A Garden for Peace', Vol. 21, *North Dakota Horizons*, No. 3 (1991); See also Sonja Rossum, 'International Peace Garden Centre for Great Plains Studies, University of Nebraska, Lincoln', available at http://www.unl.edu/plains/publications/egpentries.html#peace, accessed 14 January 2011.
44 The Association of European Border Regions (AEBR) was founded in 1971. It acts for the benefit of all European borders and cross-border regions. The aims of the AEBR include making their particular problems, opportunities, tasks and projects intelligible; representing their overall interests to national and international parliaments, organs, authorities and institutions; initiating, support and co-ordinate their cooperation throughout Europe (creation of a network); exchanging know-how and information in order to formulate and co-ordinate common interests on the basis of the various cross-border problems and opportunities, and offering adequate solutions. Visit http://www.aebr.net/, accessed 21 June 2014
45 African Union, "Report of the Commission on the Implementation of the African Union Border Programme", Executive Council 14th Ordinary Session, 29–30 January 2009, Addis Ababa, Ethiopia EX. CL/459 (XIV), p. 1.

In order to launch the AUBP in accordance with the decisions as adopted by the Conference of African Ministers in charge of Border Issues held on 7 June 2007, a number of initial measures to be taken by the Commission were identified. These include: launching of a Pan-African survey of borders, through a questionnaire to be sent to all member states, in order to facilitate the delimitation and demarcation of African borders (see Appendix I Questionnaire/Boundary Survey for African Union Border Programme); identification of pilot regions or initiatives for the rapid development of regional support programmes on cross-border cooperation, as well as support for the establishment of regional funds for local cross-border cooperation; working out modalities for cooperation with other regions of the world to benefit from their experiences and to build the necessary partnerships; initiating an assessment with regard to capacity-building; preparation of a continental legal instrument on cross-border cooperation; and the launching of a partnership and resource mobilisation process for the implementation of the AUBP. These measures and strategies appear to be in line with good practice. However, whether they are effective and sufficient to achieve the purposes of this elaborate project remain to be seen considering the time-frame remaining for performance.

It has been mentioned that a number of years were initially lost after the announcement of the AUBP. Inaction in the next few years after the Assembly of Heads of State and Government announcement of January 2002 has been as disruptive of the process as it has perhaps been surprising given the tight schedule of the initial completion date and the apparent enormity of the tasks. It is hardly possible to overestimate the negative effect of these lost years on the possibility of a comprehensive and qualitative attainment of the tasks set before the AUBP, certainly within the regulation time. The most obvious reason for the delay appears to be the difficulties of raising enough monetary support for the programme. It may be fair to say that preliminary activities only started in 2007 when the AU Commission, with the financial support of the German Technical Cooperation (GTZ),[46] organised a workshop in Djibouti (on 1 and 2 December 2007), to assist it in elaborating a three-year plan of action for the implementation of the AUBP. Representatives of RECs and other African integration organisations, African river basin institutions, the African Development Bank (AfDB),[47] the UN Secretariat and other UN institutions, the European Union (EU), the Organisation of American States (OAS) and a number of specialised institutions and experts brainstormed the programme.[48] It is not insignificant that the period after this

---

46 The *Deutsche Gesellschaft für Technische Zusammenarbeit* (GTZ) GmbH is an international cooperation enterprise for sustainable development with worldwide operations. It supports the German government in achieving its development-policy objectives and provides viable, forward-looking solutions for political, economic, ecological and social development in a globalised world. GTZ has operations in more than 130 countries in Africa, Asia, Latin America, the Mediterranean and Middle Eastern regions, as well as in Europe, Caucasus and Central Asia. It maintains its own offices in 87 countries. The enterprise employs nearly 13,000 staff, almost 10,000 of whom are national personnel. Materials and information about the GTZ are available at http://www.gtz.de/en.
47 Visit http://www.afdb.org.
48 The workshop made it possible for the Commission to elaborate an implementation matrix, which covers a number of areas: capacity-building; popularisation; delimitation and demarcation,

successful workshop represents the beginning of real implementation as the vigorous discussions helped to develop strategies based on a synergy among the African and foreign experts and technocrats. Experience shared with those outside the continent focused the attention of decision makers within the AU and African governments to the financial and logistic requirements of their aspirations.

In pursuance of the Accra Decision[49] and based on this highly complex implementation matrix, the AU Commission has undertaken the following activities: a) Pan-African Survey of Borders involving principally the formulation of a highly detailed questionnaire that was sent to all member states, in order to facilitate the delimitation and demarcation of African borders.[50] On 15 April 2008 the erstwhile Chairperson of the AUBP, Alpha Oumar Konaré, wrote to all Ministers of Foreign Affairs/External Relations of member states, to forward the questionnaire to the appropriate ministries and/or departments in their respective national territories, highlighting its importance in the overall implementation of the AUBP. The questionnaire covers issues relating to the status of member states' continental and maritime boundaries, as well as the contact details of the institutions responsible for border issues (see Appendix I). By the end of 2009 only ten member states had responded to the questionnaire. The respondent states are: Algeria, Burkina Faso, Cameroon, Mali, Mauritius, Mozambique, Namibia, Niger, Sudan and Tunisia. It is recognisable that the rate of response to the questionnaire is slow and that this contributed to the expiration of the tight deadlines imposed by the AU on the AUBP without much being achieved. Only one out of 5 countries have filled their questionnaire (See Appendix II map of responses to the AUBP Questionnaires/Surveys as at 2012). Reasons for the slow responses that may be suggested include difficulties in pinpointing which precise governmental agencies/department is in a position to fill in responses; unavailability of required data; political interference; loss of data as a result of civil or other wars and conflicts such as in the Sierra Leonean experience and perhaps sheer disinterest.[51] Although there are not really many of such instances there are also factors such as the peculiar situation of Mauritania which would like to settle its northern lateral maritime boundary in the light of massive offshore oil resources but face the serious problem of the uncertain

---

including the survey of African borders; the mobilisation of resources and exchange of experiences; cross-border cooperation, including the elaboration of the required legal frameworks and the establishment of regional funds; partnership and resource mobilisation. African Union, "Report of the Commission on the Implementation of the African Union Border Programme", Executive Council, 14th Ordinary Session, p. 3.

49 At its 11th Ordinary Session held in Accra, Ghana, from 25–29 June 2007, the Executive Council endorsed the Declaration on the African Union Border Programme (AUBP) and its Implementation Modalities, as adopted by the Conference of African Ministers in charge of Border Issues, held in Addis Ababa on 7 June 2007.

50 See Appendix I: AU Boundary Questionnaire – Boundary Survey for the African Union Border Programme.

51 The delegate of Sierra Leone pointed out at the Regional Workshop on African Union Border Programme (Windhoek, 22–23 October 2009) held in Namibia that his country lost a lot of its geographic data during the civil war and that they are still in the process of shoring up that database by recourse to the AU records.

status of Western Sahara whose statehood has yet to be recognised internationally and especially by Morocco.[52]

The second aspect of the progression of the AUBP is the establishment of a Boundary Information System (BIS) that aims to analyse and facilitate the utilisation of the information received in response to the questionnaire. On 15 July 2008, the Commission organised, in Addis Ababa, a technical meeting on the establishment of the BIS which brought together experts from the RECs, the UN, GTZ and relevant African and international institutions. The core functions of the BIS are to provide an overview of the status of all African borders based on the questionnaire returns. The information received so far has been used to monitor progress towards the delimitation and demarcation of national boundaries *inter se*. Other functions of the BIS include the formulation of a database of African border experts and cross-border cooperation initiatives in the continent.[53] The value of such a resource is inestimable in a continent with perhaps a predictable active future of territorial determination and redetermination. The Commission has been mobilising the required expertise, as well as acquiring the IT equipment needed to facilitate the operation of the BIS. The value of a centralised database of boundary positions and markers in the possession of the AU cannot be overestimated. In a continent that has been prone to destabilising internal and international conflicts and wars, a dependable and trustworthy custodian of important territorial records is inestimable.

The third aspect of the AU Commission's work involves the sensitisation of the governments and institutions of African states to the goals and aspirations of the AUBP. This aspect has taken the shape of: (i) regional workshops on the AUBP; ii) publication of a brochure on the AUBP;[54] and (iii) elaboration of an outreach strategy. Between 2008 and 2009 five regional workshops have been hosted; the workshops targeted the various stakeholders across the continent on the AUBP and sought to mobilise their support for its implementation. The eight African RECs were particularly targeted in order to elaborate regional action plans within the framework of the implementation of the programme. The RECs are expected under the process by the AU to have security plans to assist with the prioritisation of boundaries marking and management. The security plans are expected to be

---

52 Daniel, op.cit., p. 3429.
53 African Union, "Report of the Commission on the Implementation of the African Union Border Programme" op. cit., p. 5. The Geographical Information System (GIS)-section has been coordinating the demand and receipt of the questionnaires and surveys sent to member states by the African Union Commission. The BIS was set up for the storage, presentation and retrieval of various pertinent datasets and information relating to African borders. These include: status of a given boundary; background data, maps and satellite imagery; agencies for border management; position of demarcation marks; border land infrastructures, etc.; processing boundary records, e.g. coordinate transformations and analysis; datasets of cross-border cooperation and the recording of border activities.
54 In mid-August 2008, the Commission, with the assistance of UNHCR, published in a booklet format the Declaration on the AUBP and its Implementation Modalities. This booklet was circulated to all diplomatic missions in Addis Ababa, as well as to a number of institutions on the Continent and outside Africa. It has also been posted on the AU website.

presented before the council of ministers in the near future and to receive approval. After such ratification each of them are expected to sign the plan and the process will be accelerated. The problem with this is the principle of subsidiarity operating within the AU which devolves responsibilities to states and therefore, the bulk of the work can only take place in a meaningful way bilaterally.[55] The goal of the outreach programme is to create awareness and support for the AUBP among member states and other actors, including civil society organisations and border communities. The strategy, thus, aims to build a sustainable dialogue with key stakeholders by highlighting the potential benefits of the programme as a platform to transform African borders from barriers to bridges. The elaborate plans for information dissemination, some of which are clearly unique in the history of territorial demarcation law and practice are perhaps summed up in the following statement:

> In the coming months, the Commission will embark on the implementation of the pan-African aspects of the strategy. Among other activities, it is planned to feature articles and place adverts in in-flight magazines of major African airlines, especially given their role in connecting the African countries and allowing exchanges between nations; carry out specific activities with pan-African TV broadcasters; and work with existing African film festivals to introduce awards for film-making competitions on border issues.[56]

One of the ways the AUBP has been presented to stakeholders is that it contains measures to facilitate cross-border cooperation of local initiatives. The basic framework for a database on legislation relating to border cooperation and the outlines of a continental legal framework for the engagement of cross-sector initiatives involving both the public and private sector is gradually emerging for the first time in African history. The AU Commission has also taken steps aimed at facilitating the communication by the former colonial powers of all information in their possession concerning the delimitation and demarcation of African boundaries, in line with paragraph 5 (a(iii)) of the Declaration on the AUBP and

---

55 The first regional workshop took place in Kampala, from 24–25 September 2008, under the joint auspices of the AU and the EAC. The workshop was attended by the following members of the Eastern Africa region: Comoros, Djibouti, Ethiopia, Kenya, Mauritius, Seychelles, Somalia, Sudan, Tanzania and Uganda. Other participants included CENSAD, COMESA, ECCAS, ECOWAS and IGAD, the United Nations, GTZ and other partner organisations. The second regional workshop took place in Algiers, for the Northern African Region, from 16–17 October 2008. Algeria, Egypt, Libya, SADR and Tunisia participated in the workshop. Other participants included representatives of CENSAD, COMESA, EAC, ECCAS and ECOWAS, as well as the UN, GTZ and other institutions. The three other regional workshops were held in 2009. The workshop for Central Africa took place in Libreville from 19–20 February 2009; that for Southern Africa in October 2009 and for West Africa, in Ouagadougou in April 2009. African Union, "Report Of The Commission on the Implementation of the African Union Border Programme", Executive Council 14th Ordinary Session 29–30 January 2009, Addis Ababa, Ethiopia EX. CL/459 (XIV), pp. 5–6.
56 African Union, "Report of the Commission on the Implementation of the African Union Border Programme", Executive Council, 14th Ordinary Session, 29–30 January 2009, op. cit., p. 7.

its Implementation Modalities. Certain preliminary conclusions may be reached on these developments. Whether or not the AUBP succeeds in its objectives within the specified time even with the luxury of revised dates is certain to be a subjective assessment but the continent cannot but benefit tremendously from the strategic and systematic exercises conducted under the AUBP. The law, diplomacy and politics of the AUBP and its current direction is an indication of the political maturity and coming of age of African states. This process and its modest achievements deserve closer study and attention than is currently accorded to it by lawyers, social scientists and other scholars – even on the African continent itself.

Although we will be discussing the general problem of cost of delimitation and demarcation activities below, and particularly the prohibitive nature of costs to developing states, we will need to highlight the way that legal aid has taken pride of place in the ongoing AUBP processes. It is only appropriate that the very states that are blamed for the balkanisation of the African continent and its carving up into sometimes inconvenient and/or indefensible political units are those states that have contributed most to the UN Fund and also financially aided the AUBP process. It is particularly gratifying that the Federal Republic of Germany, host nation of the historical Berlin Conference which carved Africa into colonial fiefdoms, is at the vanguard of the financial rescue of the AUBP.[57] The German aid which was structured through the GTZ is designed to provide financial and technical support for the development of the BIS; human resource capacity of the Commission; development of a handbook covering methodology and best practices in the area of delimitation and demarcation;[58] convening of meetings and workshops relating to the AUBP; and financial as well as technical support to relevant African institutions and individual AU member states for the implementation of the AUBP.

In 2008, the German government, through the GTZ, allocated about €3.35 million to support AUBP related activities; of this amount, €800,000 was directly allocated to the AU. These resources were used to support the convening of activities such as the preparatory meeting with the RECs held in Addis Ababa on 13 and 14 July 2008; the technical meeting on the BIS held in Addis Ababa on 15 July 2008; the two regional workshops held in Kampala and Algiers; and the 2nd International Symposium on Land, River and Lake Boundaries Management, held in Maputo from 17–19 December 2008.[59] GTZ has also provided equipment and financial support for the payment of salaries of staff working on the implementation of the AUBP. Additional funds were allocated in 2009 with some

---

57 On 13 February 2008, the German Minister for Foreign Affairs, Dr Frank-Walter Steinmeier, extended the German state's offer of technical and financial support towards the AUBP. In his letter to the AU, the minister stressed the importance of the delimitation and demarcation of African borders, as well as the promotion of cross-border cooperation, for the overall efforts aimed at preventing conflicts and ensuring the economic development of the continent. African Union, "Report of the Commission on the Implementation of the African Union Border Programme", op.cit., pp. 8–9.
58 This publication has already being completed and is well received; see supra note 5.
59 See the AU, "Conclusion of the 2nd International Symposium on Land, River and Lake Boundaries Management", Maputo, Mozambique, 17–19 December 2008, AUBP/EXP/3(VI).

part of the budget having been provided as direct support to individual AU member states. These include monies for the demarcation of parts of the Mali/Burkina Faso boundary, as well as activities relating to the delimitation and demarcation of Mozambican borders with some of its neighbours. Financial aid has also been offered and received from Italy, another state with a controversial and irredentist past in relation to Africa with the dubious record of having invaded a fellow League of Nation member. As part of the implementation of the Italian–African Peace Facility (IAPF), the Italian government committed itself to funding some components of the AUBP in the amount of around US$1.8 million.[60] Aside from individual state donations from some of the erstwhile colonial powers, the EU has allocated a total amount of around €8 billion for cross-border cooperation. It is particularly comforting to note that support has also been promised in principle by the International Monetary Fund and the World Bank for border area initiatives in furtherance of the aims of the AUBP. In addition to all these the UN itself has committed extra budgetary resources to the process.[61]

There is much scope for further assistance from all friendly states and regions of the world in relation to completion of the important tasks of the AUBP. It is not money that is required in all cases, but there is certainly much need for targeted or purpose-built technical aid. For instance, those African states that have as a result of many years of civil and/or international crises faced particular challenges in boundary demarcation due to the presence of landmines in border areas need urgent assistance and aid from the international community. Scientific and other targeted assistance are required to clear mined areas in order to facilitate demarcation exercises and other cross-border activities. It is commendable that as a result of the AUBP programme the AU received in 2013 the true and complete copies of 45 Agreements relating to African borders. These consist of maps and plans, signed by France between 1845 and 1956. Germany has also transmitted some relevant data in its possession, while other colonial powers such as Belgium, Portugal and the UK have confirmed their willingness to participate in the voluntary transfers of archives in the near future.[62] A very simple but important form of aid that will be very useful to smaller African states that are presently charged with the task of demarcation of their boundaries under the AUBP may take the simple form of assistance in the acquisition of documents relevant to

---

60 An exchange of letters to this effect took place (on 30 June 2008) on the margins of the sessions of the Executive Council and the Assembly of the Union in Sharm El Sheikh, Egypt, in June 2008.
61 Letter by UN Secretary General Ban Ki Moon to the President of the Security Council Mr Neven Jurica in 2008 in UN Secretary General's Memoranda to the Security Council. See A.I. Asiwaju, "Getting Bordered to be De-Bordered: The African Union Border Programme in Global Focus", paper presented at the 2nd International Symposium on Land, Maritime River and Lake Boundaries: Maputo, Mozambique, 17–19 December 2008, p. 4.
62 AU, "Conclusion of the 2nd International Symposium on Land, River and Lake Boundaries Management", op.cit., see paragraph VII, pp. 3–4. See also Ackel Zwane, "Border restoration: more work ahead of 2017 Deadline", *Swazi Observer*, 2 August 2014, available at http://www.observer.org.sz/news/64579-border-restoration-more-work-ahead-of-2017-deadline.html, accessed 23 November 2014.

boundary delimitation and demarcation exercise from colonial archives. For smaller African states and their scholars and researchers the provision of accommodation and/or free access to archives including copying or borrowing facilities will go a long way to granting access to much needed information without which sourcing the necessary documents that are needed for dispute resolution and demarcation exercises will be difficult or even impossible.

6 African regional economic communities and the management of boundary disputes

The occurrence of territorial and boundary conflict is one of the problematic features of African international relations. The problem arises out of a triple inheritance in historical and socio-economic terms. First, it arises out of precolonial ethnic and national competition over African territories mostly between neighbouring nations and states. Second, the insensitive and mostly incompetent delimitation efforts by the various colonial powers has made it inevitable that attempts will be made to address perceived past injustices, thus creating fresh and recurring conflict over land and boundaries. Third, the widespread (but by no means uniform) failure of bureaucratic and political leadership across the continent since the independence era has led to careless, lackadaisical and incompetent approaches to the important tasks of diligent maintenance of boundary records as well as continuous boundary management. Furthermore, foreign intervention and diversionary politics fomented especially by the military and dictatorial elites in many countries has produced much ill-advised conflict over land. In this regard it becomes clear that the number of flashpoints is not only alarming but that it is indeed a miracle that there is not a more widespread breakdown of relations and war between African states. On the whole, boundary conflicts will occur in all human interactions in a geopolitical setting. As a result preparation for the resolution of boundary and territorial conflicts should be one of the key specialisms of any regional political institutional collaboration.

Certain successful political and legal mechanisms already exist among African states and in the various RECs that have been used to prevent many problematic situations from becoming aggravated or consummated into larger disputes. These systems, mechanisms and political cultures are deserving of further study and recognition if there is to be any meaningful strategy to the development of mechanisms to prevent and/or manage boundary disputes in Africa.

Unfortunately, however, there are varying levels of competence in the different RECs. Furthermore the kinds of boundary problems prevalent in the various RECs vary due to their differing socio-economic and legal conditions and the pertinent colonial histories at play. Apart from the many disputes that arose out of dissatisfaction with colonial delimitation and demarcation efforts, conflicts over ownership and control over natural resources appear to be the leading cause of boundary disputes across the various RECs in at least the last two decades. In many of these instances it is not even the major energy products such as hydrocarbons or precious metals that are at play but local resources that are crucial to the socio-economic survival of boundary communities.

6.1 Conflict resolution and management in the East African sub-region (IGAD area)[1]

The Intergovernmental Authority on Development (IGAD) in Eastern Africa was created in 1996 to supersede the Intergovernmental Authority on Drought and Development (IGADD) which was founded earlier in 1986.[2] In 1983 and 1984, six countries in the Horn of Africa – Djibouti, Ethiopia, Kenya, Somalia, Sudan and Uganda – took action through the United Nations to establish an intergovernmental body for development and drought control in their region.[3] Although IGADD was originally conceived to coordinate the efforts of member states to combat drought and desertification, it became increasingly apparent that the authority provided a regular forum where leaders of the Eastern African countries were able to tackle other political and socio-economic issues in a regional context. Realising this, the Heads of State and Government of Djibouti, Eritrea, Ethiopia, Kenya, Sudan and Uganda, at an extra-ordinary summit on 18 April 1995, resolved to expand the mandate of IGADD and made a declaration to revitalise IGADD and expand co-operation among member states. The revitalised IGADD was renamed the Intergovernmental Authority on Development (IGAD).

IGAD consists of the following institutional organs: Assembly of Heads of State and Government; Council of Ministers; Committee; Secretariat, headed by an Executive Secretary; and Executive Secretary, assisted by 4 Directors heading Divisions of Economic Cooperation & Social Development; Agriculture and Environment; Peace and Security; and Administration and Finance plus 22 regional professional staff and various short-term project and technical assistance staff.

6.1.1 Role of CEWARN in detecting and managing cross-boundary disputes

The seven IGAD member states (Djibouti, Eritrea, Ethiopia, Kenya, Somalia, Sudan and Uganda) created the Conflict Early Warning and Response Mechanism

---

1 Interviews were conducted among others with Tigist Haliu, CEWARN public relations and communications officer and head of CEWARN, Ms Catherine Gitahi.
2 The recurring and severe droughts and other natural disasters between 1974 and 1984 caused widespread famine, ecological degradation and economic hardship in the Eastern Africa region. Although individual countries made substantial efforts to cope with the situation and received generous support from the international community, the magnitude and extent of the problem argued strongly for a regional approach to supplement national efforts.
3 The Assembly of Heads of State and Government met in Djibouti in January 1986 to sign the Agreement which officially launched IGADD with Headquarters in Djibouti. The State of Eritrea became the seventh member after attaining independence in 1993.

(CEWARN) as a collaborative effort targeted at mitigating and preventing violent conflicts in the sub-region. Since its establishment in 2002, CEWARN has had a particular focus on cross-border pastoralist and related conflicts. Its mandate is to 'receive and share information concerning potentially violent conflicts as well as their outbreak and escalation in the IGAD region, undertake analysis of the information and develop case scenarios and formulate options for response.'[4] The CEWARN field monitors picked up the hostilities between groups within Kenya and Uganda quite early and made appropriate reports, helping to douse the flames of an open dispute. CEWARN is divided into zonal offices in each member state. The CEWARN system also depends on Civil Societies Organisations (CSOs) which collect information using field monitors. Information collected in this way is analysed at the national level and then synthesised into a regional response. It is particularly important to note the existence of *peace committees* at the local level in each district and at village level. This bottom-up approach is commendable and may be particularly suitable in the prevention of tensions and conflicts along boundary lines and in border communities. IGAD's CEWARN has received impressive feedback and its successes include the fact that the participating governments continue to give the organisation unimpeded operational access at local level in each other's territories. Commendations have also emerged from various high level meetings held by IGAD particularly after the activity reports submitted by CEWARN to that organisation.

6.1.2 IGAD's relevance in border and boundary disputes

Boundary and border disputes and tensions in the IGAD area have traditionally been picked up at the local level and through individuals known as *field monitors*. It has been suggested during interviews that IGAD is mostly faced with human security issues. Thus, in theory boundary tensions could be addressed through the various local structures such as the *peace committees* and use of elders. If it became more serious it would be taken up by the Conflict Early Warning and Response Unit (CEWARU). CEWARU, in the first instance, can attempt to manage the conflict. It is, however, unlikely that actual delimitation and demarcation can be handled at any stage without involving bilateral commissions and/or reference to the sub-regional body itself.

The prognosis for boundary disputes in the IGAD area is quite high. In May 2011 communities between Ethiopia and Kenya attacked each other leading to

---

4 CEWARN, "About CEWARN" available at http://www.cewarn.org/index.php?option=com_content&view=article&id=51&Itemid=53 accessed 12 March 2012. Through its national network of governmental and non-governmental stakeholders – Conflict Early Warning and Response Units (CEWERUs); National Research Institutes (NRIs) and Field Monitors (FMs), CEWARN undertakes its conflict early warning and response function in three clusters or pilot areas. These are the Karamoja Cluster (covering the cross-border areas of Ethiopia, Kenya, Sudan and Uganda); the Somali Cluster (covering the cross-border areas of Ethiopia, Kenya and Somalia) as well as the Dikhil Cluster (covering the cross-border areas of Djibouti and Ethiopia).

about 24 fatalities. There are problems in relation to the Mindingo Islands in Lake Victoria between Kenya and Uganda.[5] The Prime Minister of Kenya tried to visit the territory but was prevented from doing so. This has led to the building of new posts on the Islands. Kenya and Ethiopia eventually settled the matter later through diplomatic responses. CEWARN field monitors picked the incident up quite early in 2009 and made appropriate reports. Later analysis showed that it arose from misunderstandings over grazing rights. Indeed by the time governments waded in (according to CEWARN officials), the local peace committees had swung into action to prevent further deterioration of the situation.

A notable failure of the IGAD so far might be seen in the inability to achieve a conclusive solution to the dispute between Ethiopia and Eritrea. However, it is also notable that IGAD has demonstrated strong political resolve in prevention of cross-border conflicts within the region, and it was as a result of the organisation's persistent efforts that the Eritrean state had to suspend her IGAD membership in 2007. Eritrea had been accused by the regional bloc of siding with forces hostile to her neighbour Ethiopia.[6]

Because of its focus on pastoralist issues, IGAD is particularly useful in detection and understanding of border and cross-border conflicts whether they arise out of shared amenities or resources or struggles over natural resources around the border areas between IGAD states. The CEWARN mechanism has been able to develop a primary source of early warning capacity and is in the process of enhancing its link with the early response. The CEWARN's five year strategy (2007–11) articulated how the mechanism intends to link this capacity with an appropriate 'response component' in order to proactively and pre-emptively tackle the scourge of pastoral and related conflicts in the region. CEWARN has also developed the concept of the Rapid Response Fund (RRF) to help finance short-term projects which aim to prevent, de-escalate or resolve pastoral and related conflicts in the region.

Our research into the work of IGAD shows that most disputes involving grassroots indigenous communities relate to shared resources, particularly farmlands and grazing grounds. Particular expertise has been developed in these areas by IGAD in its attempts to defuse the tensions and immediately address boundary problems. A particularly impressive practice discovered in the work of IGAD is its institutionalisation of the mechanism of the 'councils of elders' who mediate the disputes that arise out of the interaction of boundary communities. The council of elders endeavours to ascertain as quickly as possible the facts of the developing situation or actual crisis. On the basis of their findings and reports, or evidence supplied to them, they offer solutions and recommendations to bring

---

5 See also Emmanuel Kisiangani, "Dispute over Migingo Escalates", News on ISS Africa, available at http://www.iss.co.za/iss_today.php?ID=1336 accessed, 12 March 2012.
6 Argaw Ashine, "Eritrea applies to rejoin IGAD bloc", *African Review* (April 2012), http://www.africareview.com/News/Eritrea+ready+to+rejoin+Igad+bloc/-/979180/1210070/-/107ota6z/-/index.html, accessed 10 May 2012.

a situation under control or resolve a conflict and have been successful in doing so on many occasions.

It is particularly commendable that African RECs have continued to take this rational and traditional approach to the delivery of localised international justice. In many instances the dispute will involve conflicts over grazing rights and the exercise of or continuance of the right of pasturage. Pasturage in many African countries pays little respect to the existence of artificial international boundaries. The jurisprudence of the council of elders has overwhelmingly supported cross-boundary grazing rights. Concern for the rights of opposing groups to use the territory for farming or other legitimate purposes are also factored into the solution. Strict adherence to 'lines in the sand' for academic or official purposes are often waived in favour of artisanal and traditional rights many of which pre-date modern delimitation of national territories in that area of Africa. Political solutions imposed from the capitals of the states concerned, or even more so by an international court or tribunal, will often be ignored. The utilisation of local justice even in this sort of factual international situation has proven to be very wise indeed. It is noteworthy that international judicial practice conforms to this pragmatic and humane approach to the sharing of cross-boundary amenities. Although it must be said that cross-boundary grazing rights should perhaps ideally be further reduced into treaty provisions, the principle that such rights do not necessarily have to die with the incorporation of new boundaries into law is at least being upheld in practice.[7] Hence the rights of nomadic Lapps to graze reindeer across borders were confirmed in an Arbitration Award between Norway and Sweden.[8] The important thing is to recognise the need for boundary justice to embrace legal pluralism and develop the judicial instinct of indigenous African communities in managing cross-boundary justice. In other words, the job of delivering justice in Africa's border areas must extend to real-life application in the many areas of border community life. Other international examples in relation to disputes over natural resources worthy of closer scrutiny include national schemes such as the Mongolian Tripartite Committee on Mining and Natural Resource Dispute Resolution[9] and Regional schemes such as the European Consumer

---

7 See the historical Sámi Codicil (*Lappekodicillen*) 1751 which is the supplement to the Frontier Treaty between Denmark–Norway and Sweden which provides in Art. 10, 'As the Lapps might need the land of both states, they shall, according to old practice, each autumn and spring be allowed to move with their flocks of reindeer across the frontier into the other state'. The Codicil confirms, moreover, that 'the Sámi as hitherto are entitled to use land and shore for the subsistence of their animals and themselves, even in times of war'.
8 See Arbitration Award of 16 December 1909 between Norway and Sweden: De Martens NRG 3 ser., Vol. 4, p. 736; Boggs, op.cit., p. 97; Tom G. Svensson, "Interlegality, A Process for Strengthening Indigenous Peoples' Autonomy: The Case Of The Sámi in Norway", Vol. 21, *Journal Of Legal Pluralism* (2005), pp. 54–5, available at http://www.jlp.bham.ac.uk/volumes/51/svensson-art.pdf, accessed 26 August 2014.
9 The organisation is based at Ulaan Bataar in Mongolia. It entertains disputes relating to mining and natural resource complaints and grievances from local to national levels. It is open to all Mongolian citizens. See http://baseswiki.org/en/Mongolian_Tripartite_Committee_on_Mining_and_Natural_Resource_Dispute_Resolution, accessed 12 March 2012. Mongolia is

Centres Network,[10] European Ombudsman[11] and European Financial Dispute Resolution Network.[12]. Where natural resources are straddling boundaries, a jointly maintained dispute resolution body like these may be of immense benefit to the relevant states.

6.2 ECOWAS[13]

The Economic Community of West African States (ECOWAS) consists of 15 countries in the West African region. ECOWAS was founded in 1975. Its mission is to promote economic integration in 'all fields of economic activity, particularly industry, transport, telecommunications, energy, agriculture, natural resources, commerce, monetary and financial questions, social and cultural matters … '.

---

emerging as a potential powerhouse in its own right through the immense mineral wealth found under thousands of kilometres of grasslands, steppes and the great Gobi Desert. Traditionally a nomadic people with livelihoods largely dependent on animal husbandry, Mongolia's nascent market economy stands on the verge of a major shift to a mining-based economy. The world's largest copper deposit to date Oyu Tolgoi is currently under construction in the South Gobi. Currently there are some 5,000 active exploration and extraction licences in Mongolia. This increased focus on Mongolia's mineral wealth and the push for mine development as well as generally limited opportunities for public participation as well as lack of shared basic knowledge on mining issues present increased potential for conflicts and pose a real threat. Not addressing these issues could have a detrimental direct, indirect and cumulative impact on the Mongolian mining sector as well as stakeholders at large. In a preventative response to these issues a multi-stakeholder Mongolian National Tripartite Committee (MNTC) has been founded. Multi-stakeholders represent Mongolian civil society, industry and government; representing their respective constituents. The current MNTC will provide public outreach and education, a space for public dialogue and engagement and implement a local to national grievance handling mechanism.

10 The Network was created by merging two previously existing networks: the European Consumer Centres ('*Euroguichets*') which provided information and assistance on cross-border issues; and the European Extra-Judicial Network ('EEJ-Net') which helped consumers resolve disputes through alternative dispute resolution schemes (ADRs) using mediators or arbitrators. See http://baseswiki.org/en/European_Consumer_Centres_Network, accessed 21 March 2012.
11 The European Ombudsman investigates complaints about maladministration in the institutions and bodies of the European Union.
12 FIN-NET is a financial dispute resolution network of national out-of-court complaint schemes in the European Economic Area countries (the European Union Member States plus Iceland, Liechtenstein and Norway) that are responsible for handling disputes between consumers and financial services providers, i.e. banks, insurance companies, investment firms and others. This network was launched by the European Commission in 2001. Within FIN-NET, the schemes cooperate to provide consumers with easy access to out-of-court complaint procedures in cross-border cases. If a consumer in one country has a dispute with a financial services provider from another country, FIN-NET members will put the consumer in touch with the relevant out-of court complaint scheme and provide the necessary information about it. Available at http://baseswiki.org/en/Financial_Dispute_Resolution_Network,_Europe, accessed 21 March 2012.
13 The interviewer spoke to Kinsa Jawara J'ai, principal programme officer of cross-border cooperation in the ECOWAS Commission in the Free Movement Directorate; Florence Iheme, Director of the Early Warning Department; Mrs Henrietta Didigu (Ag. Director, Legal Affairs); Dr Hemou Jonas Director, Political Affairs Department. Staff of the Early Warning Situation Room spoken to include Onyinye Onwuka, Claude Kondo, Valance K. Kadja, Mautene Coulibaly, Ebenezer Asiedu.

ECOWAS consists of the following institutional organs: Commission, Community Parliament, Community Court of Justice and ECOWAS Bank for Investment and Development (EBID).

Perhaps the most crucial framework for preventing and addressing conflict and disputes in the region is the ECOWAS Conflict Prevention Framework (ECPF).[14] The ECPF is intended as a comprehensive operational conflict prevention and peace-building strategy that enables the ECOWAS system and member states to draw upon human and financial resources at the regional (including civil society and the private sector) and international levels in their efforts to creatively transform conflict. It is also intended as a guide for enhancing cohesion and synergy between relevant ECOWAS departments on conflict prevention initiatives to ensure a more active and operational posture on conflict prevention and sustained post-conflict measures. Conflict prevention in this context involves: (a) operational prevention, including early warning, mediation, conciliation, preventive disarmament and preventive deployment using interactive means, such as good offices and the ECOWAS Standby Force; and (b) structural prevention, often elaborated under peace-building initiatives and comprising political, institutional (governance) and developmental reforms, capacity enhancement and advocacy on the culture of peace.

The ECPF comprises 14 components designed to strengthen human security and incorporate conflict prevention activities (operational and structural) as well as aspects of peace-building. These are:

1. early warning
2. preventive diplomacy
3. democracy and political governance
4. human rights and the rule of law
5. media
6. natural resource governance
7. cross-border initiatives
8. security governance
9. practical disarmament
10. women, peace and security
11. youth empowerment
12. ECOWAS standby force
13. humanitarian assistance
14. peace education (the culture of peace).

Whereas all these 14 components could be useful in various ways in addressing boundary disputes and situations, it appears that the most important for

---

14 Regulation MSC/REG.1/01/08 The ECOWAS Conflict Prevention Framework available at http://www.comm.ecowas.int/dept/index.php?id=p_p1_commission&lang=en accessed 14 March 2012.

boundaries are early warning; preventive diplomacy;[15] natural resource governance; cross-border initiatives; and security governance. These five concepts have a unique usefulness particularly for conflict prevention and are very useful structures upon which the ECOWAS region may rely in relation to any future commitments that may be imposed on their members under the AUBP. It is arguable that later on, once conflict has commenced and there is presumably a hardening of positions and/or actual hostilities, the components that will be of immediate importance may include: practical disarmament; ECOWAS standby force; and humanitarian assistance.

6.2.1 Conflict resolution and management in the West African sub-region: ECOWAS area[16]

From the late 1980s onwards a new phenomenon of grave incidents of internal conflicts that were not confined to the borders of individual states arose in the ECOWAS region. These conflicts had serious regional implications, both in terms of their causes and effects. Thus, it became clear that security in West Africa, like elsewhere, was indivisible. It is not surprising; therefore, that security became one of the central focuses of ECOWAS legal protocols and rules.

At the time the Liberian conflict became full-blown there was still a marked absence of any established and functional legal and institutional framework for intervention. As a result, the ECOWAS conflict resolution process at that time was based on a series of *ad hoc* mechanisms. It is acknowledged that:

> the conflict threatened the stability of the region as it led to mass exodus of refugees, influx of small arms and light weapons across the region, the infiltration of former rebels across borders leading to further instability in other member states.[17]

To resolve the problem, some member states intervened under the mandate of the 1981 Protocol Relating to Mutual Assistance on Defence, even though this

---

15 Preventive Diplomacy: Aimed at operationalising the relevant provisions of Article 58 of the Revised Treaty; Articles 3, 8–27, 31–32 of the Mechanism; and Article 36 of the Supplementary Protocol on Democracy and Good Governance; the objective of Preventive Diplomacy shall be to defuse tensions and ensure the peaceful resolution of disputes within and between Member States by means of good offices, mediation, conciliation and facilitation based on dialogue, negotiation and arbitration. Usually applied in the face of imminent crisis, preventive diplomacy shall also be applicable in the management, resolution and peace-building phases of conflict.
16 Interviews for the completion of this chapter were conducted at the Secretariat of the ECOWAS Commission at its headquarters in Abuja particularly with officers of the organisation in the departments of Political Affairs Peace and Security Trade as well as Custom and Free Movement.
17 Emmanuel Kwesi Aning, Emma Birikorang and Thomas Jaye, *Compendium of ECOWAS Peace and Security Decisions: Protocols, Declarations and Peace Agreements* (Accra: Kofi Annan International Peacekeeping Training Centre (KAIPTC) and the German Development Cooperation with support from the Training for Peace Programme, 2010) p. 8.

protocol particularly specified that such an intervention could only take place in a conflict between two member states.

6.2.2 Rules of the ECOWAS Treaty and Protocols

The ECOWAS Treaty and its protocols are quite relevant in various ways in relation to boundary matters and its rules allow the REC to intervene at all stages in the life of a boundary situation. Border conflict prevention rules in the ECOWAS Treaty include:

(a) a mandate on member states to maintain periodic and regular consultations between national border administration authorities;
(b) promotion of the establishment of local or national joint commissions to examine any problems encountered in relations between neighbouring states;
(c) encouragement of exchanges and cooperation between communities, townships and administrative regions;
(d) emphasis on the appropriateness of organising meetings between relevant ministries on various aspects of inter-state relations.

Where boundary disputes have already occurred or to avert disputes, states should in accordance with the Treaty:

(a) employ where appropriate, good offices, conciliation, meditation and other methods of peaceful settlement of disputes; or
(b) establish a regional peace and security observation system and peace-keeping forces where appropriate.

Confidence-building mechanisms that attempt to reduce the significance of borders or rebuild trust after conflict may be entrenched, for instance, in:

(a) the aims and objectives of ECOWAS as stated in Article 3(f) of the ECOWAS Treaty that the body shall promote joint ventures by private sector enterprises and other economic operators, in particular through the adoption of a regional agreement on cross border investments.
(b) Other useful innovative measures as set out in the ECPF are as follows:
  (i) 'ECOWAS shall, with the active involvement of Member States, promote the establishment of "EcoPeace" Community Radios along sensitive borders to promote community spirit, regional integration and combat cross-border crime' (Arts 61(f) and 63(d)).
  (ii) ECOWAS is to promote the establishment of model 'common border settlements' built around quick impact employment opportunities for young people.
  (iii) Cross-border initiatives are also expected to reduce tensions, fight cross-border crime and enhance communal welfare and harmony, as well as community citizenship (Arts 68 and 69).

6.2.2.1 Relevance of the Protocol relating to the mechanism for conflict prevention, management, resolution, peace-keeping and security

The Protocol Relating to the Mechanism for Conflict Prevention, Management, Resolution, Peace-Keeping and Security as explained in its preamble, concerns itself with cross-border crimes and the proliferation of small arms and all illicit trafficking that may contribute to the development of insecurity and instability or jeopardise the economic and social development of the sub-region. Similarly the mechanism created under the protocol has as an objective to strengthen cooperation in the areas of conflict prevention, early warning, peace-keeping operations, the control of cross-border crime, international terrorism and proliferation of small arms and anti-personnel mines (Art. 3). The authority created under this Protocol has powers to act on all matters concerning conflict prevention, management and resolution, peace-keeping, security, humanitarian support, peace-building, control of cross-border crime (Art. 6). Where the matter relates to boundary or border issues the heads of:

i) immigration
ii) customs
iii) drug/narcotic agencies
iv) border guards and
v) civil protection force

may be invited to assist the Defence and Security Commission (Art. 18). The problem of cross-border crimes receives particular attention in Article 46 and it is one of the preventive measures against the illegal circulation of small arms provided for in Article 51 (which states that member states may be required to act by enhancing weapons' control at border posts).

6.2.2.2 Importance of the ECPF to boundary and cross-boundary issues and conflicts

Clearly boundary problems in the ECOWAS region were seen at the time the existing rules were made to mostly involve cross-border crime and security issues. Certainly within the context of the ECPF, issues of crimes and security have been the prisms through which boundary issues have been looked at in the ECOWAS region. As Section V Context of the ECPF Protocol explains:

> Barely a decade after the creation of ECOWAS, violent internal conflicts erupted in Liberia (1989) and Sierra Leone (1991) as a new phenomenon not confined to the borders of individual [West African] nation states, but with serious regional implications, both in their causes and effects. Later, ECOWAS was to be confronted with similar conflicts in Guinea Bissau and Côte d'Ivoire (2002). Starting off as internal struggles for power and control over resources, these devastating conflicts soon took on a regionalized character, fuelled by the proliferation of small arms and light weapons, as well as private armies of

warlords, mercenaries, dispossessed youths and bandits who fed off the illegal exploitation of natural resources. The ripples of these so-called internal conflicts were instantly felt far beyond national borders in the form of refugee flows; severe deterioration of livelihoods, health and nutrition standards; disrupted infrastructure; and the proliferation of weapons, violence and trans-national crime.

It is important that ECOWAS pays attention to borders not only because of the past but also given the regional interest to create a borderless region under the Protocol on Free Movement of Persons, the Right of Residence and Establishment.[18] It is a historical fact that straddling resources along boundary lines are a source of boundary conflicts It is for this reason that there is much credit in the provisions of this Protocol that states that:

> Member States shall undertake to establish community resource governance committees, particularly in sensitive internal enclaves and common border areas, to promote the transparent, equitable and environmentally friendly use of land, water and forest resources, and enhance inter-communal harmony.
> (Article 65 (h))

Another provision of direct relevance to boundary problems is contained in Article 69, which provides that ECOWAS set up an inter-departmental committee within the Commission to map out the challenges at sensitive borders and identify specific threats to peace, security and human wellbeing in different cross-border zones in the Region, with special attention to the situation in island and landlocked member states, criminality and threats to women's livelihoods.

It may be suggested that this sort of inter-departmental committee may be seised of matters quite early to determine facts in relation to contested, disputed or problematic borders. The provision in Article 69 which allows decentralised ECOWAS institutions such as the 'Panel of the Wise' to be involved in the design, implementation and monitoring of cross-border initiatives means that they can also be mandated to be involved in resolving a boundary problem widely construed.

Under the framework of its ECPF, ECOWAS has also undertaken to establish community projects, including community 'peace radio stations', social, health and educational centres, to serve as rallying points for inter-communal and cross-border communities on resource governance. The peace radio station initiative is a particularly innovative mechanism of people diplomacy in border areas.[19]

---

18 Note also that interviews and discussions were held with officials of the Free Movement Directorate by the author.
19 In September 2006 the Cross-border Radio Stations Network of Guinea Bissau, Senegal and the Gambia was created in Djalicunda in Guinea Bissau. It is composed of eleven (11) radio station members. The Cross-border radio stations network of Guinea Bissau, Senegal and the Gambia (RETRARC GUISENGAM) are as follows: Voz de Djalicunda Djalicunda – Guinea Bissau; AD Kassoumay Sao Domingos – Guinea Bissau; Endham FM Dioulacolon – Senegal; Awaña FM Bignona – Senegal; Radio de la paix Sindian – Senegal; Kairaba FM Diouloulou – Senegal;

There is every reason to believe that this sort of conflict preventive strategy would prove very useful across the Continent and ought to be adopted as AU-wide strategy in suitable cases.

The benchmarks to be used under the ECPA to assess progress in the implementation of cross-border initiatives very importantly includes: elimination of, or reduction in 'no man's lands' or border zones considered as safe havens for lawlessness and crime (Art. 70).

It is significant that the ECOWAS ECPA envisages that ECOWAS members should in their efforts to maintain territorial integrity and border security also aim to 'promote good neighbourliness with countries bordering ECOWAS territory' (Art 69 (i)). They are also obliged to aim at '[i]ncreased security of the external borders of the Community' (Art. 70(c)). These provisions are particularly forward-looking and can be useful tools given the right leadership within the ECOWAS organisation and, perhaps more importantly, political will at government level within the ECOWAS region.

6.2.2.3 The work of the ECOWAS Free Movement Directorate

It is important to highlight the existence and work of the Free Movement of Persons Directorate. Very many border problems in Africa emanate from problematic restrictions on the freedom of persons to traverse border areas or move across boundaries with their goods and services. Had this aspect of regional regulation been previously sufficiently and successfully elaborated upon in law and practice many border conflicts could have been averted before they occurred. This ECOWAS directorate deals extensively with border issues. The Protocol introduced by a decision of Heads of State Summit in 2006 was intended to promote the concept of border regions within West Africa through cross-border cooperation. This was spearheaded by the former Mali's President Amadou Toumani Touré. Inspiration for the creation of the Directorate is said to have come from observation of the work of the European Union in the area of informal efforts at promoting cooperation in the border regions. The idea is for ECOWAS to build upon existing interests and promote cross-border marriages and successful engagements between its border communities. It was observed that that some of these interests have already existed for centuries and may have suffered a regression as a result of Westernisation and modern manifestation of the doctrine of sovereignty.

In trying to formalise this, ECOWAS has adopted a framework which includes working closely and cooperating with intra-regional partners, such as: (a) the Boundary Commissions of Nigeria, Mali and Burkina Faso, (b) the Nigeria–Niger

---

Brikama's radio Brikama – The Gambia; Kassoumay Ziguinchor – Senegal; Kouma FM Samine Escale – Senegal; Radio Kerewan Kerewan – The Gambia; Farafenni's Radio Farafenni – The Gambia. See WABIF, "Creation Of A Cross-Border Radio Stations Network in Sénégambie Méridionale" (April, 2007) pp. 1–2; available at http://www.oecd.org/swac/publications/38768082.pdf accessed 26 August 2014.

Joint Commission and (c) Non-governmental organisations such as the West African Borders and Integration Network. A regional programme of action has been developed with Civil Society Organisations (CSOs) community leaders, gender groups etc. To enhance implementation of cross-border cooperation within West Africa, the entire region was broken up into four pilot projects and zones. Two of the more important include:

(1) the zone consisting of towns bordering Mali; Burkina Faso and Côte d'Ivoire: our interviews indicate that the issues in this sub-region include food security, free trade and sub-regional plans of actions, national plans of actions and priority projects.
(2) Senegal–Gambia–Guinea: our interviews also reveal that the zone consisting of Senegal–Gambia–Guinea Bissau has experienced many issues of insecurity. In the Southern Sene–Gambia, this has sometimes taken the shape of severe secessionist group activities. Other issues that dominate the sub-region include trade and development, leading to the design of national and zonal plans of action.

In all zones within the pilot projects there is considerable experience of cross-boundary cooperation including innovative processes such as establishment of community radio stations (ECOPEACE Radio stations) and 'peace newspapers' involving young people.[20] Community leaders are also frequently brought together as ECOWAS tries to develop joint initiatives to bring the state parties and their peoples together.

These strategies are reported to have been very useful in assisting Burkina Faso and Mali to keep their border differences within check both before and after the judgment of the ICJ (dealt with below). The Free Movement Directorate helps to concretise ECOWAS action plans and help with their implementation. The Directorate does not interfere where conflict has actually begun but steps in to help with confidence-building measures that will help bring the parties to a closer relationship. During conflict the community radio stations may continue to operate and report issues. During a crisis the Directorate works with existing stakeholders. In situations such as the border closure between Nigeria and Niger in February 2012, the Directorate became particularly concerned and worked assiduously behind the scenes to bring the situation back to normalcy.[21]

---

20 Note also the important work carried out by the Sahel West Africa Club (SWAC) and its WABI network partners over the past many years. Engagement by these institutions has involved use of concrete field-level experiences including the great potential of cross-border radio station networks to strengthen West African integration. In June 2006, the 'Kurumba' network was launched with the support of the MDP in the Sikasso-Korhogo-Bobo-Dialouasso zone. See SWAC News, "Cross Border Radios for Regional Integration", at http://www.oecd.org/dataoecd/32/6/39458523.pdf, accessed 12 March 2012.
21 The border between Nigeria and Niger divides a zone with very many linguistic, religious, social, cultural and ethnic linkages, and under normal circumstances thousands of border crossings are made on a daily basis by citizens of both states. The Boko Haram uprising in Northern Nigeria,

As previously stated many border tensions arise from the actions of private persons and groups. Senegal and Gambia had problems involving transport unions that were at loggerheads, with one union wanting a border between both states closed.[22] The border was indeed briefly closed but the situation was brought under control by close involvement of ECOWAS. Related problems had occurred between Senegal and Mauritania in the past when the latter country was still formally in the ECOWAS as a state member. Mauritania has withdrawn its members and joined another economic bloc – the Northern African Community.

The work of the Directorate has been important in ensuring trade across borders despite the many impulses to restrict cross-border movement. An interviewee based in the Directorate related an instance where he personally ensured that a border was kept open during an impromptu visit; he witnessed an illegal restriction of right of free movement of goods across a particular border by apparently corrupt immigration staff. After he left the border post, however, the illegal closure was reinstated. Experts within the Directorate note regretfully that such difficulties unfortunately disproportionately affect women. The work of the Free Movement Department is, further, reported to be hampered by inadequate staffing as more borders ought to be monitored directly by staff from the Directorate. Other observable problems include inadequate training of immigration staff particularly in relation to the applicable treaties and protocols; issues relating to official corruption and low motivation of staff and security personnel. All these issues inevitably impinge on the ability of national agencies to perform their functions and also adversely affect the work of the Directorate negatively. It was suggested by one interviewee that a harmonised curriculum of immigration and custom authorities in the entire region may be helpful in removing some of these difficulties. Successes and innovative strategies of note include the award of 'Best Free Movement Member State' which has been

---

however, brought attention to the porousness of the border and its regional security implications (see Appendix III for pictures of formal but ineffectual and porous borders). Suspected Boko Haram members were arrested in Diffa, Niger in January/February 2012. As a result the Nigerian government imposed a state of emergency in the North-eastern states of Yobe and Borno that included the closure of this border among others in the area. In the same period the two countries also agreed to equip their National Boundary Commissions with requisite logistics to ensure fast re-demarcation of the Nigeria–Niger International boundary. The two states further implemented a bilateral agreement on defence and security. See Muhammad Bello, 'Boko Haram: Nigeria, Niger Begin Joint Border Patrol', *This Day*, 18 October 2012; available at http://www.thisdaylive.com/articles/boko-haram-nigeria-niger-begin-joint-border-patrol/128075/accessed 26 August 2014. In a communique issued at the end of the sixth session of the High Authority of the Nigeria–Niger Joint Commission for Cooperation, held in Niamey, the capital of Republic of Niger, the Heads of State of both countries expressed worries over the danger of terrorism in the region and emphasised the need to jointly tackle the security challenge in the sub-region which is a big threat to peace and stability in the West African sub-region.

22 Isatou Bittaye, "Gambia: Senegal Civil Society Speaks on Border Closure", *FOROYAA Newspaper*, 4 May 2011, http://allafrica.com/stories/201105050309.html, accessed 21 March 2012. To put these particular border problems in perspective see also European Union, "EU Presidency Statement on Senegal-Gambia Border Dispute," CL05–253EN, EU source: Council UN forum, 19 October 2005, available at http://www.europa-eu-un.org/articles/en/article_5154_en.htm, accessed 21 March 2012.

presented since 2010. The award gives recognition for states that diligently observe their obligations in accordance with treaties and rules of free movement applicable in the region. The first of these was awarded to Burkina Faso, crucially in consultation with private sector initiatives.[23] It is hoped that through such 'carrot'-offering strategies there will be better acceptance of the legal position in relation to free movement of persons and goods.

6.2.3 Actual and potential role of the Court of Justice of the Economic Community of West African States

It has been suggested by several interviewees that if the parties agree to it, the Court of Justice of the Economic Community of West African States is empowered to deal with disputes involving boundary and cross-boundary issues.[24] This position upon further research does indeed appear plausible. Although the Court has traditionally had a narrow field of access in that only the Authority of Heads of State and Government (the executive of the Community comprised of all the member states) and the member states acting individually were permitted to initiate a contentious case in the Court, it is possible that a boundary issue between states may also be referred to the Court by either party. There is also the possibility that advisory opinions on the Treaty relating to powers and competences in relation to boundary and cross-boundary issues may be submitted to the Court by authorised persons. The power to request advisory opinions in this manner rests on the ECOWAS Authority of Heads of State and Government, the Council of Ministers, Member States, the Executive Secretary and other institutions of the Community.

Despite these possibilities or indeed because of them, the Court more or less remained idle until 2003 and it is instructive that the first case brought before the Court was in relation to a border situation. This landmark case was that of *Olajide Afolabi v Federal Republic of Nigeria*.[25] The matter was brought by an individual businessman against the government of Nigeria for a violation of Community law

---

23 The Federation of West African Chambers of Commerce and Industry (FEWACCI) is involved in the selection process for Best Free Movement Member State of the Year. FEWACCI requests each National Committee to fill a questionnaire to evaluate the attitude of government officials and agents on promoting free movement of persons and goods. The National Committee then conducts interviews of a cross-section of cross-border businessmen/women, including truckers, on their experience on free movement. See Modou Joof, "ECOWAS Announces 'Private Sector Awards'", 27 August 2010, available at http://www.pir-rip.ecowas.int/index.php?option=com_content&view=article&id=22-3eme-forum-des-affaires-de-la-cedeao&catid=7&lang=en accessed 18 March 2012; See also Lynays, "Recipient of the 2010 ECOWAS' Innovation Awards" available at http://www.lynays.com/?cat=12 accessed 23 March 2012.
24 The Court is composed of seven judges appointed by the Authority of Heads of State and Government from a list of up to two persons nominated by each member state. The Court was seised of its first case in 2004. Project on International Courts and Tribunal, "Court of Justice of the Economic Community of West African States", available at http://www.aict-ctia.org/courts_subreg/ecowas/ecowas_home.html accessed 12 March 2012.
25 2004/ECW/CCJ/04 (ECOWAS, Court of Justice, 2004).

in the closing of the border with Benin. The Court, however, found that under the Protocol only member states could institute cases. It therefore ruled that the plaintiff had no *locus standi* to bring the action. The ruling provoked heated legal and political discussion – which, very significantly, was led by judges of the ECOWAS Court themselves – over the need to amend the Protocol to allow for legal and natural persons to have a right of appearance and *locus standi* before the Court. As a result in January 2005 the Community adopted the Additional Protocol to permit persons to bring suits against member states. Another important development was that with this monumental change, the Council took the opportunity to revise the jurisdiction of the Court to also include review of violations of human rights in all member states. In this way boundary or border situations that lead to claims of human rights violations against persons and property (e.g. affecting access to farmlands or water sources) may become directly actionable by individuals.

6.2.4 ECOWAS Early Warning System

The Early Warning System was established in line with Article 58 of the revised Treaty and Protocol relating to the Mechanism for Conflict Prevention, Management, Resolution, Peace-keeping and Security. It is currently organised into two main components: first, the Observation and Monitoring Centre at the ECOWAS Commission, Abuja; and second, zonal bureaus of which there are four established in Banjul (The Gambia), Cotonou (Benin), Ouagadougou (Burkina Faso) and Monrovia (Liberia).

It is the responsibility of the Early Warning Directorate to observe and monitor sub-regional peace and security indicators, including humanitarian, political and other human security issues within the framework of conflict prevention. The Directorate works in partnership with representatives of ECOWAS member states and civil society organisations and research institutes. The list of CSOs is not closed but is presently typified by organisations such as the West Africa Network for Peacebuilding (WANEP)[26] and West African Civil Society Forum (WACSOF).[27] The ECOWAS Early Warning System also collaborates with other RECs and the AU in the establishment of the Continental Early Warning System (CEWS).

The Directorate's activities include collecting open-sourced information and analysing and submitting timely reports making recommendations to the Office of the President through the Office of the Commissioner, Political Affairs, Peace and Security for all necessary action.

---

26 WANEP is a leading Regional peace-building organisation founded in 1998 in response to civil wars that plagued the West African Region. WANEP works with grassroots organisations doing peace-building work. See http://www.wanep.org/wanep, accessed 10 April 2012.
27 WACSOF aims to be a forum that avails an institutionalised dialogue between regional civil society organisations (CSOs) and the ECOWAS Secretariat. It is based on the recognition that civil society members from throughout West Africa have extensive experience in their various fields of expertise and are able to make valuable contributions to ECOWAS, thereby enhancing the human security capacities of ECOWAS.

The system achieves its important tasks through a network of 30 field monitors (and 15 alternates) situated in member states. Their primary responsibilities include the gathering of on-the-ground information, which is forwarded to the heads of the zonal bureau for quality control and initial analysis before transmission to the Observation and Monitoring Centre, Abuja. The field data is further verified and analysed at the Observation and Monitoring Centre and forwarded to the policymakers at the ECOWAS Commission.

Reports generated in this manner include: Daily Highlight; Incident and Security Situation reports; Weekly Situation Report; Quarterly Security Situation; Yearly Security Situation; Early Warning Report and Policy Briefs.[28]

It is recognised that early detection of border disputes is enhanced when the EWD shares information quickly with appropriate authorities within the ECOWAS organisation. The first step is to share the information with the Peace and Conflict Department. The PCD then sends a report to the ECOWAS President who decides upon all and any further action(s) to be taken. This may take the following forms: constitution of a diplomatic mission to examine the issues; working through the PCD; or references to the Council of the Wise. It is also notable that EWD may decide to exchange information it receives with other concerned departments within the ECOWAS organisation such as the Free Movement Directorate. They may also decide to communicate directly with African Union mechanisms. It may even be recommended that pertinent information may, within reason and confidentiality requirements, be shared with requisite national authorities and perhaps even the United Nations.

6.2.5 ECOWAS experience in boundary disputes

ECOWAS experience in terms of actual border conflict resolution has been relatively low and while ECOWAS has been impressive in developing institutions, it has kept a relatively low profile in response to declared open border disputes between states. Yet boundary issues do come up from time-to-time. Ongoing situations include that between Sierra Leone and Guinea over a relatively small piece of land between them.[29] The 40th Ordinary Session of ECOWAS Summit in Abuja on 14 February 2012 (Abuja–Nigeria) and the 29th Ministerial Meeting of ECOWAS Mediation and Security Council in Abuja on 14 February 2012 (Abuja–Nigeria) were largely dominated by issues surrounding the closure of the Niger–Nigerian Border which was closed down by the Nigerian authorities as a result of fears of infiltration by Islamic terrorist groups. Note may also be taken of the notable absence of ECOWAS in dealing with the Nigeria–Cameroon dispute

---

28 The Early Warning Tools and Databases primarily consist of www.ecowarnorg and www.ecowaspeaceexchange.org.
29 Rongxing Guo, *Territorial Disputes and Resource Management: A Global Handbook* (Nova Publishers, 2007), pp. 260, 275. See also Sim Turay, "Yenga Border Dispute Sierra Leone/Guinea", available at http://www.awoko.org/2009/09/29/yenga-border-dispute-sierra-leoneguinea, accessed 9 April 2012.

and the post-judgment implementation process. Despite its notorious nature within the subregion the *Cameroon v Nigerian* dispute was ultimately decided upon by the ICJ at The Hague as it involved a state outside ECOWAS territory. Thus, ECOWAS has also not been closely associated with the implementation processes. It did, however, intervene in the dispute between Gambia and Senegal in 2006, where ECOWAS helped in soliciting donations from the EU to fund the construction of a bridge between the two countries to remove the bone of contention in respect of a body of water between both states (being used for boat crossing, leading to intermittent tensions). Our interviews reveal that the favoured route by the ECOWAS in responding to boundary disputes is to urge direct negotiations between the parties. ECOWAS may also advise reference of the dispute to the ECOWAS Mediation and Security Council where it is important to do so.

During the life of the Liberian War with its attendant cross-border rebel activity ECOWAS implemented a peace plan and set up a committee to facilitate the restoration of normalcy in the border areas of Sierra Leone and Liberia. The Committee requested and secured agreement that all hostile forces should be withdrawn immediately from the territory of Sierra Leone and created a buffer zone on the Liberian side of the border which was monitored by ECOMOG (Economic Community of West African States Monitoring Group).[30] In the Agreement between the Government of Guinea Bissau and the Self-Proclaimed Military Junta (1998),[31] ECOMOG deployed an interposition force to guarantee security along the Guinea Bissau–Senegal border, keep the warring parties apart and guaranteeing free access to humanitarian organisations and agencies to reach the affected civilian population.

6.3 Conflict and dispute management in the Economic Community of Central African States (ECCAS)

At a summit held in December 1981, the political leaders of the UDEAC (Customs and Economic Union of Central African States) agreed in principle to the formation of a wider Economic Community of Central African States (ECCAS). ECCAS was thus established by a constituitive treaty on 18 October 1983 by the members of UDEAC, Sao Tome and Principe and members of the Economic Community of the Great Lakes Countries (CEPGL) created in 1976 by the Democratic Republic of Congo, Burundi and Rwanda.[32] The

---

30 See Declaration 7 of the Final Communiqué of the 4th Meeting of the Committee of Five of the Economic Community of West African States on the Liberian crisis, held in Yamoussoukro on 29 and 30 October 1991. Note also the Cotonou Accord made on 25 July 1993. ECOMOG also created zones and sealed borders (Liberia–Guinea; Liberia–Sierra Leone; and Liberia–Côte d'Ivoire) to prevent cross-border attacks, infiltration and importation of arms.
31 Agreement between the parties to the conflict in Guinea Bissau meeting in Abuja, Nigeria on 21 October and 1 November 1998 in the context of the efforts of the 21st Summit of the Authority of the Heads of State and Government of ECOWAS.
32 See the Treaty Establishing the Economic Community of Central African States, 19 October 1983, 23 ILM 945 (1984), adopted 18 October 1983 at Libreville, entering into force 18 December 1984.

current member countries are: Angola, Burundi, Cameroon, Congo, Democratic Republic of Congo, Gabon, Equatorial Guinea, Chad, and Sao Tome and Principe. ECCAS has its headquarters in Libreville, Gabon and in addition to its traditional role of regional cooperation and integration, pursues among other things the promotion of peace and stability in Central Africa.[33] The combined land mass area of the ECCAS territory includes 6,641,500 square kilometres (approximately 22 per cent of the African continent) and it has a total population of 138.5 million – approximately 13 per cent of the African population.[34]

ECCAS' institutions are: the Conference of Heads of State and Government, which is the supreme body of ECCAS; Council of Ministers; Court of Justice; General Secretariat (executive organ of the Community); Advisory Commission; and Specialised Technical Committees.

The Community's fundamental objective is the promotion and strengthening of harmonious cooperation and a dynamic, balanced and self-sustaining development in all areas of economic and social activity. It was envisaged that these factors would help the community achieve collective self-reliance and raise the standard of living of the population.[35]

The major treaties and protocols determinative of the relevance of ECCAS to maintenance of peace and security in the region are many and include: the Treaty Establishing the Economic Community of Central African States; Protocol Establishing the Network of Parliamentarians of ECCAS (REPAC); Mutual Assistance Pact Between Member States of ECCAS; and Protocol Relating to the Establishment of a Mutual Security Pact in Central Africa (COPAX).[36] Many other agreements were concluded as appendices to the ECCAS Treaty most of which may become relevant in certain circumstances in relation to the

---

33 United Nations Economic Commission for Africa, ECCAS – Economic Community of Central African States, available at http://www.uneca.org/oria/pages/eccas-economic-community-central-african-states-0, accessed 22 October 2014.
34 See Angela Meyer, "Economic community of Central African states", in Giovanni Finizio, Lucio Levi, Nicola Vallinoto (eds), *The Democratization of International Organizations: First International Democracy Report*, (Moncalieri: Centre for Studies on Federalism, 2011), p. 3.
35 Ibid.
36 COPAX is tasked with the promoting, maintenance and consolidation of peace and security and its Protocol defines the objectives of preventing, managing and resolving conflicts; undertaking actions that are aimed at promoting, maintaining, and consolidating peace and security within the sub-region; working toward strengthening regional peace and security; reducing areas of potential tensions and prevent the eruption of armed conflicts; formulating confidence-building measures among member states; promoting policies to assist in the peaceful resolution of disputes; implementing crucial provisions that relate to non-aggression and mutual assistance in areas of defence; strengthening sub-regional cooperation in defence and security; contributing towards mediation of crises and conflicts within and among member states as well as with other non-member states; formulating common policies that have regard to peace maintenance and consolidation within the sub-region; co-ordinating member states' efforts in addressing illegal migration; co-ordinating member states' policies with regard to the management of refugees, internally displaced persons and ex-combatants in accordance with the provisions of relevant international legal instruments; proposing measures that regulate coordination and dispensation of humanitarian assistance; and setting up relating structures. See ECCAS, COPAX Protocol 2000, Articles 2 and 4. For pictures of refugees on the move in Africa see Appendix III.

determination of rights and duties of states and individuals or corporate persons in boundary conflicts.[37]

The AUBP's continental project feeds in very well into the needs of this region and its severe issues of insecurity caused by poorly defined borders, cross-border crime and the presence of armed groups in these areas. Experts in the region have conducted field research that indicates that the lack of co-operation between its national border control services causes insecurity. As a result six border zones have been chosen as targets for intervention. They are: Chad–Sudan–CAR; Chad–Cameroon–CAR; Cameroon–Equatorial Guinea–Nigeria; Angola–Congo–DRC; CAR–Congo–DRC and the River Congo; and DRC–Burundi–Rwanda.[38]

The October 2009 ECCAS summit validated the ECCAS Border Programme. A programme document validated by the Council of Ministers in June 2009 recommended that ECCAS moves steadily in the direction of defining all its borders where boundaries are still vague, and that member states should build the capacity of border control authorities and encourage the development of a regional border management policy. The fate of the programme, very much as would be expected, is tied up with the general state of development of the organisation and consequently achievements have been quite modest.[39]

It is recognisable that political and security cooperation in Central Africa is in urgent need of revival. The AU has for a long time tasked the Economic Community of Central African States (ECCAS) to give life to its peace and security architecture and despite the existence of relevant treaties and protocols, ECCAS has more or less struggled to shape and implement an impressive regional policy. In such circumstances the spiral of conflict that unfortunately engulfed Central Africa in the 1990s was not entirely unexpected as the ECCAS

---

37 Protocol on the Rules of Origin for Products to be Traded between Member States of the Economic Community of Central African States; Protocol on Non-Tariff Trade Barriers; Protocol on the Re-Export of Goods within the Economic Community of Central African States; Protocol on Transit and Transit Facilities; Protocol on Customs Cooperation within the Economic Community of Central African States; Protocol on the Fund for Compensation for Loss of Revenue; Protocol on Freedom of Movement and Rights of Establishment of Nationals of Member States within the Economic Community of Central African States; Protocol on the Clearing House for the Economic Community of Central African States; Protocol on Cooperation in Agricultural Development Between Member States of the Economic Community of Central African States; Protocol on Cooperation in Industrial Development between Member States of the Economic Community of Central African States; Protocol on Cooperation in Transport and Communications Between Member States of the Economic Community of Central African States; Protocol on Cooperation in Science and Technology Between Member States of the Economic Community of Central African States; Protocol on Energy Cooperation between Member States of the Economic Community of Central African States; Protocol on Cooperation in Natural Resources between Member States of the Economic Community of Central African States; Protocol on Cooperation in the Development of Human Resources, Education, Training and Culture between Member States of the Economic Community of Central African States; Protocol on Cooperation in Tourism between Member States of the Economic Community of Central African States; Protocol on the Simplification and Harmonization of Trade Documents and Procedures within the Economic Community of Central African States; Protocol on the Situation of Landlocked, Semi-Landlocked, Island, Part-Island and/or Least Advanced Countries.
38 "*Feuille de route 'Paix et Sécurité' de la CEEAC*", ECCAS, 5 April 2010, p. 15.
39 See ICC Group, ibid.

states were lacking a user-friendly, effective organisation to pilot it through the difficult times. Even today it has been noted that human resource management is a constant problem, as is the body's financial dependence on outside backers.

It has been stated persuasively that 'on paper, ECCAS looks good'.[40] Central African states indeed signed a mutual assistance pact and a protocol establishing the Peace and Security Council for Central Africa (*Conseil de paix et de sécurité de l'Afrique centrale*, COPAX). They also set up a Regional Staff Headquarters (*État-major régional*, EMR) that runs multinational military training exercises and the Peace Consolidation Mission in the Central African Republic (*Mission de consolidation de la paix en Centrafrique*, MICOPAX). It has also been correctly observed that, the reason regional leaders have been reluctant to create and invest in this institution is that ultimately it has the potential of constraining the way they cooperate in security matters.[41]

The serious problem that ECCAS faces is that of the considerable scepticism of many experts on African international relations. Indeed it appears that confidence in effectiveness and general performance of ECCAS in resolving regional transnational security problems is one of the lowest among African RECs. Arguably therefore, the shortcomings of the REC has perhaps contributed to the severe nature of transnational criminal activity and rampant border problems within the region.[42] For instance, the Institute for Security Studies (ISS) concluded that key ECCAS institutions created by the Council for Peace and Security in Central Africa (COPAX) such as the Multinational Peace-Keeping Force in Central Africa (FOMAC) and the Early Warning Observation and Monitoring System for Central Africa (MARAC)[43] have been largely ineffective. It is believed that:

> Conflicts have continued uncontrollably among ECCAS member states, while funding to the organisation has shown little result. Could this account for Rwanda and Burundi looking to other regional organisations? Are other countries likely to follow suit? At a time when ECCAS should be playing a

---

40 ICC Group, Implementing Peace and Security Architecture (I): Central Africa Africa Report No. 1817, November 2011, available at http://www.crisisgroup.org/en/regions/africa/central-africa/181-implementing-peace-and-security-architecture-i-central-africa.aspx, accessed 31 October 2014.
41 ICC Group, Implementing Peace and Security Architecture (I): Central Africa Africa Report No. 1817, November 2011, available at http://www.crisisgroup.org/en/regions/africa/central-africa/181-implementing-peace-and-security-architecture-i-central-africa.aspx, accessed 31 October 2014.
42 The conclusions of the International Crisis Group in this area are pretty damning. It states that: 'For Central African states, loosely controlled borders, cross-border ethnic allegiances and antagonisms, ideological affinities and the unequal distribution of natural resources are reason enough to interfere in the internal wars of their neighbours. These factors transform simple conflicts between neighbouring countries into political and security risks and justify helping allies to acquire and safeguard material gains. Governments have therefore frequently provided financial, logistic and military support to one or more of their neighbours' opponents, thereby linking civil wars', International Crisis Group, ibid., p. 2.
43 There is a fuller discussion of the early warning system below.

central role in conflict intervention among its member states, the organization remains feeble and disempowered as member states continue to defect. It is very much true that only decisive political commitment by its members can breathe new life into ECCAS.[44]

As a result Gabon and Equatorial Guinea decided against settlement of the problem of Mbanie Island largely by reference to political and legal *fora* outside ECCAS' border. Similarly Angola and the DRC decided against ECCAS involvement in its settlement of the demarcation of their maritime border. Angola has also strenuously refused regional involvement in the problem posed by the Front for the Liberation of the Enclave of Cabinda (*Front de libération de l'enclave du Cabinda* (FLEC)).[45]

Furthermore it is difficult not to agree with the view that:

> The region's governments should urgently deepen their political commitment to ECCAS's structures and projects and sort out their common priorities. They must decide if they really want to be members of ECCAS. If so, they should prove their will by undertaking several crucial steps: respect their financial obligations to the organisation; name their representatives to it; and organise a summit as soon as possible. A reform agenda should focus on the decision-making system, ensuring smooth running of the secretariat in Libreville and greater involvement of civil society. Security priorities should seek practical implementation and concrete results.[46]

It has been persuasively argued that over the next few decades, the fundamental challenge facing ECCAS will be to give political meaning to the organisation while its members exist in a tangle of mistrust, rivalries and thinly veiled hostility. The geopolitical relations between the states in the region are perceptively zero; especially in relation to territorial and cross-boundary matters. As a result it has been predicted that Central African countries will continue to put their own narrow interests above the project of peace and security architecture. Political and security integration may therefore follow in the tragic footsteps of economic cooperation.[47]

To reinforce the capability of ECCAS to effectively deal with boundary disputes in the region member states must further develop dedicated legal and political processes aimed at resolving political and border disputes between member states. It will be important to implement strategies to improve the performance and capacities of the Department for Human Integration, Peace, Security and Stability (*Département de l'intégration humaine, de la paix, de la sécurité et de la stabilité*

---

44 Institute for Security Studies (ISS), "Is There Hope for ECCAS?", 19 October 2007 available at http://www.issafrica.org/iss-today/is-there-hope-for-eccas, accessed 6 November 2014.
45 *Affaire Kahemba : l'Angola rejette la thèse de l'occupation*, Radio Okapi, 13 March 2007.
46 International Crisis Group, op.cit.
47 Ibid.

(DIHPSS). Painstaking and effective communication campaigns involving the ECCAS general secretariat and pertinent boundary-related national authorities are needed to make plain ECCAS' role and functions in maintaining peaceful relations between boundary communities to the general public. There is the need for recruitment of dedicated staff with adequate training and experience in boundary management projects and international law as well as provision of the DIHPSS with an AUBP desk. This may involve enactment of strategies to increase civil society involvement in ECCAS programmes devoted towards attainment of the AUBP.[48]

6.3.1 Assessing the early warning capabilities and performance of MARAC

MARAC is the department within ECCAS tasked with collecting and analysing data for the early detection and prevention of conflicts and crises. Located at the ECCAS Executive Secretariat in Libreville (Gabon), it currently consists of the Central Structure and 31 decentralised correspondents spread throughout the ten member states of ECCAS.[49]

By their very nature early warning and early response systems are designed to provide timely and useful alert to a sophisticated institution or group of institutions about oncoming threats in order to provide crucial triggers and early and effective responses and to prevent the onset of full-blown crisis. As one African commentator neatly put it 'the relevance of such a system arises from the reality that conflict prevention is far more cost effective than conflict resolution and management, let alone transformation, especially for underdeveloped African countries'.[50] It has also been correctly noted that the establishment of MARAC flowed strongly from the logic and context of the establishment of similar mechanisms on the African continent during the same period as its establishment.[51] Yet its establishment and continuous operation, especially in recent times, is quite commendable and it would prove crucial to any plans to make ECCAS central to the prevention, resolution and management of boundary conflicts and cross-border cooperation.

The challenges to peace and security in Central Africa have been described to include:

> civil wars and unconstitutional changes of government; autocratic rule; external interference; the proliferation of small arms and light weapons; maritime insecurity along the Gulf of Guinea; election-related violence; spillover of conflicts from neighbouring regions; inadequate security sector

---

48 Ibid.
49 Sadiki Koko, "Warning Whom, for Which response? Appraisal of the Early Warning and Early Response Mechanism of the Economic Community of Central African States", Vol. 22, *African Security Review Special Issue: The State of the Art in Conflict Early Warning in Africa*, Issue 2 (2013), p. 54.
50 Ibid., p. 64.
51 Ibid., p. 54.

reform and post-conflict reconstruction; poverty, inequality and underdevelopment; environmental degradation, food insecurity and tensions borne out of unequal access to scarce resources (including land); high youth unemployment; uneasy cohabitation among social/ethnic groups leading to inter-ethnic conflicts; and chronic diseases and inadequate access to healthcare.[52]

It is precisely because MARAC has to satisfy such onerous requirements that it is so unsatisfactory that it shares many of the shortcomings and constraints that afflict its parent body. It took up to seven years for MARAC to be kick-started, and according to observers it remains inadequately staffed. In a sense therefore MARAC mirrors and reinforces the overall institutional weakness of ECCAS.

6.4 Law and practice of conflict and dispute management in the SADC

The Southern African Development Community (SADC) was set up by Treaty with the mission to promote sustainable and equitable economic growth and socio-economic development through efficient, productive systems, deeper cooperation and integration, good governance and durable peace and security so that the region emerges as a competitive and effective player in international relations and the world economy.[53] The Treaty binding upon member states is based on the following major principles: sovereign equality of all member states; solidarity, peace and security; human rights, democracy and the rule of law; equity, balance and mutual benefit; and peaceful settlement of disputes. The organisation currently has a structure consisting of eight principal institutions and organs.

The objectives of SADC are to:

- achieve development and economic growth, alleviate poverty, enhance the standard and quality of life of the people of Southern Africa and support the socially disadvantaged through regional integration;
- promote and defend peace and security;
- evolve common political values, systems and institutions;
- promote and maximise productive employment and utilisation of the Region's resources;
- promote self-sustaining development on the basis of collective self-reliance, as well as the interdependence of member states;
- achieve sustainable utilisation of natural resources and effective protection of the environment;

---

52 Ibid., p. 58.
53 Treaty of the Southern African Development Community (adopted 17 August 1992 at Windhoek, entered into force 30 September 1993) 32 ILM 116 (1993), as amended by the Agreement Amending the Treaty of SADC 2001 (entered into force 30 September 1993) 32 ILM 116. Amended by the Agreement Amending the Treaty of 2001 (entered into force 14 August 2001). See http://www.sadc.int/, accessed 14 Novemeber 2014.

- achieve complementarity between national and regional strategies and programmes;
- strengthen and consolidate cultural affinities and the long-standing historical and social links among the people of the region.

6.4.1 Political mechanisms for the resolution of boundary disputes in the SADC region

Conflicts arising out of boundary disputes will in the first instance be treated within the SADC Organ on Politics, Defence and Security. This organ is uniquely managed on a Troika basis and is responsible for promoting peace and security in the SADC region. It is mandated to steer and provide member states with direction regarding matters that threaten peace, security and stability within the region. It is coordinated at the level of summit, consisting of a chairperson, incoming chairperson and outgoing chairperson, and reports to the SADC summit chairperson.

The SADC Summit and Organ Troika Summit are mutually exclusive; and, the chairperson of the organ does not simultaneously hold the chair of the summit. The organ structure, operations and functions are regulated by the Protocol on Politics, Defence and Security Cooperation. Both the summit chair and the organ chair rotate on a yearly basis.

6.4.1.1 SADC tribunal and the judicial route

Boundary conflicts in theory can be submitted to the SADC tribunal. The Protocol providing for its establishment was signed in Windhoek, Namibia during the 2000 Ordinary Summit, and the tribunal was officially established on 18 August 2005 in Gaborone, Botswana. The SADC tribunal is set up to ensure adherence to, and proper interpretation of the provisions of, the SADC Treaty and subsidiary instruments. The tribunal based in Windhoek, Namibia adjudicates upon disputes referred to it and has a Bench of judges appointed from the member states.

The unique socio-legal and political mileau in Southern Africa became apparent when the SADC tribunal gave several judgments that ruled against the Zimbabwean government in the late 2000s.[54] The limits of tolerance of African interdependence sovereignty had apparently been breached. Consequently the tribunal was *de facto* suspended at the 2010 SADC Summit. The SADC Summit held in 2012 at Maputo resolved that a new tribunal should be negotiated and that its mandate should be confined to interpretation of the SADC Treaty and

---

54 Frederick Cowell, "The Suspension of the Southern African Development Community Tribunal: A threat to Human Rights", *Consultancy Africa Intelligence*, 17 October 2010, available at http://www.consultancyafrica.com/index.php?option=com_content&view=article&id=583:the-suspension-of-the-southern-african-development-community-tribunal-a-threat-to-human-rights&catid=91:rights-in-focus&Itemid=296, accessed 9 November 2014; Open Society Initiative of Southern Africa, "SADC Tribunal: Will regional leaders support it or sabotage it?", available at http://www.osisa.org/sites/default/files/sup_files/SADC%20Tribunal.pdf, accessed 9 November 2014.

Protocols relating to disputes between member states. The 34th Ordinary meeting of the Summit of the Heads of State and Government of the Southern African Development Community (SADC) held in Zimbabwe on 17 and 18 August 2014 received a report from the Committee of Ministers of Justice/Attorneys General relating to progress on negotiating a new Protocol on the SADC tribunal, and adopted a draft Protocol on the Tribunal in the Southern African Development Community.[55] As expected, the summit 'neutered' the court by stripping it of its real power – which is to hear complaints by SADC citizens against their own governments.[56] The significance of this is that boundary disputes will probably still qualify for interpretation but not boundary-related disputes brought by indigenous groups or non-independent states. There has, therefore, been a narrowing of the potential usefulness of this important African tribunal even before it has found its feet.

6.4.1.2 SADC Organ for Politics, Defence and Security

The SADC Organ for Politics, Defence and Security was created as a result of a decision contained in the Garborone Communique of 28 June 1996.[57] The SADC Secretariat provides secretariat services to the Organ. The specific objectives of the organ as stated in the Protocol on Politics, Defence and Security Cooperation[58] is to protect the people and safeguard the development of the

---

55 Communiqué of the 34th Summit of SADC Heads of State and Government, Victoria Falls, Zimbabwe, 17–18 August 2014, available at http://www.dfa.gov.za/docs/2014/sadc0819.html, accessed 9 November 2014.
56 Nicole Fritz, "Quiet death of an important SADC institution", *Mail & Guardian*, 29 August 2014, available at http://mg.co.za/article/2014-08-29-quiet-death-of-an-important-sadc-institution, accessed 9 November 2014. This position has been criticised by many observers and legal experts. The SADC Lawyers' Association has persuasively stated that this development is negative because it: (i) denies access to the court by, and access to justice for, people in the SADC region; (ii) derogates from internationally recognised tenets on independence of the judiciary and the doctrine of separation of powers; (iii) derogates from basic tenets of human rights and the rule of law as enshrined in the SADC Treaty; and (iv) represents an antithesis of both the Strategic Indicative Plan for the Organ on Politics, Defence and Security (SIPO) and the progressive vision contemplated by the SADC Treaty, SADC Lawyers' Association, 'SADC Tribunal Petition', letter of 18 August 2014 written to SADC Heads of State and Government c/o His Excellency, Comrade Robert Gabriel Mugabe, available at https://freedomhouse.org/article/sadc-tribunal-petition#.VGFyDrdyZdg, accessed 11 November 2014; Ray Ndlovu, 'SADC Tribunal Back with Mandate Reduced to Interstate Cases', *Business Day*, 20 August 2014, available at http://www.bdlive.co.za/africa/africannews/2014/08/20/sadc-tribunal-back-with-mandate-reduced-to-interstate-cases, accessed 11 November 2014.
57 See Extraordinary SADC Heads of State and Government Summit Communique Botswana - Gaborone: 28 June 1996, available at http://www.issafrica.org/AF/RegOrg/unity_to_union/pdfs/sadc/communiques/HoS%2096x.pdf, accessed 12 November 2014.
58 Protocol on Poliitics, Defence and Security Cooperation, available at http://www.sadc.int/files/3613/5292/8367/Protocol_on_Politics_Defence_and_Security20001.pdf, accessed 12 November 2014. Specific objectives of the SADC Organ on Politics, Defence and Security that were designed for it by the Community's leaders in the Gaborone Communique and which will be of use in boundary dispute management include the following: protect the people and safeguard the development of the region against instability arising from the breakdown of law and order, inter-state conflict and external aggression; cooperate fully in regional security and defence

region against instability arising from the breakdown of law and order, intra-state conflict, inter-state conflict and aggression. The organ promotes regional coordination and cooperation on matters related to security and defence and establishes appropriate mechanisms to this end (Art. 2(2)(a)–(d)); to

(e) prevent, contain and resolve inter-and intra-state conflict by peaceful means;
(f) consider enforcement action in accordance with international law and as a matter of last resort where peaceful means have failed;
(h) consider the development of a collective security capacity and conclude a Mutual Defence Pact to respond to external military threats; and
(i) develop close cooperation between the police and state security services of State Parties in order to address: (1) cross-border crime; and (2) promote a community-based approach to domestic security.

Should conflict over territorial integrity of any sort breakout suddenly the Protocol on Politics, Defence and Security Cooperation provides useful guidance. Any state party may request the chairperson to table any significant conflict for discussion in the Organ and in consultation with the other members of the Troika of the Organ, the chairperson shall meet such a request expeditiously. The Organ shall respond to a request by a state party to mediate in a conflict within the territory of a state and the Organ shall endeavour by diplomatic means to obtain such request where it is not forthcoming (Art. 11(4)). In interstate disputes, one or both of the Inter-State Politics and Diplomacy Committee (ISPDC) and the Inter-state Defence and Security Committee (ISDSC) may be seised of the matter. Both the ISPDC and the ISDSC can convene meetings based on the request of their respective ministers or the Chairman of both bodies. They must, however, at least meet on an annual basis. Both bodies can also establish substructures as they may deem necessary to perform necessary functions (Arts 6(6–8) and 7(6–8)).

The aim of putting the Organ in place has always been to ensure close cooperation on matters of politics, defence and security. This of course includes boundary issues and the guiding principle as enshrined in the Protocol is that the Organ shall at all times promote the peaceful settlement of disputes by negotiation, conciliation, mediation or arbitration.

It is certainly valuable that the Organ is empowered by Article 10 to enter into: cooperation with non-state parties and international organisations. This puts the

---

through conflict prevention management and resolution; mediate in inter-state disputes and conflicts; use preventive diplomacy to pre-empt conflict in the region, both within and between states, through an early warning system; where conflict does occur, to seek to end this quickly as possible through diplomatic means. Only where such means fail would the Organ recommend that the Summit should consider punitive measures. These responses would be agreed in a Protocol on Peace, Security and Conflict Resolution: promote peace-keeping in order to achieve sustainable peace and security; promote the political, economic, social and environmental dimensions of security; develop close cooperation between the police and security services of the region, with a view to arresting cross-border crime, as well as promoting a community-based approach on matters of unity. See the Garborone Communique of 28 June 1996.

SADC laws in line with those of ECOWAS and ECCAS. The ability to work with border communities in times of crisis and in a sustainable manner to provide for peaceful and qualitative cross-border cooperation will very often require collaboration and consultation with non-state parties sharing boundaries with the SADC and international organisations such as the African Union.

In terms of conflict prevention, management and resolution Article 11 obliges state parties to refrain from the threat or use of force against the territorial integrity or political independence of any state, other than for the legitimate purpose of individual or collective self-defence against an armed attack.

In relation to all disputes, including of course territorial and boundary conflicts, State Parties are obliged to manage and seek to resolve such disputes between two or more of them by peaceful means (Article 11 (b)). The Organ itself is mandated to seek to manage and resolve inter- and intra-state conflict by peaceful means. The protocol readily identifies conflicts over territorial boundaries or natural resources between State Parties as 'significant inter-state conflict' (Article 11 (2) (a) (i)). It is perhaps significant to mention that the specific peaceful means that are envisaged include preventive diplomacy, negotiations, conciliation, mediation, good offices, arbitration and adjudication by an international tribunal (Article 11 (3)). It is also significant that the power is granted in this instrument to the Organ whereby the Organ may seek to resolve any significant intra-state conflict within the territory of a state party (Art. 11(2)(b)). A 'significant intra-state conflict' shall include:

(i) large-scale violence between sections of the population or between the state and sections of the population, including genocide, ethnic cleansing and gross violation of human rights;
(ii) a military coup or other threat to the legitimate authority of a State;
(iii) a condition of civil war or insurgency; and
(iv) a conflict which threatens peace and security in the Region or in the territory of another State Party.

The chairperson, in consultation with the other members of the Troika, may table any such significant conflict for discussion in the Organ. It is important to note that in respect of both inter- and intra-state conflict, the Organ shall seek to obtain the consent of the disputant parties to its peace-making efforts (Art. 11(4)(a)).

The provision of such powers is of crucial importance and usefulness in relation to the SADC Organ's ability to deal with developments in the region along the lines of separatist activity and secessionist conflicts. As we will show later, there is significant evidence of present and potential developments of separatism in the SADC region and the ability of the entire SADC body to cope with these in the future will certainly rely on the efficient engagement with the use of these powers by the Organ.

Of particular interest to our analysis is the provision allowing the Organ to act in consultation with the pertinent bodies within the United Nations Security

Council and the AU in offering mediation in significant inter-or intra-state conflict that occurs outside the Region. This provision in many ways strengthens the overall architecture of peaceful diplomatic resolution of disputes in Africa. The opportunity offered under the SADC laws ought to be taken up on more occasions by African states in other regions in the future. Where, for instance, a dispute involves Northern African states, the independence and unconnectedness of the SADC Organ to the politics of the region will be of unique value to the disputants and African diplomacy and dispute resolution capabilities will be further enriched. Indeed it must be recommended that similar reciprocal rules ought to be made available in the other RECs as a further consolidation of our recommended policy of African ownership of its own dispute resolution requirements.

The methods to be employed by the Organ in its efforts to prevent, manage and resolve conflicts by peaceful means to include preventive diplomacy, negotiations, conciliation, mediation, good offices, arbitration and adjudication by the SADC tribunal (Art. 11). The Organ was empowered to establish an early warning system in order to facilitate timeous action to prevent the outbreak and escalation of conflict.

6.4.1.3 Assessing the SADC early warning system

Early warning systems are crucial to the detection of stress points in the international relations of any region. Just a year after a similar development in Eastern Africa–CEWARN, the SADC began steps towards the gradual establishment of its own much needed early warning system. On the recommendation of the Inter-State Defence and Security Committee (ISDSC), the Ministerial Committee of the Organ (MCO) at its meeting held in July 2003 in Maputo, Mozambique directed the Inter-State Defence and Security Committee to initiate the establishment of the Regional Early Warning System.[59] The centre was not, however, officially launched until 12 July 2010. The principles underlying the concept of the Regional Early Warning System and its operationalisation is in many ways close to the early warning systems in the other RECs, including ECOWAS, CEWARN and at the Continental level as discussed earlier. Furthermore, it is designed as a hub which links with National Early Warning Centres in all the Member States in the SADC as well as the Continental Early Warning Centre at the African Union.

---

59 The mandate and approval for the establishment of the SADC Regional Early Warning Centre (REWC) is to be found within the Strategic Indicative Plan of the Organ (SIPO) on Peace, Security and Defence. The MCO at its meeting held in July 2004 in South Africa, mandated the Troika of the Organ to initiate steps towards the phased establishment of the REWC. Phase I consisted of the development of the concept, the structure, working system, administrative and financial issues. Phase II comprised the operationalisation of the Centre. See SADC, "Regional Early Warning Centre", available at http://www.sadc.int/sadc-secretariat/services-centres/regional-early-warning-centre/, accessed 12 November 2014.

7 Manifestations of boundary disputes in the African geopolitical zones

African boundaries are largely superimposed and are therefore very susceptible to conflict. Superimposed boundaries generate conflict by creating a disjunction between the interactions of the sociocultural system on the one hand, and the political system on the other. Since nearly all of Africa succumbed to the affliction of colonialism it is not surprising that all sub-regions of Africa are nearly evenly afflicted with the scourge of boundary conflicts. The real surprise is that 'despite the extensive divisions of cultural identities by boundaries, the level of irredentism has been low in Africa.'[1]

For ease of analysis we will adopt the methodology of a zonal approach to the analysis of African international boundaries disputes. This involves an examination of the history and developments of boundary disputes within the area of membership of the African Regional Economic Communities (RECs). There are elaborate rules in place in the RECs we have discussed for the prevention and management of disputes relating to their member states. The RECs are also important players within the African Peace and Security architecture.[2] It is important, however, to note that these may be regarded as rough classifications considering that there are disputes that overlap, existing between countries that are contiguous but which belong to different zones or economic and political organisations. The zones as discussed roughly follow the membership of states to the following regional RECs that exist on the continent. They are: the Economic Community of West African States (ECOWAS);[3] South African Development Commission (SADC);[4] in East Africa – the Intergovernmental Authority on

---

1 Okomu (2010), p. 39.
2 See Memorandum of Understanding on Cooperation in the Area of Peace and Security Between the African Union, the Regional Economic Communities and the Coordinating Mechanisms of the Regional Standby Brigades of Eastern Africa and Northern Africa. Particularly useful in relation to boundary disputes are the obligations in Articles II, V–VII, IX and X.
3 The 15 West African states that constitute ECOWAS are: The Republic of Benin; Burkina Faso; The Republic of Cabo Verde; The Republic of Côte d'Ivoire; The Republic of Gambia; The Republic of Ghana; The Republic of Guinea; The Republic of Guinea-Bissau; The Republic of Liberia; The Republic of Mali; The Republic of Niger; The Federal Republic of Nigeria; The Republic of Senegal; The Republic of Sierra Leone; and Togolese Republic. See http://www.ecowas.int.
4 SADC member states and parties to the Treaty of the Southern Africa Development Community are as follows: The Republic of Angola; The Republic of Botswana; The Democratic Republic of

Development (IGAD);[5] the Economic and Monetary Community of Central African States (CEMAC);[6] and the Arab Maghreb Union for North Africa.[7]

7.1 East African boundaries: border disputes

Border disputes continue to pose a real security threat in the East African region. Wafula Okomu persuasively writes on this phenomenon that:

> each of the countries in Eastern Africa has had at least one border dispute with a neighbour, mainly over territorial claims, mostly over lack of clearly defined and marked boundaries, the availability of trans-boundary resources, and security-related matters.[8]

Burundi and Rwanda quarrel over sections of border along the Akanyaru-Kanyaru and Kagera-Nyabarongo Rivers.[9] Uganda and its CEMAC neighbour, the Democratic Republic of Congo (DRC), disputes Rukwanzi Island in Lake Albert and other areas of Semliki River.[10] Kenya and Uganda wrangle about Migingo Island in Lake Victoria.[11] Tanzania and Mozambique observe the 1936–7 agreement between Britain and Portugal along the Ruvuma River which stipulates that: 'The boundary should go along the Thalweg in the places where there are no islands; and in case of disagreement consultation should be made with the Permanent Court of International Justice (PCIJ)'. Another disputed border is the Songwe River that forms the boundary between Malawi and

---

Congo; The Kingdom of Lesotho; The Republic of Madagascar; The Republic of Malawi; The Republic of Mauritius; The Republic of Mozambique; The Republic of Namibia; The Republic of Seychelles; The Republic of South Africa; The Kingdom of Swaziland; The United Republic of Tanzania; The Republic of Zambia; and The Republic of Zimbabwe. See http://www.sadc.int/index.php?cID=528.

5 IGAD's membership comprises of Djibouti, Eritrea, Ethiopia, Kenya, Somalia, Sudan, South Sudan and Uganda. See http://igad.int.
6 Member States of this CEMAC are Cameroon, Central African Republic, Chad, Gabon and Equatorial Guinea. See http://www.cemac.int.
7 The AMU consists of Algeria, Libya, Mauritania, Morocco and Tunisia. See http://www.maghrebarabe.org/en.
8 Wafula Okomu, "Colonial Errors Border Disputes in East African Region", *Diplomat East Africa*, http://diplomateast africa.com/index.php?option=com_content&view=article&id=360:colonial-errors-border-disputes-in-ea-region&catid=1:dna&Itemid=66, accessed 13 January 2011.
9 Burundi and Rwanda dispute a farmed area in the Rukurazi Valley of Sabanerwa comprising 2 sq km (0.8 sq mi), where the Akanyaru–Kanyaru River shifted its course southward after heavy rains in 1965. Cross-border conflicts persist among Tutsi, Hutu, other ethnic groups, associated political rebels, armed gangs and various government forces in the Great Lakes Region (GLR). See Appendix III for pictures of rebels on borders/borderlines in the GLR.
10 "International Disputes", CIA, *The World Factbook–Field Listing*; See also Fulgence S. Msafiri, "Escalation and Resolution of Border Disputes and Interstate Conflicts in Africa: The Malawi-Tanzania Case", unpublished thesis, Naval Postgraduate School, Monterey, California June 2011, pp. 26–28. Available at http://edocs.nps.edu/npspubs/scholarly/theses/2011/June/11Jun_Msafiri.pdf, accessed 23 April 2012.
11 Msafiri, ibid., Reuben Olita, "Kenya: Moi Speaks Out on Migingo Dispute", *The New Vision*, 18 May 2009, http://allafrica.com/stories/200905190177.html, accessed 23 December 2010.

Tanzania and shifts from one country to another due to flooding during the rainy season.[12] Malawi and Zambia have been arguing about their 600-kilometre border for decades. In May 2005, the two countries met to discuss the issue. Today the subject is still unresolved.[13]

Aside from post-colonial disputes arising out of erstwhile colonial delimitation efforts of which there are also many, East African border disputes are notoriously related to pastoralist and rural issues. They are also often concerned with access to and control over natural resources. They would typically involve tensions between border communities and cross-border cattle and livestock rustlers and other armed bandits. These issues, therefore, require peculiar approaches to their conflict prevention and resolution. The prognosis for boundary disputes in the IGAD area is currently quite high. In May 2011 communities between Ethiopia and Kenya attacked each other leading to the death of about 24 persons. Other notable ongoing disputes involving loss of very many lives include Ethiopia–Eritrea; Eritrea–Djibouti; Sudan–South Sudan.[14]

7.1.1 Sudan–Kenya: the Ilemi Triangle

Kenya appears to claim sovereignty over a disputed territory at the corner of Kenya–Sudan–Ethiopia boundary.[15] There is an apparent absence of a treaty or legislative mandate for this claim. The claim is expected to continue to be challenged by Khartoum on the basis of principles of international law. Kenya's occupation of the Ilemi Triangle arose by default as a result of the disinterest of Sudan – which was then under joint Anglo-Egyptian rule. The erstwhile Sudanese authorities were not interested in the area because, according to the preliminary

---

12 Msafiri, ibid., p. 28; "Songwe River Sours Malawi, Tanzania Environment", Malawi,Tanzania, *Afrol News*, 18 May, http://www.afrol.com/articles/12447, accessed 23 December 2010.
13 Msafiri, ibid., p. 27; "Zambia Malawi in Border Talks", News24.com: Africa News, 17 May 2005, http://www.news24.com/Africa/News/Zambia-Malawi-in-border-talks-20050517, accessed 23 December 2010.
14 Recent field report statistics for CEWARN, the IGAD authority in charge of raising alert and dealing with border area incidents that affect the member states, reveals quite shocking facts for the period October–December 2011. In this period violent incidents, human death and livestock loss due to transboundary problems in the Somali, Karamoja and Dikhil Clusters include: Somali Cluster, Ethiopia: violent incidents, 1; human death, 3; livestock loss, 0; and Kenya: violent incidents, 23; human death, 1; livestock loss, 751. this gives a total of violent incidents, 24; human death, 4; livestock loss, 751. In the Karamoja Cluster the following were recorded. Ethiopia: violent incidents, 8; human death, 1; livestock loss, 207; Kenya: violent incidents, 86; human death, 66; livestock loss, 3354. South Sudan: violent incidents, 6; human death, 7; livestock loss, 110. Total figures for this cluster: violent incidents, 100; human death, 74; livestock loss, 3671. In the Dikhil Cluster for which only the figures of Djibouti are given the following is reported: violent incidents, 1; human death, 0; livestock loss, 1. See CEWARN, "CEWARN Field Data for October–December 2011", *CEWARN Quarterly*, Jan–April Issue No. 35 (special edition), p. 4.
15 The Ilemi Triangle is said to be named after a famous chief of the Anuak community that lives along Sudan's eastern border with Ethiopia. The size of the area is roughly larger than the Republic of the Gambia. It has also been described as 'the gateway to the unexplored oil reserves in southern Sudan and is itself suspected to have minerals'. Peter Mwaura, "Kenya's Claim over Sudan, Ethiopia Border Triangle Precarious", *The Daily Nation*, 17 July 2005, available at http://www.sudantribune.com/Kenya-s-claim-over-Sudan-Ethiopia,10663, accessed 12 April 2012.

expedition that tried to occupy and administer the territory around 1930, it appeared to be 'entirely useless'.[16] The dispute now, however, appears to arise as it does in many of these cases from 'competition for natural resources, the discovery of oil or from inter-ethnic conflicts'.[17]

In 1928, Khartoum gave Kenya permission to send military units across the border in 'hot pursuit' in order to protect the Turkana.[18] Units of the King's African Rifles (KAR) then moved into the triangle and by 1947 Kenya had seven police posts in the territory. Ilemi is currently solely controlled and administered by Kenya. Pre-1978 maps of Kenya showed the country's northern boundary with Sudan as a straight line drawn from the tip of Lake Rudolf (now Turkana) westwards to the north of Lokichoggio. Named the Maud Line, after Captain Philip Maud of the British Royal Engineers who delimited the boundary in 1902–03, the straight line was recognized in 1907 and 1914 as the international boundary between Sudan and Kenya. Above the Maud Line, the maps also showed the Ilemi Triangle in dotted lines with the words 'Provisional/administrative boundary'.

After 1978, however, the dots disappeared from official Kenya maps and have been replaced by a continuous line, suggesting that the frontier territory now belongs to Kenya. But the Maud Line, some writers claim, is the only recognised international border. Not everybody agrees that the Maud Line is the international boundary. It has been predicted that if the parties do not pay enough attention 'the triangle is going to be another Bakassi Peninsular'[19]. Reference is being made here to the seemingly intractable Bakassi dispute between a West African and Central African state which spanned many decades.

7.1.2 Kenya–South Sudan (Nadapal boundary)

Nadapal is a border point that has in more recent times generated severe disputes between the Sudan and Kenya and disturbed the relations between the people living along the common border. The conflict has forced the Government to deploy military personnel and police officers to the border and led to loss of over 40 lives. Things came to a head after the signing of the Comprehensive Peace Accord (CPA), which ushered in peace in South Sudan. The situation changed as

---

16 Rongxing Guo, *Territorial Disputes and Resource Management: A Global Handbook* (Nova, 2006), pp. 139–140.
17 Cf. the Written Answers Monday 18 May 2009, "Africa: Ilemi Triangle Question", Asked by Lord Alton of Liverpool, 18 May 2009: Column WA243, http://www.publications.parliament.uk/pa/ld200809/ldhansrd/text/90518w0001.htm accessed 28 April 2012. Hansard and written answers are available at www.parliament.uk.
18 The Turkana are basically a Nilotic people who are native to the Turkana District in northwest Kenya. They are located in the semi-arid climate region that borders Lake Turkana which lies in the east, as well as Pokot, Rendille and Samburu to the south, Uganda to the west, and South Sudan and Ethiopia to the north. They refer to their land as Turkan. According to the latest Kenyan census held in 2009 the Turkana population is estimated at about 855,399, or 2.5 per cent of the Kenyan population. This makes the Turkana the third largest Nilotic ethnic group in Kenya, after the Kalenjin and the Luo. They are, thus, slightly more numerous than the Maasai, and have the tenth largest ethnicity in Kenya.
19 Mwaura op.cit., quoting Maurice Amutabi in an interview with the *Daily Nation*.

the then semi-autonomous Southern Sudan Government sought to establish its boundary hence allegedly encroaching into Kenya's territory. A set of maps, reportedly released by South Sudanese authorities on 5 October 2011 appear to lay claim to a large tract of land that Kenya asserts is within its national borders. This has led to protests from the Turkana people.[20] High level governmental delegations from Kenya have since held meetings with their Sudan counterparts without success.[21] Kenyan Ministry of Lands officials have accused their South Sudanese counterparts of attempting to annex part of Kenya. The area in dispute is widely seen as a goldmine for the pastoralist communities due to availability of plenty of pasture and water.[22]

7.1.3 Tanzania–Malawi: Lake Malawi (Nyasa)

Since Malawi became independent on 6 July 1964, diplomatic relations with her eastern neighbour Tanzania has been fraught with severe difficulties. This is largely in relation to a dispute over the delimitation of the boundary between the two states along Lake Malawi (Nyasa). President Nyerere of Tanzania brought the issue of the dispute over the Lake out into the open in 1967.[23] Malawi's claim over the whole body of Lake Nyasa remains contested by its neighbour and continues to have serious effects of military, environmental and commercial nature in relation to the area of dispute.[24] The long-lasting dispute remains unresolved and direct negotiations involving joint teams of experts and senior government officials that the parties initially adopted to cope with it have failed and the dispute has been submitted to international mediation.[25] We will consider the legal and political aspects of the dispute in more detail below in order to highlight the workings of the mediation route.

7.1.4 Kenya–Uganda: Migingo Island

In June 2004, Kenya alleged that, Ugandan marine police invaded and pitched tent on the island, raising the Ugandan flag and that of their police department. Further diplomatic dispute ensued in February 2009 when Kenyans living on

---

20 Isaiah Lucheli, "Boundary Dispute that's an Embarrassment to Kenya", available at http://www.standardmedia.co.ke/archives/mag/InsidePage.php?id=2000000285&cid=459& accessed 21 March 2012.
21 Ibid.
22 "Tension Increases as South Sudan Declares Border", Future Directions International (12 October 2011) available at http://www.futuredirections.org.au/publications/indian-ocean/29-indian-ocean-swa/261-tension-increases-as-south-sudan-declares-borders.html, accessed 27 August 2014.
23 James Mayall, "The Malawi–Tanzania Boundary Dispute", *Journal of Modern African Studies* 11, 4 (1973), pp. 611–628.
24 Fulgence S. Msafiri, "Escalation and Resolution and Resolution of Border Disputes and Resolution of Border Disputes and Interstate Conflicts in Africa: The Malawi–Tanzania Case", June 2011, (Monterey, California: Naval Graduate School), pp. 1–2 and 55.
25 Faraja Jube, "Tanzania: Discussions to Solve Malawi Border Conflict Soon", 4 February 2010, available at http://allafrica.com/stories/201002050139.html, accessed 12 March 2012.

160 *Manifestations of boundary disputes*

Migingo were required to purchase special permits from the Ugandan government. On 12 March 2009, Uganda proposed that the matter be resolved by a survey, using as a guideline the boundaries set by the Kenya Colony and Protectorate Order in Council, 1926[26] which is copied into the Ugandan constitution and which identifies the boundary line as tangentially linking with the western tip of Pyramid Island. From that point it runs in a straight line just west of due north to the western tip of Kenya's Ilemba Island.[27]

On 13 March 2009, several government ministers, including the foreign-affairs ministers of both states successfully reached an agreement in Kampala, Uganda guaranteeing the right of fishermen from both states to continue conducting business as usual, until the boundary was determined by experts. They also agreed on Ugandan police troop withdrawal from Migingo. In reality both Ugandan and Kenyan police departments have since occupied the island at various times since 2004.

Negotiations in late March 2009 ended in deadlock and the Kenyan delegation demanded that Uganda withdraw its police. The joint verification team of surveyors that was appointed by both countries in 2009 to define its location also disagreed on the survey methodology and abandoned the exercise. It is, however, significant that the Presidents of both states have over time expressed confidence that the dispute, including the aspect relating to fishing rights, will be resolved amicably. In 2011 Uganda and Kenya agreed to jointly police the Migingo Island. The joint security operations marked the end of the domination of the one square acre rock by the Ugandan police since 2004. The Kenyan flag was also hoisted on the Island following the agreements.[28]

Essentially the problems in relation to the Migingo Island in Lake Victoria between Kenya and Uganda are ongoing.[29] After the latest breakout of hostilities between groups within the states, the Prime Minister of Kenya where the incident apparently occurred tried to visit the territory but was prevented from doing so. This has led to the building of new posts on the Islands. Kenya and Ethiopia eventually settled that particular matter later through diplomatic responses.

7.1.5 Eritrea–Ethiopia

The long-lasting disputes between Eritrea and Ethiopia have taken a heavy toll on the relationship between the two states. The Eritrea–Ethiopia dispute has also

---

26 See *London Gazette*, 3 March 1939, 1459.
27 "Kenya, Uganda to withdraw from disputed island: Nairobi", Reuters, 17 March 2009, available at http://af.reuters.com/article/topNews/idAFJOE52G0DI20090317, accessed 3 May 2012.
Nick Oluoch, "Uganda slaps work visas on Kenyans in Migingo", *The Standard* (Kenya) 7 March 2009, available at http://www.eastandard.net/InsidePage.php?id=1144008248&cid=159&, accessed 3 May 2012; Fred Opolot, "Migingo Island Press Release", 12 March 2009, Uganda Media Centre, available at http://www.mediacentre.go.ug/details.php?catId=3&item=343, accessed 3 May 2012.
28 Risedel Kasasira, "Uganda, Kenya Reach Accord Over Rocky Migingo Island", *The Monitor*, available at http://allafrica.com/stories/201108240819.html, accessed 28 April 2012.
29 Reuben Olita, "Kenya: Moi Speaks Out on Migingo Dispute", *The New Vision*, 18 May 2009, http://allafrica.com/stories/200905190177.html (accessed 23 December 2010).

been a source of deep concern for states in the region and indeed the international community. A very strong and unfortunate feature of this dispute in comparison with other boundary disputes in the region and elsewhere in Africa has been the militarisation of the dispute and the borders between both states. Consistent with the provisions of the Framework Agreement and the Agreement on Cessation of Hostilities, the parties reaffirm the principle of respect for the borders existing at independence as stated in resolution AHG/Res. 16(1) adopted by the OAU Summit in Cairo in 1964. In this regard they agreed to determine their common boundary on the basis of pertinent colonial treaties and applicable international law. The parties also agreed that a neutral Boundary Commission composed of five members shall be established with a mandate to delimit and demarcate the colonial treaty border based on pertinent colonial treaties (1900, 1902 and 1908) and applicable international law. The Commission was expressly forbidden from making decisions *ex aequo et bono*.

The Eritrea–Ethiopia Boundary Commission delivered its Decision on Delimitation of the Border between Eritrea and Ethiopia to representatives of the two governments on Saturday, 13 April 2002.[30] Similar to the Nigerian situation, the delimitation attained by the demarcators of the EEBC produced a situation whereby large numbers of people were cut off from their rivers, farms and other means of livelihood. Despite this fact, the EEBC stated in paragraph 14A of the Commission's Demarcation Directions of 8 July 2002 that with respect to the division of towns and villages:

> The Commission has no authority to vary the boundary line. If it runs through and divides a town or village, the line may be varied only on the basis of an express request agreed between and made by both Parties.[31]

What, however, is increasingly clear is that the implementation of the Eritrea–Ethiopia Decision has suffered serious prevarication and increasing reluctance of the parties to cooperate with the commission in the demarcation phase of its work. A view has it that this is mainly as a result of Ethiopian dissatisfaction with the loss of parts of its territory.[32] Notably after five years of the award Ethiopia

---

30 The Commission's Eritrea/Ethiopia Boundary (Merits), Decision on Delimitation, 13 April 2002 was followed by demarcation arrangements, paralleled by the Eritrea/Ethiopia Boundary (Interpretation) Decision of 24 June 2002, which dismissed Ethiopia's Request for Interpretation of the former Decision, as well as by the Eritrea/Ethiopia (Interim Measures) and Eritrea/Ethiopia (Demarcation) Orders of 17 July 2002, and the Eritrea/Ethiopia (Determinations) Decision of 7 November 2002. Copies of all of the Commission's Decisions were deposited with the Secretaries-General of the African Union (formerly the OAU) and the United Nations. For the texts and related UN Statements, see the websites of the PCA (www.pca-cpa.org) and of the United Nations (www.un.org/NewLinks/eebcarbitration).
31 Eritrea–Ethiopia Boundary Commission, Observations, 21 March 2003, published as an addendum to the Progress Report of the Secretary-General on Ethiopia and Eritrea, UN doc. S/2003/257, 6 March 2003. (www.pca-cpa.org/PDF/Obs.EEBC.pdf).
32 John Donaldson and Martin Pratt, "International Boundary Developments International Boundary Developments in 2003", 9 *Geopolitics* (2004), pp. 501–03; "Ethiopian, Eritrean Border

accused Eritrea of sending troops across the boundary, 'with the express aim of destabilizing Ethiopia'.[33] The parties have also expressed concern that with the levels of hostilities between them it is still unlikely that the United Nations Mission in Ethiopia and Eritrea (UNMEE) will not be able to ensure sufficient security within the Temporary Security Zone set up along the boundary for the demarcation to take place. There is no effective buffer zone in place and the two armies remain at least in the words of the Ethiopian governments 'eyeball to eyeball'.[34]

7.1.6 Sudan–South Sudan border disputes

After the split between North and South Sudan in 2012, South Sudan became Africa's newest nation state. Yet the entire boundary between the two Sudans is neither delimited nor demarcated. While a series of agreements were signed in Addis Ababa on 27 September 2012, the status of the contested areas of the boundary and particularly the explosive question of Abyei has been largely unresolved. Oil reserves and some of the most fertile land between the two countries are in the contested zones. Seasonal pastoralist routes that cut across and are between both states are some of the central tensions between the two states.

The disputes between Sudan and South Sudan are, thus, multifaceted and have had a long period of gestation. The problems have become compounded in certain border areas where the presence of strategic mineral resources has become a catalyst for national contestation over border demarcation. The Sudan Comprehensive Peace Agreement (CPA) that was concluded in January 2005 ended more than 20 years of civil war between the Government of Sudan and the Sudan People's Liberation Movement (SPLM). However despite its commitment to the CPA, the Government of Sudan opted not to implement the Abyei Protocol, one of the six protocols of the agreement. While the Government of Sudan rejected the report of the Abyei Boundaries Commission (ABC), the SPLM accepted it as final and binding as per the provisions of the CPA. Dispute over the CPA continued over up to four years and war ensued in the Abyei Area leading to massive displacement and loss of innocent lives. In an effort to avoid further conflict, the parties agreed to take their dispute to the Permanent Court of Arbitration (PCA). The Abyei Arbitration Tribunal issued its final and binding decision over the boundaries of Abyei Area, but its implementation has faced enormous challenges including the reluctance by Government of Sudan to respect the award.[35]

Since the Permanent Court of Arbitration (PCA) ruling respecting the Abyei area, other areas such as Heglig (between Unity and Southern Kordofan) have

---

Conflict Resolution Deadlocked", *The Guardian* (Nigeria) available at http://community.nigeria.com/newsroom.html, accessed 12 September 2007.

33 IBRU, "Eritrea and Ethiopia agree to discuss demarcation", *Boundary News*, available at http://www.dur.ac.uk/ibru/news/boundary_news, visited 2 October 2007.

34 Ibid.

35 L.B. Deng, 'Justice in Sudan: Will the Award of the International Abyei Arbitration Tribunal be Honoured?', *Journal of Eastern African Studies* (2010), pp. 298–9.

also joined the list of significantly contested border areas, largely owing to the scale of reserves, oil infrastructure, and lack of clarity in the border demarcation process.[36] In addition to oil, the borderlands are rich in agricultural schemes (Upper Nile pick, White Nile, Blue Nile), copper and potentially uranium (Western Bahr al Ghazal/South Darfur), and gold (Mabaan/Kurmuk). As a result the civilian population living in or near the contested areas have faced grave dangers.[37] The United Nations High Commission for Refugees (UNHCR) confirmed in April 2012 that up to 35,000 people have been displaced by the Sudan/South Sudan border crisis. The areas of Heglig, Talodi and other parts of the state of South Kordofan, located in Sudan, had been particularly affected by the crisis.[38]

Multifaceted approaches have been deployed to cope with the severe nature of the dispute between North and South Sudan. Under the draft 2010–14 Peace and Security Strategy, the Intergovernmental Authority on Development (IGAD) set as a high priority the establishment of a Mediation Support Unit. IGAD has considerable experience in mediating conflicts. The Comprehensive Peace Agreement (CPA) between North and South Sudan and the current Transitional Federal Government (TFG) are two of the most notable examples of its role in mediation efforts in the region. However, currently it appears to have little institutional capacity beyond its facilitators/envoys monitoring these two peace processes.[39] The AUBP has played a strong role in managing the dispute and has developed a useful document to enable the parties achieve their task. This is in the form of introduction of the so-called Guiding Principles for the Settlement of Disputed Areas on the Sudan-South Sudan Border' African Union Border.[40]

The AUHIP led by former South African president Thabo Mbeki has been assisting the parties to come to pacific settlement of the various contentious issues. In June 2010, the parties signed the Mekele Memorandum of Understanding. The agreement established 'cluster groups' to address the remaining CPA issues, facilitated and overseen by President Mbeki and the AUHIP. The

---

36 Arrangements regarding the Melut basin in a politically fractured Upper Nile State, not currently contested, are likely to be of increasing importance as its relative share of Sudan's oil production continues to grow vis-à-vis the Muglad basin.
37 Concordis, "More than a Line: Sudan's North-South Border", *Concordis International Sudan Report*, September 2010, pp. 9, 10 and 94, at http://www.usip.org/files/Grants-Fellows/GrantsDownloadsNotApps/More%20than%20a%20line,%20Sudan's%20N-S%20border,%20092010.pdf, accessed 15 April 2012.
38 UN agency: "35,000 People Displaced by Sudan/South Sudan Border Crisis", PANA Press Release 0- PANA AA/MA, 24 April 2012, available at http://www.panapress.com/UN-agency--35,000-people-displaced-by-Sudan-South-Sudan-border-crisis--12-826692-101-lang2-index.html, accessed 3 May 2012. See also Ulf Laessing and Alexander Dziadosz, "South Sudan Withdraws from Oil Area, Easing Border Crisis", available at http://af.reuters.com/article/topNews/idAFJOE83K01I2012042, accessed 5 May 2012.
39 L. Matshenyego Fisher, Sarjoh Bah, A. Mniema, H.N. Okome, M. Tamba, J. Frederiksen, A. Abdelaziz, R. Reeve, "African Peace and Security Architecture (APSA) 2010 Assessment Study" (Addis Ababa: AU Secretariat), pp. 54–5. Held on File.
40 AUBP Programme Document, Held on File. See also A. I. Asiwaju "Overarching Inter-Governmental Frameworks: Comparative Reflections on Nigeria's Tested Mechanisms", *Sudan Border Management and Security*: *Concordis Briefing* No. 1, June 2011.

cluster groups cover: Citizenship; Security; Financial, Economic and Natural Resources; and International Treaties and Legal Issues.[41] In addition various friendly states and groupings of donors have been helping the parties to cope with the disputes surrounding the breakup of North and South Sudan including their border disputes.[42]

7.2 West African boundaries and borders disputes

The geopolitical definition of West Africa includes the seventeen current members of the Economic Community of West African States (ECOWAS): Benin, Burkina Faso, Island of Cape Verde, Gambia, Ghana, Guinea, Guinea-Bissau, Ivory Coast, Liberia, Mali, Mauritania, Niger, Nigeria, Island of Saint Helena, Senegal, Sierra Leone and Togo. The United Nations official record of Africa describes West Africa as comprising of an area of approximately 6.1 million square km which in addition to the member states of ECOWAS includes Mauritania (which withdrew from ECOWAS in 1999) and the island of Saint Helena, a British overseas territory in the South Atlantic Ocean.[43] West African states have a very lively history of litigation at the ICJ on boundary-related matters. It is also true that some of the most significant maritime boundary disputes are likely to come from this region given the pre-eminent position of the West African coastline on the Gulf of Guinea.

The sub-regional zone consisting of Senegal–Gambia–Guinea-Bissau has experienced many issues of insecurity sometimes involving secessionist groups. Gambia and Guinea-Bissau have for long attempted to stem separatist violence, cross-border raids, and arms smuggling into their countries from Senegal's Casamance region. In 2006, they respectively accepted 6,000 and 10,000 Casamance residents fleeing the conflict. Approximately 2,500 Guinea-Bissau residents fled into Senegal in 2006 to escape armed confrontations along the border.[44] Sierra Leone disputes

---

41 The details of the agreement can be found at: http://www.cmi.no/sudan/doc/?id=1283, accessed 23 February 2012. House of Lords, "The EU's Conflict Prevention and Peace-keeping role in Sudan", Written Evidence Foreign Affairs, Defence and Development Policy (Sub-Committee C), Memorandum by the Associate All Party Group on Sudan (SUD 11). Note from the Associate All Party Group on Sudan, 21 March 2011, p. 11. Available at http://www.sipri.org/research/armaments/transfers/publications/other_publ/other%20publications/SudanWrittenEvidence.pdf, accessed 13 April 2012.
42 The EU has a close relationship with the African Union on Sudan and has provided financial and technical assistance to the AUHIP. This support has been provided through the EU's Instrument for Stability. The EU has provided experts for six months each (extendable) to the AUHIP: one expert each in minority rights, security and borders. However, the AUHIP requested an economic advisor instead of a borders expert; ibid. p. 15. The GTZ has also been at the forefront of assistance to the two states.
43 For more information on ECOWAS see supra note 6; see United Nations Statistics Division, "Composition of Macro Geographical (continental) Regions, Geographical Sub-regions, and Selected Economic and other Groupings", available at http://millenniumindicators.un.org/unsd/methods/m49/m49regin.htm, accessed on 29 August 2014.
44 See Globalsecurity.org, "International Disputes", available at http://www.globalsecurity.org/military/world/war/disputes-s.htm, accessed 23 April 2012.

Guinea's definition of the flood plain limits and holds the view that it includes the left bank boundary of the Makona and Moa rivers. Sierra Leone considers this claim excessive and protests Guinea's continued occupation of these lands, including the hamlet of Yenga, occupied since 1998. The zone indeed has many dormant disputes and a number of unresolved boundary situations. The location of the Benin–Niger–Nigeria tripoint is unresolved and a number of Gulf of Guinea maritime delimitations are yet to be achieved.

Perhaps the most crucial framework for preventing and addressing conflict and disputes in the region is the ECOWAS Conflict Prevention Framework (ECPF).[45] For instance, the strategies reported to have been very useful in helping Burkina Faso and Mali to resolve their border issues amicably include resorting to ECOWAS processes. Conflict prevention in this context involves (a) operational prevention, including early warning, mediation, conciliation, preventive disarmament and preventive deployment using interactive means, such as good offices and the ECOWAS Standby Force; and (b) structural prevention, often elaborated under peace-building initiatives and comprising political, institutional (governance) and developmental reforms, capacity enhancement and advocacy on the culture of peace.

Furthermore the Protocol relating to the Mechanism for Conflict Prevention, Management, Resolution, Peace-Keeping and Security has been useful in dousing some of the boundary conflicts in the region. An ECOWAS inter-departmental committee may be seised of matters quite early to determine facts in relation to a boundary dispute. The provision in Article 69 which allows decentralised ECOWAS institutions such as the 'Panel of the Wise' to be involved in the design, implementation and monitoring of cross-border initiatives means that they can also be mandated to be involved in resolving boundary problems widely construed. ECOWAS, under the framework of its ECPF, has also reduced tensions of cross-boundary nature by establishing community projects, including community 'peace radio stations', social, health and educational centres, to serve as rallying points for inter-communal and cross-border issues and especially on resource governance. During ongoing border conflicts the community radio stations may continue to operate and report on legitimate issues. In situations such as when Nigeria closed its borders with Niger in February 2012 to forestall entry of suspected terrorists, the ECOWAS Free Movement Directorate becomes particularly concerned. ECOWAS indeed worked assiduously behind the scenes to bring the situation back to normalcy.

Sometimes border tensions in this area have arisen out of the actions of private persons and groups. Senegal and Gambia had problems involving transport unions that were at loggerheads and one of the Unions wanted a border between both states closed. The border was indeed briefly closed but the situation was brought under control by close involvement of ECOWAS.

---

45 Regulation MSC/REG.1/01/08, "The ECOWAS Conflict Prevention Framework", available at http://www.comm.ecowas.int/dept/index.php?id=p_p1_commission&lang=en, accessed 14 March 2012.

In the event of outright outbreak of military hostilities ECOWAS has a rich history of employing peacekeeping forces. During the life of the Liberian War with its attendant cross-border rebel activity, ECOWAS implemented a peace plan and set up a committee to facilitate the restoration of normalcy in the border areas of Sierra Leone and Liberia. The Committee requested and secured agreement that all hostile forces should be withdrawn immediately from the territory of Sierra Leone and created a buffer zone on the Liberian side of the border which was monitored by ECOMOG. In the Agreement between the Government of Guinea-Bissau and the Self-Proclaimed Military Junta (1998), ECOMOG deployed an interposition force to guarantee security along the Guinea-Bissau–Senegal border, in order to keep the warring parties apart and guarantee free access to the affected population by humanitarian organisations and the agencies concerned.

7.2.1 Cameroon–Nigeria: land and maritime dispute

This dispute led to one of the most celebrated cases concerning Africa emanating from the Bench of the World Court in recent years. We will be looking at the entire case and the implementation process designed for it by the parties below. This would constitute our case study for the adjudicative route for the settlement of boundary disputes. Relations between Cameroon and Nigeria have long been strained due to problems along their common border, which is approximately 2,000 kilometres long and extends from Lake Chad to the sea. These problems were aggravated by the mutual challenge of sovereignty over the Bakassi Peninsula and Lake Chad. On 29 March 1994 the Republic of Cameroon filed an Application in the Registry of the Court instituting proceedings against the Federal Republic of Nigeria.[46] The questions posed to the Court were:

(i) Does the Bakassi Peninsula with an estimated population of 156,000 people belong to Nigeria or Cameroon?
(ii) Do the 33 disputed Nigerian Villages in the Lake Chad Area (with an estimated population of 60,000 people) belong to Nigeria or Cameroon?
(iii) Do the existing boundary treaties and other instruments adequately define the land boundary between the two countries from Lake Chad to the sea?
(iv) Where does the maritime boundary between Nigeria and Cameroon lie?
(v) Would the Court grant Cameroon's plea that Nigeria should pay some reparations relating to alleged wrongful acts concerning the boundary issues?

---

46 See Land and Maritime Boundary between Cameroon and Nigeria (*Cameroon v Nigeria: Equatorial Guinea Intervening*), Judgment, Preliminary Objections [1998] ICJ 2, 11 June 1998 (www.worllii.org/int/cases/ICJ/1998/2.html); Request for Interpretation of the Judgment of 11 June 1998 in the Case Concerning the Land and Maritime Boundary between Cameroon and Nigeria (*Cameroon v Nigeria*), Preliminary Objections (*Nigeria v Cameroon*) (www.icj-cij.org/icjwww/idocket/icn/icnjudgment/icn_ijudgment_19990325_frame.htm); Land and Maritime Boundary between Cameroon and Nigeria (*Cameroon v Nigeria: Equatorial Guinea Intervening*), Judgment, Merits, 10 October 2002 (www.icj-cij.org/icjwww/idocket/icnjudgment).

In answering the above questions, the Court addressed the various issues in the following sequence viz.:

i. Lake Chad area
ii. land boundary
iii. Bakassi Peninsula
iv. maritime boundary
v. state responsibility.

Their Excellencies former President Olusegun Obasanjo, former Secretary-General of the United Nations, Mr Kofi Annan and President Paul Biya of Cameroon in the adopted Communiqué of 15 November 2002, set up a 'Mixed Commission' to: consider the implications of the decision of the two Presidents and the Secretary-General of the United Nations; protect the rights of the affected populations; and demarcate the land boundary between the two countries.[47]

The Mixed Commission found it necessary to establish the following sub-committees to handle the various facets of its assignments:

i. sub-commission on affected populations
ii. sub-commission on demarcation
iii. Joint technical team (JTT)
iv. Working group on maritime boundary
v. Mixed Commission observer personnel
vi. Working Group on the withdrawal and transfer of authority.

The inaugural meeting of the Mixed Commission was held from 2–3 December 2002 in Yaoundé. The Mixed Commission has met about 50 times (as at 2013). Despite the existence of a judgment on this case the dispute continues in some important respects not least because the governments of both states continue to face intermittent pressures from dissatisfied sections of the affected populations that still find portions of the judgment unacceptable. This is particularly true of the Nigerian Bakassi population now carved out of the country by virtue of the ICJ judgment. Manifestation of this dissatisfaction includes intermittent calls on the government of Nigeria to seek review of the ICJ judgment.[48]

---

47 For critical views of the Court's judgment in this case, as well as wider enquiries into the theme that Eurocentric international courts and tribunals are ill-suited for the task of resolution of African boundary and territorial dispute, see Gbenga Oduntan, "Africa Before the International Courts: The Generational Gap in International Adjudication and Arbitration", Vol. 5 *Journal of World Investment and Trade*, No.6 (December 2004), p. 975.
48 Tobi Soniyi, "Bakassi: Nigeria Can Still Seek Review of ICJ Judgement, Insists NBA", *This Day*, 1 Sep 2012, available at http://www.thisdaylive.com/articles/bakassi-nigeria-can-still-seek-review-of-icj-judgement-insists-nba/123778/ accessed 28 August 2014; Anon, "Senator faults ICJ judgment on Bakassi", *Premium Times* available at https://www.premiumtimesng.com/news/100801-senator-faults-icj-judgment-on-bakassi.html#sthash.kTRMbny0.dpbs, accessed 28 August 2014.

7.2.2 Gabon and Equatorial Guinea: territorial disputes on the Island of Mbanié

The maritime and territorial dispute between Gabon and Equatorial Guinea centres upon the ownership of three islands in Corisco Bay: Mbanié, Cocotiers and Congas. The Corisco border dispute was resolved by an agreement signed with the help of UN mediation in January 2004 but the small island of Mbanié and potentially oil-rich waters surrounding it remain contested. The case was submitted to the International Court of Justice.[49] The territorial dispute over the Island of Mbanié had a long period of gestation. The dispute resurfaced in 2003 between both states in connection with the island of Mbanié. Mbanié is actually a very small island (about 30 hectares) located in the Bay of Corisco to Gabon, about 30 kilometers from Pointe Mdombo. Several claims to the Island have been made by Equatorial Guinea, even though Mbanié is alleged to have been attributed to Gabon by an agreement between the two countries in September 1974. Equatorial Guinea appeared later to challenge the validity of the agreement. This very complex dispute is further exacerbated by the supposed presence of important oil fields near Mbanié. The waters around the islands are believed to be rich in hydrocarbons. Fortunately, the two Central African states have agreed to jointly exploit the area until the dispute has been resolved.

Strategies adopted for managing and resolving this dispute has included direct negotiations between the heads of states of both states, and other high level meetings between the states.[50] The dispute was also submitted to the Secretary-General of the United Nations, who appointed a special representative in the person of an eminent Canadian lawyer, Mr Yvon Fortier, to attempt a mediation of the dispute. President Obiang, of Gabon for a while also canvassed the possibility of contesting the claims before an international judicial body.

7.2.3 Burkina Faso–Niger frontier dispute

Burkina Faso and Niger suffered a long-lasting dispute over their common border involving over 650km. Origins of the dispute relate to the imprecise delimitation of the boundary between both states as attempted during colonial times. The central portion of the boundary between the two states was initially delimited in accordance with two French administrative arrêtés in 1927. Both states were, however, unable to agree upon the interpretation of the content of the arrêtés. The 1987 agreement between Burkina Faso and Niger contained a provision that if the arrêtés proved insufficient to demarcate the boundary on the ground,

---

49 US Department of State, "Background Note: Equatorial Guinea", available at http://www.state.gov/r/pa/ei/bgn/7221.htm, accessed 29 May 2012.
50 MENAS Borders, "Ban Meets Gabon, Equatorial Guinea Leaders on Border Dispute", 28 February 2011, http://menasborders.blogspot.com/2011/02/ban-meets-gabon-equatorial-guinea.html, accessed 28 April 2012; Antoine Lawson, "Gabon and Equatorial Guinea to End Land Row", *IOL News*, 23 January 2005, available at http://www.iol.co.za/news/africa/gabon-and-equatorial-guinea-to-end-land-row-1.232134, accessed 28 April 2012.

the demarcation should be guided by the line depicted on the 1960 edition of the 1:200,000 topographic map series by the *Institut Géographique National*. The dispute was on 20 July 2010 submitted to the ICJ in order for the Court to determine the course of the Burkina Faso–Niger boundary based on the description of the line in the 1927 arrêtés, supplemented by the 1960 versions of the 1:200,000 IGN maps.[51]

7.2.4 Benin–Niger frontier dispute

The Republic of Benin and the Republic of Niger had on April 1994 entered into an agreement creating a joint commission for the delimitation of their common boundary. Upon unsuccessful negotiations the two states by a joint letter of notification dated 11 April 2002 transmitted to the Registrar on 3 May 2002 a Special Agreement whereby the governments of the two states agreed to submit to a Chamber of the Court a dispute concerning 'the definitive delimitation of the whole boundary between them'. The dispute was over a decade old by the time it was submitted by the parties to the ICJ for adjudication. Their request was that the Court should '(a) determine the course of the boundary between the Republic of Benin and the Republic of Niger in the River Niger sector; (b) specify which state owns each of the islands in the said river, and in particular Lété Island; (c) determine the course of the boundary between the two states in the River Mekrou sector.'

The parties agreed that the course of the common boundary to be determined by the Chamber of the Court should be in accordance with the *uti possidetis* principle by reference to the physical situation to which French colonial law applied and as the situation in a geophysical sense was as at the dates of independence. Neither of the parties was able to provide convincing evidence of their title. The Chamber as a result paid particular attention to *effectivités* as the basis to determine the course of the river frontier. The dispute between Niger and Benin was resolved by the ICJ in 2005 in Niger's favour. On the basis of evidence, the Chamber took the view that the main navigable channel of the River Niger was considered by both sides to be the boundary and administrative boundary was accordingly exercised. In relation to the River Mekrou, the Chamber recalled the principle of 'thalweg as the boundary' when the watercourse is navigable and 'to the median line between the banks when it is not' expressed in the *Kaskili/Sedudu Island case* (Botswana–Namibia).[52] Accordingly the view was taken that the river did not appear to be navigable. A boundary following the median line of the Mekrou was then decided upon as the boundary between Benin and Niger in that sector.

---

51 The two identified endpoints the Court was invited to decide upon are the survey pillar at Tong Tong (14 deg 25' 04"N, 00 deg 12' 47"E) in the north to the Boutou curve in the south (12 deg 36' 18" N, 01 deg 52' 07"E); Julius Martin Thaler, "Burkina Faso and Niger Refer Border Dispute to International Court of Justice", http://web.worldbank.org/WBSITE/EXTERNAL/TOPICS/EXTLAWJUSTICE/0,,contentMDK:22685713~pagePK:148956~piPK:149081~theSitePK:445634,00.html, accessed 28 April 2012.
52 ICJ Reports 1999 (II), p. 1062 para 24. See also Junwu Pan, *Toward a New Framework for Peaceful Settlement of China's Territorial and Boundary Disputes* (Leiden: Martinus Nijhoff, 2009), pp. 204–6.

7.3 North Africa: boundary disputes and contested territories

The northernmost region of Africa includes seven countries or territories: Algeria, Egypt, Libya, Morocco, Sudan, Tunisia and Western Sahara. The Maghreb is used as a sub-classification to refer to Algeria, Morocco, Tunisia, Libya and often Mauritania, all members of the Arab Maghreb Union, formed in 1989. Sudan and Egypt comprise the Nile Valley (named after the Nile River, with its two tributaries, the White Nile and Blue Nile). Egypt is Africa's only transcontinental country because of the Sinai Peninsula, which is part of West Asia. North Africa also includes a number of contested Spanish possessions, Ceuta and Melilla (which are very small exclaves or islets off the coast of Morocco which are politically controlled by Spain). It may be considered notable that in older maps and writings the Canary Islands and the Portuguese Madeira Islands, in the North Atlantic Ocean northwest of the African mainland are sometimes included in representations of the region. A school of thought postulates that North Africa rather than East Africa served as the exit point for the modern people who first trekked out of the continent in the Out of Africa migration.[53]

Border tensions, boundary and territorial disputes are rife in the region of North Africa. Sometimes the boundary problems are further complicated by personal antipathies, ideological antagonisms and differing alignments with bases outside the region. In the case of the struggle over the decolonisation and final disposition of the Western Sahara, all the above features seemingly come into play almost at once and with great intensity.[54] The North African region may be broadly described to include Mauritania in the West and Libya in the East. These have involved largely the states within the Union du Maghreb Arabe, AMU. It appears that four of the five states in the area have indeed been heavily involved in the Western Sahara conflict. The fight over territory at many points in their post-colonial history involved Morocco and Mauritania against the Polisario Front, while Libya and Algeria have intervened in favour of the Saharan National Liberation Movement. The AMU is in fact rendered inactive and frozen due to deep political and economic disagreements between Morocco and Algeria regarding, among other matters, the issue of Western Sahara.[55]

Algeria and many other states reject Moroccan administration of Western Sahara; the Polisario Front, exiled in Algeria, represents the Sahrawi Arab

---

53 See United Nations Statistics Division, op. cit.; Krista E. Wiegand, *Enduring Territorial Disputes: Strategies of Bargaining, Coercive Diplomacy, and Settlement* (Georgia: University of Georgia Press, 2011), pp. 195–6. See also Tanya M. Smith, Paul Tafforeau, Donald J. Reid, Rainer Grün, Stephen Eggins, Mohamed Boutakiout, Jean-Jacques Hublin, "Earliest Evidence of Modern Human Life History in North African Early Homo Sapiens", vol. 104, *Proceedings of the National Academy of Sciences of the United States of America*, No. 15, 10 April 2007.
54 John Damis, "The Western Sahara Dispute as a Source of Regional Conflict in North Africa", *Contemporary North Africa: Issues of Development and Integration*, p. 137.
55 *La Première Edition des Jeux de la CEN-SAD en Février 2009 au Niger*, APANEWS, 17 June 2008; "Maiden CEN-SAD Games Ends in Glory in Niamey", APA News. 15 February 2009.

Democratic Republic; Algeria's border with Morocco remains an irritant to their bilateral relations, with each state accusing the other of harbouring militants and condoning the activity of arms smuggling. Dormant disputes in this area include Libyan claims of about 32,000 sq km that are still reflected on its maps of south-eastern Algeria. Libya also claims against Niger about 25,000 sq km in a currently dormant dispute in the Tommo region. The Algerian National Liberation Front (FLN) also maintains assertions of a claim to Chirac Pastures in south-eastern Morocco.[56] Sudan claims, but Egypt *de facto* administers, security and economic development of Halaib region north of the 22nd parallel boundary. However, Egypt no longer shows its administration of the Bir Tawil trapezoid in Sudan on its maps;[57] the FLN's assertions of a claim to Chirac Pastures in south-eastern Morocco is a dormant dispute.

Aside from the severe disagreement over the Sahrawi Arab Democratic Republic, another notable feature of North African Boundaries has been the occurrence of disputes with states outside of the African continent. For instance, Egypt and Saudi Arabia are in dispute over Egyptian-administered islands of Tiran and Sanafir. Gazan breaches in the security wall with Egypt in January 2008 highlight difficulties in monitoring the Israeli–Sinai border. Morocco and Spain also remain at loggerheads over Plazas de Soberanía – formerly known as Spanish North Africa. The Morocco–Spain dispute over coastal enclaves and certain islands involves unresolved territorial sovereignty. Morocco continues to protest Spain's control over the coastal enclaves of Ceuta, Melilla and Penon de Velez de la Gomera, the islands of Penon de Alhucemas and Islas Chafarinas, as well as their surrounding waters. Both countries also claim Isla Perejil (Leila Island) and discussions have not progressed on a comprehensive maritime delimitation. Delimitation is needed in these areas to set limits on resource exploration and refugee interdiction, since Morocco's 2002 rejection of Spain's unilateral designation of a median line from the Canary Islands. It continues to be alleged that Morocco serves as one of the primary launching areas of illegal migration into Spain from North Africa. Morocco's uncooperative attitude vis-à-vis Spain is not very surprising as non-cooperation to optimal levels over immigration and policing matters is a usual fall-out of boundary problems between states.

7.4 Southern Africa: boundary disputes and contested territories

The sub-region of Southern Africa is constituted by the countries occupying the southernmost region of the African continent. The list of countries in the region is variably defined by geography and geopolitics. According to the United Nations

---

56 Index Mundi, "Morocco Disputes–international", available at http://www.indexmundi.com/morocco/disputes_international.html, accessed 29 April 2012.
57 See *CIA World Fact Book* available at https://www.cia.gov/library/publications/the-world-factbook/fields/2070.html.

classifications the region consists principally of Botswana, Lesotho, Namibia, South Africa and Swaziland. However, by virtue of membership in the SADC which was established in 1980 to facilitate cooperation in the region, the region also includes the following independent states: Angola, Democratic Republic of the Congo, Madagascar, Malawi, Mauritius, Mozambique, Seychelles, Tanzania, Zambia and Zimbabwe.[58]

The boundary disputes in the southern Africa region are some of the most extensive in the African continent. Some of them have remained intractable for a long period of time running into decades. The Namibia–South Africa border dispute over the Orange River has been described as one of the oldest boundary disputes in the world. The disputes range from boundary alignment issues (the Democratic Republic of Congo accuses Angola of shifting monuments)[59] to territorial and border disputes. A notable feature of this region is that one single state may have several boundary disputes and tensions with many states at once, yet some of the most inspiring innovative approaches to shared resources and natural features in Africa such as water bodies and wildlife parks are also to be found in the region. To illustrate, example may be made of how Namibia has had to carefully negotiate various concessions with its neighbours. There are concerns from international experts and local populations over Namibian exploitation of the Okavango River and its effects on the Okavango Delta ecology in Botswana.[60] Similar problems of environmental impact are raised with respect to human displacement and indeed this scuttled Namibian plans to construct a hydroelectric dam on Popa Falls along the Angola–Namibia border. Namibia managed a dispute with South Africa over the location of the boundary in the Orange River. Namibia has supported, and in 2004 Zimbabwe dropped objections to, plans between Botswana and Zambia to build a bridge over the Zambezi River, thereby *de facto* recognising a short, but not clearly delimited, Botswana–Zambia boundary in the river. Unresolved boundaries do in fact continue to exist along the Namibia–Zimbabwe–Zambia borders.

Maritime disputes in this area include the Tanzania–Mozambique–Comoros delimitations which have recently been resolved by direct negotiations between the parties.[61] Tanzania and Madagascar attained delimitation earlier through

---

58 McArthur, Tom, ed., "Africa", *The Oxford Companion to the English Language* (New York: Oxford University Press, 1992), p. 19; see also http://www.sadc.int.
59 *CIA World Fact Book*.
60 See further, "International Rivers: The Okavango Delta", available at http://www.internationalrivers.org/resources/the-okavango-delta-3629, accessed 30 April 2012; see also Cornelis VanderPost, Susan Ringrose and Mary Seely, "Preliminary Land-Use and Land-Cover Mapping in the Upper Okavango Basin and Implications for the Okavango Delta", Vol. 37, *Botswana Notes and Records Special Edition on Human Interactions and Natural Resource Dynamics in the Okavango Delta and Ngamiland* (2005), pp. 236–52.
61 GTZ, "Support to the African Union Border Programme" http://www.gtz.de/en/aktuell/31046.htm, accessed 30 April 2012; African Press Organisation, "Signing Ceremony of the Agreements on the Delimitation of Maritime Borders between the Union of the Comoros, the Republic of Mozambique and the United Republic of Tanzania", available at http://appablog.wordpress.

an Agreement between both states which was concluded on 28 December 1988 in Maputo.[62]

7.4.1 Swaziland–South Africa

The antecedents of this dispute, like many others in the region, arose out of the history of colonialism and its interactions and permutations with the indigenous lands and people. Swaziland lays claim to large swatches of South African land that surrounds and nearly enclaves her on three sides. Swaziland historically has protested at the way British colonial authorities ceded or gifted half of the nation's territory away to Britain's Indian Ocean Natal colony and the Boer Republics (both in present-day South Africa) in the late nineteenth century. British miners and Boer farmers laid claim to Swazi territory in the late nineteenth century. By 1902, Britain had portioned off large sections of land previously ruled by Swazi kings into the Boer Republic of Transvaal (today's Mpumalanga Province) and Britain's Natal Province, leaving the landlocked territory that today remains as Swaziland. The dispute between Swaziland and South Africa is one of those African territorial disputes that has a very long gestation but nevertheless receives sparse and sporadic political attention from the concerned parties. In essence, Swaziland claims large parts of what is currently South African territory (Mpumulanga and parts of KwaZulu-Natal (KZN) including Durban) on the grounds of historical title and existence of a large population of Swazi-speaking people. While successive, recent South African governments appear to have been dismissive of Swazi claims as not serious, it is unlikely that this dispute will go away without some form of comprehensive and systematic negotiated solution. For instance, there has not been a single bilateral session on this since 2006. Swaziland on its part appears to be growing impatient with the slow response of South Africa to the contested territories. As a Swazi prince explained; 'This is Swazi land, historically and culturally. We have had commitments in the past from South African governments, most notably Nelson Mandela, that the matter will be resolved. But since [President] Thabo Mbeki took office, there has been silence from Pretoria'.[63] According to Swaziland, the areas involved consist of lands illegally confiscated during the colonial era and later on allegedly wrongfully incorporated into South Africa.

---

com/2011/12/07/signing-ceremony-of-the-agreements-on-the-delimitation-of-maritime-borders-between-the-union-of-the-comoros-the-republic-of-mozambique-and-the-united-republic-of-tanzania, accessed 30 April 2012.

62 In Mozambique this agreement was ratified by the People's Assembly through Resolution No. 11/89, 18 September 1989, Published in the *Official Journal*, No. 37, 1st Serial, 6th Supplement. See also Elisio Benedito Jamine, *Maritime Boundaries Delimitation, Management and Disputes Resoultion Delimitation of the Mozambique Maritime Boundaries with Neighbouring States (including the Extended Continental Shelf) and the Management of Ocean Issues* (United Nations, NY, USA: Division for Ocean Affairs and the Law of the Sea Office of Legal Affairs), p. 11 available at http://www.un.org/depts/los/nippon/unnff_programme_home/fellows_pages/fellows_papers/jamine_0607_mozambique.pdf accessed 4 May 2012.

63 Prince Khuzulwandle, brother to King Mswati III, quoted in IRIN, "Swaziland: Land Claim Falls on Deaf SA Ears", Mbabane, 16 June 2003, available at http://www.irinnews.org/fr/report/44343/swaziland-land-claim-falls-on-deaf-sa-ears, accessed 24 May 2014.

So far several national diplomatic and technical institutions have addressed the issue and these include high level bilateral meetings. The Swazi Border Adjustment Committee was set up in 1994 (although even this committee meets infrequently). The Mbeki administration's decision to consider Swaziland's border adjustment claim gave the claims more visibility in diplomatic terms. The territory under contestation by Swaziland consists of three sections, the first being the KaNgwane area which extends up to 40km from Swaziland's west to the northeast border.

Second is the territory consisting Ngavuma, the whole of which is in dispute. The significance of this claim if successfully maintained is that Swaziland would as a result become a coastal state and would no longer be a landlocked country, but would abut the Indian Ocean. Swaziland would, thus encompass what is now South Africa's KwaZulu-Natal Province south from the Mozambique border to Lake Sibaya.

Third, Swaziland lays claim to a 65km by 30km banana-shaped strip, known as the Nsikazi Area. The area in dispute extends northwards from the White River in South Africa's northern Mpumalanga Province. A unique feature of this claim is that the contested area is not physically contiguous with Swaziland or any of the other disputed lands.[64] This strip has been described as 'floating like an island of Swazidom'.

During his 60-year reign, the erstwhile Swazi King Sobhuza continuously maintained this particular claim and sought national reunification of the populations. South Africa's case is complicated by the diplomatic record of the erstwhile Apartheid regime cooperation with Swaziland on the issue during the 1980s. In an attempt to prove to the world it had an ally in a black African state the erstwhile Apartheid governments of South Africa seriously engaged with the idea of using Swaziland as a 'Bantustan' homeland of which all South African Swazis would become citizens, wherever they lived, effectively transforming them into legal aliens in the country of their birth.[65] This factor coupled with the historical fact that Swazi warriors had assisted the British to defeat neighbouring ethnic groups like the Pedi who robustly defended their lands against the colonialists may have given life to a general international disinterest in the region to assist Swaziland with its claims.[66] A government-to-government agreement was nearly concluded in 1982, but the KwaZulu legislature successfully sued to block the land transfer. The current King Swazi monarch Mswati III, sought to revive border adjustment talks upon South Africa's democratisation in 1994.

There are some interesting features of this dispute worthy of mention. Power differentials play a quite prominent role in the providence of its resolution. The determination shown by Swazi kings to continuously protest the removal of the

---

64 James Hall, "Politics. South Africa: Swaziland Seeks Border Adjustment", 13 January 2005 (Inter Press Service (IPS)) News Agency, http://www.ipsnews.net/2005/01/politics-south-africa-swaziland-seeks-border-adjustment, accessed 22 April 2014.
65 IRIN, op.cit.
66 Indeed the British did not dismantle Swazi leadership, the way they subjugated the Zulu under the Natal Colonial government. Swaziland became a British protectorate, and Swazis retained their national identity intact until independence in 1968. Hall, op.cit.

lands, and the laying of claims of ownership appears only to be matched by an apparent unwillingness by successive South African governments to seriously engage with the claims. Although flashes of interest are shown, the general impression of commentators in the region is that there is little political will to comprehensively address Swaziland's claims. It needs to be noted that the power differentials between the two states has been and is bound to continue to have an effect on the mechanics of conflict resolution of this dispute. Another interesting feature to consider in analysing this case study is the effect that massive South African investments in and around the areas subject to the dispute will have on the prospects of dispute resolution. Infrastructural development has been undertaken in recent years in the disputed Mpumalanga and KwaZulu-Natal areas. Some of the disputed areas also straddle the Lubombo Mountain Range, which has been targeted for economic revival under the Lubombo Spatial Development Initiative agreed upon by Mozambique, South Africa and Swaziland (LSDI).[67] South Africa has already spent over R73 million (US $7.3 million) on hospitals, clinics, schools and crèches, and R20 million (US $2.7 million) on new roads in KwaZulu-Natal. Under the LSDI, R80 million (US $11 million) in private investment has gone into the Greater St Lucia Wetland Park, South Africa's first World Heritage site. Significantly two new highways connecting South Africa and Mozambique pass through the disputed land.[68]

In 2006, Swazi King Mswati III advocated resorting to the ICJ to claim parts of Mpumalanga and KwaZulu-Natal from South Africa. It is suggested that mutual negotiations will be the best route for the resolution of this dispute. Of course there is the danger that as a result of the power differentials between both countries direct negotiations may be stymied irrevocably. There is, however, no reason why this must be so. South Africa would need to impose upon itself a self-enacting code of modesty for any meaningful negotiations to take place. Swaziland on the other hand cannot but be very much aware of its larger interests being a landlocked state with about 535km of boundaries with two states, Mozambique (105km) and South Africa (430km). The economic dependence of Swaziland on South Africa is manifest as it receives more than 90 per cent of its imports and up to 60 per cent of its exports also go to its larger neighbour. The Swazi currency is pegged to the South African Rand, and its government is heavily dependent on customs duties from the Southern African Customs Union (SACU), and worker remittances from South Africa which go a long way in supplementing domestically earned income. With all these in view it would appear quite unsuitable for a

---

67 The LSDI aims to maximise investment into the development of tourism, agriculture and mining industries in the region with subsequent accelerated economic and social upliftment of the local residents. Aspirations include the development of the intrinsic economical potential and sustainable employment through the concentration of investment and progression of public–private partnerships (PPPs). The protocol for the LSDI was signed in 1999 by President Mbeki, President Chissano and King Mswati III of South Africa, Mozambique and Swaziland respectively. See "Lubombo Spatial Development Initiative Maputo Province", *Annual Report 2009*, available at http://www.malaria.org.za/lsdi/Reports/2009/LSDIMaputoAnnualReport2009.pdf, accessed 24 April 2014.
68 IRIN, op.cit.

litigious route to be embarked upon particularly at the instance of Swaziland, despite its attractions as a levelling dispute resolution procedure. Mediation, conciliation, good offices and/or expert determination are also mechanisms that the parties may avail themselves of sooner rather than later as it is best that the dispute should not be allowed to fester on over the following years.

7.5 Central African states (CEMAC): boundary disputes

Central Africa or Middle Africa (by UN terminology) consists of the state members of the ECCAS: Angola, Burundi, Cameroon, Congo, Democratic Republic of Congo, Gabon, Equatorial Guinea, Chad, Rwanda and Sao Tome and Principe.[69] It is significant to mention that the CEMAC states do in fact share some land and maritime boundaries with ECOWAS states and some of the most interesting developments in boundary resolution and management in the last two decades have involved states from both regions.

Cameroon, for instance, maintains an ongoing joint border commission with Nigeria that is charged with implementing the 2002 ICJ ruling on the entire land and maritime boundary between both states. The Bakassi situation has also been implemented in accordance with the Court's decision and the resulting June 2006 Greentree Agreement that finally ceded sovereignty of the Bakassi Peninsula to Cameroon with a full phase-out of Nigerian control and partition of residents in 2008. Cameroon and Nigeria agreed on maritime delimitation in March 2008. Disputes over sovereignty still persist between Equatorial Guinea and Cameroon over an island at the mouth of the Ntem River. Nigeria and Cameroon have, however, heeded the Lake Chad Commission's admonition to ratify the delimitation treaty, which also includes the Chad–Niger and Niger–Nigeria boundaries. The maritime border between Equatorial Guinea and Nigeria was settled in 2000, allowing Equatorial Guinea to continue exploitation of its oil fields and to maintain a unitisation scheme with Nigeria. Chad played a role in mediating the Darfur conflict and in 2010 it established a joint border monitoring force with Sudan, which has helped to reduce cross-border banditry and violence.

Ongoing boundary problems in the CEMAC area include location of the boundary in the broad Congo River as between Republic of Congo and the Democratic Republic of the Congo. This riparian boundary remains undefined except in the Pool Malebo–Stanley Pool area.[70] Uganda and the DRC continue to dispute over the Rukwanzi Island in Lake Albert and other areas on the Semliki River with hydrocarbon potential. A boundary commission continues discussions over a Congolese-administered triangle of land on the right bank of the Lunkinda River claimed by Zambia near the DRC.

---

69 UN Statistics Division op.cit.; U.N Economics Commission for Africa, "ECCAS – Economic Community of Central African States", available at http://www.uneca.org/oria/pages/eccas-economic-community-central-african-states-0, accessed 30 August 2014.
70 *CIA World Factbook*, "Africa: Congo, Republic of the", https://www.cia.gov/library/publications/the-world-factbook/geos/cf.html, accessed 30 April 2012.

8 Case study: the arbitral route to settlement of African boundary disputes

This chapter deals with the arbitration of the Ethiopia–Eritrea Boundary dispute, the first of three to critically evaluate celebrated boundary cases involving six African states. Our aim in Chapters 8 to 10 is to examine the dynamics of African boundary disputes through the lenses of the three leading routes of pacific dispute settlement. The three case studies differ in many respects but coalesce on the essential feature shared by most African boundary disputes which is that their origins lie in the inherent inequities of boundaries formed under colonialism. They also draw attention to the not often acknowledged fact that much of the delimitation attempted by the colonial powers of the period was quite unsuccessful even by the standards of the period. Particular attention is drawn to the sheer scale of the power and real politik characterising the international relations of the erstwhile colonial administrations of Britain, France, Germany and Italy. It is hoped that the strengths and weaknesses of the different dispute resolution routes adopted for the three different cases would emerge in the following analysis. Consideration of the combination of the facts, legal arguments, treatment of issues, diplomatic conduct and implementation processes of the cases may be of use to future researchers, boundary commissioners and dispute resolution experts in relation to Africa and other parts of the developing world.[1]

8.1 The arbitral route: the *Eritrea–Ethiopia Boundary Commission Case*

The EEBC was established as a result of the protracted Eritrea–Ethiopian border crises and in accordance with the Algiers Peace Agreement of 12 December 2000 (Art. 4).[2] The Commission's Registry is located at the PCA and the case is largely

---

1 At least two of the case studies show that the decisions imposed have been backed up by a rich practice of implementation processes and procedures. The Malawi–Tanzania dispute is still undergoing mediation.
2 Also referred to as the December Agreement. See UN Docs S/1999/32 and S/RES/1227 (1999); K. Vick, "War Erupts Along Border of Ethiopia and Eritrea", *International Herald Tribune* (IHT) of 8 February 1999, 2; "Battles Erupt on a 3d Front Between Ethiopia and Eritrea", *IHT*, 9 February 1999, 2; "Addis Ababa Rules Out Border War Cease-Fire", *IHT*, 11 February 1999, 7; K. Vick,

178 *Arbitral route to settlement*

associated with the PCA although it adopted its own Rules of Procedure and the UN Cartographer served as its Secretary.[3] The five-member *Commission* comprising Judges Stephen M. Schwebel, Bola Ajibola, Arthur Watts and W. Michael Reisman was presided over by Elihu Lauterpacht. The Commission delimited the three-sector international boundary in the milestone *Eritrea/Ethiopia Boundary (Merits)* decision delivered on 13 April 2002.[4]

The task of the Commission is prescribed in Articles 1 and 2 of the December Agreement as follows:

> the parties affirm the principle of respect for the borders existing at independence as stated in resolution AHG/Res. 16 (1) adopted by the OAU Summit in Cairo in 1964, and in this regard, that they shall be determined on the basis of pertinent colonial treaties and applicable international law.
>
> The parties agreed that a neutral Boundary Commission composed of five members shall be established with a mandate to delimit and demarcate the colonial treaty border based on pertinent colonial treaties (1900, 1902 and 1908) and applicable international law. The Commission shall not have the power to make decisions *ex aequo et bono*.

8.1.1 Synopsis of the Eritrean Case: statement submitted to the EEBC

The following is a summary of the Eritrean case as presented to the EEBC in furtherance of the prosecution of the arbitration.[5]

"Ethiopians Claim Victory in Border War with Eritrea", *IHT*, 1 March 1999, 8; S/1999/247, 250, 258–60, 696, 731, 762, 789, 794 and 857; S/2000/389, 413, 421, 422, 430, 435, 437 and 568. Note also UN Docs S/2000/610, 612, 619, 643, 676 and 793, S/PRST/2000/22 and S/RES/1312 of 31 July 2000, establishing the United Nations Mission in Ethiopia and Eritrea (UNMEE).

3 See J.-L. Péninou, "The Ethiopian-Eritrean Border Conflict", 6 *IBRU Boundary and Security Bulletin*, 46–50 (1998 No.2); Statement of the Foreign Ministers of the Five Permanent Members of the Security Council, UN Doc. S/1998/890, para.9 *in fine*, and Statements on the New Ethiopia n Map, UN Docs S/1998/956, 977 and 998. See also *100th PCA Annual Report*, para. 35 (2000) and *101st PCA Annual Report*, paras 32–4 (2001).

4 The Commission's *Eritrea/Ethiopia Boundary (Merits)* Decision on delimitation of 13 April 2002 has been followed by demarcation arrangements, paralleled by the *Eritrea/Ethiopia Boundary (Interpretation)* Decision of 24 June which dismissed Ethiopia's Request for Interpretation of the former Decision, as well as by the *Eritrea/Ethiopia (Interim Measures)* and *(Demarcation)* Orders of 17 July, and *Eritrea/Ethiopia (Determinations)* Decision of 7 November 2002. Copies of all the Commission's Decisions were deposited with the Secretaries General of the African Union (formerly OAU) and the United Nations. For the texts and related UN Statements, see websites of the PCA (www.pca-cpa.org) and UN (www.un.org/NewLinks/eebcarbitration). See also UN S/RES/1398 of 15 March 2002, which extended the UNMEE to 15 September 2002 with a view to facilitating the implementation of the *Eritrea/Ethiopia Boundary* Decision; A/57/1, para.39 (2002); S/2002/744; S/RES/1430 and A/RES/1434 of 14 August and 6 September 2002, which further extended the UNMEE until 15 March 2003; S/2002/977. See also Jon Abbink, 'Badme and the Ethiopian-Eritrean Conflict: Back to Square One?', at www.erpic.org/Badme.html.

5 Synopsis of "Eritrean Submission to The Secretary of the Boundary Commission to be created pursuant to the 12 December 2000 Agreement Between the Government of the State of Eritrea

8.1.1.1 The colonial treaty border and its origins

Eritrea expressed the view that a finding should be made by the Secretary that there is no good faith dispute between Eritrea and Ethiopia over the location of the colonial treaty border. This is because, as Eritrea has maintained for over the last century or thereabouts, Ethiopia has time and again recognised and confirmed the location of this boundary but never made claims of sovereignty over areas lying on the Eritrean side. Ethiopia is said to have accepted the colonial border in proceedings before the League of Nations during its participation in the UN process that resulted in the formation of the Ethiopian/Eritrean federation.

The 1900, 1902 and 1908 boundary conventions to which the Peace Agreement explicitly refers establish a clear boundary between Eritrea and Ethiopia. The central portion of the colonial border was fixed by the 1900 Convention, which specified a boundary following the Mereb, Belesa and Muna Rivers. The Mereb–Belesa–Muna line had been put in place as a provisional border four years earlier in the Treaty of Addis Ababa.[6] In that agreement, Italy and Ethiopia agreed to 'establish definite frontiers' and until such frontiers were established, to 'refrain from crossing the provisory frontier which shall be determined by the flow of the Mareb, Belessa and Mouna Rivers.'

The western portion of the border, near the Sudan, was fixed by the 1902 Convention. This Convention specified that the border should follow the Setit River to the Maiteb, and then proceed to the confluence of the Mai Ambessa and the Mereb. From there it continues along the Mereb–Belesa–Muna line already established by the 1900 Convention. The line connecting the Setit River to the Mereb was to be defined in such a way as to leave all Cunama territories to Eritrea.

The south-eastern portion of the border was the last to be determined. This was achieved through the 1908 Convention between Italy and Ethiopia. The border so established starts at the easternmost point of the Mereb–Belesa–Muna line and 'proceeds in a south-easterly direction, parallel to and at a distance of 60 kilometres from the coast until it joins the frontier of the French possession of Somalia' (i.e. present Djibouti).

8.1.1.2 Eritrean view of Ethiopia's practice in the League of Nations era

Eritrea pointed out that it was a condition for the admission of Ethiopia to join the League that it should have 'well-defined frontiers', and that Ethiopia's admission to membership was based on the League's findings that this condition

---

and the Government of the Federal Democratic Republic of Ethiopia", (State of Eritrea, 26 January 2001). Some of the materials refered to in this chapter are held on file by the author. They may also be consulted from the services of the Registry of the PCA in the Hague.

6 Treaty Between Italy and Abyssinia, Art. IV, 26 October 1896, reproduced in Herstlet, *The Map of Africa by Treaty 458–9* (3d edn, 1967) (App. 1, Exh. 4).

had been met.[7] Indeed when Italy, in 1935, alleged incursions from Tigray in northern Ethiopia, the League specifically affirmed that Ethiopia's border with Eritrea was fully specified by the three colonial treaties of 1900, 1902 and 1908.[8]

8.1.1.3 Ethiopia, Eritrea and the era of the United Nations

The precise question of Ethiopia's correct legal boundary with Eritrea came before the United Nations at the point when Italy relinquished its three African colonies after World War II: Eritrea, Libya and Somalia. Eritrea alleged that Ethiopia participated in the UN Secretariat process of studying the treaty border and that, like Egypt, it hoped to acquire Eritrean territory. It is, however, claimed that neither Egypt nor Ethiopia found fault with the treaty border as it then existed. Attention was drawn to a UN Secretariat report which notes quite significantly that 'Egypt and Ethiopia have claimed that at least a large part of Eritrea should be united with the Sudan or Ethiopia, respectively, but have not asked for boundary adjustments as such'.[9]

Eritrea finds it noteworthy that the Secretariat Study did identify a treaty ambiguity regarding the border between Ethiopia and the former Italian Somaliland. This is displayed in a map prepared by the Secretariat marked with rows of question marks between Ethiopia and Somalia but none between Ethiopia and Eritrea. Thus, Eritrea concluded that, 'the Secretariat Study had no doubts about the border between Ethiopia and Eritrea'.[10] When it was decided that Ethiopia and Eritrea should be united in a federation the resulting Eritrean Constitution stated *inter alia* 'the territory of Eritrea, including the islands, is that of the former Italian colony of Eritrea'.[11] Eritrea claimed that Ethiopia reconfirms its acceptance of the colonial borders when it incorporated the Eritrean Constitution into its own laws by virtue of an imperial decree of 11 September 1952, which stated, 'the territory of Eritrea, including the Islands, is that territory defined in Article 2 of the Constitution for Eritrea'.[12]

---

7 "Admission of Abyssinia to the League of Nations and Report of the Second Subcommittee of the Sixth Committee on Abyssinia's Application for Admission to the League", League of Nations Doc. A.105.1923 VII (1923) (App. 1 Exh. 7).
8 See "Report of the Council under Article 15, paragraph 4 of the Covenant, Submitted by the Committee of the Council on October 5, and adopted by the Council on October 7, 1935", in *Documents and Proceedings of the League of Nations in Regard to the Dispute Between Italy and Ethiopia, No. 1 (1935)*, PRO FO 371/19163, S6768 (App. 1, Exh).
9 See UN Secretariat, "Study of Procedures to Delimit the Boundaries of the Former Italian Colonies", at p. 7, UN Doc. A/AC.18/103 (1950) (App. 1 Exh. 10) (emphasis added).
10 Eritrean Statement, p. 8.
11 App. 1, Exh. 11.
12 "An Order to Provide for the Federal Incorporation and Inclusion of the Territory of Ethiopia Within our Empire", 12 *Negarit Gazeta*, No. 1, Order No. 6/1952 (11 September 1952) (App. 1 Exh. 13).

8.1.1.4 Eritrean view of Ethiopian administrative legislation

Eritrea's assertion is that almost immediately after the formation of the Ethiopian/Eritrean federation, Ethiopia had started violating the terms of the federal arrangement and illegally dissolved the federation and annexed Eritrea to Ethiopia, thereby setting off a war of independence that lasted until 1991. During this entire period, however, Ethiopian governments were said to have respected Eritrea's territorial boundaries.[13]

A year and a half after the 1991 defeat of the Ethiopian military government of Colonel Haile Mariam Mengistu, Ethiopia reaffirmed the historic boundary once again. This was done by adopting administrative legislation that expressly defined its internal administrative boundaries in terms of the internal administrative borders that were in effect as of 1974. These are the precise points to which Eritrea claims to have held its popular independence referendum and asserted its independence. In fact writing in 1997, eminent jurist Professor Malcolm Shaw cited Eritrea as an example of state succession to boundaries. Eritrea was a paradigm example of a succession of states in which 'the existing administrative line . . . reflected an earlier international boundary, which then resumes its former status.'[14]

8.1.1.5 Eritrean view of the period of Eritrean Independence (1993–Present)

Eritrea asserted its independence from Ethiopia in 1993, following a United Nations supervised referendum in which over 99 per cent of voters favoured this result. Eritrea maintained that cartography from Eritrea, as well as from the UN Observer Mission to the Eritrean Referendum, UNOVER, depicted the Eritrean/Ethiopian border in accordance with the three colonial treaties.

Accordingly Eritrea argued that Ethiopia must be taken as having being very well aware that these maps all depicted the colonial treaty border between Eritrea and Ethiopia. The Eritrean independence referendum was an event of tremendous significance to Ethiopia, and was closely watched by both the Ethiopian government and the Ethiopian population. It was to have been taken for granted that the Referendum would eventually lead to the re-establishment of the colonial treaty boundary between the two countries. Nonetheless, Ethiopia is said never to have suggested that it had any objections to the numerous maps that depicted the border in its familiar location.

It is noted significantly that after Eritrea became independent, Ethiopia endorsed the colonial treaty boundary in its new constitution and, repeatedly, in its official cartography. The new Ethiopian Constitution, ratified in 1994, contained an explicit definition of Ethiopia's territorial borders. The Constitution

---

13 Eritrean Statement, p. 12. See also map on p. 13: "Enlarged Excerpt from Administrative Map of Ethiopia" (Geography Division of Ethiopian Ministry of Land Reform and Administration).
14 Malcom N. Shaw, "The Heritage of States: The Principle of *Uti Possidetis Juris* Today", 67 *British Yearbook of Int'l Law* (1997) (App. 1 Exh. 16) pp. 75–154, at p. 118.

states in Article 2 that 'The territorial jurisdiction of Ethiopia shall comprise the territory of the members of the Federation and its boundaries shall be *as determined by international agreements.*' (emphasis added).[15] Quite consistent with this constitutional provision, Ethiopia's official maps in the post-Eritrean independence period are said to have shown the border with Eritrea as being the colonial treaty border.[16]

8.1.1.6 *Bilateral agreements recognising the Colonial Treaty Border*

Eritrea asserts that during the years between the formal assertion of its independence and the Ethiopian incursion into the Badme and Adi Murug/Bada regions of Eritrea in 1997, both countries had entered into numerous bilateral agreements. All of these are said to reaffirm the colonial treaty border. Examples of these supplied include a bilateral agreement for an internationally supported cooperative project to document elephant population figures and migration patterns in the Mereb–Setit border region[17] and the geological bilateral study of the 'Axum Sheet' area (this is the area containing the straight line connecting the Mereb and Setit rivers).[18]

8.1.1.7 *Assertion that Ethiopia reaffirmed the Colonial Treaty Border throughout its War on Eritrea*

Eritrea maintained that even during the entire two-year war between both countries, Ethiopia continued to represent that it had no designs on Eritrean territory. Ethiopia as a matter of fact reassured the international community about its commitment to the colonial treaty border in several ways. It is also

---

15 "A Proclamation to Pronounce the Coming into Force of the Federation of Eritrea with Ethiopia", 12 *Negarit Gazeta*, No 1, Proc. No. 1/1995 (21 August 1995; App. 1 Exh. 17).
16 To buttress this point Eritrea includes maps 10–14 on pp. 16–21 of the *Eritrean Statement*. They are: Map 10 Eritrea (UN (1996) from United Nations Department of Public Information, The UN and the Independence of Eritrea); Map 11 Ethiopia (UN, 1993; Map No. 3723 UN); Map 12: Eritrea United Nations, 2000 (Map 3790 Rev. 4 UN Dept of Public Information Cartographic Section); Map 13 Composite Maps of Boundaries of Eritrea and Ethiopia (Governments of Eritrea and Ethiopia in Cooperation with the University of Berne, 1995); Agro ecological map of Ethiopia (Ethiopian Mapping Authority and Institute of Geography, University of Berne, Switzerland, 1995); Map 14 Excerpt from Ethiopia (Ethiopian Mapping Authority, 1996).
17 See maps on p. 23. Map 15: Map of The Study Area, in Moses Litoroh, Elephant Aerial Census of South Western Eritrea and Northern Ethiopia: Report to the Governments of Eritrea and Ethiopia, The African Specialist Group and USFWS (1997); Map 16: Counting Block (Sheraro Area), in Moses Litoroh, Elephant Aerial Census of South Western Eritrea and Northern Ethiopia: Report to the Governments of Eritrea and Ethiopia, the African Specialist Group and USFWS (1997).
18 See map supplied on p. 25; Map 17: Simplified Geological Map of Axum Sheet, in Ethiopian Institute of Geological Surveys, Geology of the Axum Area (Tarekegn Tadesse, Memoir No. 9; 1997). See also Documents relating to abstracts and scientific and field excursion program, International Geological Correlation Project 348 (the Mozambique & Related Orogens) International Field Conference Held in Northern Ethiopia and Eritrea, 15–25 March 1996 (App. 1, Exh. 22).

concluded that at the end of the twentieth century, the colonial treaty border between Eritrea and Ethiopia remained precisely where it was established at the beginning of the century. Again it is concluded, 'Clearly Ethiopia has no good faith boundary dispute with Eritrea.'[19]

8.1.1.8 Arguments relating to territorial claims in derogation of the three colonial treaties

The Eritrean view of the mandate of the Boundary Commission as set out in the December 12 Agreement is that it must delimit and demarcate the colonial treaty border with reference specifically to the 1900, 1902 and 1908 treaties. Thus, Eritrea maintained that the Peace Agreement does not allow Ethiopia to submit claims in derogation of treaty rights. Indeed it is argued: 'For Ethiopia to submit claims running contrary to the three colonial treaties would be to ask the commission to exceed the authority bestowed on it by the agreements that the two countries signed.'

If however, the Commission were to deem it fit to accept that Ethiopian arguments running contrary to the three colonial treaties would be considered, then Eritrea insisted that the Commission would have to consider arguments based on Eritrean physical occupation and control as well.[20] The areas involved are those to the south of the border specified by the text of the three treaties. In these areas Eritrea claimed to have built schools, health clinics and roads; administered development projects; collected taxes; and maintained law and order through courts as well as police and militia forces. Furthermore in those areas, which were inhabited almost exclusively by Eritreans, voting stations were said to have been set up by the Provisional Government of Eritrea for the purposes of the Eritrean independence referendum of 1993. After the referendum, representatives from these areas were said to have been elected to the Eritrean Parliament.

Eritrea argued that claims in derogation of the three colonial treaties are not only inadmissible before the EEBC, being that they are contrary to the June 18 Algiers Cessation of Hostilities Agreement[21] and the December 12 Peace

---

19 Eritrea supports these assertions with two curious illustrations. In the first instance it is claimed that the Ethiopian Minister of Foreign Affairs held a meeting of foreign ambassadors in Addis Ababa on 19 May 1998, two weeks after the start of the war. At the end of the meeting a map was made available to the diplomatic community, which in comparison to other official Ethiopian government maps from the period after Eritrean independence discloses no tangible or significant difference (see Map 18: Map Distributed To Diplomatic Community by Ethiopian Foreign Minister (May 1998) on p. 27, *Eritrean Statement*). In the second instance Eritrea insists that as recently as April 2000 (a few weeks prior to the third Ethiopian invasion of Eritrea) the Head of Mission at the Ethiopian Embassy in Eritrea still displayed a map produced in 1994 by the Ethiopian Mapping Authority on the wall behind his desk. A photograph of Mr Wendemu the Head of Mission at his desk, and a close-up of the map (Map 19) supposedly displayed are contained at pp. 28 and 29. The said map is in alignment with Eritrea's position and claims.
20 Eritrea thus set up the basis for introducing acts of *effectivités*.
21 "Agreement on Cessation of Hostilities between the Government of the Federal Democratic Republic of Ethiopia and the Government of the State of Eritrea", 18 June 2000 (App. 1 Exh 26).

184 *Arbitral route to settlement*

Agreement,[22] but also for the reason of incompatibility with the principle of *uti possidetis* as contained in the 1964 Cairo Declaration.[23]

8.2 Synopsis of Ethiopia's statement in accordance with paragraph 4(8) of the Agreement concluded on 12 December 2000

The Ethiopian Submission[24] to the EEBC purported to (1) identify in accordance with Paragraph 4(8)[25] of the Agreement the portions of the boundary with respect to which the treaties of the colonial era appear to allow no dispute regarding the location of the boundary and; (2) address the other portions of the boundary, with respect to which there are disputes between the parties.

8.2.1 Ethiopia's historical account of the background of the territory

Ethiopia traced its history back several millennia ranging from mention in the Old Testament and Homeric poems through the arrival of Christianity (330 AD), the Ottoman occupation (1557), Egyptian encroachment (1872, 1875 and 1876) and British involvement through occupation of Egypt and eventual Italian presence (1882–1941). In all these cases Ethiopia successfully fought and won back its territory.

Pertinent claims were that the Emperor of Ethiopia (King of Kings) appointed rulers over large areas that extend to some areas in what is today the Eritrea. One of such regions is *Tigre*. The territory traditionally under the rule of the *Ras* of *Tigre* (a ruler within the Ethiopian empire) covered a vast area now constituting part of the Ethiopia–Eritrea border. There still remains to date the names of sub-provinces ruled by the *Ras* of *Tigre*; some now in Eritrea, others in Ethiopia. An example is *Hamasen* now located in western Eritrea just inland from the city of *Massawa*.[26]

Although Italy and Ethiopia proceeded to sign a series of boundary agreements from 1889 to 1908, the long-term expansionist objectives of Italian policy were

---

22 App. 1, Exh. 1.
23 App. 1, Exh. 2.
24 Hereafter cited in the footnotes as *Ethiopian Statement*.
25 'Within 45 days after the effective date of this agreement, each party shall provide to the Secretary its claims and evidence relevant to the mandate of the Commission. These shall be provided to the other party by the Secretary' (Art. 4(8): Agreement between the Government of the Federal Democratic Republic of Ethiopia and the Government of the State of Eritrea: see Annex 1 Documentary Annexes, Vol. II, 26 January 2001).
26 Others include Saraye, north of the Mareb River in the vicinity of the city of Massawa; Saraye, north of the Mareb River in the vicinity of the city of Aksum; Akele Guzay, east of Saraye and on the other side of the Mareb River, which at that point turns to the north; Agame, south of Akele Guzay and containing the major city of Adigrat; Adiabo and Shire, located south of the Mareb and north of the Tekkeze and Welqayit and Waldibba, located south of the Tekkeze. These areas are identified on Map 1.1 on p. 5 of the *Ethiopian Statement*.

always maintained in principle. This policy culminated in Italy's invasion of the whole of Ethiopia in 1935.

After the expulsion of the Italian forces in 1941 and a transitional period under the British Military Administration, Eritrea was reunited with Ethiopia and governed from Addis Ababa. This continued until 1993, when Ethiopia formally agreed to Eritrean independence. Upon Eritrean independence, the two states recognised the existence of disputes over their mutual boundary, given the lack of clarity in the language and implementation of the treaties signed in the colonial era. Ethiopia and Eritrea proceeded from 1993 to 1998 to discuss methods for resolving the location of their boundary. Ethiopia claimed that discussions ended in May of 1998, when Eritrea's army invaded and occupied the Badme region and subsequently Zalambessa and the Irob region among other places.

8.2.2 Ethiopian view of applicable law

Ethiopia referred to express provisions in five instruments relating to the dispute and sought to demonstrate that they all refer 'with reasonable consistency', to the fact that the dispute is to be resolved and determined on the basis of 'pertinent colonial treaties' and 'applicable international law'[27]. These are:

(1) 12 December Agreement (Art. 4);
(2) Framework Agreement, mandated by the Assembly of Heads of State and Government of the Organisation of African Unity (OAU);
(3) Agreement on the Cessation of Hostilities of 18 June 2000;
(4) technical arrangements for the implementation of the OAU Framework Agreement and its Modalities; and
(5) Clarifications of the OAU in response to the questions raised by Ethiopia relating to the technical arrangements.

Ethiopia noted that the instruments also reject the use of force and invoke the principle of respect for the borders existing at independence as stated in Resolution AHG/Res. 16 (1). Ethiopia urges that 'applicable international law' particularly must be given effective meaning. Authority for this was found in *Case concerning Kaskili/Sedudu Island* where the Court held against Botswana's contention that the Court cannot take into consideration Namibia's arguments relating to prescription and acquiescence because reference in the Special Arrangement to the 'rules and principles of international law' is 'pleonastic'. In the Court's view the Special Agreement, in referring to the 'rules and principles of international law' not only authorises the Court to interpret the 1890 Treaty in the light of those rules and principles but also to apply those rules and principles independently. Ethiopia in effect wishes that the principle of *uti posssidetis* should be presented with particular

---

27 *Ethiopian Statement*, op.cit., Supra note 24.

emphasis on the resolution adopted at the OAU Summit in Cairo on 17 July 1964.[28] This principle Ethiopia argued for forms part of the applicable law in this dispute by virtue of Article 4 of the Agreement. Three arguments are advanced in relation to this principle: (1) the principle applies to boundaries brought into being before 1964;[29] (2) the inherited alignment comprise boundary sectors that are flawed by uncertainty deriving from problems of interpretation and identification of relevant geographical features; (3) the conduct of the parties (the *effectivités*) may be referred to in order to confirm the exercise of rights derived from a legal title or where the exact territorial expanse is in doubt they may reveal the interpretation of the title in practice.[30]

8.2.3 Ethiopian view of the methodology: the five sectors

The Ethiopian approach is to divide the Ethiopia–Eritrea boundary into five sectors[31] 'for the purposes of convenience' and based on the language of the treaties of 1900[32], 1902[33] and 1908[34] which are expressly referred to in the 12 December 2000 Agreement. It is noted that this view which was adopted by the EEBC is in agreement with much of international delimitation practice. From a brief description of the sectors given it would appear that Ethiopia believes that as regards Sectors I and III, the language used in the relevant treaties is clear and that the geographical features referred to namely the Setit, Maiteb and Mareb Rivers respectively are still well known today and apart from 'certain subsidiary issues' there would be no material dispute over the location of the boundaries.

Sectors II, IV and V, however, according to Ethiiopia, require separate treatment either because the intended delimitation never occurred[35] or there are significant ambiguities and gaps including references to rivers that may not exist (as in Sector IV).

---

28 Each member state '(1) Solemnly affirms the strict respect by all Member States of the Organisation for the principles laid down in paragraph 3 of Article III of the Charter of the OAU; Solemnly declares that all Member States pledge themselves to respect the borders existing on their achievement of independence.'
29 Separate Opinion of Judge *ad hoc* Ajibola in the *Case Concerning the Territorial Dispute (Libyan Arab Jamahiriya/Chad)*, ICJ Rep. 1994, pp. 83–92.
30 *Case Concerning the Frontier Dispute (Burkina Faso/Mali)*, ICJ Rep. 1986, pp. 586–7, para. 63.
31 Numbered 1–5 and depicted on Sector map No. 2.1 following p. 14.
32 Treaty between Italy and Ethiopia for the Delimitation of the Frontier between Eritrea and Ethiopia (Annex 6).
33 Note Annexed to the Treaty of 10 July 1900 regarding the Frontier between Ethiopia and Eritrea, and the Treaty of 15 May 1902 regarding the frontier between the Sudan and Ethiopia (Annex 7 of the Ethiopian Statement).
34 Convention between Italy and Ethiopia for the Settlement of the Frontier between the Italian Colony of Eritrea and the Provinces of the Ethiopian Empire (Annex 8 of the Ethiopian Statement).
35 As in the case of Sector II (tribal locations and certain geographic features ending at the junction of *Mai Ambessa* and the *Mareb*) and Sector V (the line located parallel to and at a distance of 60km from the coast).

8.2.4 The Agreements pre-figuring the Treaties of 1900, 1902 and 1908

Ethiopia traced the history of political, military and legal developments (primarily between Ethiopia and Italy and sometimes involving Great Britain) leading to the adoption of agreements, which later led to the treaties of 1900, 1902 and 1908. Ethiopia asserted that from the initial presence of Italy in Massawa in 5 February 1885 to 1935 when Italy invaded and purported to annex Ethiopia, the Italian colonial policy and manoeuvres was one of duplicity and gradual encroachment. Ethiopia claimed that by the close of the year 1898 the settlement on the Eritrean–Ethiopian boundary had yet to be reached. Pertinent agreements showing the volatile relationships between Italy, Ethiopia and Britain as well as the shifting boundary positions they represent include:

(1) A secret treaty of amity and alliance with the Ras of Shoa in which Italy undertook not to annex any Ethiopian territories.
(2) A Treaty of Amity and Commerce, which was signed at Uccialli on 2 May 1889 (the Uccialli Treaty). Article III of this Treaty contains a significant territorial clause.[36]
(3) An Additional Convention to the Treaty of Uccialli signed in Naples on 10 October 1889 by Francesco Crispi (Prime Minister) and a local Abyssinian representative, Ras Makonnen. Ethiopia claimed this was done without the knowledge or participation of the reigning Monarch, Menelik. Article III of this Convention announced, 'a rectification of the territories shall be made, taking as a basis the actual state of possession . . .'. The Italian government thus wished to push the border further south to the Mareb River and to occupy the districts of Saraye and Akele Guzay.
(4) On 24 March and 15 April 1891, Italy concluded two Protocols with Great Britain defining respective spheres of influence in East Africa and assigning to Italy, *inter alia*, the Ethiopian territories contemplated by the Uccialli Treaty. Ethiopia's reaction to this was to assert her absolute independence and defined the Empire's boundaries as reaching on the west side, the Nile and Lake Rudolf and on the east the Dankali coast.[37] Eventually on 27 February 1893 Ethiopia denounced the Uccialli Treaty.[38]

---

36 It reads: 'In order to remove any doubt as to the limits of the territory over which the two Contracting Parties exercise sovereign rights, a Special Commission, composed of two Italian and two Ethiopian Delegates shall trace with permanent landmarks a boundary-line, the leading features of which shall be as follows (a) The boundary between Italy and Ethiopia shall follow the high table-land. (b) Starting from the country of *Afrafali* [sic], the villages *Halai*, *Soganeiti* and *Asmara* shall be within the Italian boundary. (c) *Adi Nefas* and Adi Johannes in the direction of the *Bogos* tribe shall be within the Italian boundary. (d) From *Adi Johannes* the boundary between Italy and Ethiopia shall be marked by a straight line running east and west', pp. 16 and 17, *Ethiopian Statement* quoting Herslet Sir E.: *The Map of Africa by Treaty: Abyssinia to Great Britain and France*, 3rd edn, Vol. 2, (London: Frank Cass & Co., 1967).
37 Letter from Emperor Menelik II to the King of Italy, 21 April 1891, published in DDI, *Seconda Serie:* 1870–96, Vol. XXIV, pp. 181–2. See Annex 10.
38 Ibid., Vol. XXV, p. 244. Annex 11.

188 *Arbitral route to settlement*

(5) A Peace Treaty of 26 October 1896 was signed between Italy and Ethiopia. Significantly, Article V of this Treaty stipulated that the parties had jointly agreed to the settlement of their definitive boundaries, and the Italian government undertook not to cede any territory to any third party.

(6) On 24 June 1897, the Italian resident at Harar, Major Cesare Nerazzini put the Italian government's seal on a map on which King Menelik of Ethiopia had drawn his boundary proposal. Although the map in question (which also bore Menelik's seal) has yet to be found, a report issued by an Italian press agency in August 1897 describes Menelik's proposal of 24 June 1897 as a line which, starts on Tomat along the Atbara.[39] Notably Ethiopia claims that the proposal of 24 June 1897 represented for Italy the loss of the territories of Saraye, Akele–Guzay and Hamasien.

8.2.4.1 Ethiopian interpretation and application of Agreements of 1900, 1902 and 1908: Sector 1 – from the Sudan Tripoint to the Maiteb River (Ethiopia–Italy Treaty 1900)

Regarding this treaty, Ethiopia noted that Article 1 provides the line Tomat–Todluc–Mareb–Belesa–Muna which is recognised by the two contracting parties as the boundary between Eritrea and Ethiopia.[40] Ethiopia claimed that the Tomat–Todluc–Mareb line can be seen on a certain sketch no. 3 prepared by Ciccodicola the Italian Representative in Ethiopia in 1902 which was annexed to its submission to the EEBC.[41]

8.2.4.2 Impact of boundary with Anglo–Egyptian Sudan on Sector I of the Ethiopia—Eritrea boundary

Ethiopia argued that the settled boundary situation between Ethiopia and Eritrea according to the Treaty of 1900 was disturbed by Anglo–Italian negotiations between 1900 and 1901, which led to the Anglo–Italian Declaration of 22 November 1901. Apart from replacing the previously existing frontier line between Anglo–Egyptian Sudan and Eritrea, the declaration provided for far reaching territorial reorganisation between Italy and Great Britain which also

---

39 'This line reaches the Mareb at Todluc, goes up the Mareb to the confluence of the Mai Ambessa, then the Mai Ambessa up to its sources; goes down the Mai Feccia to the high Mareb whose course it follows up to the confluence of the Mai Meretta; goes up the Mai Meretta and then, passing south of Gura, Digsa, Halai and Mahio, goes down to the Plane of the Guinea Fowls then following parallel to the Red Sea at sixty kilometres from the coast', *Agenzia Stefani, Bollettino*, 9 August 1897, Annex 13 (*Ethiopian Statement*, p. 22).

40 In Article II it is stated that 'The Italian Government binds itself not to cede or sell to any other Power the territory comprised between the line Tomat-Todluc-Mareb-Mai, Ambessa-Mai, Feccia-Mai, Marella-Mai, Ila-Mahio, Piano galline Faraone [Plane of the Guinea Fowls], and the line Tomat, Todluc, Mareb, Belesa, Muna, left by His Majesty Menelek II, King of Kings of Ethiopia to Italy.'

41 Annexes 6 and 17.

included the cession of territories between Eritrea, Anglo–Egyptian Sudan and even Ethiopia.[42] Most importantly the Abu Gamal Setit–Khor–Um Hagar line agreed upon by Great Britain and Italy – insofar as it cut through territory south of the Tomat–Todluc line (contained in the Treaty of 1900) represented an encroachment on the territorial integrity of Ethiopia.

Subsequent negotiations to seek the consent of Ethiopia led to the conclusion on 15 May 1902 of the tripartite treaty between Ethiopia, Great Britain and Italy, which modified the 1900 Ethiopia–Eritrea agreement. Thus, the frontier treaty between Ethiopia and Eritrea, previously determined by the Tomat–Todluc line was mutually modified in Article I (the portion relating to Sector I) as commencing from the junction of the Khor Um Hagar with the Setit. The new frontier follows this river to its junction with the Maiteb, following the latter's course so as to leave Mount Ala Takura to Eritrea, and joins the Mareb at its junction with the Mai Ambessa.

8.2.4.3 The fixing of the boundary in Sector I

In Ethiopia's submission, the starting point of the boundary line between Ethiopia and Eritrea was on the Setit River, at the 'junction of Khor Um Hagar with the Setit'. Furthermore, that the starting point of the Ethiopia–Eritrea boundary is on the Setit River at the tripoint with Sudan. However, Ethiopia claims that it remains to be verified where the boundary lies within the Setit and Maiteb Rivers and to determine the question of sovereignty over any river islands.

8.2.4.4 Interpretation and application of arrangements: Sector II – from the Maiteb River to junction of the Mareb and Mai Ambessa Rivers

Ethiopia claims that although precise in its indication of geographic factors to be considered in delimiting the boundary[43] the treaty of 1902 contains certain ambiguities which do not lend themselves to a clear identification of the boundary because:

(1) It does not specify precisely how the boundary should be drawn between the Maiteb and the junction of the Mareb with the Mai Ambessa, and
(2) The treaty does not delineate exactly where the Cunama tribe is located.

---

42 e.g., 'the cession from Ethiopia to the Italian colony of Eritrea "of a zone of territory to the east of the Todluc-Maieteb line, which will give Erithraea the whole of the Cunama tribe up to the Mareb"' (para. 5), p. 27, *Ethiopian Statement*.
43 Article I states that 'the new frontier follows this river [the Setit] to its junction with the Maieteb following the latter's course so as to leave Mount Ala Tacura to Eritrea, and joins the Mareb at its junction with the Mai Ambessa. The line from the junction of the *Setit* and *Maieteb* to the junction of the *Mareb* and *Mai Ambessa* shall be delimited by Italian and Ethiopian delegates, so that the Cunama tribe belong to Eritrea.'

8.2.5 Ethiopian view of the pertinent geography

Ethiopia insisted in its submissions that the existence and location of both the Setit and Maiteb Rivers are well established. That the treaty of 1902 leaves no basis for doubt regarding the present-day location of the Eritrea–Ethiopia boundary as running a short distance upstream along the Setit River 'to its junction with the Maie' and that cartographic evidence supports the wording of Article I where the boundary line is stipulated as following the Setit River 'to its junction with the Maieteb following the latter's course as to leave Mount Ala Tacura to Eritrea'.

8.2.6 Ethiopian view of the changing and opportunistic attitude of Italy during key periods

Ethiopia maintained that contemporaneous Italian diplomatic documents show that the geographical references contained in the treaty of 1902 were also reflected in seven illustrative sketches shown to Menelik and prepared by Ciccodicola during the boundary negotiations.[44] Significantly, and crucial to subsequent Italian argument, sketch no. 7 is a reproduction of a sheet entitled Mai-Daro issued by the Geographic Military Institute in 1900. This sketch shows among other things a river called 'T. Meeteb'. Ciccodicola himself is said to have admitted in a report that the 'few points designed on the [Mai Daro sheet] are wrong; it was almost impossible to discuss rationally based on knowledge of the places . . .'. But Ethiopia insists that there was no ambiguity as to the location of the Maiteb River.

Ethiopia maintained that shortly after the Treaty of 1902 was concluded Italian authorities appeared to realise that the geographic reality reflected in the Treaty of 1902, the Ciccodicola sketches and the sketch map presented to the Italian Parliament on 10 December 1902 did not correspond to their expansionist ambitions. Since then Italy was said to have unilaterally sought to rectify its mistake. Indeed from 1907 onwards, Italian maps represented the Ethiopian–Eritrean boundary as a straight line running north-east, sometimes from the junction of the Tekkeze with a newly created 'Meeteb' river, both the Tomsa and 'Meeteb' lying over 100 kilometres to the east of the Maiteb and also east of the Sittona.

8.2.7 Ethiopia's position

Ethiopia rejected the revisionist approach of the Italian maps and the conclusions based on them as inconsistent with the terms of the Treaty of 1902. The Ethiopian position is that the Treaty of 1902, when interpreted in the light of Italy's own contemporaneous views and maps places the boundary between Ethiopia and Eritrea in the sector which starts at the junction of the Setit and Maiteb

---

44 A copy of the report with the enclosed sketches were annexed to the Ethiopian submission.

Rivers passing to the east of the Ala Takura mountainous region to join up with the junction of the Mareb River with the Mai Ambessa. Self-serving Italian actions and *ex post facto* unilateral activities it was argued cannot displace the legal title acquired by Ethiopia. The Ethiopian claim is that in the years immediately preceding the Italian invasion of Ethiopia, the area was still under Ethiopian rule.[45]

8.2.8 The disposition of the Cunama (Sector II)

The text of the Treaty of 1902 stipulated that the line running 'from the junction of the Setit and Maieteb to the junction of the Mareb and Mai Ambessa shall be delimited by Italian and Ethiopian delegates so that the Cunama tribe belong to 'Erythraea'. Pollera, – Head of the Gasc and Setit Residence, observed to the Governor of Eritrea observed that the Cunama region extended further east of the boundary fixed by the 1902 treaty. He thus, suggested that, rather than proceed to boundary delimitation pursuant to the Treaty of 1902, the parties should conclude an additional convention to the Treaty of 1902. This is in order to establish that all the Cunama tribes be left in Eritrean territory. The Italian government as a result was said to have undertaken the administration and command also of those groups which are still situated in Abyssinian territory including carrying out evacuations and placing the populations within the Eritrean borders within a period of two years. However, no additional convention was ever concluded. Ethiopia concluded that Italy preferred to adopt a different course of action; that of distorting the cartographic evidence so as to include within the Italian colony of Eritrea territory, areas which pursuant to the Treaty of 1902 lawfully belonged to Ethiopia. Ethiopia also concluded that from the documentary evidence contemporaneous with the signature of the Treaty of 1902 it is clear that the Cunama tribe west of the boundary accepted by Menelik and reflected by the Treaty of 1902 were included within the Italian colony of Eritrea.

8.2.9 Interpretation and application of the Agreements: Sector III – along the Mareb River from the Mai Ambessa to the Belesa River

The government of Ethiopia expected that there will be no material dispute over the location of the boundary in Sector III. The Mareb is a well-known seasonal waterway today and it is, therefore, easy to apply the language of the Treaty of 1900. Ethiopia recognised, however, that there are subsidiary issues such as the definition of the boundary within the river itself as well as the question of sovereignty over any river islands.

---

45 *Ethiopian Statement*, p. 36 and the entire Chapter A.

192 *Arbitral route to settlement*

8.2.10 Interpretation and application of the Agreements: Sector V – from the confluence of the Mareb and Belesa Rivers to the easternmost point defined by the Treaty of 1900

Sector V is the final portion of the boundary between both states moving from west to east, and is thus defined as the portion of the boundary continuing from the endpoint of the portion defined by the Treaty of 1900 and continuing to the tripoint boundary among Eritrea, Ethiopia and Djibouti. Sector V is addressed by the Agreement of 1908, but it states a condition which was never fulfilled which is that 'the two governments undertake to fix the . . . frontier line on the ground by common accord and as soon as possible . . .'. Ethiopia insisted that Italy and Ethiopia never worked out a precise method of marking out a 60 kilometre base line, nor did they proceed to 'fix' that line in according with ground feature variation or to implement the other listed features.

8.2.11 Ethiopian view of the period 1908–present

Italian policy towards Ethiopia has undoubtedly been perceivably expansionist, but in the period 1908 to 1935, it was based to a considerable degree upon 'positive diplomacy'. Thus, in 1928 a Treaty of Friendship was concluded with Ethiopia. The changed attitude towards Ethiopia in 1935 is thought to be due to a general realignment of European politics, the rise of Fascism, and the increase in French acceptance of Italian ambitions in Africa.[46] In 1936, Italy illegally annexed Ethiopia after a brief armed struggle. Although the war continued after the Italians had entered Addis Ababa, the United Kingdom and many other members of the League of Nations recognised the Italian conquest 'in one form or another'.[47]

In the event, during the course of the Second World War the UK and other members of the anti-Axis coalition withdrew their recognition of the annexation. Eventually upon the return of the exiled Emperor Haile Selassie to Ethiopia the position of foreign governments as reflected in the White Paper on the British Military Administration of Occupied Territories in Africa was that '. . . The Emperor in returning to his country and thus resuming contact did so in his own view, and in that of the world as the rightful sovereign of the country'.[48]

Ethiopia concludes that in view of these considerations and in accordance with the General Treaty for the Renunciation of War, Italy had no capacity to modify the boundaries between the Italian Colony of Eritrea, as it then was, and Ethiopia. If any doubt remains to the legal effects of the annexation Italy expunges it by

---

46 See H. Hearder and D.P. Waley, *A Short History of Italy* (Cambridge, 1963), p. 221. See also *Ethiopian Statement*, p. 48. In any event from 1909 onwards Ethiopia kept a wary eye on events that might affect the boundary with Eritrea and necessary protests were made to the Italian authorities. Several of these protests were included as Annexes 24, 27, 28, 29 and 30.
47 M.M. Whiteman, *Digest of International Law*, Vol. 5, USGPO, (Washington, June 1965), pp. 898–9, K. Marek, *Identity and Continuity of States in Public International Law*, (Geneve, 1968), pp. 269–70.
48 *Ethiopian Statement*, p. 50.

reference to the provisions of the Treaty of Peace with Italy, which states *inter alia* in Article 35 that Italy recognises the legality of all measures, which the government of Ethiopia has taken or may hereafter take in order to annul Italian measures respecting Ethiopia taken after 3 October 1935 and the effects of such measures. The general and specific effect of these provisions it is argued is for the purpose of restoration of the *status quo ante* and shows the incapacity of Italy to modify the boundaries of Ethiopia.

Subsequent transactions at the General Assembly which led to the adoption of the 2 December 1950 Resolution 390 A (V) ultimately led to the transfer of Eritrea to Ethiopia in 1952. Thus, rather than any thing at this stage modifying the Ethiopian boundaries with Eritrea, it was recommended; '(1) Eritrea shall constitute an autonomous unit federated with Ethiopia under the sovereignty of the Ethiopian Crown.'[49]

The end of Italy's African Empire led to the establishment of the British Military Administration in the former Italian colonies. Eritrea was cleared of Italian troops and placed under British Military Administration in 1941, ending a 51-year period of colonial rule by Italy. Eritrea remained under British Military Administration until September 1952. In the view of the UK, as stated by Lord Rennell of Rodd who served as controller of finance and accounts, '[t]he Eritrea of the British Administration was the old Italian colony of Eritrea as it had been before the Abyssinian war, shorn of its accretions from Ethiopia under the Italian East African Empire'.[50] While the British Military Administration noted that there may be some overlapping and confusion between Ethiopian and colonial boundaries, the British Military Administration did not concern itself with ascertaining the rightful boundaries. Rather, it was concerned with maintaining the status quo so as to avoid transitional problems and to facilitate the Ethiopian Emperor's ability to modify the Italian administrative divisions as he saw fit.[51]

The Peace Treaty and the Four Powers Commission established to investigate and make recommendations regarding the erstwhile Italian Possessions gave way to the reference of the question of disposal of the territories to the United Nations Commission for Eritrea created in November 1949.[52] The General Assembly instructed that the commission should consider various factors, such as the wishes and welfare of the local population and the rights and claims of Ethiopia based on geographical, historical, ethnic or economic reasons. The members of the commission had two broadly opposing views.[53] Subsequently, however, a UN

---

49 Ibid., p. 52; See also M.M. Whiteman, *Digest of International Law*, Vol., 3, (Washington, October 1964), pp. 24–6.
50 Lord Rennell of Rodd, *British Military Administration of Occupied Territories in Africa During the Years 1941–7* (London: His Majesty's Stationery Office, 1948), p. 98.
51 *Ethiopian Statement*, op.cit., p. 55.
52 The Commission was composed of delegates from Burma, Guatemala, Norway, Pakistan and the Union of South Africa.
53 This led to the submission of two memoranda; one submitted by Burma, Norway and the Union of South Africa and the other by Guatemala and Pakistan. The former group were largely of the opinion that Eritrea's complete independence was precluded by its poverty, dependence upon

194 *Arbitral route to settlement*

Commissioner in Eritrea[54] was elected to oversee the adoption of a federation plan. The UN Commissioner with a panel of legal consultants prepared a provisional draft constitution which was eventually ratified by the Emperor of Ethiopia on 11 August 1952 followed by a Federal Act on 11 September 1952 which formally established the federation of Eritrea with Ethiopia.

The thrust of the legal analysis offered by Ethiopia in relation to the highlighted constitutional developments is that nothing in them discloses any consequences with respect to the question of boundaries. Significantly it is concluded that 'the United Nations General Assembly may have had a power to modify boundaries, but the key resolution did not address the question of the boundaries of Ethiopia. This is hardly surprising, given that in the end Eritrea was to be incorporated into Ethiopia. In addition, the United Kingdom, like its allies, had no legal power to constitute or to modify the boundaries of Ethiopia. This position remained the same for each phase of the British military presence in Eritrea.'[55]

The reunification, which was finalised in 1952, lasted until 1962 when Eritrea became a province of the United State of Ethiopia. On 27 April 1993 Eritrea became independent and became a member of the United Nations. On 30 July 1993 an Agreement of Friendship and Co-operation between the Government of the State of Eritrea and the Transitional Government of Ethiopia was concluded.[56] Ethiopia argued that in accordance with the applicable principles of general international law, these changes in the status of Eritrea could have no effect on the original colonial boundaries of Eritrea and that 'the entity known as Eritrea' transferred to Ethiopia by the General Assembly in 1952 was also the entity which became independent in 1993. It is also claimed that none of the interested parties has sought to assert that the political changes of 1952, 1962 and 1993 have had any effect on the boundaries upon the original colonial treaties.

8.2.12 Incidence of disputes between the parties

Ethiopia attempted a technical formulation of the incidence of the dispute between it and Eritrea in the light of the classical and modern definitions of the word and in relation to Article 4, paragraph 9 of the December 2000 Agreement. Ethiopia, therefore, concludes that in defining the present dispute it is necessary to emphasise that many existing definitions (of dispute), whilst usefully indicative, do not necessarily provide an exhaustive guide to the application of the provisions of Article 4, paragraph 9, of the Agreement. Thus, in the case of the Agreement of 1908, the criteria specified in the colonial treaty have not been applied by the parties, and the 'dispute' concerned involves the application *de novo* of the treaty provisions, and the settlement of the totality of the unresolved issues. Clearly

---

Ethiopia's resources and historical affinities. Whereas the latter argued that 'no general or important affinity existed between Ethiopia and Eritrea' and suggested that the Eritreans were in fact hostile toward Ethiopia.
54 Mr Eduardo Anze Matienzo of Bolivia.
55 *Ethiopian Statement*, op.cit., p. 60.
56 Annex 31.

certain sectors of the boundary between the two states are in dispute for purposes of paragraph 9 of Article 4 of the Agreement of December 2000.

SECTOR I: Regarding this sector Ethiopia anticipated the Eritrean argument that the initial course of the boundary should follow the Setit River, but that the boundary thereafter should not follow the Maiteb River, as provided for in the Treaty of 1902, but rather should deviate from the Setit at its junction with a river known as the Mai Tomsa lying over 100 kilometres east of the Maiteb River. Ethiopia bases this belief on maps published by Eritrea, which suggests that Eritrea will adopt this line of argument. To the extent that Eritrea adopts a position at variance with that of Ethiopia, there was clearly a dispute between the Parties, at least to the east of the confluence of the Setit River with the Maiteb.

SECTOR II: The Treaty provides that the boundary line up to the junction of the Mareb with the Mai Ambessa shall be determined so that the relevant part of the Cunama people belongs to Eritrea. A precise determination of this sector of boundary in part hinges, therefore on the disposition of the Cunama in 1902. Ethiopia aimed to demonstrate to the EEBC evidence showing that as of 1902, the Cunama were identified as being located to the north and west of the Maiteb and the Ala Tacura region. Given that Eritrea relies on a straight line 'boundary' between the junction of the Tekkeze with the Mai Tomsa and the junction of the Mareb with the Mai Ambessa, Ethiopia identified a clear dispute between the parties.

SECTOR III: Subject to a precise determination of where along the course of the Mareb the boundary lies and the task of regulating the legal status of mid-river islands, Ethiopia insisted that this aspect of the boundary is out of controversy.

SECTOR IV: Ethiopia considered that the fourth sector is bound to be in dispute and insisted that contemporary evidence reveals that the parties' knowledge of some of these features was incomplete at the time of the treaty's conclusion. Thus, there are problems of interpretation and application necessitating recourse to other kinds of evidence to establish the parties' intentions, the situation on the ground and how in practice, this sector of the boundary was interpreted.

SECTOR V: This is the easternmost sector of the boundary covered by the provisions of the Agreement of 1908. Ethiopia simply concluded that the parties to the agreement never carried out their undertaking, recorded in Article II of the agreement, to fix the frontier on the spot, adapting it to the nature and variation of the terrain. Nor did the parties ever implement the other undertakings set forth in Articles III to VI of the agreement.

8.3 Critiquing the EEBC decision and understanding the difficulties of implementation

The EEBC concluded a very complex arbitration which the parties ought to have immediately implemented. The popular view is that enforcement of judicial and arbitral decisions become concretised by the involvement of the Security Council and the possibility of coercive actions under the banner of the United Nations. Furthermore the opinion of the international community and the possibility of self-help are also thought to help gravitate the parties towards effective and complete implementation. As it happened, the EEBC process also enjoyed a close association with the United Nations. At least 30 formal reports on the activities of the Boundary Commission were provided by the President of the Commission to the Secretary-General of the United Nations and passed on to the Security Council.[57] Yet the implementation of the Award has been quite unimpressive. The process of implementation has been slow and essentially ineffective in many areas and may have in fact stalled.

The military situation in the Temporary Security Zone and adjacent areas remained tense during the period leading up to the Eritrea–Ethiopia Boundary Commission deadline of 30 November for demarcation of the boundary. Both Eritrea and Ethiopia continued to reinforce their military deployments in the border area. Eritrea continued to induct troops into the Temporary Security Zone. For their part, the Ethiopian Armed Forces began conducting training and advancing some thousands of additional troops deeper into the border areas in Sector West. Aerial border reconnaissance and illegal border crossings by personnel of both states, as well as direct military engagement and abductions are common long after final demarcation was expected. Despite all the lingering problems, the view has been taken by the UN that demarcation must be taken to have been completed because:

> In its 26th and final report the EEBC affirmed that: the boundary between Ethiopia and Eritrea now automatically stands as demarcated by the boundary points (coordinates) listed in the annex to the Commission's Statement of 27 November 2006, and that it considers this decision binding on the parties. The Commission further asserted that it 'has fulfilled its mandate and remains in existence in order to deal with any remaining administrative matters.'[58]

The 'elephant in the room situation', however, is that there is a continuing line of disagreement which includes the opposing views of both parties in relation to some portion of their common boundary as envisaged in the award. By 2008 Eritrea had settled for the position that the demarcation coordinates stipulated by the Commission is final and binding, and that is 'an important step forward towards the demarcation on the ground', Eritrea expected that the Commission should arrange placement of pillars on the ground.[59] Ethiopia, however, maintains that the coordinates are invalid 'because they are not the product of a demarcation process recognised by international law'.[60]

---

57 The Security Council had itself requested the Secretary-General to keep it closely and regularly informed of progress towards the implementation of the Award as well as developments in the Mission area and activities of the UN Mission in Ethiopia and Eritrea (UNMEE (para. 12 of Security Council resolution 1320 (2000) of 15 September 2000)).
58 Report of the Secretary-General on Ethiopia and Eritrea, 23 January 2008, UN Doc. S/2008/40.
59 UN Doc. S/2008/40, para 17.
60 Ibid.

On the issue of whether demarcation has actually occurred it would appear that the parties are closer to the law than the arbitral tribunal. The EEBC's 'automatic demarcation by coordinates' position is indeed strange to international boundaries law. It may in time be found that the EEBC has indeed created a precedent on this issue but the chances of doing so is very much challenged by the position of the parties. Even the Eritrean stance recognising coordinates as an important step forward towards demarcation falls short of the audacity of the EEBC's position. As at date of publication of this work there has been no further progress on demarcation of the Eritrea–Ethiopia boundary. In essence, the parties are in many ways back right where they started. First, there is no clear continuous line of demarcation throughout their contested and common boundary. Second, there is a continuous situation of clear and present danger of armed hostilities as a result of differences over their common boundaries. Although it is admitted that the precise areas in dispute have been significantly reduced, international arbitration, at least in this case, has not succeeded in resolving the dispute as submitted despite the many declarations that it has done so even by the parties themselves.

Interestingly when the EEBC delivered its 125-page verdict on 13 April 2002 both states and their national press enthusiastically proclaimed the ruling as a 'victory' for them. Not surprisingly, however, bitter acrimony towards the verdict erupted within weeks of the decision and serious controversies have indeed continued until this day.[61]

A closer look at the provisions of the arbitration agreement discussed above would, however, reveal that the very seeds for the failure of the Commission's work were already laid in the formulation of the task given to the Commission. There is arguably a relentless effort to exclude anything that allows the application of initiative or discretion in line with the peculiarities and realities of the creation and maintenance of Africa's largely artificial borders. It was as though there was a determination by the parties to exclude any form of originality in the work of the Commission.

To begin with it may be observed that an unfortunate hierarchical order appeared to have been embedded into Article 1. First the Commission must

---

61 The controversy surrounding the decision is reflected in a letter written to the EEBC arbitrators to mark the first anniversary of the verdict. It reads *inter alia*: 'On April 13, 2001, when the governments of Ethiopia and Eritrea announced their victory regarding their common border, thousands of Irobs woke up to find their history and their heritage suddenly altered by five judges that had never set foot in the boundary region. They were initially confused by the Commission's decision because the decision placed the term "Irob" entirely in Ethiopia, yet numerous Irob villages and hamlets were now placed in Eritrea. They were confused as to why Ethiopia declared absolute victory because Eritrean radio stations in the Washington DC area and apparently in Eritrea were bragging that they won one-third of Irobland. Slowly, our fears became true. It became clear that despite the many pleas made by the people of Irob, the Eritrea–Ethiopia Boundary Commission had shockingly sacrificed the people of Irob for the sake of political compromise', Tesfamariam Baraki, "Beyond the Badme Debate: The Forgotten Case of Irobland", 10 March 2003, available at http://www.unitedethiopia.org/BeyondtheBadmeDebate.html accessed 16 November 2014.

reaffirm colonial borders. Second, pertinent colonial treaties must be respected and given effect to. Lastly, applicable international law (whatever that might be in this case) may then be applied. It is interesting to note also that the agreement repeats unimaginatively a complete adherence to the *uti possidetis* principle even with the long history of confusion surrounding the true nature and extent of the principle. Without delving too deeply into the jurisprudence of this principle, it suffices to argue that *uti possidetis* ('as you now possess') breaks down in some cases on grounds of logic alone, since it is the extent to which the *res* is held or possessed at all that may be in issue. The principle as expressed in resolution AHG/Res. 16(1), once regarded as the recipe for peace and territorial stability in Africa, has revealed itself to be no more than a political 'time bomb', which is threatening to detonate with resounding resonance across many regions all over Africa in this new century.

It is probably necessary to assert that the time is ripe for the jettisoning of *uti possidetis* in relation to the resolution of certain types of African disputes. To begin with, the origins of the concept are foreign to the continent and present certain types of problems for the principle of self-determination of peoples. At any rate *uti possidetis* was designed to have a different effect from its present stifling limitations and manifestations.[62] Current analysis invariably ignores the existence of at least two schools of thought in relation to the concept. There is the school that argues that *uti possidetis* must mean merely a juridical line or constructive line or constructive occupation – *uti possidetis juris* or *de jure*; while another considers that the principle must be based on a rightful and actual occupation of the territory – *uti possidetis de facto*. It is only in this latter sense that the *uti possidetis* theory can have any meaningful relevance in the context of certain African disputes. Unfortunately it is in the former sense that the case in question was determined and it appears to be the only interpretation that international courts have followed in deciding African cases. The principle ought to be exposed as an ambitious plasterwork to cover deep injustices that have been done to African societies and to perpetuate unrealistic geopolitical creations. It is true that the principle may have bought a few years of peace but it is ultimately based on a legal fiction. The fiction being that colonial borders were created on the basis of pre-existing natural or national geopolitical realities or indeed with the interests of the various African peoples and precolonial states in mind. In reality the existing boundaries were in fact drawn up to preserve ethnic incoherence based on deliberate policies to divide and rule. In many cases the colonial delimitation was achieved seemingly in total devotion to the letter and spirit of Machiavelli's *The Prince*. Therefore, the politico-legal fixation upon the operation of *uti possidetis* in relation to Africa may have to be abandoned in appropriate cases otherwise genuine resolution of disputes may be sacrificed on the altar of bare legal rulings.

---

62 The doctrine formed part of the constitutional and international law of the states in Latin America largely as an extension of the Monroe doctrine, in order to ward off possible re-colonisation of the Latin American territories by declaring that there was no *res nullius*, and it also served as a just and equitable foundation for the settlement of all their boundary disputes.

The parties to the Eritrea–Ethiopia dispute and the Commission have failed to perceive the reality that the *uti possidetis* principle could not be of use in resolving the dispute when the way in which the concept is operated is in fact a major part of the problem. In the Ethiopia–Eritrea case for instance, it was because the colonial borders were not equitably and realistically formulated that the conflicts between the parties broke out periodically as it did.

Second, 'pertinent colonial treaties' occupied a pre-eminent status in the scheme of applicable laws that the Commission had to apply in the arbitration. Again this is based on the very much-undeserved assumption that colonial treaties always possess legitimacy, that their creation was 'regular' in all respect and that they are beyond reproach in terms of scope as well as content. In reality things cannot be further from the truth. The Treaties and instruments dressed up as definitive of the ownership of the Bakassi Peninsula, in the *Land and Maritime Case*, for instance, were drawn up on the basis of work done by under-funded visiting colonial cartographers with little or no local knowledge. As alleged by Nigeria in its written submissions to the court in the *Land and Maritime Case* such colonial officers often agreed 'to round things up' in order to save themselves from further bother or embarrassment at doing a shoddy job and coming up with unsupportable maps.[63]

Third, the reference to applicable international law in the last limb of Article 1 nearly suggests that it was only to be resorted to as a last resort. This is clearly unsupportable since post-colonial developments in public international law should form the very basis of the application of the principle of *uti possidetis* as well as the basis of interpretation of any relevant treaties. Probably the most damaging fact is the specific exclusion of the *ex aequo et bono* principle. This principle was perhaps the only hope of the arbitration to produce a realistic, equitable and just resolution of the dispute and such powers normally fall within the competence of any self-respecting modern international court performing the type of task that was before the EEBC.[64] It is probably true that both Eritrea and Ethiopia were

---

63 The instruments referred to in the Court's decision are the Thomson–Marchand Declaration of 1929–30, as incorporated in the Henderson–Fleuriau Exchange of Notes of 1931; the Anglo-German Agreements of 12 April 1913 by the British Order in Council of 2 August 1946; and the Anglo–German Agreement of 11 and 12 April 1913. See para. 325 of the Court's judgment. Note that Nigeria and Cameroon gained political independence in 1960.
64 Article 38(2) of the Statute unequivocally confers on the Court 'the power . . . to decide a case *ex aequo et bono*, if the parties agree thereto'. In that case the Court need not confine itself to applying the existing law but could, if it deemed the existing law to operate harshly inefficiently or unjustly, give a judgment which aligns more with the essentials of equity and justice. Similarly international arbitrators are usually allowed to decide *ex aequo et bono*. For example in the dispute that occurred between Colombia and Ecuador in 1907, arbitrators were requested to determine the dispute boundary line between the two countries in accordance with existing treaties and modifications established by the convention under which the arbitrators were appointed. There was, however, added the significant proviso that they might, 'leaving to one side strict law, adopt an equitable line in accordance with the necessities and convenience of the two countries': Case No. 285 in A. Stuyt, *Survey of International Arbitrations*, 2nd edn (1976), pp. 1794–970. See also Alan Redfern & Martin Hunter, *Law and Practice of International Commercial Arbitration* (London: Sweet & Maxwell, 1997), p. 40.

convinced that they had a legal case and one which can only be resolved or best interpreted based on considerations of 'substantive treaty law'. In truth, however, the particular genre of substantive law that is applied in many such African boundary disputes are colonial treaties designed to settle scores and grant privileges among European princes and royal families. As revealed in several areas of the detailed Ethiopian statement, sometimes such treaties are also drawn up in furtherance of treacherous relations with African monarchs and on carefully constructed falsehoods.

The sanctity of colonial treaties in many international proceedings is an unfortunate legal fiction. In many cases the insufficiency or unreliability of these very treaties are the causes of the entire disagreement or conflict. In relation to the colonial treaties considered definitive in this case, one commentator notes:

> These treaties or agreements carried annexes with unclear maps sketching the rough outlines of the border. None of the proposed borders was ever marked on the ground. There was great ambiguity on the names of places and rivers on the maps, some of them occurring more than once.[65]

It must be conceded that the fault does not squarely lie with the Court or PCA, since under the law and practice of international adjudication and arbitration the parties themselves usually formulate the basis of the resolution of their dispute. In this way, responsibility for this fallacy lies with African states. However, two things may be noted. First the source of the legal advice that is available to most African disputants is more often than not foreign and their international legal advisers are mostly based in Western Europe. These so-called international law firms keep recycling the same failed legal advice that contemporary African disputes should be resolved by reference to resurrected colonial treaties of doubtful providence. Second, it may be wondered whether it is not incumbent on international courts to refuse to apply anachronistic or 'illegal treaties'. At the very least an international court should indicate quite clearly in its decision the provenance it attaches to the treaties and/or their contents as presented to it by the parties.[66] The argument here is that in reality both the World Court and the PCA are slavish in their acceptance of the bulk of colonial treaties and in according undue respect to their contents. This appears to be the case even in the clearest of instances where colonial treaties ought to be excluded for various formal and substantive inconsistencies. Even the clearest geodetic data obtained by GPS or cartographic evidence which contradicts a colonial treaty provision

---

65 Abbink, op.cit.
66 In the *Land and Maritime Boundary Case*, e.g. in response to the Cameroonian application 'to specify definitively' the course of the land boundary as fixed by the relevant instruments of delimitation the Court had no problem in deciding that: 'contrary to what Cameroon appeared to be arguing at certain stages in the proceedings, the Court cannot fulfil the task entrusted to it in this case by limiting itself to such confirmation. Thus, when the actual content of these instruments is the subject of dispute between the parties, the Court in order to specify the course of the boundary in question definitively, is bound to examine them more closely'. *Supra*, note 13.

would appear not to be enough ground to offset the apparent bias in favour of the latter. In the *Case Concerning the Frontier Dispute Case (Burkina Faso/Republic of Mali)* the Chamber of the International Court observed that: 'The Chamber cannot uphold the information given by the map where it is contradicted by *other trustworthy information concerning the intentions of the colonial power*' (emphasis added).[67] It is clear then that the judicial instict of the ICJ Bench has been to protect the intentions of colonial powers nearly at any costs.

The problems with this approach are many. As Ethiopia stated in this case although Italy and Ethiopia proceeded to sign a series of boundary agreements from 1889 to 1908, the long-term expansionist objectives of Italian imperialism were always maintained in principle. This policy culminated in Italy's eventual invasion of the whole of Ethiopia in 1935. To begin with, this shows that even the colonial powers were never as punctilious about the treaties they signed in relation to Africa especially when signed with African peoples and states. The question then is why does there continue to exist an abiding respect for treaties that ultimately had very little to do with the good of African states? Second, is there not a highly persuasive argument that can be made that the sheer fact of the Italian invasion and annexation of Ethiopia in 1935 is sufficient basis to consider as null and void all treaties and unilateral maps that are now propped up? Indeed after the Second World War, Emperor Haile Sellassie confirmed the invalidity of many of the previous treaties and Italy renounced them in 1947 with the Peace Treaty.

It is no surprise that serious problems still beset the acceptance of the Commission's verdict in this case. That there are controversies attending the implementation of the EEBC decision over a full decade after the PCA decision of April 2002 is also unsurprising. This is because, among other reasons, the verdict is sterile and incomplete in the issues taken into account. It must be admitted that in many cases the inability of such an international arbitration to resolve the dispute is due to factors extrinsic to the arbitration itself. Professor Abbink noted for instance, that the decisions of the EEBC ignore 'the deep-rooted mutual suspicion still reigning between the two countries as well as the scepticism and distrust of citizens of their national governments on the issue'.[68] He identified Badme, an apparently insignificant village, as the *fons et origo* of the Ethiopia Eritrea Conflict and describes how it has acquired the status of a highly symbolic prize. Badme was to Ethiopia what Bakassi was to Nigeria. President Isayas Afeworqi of Eritrea is quoted, as having said after the conquest of the village of Badme in May 1998 that giving up Badme would be like saying that the sun would set in the east. For the government and people of Ethiopia, however, serious damage to national pride has been perceived by the potential loss of a territory that has been administered as part of national territory since the founding of the state. This is why Badme continues to be a serious sore point of dispute and hostility between both states. These are problems, which a legalistic arbitration award *simplicta* cannot resolve.

---

67 *Case Concerning the Frontier Dispute* (Burkina Faso/Republic of Mali), 1986, ICJ. Rep., *supra* note 13.
68 Abbink, op.cit., p. 1.

The existence of corrupt military regimes, in some cases with a vested interest in continuation of military hostilities increases the chances of recalcitrance. Therefore, a more holistic approach to ADR is needed for Africa in this century.

The question that ought to be asked is whether the imposition of one particular map (inadequacies and all), on a party to a demarcation exercise is fair and equitable. Sight must never be lost of the acquired wisdom of writers who have concluded with respect to boundary making and marking that:

> The best means to ensure stability in general is to rely upon the consent of the parties themselves, so that once the relevant parties have by whatever means agreed upon a boundary line, that agreement constitutes a binding obligation ... the key to boundary delimitation lies in the consent of the relevant states.[69]

Further ingredients for chaos were created in the Ethiopia–Eritrea dispute as a result of the unusual situation whereby the EEBC was required to continue its work by demarcating the boundary without provision for formal pleadings by the parties or full oral hearings. The formalistic approach adopted by the EEBC to its demarcation task, which disregarded local realities was bound to produce bizarre consequences. It created even more resentment from local populations that were cut off from their rivers, farms and other means of livelihood. This conclusion is supported by paragraph 14A of the Commission's Demarcation Directions of 8 July 2002, which states that with respect to the division of towns and villages; 'The Commission has no authority to vary the boundary line. If it runs through and divides a town or village, the line may be varied only on the basis of an express request agreed between and made by both Parties.'[70] The written comments submitted by Ethiopia on the draft of this provision expressed the hope that it could be made more flexible so that demarcations could be more practical and mitigate hardships. The Commission, however, rejected this suggestion, largely based on the expectation that aggrieved states must still respect the finality which the Parties had agreed to attach to the Delimitation Decision. This is, however, difficult to reconcile with the Commission's view that:

> A demarcator must demarcate the boundary as it has been laid down in the delimitation instrument, but with a limited margin of appreciation enabling it to take account of any flexibility in the terms of the delimitation itself or of the scale and accuracy of maps used in the delimitation process, and to avoid establishing a boundary which is manifestly impracticable.[71]

---

69 Shaw (1996), op.cit., p. 84.
70 Eritrea–Ethiopia Boundary Commission, "Observations" (21 March 2003), available at http://www.pca-cpa.org/PDF/Obs.EEBC.pdf.
71 Eritrea–Ethiopia Boundary Commission, "Observations" (21 March 2003), published as an addendum to the Progress Report of the Secretary-General on Ethiopia and Eritrea, UN Doc. S/2003/257, of 6 March 2003.

Despite this the Commission appeared to have determined *a priori* that there would be no need for it to be flexible in the case because it is 'not of the view that there is to be derived from that practice a settled rule of customary international law to the effect that demarcators not so expressly empowered nonetheless possess such power'.[72] In other words, the indications were indeed always there that demarcation in line with the decision reached in this case would face immense difficulties. To begin with the same rigidity and commitment to formalism that typified the delimitation stage (and which has exposed the Commission's work to the strongest criticism by all sides to the dispute) continued unperturbed during the demarcation phase. It is suggested that the Commission's work would have better chances of success had it adopted the more holistic view of the entire exercise as a process.

8.4 Eritrea–Ethiopia Claims Commission (EECC)

Despite the criticisms discussed above, the Eritrea–Ethiopia dispute provides a rich jurisprudence in many respects. One aspect of the case which will prove of enduring value to African international law is the EECC's handling of claims of responsibility for damage and loss of life as a result of the boundary dispute. After several hearings in addition to substantial memoranda filed by the parties on significant questions related to jurisdiction, procedures and possible remedies, the EECC, issued its Decisions Numbers 1–5.[73] The modus operandi of the EECC included formal and informal meetings with international organisations such as the International Organization on Migration (IOM) and the Red Cross to discuss technical issues relating to the design and implementation of possible mass claims filing systems as well as the gathering and presentation of evidential proof of aspects of the claims. The EECC adopted its own Rules of Procedure

---

72 Ibid., p. 23. In classic and unrelenting fashion symptomatic of the conservative jurisprudence of the main international courts and tribunals it is stated that 'the Commission is, as already noted, constrained by the terms of the December 2000 Agreement. The Commission is unable to read into that treaty language, either taken by itself or read in the light of the context provided by other associated agreements concluded between the Parties, any authority for it to add to or subtract from the terms of the colonial treaties or to include within the applicable international law elements of flexibility which it does not already contain'. This is very difficult to reconcile with paras 1. and 2 of the Eritrea–Ethiopia Boundary Commission Determinations, 7 November 2002, available at http://pca-cpa.org/PDF/EEBC/Determinations071102.pdf.

73 The EECC (established pursuant to Art. 5 of the Agreement signed in Algiers 12 December 2000) was directed to 'decide through binding arbitration all claims for loss, damage or injury by one Government against the other, and by nationals (including both natural and juridical persons) of one party against the Government of the other party or entities owned or controlled by the other party that are (a) related to the conflict that was the subject of the Framework Agreement, the Modalities for its Implementation and the Cessation of Hostilities Agreement, and (b) result from violations of international humanitarian law, including the 1949 Geneva Conventions, or other violations of international law'. Pursuant to the December Agreement, the Commission is an independent body. Its seat is in The Hague, although it did meet informally with the parties elsewhere. The Commission's composition was as follows: Prof. Hans van Houtte (President); Judge George Aldrich (appointed by Ethiopia); Mr John Crook (appointed by Eritrea); Dean James Paul (appointed by Ethiopia); Ms Lucy Reed (appointed by Eritrea).

which are based on the PCA's Optional Rules for Arbitrating Disputes between States. In December 2001, both parties filed their claims in compliance with the 12 December 2001 filing deadline established by Article 5(8) of the December Agreement. Neither party utilised the possibility, created by Chapter Three of the Commission's Rules, of filing claims utilising possible mass claims procedures. State-to-state claims were filed on behalf of the government of Ethiopia against Eritrea. Eritrea on the other hand also filed claims on its behalf, as well on behalf of certain named individuals. The mutual claims related to such matters as the conduct of military operations in the war front zones, the treatment of Prisoners of War (POW) and of civilians and their property, diplomatic immunities and the economic impact of certain government actions during the conflict.

The EECC bifurcated its work, dealing first with issues of liability and subsequently with the determination of damages. It began with the two parties' claims alleging mistreatment of their respective prisoners of war, followed by their claims of misconduct relating to the armed conflict in the Central Front and the allegations of mistreatment of civilians. In August 2002, the President of the Commission met in Geneva with officials of the International Committee of the Red Cross to determine whether the ICRC would consent to the parties' use of certain materials originated by the ICRC but in the possession of the parties in relation to their POW claims. Although the ICRC made available to the Commission and the parties copies of all relevant public documents, it nevertheless concluded that it could not permit access to other information. That decision reflected the ICRC's deeply held belief that its ability to perform its mission requires strong assurances of confidentiality.[74] The Commission was not very appreciative of this principled stance and wrote that; 'the Commission believes that, in the unique situation here, where both parties to the armed conflict agreed that these documents should be provided to the Commission, the ICRC should not have forbidden them from doing so'.[75]

On 1 September 2003, the Federal Democratic Republic of Ethiopia asked the Commission to provide an interpretation of the partial award in Ethiopia's claim under Article 21 of the Commission's Rules of Procedure. However, after consideration of the views submitted by both parties, the Commission declined the request and expressed doubts as to whether it involved a matter of interpretation for purposes of the Rules. The Commission held hearings *in camera* at the Peace Palace on the Central Front claims,[76] Home Front claims,[77] liability claims,[78] first[79] and second damages phases between November 2003 and May 2008. Several partial awards, thus, were given by the EECC over

---

74 See Gabor Rona, "The ICRC Privilege Not to Testify: Confidentiality in Action", 84 *Int'l Rev. Red Cross* (2002), p. 207.
75 Partial Awards, Prisoners of War – Eritrea's Claim 17, para. 53, p. 13.
76 Partial Awards, released 28 April 2004.
77 The Partial Awards, released 17 December 2004.
78 The Partial Awards, as well as the Commission's Decision No. 6, released 19 December 2005.
79 Ibid.

the years.[80] The Commission rendered its final awards on damages in each party's claims on 17 August 2009.[81]

The EECC in many ways has been a unique contribution to the law and practice of boundary dispute settlement. A myriad of issues were dealt with that may prove instructive to future disputants on the continent. For instance, the fact that the existence of war over territory does not exempt combatants and state parties from their obligations under international law even in relation to the treatment of POWs is a valuable lesson for African states. The fact that the specific issue of POWs (involving approximately 2,600 Eritrean POWs in Ethiopia and 1,100 Ethiopian POWs in Eritrea (between the start of the conflict in May 1998 and August 2002)) was extensively considered and appropriate blame pronounced upon by the EECC contributes to making future wars in Africa less dangerous both for combatants and the general population as well.

---

80 The Partial Awards as indicated by the EECC are as follows: Prisoners of War – Eritrea's claim 17; Prisoners of War – Ethiopia's claim 4; Central Front – Eritrea's claims 2, 4, 6, 7, 8 and 22; Central Front – Ethiopia's claim 2; Civilians claims – Eritrea's claims 15, 16, 23 and 27–32; Civilians claims – Ethiopia's claim 5; Western Front, Aerial Bombardment and Related claims – Eritrea's claims 1, 3, 5, 9–13, 14, 21, 25 and 26; Western and Eastern Fronts – Ethiopia's claims 1 and 3; Diplomatic claim – Eritrea's claim 20; Diplomatic claim – Ethiopia's claim 8; Loss of Property in Ethiopia Owned by Non-Residents – Eritrea's claim 24; Economic Loss throughout Ethiopia – Ethiopia's claim 7 and *jus ad bellum* – Ethiopia's claims 1–8.
81 Final Awards: Pensions – Eritrea's claims 15, 19 and 23; Ports – Ethiopia's claim 6. See further Progress Report of the Secretary-General on Ethiopia and Eritrea, 4 September 2003; UN Doc. S/2003/858; Progress report of the Secretary-General on Ethiopia and Eritrea, 19 June 2001, UN Doc. S/2001/608.

9 Case study: mediation route to settlement: the dispute between Malawi and Tanzania over Lake Nyasa

Since Malawi became independent on 6 July 1964, diplomatic relations with Tanzania its north-eastern neighbour have been strained.[1] The open dispute between the Republic of Malawi (Malawi) the United Republic of Tanzania (Tanzania) concerns the location of the border between the two states on or at the perimeter of Lake Nyasa/Malawi (the Lake). The Lake is recognised as the third largest in Africa, and is located at the bottom of the Great African Rift Valley where it covers an estimated 29,600 square kilometres.[2] The Lake's shoreline borders western Mozambique, eastern Malawi and southern Tanzania. The main issue of contention is whether, as Tanzania claims, the boundary demarcating the two states should be placed along the middle of the Lake; or, as Malawi claims, it should run along the Lake's eastern shoreline of the territory of Tanzania. Essentially, therefore, the dispute 'relates to whether Tanzania or Malawi exercise sovereignty over the eastern half of the northern part of the Lake separating Tanzania and Malawi.'[3] The border issue is further complicated by a recent history of grants of exploration licences by Malawi over the same Lake.[4]

---

1 Some of the materials referred to in this section of this chapter are held on file by the author but all other materials are in the public domain.
2 James Mayall, "The Malawi–Tanzania Boundary Dispute", Vol. 11, *The Journal of Modern African Studies*, No. 4 (December 1973), p. 611.
3 Chris Mahony, Hannah Clark, Meghan Bolwell, Tom Simcock, Richard Potter and Jia Meng, "Where Politics Borders Law: The Malawi-Tanzania Boundary Dispute", *New Zealand Centre for Human Rights Law, Policy and Practice – Working Paper* (2014), p. 1. The writers note that: 'The dispute is complicated by historical shifts in the positions of the parties and the former colonial powers. Tanzania was a German colony until 1919 when it was awarded to Britain under the Treaty of Versailles, making it, like Malawi (then Nyasaland), a British territory. While the British colonial view of the boundary may have been inconsistent, the German and British authorities had formally agreed under the 1890 Heligoland Treaty ... that the border ran along the Lake's eastern shoreline'. "Two Additional Companies Awarded with Exploration Rights by Malawi amid Unresolved Lake Dispute", *Mining in Malawi* (15 November 2013) available at http://mininginmalawi.com/2013/11/15/two-additional-companies-awarded-with-exploration-rights-amidunresolved-lake-dispute/accessed on 2 September 2014.
4 Malawi has indeed awarded oil exploration licences covering the disputed part of the Lake to Surestream Petroleum. Currently four companies have been awarded exclusive prospecting licences for six blocks on the Lake: Block 1: SacOil (awarded in 2012, 12,265 sq. km, north-western block bordering Tanzania and Zambia, all environmental work expected to be complete by the third quarter of 2014); Blocks 2 and 3: Surestream Petroleum (awarded in 2011, 20,000 sq. km,

The dispute was submitted for mediation by the High Level Mediation Team on the Boundary Dispute between Tanzania and Malawi over Lake Nyasa/Malawi (HLMT) which operates within the Forum for Former African Heads of State and Government (the Africa Forum).[5] The body was established on 11 January 2006 in Maputo, the Republic of Mozambique as an informal network of former African Heads of State and government and other African leaders. The mediators of the Africa Forum are former African Heads of State and government and other African leaders whose individual and collective experiences are considered 'treasures that must be tapped and used for the benefit of the African peoples.'[6] It is designed essentially to support the implementation of the broad objectives of the African Union (AU) and its New Partnership for Africa's Development (NEPAD) initiative, at national, regional and sub-regional levels.[7]

On 21 December 2012 its chairperson, Joaquim Alberto Chissano, former President of the Republic of Mozambique, received an official joint application requesting the Africa Forum to mediate between Tanzania and Malawi concerning their dispute. Following the submission, the Executive Secretariat of the Africa Forum (ESAF) supported the Chairperson in identifying and selecting the HLMT from members of the Africa Forum within the Southern African Development Community (SADC) sub-region to conduct the mediation process. Following necessary consultations it was decided that the HLMT would be composed of three members including Joaquim Alberto Chissano, former President of the Republic of Mozambique and Chairman of the AF; Thabo Mbeki, former President of the Republic of South Africa and member of the AF; and Festus Mogae, former President of the Republic of Botswana and member of the Africa Forum. Subsequently, it was agreed that HE Joaquim Chissano should lead the HLMT.

Members of the HLMT agreed to be guided by the principle that the HLMT should be independent, autonomous and totally neutral without bias or prejudice to any party. The HLMT is supported by a team of Legal and Other Experts (LOE), who advise them on legal and other technical issues based on their individual and collective expertise in the area of international boundary disputes. Additionally, the HLMT is assisted by the Africa Forum *ad hoc* secretariat based in Maputo which provides technical, logistic and administrative support. Initially,

---

north and central blocks on Lake Nyasa/Malawi); Blocks 4 and 5: RAKGAS (awarded in 2013); Block 6: Pacific Oil and Gas (awarded in 2013); Surestream Petroleum, the company holding the largest licence on the Lake, is an independent UK-based oil exploration company founded in 2004.

5 M. Banda, "Two Million People Hold their Breath Over Lake Malawi Mediation", in Inter Press Service News Agency, 3 March 2013, viewed on 10 December 2013, http://www.ipsnews.net/2013/03/two-million-peoplehold-their-breath-over-lake-malawi-mediation/; "The Malawi-Tanzania Border Dispute, Voices from the frontiers", in *Nation on Sunday*, 14 April 2013, viewed on 18 January 2014 http://www.scribd.com/doc/135817434/The-Malawi-Tanzania-Border-Dispute-Voices-from-the-frontiers.

6 See the Mission statement of the Africa Forum at www.africaforum.org.

7 Ibid.

ESAF also established a Support and Technical Advisory Group (STAG) as the Secretariat of the HLMT.

In their joint application, the parties proposed that the African Forum should incorporate eminent jurists, preferably from the SADC region, as well as recognised international experts, for expert guidance. Thus, the selection of the LOE was based on their expertise in the area of border disputes and international boundary issues.[8] It is pertinent to add here that this dispute is still ongoing as at the date of publication of this book and the HMLT is still seised of the matter.

9.1 The applicable treaties and instruments

Both parties agree that the Anglo–German agreement of July 1890 or Heligoland-Zanzibar Treaty (hereafter the 1890 Treaty) is binding on them. Malawi argues on the strength of Article 1(2) of the text of the treaty and on the basis of subsequent practice as a tool for interpretation. Tanzania notes that Article VI allows for rectification. It emphasises that the Article provides for rectification of the delimitation set out in Articles I to IV. As a result, it maintains, that the delimitation described in Article I(2) is not conclusive. Other applicable laws and key legal texts governing the dispute include the following; Boundary Treaty between Britain and Portugal of 1891, which delimits, *inter alia*, the boundary between Malawi and Mozambique in the area of Lake Malawi; Treaty of 1901, between the United Kingdom and Germany, which addresses the boundary 'between Lakes Nyasa and Tanganyika'; The Organisation of African Unity Charter of 1963, especially Article III (3) and (4) which require, respectively, the respect for the territorial integrity of each state as well as the peaceful resolution of disputes (including boundary disputes); Resolution of the Organisation of African Unity (OAU) AHG/Res. 16(1), Border Disputes Among African States, First Ordinary Session of the Assembly of Heads of State and Government Held in Cairo, UAR of 1964 ('the 1964 OAU Cairo Declaration'); Article 3, Settlement of Disputes with Third Parties, Vienna Convention on Diplomatic Relations of 18 April 1961; The Vienna Convention on the Law of Treaties, 1969, especially article 62 on Fundamental Change of Circumstances, Tanganyika Legislative Council, Official Report (Dar es Salaam), 12 October 1960; German Joint Boundary Commission (JBC) of

---

8 Accordingly, the following names were identified to compose the LOE team: Judge Raymond Ranjeva, former Judge of the International Court of Justice (ICJ); Prof. George Kanyeihamba, former Judge of the Supreme Court of Uganda, Presidential Legal Advisor, AG and Ministry of Justice; Dr Gbenga Oduntan, senior lecturer of International Commercial Law at Kent Law School and member of the Nigerian team at the ICJ on the *Bakassi Peninsula Case*; Dr Dire David Tladi, Counsellor and Legal Advisor of the Permanent Mission of South Africa to the UN, Department of International Relations and Cooperation (DIRCO), Republic of South Africa and current member of the UN International Law Commission (UNILC); Judge Barney Afako, legal advisor at the AU high level implementation panel on Sudan (AUHIP), private consultant, part-time Immigration Judge in the United Kingdom; Prof. Martin Pratt, director of research, International Boundaries Research Unit (IBRU) in the Department of Geography, Durham University; Dr Miguel Alberto Chissano, President of the National Institute for Maritime and Border Affairs, Republic of Mozambique; and Judge Abdul Koroma, former Judge at the ICJ.

1898; Anglo-German Joint Commission (1904–6); German–Portuguese Joint Boundary Commission (1909); Anglo-Belgian Boundary Commission (1923); and Anglo-Portuguese Boundary Commission (1954).

9.2 Malawi's position

In the view of Malawi, the 1890 Treaty between Britain and Germany, which delimited spheres of influence between them across Africa became the *de jure* boundaries between the two territories now known as Malawi and Tasmania. Article I(2) of the Treaty states as follows:

> To the south by a line starting on the coast at the northern limit of the Province of Mozambique ... till it reaches Lake Nyasa; *thence striking northward, it follows the eastern, northern, and western shores of the Lake to the northern bank of the River Songwe.*

Therefore, for Malawi the boundary between the two countries in relation to Lake Malawi is on the shoreline leaving the whole lake to Malawi. Malawi also crucially believes that the relevant subsequent practice between both states confirms its interpretation of Article I(2) of the Agreement. In this regard, Malawi relies on two later treaties in support of the 'shoreline boundary'. The first is the boundary treaty between Britain and Portugal of 1891, which delimited, *inter alia*, the boundary between Malawi and Mozambique in the area of Lake Malawi. Adopting the same approach as the 1890 Treaty, it delimited the boundary in the area of the Lake in Article I(2) in accordance with a shoreline boundary as follows:

> To the west by a line, which starting from the above-mentioned frontier on Lake Nyasa, follows the eastern shore of the lake southwards as far as the parallel of latitude 13 degrees 30' south; thence it runs in a southerly direction to the eastern shore of Lake Chiuta, which it follows...[9]

The second treaty is the treaty of 1901, between the United Kingdom and Germany which addressed the boundary 'between Lakes Nyasa and Tanganyika'. In relation to the 1901 Treaty, Malawi notes that there are two points of significance. First that it concerned only the boundary between Lake Nyasa and Lake Tangayika and did not address any aspect of the boundary between Malawi and Tanzania. Second, the fact that this particular instrument of rectification exists is an indication that rectification of the boundary could occur only by treaty and by no other means.[10]

---

9 It is to be noted that the 1891 Treaty between Britain and Portugal contained, at Article VII, an equivalent to Article VI of the 1890 Treaty.
10 The possibility of rectification of the pertinent boundaries was explicitly envisaged and there were indeed five separate rectifications of this sort although only one concerned the Malawi–Tanzania boundary. The other four rectifications concerned the boundaries as between Tanzania–Zambia;

Malawi, maintains that Tanzania in both its pre- and post-independence political and official statements has always accepted the 1890 Treaty as the basis of the boundary between the two countries in relation to Lake Malawi/Nyasa. Malawi particularly draws strong support for its views on a statement made in 1960 by Julius Nyerere, the former Tanzanian Chief Minister who stated as follows:

> ...but one point which I think I must emphasize again, which was raised by my Hon. Colleague the Minister for Information Services and repeated by the Attorney General is there is now no doubt at all about the boundary. We know that not a drop of the water of Lake Nyasa belongs to Tanganyika under the terms of the agreement, so that in actual fact we would be asking a neighbouring Government as the Attorney-General said, to change the boundary in favour of Tanganyika. Some people think this is easier in the case of water and it might be much more difficult in the case of Land. I don't know the logic of this.[11]

Malawi has also referred to what it regards as objective third-party evidence supporting the shoreline boundary position. Examples relied on include the OAU Declaration of 1964 on the inviolability of African boundaries inherited at independence.[12] As a result Malawi believes that the position taken by Tanzania necessarily calls into question the stability of many African boundaries including in some cases, those that have since assumed the status of internal administrative boundaries within states.

Malawi is of the firm view that equity is in its favour in relation to the facts of this dispute. To demonstrate this claim Malawi has pointed out and emphasised the lop-sided nature of the general geography of the sub-region which apparently is in the favour of Tanzania. Malawi's status is that of a small, landlocked and densely populated small state, which actually is one of the most economically and geographically disadvantaged in Africa. In contrast, Tanzania is described as a vast country with access to the sea along a long Indian coastline. Malawi is thus of the opinion that even arguments of equity will militate in its favour as Tanzania is better endowed geographically than Malawi.

In the light of the foregoing, Malawi is strongly of the view that the delimitation of a shoreline boundary in the Lake by the 1890 Treaty was not a mistake or an oversight, whether by the standards of the time or those of the modern times. In other words the preservation of the waters of the Lake as part of the sovereign

---

Uganda–Rwanda; Uganda–Tanzania and Kenya–Tanzania. The treaty rectifying the Kenya–Tanzania boundary was, however, not signed due to the outbreak of the First World War in 1914.
11 Tanganyika Legislative Council, Official Report (Dar es Salaam), 12 October 1960.
12 Resolution AHG/Res. 16(1), Border Disputes Among African States; Organisation of African Unity, Resolution Adopted by the First Ordinary Session of the Assembly of Heads of State and Government Held in Cairo, UAR from 17–21 July 1964, Resolutions AHG Res. 1 (1) – AHG Res.24(1).

territory of Malawi was intended by the colonial powers, and recognition of the importance to Malawi of the Lake, in the sense of deliberate preferential advantages in favour of the then German colony of Tanganyika had already also been taken into consideration.

A significant issue in the Malawian position in this dispute is that it believes that the only route for revision of the boundary is through a subsequently agreed treaty. Malawi has, therefore, maintained that any revision of the boundary between Malawi and Tanzania would have to follow the same principle adopted in the case of the Malawi–Mozambique boundary, which is that a boundary based on a treaty can only be modified by a subsequent treaty. In the absence of such a treaty it is denied that Tanzania can secure a variation of the 1890 boundary by reason of unilateral assertion of a claim.

A very serious issue between the parties has been the right of access of the affected local population to the Lake. Malawi has acknowledged the importance of the Lake to the local Tanzanian population along the shoreline. Malawi has thus committed itself to do everything to ensure access to the Lake by the Tanzanian local population for their livelihoods. This position Malawi admits is in consonance with the 1890 treaty to the extent that it incorporated important elements of the Act of Berlin of 1885 (concerning free trade) and also addressed other elements of access to the Lake by the inhabitants of both sides.[13] Malawi indeed hopes that the Forum handling the mediation between both states will assist the two sides in 'ensuring mutually agreeable arrangements for access to the Lake for the benefit of all those who live along its shores under the umbrella of Malawian sovereignty'.

9.3 Tanzania's position

In identifying the applicable treaties to rely on in its legal dispute, Tanzania has also accepted the 1890 Anglo-German Agreement (Heligoland Treaty) as crucial to the understanding of the boundary between both countries. The treaty with a dozen provisions is divided into Articles I–IV (containing descriptions of bounds or limits of spheres of influence of Great Britain and Germany in parts of Africa); (ii) Articles V–XI and (iii) Article XII (which describes cessation of the Anglo-German Agreement of 1890). It also dealt with conditions to be observed by both parties in different parts of their territories.

A central pillar of Tanzania's case has been its insistence upon what is seen as the crucial obligation upon the parties to engage with and fulfil the provisions on rectification within the Heligoland Treaty. Tanzania's case rests upon an emphasis on the importance of the provisions contained in the process of rectification wherein Britain and Germany in Article VI agreed that 'All the lines of demarcation traced under Articles I to IV shall be subject to rectification by agreement between the powers in accordance with local requirements.'

---

13 At Article VII of the 1890 Anglo-German Treaty.

Tanzania has identified several joint boundary commissions formed subsequent to conclusion of agreements between European powers describing their spheres of influence in Africa. These include the Anglo–German Joint Boundary Commission (JBC) of 1898;[14] the Anglo-German Joint Commission (1904–06);[15] the German-Portuguese Joint Boundary Commission (1909);[16] Anglo-Belgian Boundary Commission (1923);[17] and the Anglo-Portuguese Boundary Commission (1954) (which it is claimed shifted the boundary between Mozambique and Malawi from the shore line to the median line in Lake Nyasa). This particular instance is significant in its similarity to the desires of Tanzania in this case.

Tanzania has argued quite strongly that the cessation of the Anglo–German Joint Boundary Commission was a result of the occurrence of the First World War, the eventual defeat of Germany and the relinquishment of German properties abroad to the allied powers. Tangayika and Nyasaland, thus, came under British administration. The Tanzanian view, therefore, is that the boundary over Lake Nyasa between Tanzania and Malawi was not delimitated and demarcated.

Tanzania has at various points acknowledged Article III (4) of the OAU Charter on Peaceful Settlement of 1963 which mandates that all disputes arising out of the inconclusively settled African boundaries should be resolved by peaceful means. Specifically in relation to the Tanzania–Malawi Boundary, Tanzania notes that the boundary between Tanzania and Malawi on Land, Songwe River and over Lake Nyasa was described by the provisions of Article I(2) of the Anglo-German Agreement of 1890. The Article states *inter alia*:

> To the South by a line which, starting on the coast of the Northern limit of the province of Mozambique, follows the course of the river Rovuma to the point of confluence of the Misinje: thence it runs westwards along the parallel of that point till it reaches Lake Nyasa; thence striking northwards it follows the eastern, northern and western shores of the lake to the northern bank of the mouth of River Songwe; it ascends that river to the point of the intersection by the 33rd degree of east longitude; thence it follows the river to the point where it approaches most nearly the boundary of the geographical Congo basin.

However, according to Tanzania, the boundary was subject to rectification by virtue of Article VI which states:

> All the lines of demarcation traced in Articles I to IV shall be subject to rectification by agreement between the two powers in accordance with local requirements.

---

14 This treaty carried out rectification of the frontier between German and British Territories from Lake Nyasa to Lake Tangayika.
15 This body carried out rectification of the boundary from Mount Sabinio to Lake Jipe.
16 This body carried out rectification of the boundary section between the confluence of River Misinje with Rovuma to the shore of Lake Nyasa.
17 Which is said to have demarcated the boundary between Urundi–Rwanda and Tangayika.

As a result the 1898 JBC which came up with a Protocol on the Land Boundary between Tangayika and Nyasaland in 1901, introduced what Tanzania understands as a radical departure from the former frontier in the form of its Article 2 which introduced the Thalweg principle for river and stream boundaries. It states:

> In all cases where a river or a stream forms the boundary, the Thalweg of the same shall be the boundary; If however, no actual 'Thalweg' is to be distinguished, it shall be the middle of the bed...

This departure, according to Tanzania, signifies that the rectification process can involve major modifications. Tanzania states that but for the occurrence of the First World War and the eventual dispossessions affecting Germany, Lake Nyasa would also have been conclusively dealt with. Despite this, Tanzania believes that there is a wealth of documentary evidence including maps during the 1918 to 1949 period that indicate the median line as the boundary between both territories. Furthermore Tanzania relies on the opinion expressed by the office of the Attorney-General of the British government in response to an advisory opinion sought by the Governor of Tangayika in 1959. Paragraph 11 at page 15 of the opinion stated that:

> In my opinion, therefore, both for the historical and legal reasons set forth above and on the analogy of the Anglo–Portuguese Agreement of 1954, there are good grounds for demarcating a definitive boundary on the median line of the lake between the Ruvuma River line and the Songwe River.[18]

In relation to the importance of the affected population and their socio-economic activities, Tanzania has emphasised the importance of the Lake for its shoreline population and as a natural common triple heritage to the peoples of Tanzania, Malawi and Mozambique since time immemorial. Accordingly the Lake Nyasa shoreline is said to form part of Tanzania and is about 318 kilometres long comprising of several districts namely, Ludewa, Kyela, Nyasa and Mbinga. A recent Tanzanian national population census of 2012 recorded a total population of 834,296 people living along these shoreline districts.

Tanzania on the whole accepts that the 1963 AU Charter provides for peaceful settlement of disputes by various methods including negotiation and has acknowledged numerous efforts between the parties to resolve the boundary dispute after independence, including an acknowledged *Note Verbale* by which Tanzania stated its median line claim. There was also Malawi's request for a joint boundary commission in 2005. Tanzania is, therefore, of the belief that on the basis of Article I(2) and VI of the Anglo-German Agreement of 1890, the

---

18 Annex 9 of the Tanzanian Submission.

boundary between the two countries along Lake Nyasa has to be delimited and demarcated jointly by the two states. Tanzania suggests that this should be done by way of a Joint Boundary Commission as provided by the Anglo-German Treaty, which will continue the rectification process initiated by the powers (Britain and Germany).

9.4 HLMT: challenges, achievements and prospects

Although the mediation in relation to this dispute is ongoing as the time of publication of this book, there are certain issues of process worthy of attention and certain conclusions may be hazarded. The Africa Forum Mediation Panel by its very nature is not a standing institution and its capacity to function as a mediation panel is considerably *ad hoc*. Thus, for instance, the body has no standing mediation rules. The procedure adopted by the Joaquim Chissano panel has involved separate and joint sessions with the parties. The parties have indeed exchanged their submissions for further clarification of each other's views to enable them to conclusively determine the central issues on which they disagree. Before and after the closed sessions the international press is usually allowed into the mediation venue which has been within the prestigious Joaquim Chissano International Conference Center located in Maputo, Mozambique. Both oral and written evidence have been presented by the parties before the panel.

In the light of the submissions by both parties upholding the validity of the 1890 agreement, it is near certain that the mediation panel would uphold the agreement as the legal basis of the boundary between the two states. This would be consistent with the OAU Declaration of 1964 mandating the respect by African States of boundaries inherited at independence.

It is indeed encouraging to note that there is clear evidence of strong commitment and determination, on the part of African leaders, who have vacated office, to address decisively the present internal scourge of boundary conflicts in Africa. The wealth of knowledge and experience these leaders have accumulated during their tenures in office and also considering their individual and collective knowledge is bound to be uniquely relevant to disputing countries. The involvement of the current former African leaders as mediators in this case should also contribute greatly towards a possible adoption of African solutions to this long-standing dispute. The fact that a formidable team of legal and other experts assembled across Africa have been assisting and advising the three man mediation panel engenders much confidence in the capacity of the panel to discharge its duties meritoriously.

The mediation has, however, experienced unique challenges. First, in April 2013 Malawi withdrew from the process, citing a perceived bias by one of the SADC officials: Malawi accused John Tesha, a Tanzanian diplomat at SADC, of forwarding Malawi's submission outlining their arguments to the dispute resolution mechanism prematurely to the Tanzanian government.[19] Although

---

19 John Tesha incidentally is also the Executive Secretary of the Africa Forum.

Malawi returned to the mediation table in early May, following Tesha's recall by Tanzania, Malawian scepticism is rife and its Press continues to express a belief that the process will not be free from political bias.[20]

Second, certain aspects of the provisions in the bilateral agreement between Malawi and Tanzania that was signed in November 2012 make it possible for either party to refer the matter to the International Court of Justice. It is perhaps unhealthy for the process that the shadow of the ICJ is so openly cast on the Africa Forum. It is very important that a mediation or ADR mechanism be imbued with the utmost prestige possible in international matters. The perceived threat that one of the parties may pull out of the mediation at any time or that no matter how the mediation goes, one of the parties is likely to proceed to the ICJ is not helpful to international legal practice in this area. Such a situation does not agree with international policy in support of finality of judgments of international tribunals. Equally unhelpful to the mediation process are press reports of Tanzania's threats to resort to armed conflict over the dispute.[21]

Third, the parties have displayed little evidence of an intention to compromise –a necessary component of the mediation route. The head of the mediation panel President Joaquim Chissano openly admitted that the parties remained deadlocked after many months of formal and informal contacts under the process. A newly elected Malawian President, Peter Mutharika, in September 2014 has reaffirmed his country's claim to the full extents of Lake Malawi.[22]

The difficulties facing the mediation are thus formidable, although certainly not insurmountable. The fear of many observers is that extraneous issues to the bare legal acts are bound to impinge on the process as a result of the sub-regional history at play and affecting the stakeholders. Not least of these are the political histories, contrasting attitudes and policies of the states involved as well as the states the mediators come from towards the erstwhile white minority regimes in Southern Africa. The historical memory of African states in relation to political conflicts perhaps surpasses that of the proverbial African elephants that are said to possess a long memory.

---

20 Aditi Lalbahadur, "Malawi vs Tanzania vs SADC: Regional Dispute Resolution Bites the Dust", SAIIA website (13 August 2013) available at http://www.saiia.org.za/ accessed 2 September 2014.
21 President Jakaya Mrisho Kikwete stated in 2013 that 'Anyone who tries to provoke our country will face consequences ... Our country is safe and the army is strong and ready to defend our country... We will not allow anyone to mess with our country, or try to take away our territory. We will deal with them just as we dealt with [former Ugandan ruler Idi] Amin', Reuters, "Tanzania Raises Stakes in Border Spat with Malawi", *Voice of America* available at http://www.voanews.com/content/reu-tanzania-raises-stakes-in-border-spat-with-malawi/1710325.html accessed 02 September 2014.
22 The Editors, "Malawi-Tanzania Border Dispute Flares up over Potential Oil Discovery", 2 September 2014, *Trend Lines* available on the website of the *World Politics Review* at http://www.worldpoliticsreview.com/trend-lines/14024/malawi-tanzania-border-dispute-flares-up-over-potential-oil-discovery accessed 02 September 2014.

As James Mayall correctly put it over 40 years ago, this dispute like many other African disputes, has a multifaceted background and looking at the bare legal case alone will hardly scratch the surface of the holistic problem. He wrote:

> These issues are not easily separable: for if it had not been for Banda's outspoken policy towards the white South (which led him alone amongst African statesmen to establish diplomatic relations with South Africa) there would have been no compelling grounds for Tanzania which opposed this policy, to offer asylum and support to his political opponents; and if it had not been for Tanzania's confrontation, not only with South Africa but also with the Portuguese authorities as in Mozambique (with whom Malawi also maintained close relations), it is doubtful whether President Nyerere would have been provoked during May 1967 into bringing the Lake dispute into the open. There is no doubt that Malawi exiles in Dar es Salaam were actively campaigning against Banda's regime, at this time, over the whole range of his policies, including the question of the Lake.[23]

For the mediation to have any meaningful prospect of producing a 'resolution' and not just a 'decision' the parties and mediators must fully understand and factor-in the possible effects of these background issues on the present process. Considering the history and the dynamics of the dispute, it is necessary for the HLMT to ensure it has a deep understanding of the Parties' motivations and concerns, their internal political considerations as well as the interests and cultural practices of the local communities. The final recommendations should take all these matters into account and advice should be circumstantial and based on sound principles. Thus, the HLMT should encourage the parties to make proposals on frameworks and models of possible cooperation between the neighbouring states (e.g., possible joint production and wealth-sharing) – rather than take the litigious route by taking matters to the World Court.

In order to fully discharge of its duties, the HLMT must determine the specific interests of the parties related to the dispute by engaging with each party separately. At all points in time it would be advisable for the parties to demonstrate good faith to the mediation by avoiding utterances and positions that are inflammatory or calculated to incite negative reactions from the other. Everything said and done during the mediation should be for the sole purpose of bringing the parties to a mutual understanding of each other's case and to bridge the gap between them in order to reach an acceptable compromise based on international laws on the issues.

It is of course recommended that the HLMT should uphold the 1890 Treaty as the legal basis for the boundary between the two states, whilst recognising that it is open to the Parties to reach a settlement by mutual consent. The parties

---

23 Op.cit., p. 611. See also James Mayall, "Malawi's Foreign Policy", in *The World Today* (London), October 1970, pp. 435–45.

themselves ought to be aiming at building upon the history of cooperation between them in relation to the use of the Lake and in other areas of their bilateral relations. The parties must also realise that they are obliged to abide by the principle of settling this dispute in accordance with the principle of good faith. The HLMT would of course be guided by the OAU Declaration of 1964 specifying the primacy of boundaries inherited at independence. This instrument is still one of the guiding lights in the navigation of relations between African states in their border relations.

Commentators on this dispute have predominantly predicted that if the current third-party mediation fails and the disputants decide to submit the case to the International Court of Justice, the colonial treaty that delimited the border between the two territories is likely to prevail; thereby upholding Malawi's position on the Lake border on the basis of the principle of *uti possidetis*.[24] One such prediction reads:

> The default legal position is that the boundary runs along the North-eastern shore of the Lake, which is therefore under Malawian sovereignty in its entirety. As the claimant, the onus is therefore on Tanzania to establish that the shoreline boundary is not correct – an amendment to the legal position established by the Heligoland Treaty. This position is supported by the legal principle that at independence, nations maintain their colonial boundaries. Since the Treaty is explicit as to the shoreline boundary, giving sovereignty of the entire Lake to Malawi, Tanzania bears the burden to displace this. Whilst Tanzania may rely on various post-1890 maps indicating a median line boundary, it is unlikely to demonstrate the requisite intent for the maps to constitute a valid demarcation. The documents accompanying the maps are inadequately descriptive of the boundary or the colonial power's intent. Critically, there is a distinct lack of any explanatory text addressing a boundary change. The absence of explicit intent to change the boundary makes it particularly difficult for Tanzania to substantiate a claim of historical consolidation of title.[25]

Such predictions are ultimately inconsequential because of the unpredictability of the adjudicative route of dispute settlement and the fact that the ICJ does not operate upon a *stare decisis* basis in giving its decisions.

---

24 Mi Yung Yoon, "Colonialism and Border Disputes in Africa: The Case of the Malawi-Tanzania Dispute over Lake Malawi/Nyasa", Vol. 1, *The Journal of Territorial and Maritime Studies*, No. 1 (January 2014), pp. 75–89.
25 C. Mahony, H. Clark, M. Bolwell *et. al.*, op.cit., pp. 10–11.

10 Case study: adjudicative route – a critique of the land and maritime boundary dispute (*Cameroon v Nigeria*)

It may be acknowledged that there are few international legally significant events that manage to capture the attention of both the government and the people of independent states as successfully as the rendering of a verdict of the International Court of Justice.[1] The judgment of 10 October 2002 was the first in the twenty-first century to decide a territorial and boundary dispute on the African Continent and it served as a poignant reminder of the lingering effects of a colonial era fast receding in popular memory.[2] Because of the long gestation period of the dispute between the parties and time it took for the Court to handle the case (the better part of a decade), many questions have exercised scholarly minds in relation to the efficacy of the adjudicative route. Was the judgment fair and equitable in all respects? Would the parties accept the verdict of the Court as final and binding? Would the parties give effect to the judgment? Would there be a relapse into serious conflicts or even war? These questions are particularly significant if viewed in context of the seriously 'strained' relationship between the two African neighbouring states, the rash of international conflicts currently ravaging parts of the African continent and the traditional suspicion of the World Court by developing states in the twentieth century.

Many aspects of the *Land and Maritime Case* ruling may be of interest to international lawyers, geographers, political scientists, scholars of international relations and a host of experts in other fields, and much has been written on the

---

1 Referred to variously as the ICJ, the Court or the World Court.
2 See *Land and Maritime Boundary between Cameroon and Nigeria* (*Cameroon v Nigeria: Equatorial Guinea Intervening*), Judgment, Preliminary Objections [1998] ICJ 2, 11 June 1998. (www.worllii.org/int/cases/ICJ/1998/2.html); Request for Interpretation of the Judgment of 11 June 1998 in the *Case Concerning the Land and Maritime Boundary between Cameroon and Nigeria* (*Cameroon v Nigeria*), Preliminary Objections (*Nigeria v Cameroon*) (www.icj-cij.org/icjwww/idocket/icn/icnjudgment/icn_ijudgment_19990325_frame.htm); *Land and Maritime Boundary between Cameroon and Nigeria* (Cameroon v. Nigeria: Equatorial Guinea Intervening), Judgment, Merits, 10 October 2002 (www.icj-cij.org/icjwww/idocket/icnjudgment/); see particularly para.30. Three notable decisions of the ICJ preceded the land and maritime dispute in the new century, each generating significant interests in their own rights. They are the *Maritime Delimitation and Territorial Questions between Qatar and Bahrain* (*Qatar v Bahrain*), Judgment of 16 March 2001; *La Grand* (*Germany v United States of America*), Judgment of 27 June 2001; Arrest Warrant of 11 April 2000 (*Democratic Republic of the Congo v Belgium*), Judgment of 14 February 2002.

merits and demerits of the judgment by scholars in various fields.[3] The decision of the Court itself undoubtedly fits into an enviable tradition of rules, methods, strategies and framework of the theory of international law and its wealth of case law on land and maritime delimitation.

Lawyers and legal writers are accustomed to treat disputes that appear before the International Court and the decisions of the court themselves as solely legally relevant events. Unfortunately too little attention is paid to post-adjudication processes, whereas the later stages in the 'life of a dispute' can teach several lessons that give more depth to our appreciation of the concept of international justice. The implementation of the judgment in the *Land and Maritime Case*, therefore, presents a unique opportunity to examine and reassess the law, procedure and practice of boundary delimitation and demarcation in our modern times. The significance of this implementation process is also due to the enviable results obtained through it. Not least of these is that it has certainly brought a conclusion to a conflict dating back to the very early 1980s when fighting first broke out between Cameroon and Nigeria. However, the judgment and the consequent implementation process have also produced much wider consequences extending far beyond that of the litigation between the two parties. It certainly was also the first, widest-reaching and fastest-moving process of its kind in the twenty-first century arising out of the work of the World Court and may even set new standards for future actions (of which there are sure to be many). It will emerge from our examination of the issues that an impressive level of originality of thinking and practice has typified the actions of the parties in their effort to implement the judgment of the Court. It has arguably set a new paradigm in legal and political thinking about the strengths and limits of pacific resolution of territorial and boundary disputes particularly among developing states.[4]

10.1 Geophysical setting of the region

The states of Cameroon and Nigeria are situated on the west coast of Africa. Their land boundaries extend from Lake Chad in the north to the Bakassi Peninsula in the south. Their coastlines are adjacent; washed by the waters of the Gulf of Guinea. Four states border Lake Chad: Cameroon, Chad, Niger and Nigeria. The waters of the Lake have varied over time and it is common knowledge

---

3 For critical views of the Court's judgment in this case, as well as wider enquiries into the theme that Eurocentric international courts and tribunals are ill-suited for the task of resolution of African boundary and territorial dispute, see Gbenga Oduntan, "Africa Before the International Courts: The Generational Gap in International Adjudication and Arbitration", 5 *The Journal of World Investment and Trade*, No.6 (December 2004), p. 975.
4 See supra our comparisons with the Eritrea–Ethiopia case. Cf. Jean-Pierre Queneudec, "The Eritrea–Yemen Arbitration" in Bette Shifman ed., *The Eritrea-Yemen Arbitration awards 1998 and 1999* (The Hague: T.M.C. Asser Press, 2005), pp. 1–16.; The Eritrea–Ethiopia dispute. For useful commentary see Emmanuelle Jouannet, "Le reglement de paix Entre L'Ethiopie et L'Erythree: Un success majeur Pour L'Ensemble d' Afrique?" 105(4) *Revue Generale De Droit International Public* (2001), pp. 849–896.

that various native groups tend to follow the receding waters and cultivate the arable land it leaves behind. In its northern part, the land boundary between Cameroon and Nigeria passes through hot, dry plains around Lake Chad, at an altitude of about 300 metres. Lake Chad has been gradually drying up over the last 30 years; having exceeded 25,000 square kilometres in area in the early 1970s (previously the fourth largest fresh water lake in Africa), it has since been reduced to less than 2,000 square kilometres. The drying out of the Lake has had a huge impact on the local population. Many people depend on the lake for their livelihood, on both the fish it provides and the farmlands of the region. From the hot dry plains around Lake Chad at an altitude of about 300 metres the boundary goes southwards and passes through mountains, cultivated high grounds or pastures, watered by various rivers and streams. It then descends in stages to areas of savannah and forest, until it reaches the sea in Southern Nigeria.

10.2 Historical provenance of the boundary and territorial problem

Relations between Cameroon and Nigeria have long been strained due to problems along their common border, which is approximately 2000 kilometres long and extends from Lake Chad to the sea.[5] These problems were aggravated by the mutual challenge of sovereignty over the Bakassi Peninsula and Lake Chad. In the Lake Chad region the largely Nigerian population had been moving along with the receding river and the Nigerian Local Government Areas in the North-East which had traditionally provided administrative services and infrastructure for the 60,000 or so Nigerians living in the area simply expanded their control. Nigeria's boundary in that sector consists of a near straight line which joins two tripoints: Nigeria/Niger/Chad and Nigeria/Cameroon/Chad. The Lake Chad Basin Commission (LCBC), an international body comprising Nigeria, Cameroon, Chad, Niger and the Central African Republic proved unable to resolve many of these problems.[6] With the assistance of this international body (which Nigeria funded to the tune of over half of its operational and project costs) the area was the subject of significant cooperation among the countries bordering the Lake. All four countries had entered into an agreement to 'commonly demarcate the boundaries between them'. As a result of the IGN Demarcation Agreement,[7] the Lake Chad Basin Commission (LCBC) delimited the area between 1983 and 1993, and demarcated the boundary.[8] The IGN project was accepted and signed

---

5 For a brief pre-independence era outline of the disputed area see Mendelson, pp. 224–227. Maurice Mendelson, "The Cameroon-Nigeria Case In The International Court of Justice: Some Territorial Sovereignty And Boundary Delimitation Issues", vol. LXXV *BYIL* (2004).
6 Nigeria provides more than half of the funds for the operation of this body. Representatives of the five States meet on a regular basis in order to coordinate efforts to preserve and protect the environment and people of this ecologically fragile area.
7 The Institut Geographique National or IGN is a French firm which contracted the exercise.
8 Confidential. Nigeria-Cameroon Boundary on the Lake Chad. (cyclostyle n.d) p. 2.

by all member states of the LCBC in Abuja, Nigeria. The Nigerian government, however, had not ratified the treaty by the time rising tensions between the two countries degenerated into military confrontation at the end of 1993.[9]

On 29 March 1994 the Republic of Cameroon filed an application instituting proceedings against the Federal Republic of Nigeria in a dispute concerning the question of sovereignty over the Peninsula of Bakassi, and requesting the Court to determine the course of the maritime frontier between the two states in so far as that frontier had not already been established in 1975. As a basis of the jurisdiction of the Court in this case, the application refers to the declarations made by Cameroon and Nigeria under Article 36, paragraph 2, of the Statute of the Court, by which they accept that jurisdiction as compulsory. In the application Cameroon refers to 'aggression by the Federal Republic of Nigeria whose troops are occupying several Cameroonian localities on the Bakassi peninsula' resulting in 'great prejudice to the Republic of Cameroon,' and requests the Court to declare:

(a) that sovereignty over the peninsula of Bakassi is Cameroonian, by virtue of international law and that that Peninsula is an integral part of the territory of Cameroon;

(b) that the Federal Republic of Nigeria has violated and is violating the fundamental principle of respect for frontiers inherited colonisation (*uti possidetis juris*);

(c) that by using force against the Republic of Cameroon, the Federal Republic of Nigeria has violated and is violating its obligations under international treaty law and customary law;

(d) that the Federal Republic of Nigeria by militarily occupying the Cameroonian Peninsula of Bakassi, has violated and is violating the obligations incumbent upon it by virtue of treaty law and customary law;

(e) that in view of these breaches [. . .] the Federal Republic of Nigeria has the express duty of putting an end to its military presence in Cameroonian territory, and effecting an immediate and unconditional withdrawal of its troops from the Cameroonian Peninsula of Bakassi;

(f) that the internationally unlawful acts referred to under (a), (b), (c), (d), and (e) [above] involve the responsibility of the Federal Republic of Nigeria;

(g) that, consequently, reparation in an amount to be determined by the Court is due from the Federal Republic of Nigeria to the Republic of Cameroon, which reserve the introduction before the Court of (proceedings for) the precise assessment of the damage caused by the Federal Republic of Nigeria;

(h) in order to prevent any dispute arising between the two States concerning their maritime boundary, the Republic of Cameroon requests the Court to

---

9 Abel Orih, "Bakassi: Politics of Ceded Communities", *This Day online*, 16 November 2004, available at http://www.thisdayonline.com/archive/2003/11/23/20031123ins01.html visited 21 August 2007.

proceed to prolong the course of its maritime boundary with the Federal Republic of Nigeria up to the limit of the maritime zones which international law places under their respective jurisdictions.

Again on 6 June 1994 Cameroon filed in the Registry of the Court an additional application 'for the purpose of extending the subject of the dispute to a further dispute' described as relating essentially to the question of sovereignty over a part of the territory of Cameroon in the area of Lake Chad, while also asking the Court to definitively specify the frontier between Cameroon and Nigeria from Lake Chad to the sea. Cameroon requested the Court to adjudge and declare:

(a) that sovereignty over the disputed parcel in the area of Lake Chad is Cameroonian by virtue of international law, and that that parcel is an integral part of the territory of Cameroon;
(b) that the Federal Republic of Nigeria has violated and is violating the fundamental principle of respect for frontiers inherited from colonisation (*uti possidetis juris*), and its recent legal commitments concerning the demarcation of frontiers in Lake Chad:
(c) that Republic of Nigeria, by occupying, with the support of its security forces, parcels of Cameroonian territory in the area of Lake Chad, has violated and is violating its obligations under treaty law and customary law;
(d) that in view of these legal obligations, mentioned above, the Federal Republic of Nigeria has the express duty of effecting an immediate and unconditional withdrawal of its troops from Cameroonian territory in the area of Lake Chad;
(e) that the internationally unlawful acts referred to above involve the responsibility of Nigeria;
(f) that consequently, and on account of the material and non-material damage inflicted upon the Republic of Cameroon, reparation in an amount to be determined by the Court is due from the Republic of Nigeria.
(g) that in view of the repeated incursions of Nigerian groups and armed forces in the Cameroonian territory, all along the frontier between the countries, the consequent grave and repeated incidents, and the attitude of Nigeria in regard to the legal instruments defining the frontier between the two countries and the exact course of that frontier, Cameroon respectfully asks the Court to specify definitely the frontier between Cameroon and Nigeria from Lake Chad to the sea.

Cameroon further requested the Court to join the two applications 'and to examine the whole in a single case'.

Although most commentary on this case and the ensuing legal process is narrowed to the issue of Bakassi Peninsula, the Court was expected to find answers to certain pertinent questions in the course of defining the boundary between the states that arguably affect other vital interests of both states in terms of number of lives affected, the land area involved and resource implications. The vital questions that had to be decided include:

i. Does the Bakassi Peninsula with a land area of 612 sq. km and an estimated population of 156,000 people belong to Cameroon or Nigeria?
ii. Do the 33 disputed Nigerian villages in the Lake Chad Area (with an estimated population of 70,000 people) belong to Nigeria or Cameroon?
iii. Do the existing boundary treaties and other instruments adequately define the land boundary between the two countries from the Lake Chad to the sea (the Atlantic Ocean)?
iv. Where does the maritime boundary between Nigeria and Cameroon lie?
v. Would the Court grant Cameroon's plea that Nigeria should pay reparation relating to alleged wrongful acts concerning the boundary issues?[10]

10.3 The Judgment

The Court noted at para. 82 that both states agree that the land boundary between their respective territories from Lake Chad onwards has already been delimited, partly by the Thomson–Marchand Declaration[11] incorporated in the Henderson–Fleuriau Exchange of Notes of 1931, partly by the British Order in Council of 2 August 1946 and partly by the Anglo-German Agreements of 11 March and 12 April 1913. The Court likewise noted that, with the exception of the provisions concerning Bakassi contained in Arts XVIII et seq. of the Anglo-German Agreement of 11 March 1913, Cameroon and Nigeria both accept the validity of the four above-mentioned legal instruments which effected this delimitation. On the whole, the Court's delimitation involved some 17 points that were in dispute along the entire land boundary.[12] The interpretation and application of the Thomson–Marchand Declaration of 1929–30 constituted the major focus of the Court's work.

Without wishing to dwell extensively on the outcome of the judgment of the ICJ of 10 October 2002 on the above issues, it may be necessary to briefly highlight the following points:

i. With respect to Bakassi Peninsula, the Court decided to reject the theory of historical consolidation put forward by Nigeria and accordingly refused to take into account the '*effectivités*' relied upon. In this regard, the Court decided that pursuant to the Anglo-German Agreement of 11 March 1913,

---

10 See Dahiru Bobbo, "The Role of the Boundary Commission in Facilitating a Peaceful and Prosperous Borderland", paper presented at the Plenary Session of the 7th Conference of International Boundaries Research Unit (IBRU), UK, 5 April 2006, pp. 7–9.
11 Declaration made by the Governor of the Colony and Protectorate of Nigeria and the governor of the French Cameroons defining the Boundary between British and French Cameroons. Ian Brownlie, *African Boundaries: A Legal and Diplomatic Encyclopaedia* (London: C. Hurst & Company for the Royal Institute of International Affairs, 1979), pp. 570–8.
12 See ICJ Reports 2002, 360, para.86.

the Declaration of Yaoundé II (1971) and the Maroua Declaration of 1975 (which were essentially a re-affirmation of the Anglo-German Treaty of 1913), sovereignty over Bakassi lies with the Republic of Cameroon. This implies a loss to Nigeria of a total land mass of 612 square kilometres inhabited mainly by Nigerians for centuries and the loss of a Local Government Area with its political, social and constitutional implications for Nigeria.

ii. With respect to the disputed 33 villages in the Lake Chad, the Court decided that the boundary has already been delimited by an international colonial Treaty: the Thomson–Marchand Declaration of 1929–30 as incorporated in the Henderson–Fleuriau Exchange of Notes of 9 January 1931 between Great Britain and France. Indeed the boundary demarcation exercise carried out in the Lake Chad by Institute Geographiqué National of France (IGN) between 1988–90 at the instance of the Lake Chad Basin Commission (LCBC) to which Nigeria, Cameroon, Niger and Chad are members, was based on these colonial treaties. In consequence, the Court decided that the situation was essentially one where the *effectivités* addressed by Nigeria in its Memorials did not correspond to the Law and accordingly 'preference should be given to Cameroon, the holder of the title'. By this judgment, Nigeria lost 33 villages in the Lake Chad. These villages have since been handed over to Cameroon.

iii. On whether or not the existing boundary treaties are adequate in defining the land boundary between the two countries, it could be seen from the two situations cited above that the Court had relied heavily on the Treaties, Agreements and other legal documents entered into by Great Britain, France, Germany, Nigeria and Cameroon at different times to make its pronouncements. Thus, much as Nigeria would have expected or even deserved a different outcome on these two issues, the Court had decided otherwise.

iv. As regards the maritime boundary, the Court upheld the validity of the Declarations of Yaoundé II (1971; i.e. Points 1–12) and Maroua Declaration (1975; Points A–G), pursuant to which the Heads of State of Nigeria and Cameroon had jointly agreed upon the maritime boundary between the two countries from the Mouth of the Akwayafe River to a point G situated at 08 deg 22' 19" Longitude East and 04 deg 17' 00" Latitude North. From point X with coordinates 08 deg 21' 20" Longitude East and 04 deg 17' 00" Latitude North, the boundary line should move southwards on an equidistant line towards the tripoint between Nigeria/Equatorial Guinea/Cameroon having an Azimuth of 187 deg 52' 27". The Court in essence rejected Cameroon's claim to large areas of Nigeria's maritime zone including those included in the Nigeria–Equatorial Guinea maritime boundary Agreement/Unitisation of 2000 and of Nigeria/Sao Tome and Principe Joint Development Zone of 2000. This outcome represents a substantial victory in favour of Nigeria, although it is scarcely mentioned in literature.

v. On the question of paying reparation to Cameroon for alleged wrongful acts concerning the boundary issue, the Court unanimously rejected the claims of Cameroon for the payment of damages in respect of the alleged violation of its territory and other sundry violations. The Court, however, noted that the implementation of the judgment would sufficiently address any injuries suffered by Cameroon by reason of Nigeria's occupation of its territory and would further afford the parties a beneficial opportunity to cooperate in the interest of the peoples affected by the judgment.

In giving the judgment in this case the ICJ achieved 'resolution' of one of the longest and most complicated boundary cases in its history, lasting up to eight years. We have already traced some of the recognised distinctions in international law between boundary questions and questions of territorial sovereignty and jurisdiction; frontier disputes and delimitation disputes. All of these may apply in a land or maritime context or both.[13] What makes the dispute between Cameroon and Nigeria unique is that the Court had to grapple with all these categories within the same case. There are parallels in the length of this case and the case of Questions between Qatar and Bahrain which lasted a full decade (1991–2). Both cases experienced extraordinary procedural developments.[14]

Both sides are deeply dissatisfied with aspects of the judgment. Certainly, within Nigeria, the Court's judgment has been greeted with unprecedented national uproar, primarily because of the rejection of the ownership claims over Bakassi. Several vocal sections of the Nigerian population, including legal jurists, politicians and government officials, argued for outright rejection of the judgment of the Court, and quite ominously publicly proffered military solutions to the dispute. Although the Nigerian government immediately stated that it accepted the Court's judgment, it also on the other hand continued to maintain clearly that aspects of the Court's verdict are 'difficult to implement'.[15] However, with the assistance of the United Nations, the able leadership of the current democratically elected President Paul Biya of Cameroon and erstwhile Nigerian President Olusegun Obasanjo of Nigeria, both states successfully explored the most efficient ways and means of ensuring the peaceful implementation of the ICJ judgment.

---

13 Hugh Thirlway "The Law and Procedure of the International Court of Justice 1960–1989: Part Seven", Vol. 66, *British Yearbook of International Law* (1995) (1), pp. 19–22, 27–29; *Oppenheim's International law* (9th edition Jennings and Watts vol. 1 pp. 668–9.)
14 Maurice Mendelson, "The Curious Case of Qatar v. Bahrain in the International Court of Justice", Vol. LXXII, *BYIL* (2002), p. 183.
15 Nigeria's President Olusegun Obasanjo initially indicated he would not accept the ruling and a view holds it that this initial position helped harness national opinion giving time for the initial collective public shock to wear off and therefore, preventing what would have been violent responses in parts of the country. *BBC News*, "UN Mediates in Bakassi Dispute", Friday, 15 November 2002, http://news.bbc.co.uk/1/hi/world/africa/2481903.stm visited 19 August 2007; *BBC News*, "Nigeria Rejects World Court Ruling", 23 October 2002 (http://news.bbc.co.uk/2/hi/africa/2353989.stm); Sara McLaughlin Mitchell and Paul R. Hensel, "International Institutions and Compliance with Agreements" (http://garnet.acns.fsu.edu/_phensel/Research/ajps05.pdf); *BBC News*, 15 September 2004, "Nigeria Downplays Bakassi Delay" (http://news.bbc.co.uk/go/pr/fr/-/2/hi/africa/3652150.stm); *BBC News*, 12 November 2002, "Nigeria Rules Out Bakassi War" (http://news.bbc.co.uk/2/hi/africa/2447407.stm).

The significance of a vindication or rejection of the crux of a nation's arguments at the ICJ is perhaps suitably captured in the screaming headlines that follow the World Court's judgment in the national press of states.[16] After the favourable decision the Bahraini Prime Minister issued an edict to declare a public holiday in Bahrain because: 'this day is one of the great days in the history of Bahrain.'[17] Qatar on the other hand expressed 'pain' at the loss of what it considered national territory. In a television address to the nation after the verdict the Qatar Amir, Shaikh Hamad bin Isa Al Thani stated that the recognition of Bahrain's sovereignty over the disputed Hawar territory 'was not easy upon us'.[18]

As with the Cameroon–Nigerian situation, the decision by the Court was attended by calls by the leadership of the concerned states for the immediate resumption of the work of the joint high commission which was chaired by the Crown Princes of Bahrain and Qatar to look into implementing the decision as well as into the modalities of establishing joint development projects on either side of the borders. This included the construction of an international causeway. The hope of the Arab states as expressed in the words of the Bahraini sovereign Amir Shaikh Hamad bin Isa Khalifa that the building of an international highway will 'present a good model for cooperation' appears to have been borne true in the adoption of the idea of an international causeway by the CNMC around three years later in the Cameroon–Nigeria process.

Yet not all was gloomy news from the Nigerian perspective. The government and legal team that represented the country were quick to count their blessings. Whereas Bakassi peninsula was lost, this did not affect the right of innocent passage enjoyed under international law by all vessels, including Nigerian naval vessels, travelling to and from the sea to the west of Bakassi whether on the Nigerian or the Cameroonian side of the Maroua line. In terms of the potentially damaging loss of significant offshore oil resources the Court had done no more than to indicate to both states the direction of their international boundary south of the Maroua line. The line to be drawn between them will rapidly reach the outer limits of Equatorial Guinea's maritime space. The line so indicated apparently cut Cameroon off completely from access to Nigeria's significant offshore fields although a few oil platforms were lost.[19] The significance of these

---

16 After the judgment in the Maritime Delimitation and Territorial Questions between Qatar and Bahrain (*Qatar v. Bahrain*), The *Bahrain Tribune* carried a screaming red headline in bold type 'Victory' along with a 4-page pull-out supplement on the ICJ verdict.
17 Edict No. 7 of 2001. Thousands of Bahrainis took to the streets. Press reports recalled that 'celebrations broke out across the island with thousands pouring out into the streets . . .waving flags, blaring their car horns, cheering , congratulating and waving one another', "Hawar Stays with Bahrain HH Amir Hails ICJ verdict", *Bahrain Tribune*, 17 March 2001, p. 20.
18 "Hawar Stays with Bahrain HH Amir Hails ICJ verdict", ibid., front page.
19 Nigeria Information Service Centre, "Nigeria's Reaction to the Judgement of the International Court of Justice at The Hague (Nigeria, Cameroon with Equatorial Guinea Intervening)", 7 November 2002. Available at http://www.nigeriaembassyusa.org/110802_1.shtml, visited 21 August 2007; Tim Daniel, "International Boundary Disputes in Oil and Gas: What Lessons from Past Resolutions Can You Apply to Future Cases? The Cameroon-Nigeria Example", paper presented at the International Boundary Disputes in Oil and Gas, 23–24 October 2003

savings was not lost on the erstwhile Director General of the Nigerian Boundary Commission, Dahiru Bobbo who stated that: 'Indeed it could be said that Nigeria had successfully defended its Licensed Oil Blocks in the area claimed by Cameroon, thus saving Nigeria a loss of substantial sum of money (from oil) had the Court upheld the Cameroonian claim line'.[20]

The Cameroonian litigation strategy appeared to have involved the widening of the dispute by its application of 6 June 1994, asking the Court to specify definitively the frontier between Cameroon and Nigeria from Lake Chad to the sea, which appeared to have backfired. Nigeria made detailed submissions which identified areas of uncertainty and dispute and was able to convince the Court of its claims in some 17 areas along the boundary. The net result of this exercise was that approximately 17,000 hectares of land were affirmed as being Nigerian territory, including some significant Nigerian settlements, such as Sapeo, Tipsan, Lip and Mberogo. Various estimates of the area of land won especially in the land boundary by Nigeria are up to as much as 3,410 square kilometres.[21] By contrast, some 4,000 hectares of disputed territory were held to be within Cameroon. In some areas, such as at Turu in Adamawa State, the Court found that there has been substantial encroachment by Cameroon into Nigerian territory. It sat well with the national psyche that the Court directed Cameroon to withdraw her administration and military or police forces from all the areas along the land boundary such as Turu, Bourha Ouango and Nyaminyami.

In the Lake Chad area Nigeria lost 33 villages mainly due to the migratory habits of the villagers who simply moved along with the receding lake and thereby strayed significantly into Cameroonian territory. Thus, there were little problems for the Nigerian authorities to accept the rationale of either assisting its citizens to move back into national territory or staying in Cameroonian territory but subject entirely to the latter's territorial jurisdiction in all its ramifications.

10.4 The law and diplomacy of the Cameroon–Nigeria Mixed Commission

The terms of reference of the Mixed Commission as originally envisaged by the Joint Communiqué adopted by Presidents Paul Biya and Olusegun Obasanjo in Geneva (September 2002) was that:

> The Mixed Commission will consider all the implications of the [ICJ] decision, including the need to protect the rights of the affected populations

---

(Houston, Texas: IQPC, 2003). See particularly map on slide 13 which depicts the judgment's impact on Nigerian Licences.

20 Bobbo, op.cit., p. 11.
21 Tim Daniel, op.cit., see particularly map on slide 4 accompanying the paper which depicts the Cameroonian Claim line and areas won by Nigeria. Another estimate states: 'On the land boundary, there is no doubt that Nigeria emerged victorious because it was able to gain a total of 29,791 hectares of land spread in different locations from Borno State to Benue State', Abel Orih, op.cit., *supra* note 8.

in both countries. The Commission shall, inter alia, be entrusted with the task of demarcating the land boundary between the two countries. It will also make recommendations on additional confidence-building measures such as the holding, on a regular basis, of meetings between local authorities, Government officials, and Heads of State; developing projects to promote joint economic ventures and cross-border cooperation; the avoidance of inflammatory statements or declarations on Bakassi by either side; troop withdrawal from the relevant areas along the land boundary; eventual demilitarization of the Bakassi Peninsula with the possibility of international personnel to observe withdrawal; and reactivation of the Lake Chad Basin Commission.

At the inaugural meeting of the newly created body (sub-committees and working groups) it was decided that the body will deliberate on its Terms of Reference. This entailed a consideration of a draft Terms of Reference prepared by the UN as well as a draft Work Plan which was submitted for adoption to the Mixed Commission at its second meeting.[22] The Chairmanship of the created body is usually reserved for the incumbent Executive Secretary of the Mixed Commission. Since the creation of the CNMC and up to the third quarter of 2013 there have been five Executive Secretaries. One secretary had been removed as a result of insensitive statements he made with respect to the Nigerian side of the deliberations.

The significance and prestige of the CNMC has in many ways been due first to the quality of the persons who have comprised the Mixed Commission. Indeed among the six members of the Mixed Commission on the Cameroonian side, one has become Prime Minister and another Vice President as a result of appointments arising from the country's democratic elections. A third personality, Professor Maurice Kamto, became the Minister for Justice. The Nigerian side of the Mixed Commission equally consists of eminent membership including a former titular and *ad hoc* judge of the World Court. There is no doubt that chairmanship by seasoned, eminent and accomplished UN diplomats like Ould-Abdallah and Said Djinnit served to strengthen the prestige of the process and the integrity of the decisions reached. The Mixed Commission while not exactly styling itself as a diplomatic mission operated for all intents and purposes as a special mission.[23] This status applied to its sub-commissions and working groups as well. Both states gave firm guarantees to each other and to the requisite UN staff members to allow for the free movement of persons and for the safety of all delegates and staff

---

22 This was the procedure adopted during the establishment of the Working Group on withdrawal and transfer of authority in the Lake Chad area as well as the working group on Maritime Boundary. This procedure has the advantage of ensuring that the terms of reference of the newly created body are consistent with the objectives assigned to it by the Mixed Commission.

23 A 'special mission' according to the Convention on Special Missions adopted by the General Assembly of the United Nations on 8 December 1969 is a temporary mission, representing the state, which is sent by one state to another state with the consent of the latter for the purpose of dealing with it on specific questions or of performing in relation to it a specific task (Art. 1).

attached to them as well as contractors involved in the process.[24] It is, however, noteworthy that these assurances were repeated at the initial meetings of a newly created sub-committee and at the onset of every deployment of mixed delegations across boundaries.

In addition to these, the fact that most of the decisions reached since the more than a decade-long existence of the CNMC was achieved through consensus and agreement increases the authority of the body and the collective integrity of its membership. It also appears that the art of handling members of the press corps both national and international is one of the skills that would serve the leadership of a boundary commission well. The CNMC had to navigate the difficult course between Scylla and Charybdis in its relations with the national and international press. On the one hand there was the need to constantly disseminate information especially during and after Mixed Commission sessions, and on the other hand the need to encourage sensitive and mature reporting of the many issues without inadvertently stoking nationalistic fervour.[25]

The Cameroon–Nigeria Mixed Commission meets in Abuja (Nigeria) and Yaoundé (Cameroon) every two months on an alternating basis although the pace of the meetings schedule has slowed since 2012. For the first decade of its existence it was composed of the Delegation of Cameroon, led by Mr Amadou Ali, Ministre d'État in charge of Justice, and the Delegation of Nigeria, led by Prince Bola Ajibola, former Minister of Justice and former titular as well as *ad hoc* judge of the ICJ. It is chaired by Mr Ahmedou Ould-Abdallah, Special Representative of the UN Secretary-General. The Mixed Commission held its first meeting in Yaoundé on 1 December 2002 and has since held dozens of further meetings. As agreed at its first meeting, the Mixed Commission also holds special meetings when needed and has done so on many occasions so far.

---

24 See for instance, Report of the First Meeting of the Sub-Commission on Demarcation (2003); para. IV 'Programme of Work Of the Sub Commission On Affected Populations' in Cameroon–Nigeria Mixed Commission Sub-Commission on Affected Populations, Report of the Second Meeting Dakar, 2–3 July 2003. It is to the credit of both states that the mutual assistance extended to extraordinary circumstances fit for anecdotal recounting such as the arrival of a New Zealander UN expert at the International Airport in Lagos without any visa. Such was the camaraderie between the delegations that the visits afforded the delegations opportunity to stock up on local artwork, textiles and foodstuffs often transported duty-free or received as symbolic gifts to all members of the delegation including press and technical support staff.

25 At the height of national press interests in the Bakasssi issue in 2004, the chairman Abdallah of the commission found it necessary to encourage the press to 'keep interacting with the populace' on the peninsula while also hoping that they could help to educate the Bakassi populace on the desired result of the Mixed commissions work. As he put it, 'the idea is to ensure that the affected people become Cameroonians in mind and spirit'. Comparative practice may be found elsewhere. When the border commissions of Slovenia and Croatia met in Ljubljana on 12 January 1998 the official position to the public and the press was that the meeting was a 'get-to-know-each-other' session. Members of the press could not get the official corroboration for their suspicion that sensitive final delimitation of the boundaries around the Croatian–Slovenian–Hungarian tripoint as well certain territorial questions were being discussed. See China Economic net, "Nigeria, Cameroon get 8.5 million dollars to resolve border dispute", *Xinhuanet*, 2 June 2004, available at http://en.ce.cn/World/Africa/t20040602_981032.shtml; "Border Commissions Meet", *Radio Slovenia*, Ljubljana, 12 January 1998 (FBIS-EEU-98-012) quoted in http://www.dur.ac.uk/ibru/resources/newsarchive/search_results/, visited 18 August 2007.

A comprehensive Communiqué is usually given in public after the meetings but the meetings are usually held in private.[26]

The sensitive nature of the Mixed Commission's work is reflected in its composition. The Commission is composed of personalities from both countries and the UN, which have been described by the UN Secretary General and the Chairman of the Mixed Commission as 'very heavyweight and competent representatives'.[27] The Mixed Commission sits on top of the Organigram of the implementation process. It supervises and approves the activities and projects of all the tripartite sub-commissions and Working Groups set up under its powers. The Mixed Commission, however, reports its activities and defers to the Presidents of both countries and the Secretary-General of the United Nations. Thus, where there is a deadlock in its work the Mixed Commission refers the issue to the Presidents to decide.

Since the 'principal' judicial organ of the UN had taken nearly a decade to decide the dispute between the parties and issue a binding judgment, it may at first appear perplexing to observers that a negotiating forum of diplomacy then began a life of its own which has lasted another decade and a half.[28] What needs to be appreciated is that sometimes a judgment may in the technical sense be *dispositif* yet may not represent a resolution of the dispute. In such cases the careful management of the post-judgment period has to reflect political realities and this can be seen as a strength in international relations rather than a weakness, so long as nothing is done to detract from the crucial reputation of the judicial function. As long as the post-judgment engagements enable wise and effective choices to be made in establishing the best method to give effect to the letter and spirit of the judgment, the parties are well within their rights to pursue diplomacy and political 'resolution'. This idea appears to have been enunciated by no less an authority

---

26 Other members of the Mixed Commission are as follows: Cameroon (H. E., Maurice Kamto, Minister of State for Justice; H.E., Joseph Dion Ngute, Minister of External Affairs; H.E., Ambassador, Martin Belinga Eboutou, Permanent Rep. of Cameroon to the UN; Le General , Pierre Semengue, (Former Chief of Staff); Mr Bodo Abanda Ernest, cartographer, Nigeria; Ambassador Femi George, (Nigerian High Commission) Ottawa, Canada; Major General A. F. K. Akale, Ministry of Defence; Mrs Nella Andem-Ewa, former Hon. A. G. and Commissioner for Justice, Cross River State; Barrister Mohammed Monguno, former A. G. and Commissioner of Justice, Borno State; UN Madame Christina Meindersma, snr political adviser; Ould-Mohammed Salah, senior legal adviser; Mrs Sylvie Daoda, political adviser; Madame Myriam Dessables, information officer; M. David Rochette, surveyor; M. Ian Allen, surveyor; M. Augustin Muhizi, cartographer; Madame Josette Soumare Daffe, secretary.
27 See Opening Remarks by the Chairman of the Mixed Commission and Special Representative of the Secretary-General of the United Nations, Mr. Ahmedou Ould-Abdallah, Yaoundé, 1 December 2002 available at http://www.un.org/Depts/dpa/prev_dip/africa/office_for_srsg/cnmc/speeches/spchlist.htm).
28 Sir Robert Jennings, bringing his trademark clarity of thought to bear on the primacy of the Court, reminds us that it is not just in the first rank of international Courts but that it is 'first in rank'. In other words the ICJ is indeed *prima inter pares*–first among equals. This noble institution's prestige and authority is thus worth protecting and maintaining in very many ways. Robert Y. Jennings, "The Role of the International Court of Justice", LXVIII *BYIL* (1998), pp. 3–4. For a brief account of the procedure of the court in contentious cases as well as the traditions and conventions of the Court see pp. 11–31.

than Jennings who wrote that: 'The need for political and adjudicatory decisions to work and develop in parallel can be learned from any developed and working system ...'.[29] He urged consideration at all times of the limits of the judicial function:

> The simplistic ideas about the judicial function in international relations are very harmful to the public perception of the role of the International Court of Justice. Resort to the Court is inevitably thought of as the right way to deal with any dangerous crisis. Its role is seen in the popular mind, to quote a passage from Professor Georges Abi-Saab, 'as a panacea, a miraculous remedy for all the ills and structural weaknesses of the system, as a sort of philosopher's stone of international law'[30]

Although technically speaking the dispute has been decided upon by the ICJ, it is clear that there is no unanimity as to how to give effect to all aspects of the Court's judgment and the Court itself enjoined the state parties to enter into further negotiations with respect to certain issues. The establishment of the Mixed Commission has set a new standard for Africa and perhaps the developing world as regards the handling of post-adjudication stage international disputes. It is possible to locate this commendable development within the provisions of Article 33 (1) of the UN Charter which states that parties to any dispute, the continuance of which is likely to endanger the maintenance of international peace and security, may resolve the matter by 'other peaceful means of their own choice'. Even though the main disputes had been decided upon by the Court, further disputes emanated in relation to interpretation of the judgment.

The unique feature of this arrangement, however, is that it comes into active and sustained existence after the successful completion of judicial settlement. This perhaps attests to the limitations of the judicial settlement route, especially in relation to territorial and boundary disputes.

Since December 2002, the Mixed Commission has held over 50 very complex meetings involving many political and technical committees. The meetings have taken place alternately in Yaoundé and Abuja. As a result of these tremendous achievements as at the time of publication of this book approximately 1,947 kilometres of the 2,100 km land boundary between the two states have been surveyed and agreed on by the parties. It is, however, significant to note that actual demarcation in the form of pillar emplacement has not been achieved to any meaningful level beyond that which was inherited pre-ICJ judgment. In a sense this is a significant shortcoming. But the truth is that demarcation of a very long boundary is a very expensive affair and the devotion of the considerable resources needed to do this is of very little importance to politicians in their various capitals

---

29 Jennings, op.cit., p. 55.
30 Jennings, ibid. see also Abi-Saab in "*De L'evolution de la Cour International*", 94 *Revue Generale de Droit International public*, (1992) p. 273, at p. 274.

especially when the dispute is no longer seen as 'live'. The achievements of the CNMC are in many ways sensational. That two African states competently managed the diplomatic and legal terrain of complex boundary litigation and painstakingly implemented the judgment in full view of their national and international audiences speaks volumes of the maturity of the modern African state. Very often popular commentary glibly dismisses the usefulness and effectiveness of international law. Yet dramatic successes of international law like this largely pass unsung and unrecognised despite their massive significance. Examples include: the dramatic process of the physical uprooting of 32 villages in the Lake Chad area and the accompanying withdrawal and transfer of authority; the lowering and raising of flags ceremony and transfer of sovereignty over Bakassi Peninsula by Nigeria in favour of Cameroon;[31] and the many high-level technical meetings and negotiations pertaining to the delineation of the maritime boundary, including the maritime charts which were predominantly handled by African experts and technocrats in compliance with the judgment. The emergence of cross-border cooperation on hydrocarbon deposits straddling the maritime boundary is another commendable outcome of the ruling, and one which will likely be of didactic value for the future of African boundary dispute settlement.[32]

10.5 The structures of diplomacy, administration and implementation

The decision in the *Land and Maritime Case* judgment came barely seven months after the famous award of the EEBC in the case.[33] The fact that Ethiopia had expressed serious reservations about that decision and had appeared to disavow any possibility of giving effect to it at least in relation to certain sectors, particularly Badme, made the reactions of the parties to the Cameroon–Nigeria dispute all the more noteworthy. The initial reactions of Nigeria to the outcome of the case especially as it related to Bakassi were similar to that of Ethiopia in relation to Badme.[34] Nigeria contended that the ICJ essentially ignored the views of the local population (the majority of which reportedly did not wish to join Cameroon) and placed far too much emphasis on old colonial treaties; at least one government statement effectively accused the ICJ of being a neo-colonial entity. Both scenarios will cause much concern to observers of international adjudication not

---

31 On 15 August 2013 the UN Security Council acknowledged the successful implementation of the Greentree Agreement on the settlement of the dispute over Bakassi (SC/11094) and noted the achievement of the Mixed Commission's mediation as an outstanding initiative of preventive diplomacy. Typical sentiments have been expressed by the European Union which has also emphasised the cost-effectiveness of the Mixed Commission's demarcation process. UN Office for West Africa, "Cameroon/Nigeria Mixed Commission", available at http://unowa.unmissions.org/Default.aspx?tabid=804 accessed 02 August 2014.
32 By 2012 Cameroon and Nigeria began working on a draft agreement on the management of a straddling oilwell in the maritime sectors including joint border and security patrols.
33 The EEBC decision is discussed above.
34 Although the Nigerian Government was initially silent on the issue of rejecting the judgment, it did make it clear that the Court's verdict 'is difficult to implement'.

only because there remains a possibility of further conflict along two African boundaries, but also because of the potential impact on litigation as an effective mechanism for the peaceful resolution of international boundary disputes in general.

To what pressures and strategies Nigeria yielded in changing its policy and giving effect to the judgment will no doubt be the source of much theorising and pontificating. What is increasingly clear, however, is that while the implementation of the Cameroon–Nigeria judgment moved rapidly and more steadily, the Eritrea–Ethiopia implementation has been much slower, with the parties becoming increasingly reluctant to fully cooperate with the Commission in the demarcation phase of its work. This could be mainly the result of Ethiopian dissatisfaction with the loss of parts of its territory.[35] But given that Nigeria also lost territory (with maritime and perhaps resource implications) the question ought to be posed whether the difference in success at implementation stage is attributable to the method of dispute resolution employed in the first place.

It is arguable that the golden thread that underlies the successes and difficulties that have attended the implementation process of the ICJ decision in *The Land and Maritime Case* is the dogged utilisation of diplomacy. The wheels of diplomacy and negotiation may turn slowly but they do turn surely as attested to by the remarkable progress made in this case despite the many intricacies of the dispute and resulting judgment as well as the immense involvement of national security and interests at stake for both parties. This approach led to the establishment of the Cameroon–Nigeria Mixed Commission discussed in fuller detail below. The CNMC is an ongoing body that has performed remarkably successfully given the difficult nature of the tasks before it.[36] To assist this body in its groundbreaking work, two sub-Commissions and three other working groups have so far been created.[37]

---

35 John Donaldson and Martin Pratt, "International Boundary Developments International Boundary Developments in 2003", 9 *Geopolitics* (2004), pp. 501–03; 'Ethiopian, Eritrean Border Conflict Resolution Deadlocked', *The Guardian* (Nigeria) available at http://community.nigeria.com/newsroom.html accessed 12 September 2007.
36 The Mixed Commission was established in accordance with the decision arrived at by the heads of state of Nigeria and Cameroon in the presence of the UN Secretary-General during their Summit in Geneva, Switzerland on 15 November 2002. The task of this Mixed Commission is to ensure the implementation of the Court's Judgment of 10 October 2002. See further Nigeria First Official Website of the office of Public Communications, UN Mixed Commission (www.nigeriafirst.org/article_252.shtml). Materials relating to the activities of the Trilateral Mixed Commission are available at the official website of the United Nations Office for West Africa UNOWA. http://www.un.org/Depts/dpa/prev_dip/africa/office_for_srsg/fst_office_for_srsg.htm).
37 The first is the Trilateral Sub-Commission on Demarcation (involving boundary commissioners and legal experts from the UN, Cameroon and Nigeria) – a body which uniquely continues to perform its functions despite intermittent lulls in the work of its parent Commission. See para.8 of the Communiqué Adopted at the First Meeting of the Cameroon–Nigeria Mixed Commission Established Pursuant to the Joint Geneva Communiqué of 15 November 2002 (Yaoundé, 1–2 December 2002). The second is the Sub-Commission on the rights of the affected populations – a body which has completed its tasks and submitted a comprehensive report to the Mixed Commission. In accordance with paras 6 and 7 of the Yaoundé Communiqué of 2 December

i. The Sub-Commission on Affected Populations comprising of five officials each from Nigeria and Cameroon as well as the United Nations was created to identify, assess and recommend modalities for the protection of the rights of the people affected by the judgment. Such rights include but are not limited to rights to freedom of movement, freedom of association, customary rights etc. This Sub-Commission has since concluded its assignment and handed over its report to the Mixed Commission.

ii. The Sub-Commission on Demarcation comprising of five officials each from Nigeria and Cameroon as well as the United Nations was established for the purpose of the demarcation of the land boundary between the two countries in accordance with the ICJ judgment. It is assisted in its work by a Joint Technical Team which comprises of lawyers, surveyors and administrators from both countries as well as the United Nations. The work of this Sub-Commission is still ongoing as at the publication of this book and its members are currently engaged in the physical/field identification of the various pillar sites along the boundary.

iii. The Working Group on maritime boundary comprised of lawyers, oceanographers and oil experts from both countries as well as the United Nations. The Group is made up of five members from each country and had the task of considering all technical issues involved in the delineation of the maritime boundary in accordance with the ICJ judgment and making recommendations to the Mixed Commission. The Group considered all the charts and maps that were pertinent to the task given to them before making its final recommendation.

iv. The Working Group on the Withdrawal and Transfer of Authority on the Land Boundary was established to work out all the details involved in the physical identification of settlements and communities that can clearly be seen on either side of the boundary between the two countries after the judgment. The Working Group has concluded its assignment after handing over 33 villages in the Lake Chad hitherto under Nigerian administration to Cameroon in December, 2003. Similarly other settlements along the boundary such as Ndabakura (Nigeria), Narki (Cameroon), Dambore (Nigeria) and Burha Vamgo (Nigeria) have gone to the country whose claims have been confirmed by the judgment. It is important to note that the final and total handover of settlements between the two countries along the land boundary will only be effected after the final demarcation of the boundary between the two countries.

2002, the Mixed Commission decided to establish a Sub-Commission on Affected Populations with a mandate to consider modalities relating to the protection of their rights. See also para.7 of the Communiqué Adopted at the 2nd Meeting of the Cameroon–Nigeria Mixed Commission Established Pursuant to the Joint Geneva Communiqué of 15 November 2002 (Abuja, 4–5 February 2003) and para.4 of the Communiqué Adopted at the 3rd Meeting of the Cameroon–Nigeria Mixed Commission established pursuant to the Joint Geneva Communiqué of 15 November 2002 (Yaoundé, 2–3 April 2003).

v. With particular reference to the Bakassi Peninsula, the Mixed Commission established a Working Group on the withdrawal and transfer of authority from the Bakassi Peninsula. The Working Group was made up of ten officials each from Nigeria and Cameroon with representations from the United Nations and met severally before the completion of its tasks. Given the complex and sensitive nature of the assignment in this sector, its work moved step-by-step, with each step approved at the highest level of government particularly by the two Heads of States and the Secretary-General of the United Nations.

10.6 Identifying Eurocentricity in the jurisprudence of the World Court

Although the Nigerian government initially made it clear that the Court's verdict 'is difficult to implement', both countries went ahead to successfully implement most of the judgment. It is, however, possible to criticise the judgment on very many points and this has unsurprisingly been done by eminent jurists both from Africa and other parts of the world. However, it is sufficient for present purposes to concentrate on the Court's decision on the Bakassi Peninsula alone in order to illustrate the Eurocentricity of the jurisprudence of the Court.

The Court by 13 votes to 3 decided that sovereignty over the Bakassi Peninsula lies with Cameroon. The dispute over the Bakassi Peninsula turns out to be one of the most crucial aspects of the dispute between both states. In terms of the military conflict it has generated and the sentimental value the Peninsula holds in the minds of policymakers and the general Nigerian population, it is probably very similar to what Badme is to Ethiopian populace in the Eritrea–Ethiopia dispute. There are deep flaws in the reasoning of the majority, which again confirms the prejudices in favour of granting effectiveness to the actions of colonial powers retrospectively. The main lines of argument are briefly as follows.

Nigeria claimed original title to the territory based on the Treaty of Protection of 10 September 1884 between the Kings and Chiefs of Old Calabar and Great Britain. The crux of the Nigerian argument was that the letter and spirit of this Treaty makes it impossible for Great Britain to have ceded the Bakassi Peninsula to Germany in 1913. In other words Great Britain had neither the right nor the capacity to make the transfer, which later on became the basis of Cameroonian claims to have inherited the territory via Germany's ownership. In consequence the transfer should have been invalid, null and void and in breach of its obligations to the Kings, Chiefs and people of Old Calabar.

Surprisingly the Court found in favour of the proposition that there was passivity by the Kings and Chiefs of Old Calabar and concluded that their failure to protest rendered them *volenti non fit injuria*. This aspect of the judgment again demonstrates that the prevailing considerations by the Court remain the protection of the sanctity of colonial acts. To begin with it is possible to assert that in the face of such a flagrant breach (i.e. the parcelling out of a protectorate's land to another power without the consent of the sovereign from whom authority over the protectorate was derived), the *nemo dat quod non habet principle* – '*a person cannot grant a better title than he himself has*' – immediately becomes apposite.[38] It is also unfair and unrealistic for judges sitting in The Hague in 2002 to decide that a group of tribal chiefs in the last two centuries should have acted in the exact fashion expected of a European power operating within the context of close-knit European diplomatic and legal traditions.

The view of a judge of the court was that '[a]part from a single trip in 1913 to London, when a delegation sent on their behalf discussed matters relating to land tenure, they remained silent in the face of momentous events that had an impact on their status.'[39] The questions that suggest themselves are: how much help (legal and financial) was available to understandably naïve African Chiefs at that period? How many trips to the western capitals in the context of the difficulties of maritime transport of that period, which would have entailed many weeks of arduous travel, would have sufficed to refute the charge of acquiescence? It is important to note that there were other forms of protest, of particular significance within the then existing African cultural value systems, that were effectively ignored by the colonial authorities. An example of such indirect protestations can be seen in the way Ethiopian tribes reacted to early signs of territorial encroachment by Italy. Eritrea's arguments before the EEBC included the allegation that Ethiopia acquiesced by failing to react to a variety of peripheral cartographic materials, which threatened its sovereignty. Ethiopia, however, argued that on the contrary, there were Italian reports referring to several 'raiding' incidents by Ethiopian tribes on Italian interests. It is reasonable to conclude that these incidents were attempts by the Ethiopians to check Italian advances and restore the *status quo ante* using force. It would be unfair to dismiss the dissent to the oppression of colonial administrations just because they were channelled through unconventional means or were largely ignored by the colonial powers.

It would have been only just for the Court to hold that the role Great Britain had with respect to the Bakassi peninsula which she had undertaken to 'protect' was at best that of administration. The international legal status of local African rulers such as the 'King of Calabar' to hold ultimate sovereignty in land and to enter into treaties was described by Malcolm Shaw as follows:

> It has been seen that practice demonstrates that the European colonisation of Africa was achieved in law not by virtue of the occupation of a *terra nullius* but by cession from local rulers. This means that such rulers were accepted as being capable in international law not only of holding title to territory, but of transferring it to Parties.[40]

---

38 See G. Fitzmaurice, *The Law and Procedure of the International Court of Justice* (Cambridge: Cambridge University Press, 1986), pp. 164–65.
39 See the Separate Opinion of Judge Al-Khasawneh, *supra* note 13.
40 Malcom N. Shaw, *Title to Territory in Africa, International Legal Issues* (Oxford: Clarendon Press), p. 45.

As persuasively argued by Judge Ajibola in his dissenting Judgment, the treaty was valid and binding between Great Britain and the Kings and Chiefs of Old Calabar – *pacta sunt servanda*. Having signed this Agreement, Great Britain was under an obligation to protect Old Calabar territories without acquiring sovereignty over them, and to have entered into the Agreement of 1913 with Germany transferring what was for all intent and purposes 'territory held in trust' was a serious breach of its international obligations. At any rate the principle *nemo dat quod non habet* should have prevented Great Britain from passing a valid title to Germany. Great Britain could not give away what did not belong to it.[41] Just as in the *Island of Palmas Case*[42] where the United States was found to have no sovereignty over the Island of Palmas ceded to it by Spain, Germany equally could not claim any conventional title over the Bakassi Peninsula. Having dealt illegally with trust property, sovereignty over Bakassi should have reverted to the King and Chiefs of Old Calabar and, therefore, would have been inherited by the Nigerian State at the date of its independence. The inability of the ICJ to grapple with these truths leads to the inescapable conclusion that Courts which have a predominantly European and Western outlook to legal and political history of the world cannot or at least have not begun to accept that traditional African societies of the past had legal personality of their own. Dismantling such prejudices would be the beginning of addressing the inherent bias against developing nations in international law. It may, thus, be argued that as a result of such judicial attitudes held by a clearly Western-dominated ICJ Bench, the systematic injustices against the legal and political interests of African states which characterised European relations with Africa in the last two centuries continue to persist to the present day.

It is for these reasons that Nigeria argued for the severance of parts of the 1913 Agreement (XVII–XXII) because it deals with an area in which it holds original title earlier in time and in fact superior to the conventional title claimed by Cameroon i.e. *prior est tempore, prior est jure*. Whatever the effect of those Articles between Great Britain and Germany it cannot reasonably be said to bind Kings and Chiefs of Old Calabar and for that matter Nigeria. Judge Ajibola correctly summed up the insufficiency of the judgment in this way: 'The constant questions which counsel for Nigeria asked throughout the oral proceedings and which the Court fails to address or answer in its judgement are: who gave Great Britain the right to give away Bakassi? And when? And How?'[43] Unfortunately, the Court

---

41 See Dissenting Judgment of Judge Ajibola, paras 72 and 118 *et passim*. See also the dissenting opinion of Judge Koroma (para. 7) who took the view that the Treaty with the Kings and Chiefs of Old Calabar constitute part of the applicable treaties, which should have been taken into full consideration by the Court; and that the findings of the Court are in clear violation of the express provisions of the 1884 Treaty, contrary to the intention of one of the parties to the Treaty. He wrote: 'This finding, in violation of the applicable treaty and clearly in breach of the principle of *pacta sunt servanda*, is not only illegal but unjust'. *Supra* note 13.
42 Max Huber stated in the award: 'It is evident that Spain could not transfer more rights than she herself possessed', United Nations, Reports of International Arbitral Awards (RIAA), Vol. II, p. 842.
43 Ajibola, Dissenting judgment, para 71, *Supra* note 24.

disregarded events prior to the 1913 colonial treaty between European States; every other consideration in this case sprang from a determination to give effect to this treaty, and not to the legal limitations inherent in a treaty with African kings and chiefs.

There are other grounds on which the judgment in this case may be criticised. One such is the inconsistent manner in which the court treated the evidence of acts of administration by the Nigerian State relevant to a claim of title to the contested territory by occupation. In its judgment, particularly in paragraph 325 III(A), (B) and (C), the Court failed to take into consideration the situation on the ground in the Bakassi Peninsula. Instead the Court adopted the view that *effectivités* and historical consolidation, principles of long-standing significance even in the jurisprudence of the court, are mere theories which at least on this occasion it would choose to ignore. By so doing it dismissed one of Nigeria's strongest points in the prosecution of its claim to the territory of Bakassi Peninsula in favour of a legal title flowing from perhaps what is considered the 'purest source' of law – a colonial treaty between European nations. It is very interesting that in doing so the Court based its jurisprudence on the *Frontier Dispute Case* (Burkina Faso/Republic of Mali). The court pronounced that: the role played by *effectivités* in the *Frontier Dispute Case* is complex, and that the Chamber would have to weigh carefully the legal force of these in each particular instance. The Court, thus, delineated several eventualities. It noted that:

> Where the act corresponds exactly to law, where effective administration is additional to the *uti possidetis juris*, the only role of *effectivités* is to confirm the exercise of the right derived by a legal title. Where the act does not correspond to the law, where the territory which is the subject of the dispute is effectively administered by a state other than the one possessing the legal title, preference should be given to the holder of the title. *In the event that the effectivité does not co-exist with any legal title, it must invariably be taken into consideration* (emphasis added).[44]

Various acts of *effectivités* were established by Nigeria which were enumerated by the Court in its judgment. They include the establishment of schools, the provision of health facilities for many of the settlements and some tax collection. Indeed one of the prayers of Cameroon was for the court to put 'an end to Nigeria's administrative and military presence in Cameroonian territory'.[45] The Court went on to observe that in none of these cases did the acts refer to acts *contra legem* and that those precedents are, therefore, not relevant, concluding that where there is a conflict between title and *effectivités*, preference will be given to the former.[46] Most surprisingly, the judgment gave no consideration whatsoever in any part to

---

44 Ibid., pp. 586–7.
45 See paras 222, 318.
46 See para. 223 of the judgment. See also ICJ Reports 1986, Judgment, pp. 586–7, para. 63.

the *effectivités* that was so well established in favour of Nigeria. The inadequacy of this reasoning prompted Judge Ajibola to ask in his dissenting judgment: 'Was the Court misled?'[47] The answer is perhaps in the negative. The Court was not only deliberate in its abandonment of a principle that cuts across all the main legal traditions, which holds that 'possession is nine-tenths of the law' but it did so in order to re-establish its preference for European colonial treaties that regulate African territories or *uti possidetis*. In other words, colonial acts in relation to territorial and boundary questions would continue to trump all other equitable or traditional considerations. More importantly, the Court seems to have established the jurisprudence that there is a hierarchy of colonial treaties, and that those between Western colonial powers would take precedence over treaties with native African communities and political systems. This is the unacceptable state of international boundaries law as espoused by international courts today.

47 Ajibola, Dissenting opinion, para. 153.

11 Sociology, politics, insecurity and the psychology of power in African boundary relations

International borders are a security issue for all governments but particularly so in Africa because of its vast and porous national borders. It is significant to note that even developed western states are known to harbour serious concerns about security around their common boundaries. The 3,800-mile-long US–Canada boundary has at least in American eyes been characterised as a potential getaway for terrorists and undocumented immigrants. It is a 'widely held US view of Canada as a safe haven for terrorists and a country with lax immigration laws.'[1] Free movement across national boundaries for legitimate business and social purposes is not necessarily a negative phenomenon and should not be discouraged especially in a continent that was carved up rather insensitively as recently as the last century. The problem, however, is that many of Africa's border communities have become host to a pandora of negative developments including people smuggling, drugs, illegal weapons and contraband, organised crime syndicates, cattle rustling, wildlife poaching, insurrection, incursion and terrorist activity, auto theft, illegal and undocumented immigrations as well as illegal border crossings. It is ironic that most African states that would benefit immensely from inflow of trade and investment are the very ones with some of the toughest border crossing regimes with excessive red-tape, that slows down if not render impossible genuine cross-border trade. It is estimated that it takes an average of 40 paper documents and 200 data elements to undertake one customs transaction across an African border. While it takes one day to clear customs in Estonia, it takes 30 days on average in many African countries. The insecurity surrounding boundary posts ought, therefore, to be of paramount interest to the existing RECs and boundary researchers generally.[2] Clearly there is a need for more policing and security presence around international borders but this alone will not solve the many security problems posed by borders. The fact is that border areas also tend to be some of the most deprived areas of national territories with little access to investment and socio-economic activities and infrastructure. This is perhaps why

---

1 C. Sadowski-Smith, *Border Fictions: Globalisation, Empire and Writing at the Boundaries of the United States* (Charlottesville: University of Virginia Press, 2008), p. 1.
2 Okumu, op.cit., pp. 14, 19, 26, 36.

various shadowy and unsavoury actors tend to be attracted to border zones and communities. A more innovative and progressive approach would be one which witnesses a concerted effort by African states and the RECs to provide more investments and targeted economic help to the boundary communities to spark economic development ad higher levels of standard of living. This will make such areas less attractive to criminal elements that prey in the present shadowy 'no man's land' that many boundary areas have been turned into since the colonial era and to the present time.[3]

The enormous task before African governments and bureaucrats in monitoring and controlling migration at borders is often underestimated by governments and writers. Effective border monitoring and enforcement in modern times will require modern equipment-infrared night-vision scopes and low-light TV cameras, ground sensors, helicopters and all-terrain vehicles. Developed states such as the United States also make use of electronic identification systems such as IDENT, which store the fingerprints and photographs of apprehended persons at border areas. Saudi Arabia's 550-mile-long barrier with Iraq comprises of command posts with helipads, ultraviolet sensors with face recognition software and underground sensors that set off silent alarms.[4]

For all the idealism of African brotherhood and communalism of spirit, particularly in rural Africa, there are serious dangers capable of rendering vast national territories ungovernable. Yet there is no unified theory of boundary security management and each boundary has to be treated on its own merits. The movement of vast numbers of migrants through African boundaries produces severe strain on borders and African international relations. It has been recognised that migration not only highlights tensions and connections between centrifugal and centripetal forces but often also generates them.[5] Heisler could as well have been writing about African states when he noted:

> In some parts of the world migration is a bordering and rebordering force that affects identities and, not infrequently creates new ones. Migrants may establish temporary, if long-term enclaves on the edges of the host society, or they may enter it as smoothly and quickly as possible by assimilating. Migration often raises contentious questions about civic order in receiving countries.[6]

In quite significant ways migration vitiates state boundaries and the established Westphalian conceptualisation of sovereignty not least because of the body of international human rights law that attaches to migrants and reduces the choices

---

3 P. Andreas, *Smuggler Nation: How Illicit Trade Made America* (Oxford: Oxford University Press, 2013), p. 301.
4 Brown, (2010) op.cit., see particularly diagram on p. 17.
5 M. Heisler, "Now and Then, Here and There: Migration and the Transformation of Identities, Borders and Orders" in Albert and Jacobson *et al.* (eds), op.cit., p. 225.
6 Ibid., p. 226.

of the sovereign. It is probably for this reason that it has become observable in respect of all the sub-regions of Africa that the 'debordering' stress which migration puts on states has been responded to somewhat instinctively by even stronger expression of the instruments of sovereignty and jurisdiction. This is particularly true of the northern African states – such as Libya, Morocco and Tunisia. In many other cases where states are simply incapable of marshalling the full complements of the apparatus of state security including customs, immigration and policing powers, the states have become recognisably frayed at the edges. As a result migrants have indeed succeeded in establishing temporary and sometimes long-term enclaves on the edges of the host African societies.[7]

Politicians in many countries including developed states are known to exploit the existence of large-scale immigration for political effect, to stoke national sentiments and indeed to foment international conflict. Politicians in the United States and Britain have traditionally provided ample examples of this behaviour.[8] A description of Mexican reactions against Chinese immigration in the early part of the last century is instructive:

> Reactions against Chinese immigration took local and regional forms. Mob violence, public-health regulations, segregation provisions, and bans on interracial marriage in various municipalities during the 1910s and 1920s were designed to harass the Chinese into leaving Mexico. These measures intensified in the context of the Great Depression, when vigilante groups began to take Chinese to the Mexico-US border and when the Sonoran governor Rodolfo Calles ordered Chinese residents to evacuate their businesses.[9]

Smuggling has a rich and varied history across all cultures and contributes to the tensions and problems faced by African states along their boundary lines. The content of smuggling activity in Africa varies from sub-region to sub-region and the effect it has on national economies varies as well. The smuggling of petroleum products across the Nigerian border to other neighbouring West African Countries like Niger, Benin and Chad where the prices are higher is rife and its effect on the Nigerian economy has been perceived by successive Nigerian governments as intolerable. It is likely that this issue will long be a source of potential severe stress and tensions in the international relations of West Africa. The effect of smuggling is usually seen as economic but indeed goes beyond economics alone and often

---

7 Cf. ibid., pp. 226, 240–241.
8 Images of migrants dashing across the border and weaving through traffic are regularly broadcast across the country and this rarely fails to galvanise public support for dramatic action even leading to vigilante action that has little to do with legality on occasion. Governor Wilson, the 36th governor of California, stated back in the 1990s when Mexican immigration problems were even less than in the twenty-first century that: 'For Californians who work hard, pay taxes and obey the laws, I am suing to force the federal government to control the border and I'm working to deny state services to illegal immigrants. Enough is enough.' Andreas, op.cit., p. 300.
9 Sadowski-Smith, op.cit., p. 69.

calls into question the very core of the security of the state. The connections between smugglers and dissidents, rebels, militia and terrorists groups is always a clear and present danger and this is one of the reasons why border security is an indispensable part of statecraft. It is one thing to see borders as bridges and it is another entirely to allow a state to become subverted by reason of porous and ill-monitored borders. It is perhaps appropriate to note that the first signature on the American Declaration of Independence was that of a well-known merchant-smuggler John Hancock. Smugglers also extensively assisted George Washington's troops with desperately needed arms and gunpowder.[10] Similarly freedom fighters and liberation groups in Africa relied heavily on smuggling for the success of their operations. Unfortunately many of these same routes are still open to today's dissidents and terrorists across the African continent on a scale that is perhaps more worrying than anywhere else on earth.

Apart from the widespread sense of disillusionment with the central government that is common to many flung border communities, boundary security problems may emanate from the history of colonial experience or other historical oppression. Dissatisfaction with the boundary line and/or the demarcator has been known through the centuries to contribute to willingness of boundary communities to engage in illegal activities around the border areas. Decision makers at the centre, boundary commissioners and dispute resolution practitioners must, therefore, keep this in view and consider how perceptions of historical wrongs may be contributing to criminality in boundary areas. It must be borne in mind that the majority portion of the population or main ethnic groups do not necessarily have to share this grievance. Indeed what matters most are the views of the aggrieved border region populations. Examples of this abound even in recent history. Some of the Yaqui indigenous people in Mexico, and particularly Zeta and Calabazas (two alleged smugglers), claim that their illegal activities exemplify their refusal to give any recognition to the legitimacy of the Mexico–US border. Border smuggling is seen as a legitimate assertion of their rights over the territory and a sort of reparation over governmental theft by invaders. An interesting reported account of a certain native called Zeta goes thus:

> people had been free to go travelling north and south for a thousand years, travelling as they pleased, then suddenly white priests had announced smuggling as a mortal sin because smuggling was stealing from the government. Zeta wondered if the priests had announced smuggling as a mortal sin because smuggling was stealing from the government. Zeta wondered if the priests who told the people smuggling was stealing had also told them how they were to feed themselves now that all the fertile land along the rivers had been stolen by white men. Where were the priest and his Catholic church when the federal soldiers used Yaqui babies for target practice? Stealing from the 'government'? What 'government' was that?

---

10 Andreas, op.cit., pp. 4–5.

Mexico City? ... Washington D.C.? How could one steal if the government itself was the worst thief?[11]

The story of many African peoples is similar and effort must be expended to analyse and understand the role of such ancestral grievances in the relations of boundary communities to international borders. To blame the widespread incidences of criminality and insecurity along African borders on the existence of a criminal class alone is to recognise the symptom and not the cause. As stated earlier it is also a well-recognised phenomenon that African border communities are often neglected and poorly catered for. The scarce resources available to be shared in most countries do not meaningfully reach the geographical extremes where many borders lie. Hence criminality such as smuggling becomes attractive and may perhaps be the easiest 'employment opportunity' around in border communities. For terroristic elements looking for recruits the pervading poverty and politics of socio-economic exclusion that afflicts most border communities make for easy conversion of disgruntled youths and other extremists towards ignoble causes. By the time governments based far away at the centre then wake up to the reality of loss of territorial control and seek to reinforce national sovereignty by coercive means, the recipe for boundary tensions and disputes would be complete. Political anthropologists are, therefore, correct in noting that the crises of border skirmishes, disputes and wars are in fact the crises of political action, in which the state is perceived to be failing in its primary role as the provider of essential services in exercise of its sovereignty. This failure produces scarcity and conflicts of economic, ecological, military and political nature between various interests when they inevitably interact in the borderlands.[12] If this reasoning is followed to its logical conclusion the problem then is not with borders or sovereignty but is in fact a problem of poor accountability to sovereignty of the people.

To defuse the problems that occur in such circumstances and to ameliorate existing disputes is not a straightforward affair. The fact that the forces to deal with are usually not even the official state agents of a neighbouring state makes most of the strategies and mechanisms known to international law approximately ineffectual. The best tools for analysis and action would most likely lie in something most governments are not strong at – careful jurisprudential thought. First, the interaction between border cultures and the wider cultures of the nation and state that gives definition to the political and social anthropology at play must be studied and understood. Second, the presence of the state particularly through soft power of good governance widely construed must be painstakingly implemented.

---

11 Quoted in Sadowski-Smith, op.cit., pp. 77–78, 95. Indigenous people at US land borders have also been said to encounter similar historical and contemporary challenges. See Appendix III for pictures of Heroin and other drug seizures at Mozambique–South Africa Lebombo border – Drug and gun running routes and seizures in Nianing, Senegal, Sudan–Chad.

12 Donnan, (1998) op.cit., p. 153.

It is for this reason that we note with strong approval the emerging trend of specialised border and rural communities' development agencies, which are now being implemented by a number of African states (discussed below). In 2003, Nigeria established the Border Communities Development Agency (BCDA) as a development agency with the mandate to ensure the sustainable social, economic and infrastructural development of border communities in Nigeria through the implementation of planned and sustainable projects. The body aims to be the vehicle for the provision of people oriented, sustainable and equitable development projects in the border communities, thereby ensuring their full integration, commitment, patriotism and loyalty to the Nigerian state.[13] The establishment of dedicated bodies to take care of the border populations is a very good way of ensuring that the government is brought qualitatively closer to the people and particularly that welfare benefits that are enjoyed in the various cosmopolitan centres are brought closer to the people situated at the margins of state territory. Ideally such a body will offer only beneficial welfare presence to the border areas and be separate from any boundary commission whose job may include actual policing in any way of the boundary. Its functions may include dealing with local movements: for example nomadic tribes and herds; settling local conflicts, e.g. livestock raiding.[14] It is also suggested that concerted effort in this manner is compatible with the demands of the Millennium Development Goals.[15] Care must, however, be taken that the establishment of such bodies does not amount to more than mere tokenism and/or job for the boys approach to rulership. There must be verifiable ways of benchmarking progress and achievements of such organisations and a way of ensuring that they do deliver on the promises of bringing good governance to the border peoples. In the best case scenario a network of such national border development agencies by bringing infrastructural and socio-economic benefits to border regions will in a short time transform African border regions to the bridges between countries that are envisaged under visionary developments such as the AUBP.

On the whole boundary commissioners, experts and jurists must be multidisciplinary in their approach to the important tasks of understanding and

---

13 The Agency was created by an Act of the National Assembly known as the Border Communities Development Agency Act, 2003 (as amended in 2006). For more information see the website of the organisation: www.bcda.gov.ng.

14 See pictures in Appendix III. Cf. John Donaldson, Boundary Commissions: Functions and Structures (Durham: International Boundary Research Unit), PowerPoint available at www.dur.ac.uk/resources/ibru/conferences/thailand/ibru_2.pdf, accessed 2 January 2014.

15 In September 2000, building upon a decade of major United Nations conferences and summits, world leaders meeting at the United Nations Headquarters in New York adopted the United Nations Millennium Declaration. By this instrument they committed their nations to a new global partnership to reduce extreme poverty and set out a series of time-bound targets – with a deadline of 2015. These have become known as the Millennium Development Goals (MDGs). The eight MDGs range from halving extreme poverty rates to halting the spread of HIV/AIDS and providing universal primary education, all by the target date of 2015. It is clear that these goals cannot be fully actualised by 2015 but will remain relevant as positive standards and goals far beyond this decade. See General Assembly resolution 55/2. United Nations Millennium Declaration, available at www.un.org/millennium/declaration/ares552e.pdf, accessed 2 January 2014.

managing border security issues in Africa. They must exhibit a particularly sound appreciation of the relevance of the social sciences generally to boundary studies. Anthropology, for instance, is useful as the discipline that theorises on culture. It also offers growing theoretical interests in the analysis of power, politics and policy in everyday life of localities including rural and peripheral regions. Because anthropology offers the proceeds of long-term field research and because anthropologists have over the years acquired the results of decades of ethnographic study at the international borders of Africa, the incorporation of the results of such studies offers a solid corpus of local-level analyses of communities. Such knowledge will be crucial to preventing and resolving a lot of situations in African border areas.[16] Unfortunately very few African countries have any meaningful budgets for such specialised studies in place.

11.1 Power and political differentials in the diplomacy of African boundary disputes

The geography of power remains a component of international relations through the ages and in all regions. National vitality and potency is dependent upon economic and military strength which in turn rests upon the bases of economic and human resources (including sheer population numbers).[17] Power and political differentials between neighbouring states can make boundary conflicts difficult and rather intractable. The difference between Anglophone and Francophone traditions, democracies and military dictatorships, resource rich and resource poor states can assume profound importance in boundary issues. Experts in the field of conflict studies have repeatedly pointed out that not only does power symmetry increase the likelihood of severity in boundary and territorial conflicts because both sides believe they can win and will continue to fight instead of terminating the conflict, but that would-be third parties' mediators are influenced in their decision to offer their services by observable power asymmetry. Where the power asymmetry is pronounced, mediators and eminent persons offering good offices might preclude themselves from embarking on the tasks based on the feeling that these types of disputes might present lesser opportunities for success than disputes where power is roughly equal. As Frazier helpfully explains:

> First, potential third parties might assume that major powers will simply decline initiatives from third parties in helping to resolve its dispute. Second, potential third parties may resist initiating mediation as they may consider themselves unable to bring any significant amount of leverage to the mediation table that they can use to influence the major power.[18]

---

16 Donnan, (1998) op.cit., pp. 157–158; J. Dunn, "Introduction Crises of the Nations State?", Vol. 62 *Political Studies* (1995), pp. 4–5.
17 Carlson and Philbrick, op.cit., p. 9.
18 Derrick V. Frazier, "Third Party Characteristics, Territory and the Mediation of Militarized Interstate Disputes", Vol. 23, *Conflict Management and Peace Science* (2006), p. 276; A. F. K. Organski

In a sense, therefore, it appears that power asymmetry, thus, attracts dysfunctional boundary international relations wherever it may be found. Power differentials according to popular theory afflict all kinds of boundaries whether among developed states or not. For instance, the opinion has been expressed that since the nineteenth century, Canada has been construed by US Americans 'either as an extension of Europe (and therefore a culture in decline) or as an extension of themselves (with annexation as an inevitable consequence)'.[19] It is significant to note that virtually all the economic powerhouses in Africa have had boundary problems with their neighbours since independence. Virtually all the top ten African economies – South Africa, Egypt, Nigeria, Algeria, Morocco, Angola, Sudan, Tunisia, Libya and Ethiopia – in this century have had active boundary disputes in the last decade and their disputes tend to be quite severe in military and diplomatic terms.

Yet the destinies of big and small countries are in many ways shared when they share contiguous territories and to this extent boundary justice must be blind, except in very limited circumstances. It is, therefore, imperative that all current and future efforts at managing boundary problems in Africa (such as the AUBP) develop means and methodologies that are designed to level the playing field for smaller and economically disadvantaged states that may have to undergo delimitation and demarcation exercises or are engaged in boundary disputes with stronger African states. Examples of these abound in Africa but mention may be made of the power differentials between Malawi and Tanzania and Eritrea and Ethiopia. Both cases and their power relations have been dealt with in our discussions earlier in this book. One of the issues that has dogged the land and maritime dispute between Cameroon and Nigeria, even before it was brought before the International Court, is the political reality of the power differentials between the parties. Cameroon is a smaller state in size, population and economic circumstances, in comparison to its 'giant of Africa' neighbour with substantial oil reserves. Nigeria is the 7th leading producer of oil in the world. The delicate balance that has had to be struck by Nigerian administrations in furtherance of executing an ICJ judgment which required the loss of a sizeable population to a smaller state has, therefore, been how to adhere to the equality of the state's principle without necessarily creating disenchantment among the populace.

As geographical neighbours with an approximately 2,000-km-long common land boundary, a shared colonial history and the experience of a UN referendum which reshaped both countries it is impossible to overemphasise the fact that more factors connect the two states together than divide them. It can be recalled that despite the many years of boundary tensions in certain sectors, and particularly in relation to Bakassi Peninsula, children on both sides of the boundary communities

---

and Jacek Kugle, *The War Ledger* (Chicago: University of Chicago Press, 1981); Douglas Lemke, "Toward a General Understanding of Parity and War", Vol. 14, *Conflict Management and Peace Science* (1995), pp. 143–162; Robert Gilpin, *War and Change in International Politics* (Cambridge: Cambridge University Press, 1981).

19 W. H. New, *Borderlands: How We Talk about Canada* (Vancouver: UBC Press, 1999), p. 73.

attended schools that are based in the neighbouring country without let or hindrance and farmers relied on regular vaccination of their livestock from whichever state was close enough. In 2004, some 17,000 Nigerian refugees were reported to have fled ethnic conflicts between pastoralists and farmers in 2002 and found refuge in Cameroon where many of them still reside.[20]

Another boundary regime of long and complex history with asymmetrical power differentials between the parties that shows the importance of keeping both the less and more powerful states in full confidence of the fairness of the process and negotiations is that of Shatt al-Arab river. Kaikobad wrote:

> The history of the Shatt question has shown that the distribution of power between Iran and Iraq has frustrated a final and conclusive settlement of *all* the issues, and has on every occasion prompted an agreement which the weaker State was less inclined to accept. Yet in legal terms there were no outstanding problems: the alignment had, in every case, been 'conclusively' settled.[21]

The politico-historical provenance of a frontier question is important not only because it provides perspective to the dispute, but also because details of the political history tend to reveal the incidents that played a role in the development of the frontier.[22] Without a proper analysis of the political and power differentials between boundary disputants, the appropriate solutions may elude mediators, negotiators and those charged with resolving the territorial or boundary disputes. The role that the particular colonial experience of certain African states had on their national geographic image and their attitude towards irredentism deserves closer cross-disciplinary studies. Both sets of facts, viz. the questions of power and of the different historical colonial experiences, featured largely in the Cameroon–Nigeria process. It is to the credit of the CNMC that it minimised as much as possible these power differentials between the countries at the judgment implementation stage. In theory there is ample evidence of the protection of the equality of arms principle within the adversarial system practiced before many international courts. It is important that the influence of power asymmetry on dispute resolution should continue to be held in view at all stages even after a judgment.

It helps if the neighbouring states involved in a border implementation and/or demarcation process do their best to reassure each other of their support on the

---

20 See the discussion on Nigeria transnational issues in *World Fact Book*, available at www.cia.gov/cia/publications/factbook/geos/ni.html, accessed 2 April 2006. The ties between both states run very deep and cut across all strata of their societies. There are currently an estimated 3 million Nigerians permanently resident in Cameroon. The pattern of settlement of these Nigerians is quite diverse and spread not only in the urban centres but also in rural areas. They are engaged in many professions from trading to farming and fishing. A census conducted shortly after the ICJ judgment by Cameroonian officials revealed that out of an estimated 20,000 fishermen plying their trade in a region of Cameroon, 19,000 of them were Nigerians. It is, therefore, easy to see that both parties had to retain a view of the big picture of things in order to maintain good and cordial relations.
21 Kaiyan Homi Kaikobad, "The Shatt-Al-Arab River Boundary A Legal Reappraisal", LVI *British Yearbook of International Law* (1985), p. 103.
22 Ibid.

broadest issues of foreign and domestic policies in which they agree. After the ICJ judgment, Cameroon and Nigeria sent messages of goodwill to each other through the CNMC whenever major national events occurred such as national elections. Sessions of the CNMC were sensitively scheduled to avoid allowing the meetings to clash with national celebrations and elections. Important concessions to delay or accelerate the process were granted on both sides to coincide with major national elections in which the incumbent government sought an advantageous impression in the minds of the electorate or to manage parliamentary crisis. Similarly, after 40 years of boundary negotiations China and Russia in 2006 heightened their level of diplomatic relations with visits and favourable pronouncements at the highest levels around the period they attained the difficult task of resolving boundary disputes along their 4,300-km-long border. Russia expressed its strong support for the one China policy and opposed Taiwan joining the United Nations and other major international organisations. Russia was also in agreement with China that the Tibet Autonomous Region is an inalienable part of China.[23]

It is indeed important that states maintain the best of diplomatic relations with each other particularly after a boundary dispute since the existence of a clearly delimited and demarcated boundary does not constitute the end of cooperation in boundary matters. Diplomacy remains the all-important process behind boundary negotiations. Historical experience shows that diplomatic exchanges in themselves are one of the best ways to trace the history of boundary making processes and, therefore, *de facto* or *de jure* boundary lines.[24] The power differentials between the states should not be allowed by the states themselves or any third party intermediaries on dispute settlement to negate the basic principles of diplomacy between states such as mutual respect and equality principle. Without mutually shared submission to these principles cooperation and cross-border peace will elude even the most reticent states. As the experts to the 2nd International Symposium on Land, River and Lake Boundaries Management rightly concluded:

> Delimitation, demarcation, mapping and management are essential steps towards creating peaceful and prosperous borderlands, but on their own they will not achieve these goals. Hence, the need for sustained efforts to promote cross-border cooperation and set targets to be achieved within a specific period of time, including the establishment of joint border management mechanisms between Member States. Reaffirmation of boundaries (e.g.

---

23 The Russian President announced during a visit to his Chinese counterpart: 'The Russian side will continue to adhere to the one-China policy and recognize the government of the People's Republic of China as the sole legitimate government of the whole of China'. And 'Taiwan is an inalienable part of the Chinese territory'. See Xinhua News Agency, 21 March 2006, China Internet Information Center, "China, Russia Sign Joint Statement", available at www.china.org.cn, accessed 5 August 2007.
24 Daniel, op.cit., p. 224.

erection of intermediate markers) and their maintenance will facilitate the achievement of this objective.[25]

The lessons about the imperative of cooperation apply two fold for more powerful states. First, there is the lesson that to assure a just and peaceful world, the possession of political power implies certain germane obligations and responsibilities. While no state must compromise its national security, it is difficult not to agree with the submission that 'international relations must rest upon a spirit of justice and right rather than only upon force and strength'.[26] Second, and perhaps very importantly, if the negotiation route is adopted in the resolution of the international boundary dispute, wealth and power produce a tendency to overestimate capabilities and underestimate the adversary and the willingness to fight, resist or attack.[27]

---

25 Management and regular clearing of the vista are also reasons for which continuing peace and cooperation between neighbouring states sharing common boundaries is crucial. See the AU, "Conclusion of the 2nd International Symposium on Land, River and Lake Boundaries Management" Maputo, Mozambique 17–19 December 2008 AUBP/EXP/3(VI), p. 3. There is no reason why joint policing cannot be engaged in by cooperating states to increase transparency and '*espirit de corp*' between security services. Indeed juxtaposed control zones which are a feature of some western European states may be introduced where applicable. See generally Gbenga Oduntan, "Arriving Before You Depart: Separating Law and Fiction in the Development and Operation of International Juxtaposed Control Zones" in Shah and Prakash (eds), *Migration, Diasporas and Legal Systems* (London: Cavendish Publishers, 2006), pp. 325–352. Note also that arrangements towards joint inspection and management is standard practice all around the world. Even where boundary markers are diligently fixed teutonic plate shifts may lead to changes in the exact position of beacons. By a special Agreement the Finnish–Russian Boundary is jointly repaired and inspected. Field inspection is done every summer and boundary markers are renovated or replaced. A boundary corridor is maintained on either side and trees and bushes in this corridor are cleared. Both parties pay their own costs. See Pekka Tatila, "Inspection of the Finnish-Russian Boundary", Paper Presented at 2nd International Symposium on Land, Maritime River and Lake Boundaries: Maputo, Mozambique (17–19 December 2008), p. 5.
26 Carlson and Allen K. Philbrick, op.cit., p. 9.
27 Michael D. Swaine, "Understanding the Historical Record", available at http://carnegieendowment.org/files/swaine_introduction.pdf, accessed 11 January 2014, p. 8.

12 Pacific settlement of international boundary disputes

A critical appraisal of the International Court of Justice

12.1 Conflict resolution and cooling off mechanism functions of the ICJ in the adjudication of African boundary disputes

Perhaps the exemplar route for adjudication of international boundary disputes in relation to African states has been the prolific recourse to the contentious jurisdiction of the ICJ. Thus, the jurisdiction of the Court will be a convenient basis to examine the adjudicatory route of boundary dispute resolution.[1] The first and most important duty of an international arbitral body or court is to achieve settlement of international disputes and the international conflict resolution function of the ICJ is one of the most remarkable features of this principal judicial organ of the United Nations. As it was stated in the *Northern Cameroons* case, concrete legal rights over territory must be an issue for the ICJ to be successfully seised of a dispute.

The function of the Court is to state the law, but it may pronounce judgment only in connection with concrete cases where there exists at the time of the adjudication an actual controversy involving a conflict of legal interests between the parties. The Court's judgment must have some practical consequences in the sense that it can affect existing legal rights or obligations from their legal relations. It can, thus, happen as it was concluded in the *Northern Cameroons* case that '[n]o judgments on the merits in this case could satisfy these essentials of the judicial functions'.[2]

It is very important for a boundary or territorial claim to be capable of being framed in legal terms as political, sociological, anthropological or sentimental manifestations or a claim may be insufficient to cause the matter to be seised

---

1 In 1945 the Charter of the UN brought the ICJ a new judicial organ into being. The Statute of the Court is annexed to the Charter of which it forms an integral part. The Charter of the UN and the Statute of the Court entered into force on 24 October 1945. After the election of its members on 6 February 1946, the Court met for the first time in The Hague on 1 April of the same year. The first case entered in the General List of the Court (*Corfu Channel United Kingdom v Albania*) was submitted on 22 May 1947.
2 *Northern Cameroons* case, ICJ Rep. (1963), pp. 33–34.

(accepted and treated) by an international court. Sir Gerald Fitzmaurice correctly stated this in the *Northern Cameroons* case when he pronounced that:

> Courts of Law are not there to make legal pronouncements in abstract to, however great their scientific value as such. They are there to protect existing and current legal obligations, to afford concrete reparation if a wrong has been committed, or to give rulings in relation to existing and continuing legal situations.[3]

Despite the reality that cases submitted to the ICJ, especially in boundary cases, must have clear and specific legal aspects based on legal rights including equitable considerations, one of the most underreported functions which the World Court has been made to serve in the international society is that of being a cooling off mechanism in international relations. Especially in the highly emotive circumstances surrounding territorial and boundary disputes, it is becoming clear that international courts and tribunals have been exploited over time as a means to delay action and to pacify national or indeed international opinion. Boundary disputes particularly have a reputation of experiencing relatively long periods of gestation. The issues would typically have been discussed diplomatically over many years with a long trail of *note verbales*, diplomatic conferences, high level meetings, press reports, skirmishes between groups and/or military personnel, intermittent armed conflict and even on occasion covert actions. At some point political situations may necessitate a change in approach in one or both states concerned which escalates the dispute to heights that cannot be safely ignored. At such times it may be difficult for governments to continue pretending that the issue is under control or can be settled diplomatically. Submission of the dispute to the ICJ under its contentious jurisdiction procedures may in fact be a safe way to deposit the political problem that the legal dispute has become in order that the governments may be seen as 'doing something about it'. For the next few years, and even sometimes up to a decade, the embarrassing matter will be locked within the serene corridors of the Peace Palace at The Hague allowing other aspects of international relations and national affairs to go on unimpeded. Countries are known to have exploited this therapeutic effect in order that frayed nerves might be cooled by the lengthy judicial process. It is ironic that even a government that is not sure of the legal basis of its claims will still enthusiastically agree to the submission of a case to the Court since the public and the international community would readily assume that the Court will most probably hand down a rational and dispassionate judgment. From a judicial point of view, however, the 'cooling off' use of the Court may not be ideal and a preference has been maintained for the use of the Court only in the most non-theoretical and contentious manner to resolve actual disputes for which the parties have characterised as best dealt with under studied judicial functions.

---

3 See Fitzmaurice, Separate Opinion *Northern Cameroons* case, ICJ Rep. (1963), pp. 98–99.

The World Court, however, appears to take quite enthusiastically to its therapeutic mechanism role. Its judgments notably leave something for everyone. We have already treated earlier the way a country like Nigeria, which appeared to have lost the Bakassi case, also came up as a winner in its maritime claims as well as in various other portions of the land boundary. The judgment of the World Court also tends to create a very good platform for later cooperation to be based. Particularly where close cooperation between states is key to post-judgment implementation, the Court is usually acutely aware of its conciliatory and therapeutic roles. In the *Asylum Case* the Court found it legally incorrect for Columbia to grant diplomatic territorial asylum to Haya De La Torre, a Peruvian politician on an alleged rule of unilateral and definitive qualification of the offence. Columbia and Peru were unable to come to an agreement on the basis of the sentence laid down and the Court was requested to determine the manner in which effect should be given to its judgment and whether Columbia was, or was not, bound to hand over Haya De La Torre. In a judgment delivered in June 1951, the ICJ concluded that 'the asylum must cease, but that the Government of Columbia is under no obligation to bring this about by surrendering the refuge to Peruvian authorities'.[4] This instance has been said to be emblematic of the Court's therapeutic, conciliatory and weighted judgment.

12.1.1 Diplomatic function of international courts

The recourse to international courts and arbitration is increasingly assimilated into the diplomatic process in international relations. This is a role many commentators on the Courts' work will only grudgingly admit. Indeed it is a role completely unimaginable to earlier scholars on the adjudication process in international matters. But in recent times the procedures of international courts have proved useful in assisting national governments to focus and judge the strength of each other's case as well as determination to follow the matter through. In a sense, the adjudicative process and the drama of submission and/or challenge to the courts' authority is assimilated to diplomatic posturing often leading to a negotiated solution. This in no way derogates from the importance of the system of international adjudication. Neither should it be considered an abuse of the judicial process. It is quite usual even in domestic systems for settlements to be eventually made out of court, ordinarily at some stage before the case comes on for hearing but even occurring up to the eve of judgment. The institution of proceedings before an international court in such circumstances is not necessarily a waste of time and resources. Rather, it may be that the imminence of a judgment which may indeed go either way may offer the impetus for genuine negotiations. Situations may also arise where a case may be withdrawn in response to changes in the relevant sociopolitical equations. In other words, the eventual solution may

---

4 Nascimento E. Silva, *Diplomacy in International Law* (Netherlands: A. W. Sijthoff, 1972), p. 105. See also J. B. Syatoaw, *Decisions of the International Court of Justice A Digest* (New York: A. W. Sythoff-Leyden Oceana Publications, 1962), p. 51.

be devoid of the influence of the pendency of the matter before the Court. Such instances are not necessarily negative.

In an unusual manifestation of this function, the ICJ decided regarding the fight over the Danube between Hungary and Slovakia that Hungary was wrong to suspend and then in 1989 to abandon its obligations to a common dam project as spelled out in a 1977 treaty binding upon both states. But the Court also found that Czechoslovakia (from which Slovakia emerged after the collapse of communism) had proceeded illegally when it diverted the river through the dam in 1992. The two countries were, thus, ordered by the Court to proceed to negotiate in 'good faith'.[5] In this way adjudication directly assisted the parties to return to diplomatic negotiations. There is of course also the direct assistance towards diplomacy that occurs by virtue of the fact that the issuance of a judgment will necessitate the advent of further diplomacy towards implementation.

12.1.2 Advancing jurisprudence and elaboration of the law

The value of international courts in enriching the jurisprudence of public and private international law is in a sense inestimable considering that apart from the alternative dispute resolution (ADR) mechanisms known to international law, courts and arbitral tribunals are the major contributors to the field of pacific settlement of international disputes. International courts and tribunals, however, afford states, lawyers and academics the most authoritative opinion and views on legal principles. They help parties and their legal advisers towards formulating some level of predictability in relation to permissible courses of action out of several options.

Many legal principles codified into treaties, guiding norms and principles had first been forensically extracted from the jurisprudence of international courts in actual cases. Elaborate arguments would have been tested under judicial circumstances and the pertinent issues would have been decided upon with full awareness of their international impact. In turn the jurisprudence of courts inexorably concretises legal opinion of scholars and lawyers on legal principles. The Permanent Court of International Justice (PCIJ), for instance, laid down the constituent ingredients of effective occupation in the *Eastern Greenland Case* as (i) the intention to act as sovereign and (ii) an adequate exercise of the display of

---

5 See Jane Perlez, "World Court Leaves Fight Over Danube Unresolved", *New York Times*, 26 September 1997, p. 12. In short, the Court is beginning to be employed in closer relationship with normal diplomatic negotiation. No longer is the Court a 'last resort' to be employed when all else has failed and as a President of the Court convincingly put it, the Court procedures can sometimes form part of, and be a vector in, diplomatic negotiations. The two processes are, of course, juridically distinct, but in practice they may be employed complementarily, and not necessarily on a basis of mutual exclusivity. It is the constant jurisprudence of the Court that judicial settlement is only an alternative to friendly settlement by the parties themselves. Whenever the Court or its procedures can help in this way, the Court is, in an important sense, still productively at work. See the addresses of the President of the Court, Sir Robert Jennings at the 47th and 48th Session of the General Assembly, *The Yearbook of the ICJ (1992–1993)*, Vol. 47, pp. 249–251; *Yearbook of the ICJ 1993–1994*, Vol. 48, pp. 219–220.

sovereignty.[6] In *The Lotus Case* the PCIJ developed the concept of constructive presence on state territory in favour of a territorial state to capture persons who target the state from abroad in order to cause harm within. Judge Moore framed the principle thus:

> It appears to be now generally admitted that where a crime is committed in the territorial jurisdiction of one state as a direct result of the act of a person at the time physically present in another state, international law, by reason of the principle of constructive presence of the offender at the place where his act took effect does not forbid the prosecution of the offender by the former state, should he come within its territorial jurisdiction.[7]

By 1935 the Harvard Draft Convention formulated the principle as stating that a state may exercise territorial jurisdiction when a crime is committed 'in whole or in part' within its territory.[8]

In other words, apart from the central role of conflict resolution or perhaps in the course of achieving that aim, an international court may engage in the development of the law. Broadly there are two main possible approaches to the task of a judge whether in the international field or elsewhere. There is the approach which conceives it to be the primary if not the sole duty of a judge to decide the case in hand, with the minimum of verbiage necessary for this purpose and to confine himself to that. The other approach conceives it to be the proper function of the judge, while duly deciding the case in hand with the necessary supporting reasoning, all the while not unduly straying outside the four corners of the case, to utilise those aspects of it which have a wider interest or connotation, in order to make general pronouncements of law and principle that may enrich and develop the law.[9] The latter approach is considered better suited for the field of international law. This is more so as we have argued in various parts of this book that much of what is settled under international law presently may indeed represent the sectional interests of a few elite states in the international system and shoring up positions of domination or relationships of exploitation that are no longer relevant to the international system.

While the position advanced above might be true, one must not forget that in theory courts of law interpret the law and do not make it. Indeed judges loath to admit the increasingly popular notion that in a way they perform a law-creating role. Nevertheless as a writer notes, 'in practice . . . the law is complete only after

---

6 Norway–Denmark. PCIJ Ser A/B (1933) No. 53.
7 PCIJ Reports Ser A (1927) No. 10.
8 See Text of the Draft Convention With Respect to Crime in Vol. 29, *American Journal of International Law* (1935), p. 439. It is to be mentioned that the Harvard Draft Convention of 1935 was the product of the unofficial work of a number of American international lawyers. It is not binding upon states as a treaty and is not state practice. Yet it is widely accepted that the Draft Convention adequately reflects customary international law and its suggestions *de lege ferenda* have been accepted as being of considerable value reflecting the thorough study that was put into the preparation of the text.
9 G. Fitzmaurice, in "Hersch Lauterpacht – The Scholar as a Judge" Part 137 *British Yearbook of International Law* (1961), pp. 14–15.

the judge defines what it means and that, therefore, the judge is part of the law making process'.[10] We can also make reference to Article 38 (1d) of the ICJ Statute in that, (in order to help define what the law means) the Article provides for the application of 'judicial decisions and the teachings of the most highly qualified publicists of the various nations'. Of course this includes World Court judges and jurists of other international tribunals. Article 38 (2) also unequivocally confers on the Court 'the power ... to decide a case *ex aequo et bono*, if the parties agree thereto'. In that case the Court need not confine itself to applying the existing law but could, if it deemed the existing law to operate harshly, inefficiently or unjustly, give a judgment which aligns more with the essentials of equity and justice. There is therefore, much scope for judicial activism in the handling of boundary-related cases under international law.

In as much as there are such strong arguments in favour of the proposition that the Court performs the function of law development we must not fail to acknowledge a limitation in this direction embodied in the provisions of Article 59, which states: 'The decision of the Court has no binding force except between the parties in respect of a case.'

In other words the International Court is specifically bound from applying precedent or the doctrine of *stare decisis* in its decisions. Its decisions are to serve only as evidence for the existence of international law.[11] Levi, however, correctly notes that:

> Nevertheless, the fact is that all Courts and tribunals – international courts, municipal courts, – rely upon and cite each other abundantly in their verdicts. Decisions especially repetitive similar decisions, acquire an authority affecting the formulation of legal norms in subsequent cases. They are not merely evidence of existing law; they often become the creators of law, especially customary law by becoming part of international practice.[12]

Sir G. Fitzmaurice correctly remarked that international courts had recognised the development of law as an essential part of their function.[13] Sir Hersch Lauterpacht also noted that while it may well be an exaggeration to assert that the Court has proved to be a significant instrument for maintaining international peace, it has at least made a tangible contribution to the development and clarification of the rules and principles of international law.[14] Lauterpacht refers to this phenomenon as 'a heterogeny of aims ... where ... institutions set up for the achievements of definite purposes grow to fulfil tasks not wholly identical with those which were in the minds of their authors at the time of their creation ...'.[15]

---

10 Wener Levi, *Contemporary International Law: A Concise Introduction* (Boulder, Colorado: Westview Press, 1979), p. 53.
11 Ibid.
12 Ibid.
13 Fitzmaurice, op.cit., p. 15.
14 Ibid.
15 See also Janis, op.cit., p. 30.

12.2 International adjudication of African boundary disputes: a critical appraisal of the contentious and advisory jurisdiction of the World Court

To understand how Africa has fared before the Court, it is pertinent to examine certain facts and figures about the use of the Court in its 58-year history. It may be noted from a cursory glance at the following tables (see Tables 12.1–12.3) that for some reasons European states have made wider use of the services of the Court in its contentious jurisdiction. As at 2013, whereas 28 European states have appeared as parties in cases before the Court, only 23 have done so out of the states in Africa. The number of appearances by certain European states before the Court perhaps also reflects a higher confidence in the Court. For instance, France has appeared before the Court 12 times, the United Kingdom 13 times and the United States 21 times.[16] It is perhaps significant that in the first 50 years of the Court, African states, after attaining political independence, were very reluctant to submit their disputes to the Court and only towards the end of the last decade has there been an appreciable increase in submission of disputes involving African states. Even then the bulk of this increase arose as a result of the Democratic Republic of Congo crises, which accounts for six cases in the Court's docket within the last decade alone (involving five African states that have never appeared before the Court before). Notwithstanding this analysis, it is important to note that this period of *entente* between African states and the Court represents a positive development, in that African states are exhibiting a clear preference for pacific means of settlement of international disputes over resort to use of force in resolving those disputes arising out of domestic situations having cross-boundary effects.

Since the inception of the UN and up until 2014, 27 separate disputes involving 30 independent states have so far been litigated before the World Court in relation to Africa. In other words nearly half of all African states have litigated their boundaries. Only four non-African states – the United Kingdom, the United States, France and Belgium – were involved in these disputes. It is noticeable that the vast majority of the disputes involving African states are tied to territorial and boundary questions. It is also noticeable that the Francophone African states have litigated more among themselves than the Anglophone states. It is perhaps too early to tell whether this is as a result of diplomatic pressures from France or the result of a shared legal or diplomatic tradition. The case between Cameroon and Nigeria represents the very first case before the Court between a Francophone and an Anglophone African state.[17] There are unsubstantiated accounts in political and journalistic literature that the Cameroonian claim was instigated by

---

16 Notably these are three of the five permanent members of the UN Security Council. Between them they have put together a total of 46 appearances before the Court out of a total of 99 Contentious Disputes dealt with by the Court as at 2013.
17 It has been suggested, admittedly without much basis, in political circles that the hurried acceptance of the compulsory jurisdiction of the ICJ under the optional clause (Article 36 (2) of the Statute) by Cameroon just weeks prior to the institution of proceedings on 29 March 1994 was not without some level of consultation with France.

Table 12.1 Geographical distribution of countries that have been parties to contentious proceedings and number of appearances

Europe	Asia	North and South America	Africa	Australia
UK (13)	Iran (4)	Canada (3)	Cameroon (3)	Australia (5)
Albania (1)	Lebanon (2)	US (21)	Libya (6)	New Zealand (3)
France (13)	India (4)	Colombia (7)	Egypt (1)	Timor-Leste (1)
Liechtenstein (2)	Israel (1)	Peru (4)	Ethiopia (1)	
Italy (4)	Cambodia (2)	Guatemala (1)	Liberia (1)	
Hungary (3)	Thailand (2)	Argentina (2)	South Africa (2)	
*USSR/Russia (5)	Pakistan (3)	Chile (3)	Burkina Faso (2)	
*Czech Republic (1)	Turkey (1)	Honduras (6)	Tunisia (2)	
Norway (3)	Nauru (1)	Nicaragua (14)	Mali (2)	
Portugal (3)	Qatar (1)	Costa Rica (5)	Guinea-Bissau (2)	
Netherlands (4)	Bahrain (1)	El Salvador (2)	Senegal (3)	
Sweden (1)	Indonesia (1)	Paraguay (1)	Chad (1)	
Switzerland (3)	Malaysia (2)	Mexico (2)	Nigeria (2)	
Bulgaria (3)	Japan (1)	Bolivia (1)	Republic of Congo (1)	
Belgium (7)		Brazil (1)	Dem. Rep of Congo (6)	
Spain (4)		Ecuador (1)	Botswana (1)	
Germany (7)			Namibia (1)	
Denmark (3)			Rwanda (2)	
Yugoslavia (4)			Niger (2)	
Iceland (2)			Benin (1)	
Finland (1)			Republic of Equatorial Guinea (2)	
*Bosnia and Herzegovina (2)			Uganda (1)	
Slovakia (1)			Burundi (1)	
Greece (4)			Djibouti (1)	
Turkey (1)			Somalia (1)	
Malta (1)			Kenya (1)	
Serbia and Montenegro (10)				
Croatia (1)				
Republic of Macedonia (1)				
Georgia (1)				

* The former USSR spans Europe and Asia geographically but for the purpose of this analysis the USSR is treated as a European country; the Court regards Bosnia and Herzegovina as a Republic (see Application of the Crime of Genocide, Order of 16 April 1993, ICJ Reports 1993 p. 29; Czech Republic formerly Czechoslovakia.

Table 12.2 Contentious cases involving African countries at the ICJ

1. *Ethiopia v. South Africa, Liberia v. South Africa*: (South West Africa) 1960–1966
2. *Cameroon v. United Kingdom* (Northern Cameroon) 1961–1963
3. *Tunisia/Libya: (Continental Shelf) 1978–1982
4. *Libya/Malta: (Continental Shelf) 1982–1985
5. *Burkina Faso/Republic of Mali: (Frontier Dispute) (Case referred to a Chamber) 1983–1986
6. *Tunisia v. Libya*: (Application for Revisions and Interpretation of the Judgment of 24 February 1982 in the Case concerning the Continental Shelf) 1984–1985
7. *Guinea-Bissau v. Senegal*: (Arbitral Award of 31 July 1989)
8. *Libya Arab Jamahiriya/Chad: (Territorial Dispute) 1990–1994
9. *Guinea-Bissau v. Senegal*: (maritime Delimitation between Guinea-Bissau and Senegal) 1991
10. *Libya v. UK Questions of Interpretation and Application of the 1971 Montreal Convention Arising from the Aerial Incident at Lockerbie*: 1992
11. *Libya v. USA Questions of Interpretation and Application of the 1971 Montreal Convention Arising from the Aerial Incident at Lockerbie*: 1992
12. *Cameroon v. Nigeria* (Land and Maritime Boundary between Cameroon and Nigeria) 1994–2002
13. Request for the Interpretation of the Judgment of 11 June 1998 in the case concerning the Land and Maritime Boundary between Cameroon and Nigeria (*Cameroon v. Nigeria*), Preliminary Objections (*Nigeria v. Cameroon*) 1998–1999
14. *Botswana/Namibia: (Kasikili/Sedudu Island) 1996–1999
15. Ahmadou Sadio Diallo (*Republic of Guinea v. Democratic Republic of the Congo*) 1998–2008
16. Armed Activities on the territory of the Congo (*Democratic Republic of the Congo v. Uganda*) 1991–2001
17. Armed Activities on the territory of the Congo (*Democratic Republic of the Congo v. Rwanda*) 1991–2001
18. Armed Activities on the territory of the Congo (*Democratic Republic of the Congo v. Burundi*) 1991–2001
19. Arrest Warrant of 11 April 2000 (*Democratic Republic of Congo v. Belgium*) 2000–2002
20. *Frontier Dispute (Benin/Niger) 2002
21. Armed Activities on the Territory of the Congo (New Application: 2002) (*Democratic Republic of the Congo v. Rwanda*)
22. Frontier Dispute (Benin/Niger) 2002–2005
23. Certain Criminal Proceedings in France (*Republic of the Congo v. France*) 2002–2010
24. Certain Questions of Mutual Assistance in Criminal Matters (*Djibouti v. France*) 2006–2008
25. Questions relating to the Obligation to Prosecute or Extradite (*Belgium v. Senegal*) 2009–2012
26. Frontier Dispute (Burkina Faso/Niger) 2010–2013
27. Dispute Concerning Maritime Delimitation in the Indian Ocean (*Somalia v. Kenya*) 2014.

* Proceedings instituted by means of special agreement are separated by an oblique stroke.

France based on the calculation that the bench of the World Court around the early 1990s, when the case was submitted, was heavily Francophone. The first case between Anglophone African states before the Court is the *Kasikili/Sedudu Island* case between Botswana and Namibia (1996–1999).

Although the Court has been very active in dealing with African boundary disputes, two cogent criticisms have emerged over the years. The first is that throughout its existence the Court has either inadvertently or by institutional design been applying Eurocentric international law in a manner that compromises the interest of African and other developing states. Second, it is argued that the composition and staffing of the ICJ, just like that of the PCA, is largely unrepresentative of the developing states of Africa. This lack of representation further establishes the perceived bias against the overall interest of African and other developing states.

It is necessary to look more closely at those disputes which relate to boundary issues. It becomes clear that the predominant issues brought for judicial determination by African states are largely those relating to their common boundaries. Africa undoubtedly has produced the largest number of the most celebrated territorial and boundary disputes that have captured the attention of the World Court. Of the 27 separate contentious cases between African states submitted to the Court and highlighted in Table 12.2 above, 19 of them more or less directly concern territorial and/or boundary disputes.[18] Four of the contentious cases between African states were instituted in the same year and relate to the armed activities on the territory of Congo.[19] It is important to note that central to the declared disputes in the plethora of Congo cases is the problem of alleged flagrant breaches of the sovereignty and territorial integrity in violation of the Charters of the United Nations and the Organization of African Unity by Rwanda, Uganda and Burundi.[20]

---

18 *Ethiopia v. South Africa, Liberia v. South Africa: (South West Africa)* 1960–1966; *Cameroon v. United Kingdom (Northern Cameroon)* 1961–1963; *Tunisia v. Libya (Continental Shelf)* 1978–1982; *Libya v. Malta (Continental Shelf)* 1982–1985; *Burkina Faso v. Republic of Mali (Frontier Dispute)* (Case referred to a Chamber) 1983–1986; *Tunisia v. Libya (Applications for Revisions and interpretation of the judgment of 24 February 1982 in the case concerning the Continental Shelf)* 1978–1982; *Guinea-Bissau v. Senegal (Arbitral Award of 31 July 1989)*; *Libya Arab Jamahiriya v. Chad (Territorial Dispute 1990–1994)*; *Cameroon v. Nigeria (Land and Maritime Boundary Dispute)*; *Kasikili/Sedudu Island (Botswana/Namibia)*; *Request for Interpretation of the Judgment of 11 June 1998 in the Case concerning the Land and Maritime Boundary between Cameroon and Nigeria (Cameroon v. Nigeria), Preliminary Objections (Nigeria v. Cameroon)*; *Frontier Dispute (Benin/Niger)*.

19 *Armed Activities on the Territory of the Congo (New Application: 2002) (Democratic Republic of the Congo v. Rwanda 1999)*; *Armed Activities on the Territory of the Congo (Democratic Republic of the Congo v. Rwanda 1999)*; *Armed Activities on the Territory of the Congo (Democratic Republic of the Congo v. Uganda 1999)*; *Armed Activities on the Territory of the Congo (Democratic Republic of the Congo v. Burundi 1999)*.

20 ICJ Reports 2006. In the application to the Court in the *Congo v Burundi* case it was stated that '1. On 2 and 3 August 1998, columns of Burundian army trucks carrying heavily armed soldiers breached the eastern frontiers of the Congo and occupied the cities of Goma and Bukavu.' ICJ Application Instituting Proceedings filed in the Registry of the Court on 23 June 1999 *Armed Activities On The Territory Of The Congo (Democratic Republic of The Congo v. Burundi)*, available at www.icj-cij.org/docket/files/115/7127.pdf, accessed 21 September 2014.

Table 12.3 Territorial and boundary disputes in contentious cases involving African countries at the ICJ

	Cases	Issues
1	*Ethiopia v. South Africa, Liberia v. South Africa*: (South West Africa) 1960–1966	Territorial sovereignty and independence mandate
2	*Cameroon v. United Kingdom* (Northern Cameroon) 1961–1963	Territorial sovereignty and independence
3	*Tunisia/Libya: (Continental Shelf) 1978–1982	Maritime boundary and delimitation
4	*Libya/Malta: (Continental Shelf) 1982–1985	Delimitation of the continental shelf; the Libyan 'rift zone' argument; test of proportionality; equidistance line
5	*Burkina Faso/Republic of Mali: (Frontier Dispute) (Case referred to a Chamber) 1983–1986	Delineation of frontier line; principles of intangibility of colonial boundaries and *uti possidetis*; French colonial law; distinction between village and hamlets
6	*Tunisia v. Libya*: (Application for Revisions and Interpretation of the Judgment of 24 February 1982 in the Case concerning the Continental Shelf) 1984–1985.	Principles applicable to the delimitation of the areas of the continental shelf; interpretation; admissibility; request for an expert survey
7	*Guinea-Bissau v. Senegal*: (Arbitral Award of 31 July 1989)	Validity of the Arbitral Award of 31 July 1989; validity of agreements concerning the delimitation of their maritime areas
8	*Libya Arab Jamahiriya/Chad: (Territorial Dispute) 1990–1994	Frontier line; Treaty of Friendship and Good Neighbourliness between France and Libya; establishment of permanent boundaries; subsequent attitude of the parties
9	*Guinea-Bissau v. Senegal*: (maritime Delimitation between Guinea-Bissau and Senegal) 1991	Maritime delimitation line; negotiation over maritime territory
10	*Cameroon v. Nigeria* (Land and Maritime Boundary between Cameroon and Nigeria) 1994–2002	Sovereignty over Bakassi peninsula, maritime, river and water delimitation, straddling villages, Lake Chad Basin trespass issues, etc.
11	Request for the Interpretation of the Judgment of 11 June 1998 in the case concerning the Land and Maritime Boundary between Cameroon and Nigeria (*Cameroon v. Nigeria*), Preliminary Objections (*Nigeria v. Cameroon*) 1998–1999	Admissibility of Nigeria's request; cost of the proceedings; interpretation of the Court's judgment regarding internationally unlawful acts and frontier incursions
12	*Botswana/Namibia (Kasikili/Sedudu Island) 1996–1999	Sovereignty, jurisdiction and control over Island and maritime boundary
13	Armed Activities on the territory of the Congo (*Democratic Republic of the Congo v. Uganda*) 1991–2001	Armed intervention, territorial sovereignty, humanitarian law

(continued)

Table 12.3 (continued)

	Cases	Issues
14	Armed Activities on the territory of the Congo (*Democratic Republic of the Congo v. Rwanda*) 1991–2001	Armed intervention, territorial sovereignty, humanitarian law
15	Armed Activities on the territory of the Congo (*Democratic Republic of the Congo v. Burundi*) 1991–2001	Armed intervention, territorial sovereignty, humanitarian law
16	*Frontier Dispute (Benin/Niger) 2002–2005	Delimitation; sovereignty over islands, boundaries following rivers
17	Armed Activities on the Territory of the Congo (New Application: 2002) (*Democratic Republic of the Congo v. Rwanda*) 2002–2006	Armed intervention, territorial sovereignty, humanitarian law
18	Frontier Dispute (Burkina Faso/Niger) 2010–2013	Both states agreed to submit a frontier dispute between them over a section of their common boundary (from astronomic marker of Tong-Tong (latitude 14° 25' 04" N; longitude 00° 12' 47" E) to the beginning of the Botou bend (latitude 12° 36' 18" N; longitude 01° 52' 07" E)). The Court delimited the section fully in accordance with Institut géographique national de France, 1960 edition maps ("IGN line") and specific pertinent coordinates but rejected Burkina Faso's requests to decide upon sectors that the parties have been able to reach agreement upon earlier.
19	Dispute Concerning Maritime Delimitation in the Indian Ocean (*Somalia v. Kenya*) 2014	Establishment of a single maritime boundary in the Indian Ocean delimiting territorial sea, EEZ and the continental shelf, including the continental shelf beyond 200 nautical miles

* Proceedings instituted by means of special agreement are separated by an oblique stroke.

12.3 Role of the International Court of Justice in relation to the struggle for self-determination and independence for the mandate and colonial territories in Africa

Given the role international law has played in the subjugation of vast swathes of humanity under colonialism and imperialism it is necessary to examine whether and to what extent the ICJ particularly played any role in correcting or contributing to the situation. In the cases concerning the discharge of duties of the mandatory powers over the mandate territories, the ICJ's work has been more significant in its advisory jurisdiction than in its contentious jurisdiction.

Four advisory opinions concerning Namibia were rendered by the Court, of which the General Assembly requested three and the Security Council one. In the first opinion, the Court in 1950 declared that South Africa continued to have international obligations under the mandate despite the dissolution of the League of Nations. In 1955, the Court stated over South African objections that the Assembly was correct in treating decisions concerning South Africa as 'important questions' requiring a two-thirds majority vote. In 1956, again the Court declared the oral hearing of petitioners by the Committee on South West Africa as admissible and as a necessary means to enable the UN to perform its supervisory duties effectively. In the opinion requested by the Security Council, the Court stated categorically and unequivocally that the continued presence of South Africa in Namibia was illegal and that South Africa was under an obligation to withdraw its administration and put an end to its occupation of the territory.[21]

With respect to the colonial cases under the contentious jurisdiction, however, the Court seems to have been unduly conservative and unimaginative. It took 14 years of the Court's existence before the first African states (Ethiopia and Liberia), and indeed the first developing countries, litigated against a more developed state. That experience, as will shortly be shown, seriously damaged the confidence of developing countries in the Court; a situation, which arguably very slowly changed after the relatively recent separate proceedings instituted against the United States and the United Kingdom by Libya and against Belgium and France by the Congo.[22]

The *South West Africa* judgment was indeed a landmark decision in the history of the Court.[23] It still stands as a veritable source of suspicion of the Court by developing states. On 4 November 1960, Ethiopia and Liberia – the oldest sovereign states on the African continent – instituted separate proceedings against South Africa in a case concerning the continued existence of the mandate for South West Africa and the duties and performance of South Africa as mandatory power. The Court was requested to make declarations to the effect that South West Africa remained a territory under a mandate, that South Africa had been in breach of its obligations under that mandate, and that the mandate and hence the mandatory authority were subject to the supervision of the UN. On 20 May 1961, the Court made an Order finding Ethiopia and Liberia to be in the same interest and joining the proceedings each had instituted.[24]

---

21 J. B. Syatanw, *Decisions of the International Court of Justice: A Digest* (New York: A. W. Sijthoff-Leyden Oceana Publications, 1962), pp. 342–345.
22 *Arrest Warrant of 11 April 2000 (Democratic Republic of Congo v. Belgium)*; *Certain Criminal Proceedings in France (Republic of the Congo v. France)* 2002; *supra* Chapter 1, note 1.
23 The case was in two phases. The first phase was in the *South West Africa Preliminary Objections*. The second in *South West Africa (Ethiopia v. South Africa)*; *(Liberia v. South Africa)*. For convenience both phases of the case are treated in this chapter together. See ICJ Rep. 1966, pp. 6–319.
24 See the ICJ, *The International Court of Justice* 3rd Edition (The Hague, 1986), p. 7.

Their common demands were that: (i) the Court should declare that South West Africa had remained a mandated territory as laid down by the Court itself in its advisory opinion of 1950; (ii) South Africa had continued to be in breach of the obligations imposed upon it under that mandate in accordance with Article 22 of the League's Covenant; (iii) the mandate and hence the mandatory power continued to be under the international supervision of the UN, which has since replaced the League of Nations in this respect.

South Africa in its own response filed four preliminary objections to the Court's jurisdiction: (i) that the mandate for South West Africa has never been (or at any rate is since the dissolution of the League of Nations no longer) a 'treaty or convention in force' within the meaning of Article 37 of the Statute of the Court. This submission being advanced, (a) with respect to the mandate as a whole, including Article 7 thereof and (b) in any event with respect to Article 7 itself; (ii) neither the Government of Ethiopia nor the Government of Liberia is 'another member of the league of nations' as required for *locus standi* by Article 7 of the Mandate for South West Africa; (iii) the conflict or disagreement alleged by the governments of Ethiopia and Liberia to exist between them and the Government of the Republic of South Africa is by reason of its nature and content not a 'dispute' as envisaged in Article 7 of the Mandate for South West Africa, more particularly in that no material interest of Ethiopia or Liberia are involved or affected thereby; (iv) the alleged conflict or disagreement is as regards its state of development and not a 'dispute' which cannot be settled by negotiations within the meaning of Article 7 of the Mandate for South West Africa.[25]

For six years, not only the parties but also the rest of the world waited expectantly for the final judgment of the World Court in this case. On 18 July 1966, the Court handed down a decision, which according to scholarly opinion 'took almost everyone by surprise; for after all the time, energy and money that had been spent on these cases'.[26] The Court held that the applicants were not entitled to a judgment on their submissions because they had not established any legal right or interest in the subject matter of their claim.

The Algerian government declared that the ICJ, having been conceived in 1945 to direct international law by the standards of a bygone period, is no longer able to meet the present requirements of international relations.[27] A representative of Brazil in the UN General Assembly called the verdict a triumph of formalism and warned of the dangers of formalism in international law.[28] It is gratifying to note today that the law has eventually had its due course and it has done so in favour of the right of the Namibian people to self-determination and independence. Namibia received its independence in 1990. The ICJ, however, missed the early

---

25 T. Elias, *International Court of Justice Contemporary Problems: Essays on International Law* (The Hague: Martinus Nijhoff Publishers, 1983), p. 342.
26 B. Cheng, "The 1966 South-West Africa Judgment of the World Court", vol. 20 *Current Legal Problems* (1967), p. 181.
27 UNGA Official Records, 21st Session, item 66 Provisional Agenda 1429.
28 UNGA Official Records, 21st Session, item 66 Provisional Agenda.

opportunity to pronounce, within its contentious jurisdiction, on the illegalities perpetuated by the erstwhile apartheid machinery and by so doing probably bring it to a quicker end.

The case was certainly not the World Court's finest hour and the general handling of South West Africa and Rhodesia by the UN produced effects beyond litigation. Collateral damage arising thereof extended to other methods of peaceful resolution of disputes. When the United Kingdom in 1966 invited the General Assembly at its 21st Session to consider an item entitled 'Peaceful Settlement of Dispute', the General Assembly did not take to the idea. The UK initiative was immediately seen by delegates as suspicious and perhaps a ploy designed to indirectly secure some sort of pro-colonial aims and ambitions.[29]

The pessimism of other non-western cultures to the use of international litigation is perhaps seen in China's deep reservation from the use of international courts in the public international law arena:

> Both arbitral award and judicial settlement are legal decisions. The Chinese have been and are reluctant to submit their grievances to legal decisions. To go before a tribunal of law not only is contrary to Chinese philosophy and thinking, but also to their upholding sovereignty with a revolutionary state such as China holds dear. In addition, lacking trust in the World Court, the PRC ruled out any judicial settlement of the International Court of Justice.[30]

It is interesting that the Eastern Confucianism philosophy indeed discourages resorting to litigation to the extent that it appears to cast aspersions to the underlying character of those persons and leaders that resort to the mechanism:

> Chinese people are urged to respect one another by the Confucian code of ethics (li) only the "moral midgets" (*Hsiao-jen*) and pettifoggers (*sung-shih*) gravitate toward litigation. Therefore, the Chinese have traditionally preferred to settle their disputes by negotiation, mediation or conciliation rather than by courts.[31]

African governments tend not to be of a revolutionary nature and are in that sense different from China and regimes such as the erstwhile Soviet Union. However, the exclusion of their peoples from meaningful participation in the centres of power in international relations since the beginning of the era of international courts makes it necessary for them to be very careful in trusting their fortunes to international courts, where their representation and the contribution of their jurisprudence are barely meaningful.

---

29 Report of a Study Group, op.cit., p. viii.
30 Byron N. Tzou, *China and International Law: The Boundary Disputes* (New York: Greenwood Publishing Group, 1990), pp. 131–132.
31 Ibid., p. 131.

12.4 Prospects of the African Court of Justice as a preferred option under the adjudication route

The African Court of Justice (ACJ) was merged with the African Court of Human and Peoples' Right' to become what is now known as the 'African Court of Justice and Human Rights'. The merger occurred during the African Union Summit of Heads of State and Government on 1 July 2008 in Sharm El Sheikh, Arab Republic of Egypt.[32] The Protocol creating the African Court of Justice and Human Rights based in Arusha, Tanzania, fuses together the already established African Court on Human and Peoples' Rights (ACHPR) into the new Court which will have two chambers comprising of eight judges each – one for general legal matters and one for rulings on the human rights treaties.[33] In full operation the ACJ would have the jurisdiction as the principal judicial organ of the African Union (AU) with authority to rule on disputes over interpretation of AU treaties (Protocol of the Court of Justice of the African Union, Article 2.2). It is also possible to envisage that African states may, in the future, more frequently avail themselves of the mechanism of this Court in relation to their boundary problems.[34] Of particular significance are the provisions of the Protocol on Eligibility to Submit Cases (Article 18), Competence/Jurisdiction (Article 19), Sources of Law (Article 20), Summary Procedure (Article 55) and Special Chambers (Article 56). Article 18 would arguably also be useful to the extent that it also recognises the right of 'third parties' to submit cases to the Court of Justice under conditions to be determined by the AU Assembly and with the consent of the State Party concerned (Article 18 (d)).[35] Furthermore, the assembly is empowered to confer on the Court of Justice the power to assume jurisdiction over any dispute (Article 19 (2)).

The ACJ as envisaged is not yet in operation and this is regrettable given the tremendous tasks set before this much needed institution. It is desirable that this Court develops its practice and establishes clear jurisprudence of its own in many areas such as boundary disputes, resource exploitation, maritime delimitation and environmental disputes. If indeed judicial settlement continues to be the

---

32 A protocol to set up the Court of Justice [1] was adopted in 2003 and entered into force in 2009, available at www.african-court.org/en/images/documents/Court/Protocol%20Court%20of%20Justice/CoJ%20Protocol.pdf, accessed 21 September 2014.
33 Article 16. Protocol on the Statute of the African Court of Justice and Human Rights, available at www.african-court.org/en/images/documents/Court/Statute%20ACJHR/ACJHR_Protocol.pdf, accessed 21 September 2014. Article 1 of this Protocol deals with the replacement of the 1998 and 2003 Protocols. Article 2 (Establishment of a Single Court) and Article 3 provide for reference to the single Court in the Constitutive Act. Accordingly, references made to the 'Court of Justice' in the Constitutive Act of the African Union shall be read as references to the 'African Court of Justice and Human Rights' established under Article 2 of this Protocol.
34 The Court was established in consonance with the Constitutive Act of the Court of Justice of the African Union. See Protocol of the Court of Justice of the African Union in (2005), 13 *African Journal of International and Comparative Law* 115–128. See also Protocol of the Court of Justice of the African Union, www.africa-union.org/official_documents/Treaties_%20Conventions_%20Protocols/Protocol%20to%20the%20African%20Court%20of%20Justice%20-%20Maputo.pdf, accessed 4 May 2012.
35 It is arguable that in time this could be a basis for the eventual acceptance of multinationals into the Court's jurisdiction as parties.

favoured mechanism by which African states deal with their boundary matters, it would be desirable if not crucial that the Court of Justice makes good use of the unique provisions allowing (*inter alia*) use of the general principles of law recognised by African states (Article 20 (d)) to form part of its jurisprudence in deciding territorial and boundary matters.

It is also noteworthy that the provisions establishing the ACJ share many similarities with those that establish the jurisdiction of the ICJ. For instance, the provision on competence of the Court and sources of law are drafted largely along the lines of Articles 36 and 38 of the Statute of the ICJ. Apart from the controversial compulsory jurisdiction mechanism in Article 36 (2 a–d of the Statute), the jurisdiction of both courts includes: (a) the interpretation of treaties; (b) any question of international law; (c) the existence of any fact which, if established, would constitute a breach of an international obligation; and (d) the nature or extent of the reparation to be made for the breach of an international obligation.

Both courts have as their function the making of decisions in accordance with international law through the application of: (a) international conventions, whether general or particular, establishing rules expressly recognised by the contesting states; (b) international custom, as evidence of a general practice accepted as law; (c) the general principles of law recognised by civilised nations; and (d) the teachings of the most highly qualified publicists of the various nations, as subsidiary means for the determination of rules of law and the ability to decide a case *ex aequo et bono*, if the parties agree thereto. African scholars and critics of the perceived 'eurocentricity' of public international law would follow the jurisprudence of the ACJ very closely to see what principles it would recognise as 'general principles of law recognised by African states' and indeed how much diffidence it would pay to this invitation to enrich international judicial practice. The fusing of the human rights and general legal jurisdictions ought to have a beneficial effect on the ability of the Court to handle complex boundary cases, especially those that concern the rights and interests of indigenous peoples affected by colonial and/or post-colonial delimitation and demarcation of boundaries. The power of the Court of Justice to appoint experts and commission of enquiries under Article 30 are also potentially useful mechanisms of the Court which may assist it to quickly attain world class judicial competence. On the whole it is regrettable that the ACJ as envisaged is not yet in existence and more so that the timeline for its implementation remains unclear.

12.5 International arbitration of African boundary disputes: a critical appraisal of the Permanent Court of Arbitration

12.5.1 Arbitration

Arbitration is among the oldest methods of pacific settlement. It involves, like other forms apart from negotiation, decisions taken through third party participation. Arbitration became popular after the United States introduced it in its Jay Treaties, 1794.[36] Nevertheless, there was no widely agreed formalisation of the arbitration procedure until The Hague Convention of 1899 and 1907.[37] These two conventions gave the definition of Arbitration as 'the settlement of disputes between states by judges of their choice and on the basis of respect for law.' Hence arbitration could be by mixed commissions or by heads of third states or by any other agreed means.[38] In as much as there are similarities between arbitration and adjudication (or judicial settlement) there are certain basic dissimilarities. Whereas in judicial settlement the parties need not partake in the appointment of judges, in arbitration the parties chose the arbitrator(s). The basis of the decision must be respect for law, *but not necessarily the rules of law*. The parties to a dispute are also allowed to choose upon what principles the decision is to be made in so far as it does not violate the law. Thus the American Treaty on Pacific Settlement (Pact of Bogota) of 30 April 1948 provided that states' parties might, if they so agree, submit to arbitration 'differences of any kind, whether judicial or not'.[39] The decisions of arbitrators are, thus, known as 'awards' while those of judges in adjudication are known as 'judgments.'[40] It suffices to state here that in an international setting both are binding upon the parties, and both are final unless in very limited circumstances with respect to some international courts there emerge new facts of compelling nature which decisively affect the decisions.

> In the twentieth century other devices came into greater prominence which while calling for third-party participation, did not necessarily call for a commitment by the contending parties in advance to accept the eventual judgment. A limitation in this way of the initial commitment obviously makes it easier to accept, but equally obviously makes the prospect of ultimate decisions much less certain. In this situation the International Law Commission introduced into the General Assembly in 1958 a Convention on Arbitral Procedure based on what it called the "Principle of non-frustration".[41]

This principle attempted to ensure that once a country had agreed to arbitration, it could not later recede from that commitment. Debate over this proposition over the next five years reached no practical conclusion; on the contrary it revealed a deep difference of doctrine between those countries which were prepared to accept some such limitation on national freedom of choice at some stage in the arbitration proceedings and those (particularly the Communist countries) who argued that at any moment in the discussion the autonomy of the national will of sovereign states could become paramount.[42]

---

36 Levi, op.cit., p. 297.
37 Ibid.
38 Paul H. G.-B. Gore-Booth and Desmond Pakenham, *Satow's Guide to Diplomatic Practice* (London and New York: 1979), p. 354.
39 See Article XXXVIII of the Pact of Bogota, American Treaty on Pacific Settlement (Pact of Bogota), signed at Bogota on 30 April 1948, United Nations, Treaty Series, vol. 30, p. 96.
40 Levi, op.cit., p. 297.
41 Ibid.
42 Ibid.

Because the arbitral procedure must always be based upon respect for law, the generally accepted basic principles must be obeyed. Both sides must be given an opportunity to be heard, the arbitrator must be impartial and all proceedings must be fair. Within the limits set above, the disputants have a wide choice on the procedure. They may agree on the power and jurisdiction to be given to the arbitrator, the composition of the arbitration tribunal, the delimitation of the subject matter which is to be considered by the tribunal, the basis for the award, even possibly the interpretation of the principles to be applied in the particular case and the alternative awards the arbitrator is allowed to make. All these details are to be agreed upon in a '*Compromis*'; without this *Compromis* there can be no arbitration, even if the parties have a treaty obligation to submit their disputes to arbitration. Should any of the details of the *Compromis* be violated in the course of the arbitration procedure, the award is null and void,[43] 'though who decides such a violation if the parties cannot agree is an unanswered question.'[44]

Chile and Argentina appealed to the United Kingdom for arbitration over certain frontier disputes (*Argentine–Chile Frontier Case*), pursuant to an Agreement dated 17 April 1896.[45] Arbitration was also requested later to determine the Beagle Channel. Many of the arrangements for arbitration were inspired by those of the PCA.[46]

Some UN specialised agencies have also interested themselves in arbitration as a method of peaceful settlement of disputes. The International Bank for Reconstruction and Development (IBRD) established a Centre for the Settlement of Investment Disputes where questions can go to arbitration through the enquiry and conciliation procedures.[47]

All these point to the potency of the arbitration procedure. The question that arises at this stage is whether arbitration holds any particular advantages for boundary disputes. The answer according to the view of many writers is in the affirmative. The UN *Handbook on the Peaceful Settlement of Disputes* notes clearly

---

43 Levi, op.cit., p. 298.
44 Ibid.
45 Reports of International Arbitral Awards Argentine–Chile Frontier Case 9 December 1966 Volume XVI pp. 109–182, available at http://legal.un.org/riaa/cases/vol_XVI/109-182.pdf, accessed 21 September 2014.
46 The dispute between Argentina and Chile was with respect to territorial sovereignty over a number of islands in the Beagle Channel. The dispute had been simmering for more than 60 years. In 1967, the Chilean government invoked the 1902 Arbitration Treaty between the two countries and invited the British government to intervene as arbitrator in the dispute and a *Compromis* was signed by Argentina and Chile whereby they agreed to the Court of Arbitration appointed by the British government. The membership of the arbitration consisted of Dillard (US), Fitzmaurice (UK), Gros (France), Onyeama (Nigeria) and Petren (Sweden). (1976–1977); D. W. Greig, The Beagle Channel Arbitration, 7 *Aust. YBIL* 332; See also Gore-Booth, op.cit., p. 355.
47 For more information about the IBRD visit http://web.worldbank.org/WBSITE/EXTERNAL/EXTABOUTUS/EXTIBRD/0,,menuPK:3046081~pagePK:64168427~piPK:64168435~theSitePK:3046012,00.html, accessed 22 September 2014. ICSID is a foremost autonomous international institution established under the Convention on the Settlement of Investment Disputes between States and Nationals of Other States. It has over 140 member states. For more information about ICSID visit https://icsid.worldbank.org/ICSID/Index.jsp. accessed 22 September 2014.

that '[a]rbitration has, thus, emerged as one of the third-party procedures most frequently chosen for settling, for example, territorial and boundary disputes . . .'.[48] Yet we have already examined above the limited successes of the arbitral route in relation to one of Africa's most notorious boundary disputes decided by the Eritrea–Ethiopia Boundary Commission (EEBC). While both the EEBC and EECC have completed their tasks by making final awards, it has become clear that the rendering of awards has not led to final resolutions of all aspects of the dispute. The imperative of resolution appears to lie in the realms of political will. As a learned author notes:

> In short . . . arbitration is not an obscure or difficult resource for states which require an answer to a specific question. . . . Failure to settle does not suggest so much weakness in procedure as an absence of readiness to accept an unfavourable judgment.[49]

12.5.2 The Hague Conferences and the Permanent Court of Arbitration

There was no widely agreed formalisation of international arbitration procedure until The Hague Conventions of 1899 and 1907.[50] These two conventions gave the definition of arbitration as 'the settlement of disputes between states by judges of their choice and on the basis of respect for law.' The PCA (1899), as created by the Second Hague Conference held in 1907, existed throughout the era of the League of Nations and up until today. It suffered a period of relative inactivity for 50 years but the number of cases it handles has been rising steadily. After nearly a century of typically handling only one or two cases at a time, it has for the better part of the last two decades been having an active caseload of major and highly complex cases.[51]

During 2013, the PCA administered a total of 104 cases, 35 of which were initiated in that year. The docket comprises of 62 cases under bilateral/multilateral investment treaties and national investment laws; 30 cases arising under contracts between private parties and states or other public entities; eight state-to-state

---

48 Office of Legal Affairs Codification Division, *Handbook on the Peaceful Settlement of Disputes Between States* (New York: United Nations, 1992), p. 56.
49 Gore-Booth, op.cit., p. 354.
50 The 1907 Convention had the same name as its predecessor UKTS 6 (1971), Cmnd. 4575. 82 parties. The Convention revised the 1899 Convention in light of the Court's experience in its early cases.
51 See Report of the Secretary General CA/42.810 7 March 2003. Some of the major attempts made to revitalise the PCA include the 1962 PCA Rules of Arbitration and Conciliation for the Settlement of International Disputes Between Two Parties of which Only One is a State, first used in Sudan/Turriff Construction Ltd., (1970). The 1993 Optional Rules for Arbitrating Disputes between Two Parties of which Only One is a State replaced these Rules. See G. Wetter, *The International Arbitral Process*, vol. V (Dobbs Ferry, New York: Ocean, 1979), p. 187; see also Redfern and Hunter, *Law and Practice of International Commercial Arbitration* (1999) pp. 58, 170; PCA Conventions, PCA Rules of Procedure, UNCITRAL Rules and Procedures and other PCA Rules and Procedures are available online at www.pca-cpa.org, accessed 24 January 2015.

arbitrations; two cases arising under the PCA Optional Rules for Arbitration of Disputes Relating to Natural Resources and/or the Environment (2001); and two other disputes.[52]

At present, the PCA as an intergovernmental organisation has a membership of 115 states that are contracting powers to one or both of the conventions of 1899 and 1907. Twenty-three African states are contracting parties to the PCA (See Table 12.4). This institution, therefore, is very successful in a number of important ways and continues to occupy a unique juncture between public and private international law. Despite these realisations and without prejudice to the many achievements of the PCA in its 104 years of existence, it is possible to argue that its record with relation to Africa has been less than satisfactory on many levels. A number of indicators discussed below reveal the requisite problem and how they may be resolved.

Table 12.4 List of the African states signatory and parties to The Hague conventions of 1899 and 1907 and dates on which the convention(s) took effect for each of them (as at 15 April 2014)

State	1899	1907
Benin		2005
Burkina Faso	30–08–1961	30–08–1961
Cameroon	01–08–1961	01–08–1961
Democratic Republic of the Congo	25–03–1961	25–03–1961
Egypt	20–06–1907	04–11–1968
Eritrea	04–10–1997	
Ethiopia	2003	1935
Kenya		2006
Liberia		1914
Libyan Arab Jamahiriya	02–09–1996	
Madagascar		2009
Mauritius	03–08–1970	
Morocco	04–06–2001	
Nigeria	16–02–1987	
Rwanda		2011
Senegal	01–08–1977	30–09–1977
South Africa	21–12–1998	1978
Sudan	02–12–1966	
Swaziland	25–12–1970	
Togo		2004
Uganda	30–04–1966	
Zambia	01–01–2000	1999
Zimbabwe	19–09–1984	

---

52 113th Annual Report – 2013, available at www.pca-cpa.org/showpage.asp?pag_id=1069, accessed 23 September 2014.

Of the 54 existing states in Africa today, only 23 of them are parties to the PCA. This may or may not serve as an indicator as to the popularity of the PCA in Africa (depending on how we choose to examine the situation) but it does fit with the idea argued by some that there is a prevailing distrust exhibited by African jurists, legal advisers and diplomats towards the international arbitral process both in international commercial arbitration and in public international law. This position is compounded by the reality that foreign corporate nationals and states harbour an even greater mistrust of the systems of justice and dispute resolution in African national and regional courts. Thus, we are presented with a situation where foreign states would not settle their disputes in Africa and African states shy away from international arbitral institutions. Amazu Asouzu captured this reality as follows:

> There is also the rarely articulated but ever present feeling that African national courts are inappropriate for the resolution of international commercial disputes, leading investors and traders to insist on arbitration or alternative dispute resolution (ADR) mechanisms. . . . While some African states are parties to the multilateral treaties on arbitration and have enacted specific laws dealing with international commercial arbitration and foreign investment, these same states have misgivings about the international commercial arbitral process. They feel that arbitration runs counter to their interests, undermining national judicial sovereignty and generating considerable expense. Often, cities in these states are not chosen as venues for international arbitral proceedings, nor are their nationals frequently appointed as international arbitrators.[53]

Nevertheless, there is nothing inherently incompatible in arbitration with respect to African international relations. Arbitration and ADR methods remain popular in Africa and there are many attempts at the regional level to introduce arbitration as a component of more general and disparate dispute settlement mechanisms.[54] The main problem may be that the access of African states to the PCA is hindered by a history of alienation of the continent from active participation in the institution. This is observable through the severe deficit of Africans on the rolls of the PCA and within the executive and administrative machinery of the institution.

Arguably, the PCA Secretariat and its Administrative Council have traditionally been unfairly composed and such is the case until date. Apart from a serious underuse of African arbitrators in actual cases at the PCA which we have dealt

---

[53] Amazu Asouzu, *International Commercial Arbitration and African States* (Cambridge: Cambridge University Press, 2001), p. 1.
[54] See, e.g., the Organization of African Unity, Protocol of the Commission of Mediation, Conciliation and Arbitration, 1964, 3 *ILM* 1116 (1964); T. Maluwa, "The Peaceful Settlement of African Disputes, 1963–1983: Some Conceptual Issues and Practical Trends", 38 *ICLQ* (1989), pp. 299–320; M.N. Shaw, "Dispute Settlement in Africa", *YBWA* (1983), pp. 149–167; M. Bedjaoui, "Le règlement pacifique des différends africains", *AFDI* 85 (1972).

with above, Africa is also chronically underrepresented in the staffing of the PCA at all levels even down to internship opportunities. Indeed a basic research of the entire staffing of the PCA in 2014 reveals (at least to our knowledge) no single African national. This unfair situation remains the case even though the stated 'Recruitment Policy' of the PCA reads as follows:

> The PCA is an intergovernmental organization dedicated to serving the international community in the field of dispute resolution. It recruits and employs staff based on the highest standards of competence, integrity, and efficiency. Vacant positions are filled by nationals of member states based on the needs and available resources of the organization, particularly in relation to the nature and size of the PCA's caseload, which can vary from year to year. Due regard is given to maintaining an appropriate mix of men and women, and the need to seek geographical diversity in order to maintain the international character of the institution.[55]

The nature of the PCA as an 'intergovernmental organisation' is further undermined by the unwritten Convention which has ensured that since its inception and over a period exceeding a century it has never produced a developing state national as its Secretary-General. In fact all the Secretary-Generals have been Dutch nationals.

Table 12.5 shows a list of PCA Secretary-Generals, their nationality, period of service and qualification under the PCA since its inception.

It may be argued that there might even be an advantage in the constant use of Dutch nationals for this important office in that the neutrality of the exalted office can be easily predicted with regards to disputing African states, but there may be yet another more invidious implication of this undemocratic practice. The office of the Secretary-General is invested under several rules including national arbitration acts with the power of being the appointing authority of arbitrators in certain circumstances.[56] Also, any party may request the Secretary-General to designate an appointing authority where the parties have not agreed on the choice of an appointing authority.[57] The same procedure is applied in the appointment of a presiding arbitrator where the two arbitrators nominated by parties have not agreed on the choice of a third person to serve as presiding arbitrator.[58] What

---

55 Permanent Court of Arbitration, "Legal Counsel", available at www.pca-cpa.org/showpage.asp?pag_id=1046, accessed 2 February 2015.
56 Reference to such powers is enshrined in Section 2 of the revised UNCITRAL Arbitration Rules 2010 which concerns the composition of the arbitral tribunal under the Court. See UNCITRAL Arbitration Rules, Article 6 (1) and Permanent Court of Arbitration Rules, 2012, Article 6 (1).
57 UNCITRAL Arbitration Rules, Article 6 (2).
58 An appointing authority under Article 6 is a person or body who is mandated to appoint a sole or presiding arbitrator where both parties fail to reach an agreement on such appointment. A verbatim shared prerogative is vested on the Secretary-General under Article 7 (2) in designating an appointing authority or serving as an authority in the appointment of a sole arbitrator where the parties have failed to appoint a second arbitrator, UNCITRAL Arbitration Rules, Articles 9 (1), (2) and (3).

Table 12.5 Secretary-Generals of the Permanent Court of Arbitration

Secretary-General	Nationality	Service period	Qualification
Baron R. Melvil van Lynden	Netherland	1900–1901	A noble Dutch politician
Mr Leornard Henri Ruyssenaers	Netherland	1901–1905	Dutch self-trained Diplomat
Baron L. P. M. H. Michiels Van Verduynen	Netherland	1905–1929	Special envoy of the Dutch government
Dr M. A. Crommelin	Netherland	1929–1947	University of Oxford, England (Masters in Arts)
Jonkheer A. M. Snouck Hurgronje	Netherland	1948–1951	University of Leiden, Netherland
Dr A. Loudon	Netherland	1951–1953	
Prof. J. P. A. Francois	Netherland	1954–1968	Technical University in Delf, Netherland
Baron E. O. van Boetzelaar	Netherland	1968–1980	University of Leiden (Dutch Law)
Mr J. Varekamp	Netherland	1981–1990	
Mr P. J. H. Jonkman	Netherland	1990–1999	
Mr Tjaco T. van den Hout	Netherland	1999–2008	Leiden University (Law)
Mr Christiaan M. J. Kroner	Netherland	2008–2011	Leiden University (Advanced Law Degree)
Mr Hugo Siblesz	Netherland	2012–date	

then emerges is that the apparent low use of African arbitrators in cases may be partly explained by the unfamiliarity of monocultural Secretary-Generals of the PCA with African arbitrators. Furthermore if a look is taken at the nationality of the presiding arbitrators that have been involved with the PCA it is clear that African arbitrators are more notable in their absence rather than in their appearances.

As observed in Table 12.6, the Secretary-General tends to appoint western presiding arbitrators where one of the parties is a western state. *The frequency of the nationality of 'presiding arbitrators' shown in Table 12.6 can be compared to the total number of arbitrators who are of western nationality in the majority of PCA disputes involving a third world country.* Table 12.7 focuses more emphatically on the nationality of the party-nominated arbitrators.

From Table 12.7 it is evident that western arbitrators are predominantly appointed in cases involving developing states. Indeed only in four cases did African judges participate at all (Thomas A. Mensah (Ghanaian), James L. Kateka (Tanzanian), Prince Bola Ajibola (Nigerian) and Dr Ahmed Sadek El-Kosheri (Egyptian)). The reasons why developing countries consider themselves compelled to pick arbitrators from certain western states deserves further studies which hopefully will be done elsewhere but there is the conclusion that

Table 12.6 List of the nationalities of presiding arbitrators

Commercial and investment disputes involving a third world country under the PCA	Presiding arbitrator	Nationality and qualification of the presiding arbitrator
Republic of Ghana v. Telekom Malaysia Berhard (2013)	Professor Albert Jan van den Berg	Netherland Masters of Comparative Jurisprudence (New York) Masters of Law (Amsterdam)
The ARA Libertad Arbitration (Argentina v. Ghana) (2013)	H. E. Judge Bruno Simma	Germany Doctorate Honoriscausa (University of Macerata, Italy)
Timor-Leste v. Australia (2013)	Professor Tullio Treves	Argentina Doctor of Law (University of Milan)
The Duzgit Integrity Arbitration (Malta v. São Tomé and Príncipe) (2013)	Professor Alfred H. A. Soons	Dutch, Netherland Law Studies (Ultretch University Netherland, L.L.M University of Washington)
Dunkeld International Investment Limited (Turks & Caicos) v. The Government of Belize (2010)	Professor Albert Jan van den Berg	Dutch, Netherland University of Amsterdam
The Government of Sudan/The Sudan People's Liberation Movement/Army (Abyei Arbitration) (2009)	Professor Pierre-Marie Dupuy	France Diploma in Law (University of Paris)
Centerra Gold Inc. & Kumtor Gold Co. v. Kyrgyz Republic (2009)	Professor Albert Jan van den Berg (sole arbitrator)	Dutch, Netherland University of Amsterdam
Eritrea–Ethiopia Boundary Commission (2008)	Sir Elihu Lauterpacht, CBE QC	British LLD, Cambridge University
Guyana v. Suriname (2007)	H. E. Mr Dolliver Nelson	Grenada
Barbados v. Trinidad and Tobago (2006)	Judge Stephen Schwebel	American LLB University of Cambridge, B.A. University of Harvard
Eritrea v. Yemen (1998 and 1999)	Professor Sir Robert Jennings	American LLB University of Cambridge

suggests itself that there is an institutional bias against developing world arbitrators within the law and practice of the PCA. For this reason the usefulness of the PCA as a forum for settlement of African disputes must be subject to more scrutiny than it appears to be fashionable at present.

It is very much the case that developing states are becoming somewhat more critical of the limited choices of arbitrators that are open to them in real terms under the PCA list. This perhaps explains why the parties to the *Abyei arbitration* expanded the list of potential arbitrators beyond the PCA members of the

Table 12.7 List of the nationalities of party-nominated arbitrators

PCA arbitration disputes involving the third world	Party-nominated arbitrators	Nationality
Republic of Ghana v. Telekom Malaysia Berhard (2013)	Professor Emmanuel Gaillard (Claimant)	French
	Mr Robert Layton (respondent)	Canadian
The ARA Libertad Arbitration (Argentina v. Ghana) (2013)	H. E. Judge Awn Al-Khasawneh	Jordanian
	Judge Elsa Kelly	Argentinian
	Judge Thomas A. Mensah	Ghanaian
	Professor Bernard H. Oxman	American
Timor-Leste v. Australia (2013)	Lord Collins of Mapesbury PC, FBA	British
	Professor W. Michael Reisman	American
The Duzgit Integrity Arbitration (Malta v. São Tomé and Príncipe) (2013)	Judge James L. Kateka	Tanzanian
	Professor Tullio Treves	Argentinian
Dunkeld International Investment Limited (Turks & Caicos) v. The Government of Belize (2010)	Mr John Beechey	British
	Mr Rodrigo Oreamuno	Costa Rican
The Government of Sudan/ The Sudan People's Liberation Movement/Army (Abyei Arbitration) (2009)	H. E. Judge Awn Al-Khasawneh	Jordanian
	Professor Dr Gerhard Hafner	Austrian
	Professor W. Michael Reisman	American
	Judge Stephen Schwebel	American
Eritrea–Ethiopia Boundary Commission (2008)	Prince Bola Adesumbo Ajibola	Nigerian
	Professor W. Michael Reisman	American
	Judge Stephen M. Schwebel	American
	Sir Arthur Watts, KCMG QC	British
Guyana v. Suriname (2007)	Professor Thomas Franck	Canadian
	Professor Hans Smit	Dutch
	Professor Ivan Shearer	Australian
	Dr Kamal Hossain	Bangladeshian
Barbados v. Trinidad and Tobago (2006)	Mr Ian Brownlie CBE QC	British
	Professor Vaughan Lowe	British
	Professor Francisco Orrego Vicuña	Chilean
	Sir Arthur Watts KCMG QC	British
Eritrea v. Yemen (1998 and 1999)	Judge Stephen Schwebel	American
	Dr Ahmed Sadek El-Kosheri	Egyptian
	Mr Keith Highet	American
	Judge Rosalyn Higgins	British

Court.[59] It is, thus, suggested that despite the requirement of parties to appoint their arbitrators from among other lists of PCA Members of the Court that are compiled from the names supplied by member states, the real choices before African states, for instance, are quite poor. This perhaps explains the failure of the list procedure in the Abyei case with regards to the party-appointees. There was no common ground in the parties' respective views of the profile of the appropriate presiding arbitrator, and the list procedure accordingly failed leaving as the only option an appointment imposed by the Secretary-General of the PCA in the form of Professor Pierre-Marie Dupuy (the fifth and presiding arbitrator).[60]

The practical limitations of relying on the PCA list were perhaps competently identified by Brooks Daly who is the Deputy Secretary-General of the PCA but who in an academic article reflecting his personal views stated that:

> The PCA lists of Members of the Court stretch back over a century, therefore it was clear to the PCA that a 'full list' of former Members (i.e. including the Members appointed in the early 1900s) would be of little use to the parties. Even with the recent former Members of the Court, the PCA kept no record of their availability to serve as an arbitrator. The requirement also to include 'members of tribunals for which the PCA acted as registry' on the list raised similar concerns about availability, but had the further complication that in the majority of PCA-administered cases, the parties did not authorize the PCA to disclose any information about the case, including the identity of the parties or arbitrators. The PCA was nevertheless able to list 55 arbitrators from this last category, but many others were not subject to disclosure. The list of arbitrators from pending or past PCA cases had a higher percentage of individuals with significant experience in arbitral proceedings than the list of present and former members of the court.[61]

The whole gamut of questions about representation and composition comes to the fore when it is realised that particularly in relation to the PCA state/non-state Rules, the supervisory jurisdiction of the courts of the place of arbitration, i.e. Dutch national courts, can become exercisable. Although the PCA's state–state Rules exclude this possibility, and in most boundary cases this situation would not occur, it is possible to predict that given the high prevalence of separatist tendencies across the continent, this may not be the last time a non-state secessionist party will face a state party in such an arbitration. Potentially, therefore, the supervisory jurisdiction of the Dutch national courts may in time be exercisable against sovereign African states. In all such cases, the territorial states before the PCA would indeed have to be careful in not waiving their immunity and submitting to the jurisdiction of a national court.[62]

---

59 Brooks Daly, op.cit., p. 815.
60 Ibid., p. 817.
61 Ibid., pp. 813–814.
62 *The Government of Sudan/The Sudan People's Liberation Movement/Army* (Abyei Arbitration, 2009).

Table 12.8 ICC Court arbitrators: most frequent nationality

Country	% of arbitrators in total
United States	11.17
United Kingdom	7.80
France	7.59
Germany	10.12
Switzerland	16.02

It is important to reiterate that very few western states benefit from a high number of appointed arbitrators having their nationality just as in the case of judges on the bench of the ICJ.

Fortunately, however, the Statute of the International Tribunal for the Law of the Sea does manage to pave way for a balanced composition of the Tribunal based on nationality. Article 17 (3) of the Statute of the International Tribunal for the Law of the Sea provides that: If the Tribunal, when hearing a dispute, does not include upon the bench a member of the nationality of the parties, each of those parties may choose a person to participate as a member of the Tribunal.

Apparently Africa, with 23 member contracting parties at the PCA, has traditionally not benefited from the geographical diversity of this important intergovernmental institution. With all these in mind it will be expecting much for African states to have the much needed confidence in the readiness of the PCA to provide impartial service to its teeming peoples. Whereas these staffing and arbitral roll deficiencies can be quite easily remedied, it remains to be seen if there is the requisite political will within the leadership of the PCA to spearhead required changes in the institution's make up and guarantee equal access to justice in a holistic sense to African states. In the interim, *ad hoc* arbitration panels may be recommended as an attractive choice for African states in the event of arbitration of its boundary disputes. Although the PCA has been useful with respect to its exercise of jurisdiction over a couple of African boundary cases, principally the EEBC case and Abyei, it is important to note that this institution has not actualised itself as a viable route for routine resolution of African boundary cases and its composition also remains a core area of concern. It must, however, be conceded that there is an inherent flexibility of the PCA as an institution and the professionalism of its staff is one of the highest in the world. In essence, with appropriate tweaks to its legal instruments and with more attention to effective representation on its lists the PCA could serve as perhaps the leading institution outside the continent of Africa wherein disputes from the continent will be settled.

12.6 Evaluation of alternative forms of pacific settlement of boundary disputes

> The Parties to any dispute the continuance of which is likely to endanger the maintenance of international peace and security, shall first of all, seek a solution by negotiation, enquiry, mediation, conciliation, judicial, settlement, resort to regional agencies or arrangements, or other peaceful means of their own choice.[63]

Above we have looked at the two most discussed methods of boundary dispute resolution – litigation and arbitration. It remains therefore to discuss and evaluate the alternative dispute resolution (ADR) mechanisms in the international system that may be brought to bear upon African boundary disputes. It is our strong belief that the starting point of any enquiry into how a boundary dispute should be resolved is to consider the obligations of the state(s) involved under international law to resolve all such disputes by peaceful means. Of primary importance here are the obligations of states under Article 33 of the Charter of the United Nations. As was noted earlier on, African states are in addition bound by regional treaties and arrangements to settle their squabbles by peaceful means but by no particular peaceful method. Similarly under the Charter provision, they are presented with a plethora of choices of a pacific nature to deal with disputes. It should, however, be pointed out that the obligation to seek a solution by any of the approved procedures only arises in the cause of disputes the continuation of which will likely endanger the maintenance of international peace and security. Unfortunately good adherence to the demands of Article 33 of the Charter of the United Nations is far and between and sadly so with respect to the practices of the developed and militarily powerful states of the northern hemisphere.

It might be pertinent to mention here also that the determination of this likelihood is entrusted under Article 37 (2) of the Charter to the Security Council which is more or less the executive body of the UNO. This, however, does not mean that states on their own cannot come to the finding that they should avail themselves of dispute resolution techniques over disagreements and differences that exist among them. Indeed a friendly third state can *suo motu* observe the need to offer dispute resolution techniques to forestall, prevent or reduce conflict levels between two or more other states. As we have also previously shown there are ample provisions in the constitutive instruments of Africa's sub-regional bodies to deal with the detection, management and resolution of international disputes on the continent. Below are discussions of various forms of pacific settlement other than litigation and arbitration that may be brought to bear either individually or in a mixed manner on resolution of boundary disputes between states. The truth is that litigation and arbitration are heavily reliant on judicial format and processes. These two may also not fit the situation surrounding a particular dispute

---

63 Article 33 (1) of the Charter of the United Nations.

or the parties that are involved may be brought into the matter. In other words it is important to critique other viable forms of international dispute resolution.

Indeed it is one of the positive strengths of the non-judicial means of settlement discussed below that they may be offered in boundary related cases that cannot be said to constitute a legal dispute. As long as there is a 'disagreement and difference' any of the pacific methods may be triggered and pursued successfully to a conclusion. This is a fact to be celebrated in that by so doing states can indeed prevent the conflict over territory to calcify into a legal dispute or become a radical disagreement or intractable conflict. The editors of a special academic journal issue on disagreement and difference helpfully explain the gradations of the phenomena that may exist and which can also be applied to boundary problems. They stated:

> First, not all forms of diversity entail conflict; disagreement does. People may display markedly different characteristics without those being in any way rival characteristics; diversity takes the form of disagreement only if people are at odds in some way. Second, disagreement does not encompass every form of conflict but only conflicts of a particular sort: conflicts of belief. Two people may have different and conflicting preferences, but if these are conflicts of mere preference – conflicts of brute want or mere taste – it would be odd to describe that conflict as 'disagreement'. The normal subject matter of disagreement is belief, albeit 'belief' in its broadest sense.[64]

The pacific methods of dispute resolution dictated by current international law rely upon an assumption of availability of expertise and bona fide intention of third party actors. In relation to boundary disputes such experts are as rare as the African proverbial teeth in a chicken's mouth. The necessity to produce experts in these areas is not easily appreciated by the supranational organisations in the public international law field. Globally the need for sufficient numbers of experts that can offer services in the non-judicial methods provided for by Article 33 is very much understated. Certainly in relation to Africa the shortfall is of potentially disastrous significance. The international community of states has increased steadily since what was regarded as the end of the decolonisation period in the 1970s. Since then the number of states in the world has increased steadily at the rate of about 50 new states a decade. The creation of many further independent states, while it may be deemed regrettable in some quarters, is a statistical reality given the trend since 1945 and given that we certainly are very far from the end of history. The number and spread of separatist movements in and around Africa as well as parts of the developed world shows that the emergence of newer states is a statistical certainty. With these in mind the development of experts in pacific

---

64 P. Jones and C. Carey, "Disagreement and Difference", special issue of the Vol. 6, *Critical Review of International Social and Political Philospohy*, No. 3 (2003), pp. 154–164 quoted in Oliver Ramsbotham, *Transforming Violent Conflict: Radical Disagreement, Dialogue and Survival* (London: Routledge, 2010). p. 6.

resolution of boundary disputes is of crucial importance given that the provisions of Article 33 can only have meaningful life if there are realistic ways to give effect to them.

Success as a boundary dispute negotiator, boundary enquiry commissioner, mediator or conciliator requires a certain dexterity, tenacity of approach and diplomatic sophistication that may not ordinarily be found in the average practitioner of alternative dispute resolution. This is not to say that the door is closed to 'irregular peace practitioners' such as village, community elders and religious figures. We have already shown earlier that their services are in active demand and use in many parts of Africa for boundary related problems. Such practitioners have their place which must be encouraged and further explored and developed in academic studies and state practice. What is being advocated here is that the specific training in boundary dispute resolution must be developed to the level of a separate subfield of competence and performance within the disciplines of law, political science and international relations. Presently formal boundary commissions set up to deal with disputes or manage boundaries rely on the pooling of experts who approach the task from their various disciplinary backgrounds – surveyors, geophysicists, geographers, cartographers, historians, lawyers, armed forces, linguists, immigration, policing, etc. This is not a bad thing as multidisciplinary contributions are valuable in such important processes. However, what is advocated here is the introduction of dedicated undergraduate and postgraduate courses in 'boundary legal studies and sciences' in African universities. This would be with the aim to produce a cadre of trained specialists with disciplinary training and grounding in all the relevant areas identified above. It is also argued here that professional engagement of such specialists in national, sub-regional and Africa-wide boundary commissions should be systematic. Appropriate staffing by indigenous experts in this manner will prove invaluable to pertinent African institutions and governmental departments that engage in boundary delineation, demarcation, management and dispute resolution. The value of such bespoke holistic training would increase over time and its absence presently is one of the best examples of a disciplinary vacuum in education.

It is indeed more shocking that in this day and age the discipline of law still does not have a recognisable branch of international boundary law. Whereas the common assumption is that any lawyer would do, the need for specialisation in international boundary law should be a staple of international law departments and legal training in general. The training of boundary lawyers must be sound and shored up with adequate appreciation of relevant scientific principles. The important thing though is that such legal specialists must have imbued in them the philosophy of Mahatma Ghandi who in a famous quote stated: 'I felt it was my duty to befriend both parties and bring them together. I strained every nerve to bring about a compromise.'[65]

---

65 Mahatma Gandhi, *Gandhi An Autobiography: The Story of My Experiments With Truth Beacon* (Washington DC: Public Affairs Press, 1960), p. 167.

All the pacific means of dispute resolution discussed below require the use of independent third party persons. Alternative dispute resolution experts that are engaged in dealing with Africa's many boundary problems would be very much advised to take into account the excellent analysis of the skills they need to bring to the table to cope with the radical disagreements as offered by Robert Rotberg in the book *Israeli and Palestinian Narratives of Conflict* (2006). He wrote:

> Every conflict is justified by a narrative of grievance, accusation, and indignity. Conflicts depend on narratives, and in some senses cannot exist without a detailed account of how and why the battles began, and why one side, and only one side, is in the right. . . . The Israeli-Palestinian conflict for primacy, power, and control encompasses two bitterly contested, competing narratives. Both need to be understood, reckoned with, and analysed side by side in order to help abate violence and possibly propel both protagonists toward peace. This is an immensely tall order. But the first step is to know the narratives, the second to reconcile them to the extent that they can be reconciled or bridged, and the third to help each side to accept, and conceivably to respect, the validity of the competing narrative . . .[66]

In a similar guise an expert involved in addressing a boundary dispute in Africa must begin by juxtaposing and rationalising the narratives offered by the parties and concerned persons in order to appreciate the roots and branches of the conflict or what is known as the 'distorted prisms that fuel it'.[67] At the core of the available narratives would lie the symbolic constructions of shared identities or collective memories which may differ from the 'truth' but will portray subjective truths driving the parties. Once this is done the third party arbiter(s) stand a good chance of at least narrowing if not totally eliminating the chasm that separates the subjective truths. It is notable that the tasks and functions prescribed by Article 33 are not simple but the fundamental task is for ADR practitioners to expose the narratives of the disputants to each other. This will begin the gradual process of fostering a genuine understanding and reconciliation by all sides of the nature of the dispute and the workable strategies that may genuinely resolve the dispute in a meaningful and long-term manner (see earlier our discussions of the work of the Africa Forum mediation led by the HLMT).[68] Third party arbiters must, however, expect that their every analyses and actions will become implicated in the conflict arena and that Africa is not an easy place to practice their trade. Yet they must proceed with their important task with all sense of honour and courage.

---

66 R. Rotberg (ed.), *Israeli and Palestinian Narratives of Conflict: History's Double Helix* (Bloomington, IN: Indiana University Press, 2006), p. 134.
67 Ibid., pp. 2, 284; Ramsbotham, op.cit., p. 134.
68 *Supra* Chapter 9.

12.6.1 Negotiation

Once a dispute arises in the international system, it is normal first and foremost for negotiation to be adopted by the parties in an attempt to bring the dispute to an end. Negotiation has remained a particularly viable means of settlement of international disputes. There is a convergence of opinions among scholars as regards the potency of the use of negotiation in the settlement of international disputes. *Satow's Diplomacy* explains that negotiation means the conduct of direct talks between the parties to a dispute aimed at settling the dispute. H. G. Darwin thinks that: 'Negotiations are the simplest method of peaceful settlement of disputes, in the sense that in negotiations the parties to the dispute alone are involved in the procedure.'[69] Accordingly Levi believes, '[d]irect negotiation between the parties to a dispute is the most frequent method for the pacific settlement of international disputes.'[70] A distinctive feature and an advantage of adopting negotiation as a means of pacific settlement is that negotiations involve only parties to the dispute whereas the other methods enumerated in Article 33 (1) involve other states or people.

The primacy of negotiation to the peaceful conduct of all aspects of international relations is an aspect of settled law within international legal jurisprudence. In the *North Sea Continental Shelf Cases* (1969) the ICJ declared it an obligation for the parties to negotiate, and the PCIJ, in its *Railway Traffic between Lithuania and Poland* (advisory opinion), stated that the parties must 'not only enter into negotiation but also pursue them as far as possible with a view to concluding agreements.'[71] Though there is in fact no obligation to submit disputes to negotiation procedures first before other methods, the idea of negotiation is more closely linked with the notion of diplomacy, for every diplomatic action ends in negotiation. The effectiveness of negotiation rests on the important fact that diplomatic negotiation means at least in part compromise.[72] Public opinion to a large extent influences the kind of compromises and concessions made by a government. However, it is quite possible for the government to misjudge its public opinion in which case negotiations will fail.[73] The calibration of public opinion to necessary compromise is the bane of any boundary negotiator's task.

International disputes which require negotiations for settlement may arise out of the diplomatic protection abroad of citizens and body corporates. The protection of body corporates arose out of the facts of a shareholding dispute in the *Barcelona Traction Case*. For such cases the United States Supreme Court made

---

69 H. G. Darwin "Negotiations" in *David Davies Memorial Institute of International Studies, Report of a Study Group on the Peaceful Settlement of International Disputes* (London: Europa Publishers, 1966), pp. 67–71.
70 Levi, op.cit., p. 286.
71 PCIJ Reports, 1931, p. 116.
72 Nascimento E. Silva, *Diplomacy in International Law* (Netherlands: A. W. Sitjthoff International Publishing Company, 1977), p. 61.
73 Ibid., p. 292.

a strong case in favour of diplomatic negotiations over (national) court procedures.[74] The thinking here is that:

> A decision by the national court that the states acts were invalid might offend that state and make agreement difficult. ... If per chance the court should find the foreign states acts legal the findings could undermine negotiations between the two states aiming at redress regardless of the legal situation for the damaged nationals.

Here it is further posited that 'national interest might be settled reasonably satisfactorily for all concerned through negotiations with either side emerging as the victor.'[75]

Despite the obvious advantages of negotiation as a means of pacific settlement there are also certain unattractive qualities. Dag Hammarskjold, former Secretary-General of the UNO, stated as follows:

> This instrument (negotiation) has many advantages. ... But it has also weaknesses. There is the temptation to play to the gallery at the expense of solid construction. And there is the risk that positions once taken publicly become frozen making compromise difficult.[76]

We accept this thinking as true in some cases but do not view it as a strong disadvantage of employing negotiation in solving international disputes. This is because playing to the gallery is not a strategy that is limited to negotiation activity but can indeed be found in relation to nearly all forms of pacific resolution of disputes. It is in fact one of the games nations play.

Negotiating international boundaries is indeed a complex undertaking generally requiring input from a variety of experts. Boundary negotiations may be broken up into at least two phases:

(i) It is common for bilateral boundary negotiations, in the first instance, to be carried out by a panel of experts who concentrate on the technical aspects of the negotiations. In these cases there will be the understanding that the earlier negotiations are a prelude to the second phase.
(ii) Political negotiations take place later between diplomats, ministers, political representatives and even Presidents or heads of states. Appropriate levels of political will from all sides involved in the engagement would be needed for negotiations to succeed.

It is notable that a large number of African demarcation issues have been settled through bilateral negotiation. Importantly boundary negotiations require detailed

---

74 Ibid., p. 292.
75 Ibid.
76 Hammarskjold quoted in Gore-Booth, op.cit., p. 350.

preparation, goodwill and good faith, as indeed is the case in every other area of human endeavour.[77] Although delineation disputes are frequently also addressed by negotiation, it appears that settlement of such disputes is rarely accomplished through this method alone. The 'Guiding Principles for the Settlement of Disputed Areas on the Sudan-South Sudan Border', an African Union Border Programme Document (2011), would, however, appear to suggest that the AU, and in particular the AUBP, believes that even the delimitation of territories may be achieved in this manner and recommends that this should be more common.

It is recognised that comparatively, direct negotiations between disputing states seem to offer the widest opportunity for reaching an effective settlement in all forms of international boundary disputes. Whereas intra state boundary disputes may require the certitude of conformity with national laws by reference to court decisions, negotiation of international boundaries allows for resolution by diplomatic procedures. The adoption of diplomacy has a liberating effect from the 'constitutional limitations of adjudication'.[78] Crucially, diplomatic negotiations allow states the possibility of holistic treatment of their misunderstandings. The possibility of reciprocal gains and consideration extrinsic to boundary issues alone can be considered and even economic or other vital interests may be used in bargaining. It is recognised that bargaining and negotiations may often compensate for any territorial losses that may occur as a result of boundary changes.[79] It is a notable phenomenon that international boundary negotiators that have successfully completed complex negotiations derive some personal pride and satisfaction from the fact that an effective adjustment has been achieved by their direct efforts. Indeed it is not unusual that after a boundary dispute has been resolved by adjudication, in which a tribunal had decided the issue by splitting a territory and recommending a line of convenience, the parties subsequently agreed to modify the Court's alignment or vary it in part or whole. Examples of such post adjudication negotiation abound in the experience of the Cameroon–Nigeria judgment implementation activities handled by the CNMC discussed above.[80] Churchill and Lowe correctly identify enduring features of the negotiation procedure, particularly from the perspective of maritime delimitation and demarcation disputes.[81] They note that negotiations, whether or not they lead immediately to the resolution of the dispute, perform a vital role as they serve to identify the precise issue(s) at stake separating it from common grounds and peripheral issues as well as identifying other procedures that may be pursued in order to settle the dispute. Negotiation trumps other pacific means of settlement by the simple fact that it accompanies all aspects of international relations over a dispute in the sense that it is often required before, during and even after the completion of any other dispute resolution mechanism resorted to – even war.

---

77 Daniel, op.cit., pp. 226, 234.
78 Cukwurah, op.cit., p. 230.
79 Ibid., p. 231.
80 Ibid.
81 Churchill and Lowe, op.cit., p. 450.

12.6.2 Enquiry

> In differences of an international nature ... arising from a difference of opinion on points of fact, the signatory powers recommend that the parties who have not been able to come to an agreement by means of diplomacy should, as far as circumstances allow institute an International Commission of Inquiry to facilitate a solution of these differences by elucidating the facts by means of an impartial and conscientious investigation.[82]

The usefulness of the institution of international commissions of enquiry had been realised for as far back as the time of The Hague Convention of 1899.[83] Enquiry in a general sense encompasses all forms of search for information. In its specialised sense as a particular process of settling international disputes it is useful in that many disputes invariably stem from differences over facts. In that case, '[t]he commissions task is to find and report the facts of the situation, without evaluating them or drawing conclusions from them. The disputants can do with the report as they please.'[84] Thus, Article XIV of The Hague Convention of 1899 provides:

> The Report of the International Commission of Inquiry is limited to a statement of facts, and has in no way the character of an Arbitral Award. It leaves the conflicting Powers entire freedom as to the fact to give to this statement.

Following the reasoning in both the 1899 and 1907 Conventions, the League of Nations and the UN have accepted this method of pacific settlement. For instance, in 1932 the League of Nations appointed the Lytton Commission of Inquiry to investigate the Japanese invasion of Manchuria. However, on this particular Commission a writer notes that it is an example of how such a commission of enquiry can be used to evade rather than live up to responsibility: '[i]n fact it served as a device for the members of the league to avoid taking protective action for China.'[85]

In 1959, the General Assembly of the UN adopted a Resolution establishing the UN Panel for Inquiry and Conciliation to be directed by the Secretary-General and adopted rules for its composition and procedure.[86] Also in 1967, the General Assembly concluded its consideration of an item concerning methods of fact-finding by adopting Resolution 2329 (XXII). Thus, the General Assembly recognised the usefulness of impartial fact-finding as a means towards the

---

82 Article IX of The Hague Convention 1899.
83 *Supra* this chapter, note 49.
84 Levi, op.cit., p. 294.
85 Ibid.
86 Gore-Booth, op.cit., pp. 350–351.

settlement of disputes as well as their prevention. Pursuant to this Resolution a register of experts on legal matters and other fields, whose services states' parties to a dispute may resort to by agreement, was prepared by the Secretary-General.[87]

In speaking about Enquiry as a means of settlement of international disputes one has the giddy feeling that it might not be any better in practice than the various commissions of enquiry rampant in municipal settings, where commissions of enquiry are veritable instruments of time-wasting bureaucracy merely affording the government a cooling off mechanism. Herein lies the greatest flaw of this method of pacific settlement. This, however, needs not be the case in African international relations given the impressive record and competencies of the various platforms existing within the RECs discussed earlier.

12.6.3 Conciliation

Where negotiations fail to resolve a dispute, conciliation has a rich history of success as a third party settlement mechanism. Conciliation as a procedure to the resolution of international disputes is conceived in different lights by various authors. For instance, while Levi says that, '[c]onciliation is a composite of mediation with commission of enquiry.'[88] *Satow's Diplomacy* posits that, '[t]his word (Conciliation) can be employed very generally as an aspect of good offices.'[89] Roling, the eminent Belgian jurist, concurs with this latter description. He stated: '*l' essential de la conciliation est l'examen an fond ce qui, la differencie des bons offices (good offices) qui differencie conciliation et arbitage.*'[90]

A commission of conciliation ascertains the facts of a dispute and on the basis of its findings, proposes its settlement. However, the proposal is a recommendation only and advisory in nature.[91] Article 15 of the European Convention for the Peaceful Settlement of Disputes describes the tasks of a conciliation commission as:

> to elucidate the questions in dispute, to collect with that object all necessary information by means of enquiry or otherwise, and to endeavour to bring the parties to the terms of settlement which seems suitable to it and lay down the period within which they are to make their decision.

---

87 Ibid., p. 371.
88 Levi, op.cit., p. 295. See also Churchill and Lowe, op.cit., p. 450.
89 *Satow's Diplomacy* Gore-booth ed. Quoted in Gbenga Oduntan, *The Law and Practice of the International Court of Justice (1945–1996): A Critique of the Contentious Advisory Jurisdictions* (Enugu: Fourth Dimension, 1999), p. 26.
90 49 *A.I.D.I.* (1961), vol. 2, p. 227: quoted in Report on the Peaceful Settlement of Disputes. Annex II. para. 4, in Gore-Booth, op.cit.
91 Ibid.

Against the advantages of the conciliation procedure two arguments have been advanced:

> First, there are in fact treaties which bind the participants in advance to accept the conciliation Commission's views, creating the concept of a 'binding conciliation'. Secondly and more important, a decision arising out of what is basically a diplomatic procedure could well diverge in general or in an important particular from a judgment on a comparable matter given on a strictly legal basis.[92]

Despite these kinds of arguments, the Vienna Convention of 1969 on the Law of Treaties provides for 'compulsory conciliation' as a means of settling certain classes of disputes about the interpretation of the larger bulk of part V of the Convention.[93] This brings to the fore the dichotomy that appears to exist between conciliation in public international law and conciliation in private law. In other words the senses in which the term is used for international business disputes and conciliation under national law are different from the sense in which they are construed in diplomacy. Conciliation has a more aggressive feel in private law whereas in diplomacy a lot will depend on the terms under which the conciliation was assented to and the result of certain kinds of conciliation may be non-binding and, therefore, dependent on consent of the parties.

Under Article 13 of the UNCITRAL Conciliation Rules (1980), for instance, a conciliator can draw up a settlement agreement for the parties and once this is achieved 'the parties by signing the settlement agreement put an end to the dispute and are bound by the agreement'. Also under the Rules the parties may wish to consider including in the settlement agreement a clause that any dispute arising out of or relating to the settlement agreement shall be submitted to arbitration. Several treaties that govern maritime territorial disputes provide for conciliation. These include the 1969 Oil Pollution Intervention Convention,[94] the Agreement for the Establishment of the Indian Tuna Commission 1963[95] and of course the LOSC – Article 284 and Annex V. Under the LOSC provisions, whereupon there has been an acceptance of the invitation to conciliation, each party chooses two conciliators of which one may be one of its nationals from a list to which both states are entitled to contribute four names each. The four people eventually convened would then select a fifth person who is to act as chairman of the conciliation panel.[96]

Since 1918, several hundred conciliation commissions have been concluded and over 100 conciliation commissions have been established. Writers have recorded almost no other cases of conciliation, except in the League of Nations

---

92 *Satow*, op.cit., p. 354.
93 Ibid.
94 970 UNTS 211; 87 parties as of 13 September 2012.
95 Entered into force 27 March 1966, available at www.iotc.org, accessed 20 July 2014.
96 Churchill and Lowe, op.cit., pp. 450, 454.

and the United Nations, where it is used as part of their peace-keeping machinery. The usefulness of conciliation for boundary cases is reflected in the way the Security Council in particular has established a number of conciliation commissions to help solve difficult boundary related disputes such as the territorial sovereignty related claims for which the procedure has been used. These include the *Netherlands–Indonesia dispute over Western New Guinea* (sovereignty issues),[97] the *Greek Frontier incidents* (border issues),[98] the *India–Pakistan dispute over Kashmir* (territorial sovereignty), the long-standing Palestine issue and the dispute between the United Kingdom and Denmark (1962) following the seizure of the *Red Crusader* (concerning the question whether the UK flag fishing vessel was within or outside the Faroese fishing).[99] More recent conciliations of note include that which occurred in relation to the continental shelf around Jan Manyen Island, disputed between Norway and Iceland, who agreed to the establishment of a conciliation commission of enquiry. Conciliation in this sense remains an underused but viable means of resolving African boundary disputes. African states would benefit from resorting to this method more frequently although care must be taken to ensure that the results and decisions reached at the end of the conciliation are binding and enforceable.

12.6.4 Good Offices

[I]n order to maintain this general peace, the Signatory Powers agree to have recourse, as far as circumstances will allow, to the good offices or mediation of one or more friendly Powers.

[. . .] Powers are not more prone than individuals in controversy to listen to friendly advice, and they are accustomed to resent intermeddling. Between nation and nation the fear that the exercise of good offices and mediation may become a precedent and insensibly pass into a claim of intervention inconsistent with independence and its corollary, equality, has doubtless prevented an offer on more than one occasion. . . . If, however, the exercise of the offer of good offices and mediation be purely voluntary, and be not raised to the rank of a duty of strangers to decide the controversy, and if the effect of good offices and mediation be restricted to advice which may be accepted or rejected by either of the parties to the conflict, it is difficult to see how the offer, although it may be embarrassing, can prejudice the freedom of action of the contending parties.

[. . .] The essence of good offices consists in advice to parties in controversy to settle their difficulties. It precedes and calls into being negotiation, and when this

---

97 See Genevieve Collins Linebarger, "The Netherlands-Indonesian Dispute", Vol. 125, *World Affairs*, No. 1, Spring (1962), p. 30.
98 This concerned border incidents between Greece, Albania, Bulgaria and Yugoslavia. It was established in January 1947 and ended in September 1947. AG-047.
   United Nations Commission for the Investigation of Greek Frontier Incidents (1947) 1941–54, available at https://archives.un.org/sites/archives.un.org/files/files/Finding%20Aids/Missions/AG-047-Greek.pdf, accessed 19 November 2013.
99 Levi, op.cit., p. 295.

is done good offices as such are exhausted.... In a word, good offices begin and end in counsel....

(The Hague Peace Conferences of 1899 and 1907)[100]

The use of Good Offices in the settlement of international disputes entails the intercession of a third party (a state, an international organisation or even a private person) in a dispute between parties who refuse to negotiate with the aim of bringing such parties into direct negotiations.[101] To Darwin, 'Good Offices are sometimes held to mean the action taken to bring about or initiate, but without active participation, the discussion of the substance of the dispute.'[102]

Thus, it is clear that Good Offices will prove more important when the disputants are already at war or are on the delicate brink of one with each side not yet fully appreciative of a negotiation – settlement. It is offered 'to induce the conflicting parties to negotiate between themselves.'[103]

Instances of such situations abound; the Roosevelt role in the Israel–Egypt war in 1973; France in the US–North Vietnam war; France in the Dogger Bank crisis between Great Britain and Russia.[104] On the use of Good Offices a learned author observes that:

> Any party to a dispute may ask for good offices and no party has to accept proffered good offices. Nobody has the duty to offer good offices, even when asked to do so. The offer is always advisory, never binding and cannot be considered an unfriendly act. Presumably for this reason, the dispute continues, unaffected in any way by the offer. But an outside nation might consider the good offices services as "meddling" in other peoples affairs, as China did regarding American attempts in South Africa and Rhodesia and Soviet attempts in Lebanon in 1976.[105]

It is to be understood that special agreements in treaties may alter the voluntary nature of Good Offices. For instance, in the League of Nation's Covenant and in the Charter of the United Nations, members have to settle by peaceful means, at least those of their disputes: 'the continuance of which is likely to endanger the maintenance of international peace and security.'[106] Thus, it is proffered that such action would as a minimum include that Good Offices be

---

100 The term 'good offices', according to some authors, appears to have originated in The Hague Peace Conferences of 1899 and 1907. David J. Ludlow, "Preventive Peace-making in Macedonia: An Assessment of UN Good Offices Diplomacy", *Brigham Young University Law Review* (2003), pp. 791–762 at fn 6.
101 Ibid., p. 292.
102 Darwin, as quoted in Gore-Booth, op.cit., p. 353.
103 Brierly, op.cit., p. 373.
104 Ibid.
105 Ibid., p. 293.
106 (Article 33, Charter of the UN; Articles 4, 8, 11 and 19 Covenant) League of Nations, Covenant of the League of Nations, 28 April 1919, available at www.refworld.org/docid/3dd8b9854.html, accessed 2 February 2015.

offered and accepted. In this sense it is recommended that African states have a duty to at least consider in good faith the offer of Good Offices by African regional and sub-regional bodies. Similarly the offer of Good Offices by eminent personalities of sub-regional or regional relevance should not be regarded as meddlesome interloping. The offer of Good Offices by independent states from another region or even outside the continent should also be permitted much along the lines of Norway's intervention in the 1993 Oslo Accords relating to the age-long Israeli–Palestinian conflict.

12.6.5 Mediation

> As the most prevalent form of third party conflict management, mediation is often ascribed a special role in attempts to peacefully settle territorial issues. To date, however, the mediation process has yet to be fully explained.[107]

There appears to be a common assumption in literature that there is something about indigenous cultures that makes them particularly adaptable to the medium of mediation and that it is a particularly suitable means of developing world conflict resolution. It is, for instance, said that, '[t]he Asian way of settling disputes tends to be "consensual" rather than "confrontational".'[108] The aim of the consensual approach is to reach a 'harmonious' solution preserving the relationship between the parties, and this is what Asian cultures prefer rather than the western confrontational approach which is legalistic and formalistic and which may adversely affect the relationship between the parties involved.[109] Writers like Munir Maniruzzaman have on this basis argued for use of mediation instead of arbitration and litigation for the Asia-Pacific Economic Co-operation states.[110]

In Africa alone, over the past three decades mediation has been utilised in relation to deadly conflicts in Angola, Burundi, the Comoros, the Democratic Republic of Congo (DRC), the Ivory Coast, Kenya, Lesotho, Liberia, Madagascar, Mozambique, Rwanda, Sierra Leone, Somalia, Sudan, Uganda and Zimbabwe.[111]

---

107 Frazier, op. cit., p. 267.
108 See Pearlie M. C. Koh, "Enhancing Economic Co-operation: A Regional Arbitration Centre for ASEAN?" (2000) 49 ICLQ 390, at pp. 393–397; M. Scott Donahey, "The Asian Concept of Conciliator/Arbitrator: Is it Translatable to the Western World?", (1995) 10 *ICSID Review* 120.
109 Ibid.
110 A. F. M. Maniruzzaman, "The Problems and Challenges Facing Settlement of International Energy Disputes by ADR Methods in Asia: The Way Forward", *International Energy Law & Taxation Review* (2003), p. 193. See also APEC Secretariat, *Selected APEC Documents 1989–1994* (1995), APEC Ministerial Meetings 1994; Leaders Meetings 1994, Bogor; Leaders Declaration of Common Resolve, Jakarta Joint Statement, 1994.
111 Laurie Nathan, "Policy Directions: Towards a New Era in International Mediation" (Crisis States Research Network) May 2010, available at www.lse.ac.uk/internationalDevelopment/research/crisisStates/download/Policy%20Directions/Towards%20a%20new%20era%20in%20international%20mediation.pdf, accessed 19 November 2013.

In relation to boundary issues, mediation was unsuccessfully tried in relation to the Sino–Indian boundary question.[112]

There appears to be a grey area between what mediation is and what Good Offices are. This is more so because '[t]he rules relating to mediation are essentially the same as those applying to good offices.'[113] However, the confusion as to what the two terms mean seems to have been resolved by the wording of General Assembly Resolution 186/5/11 of 14 May 1948 which invited a committee of the Assembly to 'appoint a local and community authorities in Palestine who would use his good offices ... to promote adjustment of the future situation in Palestine.'[114] The aim of mediation is the reconciliation of the opposing views of the disputants and the appeasement of their feelings of mutual resentment. The difference between mediation and conciliation lies in the fact that while a mediator deals with the substance of the dispute and is under the obligation to suggest possible (though not binding) solutions, the organisation or individual offering Good Offices is more or less only to provide every possible facility including advice on procedure; proposals must come from the parties to the dispute themselves.

H. G. Darwin thinks of mediation thus: 'Mediation as a method of peaceful settlement of international disputes means the participation of a third state or a disinterested individual in negotiation between States in dispute.'[115]

The UN tried a number of times, especially in the early years of its existence, to use mediation in settling highly contentious questions.[116] In the case of Palestine, Count Folke Bernadotte of Sweden was appointed mediator; after his assassination, Dr Ralph Bunche (who was later to become Senior under Secretary-General) took over as acting mediator.

> Under the UN Charter mediation though used on a number of occasions is not fully exploited because a dispute must have reached the point where its continuance "is likely to endanger the maintenance of international peace and security" (Article 33) before organs of the United Nations can go into action. By that time, the positions of the disputants are likely to be rigid, and public mediation effort by the United Nation, became difficult. The practice has therefore developed that the Secretary-General or his representative

---

112 In 1962, during the first major armed conflict between the two countries, President Nasser of the United Arab Republic, who was regarded by China as a close friend of India, proposed to China and India a four-point resolution to solve the boundary problems. It consisted of a cease-fire, the demarcation of a demilitarised buffer zone, negotiation and the withdrawal of troops to positions that they held prior to clashes that began on 20 October. Before 8 September of that year, however, Indian troops are said to have occupied some areas north of the so-called "McMahon Line". China found that it could not accept the proposal leading to failure of the proposal. Tzou, op.cit., p. 130.
113 Ibid.
114 Gore-Booth, op.cit., p. 352.
115 *Report on the Peaceful Settlement of Disputes*, p. 72, para. 1.
116 Ibid.

engages quietly and discretely in mediation efforts when they are merited by the parties – states or Liberation movements to do so. This would be a means of their own choice to which they are entitled (and would be the answer to Soviet protests that peace-keeping is the Security Council's monopoly).[117]

From all these it can be submitted that at least with respect to the African continent an alternative method which the UN can make use of would be that before a conflict of interests or opinion becomes a 'dispute' it should be dealt with as long as it is a 'situation' which might lead to international friction or gives rise to a dispute (Article 34). But the possibilities of dealing with a situation are fewer and less effective and do not necessarily include – if they do not actually exclude – the afore-discussed means of pacific settlement.[118] Flexibility is said to be the keynote of mediation as a procedure for the settlement of disputes. How a mediator can act in dealing with a sensitive boundary case will in large part be a factor of the circumstances of the case and of course the path of the mediation. In essence, in such cases the course of history is partly predetermined by fate and partly determined by skill. It has been said that '[f]requently the acts of a mediator are only one element in the many factors which make up the complex changing political situation.'[119] It is, therefore, a combination of man (the mediator) and machine (the machinery of politics/formal organisation of the mediation, e.g. host administration of the mediation, forum and organisation such as the AU or UN) that will make mediation effort successful.

Mediation is particularly useful in relation to international boundary disputes and should certainly be high on the agenda of peacemakers in this field. Empirical studies in the area of conflict resolution would seem to suggest that territorial issues are attractive to potential third party mediators whereas disputants are less inclined to accept mediation in territorial disputes. Mediators are attracted towards territorial disputes because such disputes have a characteristic of tangibility with clear features that can be divided or bargained over. Third parties, thus, easily recognise that there is a high likelihood of a sensational successful mediation in territorial disputes than other types of conflicts. Interestingly third party mediators are also influenced by a sense of foreboding. While mediation may succeed to great possible effect for all parties involved, should such pacific means of settlement fail, territorial and boundary disputes also are likely much more than other international disputes to disrupt regional and/or global state peaceful interactions. In terms of mediation offered by states, two types of offerors of mediation are typical in these circumstances: major power status nations and/ or those states with strong trade ties with the disputants. In terms of individuals or non-governmental bodies, those offering mediation will include personalities of international relevance and prestige – notably former heads of states as in the

---

117 Levi, op.cit., pp. 293–294.
118 This idea is originally Levi's but we totally identify with it. Ibid., p. 293.
119 *Report of a Study Group*, op.cit., p. 84.

case of the African forum, a body with fast rising profile in international dispute settlement.[120]

The parties must, however, be extremely careful in agreeing to mediation offered as the result of mediation will mostly also relate to the quality of mediation offered. Where the mediator(s) is not up to scratch or where there is no evidence of deep enough intellect, knowledge or integrity, the result of the mediation will probably remain questionable or unacceptable. It has even been suggested that power asymmetry between the parties will influence the kind of mediators that will offer themselves for the job.[121] Perhaps the parties should also configure the power asymmetry between them in consideration of what type of mediators should come into the matter. Where the power asymmetry is skewed heavily in favour of one side it might make sense for the mediating state or personality to come from an equally strong or even stronger state than the one involved in the dispute. This caveat rings particularly true in Africa because of the paucity of genuine home grown leaders with democratic credentials and regionally recognised leadership record.[122]

Yet mediation has had its dramatic failures as well. Examples in this area in Africa include international mediation over Somalia.[123] It has been suggested that:

> Why the mediators appointed by the UN have failed may depend more on the disputes in question than on the mediator: No mediator can solve a dispute if the parties are not willing to make the necessary concessions to reach a common agreement. If the positions of the parties are for political reasons so widely separated and so firmly maintained that the persuasions and proposals of the mediator cannot bring them on to common ground, the mediation will fail, without fault of the mediator.[124]

---

120 Frazier, op.cit., p. 268; J. Wilkenfeld, K. Young, V. Asal and D. Quinn, "Mediating International Crises. Cross-national and Experimental Perspectives", Vol. 47, *Journal of Conflict Resolution* (2003), No. 3, pp. 279–301; A. Lall, *Modern International Negotiations: Principle and Practice* (New York, NY: Columbia University Press, 1966); P. F. Diehl and G. Goertz, *War and Peace in International Rivalry* (Ann Arbor, MI: University of Michigan Press, 2000); J. Bercovitch, J. T. Anagnoson and D. L. Wille, "Some Conceptual Issues and Empirical Trends in the Study of Successful Mediation in International Relations", Vol. 28, *Journal of Peace Research* (1991), No. 1, pp. 7–17; M. Ott, "Mediation as a Method of Conflict Resolution: Two Cases", Vol. 26 *International Organization* (1972), pp. 595–618.
121 Frazier, op.cit., p. 275. See also K. Waltz, *Theories of International Politics* (New York: Random House, 1979).
122 US President Obama aptly put the situation in the following way, 'Africa doesn't need strongmen, it needs strong institutions'. The White House, Office of the Press Secretary, Remarks by the President to the Ghanaian Parliament, 11 July 2009, available at www.whitehouse.gov/the-press-office/remarks-president-ghanaian-parliament, accessed 23 November 2013 (Accra International Conference Center Accra, Ghana).
123 See Laurie Nathan, "'When Push Comes to Shove': The Failure of International Mediation in African Civil Wars", Vol. 8, *Track Two*, No. 2, November (1999) pp. 1–4.
124 Report of a Study Group of the David Davies Memorial Institute of International Studies, *International Disputes: The Legal Aspects* (London: Europa Publications, 1972).

A mediation panel must, however, accept the limits of its powers. It can come to conclusions and make recommendations but it must leave the implementation of the decision to the parties and cannot command compliance. The conclusion of mediation may, however, lead to further bilateral negotiations regarding the implementation of the decisions. Practice in this direction is reflected in China's reaction to mediation findings over the Indo–China dispute:

> The task of the Colombo Conference was to mediate and not to arbitrate. Its proposals are only a recommendation for the consideration of China and India and not a verdict or arbitral award which China and India must accept in to . . . There is no need for China and India to agree to all the Colombia proposals before going to the Conference [sic] table.[125]

It is clear that whenever any or a combination of the pacific means of disputes mentioned in Article 33 of the Charter of the United Nations are competently employed with the right measure of political will on the side of the parties, very difficult territorial and boundary disputes may be resolved. However, it is not impossible that the best efforts will yet give rise to no suitable or enduring resolution of the dispute. Intractable radical disagreements are possible and international lawyers and dispute resolution experts must prepare for this eventuality not in the sense of giving up but in the form of preparing a long-term management strategy to ensure that the dispute does not get worse or lead to an actual catastrophe for the disputants and international relations in general. It is, thus, correctly observed that despite the best efforts of peacemakers, resolution may become intolerably elusive:

> Either a sovereign state is created or it is not created. Either a form of government is instituted or it is not instituted. Analysts wedded to deconstructive notions, and practitioners committed to the idea that all conflicts can be transformed, may not like this or want to recognise it. But, crude, brutal and simplistic though it may be, intractable political conflict obstinately persists.[126]

12.7 Multi-tracking and indigenising settlement of boundary disputes in Africa: a fusion of law, politics and culture

We have examined in some detail the major pacific dispute settlement mechanisms suitable for the resolution of boundary disputes. Accordingly we have highlighted the importance and particular features of negotiation, mediation, inquiry, conciliation and arbitration to the resolution of African boundary disputes.

---

125 China's official statements quoted in Tzou, op.cit., p. 131.
126 Ramsbotham, op.cit., p. xii (Preface).

The question, however, still remains as to how to choose any particular means of resolution for particular type of disputes. This chapter seeks to synthesise a specific model based upon existing practices in Africa and other multi-track approaches to resolution of territorial, boundary and cross-boundary conflicts. The aim is to identify and develop a progressive theoretical framework for resolving such disputes whilst considering adaptations that reflect African cultural and historical factors, contemporary political relations among African states as well as principles of public international law. An attempt is made to develop useful typologies that states may adapt in evaluating their options and, therefore, provide workable models for reconciling and resolving boundary disputes.

Essentially what is required is an indigenous mechanism that comprehensively addresses, and where possible settles, disputes related to the delineation and demarcation of African states and possibly boundary disputes with other non-African states that share boundaries with an African state. So far in this book we have adopted the following premises:

(i) when it comes to border disputes, on the basis of extensive African experience it is better for targeted solutions to be explored through bilateral diplomacy;
(ii) solutions and compromises may be developed through the RECs, all of which have relatively formidable and proactive legal and political structures to deal with boundary disputes;
(iii) there is ample evidence of institutional capacity and political will within the AU as an institution to address African disputes generally construed as well as boundary disputes in particular;
(iv) the relevance of other foreign mechanisms such as the UN and its organs to the maintenance of peaceful conduct of international relations between disputing African states remains manifest.

It is also often the case, as our analysis has shown, that when pre-existing cooperation over boundary delimitation and demarcation or management between states break down suddenly it usually becomes unclear what has led to the dispute and who should be handling its resolution. It is for such occasions among others that contemporary African scholars have found it necessary to canvass the creation of an African Boundaries Indigenous Dispute Settlement Mechanism (ABIDSM), which African states may readily follow. The development of such a system would be useful to disputing states, the pertinent RECs, the AU and indeed the United Nations in that they may all at any opportune time understand how best to handle the dispute at any particular stage under the indigenous dispute mechanism.

Our proposal for an African indigenous boundary dispute mechanism builds upon the African Peace and Security Architecture (APSA) and collates best practices observable in the practice of African states and the RECs. Again it must be mentioned that the practice of the ECOWAS and EGAD regions are particularly instructive. The aim is to create a set of settlement procedures that allow a sensible and flexible step-by-step approach to settling international boundary disputes in Africa. In order for the idea of an indigenous boundary dispute mechanism to succeed it must avoid the inane recommendation of creating even more institutions.

It must, however, possess two essential guiding philosophies. First, it should be based on the requirement of local ownership. The characteristic of local ownership is one which has eluded most non-bilateral approaches to African disputes resolution over the last many decades. Yet the entire diplomatic and legal processes recommended must be advised by contemporary international law but must also bear the imprimatur of African indigenous cultural diplomacy, legal thinking and practice. It should not be out of place to expect breaking of kolanut ceremonies at meetings and diplomatic conferences. Prayers in the three main African religions – traditional African faiths, Christianity and Islam – at the beginning and end of sessions are to be expected at many African formal events. African hospitality must be freely encouraged and sustained between the parties throughout the formal and informal stages of the dispute resolution. There may be the need to break sessions up sensitively to allow for observance of Muslim prayer schedules. Boundary disputes by their very nature tend to take place between neighbouring states, thus familiarity with each other's cultural mores and practices may be expected. During oral exchanges the normal course of western diplomatic protocol may have to be varied in favour of cultural realities. For instance, during oral testimonies or formal speeches the statements of an elder statesman or even local chief may have to be taken out of turn and accorded higher priority than those of current office holders. It is not unheard of that an entire clan walks out of a fact-finding meeting because it appears that a UN high representative appears to suggest that the village head is deliberately telling lies during oral testimonies.

Second, it must conform to the law and practices of the principle of subsidiarity. Third, as much as possible it should allow for the parties to shape the settlement methods under the guidance of competent persons with knowledge of the law surrounding boundaries and international law on the topic. Fourth, it can only bind parties where they have explicitly agreed to be bound. The commitment to be bound should ideally be expressed through the AU and then by commitment to the appropriate RECs to which the affected African states belong.

At the emergence of facts and a situation that can lead to territorial or boundary disputes, one or both parties, a REC or the AU, can submit the dispute for settlement. The various situation rooms in the RECs and the AU, which as we noted are already functioning well, will continue to serve as good mechanisms for detecting worrying signals upon which political actors may be asked to take decisions to act. Upon being officially informed, the matter would be discussed by the appropriate body within the REC or by the AU Peace and Security Council. With due regard to the principle of subsidiarity, the PSC should be very much alive to its responsibilities to deal with boundary problems as a specifically dangerous area of international disputes in Africa. The PSC can decide to become directly proactive in taking initiative on the dispute and/or recommend how to address the dispute if it is not in the position to settle it itself.

12.7.1 Bona fide assisted direct negotiations

At this stage, depending on the facts and on the disposition of the parties to each other, it would be desirable that direct or assisted negotiations on the dispute should be encouraged by the requisite REC or by the AUPSC. This stage of *bona fide assisted negotiations* may be considered as optional. This is because the facts of the dispute and the surrounding circumstances may be such that it is clear that all direct negotiations between the parties have failed, are impossible or ill advised because further direct negotiations are frivolous or destined to fail and/or result in a gross waste of time or worsening of the dispute. Yet this stage may be very significant not because negotiations may not have been conducted between the parties but because it offers a last minute opportunity to the parties to conclude direct negotiations to settle the matter knowing that third party settlement procedures progressively reduces the complete autonomy of the parties over all aspects of their case. The workability of direct negotiations as a policy for the most seemingly intractable processes is perhaps seen in the fact that even those in stronger position, *vis-à-vis* their weaker opponents, are known to submit to the logic. Thus, even with respect to the quagmire of the Palestinian territories it is said that 'Israel remains dedicated to direct negotiations as the only method of resolving the conflict.'[127] In this way even those disputes involving asymmetrical power relations in Africa can still be susceptible to the use of this method. African states have little problems with the original concept of equality of states in international law and indeed the strongest threats to the concept have emerged out of the so-called exceptionalism of the United States and a few other western powers. Hence the virtue of direct negotiations it will appear have not been fully utilised in respect to African continental boundary crises.

It may also be that much of what was said and done between the parties was not properly structured or did not involve the highest political authorities preferably with full powers. The nature of the assistance by the RECs and/or AU should be in the form of administrative cover of the negotiations such as fixing of venue and dates after due consultations with the parties. Further involvement would include secretarial services if needed, diplomatic presence at opening and closing stages of the negotiations, presence at any sessions that the parties wish there should be witnesses and a general guiding but non-interfering hand towards peaceful resolution of the dispute. In other words, a very light touch may in some cases be required of even the AU and the African RECs because it is not always the case that all state parties have the desirable full confidence in these supranational

---

127 This has also been the policy espoused by the United States in recent years in relation to the Arab Israeli question. In 2010, Hilary Clinton stated: 'I've invited Israeli Prime Minister Netanyahu and Palestinian Authority President Abbas to meet on September 2nd in Washington, D.C. to re-launch direct negotiations to resolve all final status issues, which we believe can be completed within one year'. See The Israel Ministry of Foreign Affairs, "US Secretary Clinton Invites Israel and Palestinians to Direct Negotiations", available at www.mfa.gov.il/MFA/ForeignPolicy/Peace/MFADocuments/Pages/Secy_Clinton_invites_Israel_Palestinians_direct_negotiations_20-Aug-2010.aspx, accessed 17 November 2013.

bodies for various reasons. It may be recalled that one of the reasons why Eritrea at various stages preferred a foreign forum in dealing with its dispute with Ethiopia was precisely because the AU headquarters is situated in Addis Ababa – the capital of Ethiopia.

12.7.2 African mediation

After the preceding stage has run its course, or alternatively without the recommended optional *bona fide assisted negotiations* stage, mediation of the dispute may be arranged for the disputant parties. Mediators may be appointed by the means identified in the RECs we have discussed earlier. If mediation is handled under the auspices of the AU, this will take the form of appointment by the PSC or by the Panel of the Wise. It is essential that such an appointed mediator should have great latitude in approaching his task but the mediator(s) ought to report regularly to supervisory authorities like the PSC on a regular basis. Mediators in the best tradition of their task should consider the wishes of the parties and try to bring them together towards a mutually acceptable solution. They may, however, take account of the rights and interests of local communities, and larger interests such as the environment, cross-border cooperation, possibilities for joint development and other considerations that may be conducive to viable, stable and long-term border relations.

In order to avoid the possibility of the process being frustrated, mediation should be given a time limit in which resolution may be completed. Such a time frame must not be too restrictive and neither must it be too extensive. Received wisdom in international relations goes to the effect that legal and diplomatic processes do take time and ought not to be overly rushed. In this case it is suggested that after a period of a year (24 months) if mediation does not reach a solution for any number of reasons the process should proceed to that of conciliation, unless of course one or both parties are opposed to the establishment of a Conciliation Commission. There must be enough scope for infusion of African mediation with appropriate African cultural flavour along the lines suggested earlier in this chapter. Yet it must be recommended that African international mediation may need to be further formalised in some of the existing fora where it has not yet received sufficient attention. The Africa Forum which has been conducting some of the celebrated mediation in recent times does not appear to have a set of formal mediation rules.[128] Of course this may not affect the quality of the services rendered by some of the best presidential minds found on the continent; but the existence of formal mediation rules will certainly engender better confidence in this important institution among African states especially at the early stages of the decision of which venue and forum should assist them in resolving the dispute.

---

128 *Supra* Chapter 9, note 3.

12.7.3 The African Conciliation Commission

In accordance with international practice, conciliation panels for the purpose of boundary disputes shall comprise one representative appointed by each of the parties, with the addition of a chairperson appointed jointly by the parties (to avoid a tie in decisions). A Conciliation Commission thus instituted can mediate the dispute just like the mediator, but will further be empowered to investigate the dispute with close involvement of the parties themselves through their representative in the Commission. Like the mediator, the Conciliation Commission may assist the parties in coming to compromise positions to resolve the dispute but the Conciliation Commission as envisaged in this case should have the powers to *suo motu* indicate a set of solutions for the parties to decide the dispute if a compromise is not reached by the parties. It is preferable that conciliation takes place within a fixed period of two years with the possibility of a further extension of six months where it is embarked upon in the first instance. If, however, the conciliation follows mediation it is preferable that the conciliation takes place within a fixed period of 18 months.

12.7.4 The underdeveloped state of indigenous African adjudication

African boundary dispute resolution at the ICJ has been quite frequent. Yet there is a deep dissatisfaction with this practice by African writers across disciplinary divides. It is suggested that the time has come for some Afrocentric social engineering of dispute resolution practice in this respect. It is hereby suggested that where any dispute has not been settled by conciliation within a maximum of 30 months of initiation within the ABIDSM (i.e. maximum period allowed for first instance conciliation) or 18 months in the case of conciliation after mediation, the matter shall be referred, at the request of any one or both of the parties to the dispute, to the Court of Justice of the requisite REC to which the parties belong. Where the parties to the dispute are members of different RECs they may agree to refer the case to the Court of Justice of the AU. Parties to a dispute who are also members of the same REC may also opt to send their dispute to the African Court of Justice as envisaged. The resulting judgment of such courts must ensure a binding settlement.

It is important to state that it is completely legitimate for African states to have to resort to the ICJ at The Hague or any of the UN tribunals such as ITLOS. It is good international policy that nothing ought to prevent parties from resorting to the venerable institutions of the United Nations. These options, however, are clearly not within the contemplated ABIDSM and the process is susceptible to all the strengths and weaknesses of judicial settlement at the ICJ discussed earlier. The Court continues to enjoy great prestige in the international system and will hopefully remain eternally very useful to the entire world. Contemporary international law remains closely associated with the UN system and no one gains anything in undermining the moral and actual authority of the UN system including any of its principal organs. The ICJ remains very relevant in settling international disputes widely construed. It is, however, the case that the proliferation of cases brought to the ICJ by African states has perceptively been opportunistic and exploitative of an institution that dispenses an international justice which is predictably Eurocentric in approach. By granting apparent sanctity to colonial acts in a completely uncritical manner and not being bothered by their moral providence or contemporary effects of inter-generational equities, the Court in respect of territorial and boundary disputes dispenses a conservative justice which does not allow Africa to heal. There also appears to be very little scope for the development of the law function that is sorely needed in the jurisprudence of international boundary law from the bench of the ICJ as it is presently construed under the Statute of the Court.

Although the World Court repeatedly delivers final and binding decisions with respect to boundary cases, it appears not to achieve 'genuine resolution' of such disputes in Africa given the excruciatingly slow implementation of its judgments and intermittent relapses into strife and violence by parties in relation to the same issues that have been decided upon. This conclusion is backed up by the number of skirmishes, tensions and killings that still attend the affected territories and their peoples even after judgments such as in relation to the Bakassi Peninsula. Hence we conclude that it is necessary to engage in targeted legal engineering of international dispute resolution of African boundary disputes. This would involve a kind of positive discrimination against judicial resolution mechanisms in the first place in favour of other ADR mechanisms including arbitration and a further positive discrimination in favour of adoption of African International Court processes where the judicial route is preferable or resorted to under the proposed ABIDSM. In this regard, the Courts of Justice of the RECs and the ACJ (as envisaged) will be proper and able forums to hear the bulk of African boundary disputes that are not resolved by international ADR processes. The use of these courts rather than the ICJ would in time increase access to international justice for African states. For instance, where preference for the litigation route has been expressed by the parties, cases relating to grazing rights and artisanal fishing are arguably more likely to be brought to courts situated in Africa than to the ICJ. An emergent culture of litigation relating to specialised issues before African international courts may help to reduce the severity of international boundary disputes as the lesser issues of resource control would have been dealt with before it emerges into full blown territorial or boundary claims. This is so because boundary disputes are rarely only about the precise location of the boundary but will usually involve, among others, the sharing of resources, migration pressures, transportation issues, environmental pressures, ethnic and cultural interactions as well as security, customs and policing issues.

In short one of the guiding aims of the proposed ABIDSM should be to reduce disputes to manageable proportions as it may be unduly optimistic to expect that all African boundary problems can be completely settled in the sense of resolving all equities and achieving complete delimitation and demarcation. To preserve beneficial relationships between African states, however, it is essential that the

ABIDSM be perceived as being capable of addressing all those disputes that seriously impair the relations between member states. In other words the philosophy behind our recommended ABIDSM has a more holistic purview than many contemporary models of boundary dispute settlement processes. This is in that the ABIDISM ought to be utilised even where a dispute is unlikely to be solved completely. It should be useful as a means of reducing the dispute into manageable parts and managing disputes over a longer period than is usual where this appears to be in the interest of international peace and security. It is also essential that in realisation of the multifaceted national and ethnic interests that are inherent in most African states, the ABIDISM must in attempting resolution of disputes ensure very wide involvement of the parties. Evidence of impressive practice has already been shown with respect to elders and village councils, in West and Eastern Africa, and the ABIDISM should anticipate widening the participation of such constituencies as *amici curiae* in all aspects of the processes leading to resolution of disputes.

Whether ethnic communities should be able to flag off dispute resolution processes would depend on which method is envisaged. With relation to the litigation route it is obvious that the constitutive instruments creating the courts of some of the RECs do not envisage the institution of proceedings other than by state actors. There is of course the exception of the ECOWAS Court which has successfully been hearing cases brought by individuals. Note must indeed be taken of the fate of the SADC Court which has been rendered impotent by political forces as a result of the purported use of the court by non-state actors. With respect to the ADR techniques, however, the road should be open for increased participation of outside expertise and third party intervention where they have a genuine connection to the dispute.

Another area where African jurisprudence ought to be allowed to express some difference is in the acceptance of third party participation in international dispute settlement proceedings. It is suggested that in the spirit of African brotherhood dispute settlement processes should have a philosophy of liberal allowance of third parties to participate as *amici* and to intervene in legal proceedings. The successful intervention of Equatorial Guinea in the *Land and Maritime Boundary Case* shows judicial toleration for third party intervention in maritime boundary disputes. This sort of toleration should only be increased in the context of ever closer sub-regional developments in areas such as the Gulf of Guinea where resource exploitation is bound to increase over the coming decades. A lot will, however, depend on the attitude of African governments themselves to continue to give adequate attention to the spirit of brotherhood that is inherent in the international relations of Africa. This toleration was unfortunately absent when Equatorial Guinea attempted to attend as *amici* during the diplomatic processes leading to the implementation of the World Court's decision in the maritime sector despite its inherent interests that may be involved in the determination of the maritime tripoint in the Gulf of Guinea between the three countries. In the absence of further Cameroonian agreement with Equatorial Guinea as to delimitation between the countries and possibly a further agreement regarding a tripoint with Nigeria, it is hard to see the value of an equidistance line between Cameroon and Nigeria. This is because the Cameroon–Nigeria line must end at a tripoint. The existing line indicated by the ICJ, however, appears to have been arbitrarily discovered from an English admiralty map. This situation presumably may already have laid the grounds for future disputes especially in relation to the existence of a tripoint where the boundaries of the three states meet in their maritime sectors in the Gulf of Guinea.

The proposed ABIDSM must be capable of considering all aspects of the disputes referred to it. Thus, differences and disputes relating to delineation or delimitation, demarcation, management, reaffirmation, renegotiation disputes, etc. must be within the competence of those institutions and authorities charged with duties under the ABIDSM. As a holistic procedure, the ABIDSM ought to be useable even where a conclusive solution may appear impossible under present circumstances. Hence if it is to succeed it should be able to cope with even theoretically more difficult situations than the Israeli–Palestinian question. The ABIDSM must be flexible and not mechanistically rigid. It should be possible to move seamlessly between the various dispute settlement procedures. It should be possible for the parties to start with mediation and by agreement move certain issues on to conciliation or even adjudication while other issues continue by mediation or even revert back to direct negotiation. It should be possible to insert expert determination into any of the procedures, save perhaps the adjudication procedure conducted by international courts. Whatever combinations that have realistic chances of success should be encouraged. The most important philosophical kernel of the ABIDSM should be resolution of the dispute as opposed to reaching bare decisions and/or judgments.

It is in this guise that we must make particular recommendation of the close involvement of a beefed up AUBP in the handling of African boundary disputes generally. As a political construct the AUBP ought to become a permanent standing institution within the AU. It should be infused with the moral and legal authority of its parent institution and well placed to ensure that the parties to African boundary disputes, whether being handled by the RECs or the AU or even by other foreign processes, keep themselves within the limits of genuine political cooperation required of them as African states. This is probably what Prof. J. G. Merrills meant when he noted that the essential point to make is that whatever type of boundary dispute is being considered, political institutions seem more capable of ensuring that such disputes do not get out of hand than actually settling them.[129]

Flexibility as a hallmark of the ABIDSM would again be reflexive of international standards. Apart from being compatible with international legal norms and the demands of the Charter of the United Nations and international law generally, a multi-track approach to settlement of international dispute can be

---

129 J. G. Merrills, "International Boundary Disputes in Theory and Practice: Precedents Established", in J. Dahlitz (ed.), *Peaceful Resolution of Major International Disputes* (UN: 1999), 95, at p. 106.

very well located in the theoretical framework of politics and international relations. Writers like Michelle Pace,[130] Nan[131] and Hottinger[132] have, for instance, explained the essence of the so-called two track system in relation to European Union practice. Track-one diplomatic activities include informal consultations, Good Offices, special envoys, mediation, negotiations, international condemnations, fact-finding missions, diplomatic and economic sanctions.[133] Track-two diplomacy involves other non-official dialogue initiatives where, for instance, communication, negotiation, mutual understanding and direct encounters are the main instruments at hand for forging a positive role for the European Union. Joseph Montville, who coined the term 'track two' in 1982, defined track-two diplomacy as:

> an unofficial, informal interaction between members of adversary groups or nations that aims to develop strategies, influence public opinion, and organize human and material resources in ways that might help to resolve their conflict . . . [It] is a process designed to assist official leaders to resolve or, in the first instance, to manage conflicts by exploring possible solutions out of public view and without the requirements to formally negotiate or bargain for advantage.[134]

Thus, track-one activities involve official government-to-government diplomatic interaction while track-two activities would typically engage conflict resolution professionals and involve dialogue with and training of influential elites, advocacy, empowerment, development and social and economic activities.[135] These include unofficial, non-governmental, analytical, policy-orientated, problem-solving efforts by skilled, educated, experienced and informed private citizens interacting with other private citizens. Examples of both may be found in the practice surrounding the Israeli–Palestinian case.[136] The adoption of track two in the Arab–Israeli process has been recognised as an historic turning point in the search

---

130 Michelle Pace, "The EU as a 'force for good' in border conflict cases?", in Yacobi and Newman, "The EU and the Israel–Palestine Conflict" in Diez, Albert and Stetter (eds), *The European Union and Border Conflicts: The Power of Integration and Association* (Cambridge: Cambridge University Press, 2008), p. 213.
131 S. Allen Nan, "Track I Diplomacy", *Intractable Conflict Knowledge Base Project*, Conflict Research Consortium (2003), University of Colorado.
132 J. T. Hottinger, "The Relationship between Track One and Track Two Diplomacy", *Accord: An International Review of Peace Initiatives*, issue 16 (2005), www.c-r.org/our-work/accord/engaging-groups/trackone-tracktwo.php, accessed 13 November 2013.
133 Nan, op.cit.
134 Hottinger, op.cit., p. 13.
135 Ibid.
136 Princeton University, "Bridging Divides: Track II Diplomacy in the Middle East Policy Workshop", Woodrow Wilson School of Public & International Affairs, (2013), pp. 5–7, 11–16; "*Joseph v. Montville*, Track Two Diplomacy: The Work of Healing History", *Whitehead Journal of Diplomacy and International Relations*, vol. 17, no. 2 (Summer/Fall 2006), p. 16; Heidi Burgess and Guy Burgess (eds), *Conducting Track II Peace Making* (US: US Institute of Peace Washington, DC and University of Colorado Conflict Information Consortium, 2010), p. 14.

for a solution. The negotiations were hammered out in complete secrecy in Oslo, Norway, by Israeli and Palestinian negotiators acting without intermediaries. This successful tactic leading to the so-called Oslo Accord forced both sides to come to terms with each other's existence. Israel agreed to recognise Yasser Arafat as its partner in peace talks, and agreed to recognise Palestinian autonomy in the West Bank and Gaza Strip by beginning to withdraw from the cities of Gaza and Jericho – essentially exchanging land for peace. On the side of the Palestinians they had to recognise the right of Israel to exist while also renouncing the use of terrorism and especially its long-held call for Israel's destruction.[137] A pointer to the progress made by this approach was that just a year after the completion of the Accord, the Israeli Prime Minister Yitzhak Rabin, Foreign Minister Shimon Peres and Yasser Arafat were awarded the Nobel Peace Prize for their roles in the Oslo Accord.[138] Track-two diplomacy in an African context will involve contacts with border community leaders, Obas, chiefs, Prefects, ethnic militia leaders (where the demands of public policy permits), market leaders, local chiefs, Imams, influential marabouts, parish priests and indeed any of the leading and organising personalities and forces with sufficient influence to bring a clear understanding to the issues causing the boundary conflict. These are not the type of actors usually dealt with according to the standards of western diplomacy but they are the very constituencies in Africa that have the closest relevance to boundary problems in Africa. In the context of Africa they usually possess the moral and actual authority to bring about a lessening of tensions. They can ensure the existence of peace in their locality given the political distance between African governments and boundary communities. Despite the usual political grandstanding that regional and national governments in Africa engage in when it comes to boundary related issues, the fact is that their relevance is often little seen by far flung boundary communities. Thus, as seen in the case of East African states, a political cease-fire in the capitals relating to boundary problems is often hardly observed by the actual warring communities in the border regions. Hence the wisdom in carrying such local opinion leaders and personalities along during negotiations and dispute settlement processes.

---

[137] Chairman Arafat sent a letter to Prime Minister Rabin, in which he stated unequivocally that the PLO:

> Recognises the right of Israel to exist in peace and security; Accepts UN Security Council Resolutions 242 and 338; Commits itself to a peaceful resolution of the conflict; Renounces the use of terrorism and other acts of violence; Assumes responsibility over all PLO elements to ensure their compliance, prevent violations, and discipline violators; Affirms that those articles of the PLO Covenant which deny Israel's right to exist are now inoperative and no longer valid; Undertakes to submit to the Palestinian National Council for formal approval the necessary changes to the Covenant.

Israel Ministry of Foreign Affairs, "The Israel-Palestinian Negotiations Background – Israel–PLO Recognition", available at www.mfa.gov.il/MFA/ForeignPolicy/Peace/Guide/Pages/Israel-Palestinian%20Negotiations.aspx, accessed 17 November 2013.

[138] *Frontline*, "The Negotiations", available at www.pbs.org/wgbh/pages/frontline/shows/oslo/negotiations/, accessed 17 November 2013.

On the whole, however, there is something to be said for 'free styling' African dispute resolution. Mechanistic approaches will not do in this particular area of international dispute resolution and the desirable philosophy should be that the end does justify the legitimate means. Whatever combination or group of combinations that works towards preventing the worsening of the dispute or actually resolves the dispute should be adopted. Of course too many cooks can indeed spoil the brew and concepts like confidentiality may be jeopardised by opening too many windows of dispute settlement. Yet there is enough international experience to indicate that combination therapy is not only relevant to biological sicknesses but also works in international dispute settlement. Particularly because of the inherent familiarity of the African and other non-western civilisations to the virtues of the older dispute resolution mechanisms, they will show better appreciation of and greater susceptibility to a combination of ADR mechanisms. Derek Roebuck has convincingly reflected this reality when he wrote:

> All the evidence I have been able to accumulate tends to show that mediation before, in conjunction with or instead of arbitration, has been available and widely used, with satisfactory methods of enforcement, by communities of all kinds in the past.[139]

12.8 Factors predictive of the failure of ADR and Tier 2 diplomacy in boundary matters

Given the increasing importance of non-adjudicative means of resolving boundary disputes and our clear preference for 'combination therapy' in the management and resolution of African boundary disputes it is important that some attention is given to the factors that will help make a success of international ADR mechanisms. We must, therefore, also strive to identify the practices that may predict the failure of international ADR. International ADR mechanisms and the efforts of those who attempt to bring a negotiated solution to a boundary problem will fail for nearly all the same reasons why dispute resolution fails in other areas of legal and political engagement and they include the issues discussed below.

12.8.1 Poor knowledge, incompetence or careless diagnosis of the crisis

Simply put, incompetence, carelessness, shallow comprehension of the law and misdiagnosis of the facts of the dispute will prove fatal to the success of any mediation effort. In an ideal scenario a mediator's duty to acquaint him or herself

---

139 Derek Roebuck, "Cultural Differences and Mediation: An Introduction", 135 *Asian Dispute Review* (2002), at p. 136; Thomas W. Wälde, "Mediation/Alternative Dispute Resolution in Oil, Gas and Energy Transactions: Commercially Superior to Formal Litigation and Arbitration", Vol. 1 *Oil Gas and Energy Law Intelligence*, No. 2 (2003).

with the facts of the case and knowledge about parties extends to what has been referred to as the intelligence requirement of international mediation whereby a mediator's strategies and tactics ought to be informed by a deep understanding of the parties' internal calculations about the conflict. It has even been suggested that UN mediation teams should have a monitoring and analysis unit that endeavours to meet this need and reduce the ignorance that commonly afflicts international mediation.[140] As long as the works of such units are not covert and the references to intelligence do not refer to clandestine activities, such reasoning will undoubtedly benefit the work of mediation. If, however, clandestine intelligence and surreptitious gathering of information by mediators is what is referred to then it is clear that such tactics will be ultimately unhelpful to the temple of justice to which all aspects of the field of ADR belongs. By the very nature of international relations, state parties would need to be confident that they are not being spied on by ADR facilitators.

12.8.2 Poor strategy and/or poorly trained mediators

Mediation is simply not for everyone. It is possible to live a perfectly fulfilled life in the highest echelons of power structures in national or international life and yet be a poor peacemaker. The job of a mediator is a skilled one and the attributes and knowledge do not come easily to everyone. There is a fear that some international mediators are simply appointed by approbation due to their prominence in official positions and through personal political connections. In many cases they are appointed regardless of any evidence of formal training or any form of meaningful exposure to the discipline of dispute settlement. In some cases it is assumed that the appointment of experts to assist a process will assure adequate standards. In the worst of cases international mediation may become exposed to ridicule as boundary management and adjustment principles are simply not for the untrained. Process matters as much as substance; whereas it has been observed in the experience of the author that some mediators are so focused on getting the substance right that they neglect or forget the very important aspect of process which goes hand in hand with their task.

12.8.3 Lack of neutrality/mediators with an interest to serve

Bias will forever remain poisonous to a mediator's role whereas manifest neutrality of a mediator is an essential ingredient in the making of an antidote to strife. Where possible distance from the region in which the dispute occurs is advised as a formal and perhaps natural marker of neutrality. Too much distance may begin to affect the ability of the mediator to retain that sense of local knowledge and perhaps closeness to the facts which is a key attribute of the task but too much

---

140 Laurie Nathan, "The Intelligence Requirement of International Mediation", *Intelligence and National Security* (London: Routledge, 2013).

closeness is far more perturbing to the sensibilities of most disputants. It may indeed be suggested that one of the ways in which both the ICJ and the PCA may not be suitable for many African boundary disputes is based on this very fact of distance of the members of the bench and the physical sit of the Court. Admittedly the PCA has been brought closer to the African continent with the establishment of a branch in Mauritius. In the Tanzania–Malawi case, for instance, although there is absolutely no tangible basis upon which bias may be shown to exist, it somehow lurks in the background that the mediation panel, constituted as it is by former Presidents of neighbouring states in the sub-region, may not be far removed enough from the politics of the region to have an easy job as mediators. Again the issue in such cases will be largely that of perception rather than fact. In international politics and relations, however, perceptions can be very potent.

12.8.4 Unable to stay the course

Successful mediation must show stamina. The job is really never complete as the parties may relapse. Thus, the mediator(s) must remain in good contact with the affected states. It was correctly noted in relation to the Somalia situation that '[a]rguably the single biggest mistake by external mediators since 1991 has been to conflate the revival of a central government with successful reconciliation.'[141] Inability to stay the course to the end of genuine resolution by the disputants and the mediators would be an expression of deficit of political will on their part.

12.9 Identification and evaluation of best practices for pacific settlement of disputes

Whichever route is adopted for the purpose of pacific settlement of disputes there are a few signposts of success which may be borne in mind by those charged with resolving the disputes. It must be realised that no two boundary problems are exactly the same and those tasked with the settlement of the dispute must follow indications of best practices without being slavish to them. In all academic honesty it must be conceded that any book which promises to advise all boundary commissions on their tasks for the rest of time must have being conceived by a fraud. Our work, thus, does not pretend to be prescriptive for all boundary work everywhere and at all times. Situations will change and exigencies will often require the adoption of solutions different from the received wisdom or international rules on the matter. As a general rule it is wise to realise that knowledge of international law and practice is crucial to achieving justice in international boundary matters. What we may choose to christen 'international

---

141 Ken Menkhaus, "Diplomacy in a Failed State International Mediation in Somalia", *Accord* Issue 21, available at www.c-r.org/sites/c-r.org/files/Accord%2021_4Diplomacy%20in%20a%20 failed%20state_international%20mediation_2010_ENG.pdf, accessed 12 December 2013.

boundary law' (many aspects of which this book has so far identified) is but an aspect of the general field of public international law, hence the imperative of appreciation and application of the latter to the settlement of international boundary disputes.

12.9.1 Flexibility

The first rule of the thumb is that boundary work is led by facts and then followed by law. Slight changes in the facts may modify the operation of law. Thus, it is impossible to calculate on the full manifestation of legal or other rules until the facts are understood and considered. The late African legal scholar with worldwide recognition on the subject – Oye Cukwurah who penned a very useful book on the *Settlement of Boundary Disputes in International Law* in 1967 – identified many of the technical issues of law that often crop up in practice. Yet this versatile scholar found it necessary to conclude as follows:

> An essential question to be considered is whether in the context of modern international law, the ancient doctrines developed in respect of international boundaries will still satisfy the needs of modern society if strictly applied. No doubt, these rules make for certainty and predictability in boundary matters. But in order to avoid inequitable results and unnecessary hardships on the populations to be separated by a boundary, adjoining States making new boundaries or rectifying established ones, should not hesitate to depart from the customary modes of boundary delimitation which we discussed.[142]

In other words there is a strong case for the humanisation of state practices in boundary regulations as well as demarcation. African demarcation ought to avoid the excesses of international boundary practice such as insensitive demarcation that splits school compounds and villages into two where such a result is undesirable or avoidable.[143]

12.9.2 Visit to locus

In many cases those called upon to resolve boundary cases are from far flung territories away from the places they are expected to make important determinations. It therefore makes sense that physical visits to the *locus* should be contemplated if at all possible. Unfortunately it is quite common for negotiators, arbitrators, mediators and judges to sit in foreign capitals and make life-changing decisions in relation to places they have not and may never visit. A visual and physical apprehension

---

142 Cukwurah, op.cit., p. 229.
143 Note the arguments in favour of varying boundary delimitation at the demarcation stage in limited circumstances which we have argued for elsewhere: Gbenga Oduntan, "The Demarcation of Straddling Villages in Accordance with the International Court of Justice Jurisprudence: The Cameroon-Nigeria Experience," Vol. 5, *Chinese Journal of International Law*, No. 1 (2006), pp. 79–114.

of the *locus* for appropriate length of time is recommended as part of the procedures for dispute settlement. As Cukwurah correctly wrote on this issue:

> Indeed it is most desirable that before entering upon any discussion of the boundary, the arbitrators, the umpire and the agents should where practicable, visit the territory in dispute. The soundness of the settlement which will follow a personal experience of the boundary area will more than compensate for the financial expense which such visits may involve.... Similarly, when a boundary dispute is submitted to adjudication, it will make for a better judgment if the tribunal (or an expert appointed by the tribunal) has a 'personal knowledge' of the character and dispositions of the border areas.[144]

The usefulness of the visit to *locus* was captured with clarity in the statement of Lord McNair as President of the Arbitral Court in the *Argentine–Chile Frontier Case*:[145]

> One of the objects of the Field Mission is to supplement from visual observation the information contained in the Memorials. The Court notes that very extensive information on land use, which is essential to complete the geographical picture, has been received from Chile but little such information has been received from the Argentine Republic.[146]

A visit to the *locus* is very desirable for the many experts involved in delimitation and dispute resolution of a boundary dispute but it is nearly inconceivable for it not to take place with respect to demarcators.[147] Visits may upon agreement be conducted to take evidence or may just be for visual apprehension. In the case of a demarcation team, demarcators may be divided into two. There are members of a demarcation team who may meet away from the boundary to interpret documents, agree on processes and procedures, draw up technical details, etc., and there are technical team members who actually have to carry out surveys, take measurements, build pillars, clear the vista, etc. For the latter, demarcation is a physical and hands on activity. See, for instance, our discussion earlier about the activities and *modus operandi* of the Sub-Commission for Demarcation set up to implement the ICJ decision in the Cameroon–Nigeria Land and Maritime dispute. This process also turns out a good example of the value of a visit to the *locus*. The parties had to demarcate their common boundary in accordance with

---

144 Cukwurah, op.cit., p. 232.
145 Reports of International Arbitral Awards, *Argentine–Chile Frontier Case*; supra this chapter, note 44.
146 Ibid., pp. 123, 146–149.
147 The Court of Arbitration, by means of a Field Mission appointed by it, in December 1965 and January and February 1966 examined the area in dispute and arranged for an aerial survey of that area to be made under the guidance of the Court of Arbitration, United Nations, Reports of International Arbitral Awards Argentine–Chile Frontier, op.cit., p. 123.

the World Court's judgment. As a result of the considerable doubts over the location of a particular village in one of the sectors under demarcation known as *Madas* and referred to in the Thomson–Marchand Declaration[148] applicable to the delimitation, the trilateral Sub-Committee on Demarcation (SCD) planned a visit to locate the village of *Madas*. The Nigerian view was that the village the Cameroonians (and the UN surveyors involved in the demarcation exercise) indicated to be *Madas* was actually another village entirely known as *Samke*. In the twilight of the day fixed for the meeting and after long inconclusive meetings with village elders paraded by the Cameroonian side to give oral testimonies to show that their village is *Madas*, the joint visiting team stumbled by providence on controverting evidence in the form of the village's only primary school premises (see pictures in Appendix V) which shows that the village school clearly bears the name of 'School of *Samke*'. This discovery proved very significant given the strong presumption that, in line with African tradition, village schools bear the name of the place they are built in.

12.9.3 Determination of locus standi

A court of law, arbitration, mediation, conciliation or negation panel must carefully determine that the parties appearing before it have sufficient legal and other interests to seek the resolution of the dispute in their respective rights. Not every state will have the right to institute proceedings in respect of a territorial or boundary contest or violation. Indeed an international tribunal would not accept a complaint by a state that some other state's rights have been infringed: the complaining state in that situation would not have *locus standi* to present such a case. *Locus standi* can also relate to the fact that a party must be at the very least a sovereign state in order to appear before a court or panel as in the case of the ICJ. Over-restrictive application of the *locus standi* criteria has in the past rendered havoc to the interest of African states such as in the denial of *locus standi* against the interests of Liberia and Ethiopia in the *South West Africa cases* discussed earlier.[149]

Sensible as this rule is in cases where at least one state is in fact directly affected, it hampers the enforcement of the law when a 'community interest' is at stake.[150] It is advocated here that those tasked with resolving international disputes should open up the *locus standi* standard to encompass significant '*actio popularis*' where, for instance, legal actions are instituted or complaints relate to sea or other atmospheric pollution such as that argued in the *Nuclear Test cases* (1974).

---

148 Thomson–Marchand Declaration of 1929–1930 (paras 2–60), as incorporated in the Henderson–Fleuriau Exchange of Notes of 1931.
149 Charles Henry Alexandrowicz, *The European-African Confrontation: A Study in Treaty Making* (Leiden: A. W. Sijthoff, 1973), pp. 113–116; Contributed, "South West Africa Cases (1966): Two Views: II. An Examination of Certain Criticisms of the South West Africa Cases Judgment", *Australian Year Book of International Law*, Vol. 2 (1966), pp. 143–148.
150 Churchill and Lowe, op.cit., p. 460.

In sum it is well within judicial tradition for the criteria of *locus standi* to guide tribunals and dispute resolution mechanisms in accepting the cases. Yet those concerned with boundary cases, particularly in relation to Africa, must remain vigilant and respect the true interests of justice and equity through which the standard of *locus standi* may have to be extended to include situations of trust as well as the general interests of third party states and peoples.[151]

12.9.4 The interpretative function in boundary dispute resolution

No matter which pacific dispute resolution mechanism is brought to bear upon a dispute, the interpretation of treaties and agreements would very commonly be required in determining the rights and obligations of the parties. As a result, practitioners, lawyers, arbitrators and mediators charged with resolving cases should be significantly familiar with the 1969 Vienna Convention on the Law of Treaties. The general rule is that all pertinent treaties that will be used in coming to a decision must be interpreted with full consideration of the good faith principle and in accordance with the ordinary meaning to be given to the terms in their appropriate context and in light of the respective treaty's object and purpose. In other words, the total context of the applicable treaty/treaties should be taken into account. Accordingly all parts of the treaty – preambular provisions and annexes as well as further protocols and even other treaties that may mention that treaty under interpretation – could be useful in understanding and interpreting an applicable instrument. Particularly in relation to territorial and boundary problems it is recognised that 'any subsequent agreement between the parties concerning interpretation must be taken into account, as may any subsequent practice of parties in the application of the treaty which establishes their (perhaps tacit) agreement concerning its interpretation'.[152]

The interpretative function in boundary disputes is one which can be quite extensive in character. For instance, where the dispute is in relation to aerial rights the true meaning of 'airspace' in certain languages as used in the major air treaties may come into issue and produce controversy.[153] Where the dispute affects rights

---

151 The ECOWAS Court of Justice has generally broad jurisdiction. It can hear disputes filed by the member states or the highest organ of the community, the authority, against another member state or another organ. Yet, private parties and ethnic or national groups do not enjoy direct *locus standi*. See Julia Lehmann, "Regional Economic Integration and Dispute Settlement Outside Europe: A Comparative Analysis", Vol. 7, *International Law FORUM Du Droit International*, No. 59 (2005), p. 59; See also W. Bray, "*Locus Standi* in Environmental Law", Vol. 22, *The Comparative and International Law Journal of Southern Africa*, No. 1 (1989), p. 33; C. Loots, "Keeping *locus standi* in Chains", Vol. 3, *South African Journal on Human Rights*, No. 66 (1987), p. 49.
152 Churchill and Lowe, op.cit., p. 460.
153 Scholars have noted that the equivalent of the expression 'airspace' in the French text of the Paris Convention is '*l'espace atmospherique*', while in the Chicago Convention the term '*l'espace aerien*' is used. Depending on particular preferences of legal writers, the height above space territory to which total and exclusive territorial jurisdiction may be argued to belong, i.e. 'airspace', may be confined to the limit where the air is found around the earth's atmosphere, as in the *l'espace*

in relation to the seas, Churchill and Lowe have alerted us to the possibility that comparisons of all the six authentic texts to the Law of the Sea Convention (Arabic, Chinese, English, French, Russian and Spanish) may have to be made by a tribunal and its lawyers. It is significant indeed to mention that at least one African state, Egypt, has signified in its declaration accompanying ratification of the LOSC (1982) that it would 'adopt the interpretation which is best corroborated by the various texts of the Convention'.[154] Furthermore, the interpretative function in deciding a boundary case includes the use of the *travaux préparatoires* (or historical rule). Here the meaning of an obscure text is clarified by reference to the drafting history or the preparatory work. At least in municipal law it has been recognised that recourse to *travaux préparatoires* should be rare. It should also be noted that for disputes in relation to maritime territory, the LOSC (1982) as a matter of fact does not have a comprehensive official record. Indeed 'some of the critical parts of the final text of the 1982 Convention were the product of unrecorded negotiations'.[155] This reality greatly reduces the scope for the resort to *travaux préparatoires* in maritime boundary cases in Africa as much as elsewhere.[156]

12.9.5 Interim measures of protection and control

A boundary commission must be particularly alive to its powers to issue interim measures of protection and control where provisions for such powers are contained in its constitutive instruments or by agreement of the parties. If the matter is to be heard by an arbitral institution, mediation, conciliation or other panel that has not been constituted, any of the parties may approach a standing judicial institution such as the ICJ (Articles 41 of the Statute of the Court and 73 of the Rules of Court), the standing regional international court (e.g. ECJ) or specialised court such as the ITLOS (LOSC Article 290) to provide provisional measures of control that will prevent an unfortunate deterioration of specific rights that are in dispute. This is to ensure that such rights do not become irrevocably compromised by the actions of one or more of the parties. In essence the power of tribunals and commissions to issue these measures is to prevent or arrest

---

atmospherique formulation much closer to the earth's surface, or it may be proposed to equate geophysical and legal limits of the whole aerial space and extend to up to 60,000 miles which the *l'espace aerien* formulation permits. See Committee on the Peaceful Uses of Outer Space, Legal Sub-Committee, "The Question of the Definition and/or the Delimitation of Outer Space: Background paper prepared by the Secretariat", available at https://cms.unov.org/documentrepositoryindexer/MultiLanguageAlignment.bitext?DocumentID=ed5223f6-9900-4244-a6b4-d050d7bbbc8e&DocumentID=de23ff7d-3886-43d2-a45b-78dd1c6cc38b, accessed 24 July 2014.

154 Declaration made upon ratification of the UNCLOS 25 *Law of the Sea Bulletins* 12 (1994); Churchill and Lowe, op.cit., p. 460.
155 Robin Rolf Churchill and Alan Vaughan Lowe, *The Law of the Sea*, Revised Edition (Manchester: Manchester University Press, 1988), p. 340.
156 See the cases of *Garland v. British Rail* [1983] 2 AC 751, at 278 and Lord Dennings's dicta in *R v. Chief Immigration Officer, Heathrow Airport, ex p. Salamat Bibi* [1976] 1 WLR 979, at 283.

the situation and fetter the discretion of the parties to undertake actions that would further prejudice the rights of the other side(s). This is to prevent a situation where vindication of one of the parties will be illusory in effect or meaningless in the context of the damage already suffered.

It will be useful to consider and grant such rights where soldiers from one state enter presumably into the territory of another and start coercive violent actions such as killing and maiming of residents. Indeed it is preferable that a tribunal should be 'trigger happy' in granting such measures especially where the safety of life is involved. It is also arguable that it is not a violation of the *ultra petita rule* (not granting more than is prayed for) for an African boundary tribunal to *suo moto* introduce and pronounce interim measures of control in the course of dealing with international boundary disputes involving African states, if it is apparent on the face of the facts that innocent lives can be lost by the actions of the parties in such disputes. This reason is borne out of the experience of past disputes on the continent which have shown that a lot of civilian lives have been lost in the prosecution of boundary rivalries and disputes;[157] whereas an opportune interim measure of protection that, for instance, freezes action in terms of troop movements across a specified portion of the contested boundary can help prevent tit-for-tat military actions that often prove very costly in terms of loss of human lives. Maritime boundary dispute resolution processes may indeed last many decades before being finally negotiated or settled. In such cases it is possible that provisional measures may be given where a party can show that irreparable damage can be caused to its interests or to the marine environment.[158] The general rule, however, is that there ought to be a clear situation of urgency for interim measures to be legally obtained by any party. This requirement was first adhered to in the *Passage through the Great Belt case* wherein the court said 'Provisional measures are ... only justified if there is urgency in the sense that action prejudicial to the party is likely to be taken before such final decision is given.'[159] The ICJ explained further in the *Land and Maritime Dispute* as follows:

> Whereas this power to indicate provisional measures has as its object to preserve the respective rights of the Parties, pending a decision of the Court, and presupposes that irreparable prejudice shall not be caused to rights which are the subject of dispute in judicial proceedings; whereas it follows that the Court must be concerned to preserve by such measures the rights which may subsequently be adjudged by the Court to belong either to the Applicant or

---

157 Note, for instance, that estimates of deaths from the Eritrea–Ethiopia boundary dispute alone run into about 300,000 lives.
158 Igor V. Karaman, *Dispute Resolution in the Law of the Sea* (Netherlands: Martinus Nijhoff and Brill, 2012), p. 199.
159 *Passage through the Great Belt (Finland v. Denmark)*. See opinion of Judges Treves and Paik, para. 17. Chandrasekhara also reiterated that the requirement of urgency is indeed imposed by Article 290 (1) of the LOSC.

to the Respondent; and whereas such measures are only justified if there is urgency.[160]

It may in fact be the case that the interim measure of protection will emanate from a process that is less adjudicative even where a judicial determination of the dispute is in process. This arose in the Cameroon–Nigeria case where the ICJ noted (in para. 37) that:

> mediation has been undertaken to bring about a cease-fire between the armed forces of the Parties and whereas, following the discussions between the Ministers for Foreign Affairs of Cameroon, Nigeria and Togo, a communiqué announcing the cessation of all hostilities was published on 17 February 1996; whereas this circumstance does not, however, deprive the Court of the rights and duties pertaining to it in the case brought before it.

The Court in course issued out its own interim measures, but it is important to note that the parties availed themselves of a mediated cease-fire before judicial authority had the opportunity to determine the interim measures. Although it is usually the case that courts are more accustomed to issuing injunctive orders and interim measures, clearly mediated interim measures can exist and the important consideration is that urgent help should be brought to bear upon the parties to prevent unnecessary and unfortunate deaths. The operative thinking is reflected in the Yoruba saying: 'If a man sees a snake and a woman kills it, all is well and in order, as long as the snake is quickly killed'. It matters very little whether interim measures emanate from courts or by means of ADR such as mediation or even negotiations. What does matter is for such necessary reliefs to be procured in good time.

---

160 *Case Concerning the Land and Maritime Boundary Between Cameroon and Nigeria (Cameroon v. Nigeria), Request for Indication of Provisional Measures Order* of 15 March 1996, para. 35.

13 Role and scope for involvement of Africa's developed northern partners in the settlement of boundary disputes

13.1 Role and scope of involvement of the European Union in African boundary dispute resolution

There is some value in examining the merit of involvement of the European Union as a whole in African boundary dispute resolution as opposed to involvement by individual states, particularly those that had a lively colonial history. We have already established the possibility of independent states mediating in boundary disputes but there is much to be said for the general reluctance of erstwhile colonial states to engage directly with territorial disputes in Africa. There is an undeniable perceived sense of perfidy about the turnaround from mutual trading arrangements and treaties of protection to a complete grab of the land, lives and souls of African peoples under colonialism which runs deeper than is acknowledged in literature. Such feelings of mistrust will remain for many more years and continue to colour the involvement of European states with Africa. This is more so since the vestiges of colonialism by European powers still exist until the present and serve as a constant reminder of the imperialism suffered by African states. For instance, Spain continues to hold and defend its right to ownership of Melilla, an African enclave bordering between Spain and Morocco.[1] The Arab world is equally viewed with suspicion as a result of their own colonial interventions in African territories predating the intervention of Western Europe and the 'missionary' fervour of the Islamic faith in Africa.[2]

In many senses the EU does see itself and is seen as a force for good in border disputes both in its own region and internationally. EU actors engage in border

---

1 Donnan and Wilson (1999), op.cit., p. 68. The truth, it will appear, is that this is the only way much of EU foreign policy plays out not only with Russia but many countries in the Middle East, Latin America and beyond. The days of hegemonic power relations based on subjectivism of western values are fast receding to a perhaps more balanced world.
2 The Yoruba description of Islam in their language is 'Imale', a derivative of 'Imo lile' or forceful faith/knowledge. Note may be taken of the role that Christian missionaries played in the preparation of the colonial project. It is ironic that the a lot of the divisions afflicting Africa today are as a result of increasing conflicts between adherents of Islam and Christian faiths in many African states today. See further Harry H. Johnston, *A History of the Colonization of Africa by Alien Races* (Cambridge: Cambridge University Press, 1899), pp. 283–284, also available at https://archive.org/stream/cu31924074488234#page/n9/mode/1up, accessed 1 February 2015.

problems typically by attempting to restrain conflicting parties through normative influences (including the normative authority of EU institutions), the legitimacy (and domestic resonance) of EU norms and identification of conflict parties with the EU. The EU's constructed 'goodness' of intervention in non-African cases of border conflict has been powerful in some cases but not in others.[3] Crucially EU actors do not merely reproduce a positive image of the EU episteme: this epistemic community works discourses out, or animates them, using narrative technique and historical and exploratory attitudes. The EU itself has a policy which stipulates that countries joining should be completely devoid of open border disputes with their neighbours. Identifiable best practices include quick and pragmatic attention to emerging tensions by EU institutions as well as the promotion of closer cultural ties between European states and investment in the rural areas of Europe. These templates could be transferred to African states via the AU. This can be done by means of technical cooperation, capacity development training and funding of delimitation and demarcation activities. There are also recognisable failures in 'the force for good' approach of the EU in boundary matters such as in relation to EU–Russian relations.[4]

13.2 Role and scope of involvement of the United States in African boundary dispute resolution

The US currently occupies a unique position in the life and development of most developing countries but even more so in relation to Africa. The position of the US as an outsider to the small circle of erstwhile European powers that engaged with Africa from the 1880s to the 1970s under stark colonial relationships allows the US to play the role of an arbiter in African affairs. The fact that anti-colonial feelings in Africa are largely unaddressed to the US can be put to great effect by the US in that it increases the scope for peaceful intervention with African boundary disputes. Thus, the US is more capable of mediating between disputing states in Africa without the awkwardness on many levels that logically follows attempts by ex-colonisers to do the same. American presidents tend to be very

---

3 Diez *et al.*, op.cit., p. 219.
4 Critics of EU foreign policy worry about the high status offered to Russia through regular EU–Russia summits. They insist that this close relationship is surely difficult to justify in light of the 'force for good' posture of the EU, given Russia's alleged deficient democratic and/or human rights performances compared with the supposedly higher standards of Western European states. See A. Makarychev, "Energy Relations in Russia: Administration, Politics and Security", Vol. 57, *International Social Science Journal* (2005), pp. 107–117. It would appear that because of Russia's strategic importance, the EU regularly puts aside its projection as a 'good' power and adopts an inconsistent strategy towards its neighbour to the north. As Timothy Garton Ash argues:

> So long as we remain dependent on their energy and raw-material supplies, our political leverage over such states will be limited. Russia is a major worry, especially for us in Europe, and we need a more coordinated EU policy towards our Eurasian neighbour . . . but we also need to keep articulating our own values, not parroting theirs.
>
> Timothy Garton Ash, "Islam in Europe", *The New York Review of Books* (5 October 2006), p. 27

popular in Africa with some like Obama and Clinton having near fervent cult following and immense moral capital. Such personalities and some former Secretaries of States would also be ideal as offerors of Good Offices when boundary disputes break out between African states.

However, the US has not been playing any significant role in African boundary dispute resolution but has chosen to be more involved in another notorious territorial and boundary conflict in the Middle East – i.e. the Palestinian–Israeli conflict. Ironically, the US has received less accolades in this area. Rather it has been stated that: 'The failed policies of the U.S. administrations are the result of an inherent contradiction in its position as Israel's strongest ally and an "honest broker" in the conflict'.[5]

---

5 Abu Marzook Mousa, "What Hamas is Seeking", *The Washington Post*, 31 January 2006, available at www.washingtonpost.com/wp-dyn/content/article/2006/01/30/AR2006013001209.html, accessed 15 December 2013; Tamimi, op.cit., p. 271.

14 The problem of costs and the relevance of legal aid in African boundary dispute resolution

Funding delimitation, demarcation and other implementation activities

No matter the preferred route adopted by African states in dealing with their boundary disputes, costs will accrue quite significantly. A legal expert put it succinctly:

> Boundary making is an expensive exercise. The need for proper budgeting is paramount if the exercise is to succeed. Detailed estimates of costs in order to arrive at budget figures are highly desirable. Members of a Boundary Commission may typically be given the responsibility for producing such estimates. The need for accurate costing will become even more accurate when dispute resolution processes are invoked.[1]

Costs are doubtless a factor deterring many African states with limited resources from addressing their delimitation and demarcation needs. Where the matter has been allowed to fester long enough to demand third party adjudication or arbitration the costs of appearing before international courts are certainly not negligible.[2] It has been recognised that 'the cost of boundary delimitation will run into the millions of dollars (US Currency) if pursued via negotiations and may exceed tens of millions of dollars if achieved via third party settlement, as in the Barbados-Trinidad and Tobago case'.[3] The AUBP must as a matter of utmost priority keep the economics of two separate sets of issues in mind. First, the cost of resolving disputes through the various mechanisms known to law discussed earlier; second, the costs of actual demarcation. The imperative actions are again two fold. First, continental bodies such as the AU may position themselves to

---

1 Daniel, op.cit., p. 222.
2 David H. Anderson, "Trust Funds in International Litigation" in N. Ando, E. McWhinney and R. Wolfrum (eds), *Liber Amicorum Judge Shigeru Oda* (Leiden, the Netherlands: Kluwer Law International, 2002), pp. 793–794; P. Bekker, "International Legal Aid in Practice: The ICJ Trust Fund", Vol. 87, *American Journal of International Law* (1993), p. 659; Charles C. Okolie, *International Law Perspectives of Developing Countries: The Relationship of Law and Economic Development to Basic Human Rights* (Lagos: MOK Publishers, 1978) pp. 50–51.
3 Clifford Griffin, *The Race for Fisheries and Hydrocarbons in the Caribbean Basin* (Kingston, Jamaica: Ian Randle Publishers, 2007), p. 152.

provide free or subsidised services in both dispute settlement procedures as well as in demarcation activities. This may involve the creation of a well-endowed trust fund for such purposes. Second, the AU may have to provide the diplomatic clout necessary to reach concerned African states in order to access the existing trust funds and/or attract fresh sources.

Just as in the municipal setting, where the financially well-to-do find it easier to institute civil action to address their grievances and defend themselves in criminal cases, so also it is in the society of nations that those with better financial resources appear to have a better chance at seeking adequate justice. It is, therefore, the case that some states cannot litigate or arbitrate for financial reasons. For as Castaneda rightly noted of litigation before the ICJ, it makes little difference whether the case is a contentious suit or one requiring an advisory opinion, the costs are comparable and frequently too high.[4] Litigation at the ICJ, depending on the nature of the dispute, may require several millions of dollars even before the cost of implementation is considered. In many cases the cost of implementation will be several times fold the cost of litigation. Maritime boundary litigation, for instance, involves exceptionally high open and hidden costs.[5] There would usually be the need for experts on geography, cartography, oceanography, geologists and other specialists in addition to costs for exhibits, memorials and lawyers. Land boundary demarcation may also be equally prohibitive. Acquisition of satellite imagery, ground surveys, mapping and erection of boundary pillars would require immense sums to accomplish. In many cases both land and maritime issues are at stake from litigation through to implementation. Even for wealthy nations there is the problem of competing priorities and considerations of opportunity cost.[6] The implications are certainly direr in relation to developing states.

The administrative cost of instituting proceedings at an International Court is just the beginning of a series of serious expenditure. Ironically in comparison to

---

[4] Max Planck Institute for Comparative Public Law and International Law, *Judicial Settlement of International Disputes: An International Symposium* (New York: Max Planck Institute, 1974), p. 30.

[5] Ironically because of the relatively daunting problem of costs facing African states, particularly in the delimitation of their maritime boundaries, decision-taking suffers from a unique double handicap. Where the maritime sea does not disclose apparent mineral riches, negotiations are hindered due to the absence of a compelling case to invest scarce financial resources and the time of few available technical experts in light of competing national and bilateral issues. Where, however, studies reveal a rise in prospects of offshore drilling for oil and other mineral resources found on the subsoil and seabed, and possibly the Extended Continental Shelf, then negotiations get bogged down in political wrangling and disputes. The net effect of this paradox, therefore, is that the delimitation of the African seas may in time prove to be the most intractable part of the work of the AUBP.

[6] The Australian government, for instance, has on many occasions resorted to US law firms to advise it on matters relating to litigation before the WTO as a result of a dearth of home grown expertise. US firms have also been resorted to where there is a need to research into domestic law aspects of the US domestic sugar programme and to prepare the lamb meat case. Department of Foreign Affairs and Trade, Australia's Relationship With The World Trade Organization (WTO): Submission to the Joint Standing Committee on Treaties by the Department of Foreign Affairs and Trade, September 2000, p. 58, available at www.dfat.gov.au/trade/negotiations/wto/aust_wto.pdf, accessed 21 August 2013.

the hidden financial cost of litigation, the administrative fees appear modest. In the PCA a non-refundable registration fee of €2,000 is accruable to the Institution to perfect the commencement of proceedings.[7] However, the cost of the services of each key staff can go up to as much as €250 per hour. Several Registry staff may be needed at a time and the hours to be paid for may run into thousands of hours. This, of course, does not include the cost of use of facilities for each period of use and of course the remuneration of arbitrators. It is usual that each party to a commercial dispute pays for the arbitrator(s) they nominate whereas the cost of the presiding arbitrator/umpire will be shared between the parties. Since the average PCA case (just like the World Court) lasts several years it becomes clear then that the costs of proceedings at The Hague is also prohibitive. For poorer and developing states, the risk of defeat might carry far greater financial weight especially since it is for sure that 'there was always a winner and a loser' in any such legal encounter.[8] Thus, the problem of costs needs urgent attention, especially as these costs are, as should be expected, on the increase.

The first 50 years of the World Court's life was characterised by a relatively poor number of appearances by developing states. It was thought that a major reason for the poor turnout at the Court is that some states just cannot afford the rising cost of justice. It is, thus, no wonder that the Secretary-General of the UN in 1989 announced the creation of a legal aid scheme to financially assist developing states in litigating before the ICJ.[9] It comes as no surprise either that the first beneficiaries of this very laudable scheme were two African states involved in a boundary dispute.[10] The trust fund idea might also have been inspired by

---

7 The designation of an appointing authority pursuant to the UNCITRAL Arbitration Rules requires a non-refundable processing fee of €750. Acting as an Appointing Authority Pursuant to the UNCITRAL Arbitration Rules requires a non-refundable processing fee of €1,500. The Schedule of Fees of the PCA including the fees structure for guest tribunals that use the PCA facilities are available at the PCA website: www.pca-cpa.org/showpage.asp?pag_id=1028, accessed 1 February 2015.

8 Max Planck Institute for Comparative Public Law and International Law, *Judicial Settlement of International Disputes*, op.cit., p. 30.

9 This was based upon a directive of the UN General Assembly. See Provisional Verbatim Record of the Forty-Third Meeting, 44 UN GAOR (43rd Mtg.) at 7–11, UN Doc. A/44/PV.43, at 7–11 (1989). It is necessary to note laudable initiatives such as the Secretary-General's Trust Fund to Assist States in the Settlement of Disputes through the International Court of Justice (UN Doc. A/59/372). The Trust Fund was established in 1989 under the Financial Regulations and Rules of the United Nations. It provides financial assistance to states for expenses incurred in connection with a dispute submitted to the Court by way of a special agreement or the execution of a judgment of the ICJ resulting from such a special agreement. The Fund is open to all states parties to the Statute of the Court, as well as non-member states that have complied with the conditions stipulated in Security Council Resolution 9 (1946).

10 The many accounts of where the greatest impetus for the introduction of the various legal aid schemes came from attest to the success of the idea. Many states, writers and jurists have been known to jostle for primacy of position in the chronology of the creation of the schemes. The non-aligned states majority of which are indigent sensibly pushed through the agenda for the creation of a trust fund in order to enhance the use of the Court by member states. Ministerial Meeting of Non-Aligned Countries, UN Doc. A/44/PV.59, at 2 (1989); The Hague Declaration of the Meeting of the Ministers of Foreign Affairs of the Movement of Non-Aligned Countries to Discuss the Issue of Peace and the Rule of Law in International Affairs, UN Doc. A/44/191

Switzerland's commendable $400,000 assistance to Burkina Faso and Mali to help them implement the ICJ boundary decision in the Frontier Dispute Case.[11] In the final analysis, however, it was the UN Secretary-General, Senor Javier Perez de Cuellar, who took the initiative in 1989 to create the Trust Fund.[12] In 2004, the Fund received one joint application from Benin and Niger to defray the expenses incurred in connection with the submission of their boundary dispute to the Court (*Frontier Dispute (Benin/Niger)*). Subsequently, on 24 May of that year, $300,000 was awarded to each applicant to defray the staffing, production and legal expenses incurred in the demarcation of the border of the two countries. In the same year, Finland, Norway and Mexico contributed $34,665 to the Fund.

Similarly the PCA has commendably created a Financial Assistance Fund for Developing States.[13] In October 1994, the Administrative Council agreed to establish a Financial Assistance Fund and approved the Terms of Reference and Guidelines for the operation of the Fund. This Fund, to which contributions are made on a voluntary basis, provides financial assistance to qualifying states to enable them to meet, in whole or in part, the costs involved in international arbitration or other means of dispute settlement offered by The Hague Conventions. Qualifying states are state parties to the Conventions of 1899 or 1907 that: (1) have concluded an agreement for the purpose of submitting one or more disputes, whether existing or future, for settlement by any of the means administered by the PCA; and (2) at the time of requesting financial assistance from the fund, are listed on the 'DAC List of Aid Recipients' prepared by the Organisation for Economic Co-operation and Development (OECD). A qualifying state may seek financial assistance from the Fund by submitting a written request to the Secretary-General of the PCA. An independent Board of Trustees decides on the request.[14]

(1989); Bien-Aime, "Enhancing the Role of the World Court: An Examination of the Secretary-General's Trust Fund Proposal", Vol. 22, *New York University Journal of International Law and Practice* (1991), p. 671.

11 *Burkina Faso v Mali* 1987 ICJ Rep. 7 (Nomination of Experts, Order of 9 April 1987). The dispute was so contentious that an outbreak of military hostilities ensued during the case. However, when the Court ruled, the two states found they could not afford the cartographers needed to actually turn the Court's decision into a useable map. Switzerland's financial help supplied the needed experts. See Mary Ellen O'Connell, "International Legal Aid: The Secretary General's Trust Fund to Assist States in the Settlement of Disputes Through the International Court of Justice", in Mark Janis (ed), *International Courts in the Twenty-first Century* (Dordrecht: Martinus Nijhoff, 1992), p. 235.

12 On the occasion of the consideration of the Report of the Court 1989, the Secretary-General announced the initiative to the General Assembly, referring to his responsibility to promote the settlement of disputes by the Court. In a very rare move whereupon there was no proposal, debate or decision in the General Assembly, the Secretary-General established by his own motion a permanent Trust Fund with its own terms of reference. Annex to UN Doc. A/47/444 of 7 October 1992. See also 28 ILM (1989) 1589.

13 Article 47 of the 1907 Convention states:

> With the object of facilitating an immediate recourse to arbitration for international differences, which it has not been possible to settle by diplomacy, the Contracting Powers undertake to maintain the Permanent Court of Arbitration, as established by the First Peace Conference, accessible at all times.

14 PCA Annual Report (2005), p. 7; documents and materials relating to the PCA are available at www.pca-cpa.org.

Since the establishment of the Fund, Norway, Cyprus, the United Kingdom, South Africa, the Netherlands and Costa Rica have made contributions, and four grants of assistance have been made: one to a Central Asian state, one to an Asian state and two to African states. These grants have allowed the parties to defray the costs of arbitration.[15]

Even after litigation is complete it is clear that the costs of implementation are significant. First, there are structures of implementation to be created and the time scale for implementation is not negligible. The normal practice is that both states contribute equally towards the entire costs of demarcation and pay incidental costs for visits to sites on their side of the border. In the *Rio Palena Arbitration*, (*Argentina–Chile Frontier Case* (1966)), the two countries split the $168,000 cost of the arbitration.[16] In the Cameroon–Nigeria process the implementation route started in December 2003 and continues until the present. The process is a good example of the high costs of post-judgment demarcation activities. On demarcation alone without reference to the costs of diplomatic activities and party controlled technical costs (surveyors, technical staff and field visits) the amounts spent are over $12 million. To ensure the demarcation of the boundary, both countries had by 2004 contributed the sum of $3 million each. The United Kingdom contributed £1 million while the European Union donated €4.4 million. The total sum so far collected is about $12 million. This sum is currently in a Trust Fund with the United Nations. The costs, however, continue to rise as the demarcation continues and the funds collected diminish in value due to devaluation of the currencies as well as rises in costs of services and equipment. The Eritrea–Ethiopia process is notably one year older and progress between the states has faltered significantly.

---

15 Ibid.
16 "Two Queens to the Rescue", *Time* Magazine, 30 December 1966, available at www.time.com/time/magazine/article/0,9171,901916,00.html, accessed 7 August 2007.

15 Settlment of international boundary disputes by use of force

> If as I believe, man's innumerable territorial expressions are human responses to an imperative lying with equal force on mocking birds and men, then human self-estimate is due for radical revision. And it may come to us as the strangest thoughts that the bond between a man and the soil he walks on should be more powerful than his bond with the woman he sleeps with. Even so, in a rough, preliminary way we may test the supposition with a single question: How many men have you known of, in your lifetime, who died for their country? And how many for a woman?[1]

Boundary conflicts tend to be 'radical disagreements'. Radical disagreements according to conflict studies tend to be located at the intersection of the three great realms of human difference, human discourse and human conflict.[2] In these types of intense conflicts the parties and other stakeholders mind very much which outcome prevails. Of these sorts of conflicts it has been said that when given the power to do so the parties would ride 'roughshod over the others dearest interests' and the conflict 'can go on for years, if not decades, during which time unimaginable destruction and damage to human lives and life-hope is – often unnecessarily – inflicted'.[3] The survival value that territory brings to all species of primates sometimes makes the defence of territory by use of force not only a possibility but unfortunately quite often a necessity. The territorial imperative applies to most biological entities and human beings are not essentially different. Fight over territory is a crucial fact of nature and it has been recognised that:

> So it goes with the Gentoo species in Grahamsland, where the male defending his four-foot territory will fight anybody including his mate, unless she makes the proper bow at the border. So it is with the chin-strap, also in Grahamsland, who like the albatross returns season after season to the same site and will evict all comers who seek to dispute him.[4]

---

1 Ardrey, op.cit., p. 18.
2 Ramsbotham, op.cit., p. 15.
3 Ibid., Preface, p. xi.
4 Ardrey, op.cit., pp. 372–373.

As James Crawford helpfully reminds us, the prohibition of the use of force enshrined in Article 2, paragraph 4, of the Charter of the United Nations against the territorial integrity or political independence of other states does not affect the right of self-defence against armed attack under Article 51.[5] In an ideal world, therefore, there will be no wars over territories and boundaries. If all states only acted defensively in their use of force there will be no aggressor that uses force to claim territory or to adjust territorial boundaries. But we are not yet living in an ideal world and on a frequent basis the use of force is still used to settle territorial, boundary and border issues.

Oye Cukwurah sums it up quite beautifully when he wrote in 1967 that '[n]otwithstanding the position in law, by far the most important lesson to be drawn from this state of affairs is that force is still, rather irresistibly, a dominant feature of territorial and boundary disputes'.[6] For this reason the right to defend state territory from encroachment by an armed aggressor is sacrosanct. As a matter of fact other states may be permitted to come to the aid of a state that is lawfully acting in the self-defence of its territory and 'assistance by (other) states to local insurgents in a self-determination unit may be permissible' (parenthesis added).[7] For these reasons the use of force in resolution of boundary issues would more likely than not continue to be a feature of international relations.

Indeed war may arise out of the need to impose a solution on one or more disputants after a REC or continental body has completed painstaking and peaceful diplomacy and has failed in its attempt to put an end to the conflict and needs to impose a solution or implement the result of a determinative process such as judgment implementation. The SADC Protocol on Politics, Defence and Security Cooperation empowers the SADC to take military action against any member states where peaceful means of resolving a conflict are unsuccessful (Articles 2 (f) and 11 (3c)). The Chairperson of the Organ on Politics, Defence and Security Co-operation acting on the advice of the Ministerial Committee may recommend to the Summit that enforcement action be taken against one or more disputant parties. The SADC Summit shall, however, only resort to enforcement action: (a) as a matter of last resort and (b) in accordance with Article 53 of the Charter of the United Nations, in which case it will act only with the authorisation of the UN Security Council (Article 11 (3d)).

If the territorial invasion comes from a state outside the region, external military action will also appear to be possible through 'collective security arrangements' to be agreed upon in a Mutual Defence Pact among the state parties (Article 11 (3e)). The exercise of the right of individual or collective self-defence shall be immediately reported to the United Nations Security Council and to the Central Organ of the Organisation of African Unity Mechanism for Conflict Prevention, Management and Resolution (Article 11 (4e)).[8]

---

5 Crawford (2006), op.cit., p. 131.
6 Cukwurah, op.cit., p. 7.
7 Crawford (2006), op.cit., p. 147.
8 See further our discussions earlier relating to the law and practice of conflict and dispute management in the SADC.

Nevertheless the presumption against the independence of entities and territory acquired by the use of force is very strong and international law is primed against the unlawful use of force in furtherance of a claim to territory and even statehood. Thus, belligerent occupation and illegal annexation does not affect in any real sense the continuity of the trespassed state.[9]

15.1 Retorsion, retaliation and war

The use of force in international boundary disputes does not always necessarily involve destructive physical force. It may involve any form of undisguised means of constraint. This may be by way of retorsion, reprisals and open warfare. Measures of retorsion are usually mild constraining events and actions; yet the development of international law (including treaty obligations) limits the scope of retorsion as well since the freedom of action of the states involved is reduced *de facto*.[10] Examples of retorsions are legion in international affairs but such actions usually do not interfere with any legal obligation and the aim generally is to reduce the facilities, easements and rights granted to a state and/or its nationals diplomatically, economically or commercially. An offended state may reduce diplomatic representation, close a border (or reduce the hours lawful passage may occur) or suspend flight agreements. Israel, for instance, has at various times imposed economic sanctions and withheld fuel supplies and electricity on the Gaza Strip.[11]

Reprisals would typically involve a coercive action which violates principles of law but which is based on alleged previous violations of the state against which it is directed. Typically in these sorts of cases the law is broken twice: first by the state against which reprisal is directed and second by the state conducting the reprisals themselves. In boundary cases reprisals may take the form of non-application of trade agreements and applicable law-making treaties, occupation of the territory of a state, bombardment by air or blockade by naval forces, temporary seizure of merchant ships.[12] In the long period of dispute over the Bakassi Peninsula both Cameroon and Nigeria engaged in various acts of reprisals.

Outright war has been described as 'an armed struggle between two or more States, implying the possible use of all weapons not forbidden by international law and imposing on other states the rights and duties of neutrals'.[13] Truth regularly becomes the first casualty of the event of boundary wars. Each side will typically claim to have a legitimate basis to have embarked upon the use of force and as a writer correctly noted: 'The main problem is to decide who is the aggressor'.[14]

---

9 Crawford (2006), op.cit., pp. 133, 688–689.
10 Reuter, op.cit., pp. 174–175.
11 Abraham Bell, "International Law and Gaza: The Assault on Israel's Right to Self-Defense", Jerusalem Center for Public Affairs, 28 January 2008, available at http://jcpa.org/article/international-law-and-gaza-the-assault-on-israel%E2%80%99s-right-to-self-defense/#sthash.u9ZhSizz.dpuf, accessed 10 July 2014.
12 Reuter, op.cit., p. 175.
13 Ibid., pp. 175–176.
14 Ibid., p. 177.

When states have advertently or inadvertently strayed into a state of military reprisals and/or war it is important that they pay attention to the full gamut of the applicable laws of war and other pertinent aspects of international law. Since the middle of the nineteenth century there has been the introduction of the *jus in bello* or the rules of the laws of war and all military operations ought to begin by a formal declaration of war.[15]

Although some writers have argued that 'it is not always in the international interest to halt armed conflict at the earliest possible moment',[16] it is usually the case that regional bodies or the United Nations will quickly step in to intervene once armed conflict begins between two or more states. We have already shown how the ECOWAS, SADC and the UN Security Council, among others, very quickly busy themselves in a range of procedures and steps to intervene for the purpose of putting an end to the hostilities.

States must cease all hostilities when competent international authorities, like the UN, regional organisations and international courts or arbitral panels issue interim orders of control. In the Cameroon–Nigeria case, provisional measures were unanimously issued by the World Court to the effect that:

> Both Parties should ensure that no action of any kind, and particularly no action by their armed forces, is taken which might prejudice the rights of the other in respect of whatever judgment the Court may render in the case, or which might aggravate or extend the dispute before it.[17]

Often the Security Council will be the body that calls for a halt to the fighting, leading the parties to issue cease-fire orders.[18] A cease-fire suspends acts of violence by military or paramilitary forces usually resulting from the intervention of competent third parties. Cease-fires are preliminary and provisional with the aim of providing breathing space so that the competent organs of the UN or any of the regional or sub-regional bodies discussed earlier in this book can negotiate

---

15 The laws of war include: The Hague Regulations of 1899 and 1907 that set out the rules guiding the conduct of hostilities; the four Geneva Conventions of 1949, which protect war victims – the sick and wounded (first); the shipwrecked (second); prisoners of war (third); and civilians in the hands of an adverse party and, to a limited extent, all civilians in the territories of the countries in conflict (fourth) – and the Additional Protocols of 1977, which define key terms such as combatants, contain detailed provisions to protect non-combatants, medical transports and civil defence, and prohibit practices such as indiscriminate attack. Note also the London Naval Declaration 1909 – See Karma Nabulsi, Jus ad Bellum/Jus in Bello available on the website Crimes of War at www.crimesofwar.org/a-z-guide/jus-ad-bellum-jus-in-bello/#sthash.qZgIxce7.dpuf, accessed 12 July 2014; Carnegie Endowment, *The Hague Conventions and Declarations of 1899 and 1907, accompanied by tables of signatures, ratifications and adhesions of the various powers, and texts of reservations*, James Brown Scott (ed.), (New York: Oxford University Press, 1915); Reuter, op.cit., p. 176.
16 Bailey, op.cit., p. 3.
17 Paragraph 49 (1) Order of 15 March 1996 Request for the Indication of Provisional Measures; *Land and Maritime Boundary* case.
18 The primacy of the Security Council is based on the Charter provisions by which the Council has been tasked with the 'primary responsibility' for maintaining international peace and security (Article 24 (1)). The Securtiy Council may, however, convoke the General Assembly if it deems it fit to do so (Article 20).

a truce of a more detailed and durable kind.[19] Although boundary dispute wars and military actions may be of ill-defined beginnings and even though there may be no clear or decisive military outcome, the demand of international law on the subject is that hostilities must be formally suspended. When competent international bodies call for the end to armed hostilities in boundary disputes there is usually a proposal or demand that forces should withdraw behind national lines and where that remains unclear back to positions occupied before the outbreak of war or other fighting, even if the territory thus vacated is not to be re-occupied by the other side.[20] Good practice will usually dictate in such circumstances that armistice lines be marked on the ground. Demilitarised zones from which all combatants, weapons, military equipment and military installations are installed may also be created as in the case of the 25-km-wide demilitarised Temporary Security Zone (TSZ) created for the Eritrea–Ethiopia process.[21] There may also be cease-fire and armistice demarcation lines, which are not initially permanent boundaries and are not intended to prejudice the rights, claims or position of the concerned parties. However, much care is to be taken when lines are demarcated, not just because it may appear indicative of the *de facto* boundary in territorial and boundary disputes but because they are certain to seem arbitrary to the local civilian population.[22] It is also good practice that armistice lines and demilitarised zones should be supervised by peace-keepers. Peace-keeping forces would typically involve police and/or military contingents who are placed within the appropriate zone/territory with the agreement of the host country/countries. Peace-keeping forces in such scenarios are 'not there to impose a solution or even to enforce the cessation of hostilities: its function is partly symbolic'.[23]

Apart from the obligations to end the use of force as soon as possible by operation of international rules (cease-fire, truce or armistice) states engaging in armed conflict over territory must, furthermore, avoid the violation of other prohibitions of *jus cogens* such as the creation of a system of apartheid or the perpetration of genocide.

The right to use force to repel territorial attacks is not an invitation to frivolous, gratuitous or malicious use of force in such circumstances. The possibility of

---

19 Bailey, op.cit., p. 37; S. Rosenne, *Israel's Armistice Agreements with the Arab States: A Judicial Interpretation* (Tel Aviv: Blumensteins, 1951), p. 25.
20 This was the case in relation to Indonesia (1947 and 1948–1949), Kashmir, Jerusalem, the Negev and Korea. Bailey, op.cit., pp. 365–366.
21 A 25-km-wide demilitarised TSZ was set up as part of the signing of the Cessation of Hostilities Agreement in 2000. Jonathan Ewing, "Ethiopia and Eritrea in Turmoil: Implications for Peace and Security in a Troubled Region", 31 March 2011 (Institute for Security Studies (ISS)), p. 2. Armistice and demilitarisation may then be followed by plebiscite. Bailey, op.cit., p. 232. Note also our recommendation below for the increasing use of plebiscites in the resolution of African boundary disputes (infra 18.6: Appropriate Recourse to the Use of Plebiscites).
22 In the Israel–Jordan armistice agreement, provision was made for possible revisions of the demarcation line by later agreement between the parties. SCOR, 4th year, Supplement no. 1 s/1302/Rev. 1, Article VIII; Bailey, op.cit., p. 229.
23 Bailey, op.cit., p. 369.

resorting to use of force is, thus, within very strict limits in international law. These rules concerning the use of force constitute part of the peremptory norms and the international community has with remarkable consistency refused to accept the legal validity of acts done or situations that are brought about by the use of force.[24] This has moved Crawford to convincingly conclude that if ever effective territorial entities were to have their status regulated by international law, it would in time be so regulated by the rules relating to the use of force.[25] In relation to at least one African situation it has been helpfully clarified that the treatment of POWs captured during a war relating to boundaries are governed by the normal rules of international humanitarian law even where one of the parties is not a party to the applicable humanitarian treaty.

Even a demarcation line within a state may become a frontier for the purpose of prohibition of the use of force. For instance, the Friendly Relations Declaration of 1970 demands of every state that they exercise:

> the duty to refrain from the threat or use of force to violate international lines of demarcation, such as armistice lines, established by or pursuant to an international agreement to which it is a party or which it is otherwise bound to respect. Nothing in the foregoing shall be construed as prejudicing the positions of the parties concerned with regard to the status and effects of such lines under their special regimes or as affecting their temporary character.

---

24 See Vienna Convention on the Law of Treaties, Articles 52 and 53. Note also the application of Article 52 in the *Icelandic Fisheries case First Phase*, ICJ Rep. (1973), pp. 3, 19.
25 Crawford (2006), op.cit., p. 132. Cf Malcolm N. Shaw, "Peoples, Territorialism and Boundaries", Vol. 8, *European Journal of International Law*, No. 3 (1997), pp. 478, 500.

16 Re-evaluation of the *uti possidetis* principle in light of the African experience

16.1 *Uti possidetis* in Africa: a problematic doctrine?

The origins of *uti possidetis* in European legal history date back to Roman law in which it designated an interdict of the *Praetor*, by which the disturbance of the existing state of possession of immovable property as between two individuals was forbidden.[1] *Uti possidetis* as a term was first coined with reference to the need to deal with the transformation of Spanish colonial possessions in South America into independent states. Devised in its inception to moderate boundary affairs 'from the Rio Grande to Cape Horn', *uti possidetis* provided convenience and expediency in maintaining the existing administrative lines and divisions applicable to the new states as at the 'critical date' of their independence. In the case of South America this was 1810 and for Central America it was 1821. Essentially, therefore, it fossilised for the emergent modern states the old administration boundaries set by Spain. The doctrine found new expression in Africa when a similar process of serial independence from European states occurred and the African leaders in their own decisiveness adopted the historic Cairo Resolution AHG/Res. 16(1) in 1964 whereby they undertook to 'respect the borders existing on their achievement of national independence'. In this way they declared their acceptance of the old colonial boundaries as sacrosanct and according to a predominant view, thus, signed up to the *uti possidetis* doctrine. Article 3, paragraph 3 of the Organisation of African Unity Charter underlies this further by mandating 'Respect for the sovereignty and territorial integrity of each State and for its inalienable right to independent existence.'

As a result the significance and crucial importance of the whole gamut of colonial acts, practices and treaties relating to African boundaries became inseparable from any legal handling of boundary and territorial issues in Africa.[2]

---

1 J. B. Moore, Memorandum on Uti Possidetis, Costa Rica-Panama Arbitration, printed at Rossalyn, Virginia, 1913 and cited in Cukwurah, op.cit., p. 113; Boggs, op.cit., p. 79 and in Charles Cheney Hyde, *International Law*, vol. I, (New York: Little, Brown and Company, 1945) p. 500.
2 See, for instance, the *Burkina Faso–Mali* case; Botswana–Namibia; Ethiopia–Eritrea; Cameroon–Nigeria. See also Daniel, op.cit., p. 245; see AU, *From Barriers to Bridges: Collection of Official Texts on African Borders from 1963 to 2012*, 2nd edition (Addis Ababa: Commission of the African Union, Department of Peace and Security, 2013), p. 17.

The majority of African states appear to have taken the view that the existing borders have to be maintained to forestall practical attempts at reshaping the map of Africa because of the fear that boundary revisionism will produce disastrous effects. The *uti possidetis* principle certainly has its values, the head point of which lies in international policy – chiefly *Quieta non movere*, by which legal reasoning dictates that it is better not to disturb quiet things. The principle is generally regarded as playing a major role in the prevention of conflicts. The 'stability of borders means peace' and this argument recognises that frequent changes to borders can lead to instability and encourage resorting to the use of force in the international system. Stability, often meaning continuation, of boundaries is in this way understood as fundamental to international order and peace.[3]

President Tsiranana of Madagascar captured the cautious mood in the following words:

> It is no longer possible, nor desirable to modify the boundaries of Nations, on the pretext of racial, religious or linguistic criteria. . . . Indeed, should we take race, religion or language as criteria for setting our boundaries, a few States in Africa would be blotted from the map.[4]

The Malian President on his part bluntly asserted: '[W]e must take Africa as it is, and we must renounce any territorial claims, if we do not wish to introduce what we might call black imperialism in Africa.'[5] In the same vein the Ethiopian Prime Minister stated: 'It is in the interest of all Africans now to respect the frontiers drawn on the maps, whether they are good or bad, by the former colonizers.'[6]

Some scholars, however, correctly note that the cautious attitude of African statesmen has not always been there and that this view is not universal. There were well-argued positions expressed in the pre-independence era that rejected what was regarded as generational wrongs expressed in European boundary delimitation.[7] Prior to independence the predominant mood of scholars and political thinkers on the continent was that of general dissatisfaction with the colonial boundaries that had created a variety of European delimited territories. Malcom Shaw acknowledged that 'It appeared that a general campaign of frontier rearrangement was under consideration.'[8] It is true that African nationalists took a very dim view of the existing frontiers and the boundary treaties that set them up. The treaties were seen as fraudulent documents and the

---

3 M. C. Johanson, *Self-Determination and Borders: The Obligation to Show Consideration for the Interests of Others* (Åbo: Åbo Akademi University Press, 2004), p. 24.
4 Proceedings of the Summit Conference of the Independent African States, vol. 1, section 2, CIAS/GEN/INF/14.
5 Ibid., CIAS/GEN/INF/33.
6 Ibid., CIAS/GEN/INF/43.
7 Susanne Lalonde, *Determining Boundaries in a Conflicted World: The Role of Uti Possidetis* (Montreal: McGill-Queens University Press, 2002), p. 115; Shaw, *Territory in Africa*, op.cit., p. 183.
8 Shaw, Ibid.

boundaries as 'humiliating reminders of the way in which their territories had been carved up by the colonial powers'.[9] Professor Allott took the view that some of the boundary treaties were outright forgeries and where they were genuine the traditional rulers that executed them had little clue, if any, as to their actions.[10] Boundary readjustment was not the undesirable concept it became soon after the era of cascading independence for African states. President Nkrumah of Ghana, a leading Pan Africanist of his era, argued forcefully for 'eradicating the artificial divisions and boundaries which are responsible for the balkanisation of our continent'.[11] A decade after both Cameroon and Nigeria had gained their independence, Chime lamented what he saw as the failure of African states to abolish the 'artificial' frontiers which the colonisers had devised for Africa.[12] In a sense modern African writers and activists arguing for a radical departure from the tradition of respect for inherited European delimitation and who champion recognition of the rights of peoples to independence irrespective of existing political boundaries are simply revisiting the premise of earlier scholars like Chime. It is in this category that calls for the independence of Bakassi may be placed.[13]

In truth, however, the sanctity of colonial treaties in many international proceedings is arguably an unfortunate legal fiction. There are indeed many convincing reasons not to support a full adherence to the *uti possidetis* principle. In many cases the insufficiency or unreliability of these very treaties are the causes of the entire disagreement or conflict. As Johanson correctly points out: 'stability is not necessarily maintained by preserving the status quo or by, as seems to have been the case so far, considering the functionality of boundaries as unrelated to peace'.[14] Indeed uniformity by reference to the *uti possidetis* principle is gradually being unmasked as a poor panacea to conflict and constituting 'a dangerous substitute for contextualisation'.[15] Authors like Johanson and Okomu helpfully invite us to consider that it is not changes to boundaries that matter as much as the methods by which changes are brought about.[16] Furthermore they correctly maintain that peace can best be brought about not by prohibiting border changes but rather by establishing 'clear guidelines as to when and how discussion

---

9 Lalonde, op.cit., p. 115; see Shaw, *Territory in Africa*, op.cit., p. 183.
10 See Olajide Aluko, "African Boundary Problems, Review", *The Journal of Modern African Studies* (1970), p. 314.
11 President Nkrumah, quoted in Lalonde, op.cit., p. 116.
12 Olajide Aluko, "African Boundary Problems, Review", *The Journal of Modern African Studies* (1970), p. 315.
13 The Bakassi Movement for Self-Determination (BAMOSD) was founded in 2006 and fights for the independence of Bakassi, a territory located between Nigeria and Cameroon. Heidelberg Institute for International Conflict Research, University of Heidelberg, *Conflict Barometer 2009: Crises – Wars – Coups d'État – Negociations – Mediations – Peace Settlements. 18th Annual Conflict Analysis* (2009); Djat Mpayon, "Les Bakassi Boys font règner la terreur", afrik.com, 8 September 2008, available at www.afrik.com/article15089.html, accessed 18 October 2014.
14 Johanson, op.cit., p. 24.
15 Ibid.
16 Ibid., pp. 24–25; Okomu (2010), op.cit., p. 37.

regarding border changes may be affected.'[17] Okomu for his part also notes that retaining a boundary does not mean that the status quo is actually preserved. The assumption that retaining a boundary is tantamount to maintaining a status quo is reflective of the entire misconception that holds borders as similar, with the same effect on all those affected by it not minding at all their status or functionality.[18]

In relation to the colonial treaties considered definitive in the Ethiopia–Eritrea case a commentator noted:

> These treaties or agreements carried annexes with unclear maps sketching the rough outlines of the border. None of the proposed borders was ever marked on the ground. There was great ambiguity on the names of places and rivers on the maps, some of them occurring more than once.[19]

It must be conceded, however, that the fault does not squarely and entirely lie with the ICJ or PCA, since under the law and practice of international adjudication and arbitration the parties themselves usually formulate the basis of the resolution of their dispute. In this way, responsibility for this fallacy lies with African states since they readily submit their dispute for resolution and identify the applicable laws as colonial treaties. However, two things may be noted. First, the source of the legal advice that is available to or requested by these countries is more often than not foreign and based in Western Europe. Prestigious international law firms keep recycling the same failed legal advice that contemporary African disputes should be resolved by reference solely or principally to colonial treaties of doubtful providence. Second, it may be wondered whether it is not incumbent on international courts to refuse to apply anachronistic or 'dubious treaties' and refuse to make use of clearly irrelevant or inappropriate legal instruments or principles. At the very least an international court should indicate quite clearly in its decision the providence it attaches to the treaties and/or their contents as presented to it by the parties.[20] The argument here is that in reality the Court and the PCA may have been slavish in their acceptance of the bulk of colonial treaties and in according undue respect to their contents. These treaties are applied even in the clearest of cases where they ought to be excluded for various formal and substantive inconsistencies. Not even the clearest contradicting geodetic data

---

17 Johanson, op.cit., p. 25.
18 Okomu (2010), op.cit., p. 37.
19 Abbink, op.cit.
20 In the *Land and Maritime boundary case*, for instance, in response to the Cameroonian application 'to specify definitively' the course of the land boundary as fixed by the relevant instruments of delimitation, the Court had no problem in deciding that:

> contrary to what Cameroon appeared to be arguing at certain stages in the proceedings, the Court cannot fulfil the task entrusted to it in this case by limiting itself to such confirmation. Thus when the actual content of these instruments is the subject of dispute between the parties, the Court in order to specify the course of the boundary in question definitively, is bound to examine them more closely.
>
> (*Supra* Chapter 1, note 1)

obtained by modern GPS or cartographic evidence would appear to be enough ground to offset this apparent bias. In the *Case Concerning the Frontier Dispute* (Burkina Faso/Republic of Mali) the Chamber of the International Court observed that: 'The Chamber cannot uphold the information given by the map where it is contradicted by *other trustworthy information concerning the intentions of the colonial power*' (emphasis added).[21]

It indeed must not be forgotten that even in the limited context of regulating the former Spanish colonies of Latin America the achievements of the *uti possidetis* doctrine has been quite moderate. The experience of the Latin American states was not in tally with the grand expectations of the statesmen who adopted the doctrine as many boundary disputes indeed broke out over time in relation to the same Latin American countries. Cukwurah clearly explains the ensuing chaos when he wrote:

> Uti Possidetis did not solve the problem of delimitation to which it was meant to apply. Uncertainty pervaded the whole proceedings. Claimant States often disagreed as to the exact limits of viceroyaties, captaincies-general, audienceias, presidencias or provincias, which constituted the complex entities of the colonial era.[22]

In the bizarre and bloody Gran Chaco dispute, for instance, Bolivia asserted that the contested territory belonged to it as successor to the Royal Audencia of Charcus and cited the *cedulas* of 1561 and 1563 in support of the claim. Portugal on the other hand disputed this and produced other *cedulas* issued between 1591 and 1789 which show that Spain had considered the territory to be Spanish.[23]

There is persuasiveness to the view that the *uti possidetis* principle ought to be exposed as an ambitious plasterwork to cover deep injustices that have been done to African societies and to perpetuate unrealistic geopolitical creations. It is true that the principle may have provided for a few years of peace but it is based on a legal fiction that colonial borders were created on the basis of pre-existing natural or national geopolitical realities or indeed with the interests of the various African peoples in mind. In reality much of the existing boundaries in Africa were in fact drawn up to preserve ethnic incoherence and to divide and rule. Therefore, the politico-legal fixation upon the operation of *uti possidetis* in relation to Africa must be much more critically applied in practice. African governments are particularly mistaken about the value of the principle. It can be helpful in straightforward cases but not in every case. *Uti possidetis* cannot trump all else. The parties to the Eritrea–Ethiopia dispute and the Commission have failed to perceive this reality.

---

21 *Case Concerning the Frontier Dispute* (Burkina Faso/Republic of Mali), ICJ Rep. (1986), *supra* Chapter 1, note 1.
22 Cukwurah, op.cit., p. 114. See further Gordon Ireland, *Boundaries, Possessions and Conflicts in South America* (Harvard: Harvard University Press, 1938).
23 Cukwurah, op.cit., p. 115.

It was because the colonial borders were not equitably, competently or realistically formulated that conflicts between the parties had broken out periodically as it did. This lack of appreciation of the limits of *uti possidetis* is pervasive; hence, for instance, the arbitrator in the *Bolivia-Peru Award* in 1902 carefully explained that he was not able to find that the line claimed by either of the parties had been established by the evidence and that in reality, the disputed territory was unexplored in 1810 and practically up to the time of the award. It is clearly difficult to see how unexplored territory could have been acquired and, thus, capable of succession.[24]

Second, 'pertinent colonial treaties' continue to occupy a pre-eminent status in the scheme of things that the Commission must employ in its dispute resolution function in this case. Again this is based on the very much-undeserved assumption that colonial treaties always possess legitimacy, that their creation was 'regular' in all respect and that they are beyond reproach in terms of scope as well as content. In reality things cannot be further from the truth. The treaties and instruments dressed up as definitive of the ownership of the Bakassi Peninsula in the *Land and Maritime* case, for instance, were drawn up on the basis of work done by under-funded visiting colonial cartographers with little or no local knowledge. As alleged by Nigeria in its written submissions to the Court in the *Land and Maritime* case they often agree 'to round things up' in order to save themselves from further bother or embarrassment at doing a shoddy job and coming up with unsupportable maps.[25]

We are, thus, in agreement with the analysis offered by Castellino and Allen to the effect that 'not only has this often constituted defeat for "order" in the longer term – so precious to the international community – but it has also negated "development" that the ICJ refers to as being essential to Africa'.[26] According to this analysis *uti possidetis* has a hidden economic cost to Africa. The force of this argument has perhaps not been subjected to intense debate but it is nevertheless a significant thesis which at least deserves serious attention considering that the economic gains that come with the perception of stability is one of the strongest arguments in favour of the adoption of *uti possidetis*. Some authors have indeed drawn a link between the economic underdevelopment faced by countries like Rwanda and Burundi and the intense crisis of ethnic identities and rivalries existing in those states.[27] In other words the inability to debate ethnic and

---

24 G. H. Hackworth, *Digest of International Law*, Vol. 1 (Washington DC, 1906–1939), p. 727.
25 The instruments referred in the Court's decision are the Thomson–Marchand Declaration of 1929–1930, as incorporated in the Henderson–Fleuriau Exchange of Notes of 1931; the Anglo-German Agreements of 12 April 1913, by the British Order in Council of 2 August 1946; and the Anglo-German Agreement of 11 and 12 April 1913. See para. 325 of the Court's judgment. Note that Nigeria and Cameroon gained political independence in 1960.
26 Joshua Castellino and Steve Allen, *Title to Territory in International Law: A Temporal Analysis* (Aldershot: Ashgate Publishing, 2003), p. 23.
27 E. Kolodziej, "Great Powers and Genocide Lessons from Rwanda, Illinois: Program in Arms Control, Disarmament and International Security", Occassional Paper 2000, p. 60 ff.

state boundaries means that the various peoples cannot move on and the only way they can raise their dissent with current boundaries is through ethnic tensions and conflicts.

Thus, it is possible to conclude that *uti possidetis* has not been the immutable solution to all the problems of territorial stability that an economic investor seeking assurances of the permanence of boundaries in Africa may be looking for. Indeed it is better to adopt the view that the doctrine can only provide useful guidance regarding prima facie evidence of boundary delimitation. Essentially an investor must remain aware that with regards to incomplete or contested boundary delimitation, especially in the maritime sector or where natural resources are involved in the area, political process looms large. Political solutions reached on the basis of principles of law and international negotiations have proven to be the most successful strategy for resolving disputes in these areas and not an avid recital or reliance on the *uti possidetis* principle. It has been aptly stated that 'The drawing of boundaries is, in itself, an essentially political event that demonstrates the agreed physical limits to state sovereignty'.[28] It is for this reason that we have considered above the limits of the litigation route to solving boundary problems.

In sum, *uti possidetis* is an idea with very simplistic aims but which has to operate in a complex world for which it is becoming increasingly unsuited. When all is well with a country's boundaries, *uti possidetis* with its snapshot on independence fiction operates like a deemed certificate of occupancy.[29] When that certificate is, however, challenged it must be set aside and some other proof(s)

---

28 Joshua Castellino and Steve Allen, op.cit., p. 24. See also S. Reeves, "International Boundaries", Vol. 38, *American Journal of International Law*, No. 4, pp. 533–545.

29 For a better appreciation of the issue, it may be necessary to compare with aspects of national land law in some African states such as Nigeria where according to the Land Use Act, 1978, two types of rights of occupancy were created. These comprise of Statutory right of occupancy and Customary right of occupancy. Both Statutory right of occupancy and Customary right of occupancy are of two classifications. The first is the Statutory right of occupancy granted by the State Governor pursuant to Section 5(1) (a) of the Act and the Customary right of occupancy granted by the Local Government under Section 6 (1) (a) of the Act. The second classification is the Statutory right of occupancy deemed to have been granted by the State Governor pursuant to Section 34(2) of the Act and the Customary right of occupancy deemed to have been granted by the Local Government under Section 36(2) of the Act. In both cases of Statutory and Customary rights of occupancy, therefore, there exist an actual grant as well as a deemed grant. An actual grant is naturally a grant made by the Governor of a State or a Local Government whilst a deemed grant comes into existence automatically by the operation of law. See *Savannah Bank (Nig.) Ltd. v. Ajilo* (1989) 1 NWLR (Pt. 97) 305 and *Alhaji Adisa v. Emmanuel Oyinwola and Others* (2000) 10 NWLR (Pt. 674) 116. It is suggested here that as at the date of independence according to the *uti possidetis* rule a deemed certificate of occupancy is granted to every African state. But again the logic of law just as in the municipal system dictates that 'the mere issuance of the Certificates of Occupancy . . . does not and cannot confer title in respect of the land in dispute on the receipient where no such title either existed or was available to be transferred to anyone' (*Alhaji Goni Kyari v. Alhaji Ciroma Alkali & Ors* (2001) 11 NWLR (Pt. 724)). It cannot humanly be possible that all actions done by all colonial administrations with respect to the mapping, delimitation, demarcation and control of African territories were legal and appropriate even with the application of intertemporal laws. Thus, the deemed certificate of occupancy granted by application or reference to *uti possidetis* can only be useful to the extent that superior title is non existent.

of title to the territorial bounds must be brought to the table to prove the states' territorial extent.

16.2 *Uti possidetis* within the equation of political separation and self-determination

The problem of determination of the legality of separatist movements across Africa goes beyond the remits of this present work and can only form the subject of a future publication. Yet it would be strange indeed if a book on African boundary disputes does not give some careful thought, no matter how brief it is, to the problem of secession and the applicability of the *uti possidetis* doctrine to the former. Secession is an attempt at the creation of a state from within a larger territory by the use or threat of force without the consent of the former sovereign. Such attempts have also shaped the direction of international relations generally and many have occurred in Africa over the years.[30] Successful secessions in Africa include Guinea-Bissau and Eritrea. African secessionist movements that have failed include Katanga, Rhodesia and Biafra. Table 16.1 reveals that there are currently approximately 58 potential secessionist territories in 29 out of the total 57 independent states of Africa. These are championed by at least 83 political groups, associations and pressure groups. This is in many ways quite deterministic of the prolific future of state creation on the continent. Traditionally just as 'every state regards the menacing presence of foreign troops near its borders as a threat to its vital interests', states react with equal vigour to the presence within their territory of centripetal forces whose intent is to break up the state.[31] In both cases it will be correct to observe, as Cukwurah noted, that such beleaguered states 'will not hesitate to take preventive action even where this may not be justified as self-defence'.[32] In this context many existing tensions and disputes between African states would inevitably relate to the redrawing of territories arising out of the creation of new states. It is also inevitable that both internal and external assistance and every act of support for the actions of secessionist movements by foreign states or groups would generate conflicts of an international nature. Hence it is important to grapple with some legal issues in this area.

Yet it is not in the African context alone that the problems of self-determination and secession have raised their heads on many occasions. Two League of Nations commissions were set up to deal with the self-determination issues arising out of the dispute involving the Aland Islands. The question was whether international law permitted a group of islands regarded as strategically essential to Finland to break away from Finland and become part of Sweden because their Swedish speaking inhabitants desired to break away. Although the Committee of Rapporteurs denied the Alanders the right of self-determination in that case the

---

30 Crawford (2006), op.cit., p. 375.
31 Cukwurah, op.cit., p. 7.
32 Ibid.

Table 16.1 History and patterns of separatist movements in Africa

Country	Proposed entity	Location within existing state	Militancy level	Political organ
Algeria	Kabyle	Mountainous region, North of Algeria, East of Algiers	Low	– RCD (Union for Culture and Democracy); – FFS (Socialist Forces Front)
Angola	Republic of Cabinda	7,284 sq km in West Central Africa with a population of 264,584 in 2006 (estimate)	Medium (Forças Armadas de Cabinda (FAC)). Note 2010 attacks on visiting Togolese Football team	– Frente para a Libertação do Enclave de Cabinda (FLEC); – Forças Armadas de Cabinda (FAC)
Cameroon	– Ambazonia – Bakassi	– Ambazonia: 42,383 sq km (16,364 sq mi) Density 49.5/sq km (128.3/sq mi approximately) 6 million; Southern Cameroon is between Cameroon and Nigeria – Bakassi: peninsula on Gulf of Guinea between the Cross River estuary, near the city of Calabar in the west and the Rio del Ray estuary on the east	– Ambazonia – Low – SCNC – Medium. Armed members of the SCNC took over the Buea radio station in Southwest Province on the night of 30 December 1999. – Bakassi – Low	– Bakassi Movement for Self-Determination; – Southern Cameroons National Council (SCNC); – Southern Cameroon Liberation Movement (SCLM); – Southern Cameroons Peoples Organisation (SCAPO)
Central African Republic	Republic of Northern Central Africa (République du nord de l'Afrique centrale)	Area of Bangui but largely yet ill defined	Séléka Coalition – High	Séléka Coalition consisting of the following: – Democratic Front of the Central African People (FDPC); – Convention of Patriots for Justice and Peace (CPJP);

			– Union of Democratic Forces for Unity (UFDR); – Alliance for Revival and Rebuilding (A2R); – Patriotic Convention for Saving the Country (CPSK)
Comoros	– Autonomous Island of Anjouan – Democratic Republic of Mwali	Mohéli – Total 211 sq km (81 sq mi) – Water (%) negligible Population – 2006 estimate 38,000 (2003 census 35,400) Anjouan is part of the Comoros Islands located in the Mozambique Channel.	Anjouan People's Movement – Medium to High Former President on Exile Intermittent secessionist history but all now unified under Comoros	– Anjouan People's Movement, (Mouvement Populaire Anjouanais); – Mawana
Democratic Republic of the Congo	– Bas-Congo Proposed Kingdom of Kongo – Katanga – Kwili – Kivu – Bukavu	Bas-Congo: Borders Kinshasa to the north-east, Kwango to the east and the Republic of Angola to the south as well as the Republic of the Congo and Cabinda to the north; – Katanga's area is 497,000 sq km. The province forms the Congolese border with Angola and Zambia. The province also borders Tanzania – although Katanga province and Tanzania do not share a land border – but the border is within Lake Tanganyika.	High sporadic violence and insurgency	Pressure group: – Bundu dia Kongo; – Confédération des Associations de Katanga Tribales; – Union of Independent Federalists and Republicans; – Mai-Mai community-based militia groups

(continued)

Table 16.1 (continued)

Country	Proposed entity	Location within existing state	Militancy level	Political organ
Egypt	– Coptic Pharaonic Republic – Bir Tawil Republic of Ababda – Republic of Nubia		Very low	– Coptic Christians living abroad; – Ababda people; – Nubian Ethnic Group
Equatorial Guinea	Bioko (Fernando Po)		Low	Movement for the Self-determination of Bioko Island
Ethiopia	– Islamic State of Afaria – Gambella Region – Republic of Ogadenia – Republic of Oromia – Independent Republic of Tigray – Republic of Sidama		Variable ranging from low to very high and war in the case of Eritrean secession	– Afar Liberation Front; – Gambella People's Liberation Front; – National Liberation Front; – Ogaden; – National Liberation Front; – Western Somali Liberation Front; – Ogaden Republican Army; – Ogaden Youth Association; – Oromo Independence Movement; – Oromo Liberation Front; – Islamic Front for the Liberation of Oromia; – Conference of Oromiya People's Liberation Front; – Oromo Youth Revolutionary Movement (Abiddaa); – The National Youth Movement for Freedom and Democracy; – Tigrayan People's Liberation Front; – Sidama Liberation Front

Ivory Coast	Republic of Gimbabwe	All rebel groups display very high levels of violence	– Patriotic Movement of Côte d'Ivoire (MPCI); – Ivorian Popular Movement of the Great West (MPIGO); – Movement for Justice and Peace (MJP)
Kenya	Mombasa Republic	Low	Mombasa Republican Council
Libya	– Semi-autonomous 'State of Cyrenaica'	High	– Movement for Federal Libya; – National Union Party; – Cyrenaica Youth Movement
	Cyrenaica is the eastern coastal region of Libya		
Mauritius	Rodrigues Island	Low	– Mauritius Labour Party (MLP); – Mauritian Militant Movement (MMM)
	Autonomous outer island of the Republic of Mauritius in the Indian Ocean, about 560 km (350 mi) east of Mauritius		
Mali	Azawad	Very high	National Movement for the Liberation of Azawad
	Territory in northern Mali		
Morocco	– Sahrawi Arab Democratic Republic – The Confederal Republic of the Tribes of the Rif	Very high	– Polisario Front; – Sahrawi People's Liberation Army; – Istiqlal Party; – National Action Bloc; – Rif Independence Movement occurred in Morocco during the 1920s and was revitalised in 2013
	Free Zone – the part of Western Sahara that lies to the east of the Moroccan Berm (the Moroccan border wall) and west and north of the borders with Algeria and Mauritania, respectively		
Namibia	Free State of Caprivi Caprivi Strip/Itenge	Low	– Caprivi African National Union (CANU); – Caprivi Liberation Army (linked to the Barotseland Liberation Front in Zambia and to UNITA in Angola)
	Narrow strip of land in the far northeast, about 400 km long. The East Caprivi bordered by the Kwando, Linyanti, Chobe and Zambezi Rivers is a region of swamps and flood plains		

(continued)

Table 16.1 (continued)

Country	Proposed entity	Location within existing state	Militancy level	Political organ
Niger	– Agadez Department – Akal N Tenere, Tenere Republic	Agadez Region (about 52% of the total area of Niger with 321,639 inhabitants)		– Revolutionary Armed Forces of the Sahara; – Taniminnak Tidot N Tenere; – Tidot Union of Tenere
Nigeria	– Republic of Biafra (defunct) – Arewa Republic – Ogoni – Niger Delta Republic – Oduduwa Republic of the Yorubas		Generally high levels of militancy (especially Boko Haram and the Niger Delta militant groups)	– Bilie Human Rights Initiative; – Biafran Congress Party (BCP); – Movement for the Actualization of the Sovereign State of Biafra; – The Indigenous People of Biafra; – Biafra Zionist Movement; – Arewa People's Congress; – Boko Haram; – Movement for the Emancipation of the Niger Delta (Ijaw); – Niger Delta People's Volunteer Force; – Movement for the Survival of the Ogoni People; – Oodua People's Congress
Rwanda	Batwaland	Indeterminate. Areas affected include: Rwanda, Burundi, Uganda and Eastern Congo Estimated population: between 86,000 and 112,000.	The Batwa are mostly victims of other ethnic and governmental violence	Association for the Promotion of Batwa
Senegal	Casamance	Casamança is the area of Senegal south of the Gambia including the Casamance River	High	Movement of Democratic Forces of Casamance

Somalia	Somaliland	Somaliland is situated in northwestern Somalia. It is bordered by Djibouti to the west, Ethiopia to the south and the Puntland region of Somalia to the east.	Very high	Somali National Movement
South Africa	– Volkstaat – Transvaal – Orange Free State – Natalia – Cape Republic – Stellaland			– Freedom Front Plus; – Front Nasionaal; – Orania Movement; – Afrikaner; – Weerstandsbeweging; – Boeremag; – Cape Party; – Thembuland
South Sudan	Nuerland	Nuer territory lies approximately 800 km (500 mi) south of Khartoum	Very high	Nuer White Army; SPLA-Nasir
Sudan	– Beja – Darfur – Eastern Sudan – Kordofan – Republic of Nubia	Indeterminate	Very high	– Beja Congress; – Darfur Liberation Front; – Eastern Front
Tanzania	Zanzibar	Zanzibar (including Pemba) about 2,460 sq km	Medium	Civic United Front
Uganda	Buganda			Buganda Youth Movement

(continued)

Table 16.1 (continued)

Country	Proposed entity	Location within existing state	Militancy level	Political organ
Zambia	Barotseland	Upper Zambezi valley region, mostly comprised in Zambia's Western Province Capital: Mongu	Low	– Barotse Patriotic Front; – Barotse Freedom Movement; – Linyungandambo; – Barotse National Council; – Barotse National Freedom Alliance (BNFA)
Zimbabwe	– Matabeleland – Mthwakazi Free State	Matabeleland-based separatist group seeking an independent Ndebele state	Low	– Mthwakazi Liberation Front (MLF); – Matabeleland Freedom Party

Table compiled from various sources, including: Dimitri Dombret, "Kabylie: Repression and a Plan for Autonomy", available at www.amazighworld.org/eng/human_rights/index_show.php?id=76, accessed 30 June 2013; International Crisis Group, "Algeria: Agitation and Impasse in Kabylie", Middle East/North Africa Report, no. 15, 10 June 2003; Amnesty International, "Algeria – A Culture of Impunity", 8 April 2009. Unrepresented Nations and Peoples Organization: Bembe to UNPO: "The Peace Process in Cabinda Must and Will Continue", 11 October 2005; James Sturcke, "Togo Footballers were Attacked by Mistake, Angolan Rebels Say", *The Guardian*, 11 January 2010.

principle survived well in many other instances including the recent and very unique reintegration of Crimea into the Russian Federation.[33] Due regard is given to the *uti possidetis* principle in several aspects of the Treaty of Versailles and the counterpart peace treaties of 1913–1923.[34]

In Africa, however, the problem appears to be of growing significance. African states with a severe history of secessionist activities include Algeria, Angola, Cape Verde Islands, Mozambique, Guinea-Bissau and Senegal. Ongoing and notorious secessionist activities in Africa include that of Somaliland.[35]

The quest for self-determination by a people or group may arise for a myriad of reasons. One of the reasons could be that as a result of a Court or arbitral decision a people have to be partitioned into another country that they have little or no affiliation with. In such cases the sense of historic grievance may be so severe that a group may begin a movement to set themselves apart as a separate nation or state against the wishes of the government of the territorial state. In relation to such situations it is possible to explore two related issues. First, it is important to consider the rights of the indigenes of this area to express dissatisfaction with the territorial boundary and division created by the colonial powers which have cut them off from their ancestry. This was perhaps what led the All-African People's Conference to declare in a 1958 resolution that it:

(a) denounces artificial frontiers drawn by imperialist powers to divide the peoples of Africa, particularly those which cut across ethnic groups and divide people of the same stock;
(b) calls for the abolishment or adjustment of such frontiers at an early date;
(c) calls on the independent states of Africa 'to support permanent solution to this problem founded upon the wishes of the people'.[36]

Second, it is necessary to consider the claims to sovereign and independent nationhood that such dissent may give rise to.

The ascendancy of the *uti possidetis* principle in the jurisprudence of African international law and relations via its manifestation as a Latin American principle and as enshrined in Article 3, paragraph 3 of the Organisation of African Unity Charter has, however, transfixed African boundaries. *Uti possidetis* indeed found new expression in the state practice of the ex-Soviet breakaway republics where

---

33 For contrasting views on this event see Roslyn Fuller, "Russian Crimea: On the Right to Secede" *Russia Today*, available at http://rt.com/op-edge/crimea-secession-international-law-861/, accessed 19 October 2014; Brad Simpson, "Self-Determination in the Age of Putin: Does Crimea Have the Right to Join Russia? The Answer Isn't as Clear as Moscow's Critics or its Defenders Think" *Foreign Policy* (21 March 2014), available at www.foreignpolicy.com/articles/2014/03/21/self_determination_in_the_age_of_putin_crimea_referendum, accessed19 October 2014.
34 Crawford (2006), op.cit., pp. 12–13.
35 Ibid., p. 375.
36 Resolution of the All-African People's Conference, 4 December 1958 (a non-governmental conference of African political parties). Saadia Touval, "Africa's Frontiers", Vol. 42, *International Affairs* (1966), at 642; see also Lalonde, op.cit., p. 116; Celestine Oyom Bassey and Oshita O. Oshita (eds), *Governance and Border Security in Africa* (Lagos: Malthouse Press Ltd., 2010), pp. 96–97.

there is a marked common commitment of Central Asian states to preserve existing Soviet-era borders and reject nationalist or irredentist claims.[37] The manifestation of this principle on the African continent makes it difficult, for instance, that Nigeria or indeed Cameroon can lawfully make irredentist designs on any part of each other's territory, again particularly in light of the ICJ Judgment of 10 October 2002. Furthermore, Nigeria's commitment under the express terms of the Greentree Agreement (2006) arguably forbids it from assisting in any way the Bakassi population to espouse self-determination rights. Any such assistance will clearly run into the sharpest criticisms from Cameroon and the international community of states. The golden question, as considered below, however, is whether in these sorts of cases this extinguishes the right of the people to espouse their claims to self-determination under contemporary or customary international law.

Suffice to mention that there are two opposing theories on the principle of self-determination. There is the school that argues that *uti possidetis* must mean merely a juridical line or constructive line or constructive occupation – *uti possidetis juris* or *de jure* – while another considers that the principle must be based on a rightful and actual occupation of the territory – *uti possidetis de facto*. It is only in this latter sense that the *uti possidetis* theory ought to have any meaningful relevance in the context of Africa. It would appear, however, that it is in the former sense that cases such as the Nigerian claim over Bakassi and that of Ethiopia over sections of its disputed boundary have been decided. It indeed also appears that this is the usual interpretation that international courts have followed in many other decided cases.

However, political philosophers, lawyers and political scientists continue to struggle with the circumstances under which secession, dissolution and unilateral declaration of independence are lawful and/or permissible. These questions were brought to a head in the Bakassi area by the advent of separatist voices ringing more loudly since the judgment of the ICJ and since Nigeria handed over sovereignty of the Peninsula to Cameroon. In essence Nigeria is placed in the unenviable position where it cannot be seen to assist the Bakassi population in any way that may be interpreted as fanning secessionist activism, yet it cannot just stand back and look if the advent of such a movement elicits a heavy-handed backlash from the Cameroonian authorities. It is in the interest of both states to ensure that (according to the letter and spirit of the Greentree Agreement) they are seen to act in a manner that prevents the alienation of the very population that the treaty seeks to protect.

There already appears to be grounds for serious concern that the Bakassi population may harbour separatist inclinations. The discussion of the Bakassi issue may in this way be placed in context of the larger questions of how the self-determination of peoples is to be accommodated in contemporary international law and relations. As an author put it:

---

37 International Crisis Group, "Central Asia: Border Disputes and Conflict Potential", op.cit., p. 6.

It is now conventional wisdom that the proliferation of ethnic-based violence constitutes the greatest threat to public order and human rights since the lifting of the Iron Curtain. The eruption of hatreds, whether suppressed or ignored for a half century or newly arisen, has unleashed centrifugal forces that are pulling states apart from Africa to Europe to South and Central Asia.[38]

Yet there is some merit to the argument that the limits of *uti possidetis* as policy must be recognised. The true target of the principle is the doctrine of protection of boundaries and borders. *Uti possidetis* was not even in the Latin American sense designed to answer back to separatists nor was it meant to trump the right of self-determination. It definitely should not be a valid incantation against well-founded exercise of the rights of a people to self-determination.[39]

As Ratner convincingly put it:

> The easy embrace by governments of *uti possidetis* and the suggestion that it is now a general rule of international law to govern the breakup of states lead to two distinct, yet opposite, spillover effects that endanger global order at this time of ethnic conflict. First, a policy or rule that transforms all administrative borders of modern states into international boundaries creates a significant hazard in the name of simplicity . . . Second, the extension of *uti possidetis* to modern breakups leads to genuine injustices and instability by leaving significant populations both unsatisfied with their status in new states and uncertain of political participation there. By hiding behind inflated notions of *uti possidetis*, state leaders avoid engaging the issue of territorial adjustments – even minor ones – which is central to the process of self-determination.[40]

The rote application of *uti possidetis*, therefore, raises practical problems in the determination of the possible merits of independence for national groups across Africa. It becomes necessary to locate the answers to possible problems with the exercise of self-independent rule by groups such as the people of Bakassi under the well-recognised principle of self-determination. The pertinent questions include: What are the permissible responses by the territorial state in reaction to groups seeking to exercise these powers under international law? What are the obligations of other states in response to the claim of self-determination?

---

38 Steven Ratner, op.cit., p. 590.
39 For critical views on *uti possidetis* see Ratner's excellent article, op.cit., See, e.g., Crawford (2006), op.cit., *et.seq*. Ardent supporters of the principle, like Santiago Torres Bernárdez, admit that the *uti possidetis* doctrine still has to be reconciled with developments in law and 'the evolution of the rules of international law governing, for example succession, self determination, acquisition of title to territory, frontiers and other territorial regimes, treaty law, intertemporal law, etc.' See, e.g., Torres Bernárdez, "The 'Uti Possidetis Juris Principle' in Historical Perspective", in K. Ginther *et al.* (eds), *Festschrift für Karl Zemanek* (Berlin: Duncker & Humbolt, 1994), p. 436.
40 Ratner, op.cit., p. 591.

It is clear that secessionist activities will inevitably produce a reaction from the territorial state. Every state has a right to defend its territorial integrity both from internal and external threats. This right is not only in line with public international law but it is also good international policy. It must, however, be realised that if overwhelming force is used, the territorial sovereign or occupier may succeed either in the short, medium or long term to stem the agitation and prevent breakup or independence but the conditions for deeper problems may have been created. Overwhelming force from experience may radicalise the struggle for independence even further. This may even take the form of emergence of a more radicalised faction or liberation movement which may confound not only the sovereign but also the pre-existing freedom fighters. This is a phenomenon which has been seen in Northern Ireland and Palestine. With the increasing frustration of the PLO, the even more militant Hamas emerged to the dismay of Israel and to the PLO.[41] Indeed the danger of emergence of a cacophony of voices and groups is always present and whilst splinter groups may weaken the separatists, it also poses a serious problem for the territorial sovereign who will not know who to deal with precisely for talks, negotiations, cease-fires, etc. Furthermore the existence of many separatist groups makes the likelihood of dismantling the group by spectacular capture or neutralisation of particular leader(s) less likely:

> It is also the case that each group will try to canvass for its own attention by various overt and covert means guaranteed to command attention even if also increasing the tensions with the territorial sovereign or other separatist or loyalist groups.[42]

There are indeed horses for courses; it is natural that a territorial state will in reaction go for every legitimate principle of international law to protect itself from disintegration but it is suggested here that *uti possidetis* will be a poor tool in such cases unless it is the case that it can be shown that behind the pull for separation in an African territory there is the orchestrating hands of an irredentist land or maritime neighbour waiting to gain any form of territorial or boundary advantage from the disintegration. In other words, other states that are not able to gain or change territorial or boundary lines are also technically immune from the *uti possidetis* defence of the territorial state even if they support the separatists

---

41 A writer explains:
> The PLO met Hamas in the beginning with total disregard, then it tried to cast doubt on its authenticity, then it endeavoured to belittle it and refused to recognise it, then it went into a stage of open confrontation followed by an attempt to contain it.
> (Khalid Mish'al quoted in Tamimi, op.cit., p. 187)

42 The late Yasir Arafat and his Fatah colleagues who were the principal faction within the PLO struggled hard for recognition both in the Arab world and internationally. The Palestinian Islamists, led by the Ikhwan and then by Hamas, refused to accept the PLO's claim insisting that the PLO had no mandate to monopolise representation outside an elective mandate. Tamimi, op.cit., pp. 89–90.

unless again they are acting in favour of another state which will make such territorial or boundary gains. On the whole, negotiation is the most appropriate pacific mechanism for dealing with separatist movements. Negotiation does not necessarily have to lead to caving in to the demands for separation but it is a necessary step towards understanding the true nature of the demands of agitators and rebel groups as well as identifying acceptable compromises or middle grounds upon which peaceful agreement may be reached. Note must, however, also be taken of the unique role that the PCA successfully played in handling the Sudanese secessionist situation in relation to the case of the Government of Sudan/Sudan People's Liberation Movement discussed earlier.[43] The uniqueness of the proceedings lies in the fact that it is very unusual for a state that is not yet in existence to arbitrate or litigate on territorial issues before a formal international institution.

---

43 *Supra* our discussion of the Sudan–South Sudan border disputes in Chapter 5 and also Chapter 7, Section 7.1.6: Sudan–South Sudan border disputes.

17 Strategies and modalities to resolve straddling communities and resources under the African Union Boundary Programme

Delimitation of boundaries is rendered more difficult where villages and communities straddle the boundaries of two states. The existence of these straddling communities in many cases complicates the situation and prevents agreement between state parties. In many ways the situation is worsened where valuable economic resources straddle the boundaries between the states. The very existence of a boundary dispute may have emanated from the discovery of valuable hydrocarbons or other such important minerals. It is likely that acceleration of delimitation and demarcation activities across the continent may precipitate the discovery or reignite these issues on a large scale. The potential for conflict or perpetuation of injustice in both cases is great. Certainly there is no unanimity in state practice on the issues and there is very little guidance in international law in dealing with the problems that may arise. In light of this it is necessary to consider the increasingly common problem of straddling communities and resources with the intention of offering Afrocentric positions and solutions which ought to guide African states in the future.

17.1 Boundary demarcation and the problem of straddling communities and enclaves

Given the high number of international straddling villages across Africa it is a wonder that there are not many more open conflicts over boundaries than is officially acknowledged.[1] In many cases the inhabitants of straddling communities continue to live peacefully side by side while the states they belong to engage in hostile diplomacy, litigation, or worse still, military skirmishes. It is perhaps also remarkable that there are not many examples of enclaves in the classical sense (i.e. territory belonging to one state in the foreign territory of another) in Africa at all. Indeed enclaves predominantly exist on only two continents:

---

1 Only further research can reveal whether this is because the existence of straddling villages and *de facto* enclaves are largely ignored by governments in the light of other pressing economic and political problems or perhaps this is as a result of the relative recentness of the making of African boundaries. See Oduntan (2006), op.cit., *et.seq.*

Europe and Asia.[2] Africa is, however, host to at least one successful case of complete enclosure of one state in another. Reference is made here to Lesotho's existence as an enclave inside South Africa.[3]

It is fortunate that African states appear to hesitate to dissect settlements into two during boundary demarcation despite the contents of the delimitation instrument. Where the main path of the boundary is parallel to a road or along a meridian/parallel, it is diverted around villages which otherwise straddled the boundary. A good instance is the Benin/Nigeria boundary which is found at 10 deg N, and which has semi-circular offsets to let Nigeria retain villages along the road the boundary follows. Similarly, the Ghana/Burkina Faso boundary along the 11 deg N parallel between 1 deg W and the Red Volta River was demarcated by rectangular offsets in order to leave straddling villages to either country.[4] As a result of the dependence of traditional African societies on communal or customary lands and property there is also the problem of straddling customary lands recognised by the customary communities but ignored or disputed by the state parties. This issue, however, is yet to receive the academic attention it deserves in African legal jurisprudence.

In a sense this approach of carefully ensuring that communities are left as an organic whole is in accordance with the African tradition of ensuring that ownership and possession are exercised as concurrent rights and in line with centuries of traditional belief that 'good fences make good neighbours'. As explained in earlier chapters the practice of completely encircling political groups behind walls sometimes running into thousands of kilometres in length dates back over a millennia in Africa. Nevertheless, it appears that the inclination not to separate or split existing communities in the name of demarcation is far more likely where the demarcation does not follow military hostilities or protracted litigation as was unfortunately the case in the recent history of some African states such as Cameroon and Nigeria. It is for this reason that the parties

---

2 In the main these have a feudal origin and date back several hundred years. B. Whyte, "Bordering on the Ridiculous? A Comparison of the World's Two Most Complex Boundaries: The Belgo–Dutch Enclaves at Baarle and the Indo–Bangladeshi Enclaves at Cooch Behar", 53, *The Globe* (2002), pp. 43–61; B. R. Whyte, "Waiting for the Esquimo: An Historical and Documentary Study of the Cooch Behar Enclaves of India and Bangladesh", PhD thesis, published as Research Paper No.8, by the School of Anthropology, Geography and Environmental Studies, Melbourne, University of Melbourne (2002).

3 Note, however, that this is a different legal and political situation from the cases discussed later relating to enclaves of independent states that are planted in another (usually neighbouring) state. Note also the ten self-governing territories for different black ethnic groups which were established as part of the apartheid policy of the erstwhile apartheid South Africa. Four of these were granted 'independence' by the infamous South Africa regimes, although they were recognised only by South Africa and each other. These former South Africans Homelands or Bantustans ceased to exist on 27 April 1994 and were re-incorporated into South Africa, and all were absorbed into the new provinces.

4 Maps and descriptions of the boundary treaties can be seen in Ieuan Griffiths, "The Scramble for Africa: Inherited Political Boundaries", Vol. 152, *Geographical Journal*, No. 2 (1986), pp. 204–216, especially pp. 207–208. For the Ghana/Burkina boundary see the Russian 1:200,000 map C-30-xii available at http://sunsite.berkeley.edu/EART/ghana/200k/03-30-12.jpg, accessed 3 February 2015.

to that process have continued to handle issues surrounding straddling villages with reasoned diplomacy and the problem remains one of the unsolved issues in a largely successful implementation process.

The implementation of post-boundary dispute decisions and awards is a desirable end in itself but a close eye must be placed on the larger picture in light of past experience on the African continent. Nothing less than a sensitive implementation of ICJ and arbitral decisions is required and concerned parties as well as demarcation commissions ought not to be limited by a slavish attitude to judicial decisions. Where decisions imply an insensitive dissection of lives and organic communities it is in line with African tradition to amend the decision towards a more African solution where mutual agreement exists. In the situations where a boundary decision or award has been given by an international court, it is advocated here that the spirit of the Yoruba philosophical and legal maxim be adopted as the guiding principle. As the maxim goes; *'bi a ba ran eniyan ni ise eru ologbon afi ti omo je'* (Where instructions are insensitive and befitting of a slave, reasonable men must amend it sensitively and deliver it in a manner befitting the free).

Even after post adjudication or other dispute resolution processes, there is much precedent for innovative thinking and cooperation among African states. In the Cameroon–Nigeria situation immediate post-litigation processes included negotiations regarding the revival of projects under the Lake Chad Basin Commission (LCBC). The CNMC is in continuous discussion relating to the reactivation of the work of the LCBC. The World Bank has also helpfully funded the LCBC in clear support for the peaceful diplomacy carried out by the states involved in relation to their international boundaries.[5] Note may also be taken of certain bilateral confidence building efforts Nigeria and Cameroon have embarked upon, such as the upgrading of the Mamfe-Abakaliki road to Kumba and Mutengene on the Cameroonian side and the development of an early warning system to alert the relevant local authorities and affected populations about potential natural or other disasters. It may be suggested that if the neighbouring states continue to exhibit high levels of political resolve, significant financial help could be expected from international donor partners and financial institutions for joint cross border projects. These may take the form of international parks and conservation gardens.[6]

It is particularly crucial that post adjudication negotiations regarding straddling villages are as comprehensive and as honest as possible given the fact that both family and economic life of the inhabitants of these villages may

---

5 See Communiqué adopted at the second meeting of the Cameroon–Nigeria Mixed Commission established pursuant to the Joint Geneva communiqué of 15 November 2002, Abuja, 4–5 February 2003.
6 See paras 8 and 11 of the Communiqué adopted at the third meeting of the Cameroon–Nigeria Mixed Commission established pursuant to the Joint Geneva Communiqué of 15 November 2002, Yaoundé 2–3 April 2003. See also Communiqué adopted at the fourth meeting of the Cameroon–Nigeria Mixed Commission established pursuant to the Joint Geneva Communiqué of 15 November 2002, Abuja, 10–12 June 2003.

become disrupted as a result of insensitive 'line in the sand' approaches to the demarcation tasks. The reasonable policy which ought to be encouraged in Africa is as follows:

(a) Post adjudication demarcation must proceed along the lines determined by the Court but where it would occasion manifest injustices or absurdities such as splitting a school compound into two halves or separating families from their means of subsistence, the legal boundary would cease to be useful and will only be indicative of the direction in which the demarcation must follow for as long as the manifest absurdity is avoided.[7]
(b) If the option of the splitting of straddling villages is eventually adopted it is necessary to point out that the right of inhabitants of straddling villages to leave the country should be guaranteed in a watertight agreement.

Human rights NGOs have for long noted discrimination in the treatment of groups wishing to exercise freedom of movement within straddling communities. Often whole populations would be punished for the activities of one individual or for actions of the opposite central government. At other times when the communities have been split up into two states the right of freedom of movement would only be extended to those regarded as coming from the favoured side.[8]

It is perhaps important at this stage to advance certain criteria by which the demarcation of straddling villages may be resolved. The extent to which a settlement straddles the state(s) in question would naturally differ from case to case. Rarely will the straddling village/community or city be geometrically spread equally over the territories involved because human settlements as organic phenomena rarely have such natural symmetry. A straddling settlement may therefore 'straddle' with respect to one of the territories with only a few dozen houses or homesteads. It is suggested that permanence of the structures that straddle into foreign territory would be a relevant factor in the consideration of the rights and interests of the affected people and states in the search for an equitable solution.

Where only tents, caravans or other moveable architectural structure are at issue, especially where they are few, it may be suggested that a court can afford to carry out delimitation exercise in a much more stricter fashion. However, it may be that a straddling settlement straddles not by virtue of human habitation but by virtue of the fact that the farmland or other economic or vital resource, such as a river, upon which the human settlement depends is to be found within the territory of another state. In such cases the appurtenance and close geographical relation to the human settlement, the crucial importance of the resources, the length of time that the settlement has spread into foreign territory as well as other

---

7 Gbenga Oduntan, "Straddling Villages", op.cit.
8 International Service for Human Rights (ISHR), "Fight Against Discrimination and Protection of Vulnerable Groups", available at www.ishr.ch/About%20UN/Reports%20and%20Analysis/Sub%2052%20-%20Discrimination.htm, accessed 2 February 2015.

'effectivité'-oriented criteria would all be relevant facts.[9] In such cases there is a strong basis for the exercise of judicial discretion to vary the line in the interest of human justice even where no single dwelling is in issue. It is argued that this view is supportable especially where there is no adjacent settlement that competes for the use of the river or fertile land on the other side. Where significant economic resources are at stake, such as oil and gas or fisheries, it is suggested that the issue is no longer that of merely protecting the indigenous people, and the territorial state into which the settlement has spread into ought to retain full rights over such resources (subject to our discussions on sharing mineral resources and fisheries discussed below).

Where just a few compounds or farmlands spread into another territory a court may decide not to treat this as an instance of the existence of a straddling settlement and strict delimitation may be exercised. But when, for instance, the majority of the village's farmland is now to be excised away into another state then perhaps this will raise the presumption that some form of exchange of coaxial or proportionate territory may be arranged. Boundary demarcators in such cases may also adopt a strict adherence to the delimitation line. Again it must be restated that where an international court has not exercised discretion along the lines suggested above, and this would lead to manifest injustice to a significant population, there is much credence for the view that those charged with the implementation of the judgment should seriously explore possibilities of ameliorating the harshness of the delimitation. However, note should be taken that the discussion so far is in relation to straddling villages the sovereignty over which is not dispute. A dispute over the determination of which state can lay claim to a straddling settlement as a whole is a territorial dispute and not a boundary dispute.

The centre of the village, the location of its religious places (such as shrines, mosques, churches, ancestral groves), the palace of the king or chiefs (in the case of the affected Cameroon–Nigeria boundary village the *Bullama*) or its oldest quarter may be a useful indication of which state may claim ownership but these features do not offer conclusive evidence of the ownership of one state or the other to the extent that the people themselves may consider themselves to be rightfully the citizens of another state in spite of where the centre of the village or its oldest parts lie. It is indeed not inconceivable that villagers may move around frequently creating confusion as to where the origins of the village or settlement began and where the locations of the many places mentioned above actually

---

9 Note should be taken that effectivité remains a potent consideration in determination of boundary and territorial issues despite the courts disregard of the principle in the Cameroon–Nigeria case. This conclusion is clear from the Court's conclusion in the *Frontier Dispute* (Burkina Faso/Republic of Mali) case that:

> where the territory which is the subject of the dispute is effectively administered by a state other than the one possessing the legal title, preference should be given to the holder of the title. In the event that the effectivité does not co-exist with any legal title, it must invariably be taken into consideration.

(emphasis added); (*Frontier Dispute* (Burkina Faso/Republic of Mali) 586–587, para. 63)

were. Natural causes (war, drought, landslides, earthquakes, infestation by locusts, wildlife, etc.) may cause a settlement to shift around in such a way that it becomes difficult, if not impossible, to determine the pattern of spread of a straddling settlement.

It is for this reason that the oral history of the particular people and their wishes as may be determined by consultation and plebiscites are crucial factors to be taken into consideration by demarcators. It is also for this reason that African international courts are perhaps more suited to hearing these sorts of cases. A court that is without close knowledge of the people and places involved or has not received extensive evidence on a straddling community and/or the workings of an African village must hesitate to prescribe a delimitation that definitively splits the community. The position has been consistently advanced in this book that those that are entrusted with the function of deciding upon boundary disputes should consider the wishes of affected people in a straddling settlement. They should equally consider other factors such as the previous history of administration and they should vary the line of delimitation in the overall interest of human justice. It hardly needs to be mentioned that the exercise of this function in any delimitation exercise must be used within very strict limits. It may in fact be that after consultation, the people of a straddling settlement may not be opposed to a strict division along treaty lines especially where the treaties concerned have an unquestionable legitimacy in the estimation of the people. The important consideration, however, is that diligent consultation with the concerned population ought to be a central task of an African delimiting tribunal and a desirable task of the demarcation team.

It is suggested that the power to vary the delimitation line around straddling settlements in Africa must be exercised very carefully and such exercise of jurisdiction is justifiable upon the existence of certain conditions:

(a) The exercise of this power is pleaded by one of the states involved and there is a finding that there is indeed a straddling community in existence.
(b) The exercise of this power is pleaded by the affected people and the request is not opposed by at least one of the states involved and there is a finding that there is a straddling community in existence.
(c) There has been no express and specific limitation by the parties that this power may not be exercised.
(d) The exercise of the power is fair, just and equitable in view of the overall circumstances and merits of the case.
(e) The ownership of the straddling settlement is not judged by the Court to be a central dispute between the parties.[10]

---

10 This differentiation in relation to the Cameroon–Nigeria dispute is perhaps discernible in the way the dispute unfolded before the Court. On 29 March 1994, Cameroon filed the suit against Nigeria and defined it as 'relat[ing] essentially to the question of sovereignty over the Bakassi' (paras 1 and 25 (a)). Later on 6 June 1994, Cameroon filed in the Registry of the Court an additional application 'for the purpose of extending the subject of the dispute to a further dispute' described in that

Relevant factors that will determine the extent to which such discretion may be exercised include the relative size of the states facing the boundary dispute. In the case of relatively large states such as Cameroon and Nigeria, the varying of a line of delimitation by a few dozen metres is good policy if it can keep settlements together where the people and at least one of the states involved are desirous of that result. Justification for this position exists in the annals of jurisprudential thinking and practice.

The fifth condition mentioned above perhaps deserves further explanation. It refers to the need to make a distinction between a settlement that forms part of the central dispute between the litigating states and those which are only to be dealt with as a consequence of the general task put before a court or tribunal. Thus, disputes over territories such as Bakassi Peninsula (Cameroon–Nigeria dispute) and Badme (Eritrea–Ethiopia dispute) would not necessarily fall within the scope of the argument presented here. In reality the entire frontier between two states may be drawn into issue whereas only specific places are crucial to the dispute between the two states. While the Court must apply all due diligence in its work of delimiting the boundaries between the two states, it is clear that varying the line with respect to small straddling villages in the interest of human justice, especially in situations where both states stand to potentially gain from this approach, for instance, by creating conditions for enduring peace. Courts of law should be held to a higher requirement and standard of justice which go beyond the demands of the litigating states at the particular point in time. An institution that arbitrates or adjudicates matters between sovereign states is first and foremost an international temple of justice and is no way obliged to maintain a positivist approach in the execution of its tasks in the face of the possibility of putting in jeopardy human and generational rights of indigenous peoples.[11]

Additional Application as 'relat[ing] essentially to the question of sovereignty over a part of the territory of Cameroon in the area of Lake Chad' (para. 3). Cameroon then also requested the Court, in its Additional Application, 'to specify definitively' the frontier between the two states from Lake Chad to the sea, and asked it to join the two Applications. It is arguable that a pecking order may be established as to the crucial areas in dispute.

11 It is notable that the ICJ approach in this matter is in no way different to the general attitude of other international courts. The refusal of international courts and international law practitioners to adopt a more flexible approach to the resolution of disputes noted by older authorities like Han Morgenthau (in relation to the PCIJ) remains unchanged until date. Morgenthau regretted the predominance of a 'time-honoured pseudo-logical method of traditional positivism which prevailed in the jurisdiction of the domestic supreme courts at the turn of the (19th) century' (parenthesis added). He wrote:

> resistance to change is uppermost in the history of international law. All the schemes and devices by which great humanitarians and shrewd politicians endeavored to reorganize the relations between states on the basis of law, have not stood the trial of history. Instead of asking whether the devices were adequate to the problems which they were supposed to solve, it was the general attitude of the internationalists to take the appropriateness of the devices for granted and to blame the facts for the failure.
>
> (Hans J. Morgenthau, "Positivism, Functionalism, and International Law", Vol. 34, *American Journal of International Law* (Apr., 1940), pp. 260, 263. See also generally, P. S. Wild, "What is the Trouble with International Law?", Vol. XXCII, *American Political Science Review* (1938), pp. 478–494)

17.2 Varying demarcation in the interest of justice and accommodating losers' interests

17.2.1 Straddling resources and hydrocarbon fields

Border disputes are often associated with the existence and actual or potential use of cross-border resources. Those charged with resolving boundary disputes are, thus, often faced with the need to allow affected states and their nationals the best options that maximise the economic development of the states concerned through resource control. For instance, the allocation of a group of islands to Yemen in the Eritrea–Yemen arbitration was done but great care was adopted by the arbitration in order not to affect the traditional artisanal fishing rights held by Eritreans.

The potential of straddling resources as flash points on the African continent is a repeating decimal in African international relations. The phenomenon deserves closer scrutiny than it gets in legal and political literature. It certainly does deserve closer study under the AUBP. The problem as accurately described by the AU is as follows:

> Since African countries gained independence, the borders – which were drawn during the colonial period in a context of rivalries between European countries and their scramble for territories in Africa – have been a recurrent source of conflicts and disputes in the continent. Most of the borders are poorly defined. *The location of strategic natural resources in cross-border areas poses additional challenges* (emphasis added).[12]

The very rationale for our argument that there is or ought to be the presumption of joint and cooperative development of straddling resources such as hydrocarbons rests on the factual geophysical nature of the minerals in their natural states as fluid substances that subsist underground without any respect whatsoever for man-made political geography. The irreverent nature of hydrocarbon deposits is further compounded by the reality that whenever a single owner extracts hydrocarbons from a point presumably within its own jurisdictional claims, the potential share of the other claimant(s) is damaged. Resorting to free for all exploitation will in most cases irresponsibly reduce the viability and vitality of the deposit(s) beyond repair. In such circumstances and for these reasons, cooperative cross-border upstream management is not only reasonable but resort to this device is fast crystallising into customary international law.[13]

---

12 African Union, "Report of the Commission on the Implementation of the African Union Border Programme", Executive Council Fourteenth Ordinary Session, 29–30 January 2009, op.cit., p. 1.
13 Writers that agree with the customary rule argument include: W. T. Onorato, "Apportionment of an International Common Petroleum Deposit", Vol. 17 *International & Comparative Law Quarterly* (1968), p. 101; W. T. Onorato, "A Case Study in Joint Development: The Saudi Arabia-Kuwait Partitioned Neutral Zone" in Valencia (ed.) Workshop II (1985); I. F. I. Shihata and W. T. Onorato, "Joint Development of International Petroleum Resources in Undefined and Disputed Areas", Paper presented at the International Conference of the LAWASIA Energy Section, Kuala Lumpor

Agreement on joint development is often a product of the tortuous process of agreement on delimitation and demarcation. Before concluding the agreement on their maritime boundary in 1997, Thailand and Vietnam had also discussed the possibility of joint development for their overlapping claims area.[14] Fortunately there is ample evidence of cooperation in the sharing of cross boundary resources in the maritime sector among African states. It may indeed be predicted that much of the practice of joint development of hydrocarbons in the immediate future will occur in Africa given discoveries of new fields and development of acreages both on land and in the sea such as the Gulf of Guinea.[15]

A specific instance has resulted out of the agreed maritime boundary formally demarcated by Cameroon and Nigeria recently in implementing the ICJ judgment concerning their common maritime boundary. It became evident that some oil fields/blocks belonging to Nigeria have been affected by the new maritime boundary. The Maritime Working Group set up by the parties very quickly identified the need to study the extent to which the existing hydrocarbon resources that overlap in the Gulf of Guinea could feasibly be regulated within a sharing regime for straddling resources.[16] There is no reason to believe that the AU cannot routinely adopt this policy as recommended practice throughout the continent both on land and sea. Areas where two or more states share

---

(18–22 October 1992), pp. 3–4. Writers that disagree with the customary rule argument include: Masahiro Miyoshi, "The Joint Development of Off Shore Oil and Gas in Relation to Maritime Boundary Delimitation", Vol. 2, *Maritime Briefing*, No. 5 Durham: IBRU (1999), p. 4. Note also the conclusion of a group of experts at the British Institute of International and Comparative Law as at 1989 that 'in contradiction to agreed boundary areas where a known field straddles the boundary, there is at present as regards disputed areas no clear rule of customary law which requires a State to inform and consult other interested parties', H. Fox *et. al.*, "Joint Development of Offshore Oil and Gas, Vol. II London: BIICL, *Joint Development I*' (1989) quoted in Miyoshi, op.cit., p. 4.

14 Joint development or what we prefer to call Cooperative Crossborder Upstream Exploitation has been ably described as 'an inter-governmental arrangement of a provisional nature, designed for functional purposes of joint exploration for and/or exploitation of hydrocarbon resources of the seabed beyond the territorial sea'. See Protocol of the first meeting of the Thai–Vietnamese Joint Committee on Culture, Economic, Science and Technical Cooperation in October 1991. Note the eventual Agreement between the Government of the Kingdom of Thailand and the Government of the Socialist Republic of Viet Nam on the delimitation of the maritime boundary between the two countries in the Gulf of Thailand, 9 August 1997, Delimitation Treaties Infobase, available at www.un.org/Depts/los/LEGISLATIONANDTREATIES/PDFFILES/TREATIES/THA-VNM1997MB.PDF, accessed 24 October 2004.

15 The development of a joint development zone (JDZ) or unitisation in the maritime sector is a time consuming and potentially politically hazardous process. The scientific determination of the extent of the oil fields alone may take years to appreciate. More and more interlocking fields may be discovered than are presently envisaged. Furthermore there is lurking in the background the fact that most scholars on the topic are of the opinion that there is no rule of customary international law that states that joint development of hydrocarbons must be embarked on even in the most apparent cases of straddling resources. See Thao Nguyen, "Joint Development in the Gulf of Thailand", Vol. 7, *Boundary and Security Bulletin*, No. 3 (1999), p. 85; Miyoshi, op.cit., p. 4–6.

16 It is important to note that the parties have, however, not yet achieved the significant task of determining the form of cooperation suitable for their purpose (unitisation or joint production zone) nor have they decided upon an exact sharing formula.

sovereign rights to explore and exploit the natural resources of the area and where the states concerned agree to engage in exploration and exploitation under some form of common or joint arrangement should in time become common on the continent.[17]

17.2.2 Straddling fisheries

Another sore point in African international relations with huge boundary repercussions is the exploitation of fisheries. In relation to fisheries the recognition of common artisanal fishing rights is clearly a favoured option for African states. The jurisprudence of the ICJ in relation to fishing rights of indigenous populations reveals that the Court is indeed sensitive to the desirability of the preservation of the livelihood and interests of indigenous populations affected by its judgments. In relation to maritime disputes, the Court strictly construes its delimitation tasks but has also always strongly expressed a view in favour of joint exercise of fishing rights. There is no reason why the ACJ as well as arbitrators and negotiators called to decide upon straddling fisheries stocks and the fate of straddling villages should depart from this jurisprudence.

It is also notable that there are important obligations under Articles 61–65 of the UN Convention on the Law of the Sea (UNCLOS)[18] that mandate states to cooperate on a global, regional or sub-regional basis in relation to sea resources. This includes in its purview instances such as the Cameroon–Nigeria situation where there are ample stocks shared by the two states along their internal boundary rivers as well as the conservation of stocks that straddle the seas between the two states. These obligations also create the imperative to protect and preserve the marine environment.[19]

There are already commendable examples of inclusive regimes, which cover oil and gas as well as living marine resources, such as that between Guinea-Bissau–Senegal in their Agreement of 14 October 1993.[20] This joint development agreement was based on a previous maritime boundary agreement between the parties' respective colonial powers signed in 1960. In essence there will be instances where it will make perfect sense to simultaneously deal with the hydrocarbon and fisheries regime in a single legislation and there will be instances where it will be wiser to have different regimes.

---

17 See Hazel Fox, *Joint Development of Offshore Oil and Gas*, Vol. II (The British Institute of International and Comparative Law, 1990), p. 55.
18 Convention on the Law of the Sea (21 ILM (1982) 1261; Misc 11 (1983), 8941; 1833 UNTS 3 (1994); Brownlie, *Basic Documents in International Affairs*, 3rd Edition, p. 129).
19 Article 197 of the LOSC. See generally Gbenga Oduntan, "Maritime Pyrrhic Victories: Evaluation of the de facto Regime of Common Fishing Rights in the Land and Maritime Boundary Case (Cameroon v Nigeria)", Vol. 37, *Journal of Maritime Law and Commerce*, No. 1 (2002), pp. 118–146.
20 See text of the Exchange of Notes in I. Charney and Lewis M. Alexander, *International Maritime Boundaries* (Dordrecht: Martinus Nijhoff, 1993), pp. 873–874.

17.3 Recognising an African customary rule in favour of sharing straddling resources

In many cases the world over, the discovery of valuable resources is what catapults sleepy frontier lands into the scene of intense territorial and boundary conflict.[21] It is also a truism that 'a boundary only becomes a source of conflict depending on how it is used, controlled and managed'.[22] This realisation is one which ought to be instructive to the jurisprudence that must inform practice of the AU. It has been correctly observed that mining investors often enter into agreements with a government to explore natural resources in the borderlands only to discover, once the exercise is under way, that they belong to other countries. Wafula Okomu, therefore, reminds us that:

> When countries sign contradictory agreements with investors to explore for natural wealth in the borderlands, the outcome could easily turn violent if the border is not agreed upon and clearly marked. When such conflicts occur, the outcome is usually negative on economic relations.[23]

When a reservoir straddles the boundary between two sovereign states, the common nature of petroleum resources dictate that the ideal strategy to undertake their development from a legal, technical conservationist and environmental perspective is either unitisation in the case of delimited and demarcated land boundaries or joint production zones in the case of undelimited/undemarcated maritime boundaries.[24] The writers who have argued that joint development could constitute a rule of customary international law base their conviction upon three main points: first, that no state may unilaterally exploit the common international petroleum deposit over the timely objection of another interested state; second, the method of exploitation of such a deposit must be agreed upon by the states concerned; and third, that concerned states must enter into good faith agreements at least of a provisional nature until full and final agreement is reached.[25] Similarly Zhiguo Gao – relying upon sections of the ICJ judgment in the *Libyan Continental Shelf* case, state practice and the general

---

21 If press reports are anything to go by the 'oil rich' nature of the Bakassi Peninsula is the *fons origo* of the Cameroonian crises and many years of litigation at The Hague. The Nigerian government has, however, been at pains to deny this idea on many occasions. The dispute between Angola and the DRC along the Cabinda coast increased in intensity after oil was discovered. See "Conflit maritime Angola-RDC: Alfred Muzito's explique devant le Sénat", Le Potentiel, 15 December 2010. Note also the role of newly discovered hydrocarbon finds in the development of the Sudan–Kenya: The Ilemi Triangle. See our discussion in section 7.1.1.
22 Ibid., p. 39. Sociological theories of conflicts can help throw light on why some boundaries are more likely than others to present a problem in international relations. Reuter, op.cit., p. 31.
23 Okomu, op.cit., p. 40.
24 A. E. Bastida, Ifesi-Okoye, Salim Mahmud, James Ross and Tjhomas Walde, "Cross-Border Unitization and Joint Development Agreements: An International Law Perspective", Vol. 29, *Houston Journal of International Law*, No. 2 (2007), p. 357.
25 See T. Onorato, "Apportionment of an International Common Petroleum Deposit: A Reprise", Vol. 26, *International & Comparative Law Quarterly* (1977), p. 324.

principles of soft law – argued that joint development has become a binding rule of international law.[26]

It suffices to say that irrespective of which school of thought eventually wins the argument on the bindingness of joint development of straddling resources, the fact is that among African states there is no evidence of *opinio juris sive neccesitatis* that will create a customary principle of law on this issue. That, however, does not mean that it is not indeed necessary for writers to argue in favour of adoption of cooperative cross-border upstream hydrocarbon exploitation in this instance. In the specific case of the Cameroon–Nigeria process, which is still ongoing as of 2015, the first important query to solve this riddle is whether the statements and acts of the parties during the ongoing negotiations of the Mixed Commission may be enough to *estoppe* any of the parties from refusing to conclude a joint development agreement.[27] Certainly there is enough in the records of the process in recent times as discussed earlier to show that the parties are seriously considering Cooperative Cross Border Upstream Hydrocarbon Exploitation, but does this mean they are bound under international law to conclude and successfully implement a JDZ or unitisation?

The answer to this question is debatable and the distinction on this issue made by a research team at the BIICL between situations where there is an agreed boundary and those where there is none is helpful, but the better view from our perspective is that the parties to the present process are not bound to do so as they may indeed not come to an agreement for varied reasons.[28] It is impossible to come to the conclusion that there may be no valid reasons why states may not be able to conclude a joint development agreement. If mutual distrust is so high between states as to make it too difficult to agree on joint development or prevent

---

26 Zhiguo Gao, "The Legal Concept and Aspects of Joint Development in International Law", Vol. 13, *Ocean Yearbook* (1998), p. 123.
27 The principle of estoppel developed principally as a rule of common law. Up until the late 1920s it was observed to have garnered little attention in the field of public international law but as MacGibbon puts it as at 1958: 'the marked increase since then in international judicial and arbitral activity has provided substantial grounds for the modern tendency to consider estoppel as one of the "general principles of law recognised by civilised nations".' The main justification and basis upon which estoppel survives in international law is the requirement that a state ought to be consistent in its attitude to a given factual or legal situation. See I. C. MacGibbon, "Estoppel in International Law", Vol. 7, *International & Comparative Law Quarterly*, No. 3 (1958), pp. *et seq*. Note also the early recognition given to this principle by Professor Bin Cheng: Bin Cheng, *General Principles of Law Recognised by International Courts and Tribunals* (Cambridge: Cambridge University Press, 1953) at p. 137 *et seq*.
28 The experts concluded:

> it would seem that international law only entails an obligation to consult and negotiate where States have broadly agreed on the delimitation of their maritime boundaries. There would seem to be no body of State practice upon which to underpin such a general obligation in the case where no boundary has been drawn in a disputed area.... It would seem in these circumstances that a disputant State may carry out unilateral prospecting in the disputed area. Our conclusion, therefore, is that in contradiction to agreed boundary areas where a known field straddles the boundary, there is at present as regards disputed areas no clear rule of customary law which requires a State to inform and consult other interested parties.
>
> (Fox (1989), op.cit, p. 35)

them from successfully concluding negotiations, then either wastage due to non-exploitation or wastage due to inefficient exploitation method whilst regrettable is a likely if not legitimate outcome. The intensity of previous rivalries and conflicting interests should not be so readily discountenanced without caution.[29] For instance, it is not to be forgotten that traditional perceptions of the immediate neighbours of Nigeria are that the country poses a deep concern because of its competitive capacity to appropriate valuable resources, particularly hydrocarbons and fisheries which abound in the maritime boundary areas. In other words, even in the case of agreed boundaries between two states, joint development may be customary practice based on what Miyoshi calls 'correct and scrupulous logic' but it has not and may not concretise into a customary rule of international law.

It is in this light that African states need to establish a consistent policy and practice. The onus to develop this presumption that joint production and sharing of hydrocarbon and fisheries resources is the African legal practice will largely fall on African arbitrators and judges. The ACJ will also have to develop jurisprudence in this area for in it arguably lays perhaps the solution to many hotly contested resource disputes which may threaten international peace. This argument is made here not without consideration of the fact that economic resources are the reason of great obstinacy by national governments. The fact, however, remains that there is something of a fascination for the communal as opposed to the allodial nature of land and in its resources in most African traditional cultures. Rivers and water resources are shared without rancour across the length and breadth of boundary lines and sometimes watering holes and infrastructure based in a neighbouring country are used by the citizens of the neighbouring state. Although there is the possibility of individualised ownership and 'propertisation' of land and resources, the central thrust of much of African understanding is that of common ownership through allocation by the sovereign or Chief.[30] Thus a principle of law that allows the governing authority to share resources without alienating some is arguably well within the 'proto-culture' of African states and societies. This presumption towards the unitisation and/or JPZ would arguably immunise African states to the deleterious activities of divisive multinational companies who may want to exploit international divisions between weaker states.

---

29 Note may be taken of the fact that the fear of the loss of Nigeria's vital offshore oil installations was one of the reasons why General Murtala Muhammad, a Nigerian Head of State, condemned the Maroua Accord, which was one of the treaties relied upon by the Court in coming to its decision. It remains true, however, that the suspicions are mutual and Cameroon, perhaps like some other neighbouring states of Nigeria, is fearful of Nigerian paternalism. With a vibrant and fast improving economic base and a population that is at least three times the size of the five states it shares boundaries with, Nigeria certainly evokes in the national memory of its neighbouring governments what an author describes as 'the potentialities of a sub-imperial state . . . masking an innate covetousness and potential threat to their territorial integrity'. Bassey E. Ate, "Introduction: Issues in Nigeria's Security Relations with its Immediate Neighbours", *Nigeria and Its Immediate Neighbours: Constraints and Prospects Of Sub Regional Security in the 1990s* Bassey E. Ate and Bola A. Akinterinwa (eds), (Lagos: Nigerian Institute of International Affairs, 1992), pp. 2, 6.

30 Olawale Elias, *The Nigerian Legal System* (London: Routledge, 1963); Olawale Elias, *Nigerian Land Law and Custom* (London: Routledge & Kegan Paul, 1962); Bonny Ibhawoh, *Imperialism and Human Rights* (New York: State University of New York Press, 2007), pp. 89–90.

18 Alternative futures

Strategies of negotiation and innovative methods to avoid deadlock in relation to territorial conflicts

It is perhaps important to begin by commending the good work done by the various peace commissions, mixed commissions, mediation panels, negotiation teams and international courts that have helped manage and bring resolution to African boundary disputes. It is worthy of note that the leaders of most African states have traditionally demonstrated enviable leadership by engaging in peaceful negotiations and thereby avoiding and bringing an end to military conflict and hostilities in relation to boundary and cross boundary disputes.

It needs to become more popular knowledge, particularly to political leaders, that the judicial instinct of boundary commissions is to reduce the possibility of winner-takes-all decisions. The jurisprudence of international courts in relation to African states is that the loss of a territory or the results of an unfavourable delimitation of boundary no longer means that nationals cut off into a winner's territory are at the total mercy of the territorial state. It is in fact the case in recent times that courts and boundary commissions have decided that the affected people do not have to lose their nationality. They are also not necessarily forced to take up the nationality of the new state. Attention must be drawn to the judgment of the ICJ in the *Cameroon–Nigeria Land and Maritime* case which unequivocally affirmed the rights of the affected Nigerian Bakassi population to continue to occupy the territory of Bakassi. The judgment and the ensuing Greentree Agreement both place onerous obligations on Cameroon to continue to provide a living standard for the Nigerian Bakassi population to an extent at least commensurate to that presumably which Nigeria has always done. Accordingly, starving the Peninsula of funds for administration and development would be an infringement of the judgment and the treaty.

In essence there are ways and means within contemporary international boundary jurisprudence by which the core interests of both states involved in a dispute may be accommodated allowing the necessary delimitation and demarcation to be done. It is our view that in many cases peaceful resolution is prevented simply because not enough was done to clearly communicate the crucial national interests to be protected and the real nature of the issues to be decided upon. Thus, it is often the case that careful articulation and presentation of the particular rights that both parties may seek to exercise will allow both states to bargain better by picking, mixing and choosing from the plethora of devices known to territorial and boundary arrangements under international law in order to resolve the problem at hand. With this in mind we may want to consider the following devices that have been successfully deployed to resolve disputes and put into practice outside the continent and for which there are extensive precedents in international relations.

These include:

(a) international territories;
(b) condominium;
(c) free cities;
(d) joint possessions;
(e) mandate and trust territories;
(f) international leases and servitudes, etc.[1]

It is indeed trite to observe that contested boundaries and territories can be resolved by using any of the above territorial arrangements in such a way as to reduce the effect of an outright grant of the contested territory to one state and to avoid zero-sum results. Indeed only the imagination can limit the possible arrangements, which can be reached to govern contested territories. Yet most of the categories listed above have not even been tested on the African continent.

The strength of these specialised legal arrangements lies in the fact that they allow great flexibility in relation to territorial boundaries through the recognition of severable rights and obligations within the totality of the doctrine of territorial sovereignty. In many cases the interest of a disputing state over a territory may be no more than retaining or exercising protection over an indigenous population within the contested territory. In such cases any of the above legal arrangements creating *sui generis* territorial entities may be created to resolve the contentious dispute.

18.1 Special territorial arrangements

Examples of *sui generis* entities created often after military hostilities in the last 50 years include the occupation and control of Germany, Taiwan, the Turkish Republic of Northern Cyprus and the Saharan Arab Democratic Republic. Apart from these, certain territories are created to account for practical situations and are often described by international lawyers as 'special cases', such as the Sovereign Order of Malta and the Holy See and Vatican City. Thus, in respect of populations that become excised into another state's territory, a territorial status may be conferred on the precise area occupied by the affected population which allows them to either be self-governing or governed under the civil and/or criminal jurisdiction and administration of the country that has lost the territory

---

1 Servitudes are rights by which something (such as a piece of land) owned by one person is subject to a specified use or enjoyment by another.

or boundary position. Yet another variant of this principle is that the lost population may remain part and parcel of the territorial state which will have its territorial sovereignty recognised, but particular competencies, such as aspects of administration, education, health, social affairs regulation and civil law, will remain under the losing state's control and regulation. It is possible that the victorious state will be satisfied to possess and exercise criminal jurisdiction over the population while ceding the civil jurisdiction to the state that lost.

18.2 Sale and purchase of territory

The sale and purchase of territory is a valid form of territorial acquisition as a form of peaceful cession. Many African boundary jurists will be surprised to learn about the history of Louisiana's inclusion into the US federation. The United States offered to purchase New Orleans, a city in Louisiana, from France. Napoleon Bonaparte, however, counter offered with the whole territory, and for a sum of $10,000,000 the US eventually bought the entire Louisiana territory in 1803 and incorporated it into the US.[2] Similarly, Spain ceded Florida to the US for $5,000,000 under the auspices of the 1819 *Adams Onis Treaty*.[3] The US thereafter relinquished its claims of parts of Texas west of the Sabine and other Spanish areas. Parts of Arizona and New Mexico were also purchased from Mexico in the Gadsden Purchase of 1853.[4] This option has not been explored on the African continent since the end of the colonial era. The option may, however, prove very useful, especially in those cases where a territorial victory will lead to the acquisition of a disgruntled population that may embark on many forms of disobedience and deleterious activities that it may make sense to sell the precise territory away. Spain, for instance, was forced to negotiate because it was losing its hold on its colonial empire, with its western colonies ready to revolt.

18.3 The establishment of free cities

The device of free cities was a common feature of the League of Nations era, which may in many ways find relevance in the resolution of many of the controversies over African territories. The establishment of a free city allows two

---

2 The idea of an offer to purchase New Orleans arose from a close relationship between France and the United States. Napoleon then had the most powerful army in Europe and saw the sale of his American territory as a goodwill gesture and a strategic move against the British. The American purchase of the Louisiana territory was not accomplished without domestic opposition. Federalist elements strongly opposed the purchase and favoured close relations with Britain rather than Napoleon. The Federalists forcefully argued that the purchase was unconstitutional.
3 Treaty of Amity, Settlement, and Limits between the United States of America and His Catholic Majesty (also known as the Transcontinental Treaty of 1819, and the Florida Treaty).
4 The purpose of this purchase was ostensibly to allow for the construction of a southern route for a transcontinental railroad, which in any case unfortunately was never built. Another rationale for the purchase was said to be to give Mexico more money in compensation for the small amount paid for the lands taken by the United States five years earlier in 1848. See further www.wordiq.com/definition/Gadsden_Purchase, accessed 1 February 2015.

contending powers to save face in a dispute over a small population by prima facie granting the people concerned considerable level of authority over that small city in such a way that each part retains some jurisdictional powers over aspects of the governance of that territory, but the city is more or less free from the strict supervision or ownership of either state and can within non sovereign limits govern itself. The classic case offered in many treaties on the subject is the Free City of Danzig.

In 1919, French Prime Minister Aristide Briand proposed the creation of the entity of the 'free city', as a sort of protectorate under the League. The city of Constantinople – strategically located at the mouth to the Black Sea and of religious importance to the Orthodox Christian countries of Europe, as well as of immense economic and cultural importance to Turkey – was the first free city to be established, in 1920. As a free city, Constantinople had its own municipal government that provided all manner of services to its population, but it was devoid of any of the central functions of government that are exercised by a sovereign state, such as defence and foreign relations.

The Free City of Danzig was a separate state established in 1919, as a territory that included the city of Danzig and its surrounding parts, previously part of Prussia (itself a part of the then German empire). The free city comprised 1,966 sq km (759 sq mi) including about 252 villages and 63 hamlets with a total population of 357,000 in 1919. With the Treaty of Versailles it was separated from Germany and created as a separate state under protection of the League of Nations with special rights reserved to Poland. The Free City of Danzig was made up of an ethnic German majority of over 90 per cent and a Polish minority of about 4 to 8 per cent. The free city was represented abroad by Poland and was in a customs union with Poland. Note also the Free City of Jerusalem which allowed Israelis and Palestinian Arabs to feel safe in their holy city; the 1948 establishment of Jerusalem as a League Free City placated Israeli nationalists and Muslims and fostered the initial productive relationship between Israel and its Arab Muslim neighbours.

Although the free city status option is an attractive option to the inhabitants of a troubled territory, it is less likely to be preferred by a party that considers that it has *de jure* sovereignty over the territory. Thus, this option would appear not to be easily attainable in the absence of a third party intervention of high significance such as by the UN, which may also have to supervise the entire arrangements. Nevertheless, there is no reason to believe that there is something about the African mind that is particularly unsuitable for this option.

18.4 Lease back options

The lease of territory between and among states is a practice with much precedence. Great Britain received a 99-year rent-free lease from China in 1898 over the territory of Hong Kong. In anticipation of the lease's 1997 expiration, China and Britain drafted the 1984 Sino-British Joint Declaration. The Joint Declaration stipulated that upon Great Britain transferring sovereignty over

Hong Kong to the People's Republic of China, the Basic Law of the Hong Kong Special Administrative Region of the People's Republic of China will come into effect as Hong Kong's constitution.[5] Ironically, despite a steadfast preference for the bare black letter interpretation of the decision of the ICJ in the *Land and Maritime* case, Cameroon very uniquely may have one of the few substantiated histories of territorial leases in the history of the continent, at least within the colonial era. Germany indeed was the first colonial power that acquired what was then known as the *Kamerun* and it leased part of its African Possessions in the *Kamerun* to France in the early part of the twentieth century. This early example displayed the main outlines of the practice of territorial lease, whereby the lessor pays a determined fee even if it is symbolic and the leasing state retains some level of jurisdiction over the leased territory.[6] The grant of a lease is always strictly construed and cannot involve the alienation of the territory by the lessor even when not so stated.[7] The general rule is that when a territory is leased it does not affect the sovereignty over the territory. Thus, when China leased Port Author to Russia in 1898 it stated that it was 'on the understanding that such lease shall not prejudice China's sovereignty' over this territory.

For leases it is crucial that the term of years is determined and the means of termination of the lease stated quite unambiguously. It is arguable that a lease arrangement over the Bakassi Peninsula between Cameroon and Nigeria could have been a suitable option in resolving the decades-long dispute between the parties.

18.5 Cession

Cession of territory from one state to another is permissible under international law. Where an African state in the face of better claims or more convincing arguments concedes the territory peaceably to another by cession, bitter disputes and heavy costs may have been so avoided.

18.6 Appropriate recourse to the use of plebiscites

It may be argued that there is much broader scope for the wider and more systematic use of plebiscites in the determination of ownership and sovereignty over contested lands in the African continent. Plebiscites are not totally unknown

---

5 Convention Between China and Great Britain Respecting an Extension of Hong Kong Territory (Convention of Peking), 29 June 1898, Gr. Brit.-P.R.C., 186 Consol. T.S. 310.
6 Para (e) of the lease states: 'It is understood that the loading and storing of Goods within said parts of the territory shall be effected in all respects in conformity with the laws then in force in the German possessions Kamerun'. See *Le Memorial Diplomatique*, 19 November 1911, p. 620. See also "The Kamerun Lease Contract", Vol. 6, *American Journal of International Law*, No. 2, Supplement: Official Documents (April 1912), pp. 111–113. In this particular case this even extends to the right of the lessor to sublease.
7 See George Grafton Wilson, "Leased Territories" in Editorial Comment, Vol. 34, *American Journal of International Law*, No. 4. (October 1940), pp. 703–704.

on the continent and were resorted to in accordance with the decision of the ICJ in the *Northern Cameroons* case to much acclaim. More recently Ethiopia and Eritrea in April 1993 separated as a result of a plebiscite. Carefully conducted plebiscites, preferably organised and monitored by the AU, will at the least offer equitable representation to the peoples caught up in a territorial dispute between states. This might prove a more pragmatic solution in comparison with the dogmatic adherence to colonial treaties upon which many such disputes are decided presently. This argument is particularly resonant for Africa and other parts of the New World due to whose collective efforts the principle of self-determination was specifically developed in the last century. It is relevant to note that even colonial powers appreciated and resorted to the mechanism of plebiscites in the resolution of territorial questions in Africa.[8] This of course is not to say that colonial treaties would have no further relevance in the determination of disputes by international courts. There is in fact no reason why colonial treaties cannot delineate the geographic scope (features and coordinates) of the territory and indicate other relevant issues while (in appropriate cases) the ultimate decision as to whose sovereignty prevails should be decided directly by the population affected.

This is probably the point that was made by the Attorney General of one of the federal states in the Nigerian federation, which is directly affected by the Bakassi decision of the Court. She stated:

> It is shocking to note that the ICJ would disregard the impact of its decision on the people of Bakassi in particular, and deliver a judgment. . . . The failure or omission to conduct plebiscites in Bakassi is not only discriminatory but offends against the Purposes and Principles of the UN and the Charter of the African Union with regard to self-determination. All persons have the right to their abode, within their ancestral territory, and should not be subjected to unjustifiable consignment of their ancestral land to a foreign government, country and alien culture without their consent or due consultation.[9]

---

8 As a result of a plebiscite conducted under the auspices of the United Nations in October 1961, the Southern Cameroons joined the Republic of Cameroon while the northern portion of the territory of the Cameroon under the administration of the United Kingdom of Great Britain and Northern Ireland joined the Federal Republic of Nigeria. T. O. Elias, *The International Court of Justice and Some Contemporary Problems* (The Hague: Martinus Nijhoff Publishers, 1983), p. 322; Note, however, Cameroun Government White Paper alleging irregularities in the Northern Cameroons plebiscite and arguing for its nullification. Republic of Cameroon, Ministry of Foreign Affairs and the Secretariat of State for Information. Position of the Republic of the Cameroon following the plebiscite of 11th and 12th February 1961 in the northern portion of the Territory of the Cameroon under the administration of the United Kingdom of Great Britain and Northern Ireland. Yaoundé, 1961, 48 pp. Cameroun Government White Paper alleging irregularities in the Northern Cameroons plebiscite and arguing for its nullification.

9 Nella Andem-Ewa, "Bakassi: Legal Options for Nigeria", *This Day* (Lagos), 3 December 2002, available at http://allafrica.com/stories/200212030216.html, accessed 1 February 2015.

18.7 Afrocentric solutions to the problems of delimitation and demarcation

It is necessary that home grown legal and judicial expertise on boundary matters must be developed. What is advocated here is not protectionism or restraint of trade but it must be realised that there is abysmal participation of African lawyers and judges in the area of boundary cases. The EEBC had only one African on board as an arbitrator. The lawyers that present cases on behalf of African countries at the World Court are invariably western lawyers; whereas the facts and incidences that will generate dispute on the continent from now until eternity will be invariably African. The potential for this skill gap to continue or grow in this century is real. The skilled gap pertains to nearly all areas of delimitation and demarcation practice but it is most revealing in the area of maritime law and scientific practice. Technical experts, notably hydrographers and cartographers, are invariably used in negotiations for a new boundary. A jurist wrote: 'it would be unthinkable to undertake negotiations for a new boundary, for instance, without first conducting a hydrographic study'.[10] Although some level of support in terms of technical expertise are supplied by intergovernmental organisations such as the UN and the Commonwealth Secretariat, the bulk of expertise needs to come from within Africa itself both as an issue of continental capacity development as well as an issue of security concern. This century ought to be the century of Africa's renaissance and since resource knowledge and exploitation will be central to this, information management needs to become more indigenised and not carelessly handled. Confidential negotiations over valuable national assets need not be exposed to the entire world just because of a dearth of qualified home grown expertise at this stage of African human development in the twenty-first century.

The AU border programme, thus, presents an opportunity to address this deficit of legal and technical skills base. Strategies ought to be put in place to encourage the training of African boundary experts in all relevant fields. It is indeed possible to plug the skills deficit and reverse the trend towards reliance on foreign experts within a generation. Particular emphasis should be made to encourage the bespoke training (in boundary studies) of lawyers and judicial officers that will form the bar and bench of the pertinent courts, particularly the ACJ. There are certain facts and elementary considerations, which a Court composed, of persons with local geographical or customary knowledge would very easily take judicial notice of. Local custom is often an important factor in land boundary disputes. Matters such as local farming patterns, fishing activities, rights of passage, easements and even religious observances may all prove to be highly significant during litigation.[11] This would save time and reduce the possibility of the Court inadvertently endorsing the disputants' claims that are

---

10 David Anderson, "Resource, Navigational and Environmental Factors in Equitable Maritime Boundary Delimitation" in Charney, Colson and Smith (eds), op.cit., p. 3219.
11 Daniel, op.cit., p. 222.

obviously unnecessary, mischievous or inflated. Africa has to put to good use its peculiar advantage of multiculturalism in its legal heritage. This rich heritage can only serve it well if it is harnessed and recognised as strength rather than a hindrance to the resolution of boundary marking and resolution of disputes. African rivers' and lakes' boundaries create special challenges in terms of: (a) delimitation and demarcation; and (b) the management of shared water and other resources. Just as there have been severe problems, there are also many instances of Afrocentric solutions and approaches to the sharing of common aquatic bodies that have to be studied. The sharing of experiences and best practices is, therefore, of paramount importance.[12]

The call for home grown expertise in all aspects of boundary making and boundary marking is justifiable on many grounds. In certain instances the close involvement of nationals is an essential part of a boundary delimitation exercise. The UN Commission on the Limits of the Continental Shelf correctly insists on the involvement of citizens from a state making submission in all phases of the Continental Shelf Claims Project. Nationals, and not the contractors or consultants they employ, are required to participate in the conduct of oral submissions and respond to interrogatories before the Commission during the examination of submissions.[13]

---

12 This was also one of the conclusions of African experts in AU, "Conclusion of the 2nd International Symposium on Land, River and Lake Boundaries Management", op.cit., para. VIII, pp. 3–4.
13 *Supra* Chapter 1, note 13.

19 Resolution of international boundary disputes involving African nations
Alternative futures and general conclusions

> I regard the territorial imperative as no less essential to the existence of contemporary man than it was to those bands of small-brained proto-men on the high African savannah millions of years ago.[1]

Sovereignty, territorial acquisition and territorial integrity are essential and integral concepts in the ordering of the international society of states. Hence they are important doctrines of international law that are worthy of interdisciplinary interest and continuous analysis. In a political sense sovereignty is the base of the influences and powers of the state, a fact recognised by Thomas Hobbes in his Leviathan where he wrote: 'A Common-wealth without Sovereign Power, is but a word, without substance, and cannot stand'.[2] The link between sovereignty and the territory and the overriding interests of the sovereign in safeguarding at all costs the territorial sovereignty is again eloquently expressed in the Leviathan; wherein Thomas Hobbes argued that 'Subjects owe to the Sovereign simple obedience, in all things, wherein their obedience is not repugnant to the laws of God'.[3] State territory is the place where that simple duty of total obedience is owed. In the normal course of international life it then becomes part and parcel of the rationale of being a sovereign that the sovereign must exercise and exert himself to account for every inch of that portion of the earth where obedience in all things is owed to him. Conversely he cannot expect obedience or exercise legitimate power over persons in foreign territory who are not bound to obey and to whom he is not sovereign. Persons and entities out of the territory of the sovereign are in that sense 'outernationals' and outside of the normal direct exercise of sovereignty. Jurisdiction, however, may follow outernationals in prescribed ways to the very ends of the earth.

The concept of territory as a genetically determined form of behaviour in many species is today accepted beyond question in the biological sciences.

---

1 Robert Arderey, *The Territorial Imperative. A Personal Inquiry into the Animal Origins of Property and Nations* (New York: Athenaeum, 1966), p. 18.
2 Thomas Hobbes, *Leviathan* (Digiread.com 2009), p. 152; see also Wendy Brown, op. cit., p. 73.
3 Ibid.

Lawyers and diplomats have to accept that which has been settled in the biological sciences, that the *homo sapien* is territorial by nature. Humans stake out property, chase off trespassers, diligently defend their territories precisely because they are sapient and this all started in Africa.[4] Hence it is impossible not to expect Africans to be conscious of territory or the need to protect and preserve to the exclusion of other sovereigns their landed territory. Territoriality is, thus, central to the human project. Territoriality is a primordial and necessary trait of any peoples even if in the case of nomadic tribes' territory it is held in a transient manner. Hence an early study of 24 different hunting groups with near paleolithic modes of existence in places like the Philippines, Congo forests, Tasmania, Tierra del Fuego in Canada, the Andaman Islands of the Indian Oceans and in the Kalahari desert of South Western Africa all formed social bands that occupy exclusive, permanent domains.[5]

In this light we make bold to submit that liberal attitudes to the notion of sovereignty to the extent that they appear to suggest that territorial sovereignty is becoming outmoded are imaginative but ultimately impractical. African states, like all states worldwide, must be prepared to ascertain and defend their territories. In Africa, boundary disputes are bound to continue to occur both as a result of colonial heritage of territorial and ethnic confusion but also as a result of sheer vicissitudes of politics and international relations. It is, therefore, important for international legal theory and practice that the rules surrounding boundary delimitation and demarcation be sufficiently elaborated upon. It is imperative for international peace and security in modern times that the rules and practices that govern this important area should be transparent and democratically collated. The days of sheer hierarchical imposition of theories, doctrines, practices and prescribed solutions by a few states in relation to boundary matters are happily over. What concerns all must be decided upon by all – *Caveat humana dominandi, quod omnes tangit ab omnes approbatur*. The legal rules surrounding boundary making, marking, reaffirmation and maintenance must be interrogated and re-interrogated continuously by modern day scholars and practitioners from the developing world. Regional solutions must be explored. This invitation to legal pluralism permits for regional colouration and understandings of international boundary law and admits of appropriate margins of appreciation.

It certainly cannot be assumed that international boundaries are not important or that African boundaries are inherently less rigid than or should be more ambivalent than any other international boundaries. There is in fact no single African understanding of the nature of international boundaries and like most other races and civilisations in the world, African boundaries tend to be more solid against neighbours than far off lands that are of no immediate physical threat to the territorial state. Respect for the precepts of territorial sovereignty and territorial jurisdiction (political independence and legal control) is one thing

---

4 Cf. Arderey, op.cit., p. 15.
5 Ibid.

and recognition of the *de facto* interdependent nature of the contemporary international system of states is another. Interdependence does not trump territorial sovereignty anywhere much less in Africa. Indeed in Africa the saying 'good fences make good neighbours' is poignant. This is, however, not to suggest ridiculous and impractical fencing mechanisms such as that experienced in other continents where fenced boundaries are becoming more rampant. The appreciation of precise coordinates and resort to valid mapping and conscientious demarcation activities are desirable features of African international law and diplomacy. This does not of course mean that ever closer unions bilaterally and sub-regionally should not be encouraged. Cooperative cross boundary ventures of all kinds must not only be permissible but encouraged. These include wider resort to commercial cooperation in the form of unitisation and joint production zones as well as cross cultural cooperation in the form of transnational parks and common fishing, grazing or hunting grounds. Such common zones must, however, not be allowed to become security black holes lacking in regulations and control. Several parts of Africa are quite easily susceptible to the horrors of piracy (Gulf of Eden and Gulf of Guinea). Insurgent groups and other local and foreign inspired terrorist militias also have an affinity for the frontier regions such as forests and desert areas that trans-border parks tend to be established. These zones should not be left uncontested and put into the hands of mischievous non state actors. Indeed the existence of transnational shared spaces should be geared towards more efficient management not only of the commercial resources that may be available but also the security and welfare interests of the sovereign states involved.

Since territorial boundaries are not only important but also inevitable, what can be done is to prepare the doctrine of law for the task of resolving in the most efficient and pacific manner the disputes that relate to and can emanate from boundaries. When liberal scholars express ideas that appear to deemphasise territorial sovereignty it may be argued that what they are really trying to do is to reduce its severity on human affairs. What then needs to be done in addition to preparing the rules and methods of resolving boundary disputes is to work out ways of ameliorating the effects of boundary delimitation on aspects of human and international relations. This would require multidisciplinary approaches and strategic management of dispute resolution. Thus, for instance, effort would be required to ensure that introduction or the redrawing of international boundaries does not lead to disappearance of languages or negatively affect human rights widely construed. Better attention to language and linguistic rights as well as other sociocultural and religious rights must accompany the making of law with respect to international boundaries. Where international boundaries become disruptive of traditional rights, such as fishing or pasturing grounds, provisions may be made in treaty or by other legal means for their continuance.

Targeted and meaningful aid, especially of a technical nature supplied by development partners including the African Development Bank, IMF/World Bank, IBRD, the European Union just to mention a few, have a place of value in assisting parties that have shown a readiness to move towards implementation of judicial and negotiated decisions as well as arbitral or other ADR awards. Development partners' assistance in socio-economic projects in African border areas would be very useful and ought to be promoted with more vigour by national governments, the RECs and international bodies.

International law, like all kinds of law, is a reflection of elitist interests. Like all laws as well it in many salient ways reflects the era it is written for and protects the interests of the most powerful forces and interests of the day.

The argument has often been made by African scholars that resort to Eurocentric adjudication and arbitrary mechanisms is unsuitable for resolving African disputes because of the inadequate attention that is paid to significant regional peculiarities and realities. Without prejudice to the importance of the main international courts and tribunals that deal with boundary and territorial disputes, there is no convincing reason to believe that many of the African boundary and territorial disputes cannot be satisfactorily resolved through other means of dispute resolution.[6]

In the short term, it is advisable that when African states enter into agreements regulating the resolution of boundary disputes and when they engage in drafting *compromis* clause submitting disputes to the main international courts they should:

(a) insist upon a regional International Court with competent jurisdiction or arbitration tribunals with their seat in Africa;
(b) infuse the applicable laws with the needed flexibility such as ability of the tribunal to decide *ex aequo et bono* or with reference to African traditional law.

Only in this way would African states escape the deleterious effects of arguing their cases before courts that at best may have demonstrated a lack of understanding of their peculiar interests and history in international relations and at worst have consistently by their jurisprudence established a bias against the collective interest of developing states.

There is the need for more frequent resort to ADR in resolving boundary disputes in particular, as opposed to full territorial contest. ADR techniques appear to be better suited for the resolution of certain kinds of disputes where what is in issue is whether a certain line should be followed where both parties claim the land, riparian or maritime space but it, for instance, splits a community

---

6 The argument has been made elsewhere that perhaps the ICJ and the PCA have in the past been incapable of handling African affairs as well as those of the developing world; it is necessary to bring certain facts, figures and historical accounts into analytical perspective. Examining two major issues or charges will do this. The first is that throughout their existence the courts have either by institutional design or inadvertently been applying a Eurocentric international law in a manner that compromises the interest of African and other developing states. Second, it is argued that the composition and staffing of these two institutions is inherently insufficient and probably biased against the overall interest of African and other developing states. Gbenga Oduntan, "How International Courts Underdeveloped International Law: Economic, Political and Structural Failings of International Adjudication in Relation to Developing States", Vol. 13, *African Journal of International and Comparative Law*, No. 2 (2005), pp. 262–313.

into two or separates the community from ancestral burial sites or important artisanal resources. At any rate as we have shown in this book there is evidence of some good practice of formal quasi-ADR involvement offered by the RECs as well as by other indigenous operators such as the use of elders. These methods need to be exploited more systematically and given greater support by all that are concerned with African peace and security. The ABIDSM proposed in this book only aims at building on these varied practices and to provide the necessary means by which better fine-tuned processes fit for the twenty-first century may be established.

The African Border programme and the law and practice it will set into motion is a veritable opportunity for African scholars, judges, lawyers and civil servants to reengineer international law and make it more user friendly to the needs of their continent. It is certainly not the time to engage in undue conservatism despite the alluring nature of the 'stability' it appears to offer. Africans do have a way of settling disputes in general and land disputes in particular and this must be reflected in the AU Border programme. It must rely on what has been achieved by the universalist sentiments/positivistic aspects of international laws but it must not be slavish to same (i.e. positivist aspects of international rules). It will not be the first time Africa has set or established trends that become acceptable worldwide. Africa may be credited with having given a new life to the concept of reconciliation after periods of national trauma. Examples exist in South Africa, Rwanda, Nigeria and others. It is easy to predict that the further development of the reconciliation method would be yet another innovation and contribution to world legal traditions emanating from the African continent.[7] It may also be envisaged that Afrocentric solutions would provide the necessary panacea to cure many of the festering boundary related disputes all over Africa.[8]

Boundary disputes are inimical to the continuous trend towards economic growth in the continent. For instance, the Kenyan and Ethiopian boundary

---

[7] The inter-ethnic fragmentation and ethnic rivalry that was produced by the colonial experience in Africa and which in many cases was carefully engineered by the colonial power makes reconciliation a particularly valuable means of dispute resolution on the African continent. There is no reason why such mechanism may not find usefulness even in disputes of an inter-continental nature. It may also be noted that the concept of reconciliation is a very important theme in Christian theology. The term reconciliation is derived from the Latin root word, '*conciliatus*', which means to come together, to assemble. Reconciliation refers to the act by which people who have been apart and split-off from one another begin to stroll or march together again. Essentially, reconciliation means the restoration of broken relationships. For a clearer exposition of reconciliation as an ADR technique, see: Kader Asmal, Louise Asmal and Ronald Suresh Roberts, *Reconciliation Through Truth: A Reckoning of Apartheid's Criminal Governance* (Cape Town: David Philip Publishers, 1996), p. 47; Joseph V. Montville, "The Healing Function in Political Conflict Resolution", in Dennis J. D. Sandole and Hugo van der Merwe (eds), *Conflict Resolution Theory and Practice: Integration and Application* (Manchester: Manchester University Press, 1993), pp. 112–127; Institute for Multi-Track Diplomacy, "Consultation on Reconciliation II: Final Report", Washington, DC: IMTD, 28–29 July 1995.

[8] See Issa G. Shivji, "Law's Empire and Empire's Lawlessness: Beyond the Anglo-American Law", International Conference on: "Remaking Law in Africa: Transnationalism, Persons, and Rights," Edinburgh, 21–22 May 2003, p. 5.

dispute spanning the years between 1963 and 1975 cost both states an estimated $44 million in bilateral trade. To put this in perspective, the loss amounted to over 11 per cent of Kenya's and about 23 per cent of Ethiopia's total overseas development assistance for the same period. The Chad–Libyan dispute between 1960 and 1994 had an estimated cumulative cost of $32 million. The Egypt–Israel dispute spanning 1950 and 1988 had a cumulative cost of $103 million.[9] Although this study is not aware of any precise studies done to determine the cumulative impact cost of the Cameroon–Nigeria dispute it may be expected that as a result of the long gestation period of this dispute and the strategic regional positons of both states across two sub-regions, the costs may be in the region of hundreds of millions of dollars.

The network of early warning systems in the various RECs covered in this book shows that there is some existing commendable capacity for quick detection of stress points and developing conflict situations across Africa. It is commendable that the existing early warning systems also tie in very well with the Continental Early Warning system. There are some differences in the workings of the various systems as well as in the rules designed for their operation. The SADC rules for the Early Warning System links very well with the national systems and the CEWs but mentions nothing about linkages with the early warning systems in other RECs. It may, however, be conceded that there are many other grounds for such collaboration between the different early warning systems within the continent.

While one must admit the inherent subjectivity of any exercise that seeks to rate the effectiveness of the various African RECs, and although this has not been the aim of this study, it can be said that they all appear to have certain identifiable areas of strengths and weaknesses. Taken together they show genuine potential as tools of multilateral diplomacy capable of providing genuine diplomatic and security assistance to their member states in times of crisis and conflict. Overall, the ECOWAS has an impressively developed institutional capacity in many key areas that is very useful for dealing with regional problems. It also has one of the oldest continuous historiographies in legal and political sub-regionalism in Africa created as it was in 1975 whereas most other RECs began their existence in a meaningful manner in the 1980s and even 1990s. ECOWAS shows a lot of potential as an avenue for political and legal settlement of the region's boundary disputes. The truth, however, is that although much progress has been shown in relation to the capabilities of ECOWAS to deal with political conflicts in general, its actual record in relation to boundary disputes has been very modest. IGAD on the other hand, with much more modest institutional capacity, has a much more active involvement in dealing with border management and boundary disputes. This is probably due to the political and legal space given to the organisation to link and collaborate with community leaders, village elders and NGOs in the boundary communities. This is an area in which other RECs may learn from as it will help douse border related conflicts and problems before they become bigger

---

9 Simmons, op.cit., p. 38; Okomu, op.cit., pp. 40–41.

and more intractable. It may be conceded, however, that the geography, ecology and pastoral nature of rural border regions in the IGAD sub-region makes it more attractive for governments in that sub-region to encourage local treatment of boundary problems as opposed to the situation in other regions such as West Africa where the various capitals tightly control every reaction to boundary problems in a more centralised manner.

Separatism as a phenomenon deserves serious attention in African international law and diplomacy given the widespread occurrence and virulent nature of secessionist movements and activities in all the sub-regions making up the continent. The effect of separatism on the future of African boundary disputes is in many ways apparent. Since we have not reached the end of history it is inevitable that newer states will emerge on the continent. Also, it cannot be impossible that existing or future independent states would find it necessary to coalesce into single units. The AU continental policy on management of separatist movements must be thoughtful, balanced and based on diligent research into the conditions that gave rise to the manifestation of the problems in the various national territories affected by the problem. The argument usually raised by national governments that the competence to deal with separatist movements are solely within their domestic jurisdiction should be challenged where there is a likelihood that cross-boundary spill overs of the situation will occur or human rights conditions will systematically breakdown. The legal provisions in certain RECs, such as the SADC allowing key organs to mediate crises and conflicts within member states, offer opportunities for the RECs to act proactively in relation to those countries facing separatist threats.

On the whole there are troubling uncertainties in relation to the effective and continuous existence of some of the key supranational judicial bodies in Africa. This situation is very unsatisfactory and will certainly have a deleterious effect on African international relations. If this situation is allowed to continue it will make the resolution of African disputes generally more difficult as it reduces the avenues for judicial resolution of international disputes. By definition the continuance of this situation also makes the resolution of African international boundaries more difficult as it reduces even further the availability of adjudicative venues for resolution of territorial and boundary disputes. The suspension of the SADC Tribunal by the Summit of Heads of State and Governments in August 2010 following representations by Zimbabwe has compounded this situation. The current unavailability of the ACJ in its envisaged form with an enlarged jurisdiction spanning human rights and other justiciable issues is perhaps the most disappointing fact from the perspective of the recommendation that African institutions should be preferable to foreign ones when it comes to the decision of where to litigate upon African boundary cases. In short, the untidy nature of the constitutive instruments of some of the political and judicial bodies of RECs leaves much to be desired. This is what has led to the quite disturbing finding in relation to the SADC that the body was not properly established and, therefore, could not be legally recognised as an institution of the SADC. A similar audit of the legal instruments in relation to all other regional courts may be recommended with a view towards fine-tuning their operative laws and making them more relevant to the needs of the African continent in the twenty-first century.

The successful implementation of the AUBP will largely depend on the Border Information System (BIS) designed by the AU, and this in turn depends on the timely feedback of participating countries. African states should, therefore, be encouraged to do all that is within their power and resources to assist in the actualisation of the aims and objectives of the AUBP. There is a balance to be struck between implementing a very detailed legal and political process and the invitation to chaos by inadvertent reawakening of irredentism and inordinate territorial and boundary claims across the continent. The danger is particularly true of the maritime boundaries and zones – areas that are usually rich in resources but very expensive and technical to decide upon. This is not to suggest that the demarcation of land boundaries is not fraught with significant difficulties. Even where all the concerned states in the AUBP move expeditiously to resolve the demarcation problems, the difficulties that may be encountered by the parties include the disappearance or obliteration of certain features that may have been mentioned in the applicable treaties; inaccuracy of the initial surveying or mapping effort; the inclusion of sensitive areas of religious,[10] traditional, ethnic[11] or economic importance in the areas of dispute and the possibility of areas of indeterminate sovereignty (such as Western Sahara).

There is a sense in which the finality of judicial and arbitral awards may have encouraged uncompromising attitudes and frequent resort to military conflicts among African states. It is recommended that there ought to be, as a feature of African boundary delimitation and demarcation practice, a presumption that the party that loses a contested territory should have a right if it so chooses to enter into lease agreements with the eventual winner of the territory. While a duty to agree to international leases will be going too far, the duty to at least negotiate on this point ought to be permitted and is good policy. There is a possible argument that the six-year-long implementation of the Cameroon–Nigeria process concerning the Bakassi area would have been halved if the negotiations had included from the beginning the possibility of an international lease of Bakassi by

---

10 This case even shows that many years after definitive judgment severe problems may flare up as a result of religious and cultural implications on the affected population. The *Temple of Preah Vihear* case concerned a boundary conflict between Cambodia and Thailand (formerly known as Siam). The disputed area contained an old temple of great archaeological significance. It had been built by the Khmer Peoples, the ancestors of the present Cambodian population, at the high point of their power; since then the Khmer Peoples have been forced back into smaller areas. The considerations the parties wished the Court to pronounce upon included: to which of the two countries' history is the temple more related. Despite the Court's decision in 1962, conflict persists between the parties in relation to the temple (ICJ Rep. (1962), p. 14). Military conflicts and skirmishes occurred as recent as 2008. See Thomas Bell, "Thailand Steps back from Cambodia Conflict", *Telegraph*, 6 January 2010, available at www.telegraph.co.uk/news/worldnews/asia/cambodia/3195213/Thailand-steps-back-from-Cambodia-conflict.html, accessed 6 January 2010; Richard Lloyd Parry, "Thailand and Cambodia Teeter on Edge of Conflict at Cliff-top Temple", *Times*, 19 July 2008, available at www.timesonline.co.uk/tol/news/world/asia/article4360257.ece, accessed 6 January 2010.
11 The Nigerians caught in the Bakassi judgment in the Land and Maritime Judgment.

Nigeria from Cameroon. Similarly the very slow progress that has typified the Eritrea–Ethiopia process would have been prevented if the possibility of leases and territorial exchanges was injected into the proceedings.

It is true that the distances across Africa's boundaries are daunting and this must be taken into account in formulating the implementation of the AU Border programme. The time scale that is required for a qualitative delimitation and demarcation process across the continent in all the areas that have not been so delimited and demarcated is significant and clearly beyond the period earmarked under the current programme. It is recommended that a 30-year plan is put into place in which a phased approach will be used to attain the aims and objectives of the African Boundaries programme. This phased approach preferably based on a sub-regional timetable will allow for more qualitative concerted effort required to analyse and formalise the process of delimiting territories in particular regions. A realistic time frame will allow the member states to cover all aspects of the best practices in boundary work such as recovery, delimitation, demarcation and reaffirmation. It also accords better with the view that boundary work is a continuous phenomenon – a means to an end and not an end in itself. In this way, supervision of boundary management according to best practices may eventually fall under the African Union Boundary programme. This is certainly not to suggest that rigorous demarcation is required along every inch. Boundary pillar emplacement programmes, for instance, may be unnecessary along previously uncontested boundaries and along inaccessible mountain ranges or other dangerous places. Boundary pillars that are 'intervisible' will be required along settlements and other border villages for ease of reference and to inform the largely illiterate population that live in the African, rural border areas.

The idea that clear demarcation of a state's boundaries is required only when economic resources are involved is counterintuitive to the prevention of conflicts, and promoting of integration. Yet African border areas ought to be assisted to become areas of opportunity and bridges between peoples rather than peripheral and divisive in all senses. Governments have to be made to realise that boundaries define both a state's rights to the resources of territory, as well as its responsibilities for the administration of populations within that territory. It ought to also be one of the aims of the African Union Boundary programme to encourage the creation in all member states of a Border Region Agency. These agencies are to have the function of bringing infrastructural, education, health and economic development to the border areas, which in most cases are located in more central parts of the states and the capital cities.

The popular conception that demarcation pre-empts an end to all cross border interaction/relationships is inherently 'un-African' and all effort must be made to keep things that way. It is hoped that the legacy of the African Union Boundary programme would be the advent of greater cooperative management by neighbouring states in the border areas not only because ambiguities causing boundary disputes would have been removed but because an era of genuine cross-border cooperation would have been created. Local stakeholders ought to be involved as direct initiators of cross-border cooperation under the auspices of states. There is the need for states to understand that they have an interest in facilitating local initiatives.[12] Cross-border cooperation remains a strong factor of peace, stability and development. Positive examples abound across the continent but these must be multiplied in the course of the AUBP processes and it must be seen as one of the aims of the AU to forge solidarity and good neighbourliness through local and national cross-border cooperation.[13] The time has come for the idea of an African Boundary Commission. This commission will, among other things, act as a depository for official maps, treaties, conventions, pacts and agreements relating to Africa's internal and external boundaries. The African Boundary Commission as a permanent institution, apart from being able to take over the management of the AUBP, may also perform several important functions including assisting national boundary commissions in attaining their goals. It may also host a world class academic and/or vocational institution – African Boundary Research Centre. This institution would engage in the provision of world standard training for delegations and professionals from African states in all areas of boundary studies.

The creation of the African Boundary Research Centre may also facilitate the training of high calibre engineers, drilling experts, geologists, marine and fisheries experts and even business and management experts to service the demands of the continent. There ought to be an interest in achieving self-sufficiency at least in the provision of skilled labour that would be engaged in the management of African Boundaries and this task cannot in good conscience of present African leadership be contracted out again to European and North American states only. The benefits of this to all states concerned are innumerable and of course include employment generation. In this way the region may also contribute to the international demand for high skilled expatriate workers in surveys, cartography,

---

12 Conference of African Ministers in Charge of Border Issues, "Declaration On The African Union Border Programme and Its Implementation Modalities Addis Ababa, 7 June 2007", Preparatory Meeting of Experts on The African Union Border Programme Addis Ababa, Ethiopia, 4–7 June 2007 BP/MIN/Decl.(II) pp. 2–3; see also Conference of African Ministers in Charge of Border Issues, "Report of the Meeting of Experts on the Border Programme of the African Union, Bamako, Mali 8–9 March, 2007", Preparatory Meeting of Experts on The African Union Border Programme Addis Ababa, Ethiopia 4–7 June 2007, p. 7.

13 *Supra* Chapter 5, note 43. See also Appendix III. The development of transfrontier parks and transfrontier conservation areas is fast becoming common on the continent. Examples include the Great Limpopo Transfrontier Park – the largest wildlife park in the world – and the Kgalagadi Transfrontier Park, which comprises the Gemsbok National Park in Botswana and the Kalahari Gemsbok National Park in South Africa; the Ai-/Ais/Richtersveld Transfrontier Park between South Africa and Namibia (approximately 35,000 sq km). These laudable initiatives are backed up by treaties that remove boundaries separating conservation areas and other protected areas in favour of integrated, jointly managed parks. Cameroon and Nigeria are also in talks to establish such a transnational park within certain areas along their newly demarcated 2,000-km common boundary. President Thabo Mbeki was quite forthright in denoting the positive effects of the African initiatives in integrating and unifying its communities towards prosperity. He stated: 'We are doing this because we have understood very well that all of us are interdependent, that the success of any one of our countries depends on the success of the others', SouthAfrica.info, "SA, Namibia Cross-border Park", available at www.southafrica.info/about/sustainable/sanamibia-park.htm, accessed 7 January 2010.

Alternative futures and general conclusions 381

boundary ethnologists and lawyers among others. If there is to be any chance at all of a successful and meaningful management of boundary conflicts by the AU, capacity building must be taken even more seriously by the organisation. This will at the very least require the injection of added specialist personnel to the Conflict Management Division of the Peace and Security Department. Without a largely indigenous army of skilled workers in these key industries there can be no meaningful control of national boundaries and perhaps resource exploitation. Delay in developing these competences may ultimately prove fatal to national economic growth and even collective security. It is necessary to continue cataloguing existing capacities within the continent and putting such capacities to use. More frequent use should, therefore, be made of existing specialist institutions such as the African Organization of Cartography and Remote Sensing (AOCRS).[14] Closer engagement should also be struck with the few private think tanks and research centres such as the African Regional Institute Imeko, Ogun State.[15]

African scholars should be encouraged to contribute to scholarly literature in this area. Such contributions would highlight best practices in/guidelines for delimitation, demarcation, maintenance and of African boundaries reaffirmation. There is no reason why African scholars and practitioners may not contribute qualitatively to the lexicon, law and practice of international boundary law. Other interesting and appropriate suggestions that deserve mention include the promotion of an 'African Border Day' to highlight the importance of the AUBP and encourage further efforts towards its implementation. To date there have been four celebrations of this border day.[16] It may, however, be suggested that a

---

14 The African Organization of Cartography and Remote Sensing (AOCRS) is an African intergovernmental organisation, established in Addis Ababa in 1988 by the merger of African Association of Cartography (AAC) with the African Remote Sensing Council (ARSC). The AOCRS is the principal national mapping and remote sensing organisation/agency representing the governments of 24 African countries: Algeria, Burkina Faso, Cameroon, Central Africa, Congo, DR Congo, Cote d'Ivoire, Ethiopia, Gabon, Ghana, Guinea, Liberia, Libya, Madagascar, Mali, Mauritania, Morocco, Niger, Senegal, Sudan, Tanzania, Togo, Tunisia and Uganda; visit www.agirn.org/documents/AOCRS_leaflet.pdf, accessed 7 January 10. See also Conference of African Ministers in Charge of Border Issues, the Report of the Meeting "Preventing Conflicts, Promoting Integration", Preparatory Meeting of Experts on The African Union Border Programme Addis Ababa, Ethiopia 4–7 June 2007. BP/EXP/RPT(II), pp. 4–5.
15 Anthony Ashiwaju, "Respacing for Peace, Security and Sustainable Development: The African Union Border Programme in European Comparative Historical Perspective", in Ulf Engel and Paul Nugent (eds), *Respacing Africa* (Netherlands: Brill, 2010), p. 105.
16 AU, "Conclusion of the 2nd International Symposium on Land, River and Lake Boundaries Management", op.cit., pp. 3–4. The last one before publication of this book was held in Addis Ababa, 6 June 2014. The Day was celebrated in the presence of AU member states, representatives of the diplomatic missions in Addis Ababa, RECs, partners, international organisations, Civil Society Organisations (CSOs), as well as staff from the AUC. The event featured a release of Part II of the Documentary titled "African Borders; From Barriers to Bridges" and the launching of new guidebooks on the introduction of the newly adopted Convention on Cross-Border Cooperation as well as a photo exhibition showcasing 'historical documents and, images from African borders'. AU, The African Union celebrates the 4th African Border Day (Newly Adopted Convention on Cross-Border Cooperation Introduced) – see more at www.peaceau.org/en/

more meaningful way of actualising the benefit of this event is for there to be simultaneous official recognition and celebration of this day across all African territories in symbolic ceremonies at recognised borders between African states. The importance of synergy and continuous dialogue between border policy makers, scholars and boundary practitioners is irrefutable. More widespread establishment by Member States of National Boundary Commissions is recommended but it is recognised that the costs of maintaining such institutions may in the nature of things be considerably prohibitive for the smaller or more indigent states.

At any rate, it is most important to reimagine the role and effect of contemporary international law in the resolution of African disputes generally. It is on this note that we align ourselves with the powerful submissions of Professor Issa G. Shivji. He wrote:

> whatever the achievements of Western bourgeois civilisation, these are now exhausted. We are on the threshold of reconstructing a new civilisation, a more universal, a more humane, civilisation. And that cannot be done without defeating and destroying imperialism on all fronts. On the legal front, we have to re-think law and its future rather than simply talk in terms of re-making it. I do not know how, but I do know how not. We cannot continue to accept the value-system underlying the Anglo-American law as unproblematic. The very premises of law need to be interrogated. We cannot continue accepting the Western civilisation's claim to universality. Its universalization owes much to the argument of force rather than the force of argument. We have to rediscover other civilisations and weave together a new tapestry borrowing from different cultures and peoples.[17]

It is possible to envisage that African states may more frequently avail themselves of the mechanism of the ACJ, which is the principal judicial organ of the AU.[18] Of particular significance are the provisions of the Protocol on Eligibility to Submit Cases (Article 18), Competence/Jurisdiction (Article 19), Sources of Law (Article 20), Summary Procedure (Article 55) and Special Chambers (Article 56). Also Article 18 would arguably be useful to the extent that it also recognises the right of 'third parties' to submit cases to the ACJ under conditions to be determined by the AU Assembly and with the consent of the state party concerned

---

article/the-african-union-celebrates-the-4th-african-border-day-newly-adopted-convention-on-cross-border-cooperation-introduced#sthash.ATMHEghl.dpuf, accessed 23 November 2014.

17 I. Shivji, "Law's Empire and Empire's Lawlessness: Beyond Anglo-American Law", Vol. 1, *Law, Social Justice & Global Development Journal* (LGD) (2003), available at www2.warwick.ac.uk/fac/soc/law/elj/lgd/2003_1/shivji2/, accessed 2 February 2015; see also Issa G. Shivji, *Where is Uhuru?: Reflections on the Struggle for Democracy in Africa* (Cape Town: Fahamu Books, 2009), p. 255.

18 The Court was established in consonance with the Constitutive Act of the Court of Justice of the African Union. See Protocol of the Court of Justice of the African Union in Vol. 13, *African Journal of International and Comparative Law* (2005), pp. 115–128.

(Article 18 (d)).[19] Furthermore, the assembly is empowered to confer on the ACJ power to assume jurisdiction over any dispute (Article 19 (2)).

It is desirable that over the next years and decades the ACJ should develop and establish clear jurisprudence in the area of boundary disputes, resource exploitation, maritime delimitation and environmental disputes. If indeed judicial settlement proves to be the favoured mechanism by African states in resolving boundary matters it would be desirable if not crucial that the ACJ should make good use of the unique provisions allowing (inter alia) the general principles of law recognised by African states (Article 20 (d)) to form part of its jurisprudence in deciding territorial and boundary matters.

It is also noteworthy that the provisions establishing the ACJ share many similarities with those that establish the jurisdiction of the ICJ. For instance, the provision on competence of the Court and sources of law are drafted largely along the lines of Articles 36 and 38 of the Statute of the ICJ. Apart from the controversial compulsory jurisdiction mechanism in Article 36 (2 a–d of the Statute), the jurisdiction of both courts includes: (a) the interpretation of treaties; (b) any question of international law; (c) the existence of any fact which, if established, would constitute a breach of an international obligation; and (d) the nature or extent of the reparation to be made for the breach of an international obligation.

Both courts have as their function the making of decisions in accordance with international law through the application of: (a) international conventions, whether general or particular, establishing rules expressly recognised by the contesting states; (b) international custom, as evidence of a general practice accepted as law; (c) the general principles of law recognised by civilised nations; and (d) the teachings of the most highly qualified publicists of the various nations, as subsidiary means for the determination of rules of law and the ability to decide a case *ex aequo et bono*, if the parties agree thereto. African scholars and critics of the perceived 'Eurocentricity' of public international law would follow the jurisprudence of the ACJ very closely to see what principles it would recognise as 'general principles of law recognised by African states' and indeed how much diffidence it would pay to this invitation to enrich international judicial practice. The power of the ACJ to appoint experts and commission enquiries under Article 30 are also useful mechanisms of the Court which may assist it to quickly attain world class judicial competence.

The African Union Border programme will in time accelerate the introduction of new boundary related treaties among African states. Dispute resolution clauses naturally constitute a crucial part of any such treaty. It is, thus, necessary that this is the stage that serious thinking must be brought to bear on the best Afrocentric procedures to encourage and promote boundaries dispute settlement mechanisms among African states. The prevalent view among African scholars and statesmen is that litigation routes that have been dogmatically adopted by

---

19 It is arguable that in time this could be a basis for the eventual acceptance of multinationals into the Court's jurisdiction as parties.

African states in the past have produced poor and unsatisfactory results in African international relations.

The inclinations for a change in direction in state behaviour are discernible. Examples may be made here of regional cooperation in the Gulf of Guinea leading to the recent establishment of the Gulf of Guinea Commission. The recently concluded Treaty Establishing the Gulf of Guinea Commission[20] outlines the framework of the Gulf of Guinea Commission and prescribes its objectives, powers and responsibilities. With the huge interests generated among the major oil producing multinational corporations (MNCs), the newer independent producers and the participating states, it was clear to the participating states that the treaty to govern this massive rich and strategic littoral zone which is largely un-demarcated must apart from facilitating a sustainable and responsive regime for the anticipated explosion of exploitative activities, prepare a reliable dispute resolution mechanism.

The parties to the Treaty stated they are '[a]nxious to settle our disputes by peaceful means' (Preamble). Article 20 of the Gulf of Guinea Treaty thus states:

> Member States shall act collectively to guarantee peace, security and stability as prerequisites to the realization of the objectives set forth in this Treaty. To this end, they undertake to settle their disputes amicably. Failing which either party shall refer the matter to the Ad Hoc Arbitration Mechanism of the Treaty or any other mechanism for peaceful resolution of conflicts stated by the Charters of the United Nations, the Organisation of African Unity and the African Union.

State members are, thus, generally enjoined to act collectively to guarantee peace, security and stability as prerequisites to the realisation of the objectives set forth in the Treaty. To this end, the member states are enjoined to settle their disputes amicably. Where a dispute persists, the state parties may refer the matter to the Ad Hoc Arbitration Mechanism of the Treaty or another mechanism for peaceful resolution of conflicts stated by the Charters of the United Nations, the Organisation of African Unity and the African Union. The formulation of Article 20, therefore, arguably suggests a hierarchy of dispute management techniques for the member states. Attempts should first be made to reach amicable settlement and by this the drafters appear to refer to *bona fide* negotiation. Second, *ad hoc* arbitration may become applicable. Third, parties to the dispute may make reference to any of the means of resolution contained in the Charter of the United Nations. The principal means as identified earlier are to be found in Article 33 of the Charter.

---

20 Hereinafter referred to as the Treaty. A Bill for an Act to Enable Effect to be given in the Federal Republic of Nigeria to the Treaty Establishing the Gulf of Guinea Commission has been placed before the National Assembly of Nigeria. The Bill is sponsored by the Executive and has had its first reading on Tuesday, 1 February 2005. See further www.nassnig.org/bills/BILLS%20 PAGE%202004.htm, accessed 6 March 2006.

It is, however, doubtful that reference is being made here to Article 33 because the provision therein largely refers to methods which form part of the 'amicable means' already envisaged in the first sentence of Article 20.[21] It appears, therefore, that reference is being made to the jurisdiction of the ICJ. The ICJ is the principal judicial organ of the UN and its basic instrument is the Statute of the Court, which forms an integral part of the Charter and is annexed to it. It must, however, be noted that reference of the dispute to the Security Council or the General Assembly of the UN under Article 34 and 35 (1) of the Charter is also a possibility.[22] Fourth, the matter may be dealt with in accordance with the African Union (AU) Charter. It is possible to also argue that the parties to the Treaty being African states themselves would have a preference for the mechanisms under the AU Charter and would prefer to seek resolution of the dispute under the AU regime before the UN regimes.

It is important to mention the pride of place that arbitration has also played in the resolution of territorial and boundary disputes. As Hazel Fox eloquently stated of the arbitration route:

> The first element, and the one which historically has induced States to submit disputes to arbitration, is the necessity for consent of the arbitrating parties to every stage in the arbitration. Selection of judges of their own choice is only one aspect of the very wide powers of supervision and control given to States under the usual arbitration agreement.[23]

The idea that consent, not only given at the beginning of the arbitration proceedings, but that which 'continues throughout the proceedings until the tribunal retires to make its award, is therefore, an essential ingredient to the completion of any arbitration' is certainly true. However, this does not assure a party that it can withdraw consent so as to disrupt the arbitration opportunistically and forestall an unfavourable award.[24]

Boundary experts are beginning to converge on the position that there is a possible hierarchy of dispute resolution mechanisms to be resorted to for territorial and boundary disputes.[25] This position falls in line with the demands

---

21 Article 33 provides that:

> the parties to any dispute, the continuance of which is likely to endanger the maintenance of international peace and security, shall, first of all, seek a solution by negotiation, enquiry, mediation, conciliation, arbitration, judicial settlement, resort to regional agencies or arrangements, or other peaceful means of their own choice.

22 Indeed Article 34 and 35 make provision for any member of the United Nations to bring any dispute, or any situation which might lead to international friction or give rise to a dispute or endanger the maintenance of international peace and security to the attention of the Security Council or of the General Assembly.

23 Hazel Fox "Arbitration", *International Disputes: The Legal Aspects* (London: Europa Publications, 1972), p. 101.

24 Fox, op.cit., p. 100.

25 Derek Smith, "Principles of Dispute Resolution: A Practical Route to Follow", International Boundary Disputes in Oil & Gas, Houston, Texas (2004); Justin Stuhldneher, "Steps You Need to

of the LOSC (1982) that negotiations should be the principal means of resolving maritime delimitation.[26] Although clearly each case would be unique and may deserve a different conclusion, it has been observed that the preponderance of practice is in favour of bilateral negotiation, conciliation and mediation.[27] The results of any of these are capable of being made binding by signature to a document or treaty. This is followed by judicial settlement, which includes arbitration and *ad hoc* tribunals. Preference for negotiation is borne out of the need to avoid the perceived arbitrariness of judicial decisions or the rigidity with which legal principles are followed in a situation, which may call for sensitivities unknown to law. Negotiation reduces or even removes the costs of legal representation. Negotiation is also viewed as being in line with the instinct of states to engage in international politics.

In many cases, even after the long and expensive route of adjudication has been completed, parties find themselves returning to the table to negotiate raising the presumption that this is perhaps where the matter would have been best resolved. Although technically speaking the dispute would have been decided upon by the ICJ, it is often clear that there is no unanimity as to how to give effect to all aspects of the Court's judgments and the Court itself often enjoins the state parties to enter into further negotiations with respect to certain issues. With these considerations in mind it is necessary that full weight is given to the recommendation of the conference of African ministers in charge of border issues that concluded that the Act must: 'encourage the States to undertake and pursue bilateral negotiations on all problems relating to the delimitation and demarcation of their borders'.[28] Clearly Africa does not lack 'very heavy weight and competent representatives' who can conduct international negotiations in the best traditions of the term.[29]

Recent examples in the Cameroon–Nigeria and Namibia–Botswana and other processes denote certain commonalities and peculiar trajectories. The parties must set up joint negotiation teams comprising of equal numbers of high level officials and experts as much as possible of coordinate grade levels.[30] One of

---

Take to Negotiate and Operate Within a Production Sharing Agreement: A Roadmap to Success", International Boundary Disputes in Oil & Gas, Houston, Texas (2004).

26 Griffin, op.cit., pp. 151–152.
27 On occasion, the UN itself will, at the request of the parties, appoint a mediator in an attempt to resolve matters (for instance in the *Guatemala/Belize; Guyana/Venezuela* disputes).
28 Paragraph 5 (a)(i), Declaration On The African Union Border Programme, *supra* Chapter 1, note 3.
29 (See Opening Remarks By The Chairman Of The Mixed Commission And Special Representative Of The Secretary-General Of The United Nations, Mr. Ahmedou Ould-Abdallah, Yaoundé, 1 December 2002 available at www.un.org/Depts/dpa/prev_dip/africa/office_for_srsg/cnmc/speeches/spchlist.htm, accessed 12 February 2005).
30 This factor does admit of the introduction of experts who may have difficulty fitting into a known governmental or civil service grade structure. The equivalence of such a person will in fact depend on their reputation or expertise value. In many cases this will be easily explicable by the nature of the specialism or added value they bring to the process. It is highly discouraged that countries use any slots available in boundary negotiation/implementation commissions to advance the course of

the first tasks that the negotiating team will have to deal with is to agree on the applicable treaty instruments and compare their interpretations of such instruments.[31] Effort must be made to identify areas of agreement. Regarding such areas, agreement may be made as soon as practicable in relation to the demarcation specifications. This includes agreement as to pillar types, pillar interval mapping corridor, map scales, etc. The attention of the teams will inexorably have to shift to areas of differences where the parties have opposing or divergent views. Consensus would have to be reached on how to delimit and demarcate these areas. Where necessary compromises and agreements have been made on the above, the parties must then produce final demarcation maps with all boundary pillars and coordinates to be domesticated by each party and circulated to all stakeholders. Parties may then set up a joint boundary management and transboundary activity related structure.[32]

Where parties have, however, taken the judicial settlement route, in all likelihood they would still have to resort to many aspects of the foregoing in that the decision of the Court or arbitration panel will in practice be referred to a joint commission with (preferably) or without a facilitator of the process who will be part of the Commission. As mentioned earlier, in the case of the Eritrea–Ethiopia process the decision was taken by the state parties to retain the same Commission that decided this process as the demarcators. Joint commissions usually work out the modalities for the implementation of the decision of the judicial process.[33] Although theoretically the Court or arbitral body should have resolved the dispute and all that should remain is a rapid implementation process, recent disputes have shown that what the Court or panel can really do is to 'decide' or make an 'award'. In other words, 'resolution' of the dispute in the true sense of the word belongs to the parties. Thus, an implementation body will in all likelihood find itself having to work out modalities to resolve knotty issues and lingering problems between the parties in the spirit of give and take where necessary. This phenomenon of post formal decision diplomacy should be seen as a strength rather than a shortcoming of boundary determination processes.

This book must conclude with an attempt to present a possible flowchart for the resolution of boundary disputes. The flowchart is derived from several sources. First, it is informed by the elaboration of the law and practice of dispute settlement in boundary matters dealt with so far in this book. Second, it is informed by the results of the interactions we have had with various officials in the RECs and the

---

nepotism or sheer political appointments as the matters at hand are of grave importance and it is in the interest of all that only competent persons of value to the process are brought on board.

31 Where the list of applicable laws has already been decided upon by a Court or other legal process, the parties may simply move towards demarcation.

32 S. M. Diggi, "Negotiation and Demarcation of International Boundaries – The Experience of National Boundary Commission of Nigeria", Paper presented at 2nd International Symposium on Land, Maritime River and Lake Boundaries: Maputo, Mozambique 17–19 December 2008, p. 4.

33 The funding for the activities of joint commissions are usually by equal contributions of the parties and/or assistance or grants from donor agencies and friendly countries, *supra* Chapter 2, note 56; see also Diggi, ibid., p. 6.

AU. Third, it is distilled from observed good practice in the African region as well as internationally. Fourth, it is based upon available or attainable dispute resolution mechanisms, institutions and facilities on the continent. The caveat must be immediately added that pragmatism is the first rule of success in the area of international dispute settlement engagements. Therefore, a linear approach to the steps may not be helpful in some circumstances and it may be necessary to mix the order up or miss out on some steps entirely. The end in this manner does justify the means as long as pacific settlement of the disputes is achieved. The following typology is thus, recommended:

- Declaration of an open dispute
- Involvement of Interstate Commissions
- Assistance of a Neutral Study Group (to discover and delineate the issues)
- Technical studies and the holding of Seminars
- Direct Negotiation
- Adoption of ADR mechanisms and techniques
- Involvement of RECs
- Continental Intervention by the AU
- African Arbitral Mechanism
- Judicial Mechanisms: ACJ; International Court of Justice.

It is also suggested that there is scope for increased participation for civil society organisations in boundary dispute management and resolution. They can be very useful in the area of preventative diplomacy and can assist in rebuilding after conflicts. It is thought that they will, however, be of little use during direct negotiations when a dispute has already commenced.

Appendix I

QUESTIONNAIRE

INSTRUCTIONS FOR FILLING UP THE DATA FOR THE AU BOUNDARY SURVEY

1.-	Each Member State should, for each boundary with a neighbouring state, choose the number (from 1 up to 9) which best represents the actual status of that boundary.
2.-	If certain types of boundaries are not relevant to a given Member State, please enter zero (0).
3.-	If found relevant, data may be exchanged between Member States that share a boundary to ensure consistency.
4.-	Specific remarks/observations may be made to provide further clarifications on the data provided.
5.-	The Commission does not expect any Member State to gather any extra data in the field. The data required for the purpose of the production of a map on the status of African boundaries should be available already in the relevant national structures, e.g. Commission of Boundary, Department of Surveying and Mapping, etc.

DELIMITATION	process of establishing a boundary in treaty or any other legal instrument.
DEMARCATION	process of physically marking the boundary on ground (e.g. constructing boundary beacons).
REAFFIRMATION	when the boundry has already been delimitated and demarcated in the past and there is need to make it more clear by placing more intermediate beacons, rebuilding misplaced, missing and/or displaced beacons, etc.

Appendix II

RESPONSES

- ALGERIA
- BURKINA FASO
- CAMEROON
- CONGO
- MALI
- MAURITIUS
- MOZAMBIQUE
- NAMIBIA
- NIGER
- SUDAN
- TUNISIA

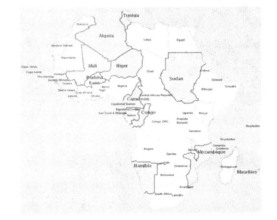

Responses to AUBP Questionnaire

Appendix III

Rebels on Borders/Borderlands

Rebels on Borders/Great Lake Regions (GLR)

Appendix III 393

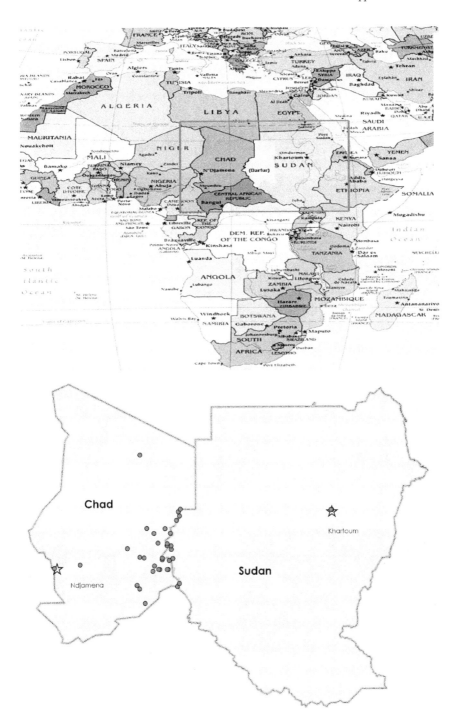

An Overview of Border Security-Hotspots

394 *Appendix III*

Border Security Hotspots-Chad-Sudan

Border Security Issues: Refugees

Heroin found at
Mozambique-SA Lebombo
Border Post

Drugs Seizure in
Nianing, Senegal

Border Security Issues: Drugs

Appendix III 395

Weapons

Border Security Issues: Gun Smuggling

Illegal Border Crossings

UPDF Patrolling
Uganda-DRC
Border

Responses to Border Insecurity

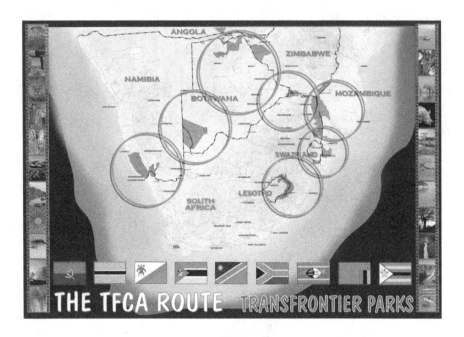

Establishment of Border Post Between Kruger National Park (KNP) and Limpopo National Park (LNP)

Appendix III 397

Banki-Amchidé Cameroon - Nigeria border

Cutting of 15 Km of Fence between KNP and LNP

Appendix IV

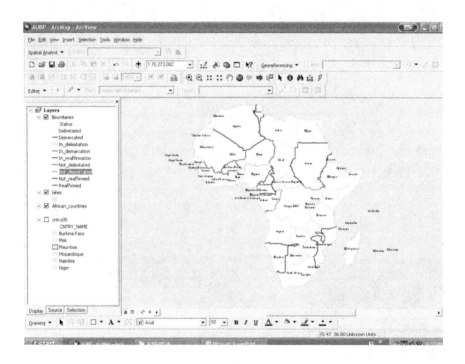

Appendix IV 399

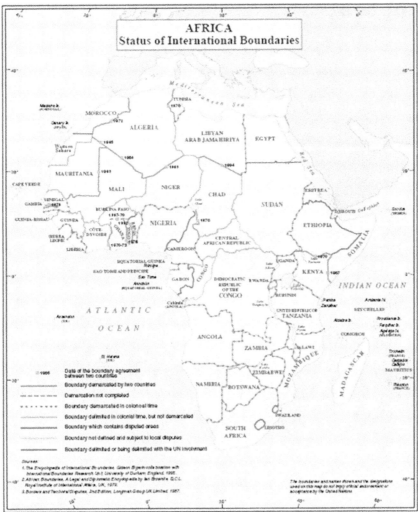

Appendix V

VISIT TO LOCUS: Meeting with villagers of Mada/Samke to determine location and nomenclature of Village

Appendix V 401

VISIT TO LOCUS: Sub Commission for Demarcation members in meeting with villagers of Mada/Samke to determine location and nomenclature of Village

VISIT TO LOCUS: Sub Commission for Demarcation in the twilight of their visit discover public primary school with contradictory name to that claimed by Cameroon.
Cameroon claims village is 'Mada' but name on school wall reads "School of Samke"

VISIT TO LOCUS: Sub Commission for Demarcation in the twilight of their visit discover public primary school with contradictory name to that claimed by Cameroon.
Cameroon claims village is 'Mada' but name on school wall reads "School of Samke"

Index

abandonment, territorial acquisition by 46
Abbink, J. 200, 201
Abi-Saab, Judge 19–20
ABIDSM 300–4, 375; *see also* indigenous boundary dispute settlement
accretion, territorial acquisition by 44
adjudication: African Court of Justice (ACJ) 266–7; territorial acquisition by 46; underdeveloped state and proposed improvements 300–6; *see also* Cameroon–Nigeria land and maritime boundary (ICJ adjudication); International Court of Justice (ICJ)
Africa: and international law 8–16; origins of law 6–8
'African Border Day' 381–2
African Boundary Research Centre 380–2
African Conciliation Commission 300
African Court of Justice (ACJ) 266–7, 382–3
African Union (AU) 102–5; Charter 104; Early Warning Unit (EWU) 105–8; High-Level Implementation Panel (AUHIP) 164; indigenous boundary dispute settlement 297, 298–9; natural resources 357, 35; and RECs 107–8
African Union Border Program (AUBP) 108; and ABIDSM 303; achievements and challenges 375, 378–80, 381–2; costs 319–20; and ECCAS 144–5, 148; implementation 118–25; law practice and diplomacy 109–18; and RECs 106–7; Sudan-South Sudan 163
Afrocentricity 369–70; critical approach 5; customary rule 360–2; oral history and local consulation 355; *see also entries beginning* indigenous
Ajibola, Judge 17–18, 237–8, 239
Algeria 120, 170–1, 247, 264

All-African People's Conference (1958) 345
Allot, A. 18, 332
alternative dispute resolution (ADR) 279–80, 374–5, 385–8; experts and 'irregular peace practitioners' 280–1; factors predictive of failure 306–8; and foreign interests 272; identification and evaluation of best practice 308–15; methods 283–95; multi-tracking and indigenising 295–306; third party role 282; training issues 280, 307
alternative futures 363–4; Afrocentric solutions 369–70; cessation 367; free cities 365–6; lease back options 366–7, 378–9; sale and purchase of territory 365; special territorial arrangements 364–5; use of plebiscites 367–8
Amman, Judge 15
Anglophone and Francophone states 257–60
Angola 147, 172
annexation, territorial acquisition by 44–5
anthropological/socio-cultural perspectives 96–99, 244, 246
Arab Maghreb Union (AMU) 170, 171
arbitration *see* Eritrea-Ethiopia Boundary Commission (EEBC); Permanent Court of Arbitration (PCA)
archaeological studies 70–1, 82
armed conflict 93, 94; civil wars 63; *see also* early warning systems; military presence/action
artificial vs natural boundaries 52–3
Asouzu, A. 272
avulsion, territorial acquisition by 44

Badme, Eritrea-Ethiopia 182, 185, 201, 232–3, 235

404 Index

Bakassi Peninsula *see* Cameroon–Nigeria land and maritime dispute
Baldersheim, H. and Rose, L.E. 64
Beale, J. 32
Benin, history of 11, 82–3, 86, 89
Benin–Niger: French colonialism 86; frontier dispute 37–8, 169
Benin–Niger–Nigeria tripoint 165
Benin–Nigeria, straddling communities 351
Benjamin, W. 85
Benjedid, C. (Algerian President) 19
Bennouna, Judge 20
Berlin Conference (1885) 88–90
best practice, identification and evaluation of 308–15
Bobbo, D. 227
Bodin, J. 24
Boko Haram 28, 95
bona fide assisted direct negotiations 298–9
border villages *see* straddling/boundary communities
borders and borderlands, definition of 73–4
Botswana 45, 77, 89; –Namibia 86–8, 260
boundaries: artificial vs natural 52–3; classification of 72; definition and types 69–78; *see also* delimitation and demarcation; frontiers and boundaries
Boundary Information System (BIS) 121, 378
British colonialism: agreements/treaties with Germany 209–14, 216–17, 223–4, 235–8; and Military Administration, Eritrea–Ethiopia 185, 188–9, 192, 193, 194; Southern Africa 71–2, 171–3, 174
Brown, C. 101
Brown, W. 26, 28, 77–8
Brownlie, I. 1–2, 41, 58, 86
Burkina Faso 88; –Ghana 351; –Mali 138, 164, 200–1; –Niger frontier dispute 168–9, 238

Cameroon: *North Cameroons* case 60, 251–2
Cameroon–Nigeria land and maritime dispute 166–7, 176; and AUBP 109; Boko Haram 95; and ECOWAS 142; geophysical setting 219–20; nationality and citizenship 68–9; territorial lease option 367, 378–9
Cameroon–Nigeria land and maritime dispute (ICJ adjudication) 218–19, 363; alternative futures 367, 368, 374; costs and funding 323; Eurocentricity in jurisprudence 235–9; Francophone and Anglophone states 257–60; historical provenance of boundary and territorial problem 220–3; interim measures of protection and control 314–15; judgement 223–7; maritime resources 226–7, 358, 358, 360–1; Mixed Commission (CNMC) 227–32, 233–4, 248, 249, 352; post-litigation processes 358; power differentials 247–9; structures of diplomacy, administration and implementation 232–5; Sub-Commissions 234, 310–11; *uti possidetis* principle 332, 346–7; Working Groups 234–5
Castellino, J. and Allen, S. 335
cease-fires 327–8
Central Africa: CEMAC 176; COPAX 144, 146–7; ECCAS 143–9; MARAC 148–9
cessation, territorial acquisition by 43–4, 367
Chagos Island 16
citizenship and nationality 68–9
Civil Society Organisations (CSOs) 128, 138, 141, 148
civil wars 21, 63, 148
collective sovereignty 24
colonial agreements/treaties: Bakassi Peninsula 223–4, 235–58 Lake Malawi 209–14, 217; *see also* Eritrea–Ethiopia Boundary Commission (EEBC)
colonialism: British *see* British colonialism; and criminality in border regions 243–4; and Eurocentric jurisprudence 16–22, 235–9, 260, 374, 382–3; and internal boundaries 64; and international law 9–16; Italian *see* Eritrea–Ethiopia Boundary Commission (EEBC); and plebiscites 368; and Westphalian sovereignty 27; *see also* delimitation and demarcation; independence/self-determination; territorial acquisition; *uti possidetis* principle
commission of enquiry 286–7
community radio stations 136–7, 138–9, 165
conciliation 287–9; African Conciliation Commission 300
Conflict Early Warning and Response Mechanism (CEWARN) 127–8, 129
Congo, Democratic Republic of (DRC) 147, 177, 257; region 15, 88–90, 260; River 177

conquest, territorial acquisition by 44–5
Continental Early Warning System (CEWS) 102, 141, 376
continental shelf: extension 112–13, 116; North Sea cases 60–1, 283
cooling off mechanisms, ICJ 251–6
COPAX, Central Africa 144, 146–7
costs 319–23, 375–9
Crawford, J. 35, 49, 97–8, 325, 329
critical approach 5
Cukwurah, O. 309, 310, 325, 334, 337
customary rule 360–2

Daly, B. 277
Darwin, H.G. 283, 290, 292
Davidson, B. 9, 33, 35, 90
delimitation and demarcation: Berlin Conference (1885) 88–90; difference between 78–9; flawed colonial project of 20–2; functions of 74–5; historical, colonial and contemporary contexts 79–88; phases 84–5; *see also* alternative futures
Democratic Republic of Congo (DRC) 147, 177, 257
Department for Human Integration, Peace, Security and Stability (DHIPSS) 147–8
dependencies and areas of special sovereignty 40
dereliction, territorial acquisition by 46
developing states and international law 18–19
Dieng, A. 7, 8
Diop, C.A. 5, 6
diplomacy 19, 22, 289; African Union (AU) 106, 107–8; African Union Border Program (AUBP) 109–18; Cameroon–Nigeria Mixed Commission (CNMC) 227–32, 233–4, 248, 249, 352; function of international courts 253–4; political and power differentials 246–50; two track system 304–5
'disagreement and difference' 280
discovery, territorial acquisition by 46
Djibouti–Eritrea 103, 192

early warning systems: AU EWU 105–8; CEWARN 127–8, 129; CEWS 102, 141, 376; ECOWAS 141–2; MARAC 148–9; SADC 154
East African boundaries 156–64
East African sub-region (IGAD) 127–8; and AU 103, 106; Conflict Early Warning and Response Mechanism (CEWARN) 127–8, 129; Mediation Support Unit 163; relevance 128–31
ECOMOG 143
Economic Community of Central African States (ECCAS) 143–8; and MARAC 148–9
Economic Community of West African States (ECOWAS) 131–3; and AU 106, 108; Conflict Prevention Framework (ECPF) 132–3, 135–7, 165; conflict resolution and management 133–4; Court of Justice, actual and potential role 140–1, 306; early warning system 141–2; experience 142–3; Free Movement of Persons Directorate 137–40; Mediation and Security Council 107; Peace and Conflict Department (PCD) 142; Treaty and protocols 134–40
Egypt: and colonial treaties 188–9; history of 7–8, 13; LOSC ratification 313; and Middle East 77, 171
elders 281, 297, 302, 311; councils of 129, 130
enclaves 350–1
enquiry 286–7
Equatorial Guinea: –Gabon: Mbanie Island 147, 168; third party intervention 302–3
Eritrea–Djibouti 103, 192
Eritrea–Ethiopia 160–2; IGAD and 129
Eritrea–Ethiopia Boundary Commission (EEBC) 177–8, 236, 270; applicable law 185–6; Badme 182, 185, 201, 232–3, 235; critique of decision and difficulties of implementation 195–6; Eritrean submission 178–84; Ethiopian submission 184–95; five sectors 186, 188–9, 191–2, 195
Eritrea–Ethiopia Claims Commission (EECC) 203–5, 270
erosion, territorial acquisition by 44
Ethiopia: historical land measurement 81; ICJ *South West Africa* judgment 263–4; *see also* Eritrea–Ethiopia
Eurocentric jurisprudence 16–22, 235–9, 260, 374, 382–3
Europe/European Union: AEBR 118; funding and technical assistance, AUBP 119–20, 122–5; *North Sea Continental Shelf Cases* 60–1, 283; role and scope of involvement 316–17
extra-territorial jurisdiction 32

'failed states' 35
farming and grazing rights 129–30
fences and walls 75–8
field monitors 128–9
fisheries 359, 362
Fitzmaurice, Judge G. 60, 252, 256
flexibility, as best practice 309
foreign states and corporations 272
Fox, H. 385
France, IGN Demarcation Agreement 220–1, 224
Francophone and Anglophone states 257–60
free cities, establishment of 365–6
free movement: ECOWAS Directorate 137–40; and globalisation 100; straddling communities 353; *see also* migration
Friendly Relations Declaration (1970) 329
frontiers and boundaries: definitional issues 50, 52–4, 71–2; functionality of 50–2
funding: bilateral and multilateral projects 352; legal costs and 319–23; and technical assistance 119, 122–5, 373–4

Gabon–Equatorial Guinea: Mbanie Island 147, 168
Gambia *see* Senegal–Gambia
game theory 15, 16
Germany: colonial agreements/treaties with Britian 209–14, 216–17, 223–4, 235–8; financial and technical assistance (GTZ) 119, 123–4
Ghana–Burkina Faso, straddling communities 351
Gibbs, Justice 16
globalisation: and boundaries thesis 73; and free movement 100; vs territorial sovereignty 27–31
God and sovereignty 26
Good Offices 289–91, 292
grazing rights 129–31
Greentree Agreement (2006) 176, 346, 363
Guinea Bissau–Senegal–Gambia zone 138, 165, 165–6, 358
Gulf of Guinea: Commission and Treaty 384–5; *Land and Maritime Boundary* case 92–3, 302–3, 358

Hague Conferences/Conventions 286, 289–90, 322; and Permanent Court of Arbitration (PCA) 270–1
Hammarskjold, D. 284

Heisler, M. 241
Heligoland Treaty 209–14, 217
Homlmes, Justice 32
Horsman, M. and Marshall, A. 74
Huber, M. 24
hydrocarbon/oil fields 226–7, 357–9, 360–1

IGAD (Intergovernmental Authority on Development) *see* East African sub-region
IGN (Institute Geographiqué National of France) Demarcation Agreement 220–1, 224
Ilemi Triangle: Kenya-Sudan 157–8
independence/self-determination: ICJ role 262–5; internal boundaries 65; power differentials 14–16; *uti possidetis* principle 332–3, 337–49
independent states 40, 41
indigenous boundary dispute settlement 295–7; African Conciliation Commission 300; African mediation 299; bona fide assisted direct negotiations 298–9; underdeveloped state and proposed improvements (ABDSM) 300–6
indigenous vs Westphalian sovereignty 33–6
indigenous zones of separation 80
insensitive judicial decisions 352
interim measures of protection and control 313–15
internal boundary disputes 63–5
international boundary disputes: classifications and nature of 90–6; range and definitional issues 55–63; vs territorial disputes 65–9
International Court of Justice (ICJ) 17–18, 19, 20, 22, 41–2, 104; colonial maps/treaties 89, 200–1, 333–4; conflict resolution and cooling off mechanisms 251–6; critical appraisal of contentious and advisory jurisdiction 257–62; definition of 'international dispute' 60; fisheries 359; and indigenous African adjudication 300–1; litigation and administrative costs 320–3; political and legal disputes 60–2; and proposed ABIDSM 300–1; and provisions establishing African Court of Justice (ACJ) 267, 384; role in self-determination/independence for mandate/colonial territories 262–5;

and Tanzania–Malawi: Lake Malawi/Nyasa 217; *uti possidetis* principle 67, 333–4, 335, 346–7; *see also* Cameroon–Nigeria land and maritime dispute (ICJ adjudication)
international courts: advancing jurisprudence and elaboration of law 254–6; diplomacy function 253–4; litigation and administrative costs 320–3
International Monetary Fund (IMF) 124
International Symposium on Land, River and Lake Boundaries Management 249–50
interpretive function of boundary dispute resolution 312–13
intra-state conflicts 63, 152, 153–4
Italian colonialism *see* Eritrea–Ethiopia Boundary Commission (EEBC)
Italian–African Peace Facility (IAPF) 124

Jennings, R. 230–1
Johanson, M.C. 332–3
Joint Border Verification and Monitoring Mission (JBVMM) 103–4
Jones, P. and Carey, C. 280
jurisdiction: principle of 36–8; and sovereignty 31–3, 50–4

Kaikobad, K.H. 248
Kavango Zambezi Trans-frontier Conservation Area (KAZA) 75
Kenya: –Ethiopia 129; –South Sudan: Nadapal boundary 158–9; –Sudan: Ilemi Triangle 157–8; –Uganda: Migingo Island, Lake Victoria 129, 159–60
Krasner, S.D. 29

Lake Chad *see* Cameroon–Nigeria land and maritime dispute
Lake Chad Basin Commission (LCBC) 220–1, 224, 352
Lake Malawi/Nyasa *see* Tanzania–Malawi: Lake Malawi/Nyasa (mediation)
Lake Victoria: Migingo Island 91, 129, 159–60
landlocked states 41
landmine clearance 125
Lauterpacht, H. 256
Law of the Sea Convention (LOSC) 26, 112–13, 116, 278, 288, 313, 358
League of Nations: Eritrea-Ethiopia 179–80; free cities 365–6; self-determination issues 337–45; *see also* United Nations (UN)
lease back options 366–7, 378–9
legal aid 321–3
legal and implementation costs 319–23
legal and political disputes 60–2
legal practice and diplomacy: AUBP 109–18; Cameroon–Nigeria Mixed Commission (CNMC) 227–32, 233–4, 248, 249, 352
legal and technical skills 369–70, 380–1
Lesotho 41, 351
Levi, W. 256, 268, 269, 287
lex lata and *lex fernada* 15–16
liberal political theory, divisions within 100–1
Liberia 133–4, 143, 166, 263, 264
local consulation, straddling communities 355
locus standi, determination of 311–12
Lorimer, J. 10

McEwen, A.C. 80
Machiavelli, N. 76
McNair, Lord 310
Madagascar–Tanzania 104, 172
Malawi *see* Tanzania–Malawi: Lake Malawi/Nyasa (mediation)
Mali–Burkina Faso 138, 165, 200–1
maritime boundaries: AU/AUBP 104–5, 108, 112–13, 116, 120; fisheries 359; LOSC 26, 112–13, 116, 278, 288, 313, 358; Mauritania 120; Morocco–Spain 171; Southern African region 171–3; *see also* Cameroon–Nigeria land and maritime dispute
Mauritania 120, 139
Mayall, J. 216
Mbanie Island: Gabon–Equatorial Guinea 147, 168
mediation 291–5; African 299; factors predictive of failure 306–8; REC councils 106–7; *see also* Tanzania–Malawi: Lake Malawi/Nyasa
Migingo Island, Lake Victoria 129, 159–60
migration: security issues 240–6; *see also* free movement
military presence/action 324–6; Cameroon–Nigeria 221, 228, 326, 327; Eritrea–Ethiopia 196, 204, 205, 328; interim measures of protection and control 314–15; retorsion, retaliation and war 326–27

monarchs *see* royalty/monarchy
Montville, J. 304
Moore, Judge 255
Morocco: –Spain 171; –Western Sahara 43, 77, 121, 170–1
Mostert, N. 71–2
Mozambique 211, 216; Tanzania–Mozambique–Comoros 102, 172
multi-track approach (ADR) 295–306
multidisciplinary approach 96–101, 245–6, 281

Namibia: –Botswana 86–8, 260; –South Africa 172–3; *South West Africa* judgment 263, 264–5
Napadal boundary: Kenya–South Sudan 158–9
nationalism 35
nationality: and citizenship 68–9; PAC staff/arbitrators 272–8; *see also* Afrocentricity
natural resources *see* resources
natural vs artificial boundaries 52–3
negative sovereignty 25, 26–7
negative strategies 117–18
negotiation 283–5; bona fide assisted direct 298–9; post adjudication 352, 386–7
neutrality, lack of 307–8
Newman, D. 95, 97
Ngenda, A. 14
Niger: boundary commission 109; *see also* Benin–Niger; Burkina Faso; Nigeria–Niger
Nigeria: –Benin, straddling communities 351; Border Communities Development Agency (BCDA) 245; boundary commission 109, 138; commissions of enquiry 287; *see also* Cameroon–Nigeria land and maritime dispute
Nigeria–Niger: border closure 138, 140–1, 142, 165; Joint Commission 138
North Africa 170–1
Nugent, P. 73

occupation, territorial acquisition by 42–3
oil/hydrocarbon fields 226–7, 357–9, 360–1
Okomu, W. 52, 79–80, 84, 157, 332, 333, 360
Open Society Justice Initiative 67, 68
oral history/local consulation, straddling communities 355

Organization of African Unity (OAU) 67, 110, 345

pacific settlement *see* alternative dispute resolution (ADR); International Court of Justice (ICJ)
Pakenham, T. 90
Pan-African survey of Borders 119, 120–1
Panel of the Wise (ECOWAS) 108, 136, 142, 165, 299
papal grant, territorial acquisition by 47–8
peace committees 128, 129, 363
Peace and Conflict Department (PCD) (ECOWAS) 142
Peace and Security Council for Central Africa (COPAX) 144, 146–7
Peace and Security Department (PSD)/Council 102, 104, 105, 106, 107, 108
peace-keeping forces 329
Pelkmans, M. 98–9
Peres, S. (Israeli President) 76
Permanent Court of Arbitration (PCA): arbitration principles 267–8; cases 67, 164, 270–1; criticisms 272, 308; Hague Conferences and 270–1; litigation and administrative costs 321, 322; member states 271–2; nationality of staff/arbitrators 272–8; Secretary-Generals 273–4
Permanent Court of International Justice (PCIJ) 254–5
plebiscites, use of 367–8
political differentials in diplomacy 246–50
political and legal disputes 60–2
political sovereignty 26
Portugal 88, 209, 216
power differentials: in diplomacy 246–50; post-colonial 14–16; Swaziland–South Africa 173–6
pre-colonial era 24, 33–4, 78, 79–84
Prescott, V. 79; and Triggs, G.D. 20–1, 71, 78
prescription, territorial acquisition by 45
prisoners of war (POWs), Eritrea–Ethiopia 204, 205, 329
privatisation 30
Protectorate Convention 44–5
protectorates 12–13, 14, 21

racialism and colonialism 9–14
radio stations, community 136–7, 138–9, 165
Ratner, S. 347

refugees 28, 52, 94–5, 163, 248
Regional Economic Commissions (RECs) 126–7, 383–4; and AU/AUBP 91, 106–7, 108, 118; indigenous boundary dispute settlement 297, 298–9, 300; security plans 121–2; *see also specific RECs*
religion: God and sovereignty 26; history of 7–8; indigenous boundary dispute settlement 297; tensions 28–9
relinquishment/renunciation, territorial acquisition by 46
res communis/res nullius concepts 37
resources 129–31, 353–4; fisheries 359, 362; hydrocarbon/oil fields 226–7, 357–9, 360–1; recognising African customary rule 360–1; Southern Africa 171–3
retorsion, retaliation and war 326–9
Rodney, W. 11
Rotberg, R. 282
royalty/monarchy: absolutism 24; Cameroon–Nigeria 235–7; Eritrean–Ethiopia 184, 192, 200, 201; kidnappings and depositions 89
rural development bodies 245

Said, E. 12
sale and purchase of territory 365
Schwarzenberger, G. 25, 26–7
security: and migration 240–6; plans (RECs) 121–2
self-determination *see* independence/self-determination
Senegal–Gambia 139, 143, 165–6; –Guinea Bissau zone 138, 165, 166, 358
separatist movements 338–44
Sharon, A. (President of Israel) 76
Shaw, M. 181, 202, 236, 331
Shivji, I.G. 382
Sierra Leone 135–6, 142, 143, 165, 166
smuggling and related crime 242–4
socio-cultural/anthropological perspectives 96–99, 244, 246
Somali territorial claims 66
Somalia 95, 180, 294, 308
South Africa: –Namibia 172; –Swaziland 173–6; Apartheid regime 18, 175; colonial era 89; *South West Africa* judgment 263–5
South Sudan: –Kenya: Nadapal boundary 158–9; –Sudan 162–4
South West Africa judgment 263–4

Southern Africa 171–6; British colonialism 71–2, 173, 175
Southern African Development Community (SADC) 149–50, 172; early warning system 155; Organ for Politics, Defence and Security 150, 151–4, 325; political mechanisms 150–4; tribunal and judicial route 150–1, 302
sovereignty: areas of special 40; concepts and forms 23–7; globalisation vs territorial 27–31; and jurisdiction 31–3, 50–4; territorial 370–2; Westphalian vs indigenous 33–6
Spain: –Morocco 171; *Western Sahara Case* 43
special territorial arrangements 363–4
stakeholders, pan-African strategy 121–2
stare decisis doctrine 256
statelessness 67–8
straddling/boundary communities 350–7; armed conflict 94; 'bad practices'/negative strategies 117–18; dedicated border and rural development bodies 245; and enclaves 350–1; migration and security issues 240–6; smuggling and related crime 242–4; statelessness 67–8; structures 353; *see also* resources
Sudan: –Kenya: Ilemi Triangle 157–8; –South Sudan 162–4; and AU 103; and colonial treaties 188–9; Western and Central 34
Swaziland–South Africa 173–6

Tanzania–Madagascar 104, 172
Tanzania–Malawi: Lake Malawi/Nyasa (mediation) 159, 206, 308; applicable treaties and instruments 208–9; HLMT challenges, achievements and prospects 214–17; HLMT membership 207–8; Malawi's position 209–11; Tanzania's position 211–14
Tanzania–Mozambique–Comoros 104, 172
technical and financial assistance 123–4, 373–4
technical and legal skills 369–70, 380–1
terra nullius 42, 43, 80, 236
territorial acquisition: types of 41–9; *see also* alternative futures
territorial vs boundary disputes 65–9
territory: concept/extent of 36–8, 371–3; definitional issues 38–9

'thematic reflection' 108
third parties: power differentials 246; role of 282
Thomson–Marchand Declaration (1929–30) 223, 284, 311
training issues 280, 307, 369–70
transborder communities *see* straddling/ boundary communities
tribalism 35
trust funds 321–3
Tsiranana, P. (President of Madagascar) 331
two track system of dispute settlement 304–5

Uganda: –DRC 176; –Kenya: Migingo Island, Lake Victoria 129, 159–60
United Nations (UN): alternative dispute resolution 269–70, 286–7, 288–9, 290, 292–3, 294, 295; AUBP funding 123–4; Cameroon–Nigeria Mixed Commission (CNMC) and related groups 228–9, 230, 231, 234, 235; Charter 25, 45, 63, 231, 279, 325, 384–5; Eritrea–Ethiopia 179–80, 181, 193–4, 196; High Commissioner for Refugees (UNHCR) 163; and ICJ 59; and IGAD 127; LOSC 26, 112–13, 116, 278, 288, 313, 358; and proposed ABIDSM 300–1; Security Council 325–6, 327–8; self-determination/independence issues 263, 264–5; Trust Fund 323
United States, role and scope of involvement 317–18

uti possidetis principle: and AUBP 113–14; Eritrea–Ethiopia 197–9; internal boundaries 65; and OAU 67, 345; origins of 330; political separation and self-determination 337–49; as problematic doctrine 330–7; Tanzania–Malawi 217

Verzijl, J.H.W. 51
visit to locus, as best practice 309–10

walls and fences 75–8
war *see* armed conflict; military presence/ action
Wedgewood, R. 35
West African region 164–9; *see also* Economic Community of West African States (ECOWAS)
Western Sahara 43, 76, 121, 170–1
Westphalian sovereignty 25, 27, 29; vs indigenous sovereignty 33–6
World Bank 124, 352
World Court *see* International Court of Justice (ICJ)

Xhosa 71–2

Yoruba: history 81–2; philosophy 352

Zaire *see* Congo region
Zambia 41; *see also* Congo region
Zimbabwe 11, 18, 77, 89, 172; SADC 150–1; *see also* Congo region

CPSIA information can be obtained
at www.ICGtesting.com
Printed in the USA
BVHW072113071218
535054BV00010B/222/P